Elizabethan Poetry

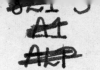

MODERN ESSAYS IN CRITICISM

Elizabethan Poetry

MODERN ESSAYS IN CRITICISM

Edited by
PAUL J. ALPERS

OXFORD UNIVERSITY PRESS
LONDON   OXFORD   NEW YORK
1967

Preface

The essays in this collection are intended to illuminate the assumptions, the variety, and the achievement of the non-dramatic poetry written in the reign of Elizabeth I. The first section is devoted to the problem of poetics that has most concerned students of this period and that most directly brings out questions about the relation between historical knowledge and critical analysis. *The Faerie Queene* is given a section of its own, not only because it presents special difficulties to the modern reader but also to emphasize its pre-eminence among Elizabethan poems.

I have limited the essays (except for the first) to those whose interest is primarily critical, even at the expense of not representing such classics of scholarship as Douglas Bush's *Mythology and the Renaissance Tradition*. I have imposed this limitation both for the sake of general coherence and to focus attention on what has been a main point of interest for me in making this selection and will be, I hope, for those who use it. Modern criticism has been uncertain how to deal with Elizabethan poetry, even though, under Eliot's influence, it has been nourished by seventeenth-century poetry and Elizabethan and Jacobean drama. While for these bodies of literature there is a coherent tradition of critical praise, analysis, and controversy, most of the essays in this volume ask fundamental questions anew: "What kind of poem or what kind of language is this?" "What value or interest does poetry of this sort have?" We still need to ask these questions, but the variety and resourcefulness of the essays in this volume show how well they have been and are being answered. Certainly the time is past when Elizabethan poetry, and Spenser in particular, can be used as a whipping boy for Donne and Jonson.

Berkeley, California
July 1966

PAUL J. ALPERS

Contents

I. Rhetoric and Poetry

II. Individual Poets and Modes of Poetry

III. "The Faerie Queene"

Elizabethan Poetry

MODERN ESSAYS IN CRITICISM

PART I

Rhetoric and Poetry

G. K. HUNTER

Humanism and Courtship

The only English work of criticism, written about John Lyly before this present one (I mean John Dover Wilson's Harness Prize essay, *John Lyly* [Cambridge, 1905]), opens with a clear statement that the interest of the subject lies not in his intrinsic merits, but in the influence he exerted and the developments he encouraged. The only other critical book written about Lyly (M. Feuillerat's massive French thesis, *John Lyly: contribution à l'histoire de la Renaissance en Angleterre* [Cambridge, 1910] begins with almost the same sentiments: "il m'a paru que Lyly avait surtout une valeur historique et philologique, et que vouloir l'offrir au délassement des simples amateurs de belleslettres c'eût été l'exposer à des affronts."

This is a depressing unanimity; yet it seems to the present writer to rest on distinctions which allow some play in their interpretation. Of course, to approach the works of Lyly by any kind of "direct method" would be ridiculous. No modern reader can be expected to enjoy *Euphues* or the plays without some preparation in the modes of thinking and writing which they exemplify. Lyly has left no works which speak directly to the human heart of the twentieth century as do many of the lyrics of the period, for example, Ralegh's "The Lie" or Wyatt's "Be still my lute." Lyly has no personal voice of this kind

Reprinted by permission of the publishers from G. K. Hunter, *John Lyly* (London: Routledge & Kegan Paul Ltd.; Cambridge, Mass.: Harvard University Press), pp. 1-35. Copyright, 1962, by G. K. Hunter.

3

which can carry across the intervening centuries and stir the responses of the sympathetic but uninstructed reader today.

Yet to say that these works have "aesthetic" value while Lyly's have only "historical" interest seems an unnecessarily sharp distinction. For if by "historical" we mean that they contribute to our understanding of the age in which they appeared, I do not know how they do this unless they make us respond to the attitudes they convey; and this *response* seems to me an aesthetic one. What is more, the response seems to work two ways. An appreciation of Lyly sharpens our awareness of what the Elizabethan Age was really like; but it is also true that an understanding of Elizabethan attitudes enables us to see the virtues of Lyly in a sharper focus.

It is along these two lines that I wish to conduct the argument of this book. I wish to approach Lyly from a historical point of view, but to dwell at the same time on his individual merits rather than his influence on others. For concentrating on what Dover Wilson (following Taine) calls his "dynamical" interest—estimating what he contributed to others, and especially to Shakespeare—seems to me to distort quite basically the qualities he had. For he is not seeking to do the same kind of thing as Shakespeare; he is not appealing to the same responses; he was, in fact, a different kind of writer. Though the gap in time and class between the two men was small, there is a historical gap of some magnitude between the points on which their separate gazes are fixed—Shakespeare looks forward where Lyly looks back.

The approach to the Elizabethan age that begins with Shakespeare is natural and inevitable; but it has its limitations, and at some stage in a closer study it has to be abandoned. Through major authors the historical situations in which they lived become universal; "any man" we suppose, "could think thus" discovering High Toryism in Dr Johnson, Christian Pessimism in Swift, Puritanism in Milton or Bunyan. But the modernity of such authors can be as misleading as illuminating, for the supposition that the whole age was really trying to achieve the "modernity" of its greatest figures often fatally distorts its minor ones. The cultural history of Elizabethan England has suffered especially from this "Whig"[1] interpretation of its tendencies, and from the assumption that its tendencies were also its principles.[2]

This standard view sees the voyages of Drake, the defeat of the Armada, the daring plays of Marlowe, the wild life of Robert Greene as different manifestations of the same central urge towards modern freedom and naturalness, the same impatience with restraints (physical or intellectual) which might impede the vigorous flow of life, released at last from the long sleep of the medieval "night" preceding —an energy which found its fullest expression in the mature plays of Shakespeare. From this point of view the "spaciousness" of Elizabeth's reign is a setting for a new-found freedom of the human spirit,[3] where (as J. R. Green long ago pointed out):

> The sphere of human interest was widened as it has never been widened before or since, by the revelation of a new heaven and a new earth. It was only in the later years of the sixteenth century that the discoveries of Copernicus were brought home to the general intelligence of the world by Kepler and Galileo, or that the daring of the Buccaneers broke through the veil which the greed of Spain had drawn across the New World of Columbus. (*Short History* (1886), p. 412)

Green may be brasher in expression than later historians, but the general view he expresses here may be said to remain a popularly accepted line in history (certainly in literary history) up to the present time. The widely influential *History of English Literature* by Legouis and Cazamian (revised edition, 1933) may serve as a convenient example of this, not because it is especially tendentious, but because its views are so coherent and well-organized. Beside Green's statement we may set Legouis' summary:

> The Renascence showed in England almost all the characteristics which it had throughout Europe: thought was liberated and broadened so that it broke its scholastic framework; destiny and morals ceased to be the matter only of dogma and became problematical; a rebellion against the spiritual authority was first incited by the Reformation . . . men looked with a new wonder at the heavens and the earth as they were revealed by the discoveries of the navigators and astronomy; superior beauty was perceived in the literature of classical antiquity. (p. 200)

We may also note his later point:

> By two successive advances [in literary production], the one made in 1578 [*Euphues* and *The Shepheard's Calendar*] while

Drake was sailing round the world, the other in 1589 [*Faerie Queene*, I suppose], on the morrow of the Armada, England caught up with her continental rivals, if indeed she did not outpace them . . . The impulse for this production was derived from patriotism. It sprang from England's growing consciousness of strength, her pride of prosperity, the spirit of adventure which animated her sons and caused them always to aspire to the first place, and her faith in her own destiny. . . . For most men, the exactions of God did not go beyond those of patriotism . . . in truth, the country was . . . eager not for religion but for games and pleasure, ambitious of the free development which is the very spirit of the Renascence. The intellectual paganism of humanism rested on the broad basis of an instinctive paganism scattered wide among the people. (pp. 250 f.)

Indeed, even though modern (non-literary) historians are more cautious of committing themselves than was Green, one may cite a paragraph from the current Oxford History of the Age of Elizabeth showing the same views:

The outgoings of the spirit are conditioned by its in-takings, and the imaginative reach of the man of letters keeps pace with the widening horizon of his experience. The countless adventures on land and sea that made England respected and feared, and opened up the world to English enterprise, produced an exaltation of soul which the poet and the philosopher by the alchemy of their genius transmuted into the unforgettable beauties and enduring strength of a great literature. Like Drake and Cavendish, Shakespeare and Bacon circumnavigated the earth and grew rich on its spoils. (J. B. Black, *The Reign of Elizabeth* [2nd edn., 1959], p. 280)

Such statements are surrounded, it is true, by qualifications, but in the absence of any other positive cultural interpretation of the period this may well be taken as the author's view. Certainly Black is at one with Legouis in seeing "the prevailing tone" of the age as "markedly secular and worldly" (p. 278)—taking the words of preachers and satirists as objective truths (speaking of "the atmosphere of egoism, paganism, and epicureanism in which the Elizabethan lived and moved and had his being") and ignoring the standpoint of piety from which such statements are made, and which they presuppose in their readers.

So long as this view of the English Renaissance is accepted, and with it the coordinate view of the relationship between England and Italy in the period (see Black, p. 279), Lyly can only appear as an awful example, the author of a work "the style of which is, perhaps, more elaborately and systematically bad than that of any work in the whole extent of literature."[4] For in so far as he shared in the new freedom of his time Lyly used this only to concoct "a style modelled on the decadence of Italian prose" (Green's words). His liberty expressed itself as licence and as all good Whigs know, this leads to the abrogation of liberty itself. He is a writer without the hearty vitality that is supposed to be typical of the age, not a sea-dog of a writer but an exquisite miniaturist, a jewel-encrusted Fabergé nightingale, not a genuine English bird in the rediscovered world of natural beauty.

Indeed, even if we abandon the distortions of these literary-history preconceptions altogether, it is not obvious what attitudes to Lyly can take their place. The latest approaches to the literature of the English Renaissance are biassed by their method in favour of the complex lyric expressing individual soul-state. Such a work as the "Pelican Guide" volume on *The Age of Shakespeare,* though the arguments against Lyly that I have indicated are dropped, does nothing to bring him into a new focus; and it is worth noting that the eclipse of Lyly is shared by Sidney, while Spenser (too large to be ignored) is given a travesty of treatment as an appendix to Chaucer. It would seem that with the decline of "lit.-hist." the sixteenth-century part of "Elizabethan literature" has vanished.

I have already suggested that the only possible approach to Lyly is through the temper of the time in which he lived; but this can hardly be seen in perspectives which emphasize the incipient "modernity" of the period, at the expense of its traditions; and these are the commonest perspectives in modern literary history and literary criticism. Fortunately, however, there is also a wealth of specialized scholarship on the period, which can be brought to bear on Lyly's position and which yields a different picture of his situation.

The English Renaissance, it appears, was never, by itself, a movement which could have condemned Lyly as "artificial"—the word was, of course, at that time a term of praise. The days of Elizabeth may have seemed "spacious" even to those who lived under the Queen, but the space was seen in very different terms from Green's

by those who occupied it. The terms in which the age seems to have
been aware of itself and proud of itself were terms which showed it
to possess a new power over the moral content of life (morals being
taken to include manners); this was coupled to a sense of release
from the muddle of the past, from the medieval tendency to spin
schemes and dreams and leave the practice to founder in the mud.[5]
The age was aware of concentrating its cleverness on *this* world, a
world of solid and colourful objects, and of using eloquence to produce a human rather than a theoretical order, by actualizing the
moral ideals that God had supplied. But this is very far from supposing that forceful action or liberty from restraint are goods in themselves.

The age sees the historical movement as one out of contemplative
idleness (pictured as a monk in Spenser, and elsewhere) and into
practical utility.[6] Religion, says Sir John Cheke (who taught King
Edward and all Cambridge Greek) has two parts, "the one of which
is placed in the searching after *knowledge* and in the tracing out of
those things which are grateful and well-pleasing unto God; but the
other is employed in *action*, which puts forward into life and performance what she understands to have the divine approbation."
That which is active, Cheke says, "we may name piety."[7] There can
be little doubt that Cheke himself, and most vocal Elizabethans,
supposed that this second was the crucial part of religion,[8] it was obviously so if the scriptures were plain, open, easy and fruitful, as they
were often said to be.

It follows that forceful action *of the right kind* could be seen as
the highest human activity by many Elizabethan theorists, and here
they were at one with continental Humanists. Man was widely admired in the period for his power to remould himself and his destiny.[9] Even the staid Erasmus says that Prometheus is a figure to be
admired and imitated.[10] But this ideal of "Promethean man" is no
late nineteenth-century anarchist or even radical vision; rather is it
part of a priggish course in self-improvement. C. S. Lewis has amusingly presented the essential difference between Renaissance *human-
itas* and medieval *humilitas*;[11] self-consciousness in virtue certainly
seems to be a recurrent feature of the Renaissance, as of its idol,
Cicero.

The energy that is admired widely and with complete orthodoxy
is the energy which is disciplined in the mind by *order,* so as to
effect and control an order in the world outside. The "Promethean,"

men of the English Renaissance—Ralegh,[12] Sidney, Burghley—are as devoted to self-conscious moral platitudes as are the "irregular" dramas of the populace. Both see energy reaching out to touch an immutable set of moral norms; the "spaciousness" of the Queen's reign was seen as stretching between the little that man had done and the great deal that man could do, but what man could do was not to be determined by the limits of human energy but was everywhere bound in by a divinely appointed frame of order. Discovery of "those things which are pleasing unto God" will lead from self-conscious probity to action—and this is seen at its highest as the kind of action which will reduce "divers cities, countries and nations . . . to civil order and politic life" (Starkey's *Dialogue between Pole and Lupset* [ed. Burton], p. 22).

Both the pleasures of self-conscious rectitude and sense of Divine Mission in the power to order secular affairs point to a truth about the Elizabethan court. Elizabeth and her establishment remained at the centre of the national consciousness throughout the "spacious days" we admire so much, and this would seem enigmatic if we were to suppose that the main national effort of the time was in the direction of freedom and naturalness. For the court of Elizabeth was neither natural nor free. Its ritual was artificial to the last degree, despotic and repetitive. The sovereign was a painted idol rather than a person; the codes of manners it encouraged were exotic, Petrarchan and Italianate. Yet this artificial and insincere world had the power to harness the diverse energies of high and low alike. Its artifice does not seem to have cut off the sovereign from her people, but on the contrary seems to have focussed more clearly what they wanted to see —a manifestation of Divine Order on earth, and a guarantee of the meaning of secular energy, in terms which recalled the ritual of divine service.

The writers of the Elizabethan court show the same characteristics, and for the same reasons. Sidney, Spenser and Lyly are "artificial" writers, but this hardly means that they were out of touch with their age. As the artificiality of the court was an efficient means of expressing its serious and indeed religious sense of the "space" that was open to it, so the artifice of these writers was part of a serious attempt to display what were generally taken to be the deepest values of the age. Exquisiteness of form in Lyly, Spenser or Sidney is no more an argument for superficiality of treatment than are the love-locks and silk stockings of the courtiers a sign of effeminateness; one supposition is as crass as the other. The common modern assumption is that the "real" Elizabethan qualities are found in popular rather than courtly literature of the time. The formality of the court writers is usually seen not as an effort to impose order on the chaos of secular experience but rather as an attempt to emasculate the "natural" vitality of the Elizabethan spirit. For Green, "wild, reckless, defiant of all past tradition, of all conventional laws, the English dramatists owned no teacher, no source of poetic inspiration, but the people itself."[13] If this were true, then Sidney, Lyly, Spenser would indeed be coterie pedants, only coming alive (if ever) when their natural vitality broke through their sense of decorum.

These assumptions, however, seem to distort both the popular and the courtly art of the time. Our ideas of court formality and of the art which is appropriate to that seem, on the whole, to belong to Versailles rather than to Whitehall. The neo-classical pronouncements of Elizabethan critics are so much more intelligible than the art-forms they use that we tend to substitute one for the other, when we wish to discuss ideals; it is much easier to see what Sidney was aiming at in the neo-classical canons of *The Defence of Poesie* than to discover the rationale of the *Arcadia*—that "pastoral-romantic-heroic-philosophical prose-poem."[14] If we pursue the "mixed wit" of the *Arcadia* or *The Faerie Queene*, however, we find a Gothic concern for variety of experience and for the different levels of meaning which links them to the "art" we discover in Shakespeare, when we cease to see him (in the Green manner) "warbling his native woodnotes wild." The popular Elizabethan drama (as Miss Bradbrook has taught us all) was just as "artful," as dependent on themes and conventions as was the court art of the time. Both kinds of writing use the same "multiple" modes of presentation; instead of concentrating on a single viewpoint, and subordinating all else, they bring together different attitudes, stories, experiences, situations, and require them to harmonize "thematically" as best they can. But in the popular work of the time, this may well seem to modern readers an art without art —may even seem to be "nature"—while in the court works it is intellectual and obviously intentional. We cannot patronize the work of Sidney and Spenser in the same way that critics often patronize that of Greene or Lodge; we must accept it as seriously artful, or not accept it at all.

The difference may be seen in terms of the distinction between the *tendency* of the age and its *self-consciousness*, already touched on.

The courtly artists are more obviously self-conscious; in consequence they reflect the sense of the need for order, which I have described, more obtrusively than their popular contemporaries; they appeal to an audience well aware of the abstract implications of their own mode of life. But the popular authors did not have a different creed; they subscribed to the same general assumptions and worked by the same artistic methods. Though we may find it easier to ignore the artfulness of *their* "Gothic" methods, they were not different in principle. If we are to understand the "Elizabethan" quality even in Shakespeare we must understand his art as well as his exuberance, his energy; and his art is an unpretentious variant on the formal art of the court. The two aspects are derived from one age and from unified individuals; they point in different directions, but they belong together, and modify one another continuously.

With this sense of the homogeneousness of Elizabethan writing, courtly and popular, in our minds, we may see why contemporaries looked on "friendly Shakespeare" and other popular writers as all right in their kind, but of a rather lowly kind. Today we may prefer the spontaneous, unfinished sketch or fragment to the laboriously polished masterpiece,[15] but we should see why, in an age which prided itself on its sense of secular Order, this judgment had to be reversed. Looking back on the period with the eyes of Romantics, and through the vistas of neo-classicism, we are liable to talk about its *freedom*; but this is only possible because we are seeing history the wrong way round; what, from our nostalgic point of view, may seem "vitality and freedom" must have seemed then more like the threat of chaos,[16] to be held in check by whatever formal means were available. And this is the achievement of the court artists of Elizabeth's reign—to have found formal means of containing the experience of the time, and so to pass on to the age following the easier task of humanizing and modifying the formal heritage.

Another way of looking at this achievement is to look at it in terms of *wit*. I have suggested that the Elizabethans modified the attitudes they inherited by concentrating the interest of their art on *this* world, and so turning the complex valuations of spiritual and worldly experiences (as in *Piers Plowman* or poems of the *de contemptu mundi* tradition) into complex valuations of different kinds of worldly experience. The ease with which a man moves among these comparative valuations may be measured by his capacity to play them off, one against the other, and this is obviously a capacity in-

volved in "witty" writing, such as we find in Lyly's *Euphues*. Indeed
I shall argue that Lyly's works are characterized throughout by a remarkable capacity to balance modes of experience against one another. It may be a coincidence, but if so it is an interesting one, that
about this time the word *wit* seems to have acquired a new sense.[17]
Dr Johnson tells us that "it was about the time of Cowley that *wit*
which had been till then used for *intellection*, in contradistinction to
will, took the meaning, whatever it be, which it now bears." (Life
of Cowley) Johnson would seem to be wrong about the date. The
Oxford Dictionary gives *Euphues* as the first source for the meaning,
"liveliness of fancy"; this is not a final dating, but it is certain that
Euphues, the Anatomy of Wit is concerned to define *wit* in an unusual way. I may quote here the note of Professor Croll:

> The word as used by Ascham in the passage which suggested
> Lyly's title [*see below*, p. 49], means simply talent for studies,
> intellectual capacity. This is the usual meaning of the 16th
> century. Lyly often places it, however, in antithesis with *wis-
> dom*, much as he contrasts *lust* and *love*. A new turn is thus
> given to the word (which it also displays in other writers).
> (*Euphues*, ed. Croll and Clemons, p. 2)

The extreme formality of the structure and the expression of *Euphues* I am suggesting to be a measure of Lyly's effort to organize
the different levels of experience in this life so that they throw light
on one another. He reflects and comments on the courtly world of
Elizabeth by organizing into witty patterns different responses to its
key ideas—"wit," "honour," "love," "royalty," etc. Seeing his work in
this way we may see how far Lyly could be himself, and also the
entertainer of Elizabeth and other vital creatures, and perhaps the
largest single influence on that "spacious" genre, Shakespearian
Comedy.

I have suggested that the formal literature of Elizabeth's court expresses the society we profess to admire in a more exact way than the
popular literature that provides our first glimpse of it. It is also worth
noticing that modern political enthusiasm for the reign of Elizabeth
does not belong even chronologically with modern taste for "Elizabethan" drama (largely the product of the last ten years of the Queen
—"the decline" as Professor Neale sees it[18]—and the reign of James).
The literature which we admire most easily belongs to a political
set-up that we do not admire. The individualistic soul-searching and

suspicion of conventionality which we meet in Bacon, Greville, Jonson, Donne, and in Shakespeare's tragedies is the mirror of a general loss of faith in society; and it speaks directly to our own individualistic suspicions of social good. But the genuinely Elizabethan works cannot make this appeal; their claim is rather to be representative of the milieu in which they first appeared, and they can most conveniently be approached through the social and intellectual presuppositions of their social background. To see the works of Sidney and Lyly only as precursors to the modern novel and drama is, I suggest, to deny them what coherence they have; we are reduced to the position of the learned historian of the novel, who complains that the Elizabethans never managed to approach the novel form, because they never had any inkling of what a novel was like.[19] Likewise to see them only as precursors to the more sympathetic writers at the turn of the century is to destroy their individual quality. Our hope must be that if we can understand an author like Lyly in relation to his original context, his works will acquire meaning in terms of our own very different context. The hope is better founded than it might seem. In their elaboration of style, their virtuoso techniques asking for expert admiration, their attempt to derive an ideal way of life from a set social system, such works are not so remote from us today as they were from the Whig historians of literature at the beginning of this century. The breakdown of belief in the individual life as the resting-place of all real goodness has thrown a corresponding weight upon our view of the institutions and systems which contain individuals. We are in consequence more prepared today to allow the seriousness of works which show ideals of living only to be realized in highly developed and to that extent artificial societies. It has become easier for us to understand that society may seem an immutable good, a divinely appointed organism and to see that flattery can be an activity that is compatible with self-respect, being indeed only the homage that the self-aware individual pays to such a society. In more purely literary terms, we have become correspondingly uncertain of the necessity for an artist to be *original;* and it follows from this that we are more prepared to accept Imitation as a legitimate approach to creative writing. If this is so, then the hope may be justified that Lyly can now be seen as more than a mine for antiquarian research; for Lyly is par excellence both flatterer and imitator. We cannot find a way into Lyly's prose-works and plays by pretending that his worlds are real worlds in which we ourselves might live. His aim is to create a mode of life which is so witty, so poised, so brilliant that we are flattered by being thought refined enough to forget real life and enjoy its ideals of love and honour; of these the characters are only mouthpieces, and these the works assume without argument to be desirable. A modern audience does not bring such assumptions to the work, but the aspiration to a life of witty elegance is sufficiently general to give us at least a point of entry.

I have suggested that the natural approach to Lyly lies through the society for which he wrote, and whose ideals he reflected. I argue also that his works stand at the end of a tradition of courtly entertainment and relate to the general entertainments or literature of Shakespeare or Marlowe only to the extent to which the terms of one tradition can be translated into another. Both of these suggestions depend for their plausibility on an understanding of the traditional notions about art and entertainment which governed the thinking of court artists and of the court itself in Tudor times. If we cannot approach Lyly through the understanding that an appreciation of Shakespeare gives to us, we must try to approach him through the tradition of what is called Humanism.

I am reluctant to use this word since it raises the fearsome question, "What is Humanism?" a question within whose murky depths whole libraries might be sunk without affording a foothold. If we restrict ourselves to England, however, a basic description is possible: the Humanists were those who promoted and engaged in the study of Greek and of Ciceronian Latin, and, as C. S. Lewis blandly remarks, followed "the critical principles . . . which ordinarily went with these studies." Unfortunately (for definition) we cannot limit the Humanist principles to those of literary criticism. Humanism, like any other seriously pursued discipline, was a way of life, defining itself by its violent antipathy to other ways of life; in this case the obvious enemy was the medieval attitude to contemplation, with its accompanying views on the function of study in *this* world, and on the purpose of elegance and order in the mind.

From this point of view the Humanist movement was, it is true, part of a general movement of secularization; but it seems an error, as far as England is concerned, to think of it as anti-religious, or at all like the modern movement of the same name. It sought to turn religious ideals and energies towards the amelioration of life in this world and to achieve an order in this life corresponding to the religious vision of man's worth. The ideals of civility were in most cases based on the civilization of pagan antiquity, but this did not seem to them to require an abandonment of Christian conscience. It is absurd to call English Humanism "pseudo-humanism—not pagan, but Christian" (as J. A. Gee does in his life of Lupset [p. 29]), not only because the humanism of Pico and Ficino shows the same bias (and if theirs is not the true Humanism, whose is?), but because there was, in fact, no contradiction between the classical literary enthusiasms of Erasmus, Melanchthon or More and their enthusiasm for a renewed and purified Christianity. They saw themselves as freeing religion from a cloistered uselessness, a concentration on theory coupled to an ignorance of practice, and there is a lot to be said on their side. Mighty though their admiration was for Greek clarity and Roman civility they had no doubt that they themselves had a basic advantage over their classical forebears in the revelation of Christian truth.

It is only in the context of this practical Christianity that their untiring pursuit of the faded elegancies of Ciceronian Latin can be seen in correct perspective. The desire for elegance, urbanity and that sophistication which instinctively recognizes the *mot juste* was part of their desire for order in this world as a whole, an order which would show itself in its fulness only when Ciceronian urbanity controlled philosophical senates or philosopher-kings and created a state where the Christian potentialities of man could be realized, where the *vita contemplativa* of the saint could enrich and enlarge the *vita activa* of the statesman. Christ himself, Richard Pace pointed out, could be seen as the type of the Humanist, for He was not only saintly but also practical, using persuasive eloquence to impart His message; this example (together with that of the Evangelists and the Fathers) imposed an obligation to do the like on all Christians:[20] "to this [end] all men are born and of nature brought forth: to commune such gifts as be to them given, each one to the profit of other (Starkey, p. 22); [for] virtue and learning, not communed to other is like unto riches heaped in corners never applied to the use of other" (ibid. p. 24). Eloquence and Rhetoric are simply the means of carrying out this duty of communication most efficiently;[21] and it was as such it was taught in the grammar schools: "so as to work in themselves [the pupils] a greater love of the virtue and hatred of the vice, and to be able with soundness of reason to draw others to their opinion" (Brinsley, *Ludus Literarius* [ed. Campagnac], p. 175).

The aim, as can be seen, was high, and the programme coherent;

but there was a fatal weakness in the position. Since Humanism was concerned to point spiritual energies and enthusiasms into this world and so to ameliorate its condition, it deprived the scholar of his natural refuge in contempt of the practical world. For this very reason, as English history moves forward, and as the Humanists seem to move nearer to their ideal of a philosophical state, so their involvement in politics becomes more crippling; their natural instinct as scholars is to remain theorists (even if theorists of practical affairs), but the philosophy of scholarship within which they are operating keeps them from retiring altogether. Their position *vis-à-vis* any opportunist politician (like Wolsey or Henry VIII) who wished to use them as official apologists was thus fatally weak, and was ruthlessly exploited; but in spite of this, the possibility of affecting human destiny in a *real* (as against a theoretical) way remained a powerful myth for humanists, from Wolsey to Milton and beyond. Certainly the history of English Humanism can be seen as an exercise in the myth of the political effectiveness of learning: we see Wolsey, Cromwell, Henry, Edward and the young Elizabeth, each for a different purpose, requiring the Humanists to use their talents in the preparation of policy statements and the persuasion of other countries. It is only by the middle of Elizabeth's reign that government becomes sure enough of itself to dispense with their sometimes embarrassing services; by this time, however, the myth of state-service as the natural end of a training in the humanities is so well established that the up-and-coming literati cannot escape from it: it controls the outlook and attitudes of a man like John Lyly, and to understand the course his life took as well as the mode in which he wrote we must trace something of its development in England.

The first generation of Englishmen who studied Greek and Latin in the new Italian manner was, inevitably, a medieval generation. Grey, Gunthorpe, Free, Flemming, Sellyng—that choice band of pioneers one can read about in Professor Roberto Weiss's *Humanism in England during the fifteenth century* (1941)—were all ecclesiastics, and their careers remained ecclesiastical: two became bishops, two became deans and one became a prior, but this can hardly be said to be a direct consequence of their knowledge of Greek. They founded no schools and left no clear tradition, and it has required modern scholarship to unearth their very names. In a tenuous way one may say there was some continuity: Sellyng taught Linacre, and Linacre is the eldest of the next generation of humanists and the "studiorum praeceptor" of Thomas More; but the demands on humanism were so altered by the historical developments of the sixteenth century that the earlier experience of Greek studies could have little to say to the later.

The next generation—of Linacre, Grocyn, Latimer, Fisher, Fox, More, Colet and William Lily, to which one may annexe the extraterritorial name of Erasmus, is the generation of pedagogues; most of these men seem to have been in orders of some kind, but their lives, and their fame now, centre upon their founding, organizing, establishing instruments of the new learning—Corpus Christi College in Oxford, St Paul's School, The Royal College of Physicians—and their elaboration of programmes and curricula. These foundations and programmes have, moreover, a severely practical aim—none the less pious for that. They aim to make learning more useful and to create in consequence an elite in learning to replace the feudal aristocracy now going rapidly out of date, and already out of key with the Tudor absolutism. The story told by Richard Pace—himself a product of humanist advancement—is well known, but is worth repeating again, so typical is it of this development.

> A nobleman of this time in contempt of learning said that it was for noblemen's sons enough to wind their horn and carry their hawk fair and to leave study and learning to the children of mean men. To whom . . . Richard Pace replied, "Then you and other noblemen must be content that your children may wind their horns and keep their hawks, while the children of mean men do manage matters of estate." (Camden's *Remains* (1605), p. 220)

There is an interesting variant in the last sentence here from the Latin which Camden is paraphrasing. Pace himself writes

> nam si veniret ad regem aliquis vir exterus quales sunt principum oratores, et ei dandum ei responsum, filius tuus sic ut tu vis, institutus, inflaret duntaxat cornu et rusticorum filii docti ad respondendum vocarent. (p. 15)

> for if some foreigner, such as are the ambassadors of princes, come to the king and a reply has to be given to him, your son, educated as you desire, may blow his horn, but it is the learned sons of mean men that are called to make the reply.

One of the most obvious uses of Ciceronian Latin was in the diplomatic service, and the Humanists were much employed as ambassadors (*oratores*). The capacity to pronounce royal messages was of course only a part of the New Learning. More important was the capacity to think out the proper content for such messages. Wolsey's foundation, Cardinal's College in Oxford, and Cromwell's (and later, Henry's) support of English scholars on the continent were aimed at a flexibility of mind and width of political and social experience so that the new world of secular law and centralized administration would not have to rely on minds entirely unprepared for it.[22] By the time of the third generation of Humanists the original impulse towards a secular piety was already being distorted by court necessities into shapes that seem to bear little likeness to their originals. By the time we reach John Lyly the Humanist impulse is so strangely altered that we would not recognize it, were it not for the clear line that carries down this far.

To study the debt that John Lyly owes to this tradition it is not necessary to go outside the history of his own family. John's grandfather and the founder of the family's scholastic fortunes was William Lily,[23] who was born in Odiham, in Hampshire, in or about 1468. We know nothing of his parentage or early life, but Anthony à Wood tells us that William Grocyn, one of the foremost scholars of the time, was his godfather; it was this cause that led Grocyn to leave Lily the sum of five shillings in his will (*Oxford Collectanea* II); and we may assume that Lily did not come from totally undistinguished stock. Like Grocyn himself, Lily went to Magdalen College, Oxford, which had been recently founded by William of Waynfleet and now served as one of the principal nurseries of Humanist learning. The same college was the home of Linacre, Grocyn (who was Divinity Reader there), Thomas Starkey, Cardinal Pole, and probably of John Colet, who was at Oxford at the same time as Lily. In 1486 Lily entered as a Demy of Magdalen; it has been suggested that he was one of those Demies who were to apply themselves "so long to grammatical and poetical and other humane arts that they could not only profit themselves but be able also to instruct and educate others"—that is, that he worked as a grammar master in Magdalen School.[24]

Like the other Humanists, Lily completed his education by travelling to the Mediterranean,[25] which he did in 1488-1492. Before attending to the secular pursuit of learning, he visited the Holy places in Jerusalem. On his return from Jerusalem he stayed some time in Rhodes where he learned Greek, no doubt as the pupil of one of the many learned refugees who had fled from Byzantium to the protection of the knights of St John, there established. From Greek in Rhodes he seems to have passed to Ciceronian Latin (the other hallmark of Humanist learning) in Italy. He studied in Rome and Venice and had as instructors Giovanni Sulpicio (Sulpicius Verulanus) and Julius Pomponius Laetus [Sabinus] (also known as Pomponio Leto). This former teacher may almost be supposed to have provided a model for Lily's own career, for he was the author of a celebrated Latin grammar and of a *Carmen Iuvenilis de Moribus*, just as Lily was to be. In view of the close relationship that was to grow up between the English grammar schools and the English drama it may be worth noticing that Pomponio Leto (also a grammarian[26]) is said to have been the first modern European to stage the works of Plautus and Terence, which he did at his Roman Academy from 1471 onward.

In making this Grand Tour of Learning, Lily was following in the footsteps of Grocyn (who had returned to Oxford in 1491 to become the first teacher of Greek in the University); in Rome he had as his companions a choice band of scholars including Linacre, Colet, William Warham, and Christopher Bambridge.[27] He is still in the same circle when he returns to England. We do not know what he is doing in this period: he is presented with a living which he subsequently resigns; he marries a certain Agnes, and we must suppose from this that he never went further than minor orders. In 1504 he is passing his time with Grocyn, Linacre and Thomas More in London, and More refers to him as his "dearest friend." Grocyn was at this time Rector of St Lawrence Jewry and was lecturing in St Paul's on the *Celestial Hierarchies* (still generally taken in this period to be the work of that Dionysius that St Paul met, though Grocyn (characteristically) came to have doubts).[28] More, no doubt under Grocyn's auspices, had been lecturing about the same time on St Augustine's *City of God*. The combination of piety and learning that is evident in these activities was much to the taste of William Lily but we do not know if he was engaged in any kind of teaching at this time. The instinct which had taken Lily to Jerusalem and was to carry More to martyrdom showed itself in the devotions which the two of them undertook in this period among the Carthusians in London. The taste for religious austerity as well as classical wit which makes

More's character a puzzle to many moderns seems to have been shared with William Lily. The two men also competed in translations from the Greek Anthology.[29]

As far as the history of English Humanism goes, the crucial event of these years is the decision of Colet (Dean of St Paul's since 1504) to devote his patrimony to the foundation of a new school; this would embody in its curriculum the new Humanist ideals of elegant Latin and ethical Greek. As early as 1508 he began building in the southeast corner of St Paul's churchyard, and he also set about looking for a man "whole in body, honest and virtuous, and learned in the good and clean Latin literature and also in Greek, if such may be gotten; a wedded man, a single man or a priest that hath no benefice . . ." to serve as headmaster. He found his man in William Lily, one who was, says Polydore Virgil, "a man such as Horace speaks of *integer vitae scelerisque purus*."[30] Lily was officially appointed as the first High Master of St Paul's School in 1510. It seems probable that by 1509 Lily and Colet were already collaborating in a new Latin grammar. In 1509 Colet produced his *Aeditio* (accidence) and it must have been about the same time that he requested Lily to write a syntax more advanced than the *Rudiments* which Lily had already written (it would seem). Lily wrote his syntax, Erasmus revised it and the *De Constructione* as it was called appeared anonymously at some date which we can hardly guess at (since the first surviving edition is dated 1527).[31] In spite of the modesty, which prevented either author from claiming the work of the other, Lily's name became attached to the whole collection of these separate parts, and "Lily's Grammar" carried his fame down through the eighteenth century.

The aim of "Lily's Grammar" was an extremely humane one: to take the pupils as quickly as possible to classical *literature* by cutting down to a minimum the rules that had to be learned. Set against the old method of "Vulgars,"[32] the grammar of St Paul's was something like a "direct method" approach to Latin; years later (1570) Roger Ascham was still complaining about the "Vulgars" of Horman and Whittington, which had allowed the pupils to approach classical Latinity via a dog-Latin which aped the order of English. Such an approach offended the Humanist conscience which saw elegant Latinity as a state of grace, not to be debased or vulgarized.[33] For this reason the framework of grammar is always to appear secondary and supplementary; ". . . all the varieties and diversities and changes in Latin speech (which be innumerable) if any man will know, and by

that knowledge attain to understand Latin books, and to speak and
to write the clean Latin, let him above all busily learn and read good
Latin authors of chosen poets and orators, and note wisely how they
wrote and spake, and study alway to follow them, desiring none other
rules but their examples. For in the beginning men spake not Latin
because such rules were made, but contrariwise because men spake
such Latin upon that followed the rules were made. That is to say,
Latin speech was before the rules, not the rules before the Latin
speech. Wherefore, well-beloved masters and teachers of grammar,
after the parts of speech sufficiently known in your schools, read and
expound plainly unto your scholars good authors, and show to them
every word, and in every sentence what they shall note and observe,
warning them busily to follow and to do like both in writing and in
speaking, and be to them your own self also speaking with them the
pure Latin very present, and leave the rules." (Colet's epilogue to his
Accidence).[34] Colet's almost clinical concern with "cleanness" of
Latinity is very evident in this extract and is embodied in the statutes
which he drew up for St Paul's.

> As touching in this school what shall be taught of the masters
> and learned of the scholars it passeth my wit to devise and de-
> termine in particular, but in general to speak and somewhat to
> say my mind, I would they were taught alway in good litera-
> ture both Latin and Greek, and good auctors such as have the
> very Roman eloquence joined with wisdom, specially Christian
> auctors that wrote their wisdom with clean and chaste Latin
> either in verse or in prose; for my intent is by this school spe-
> cially to increase knowledge and worshipping of God and our
> Lord Christ Jesu and good Christian life and manners in the
> children. And for that intent I will the children learn first
> above all the Catechism in English and after, the accidence that
> I made, or some other if any be better to the purpose, to induce
> children more speedily to Latin speech. And then *Institutum
> Christiani Hominis* which that learned Erasmus made at my
> request and the book called *Copia* of the same Erasmus. And
> then other auctors Christian, as Lactantius, Prudentius, and
> Proba and Sedulius and Juvencus and Baptista Mantuanus and
> such other as shall be taught, convenient and most to purpose
> unto the true Latin speech. All barbary, all corruption, all Latin
> adulterate which ignorant blind fools brought into this world,

and with the same hath distained and poisoned the old Latin
speech and the very Roman tongue which in the time of Tully
and Sallust and Virgil and Terence was used, which also Saint
Jerome and Saint Ambrose and Saint Austin and many holy
doctors learned in their times—I say that filthiness and all such
abusion which the later blind world brought in, which more
rather may be called bloterature than literature I utterly aban-
ish and exclude out of this school and charge the masters that
they teach alway that is the best and instruct the children in
Greek and reading Latin, in reading unto them such auctors
that hath with wisdom joined the pure chaste eloquence.
(Lupton's *Life of Colet,* p. 279 f.)

This passionate concern with wisdom of subject matter and "chastity" of expression, leading to the position, as C. S. Lewis somewhat
unfairly remarks, that "the boys were to be guarded from every
word that did not occur in Virgil or Cicero, and equally from every
idea that did" (*16th century literature,* p. 160) was a direct reflection
of the educational philosophy of Erasmus; for him, "All knowledge
falls into one of two divisions: the knowledge of 'truths' and the
knowledge of 'words' . . . They are not to be commended who, in
their anxiety to increase their store of truths, neglect the necessary
art of expressing them . . . This goes to prove that true education
includes what is best in both kinds of knowledge, taught, I must add,
under the best guidance. For, remembering how difficult it is to eradi-
cate early impressions, we should aim from the first at learning what
need never be unlearnt, and that only. Language thus claims the
first place in the order of studies . . . But I must make my conviction clear that, whilst a knowledge of the rules of accidence and
syntax is most necessary to every student, still they should be as few,
as simple, and as carefully framed as possible . . . For it is not by
learning rules that we acquire the power of speaking a language, but
by daily intercourse with those accustomed to express themselves
with exactness and refinement, and by the copious reading of the
best authors . . . Some proficiency in expression being thus attained
the student devotes his attention to the content of the ancient literatures . . . For I affirm that with slight qualification the whole of
attainable knowledge lies enclosed within the literary monuments of
ancient Greece. This great inheritance I will compare to a limpid
spring of whose undefiled waters it behoves all who truly thirst to

drink and be restored" (paraphrase of "De Ratione Studii," in Woodward, *Erasmus on Education*, pp. 162-4).

The aim of the whole process is to produce pupils who will speak
and write "pure," "clean" and "chaste" Latin of their own—the moral
connotations of these epithets are not accidental, for the clear and
elegant arrangement of words "The common word exact without vul-
garity, The formal word precise but not pedantic, The complete
consort dancing together" is seen as a symptom of an orderly mind, a
mind attuned to the orders of monarch and deity:

> Ye know not what hurt ye do to learning that care not for
> words but for matter, and so make a divorce betwixt the tongue
> and the heart. For mark all ages: look upon the whole course
> of both the Greek and Latin tongue, and ye shall surely find
> that when apt and good words began to be neglected and prop-
> erties of those two tongues to be confounded, then also began
> ill deeds to spring, strange manners to oppress good orders, new
> and fond opinions to strive with old and true doctrine, first in
> Philosophy and after in Religion, right judgment of all things
> to be perverted, and so virtue with learning is contemned and
> study left off; of ill thoughts commeth perverse judgment, of ill
> deeds springeth lewd talk, which four misorders, as they mar
> man's life, so destroy they good learning withall.
>
> But behold the goodness of God's providence for learning:
> all old authors and sects of Philosophy which were fondest in
> opinion and rudest in utterance, as Stoics and Epicures, first
> contemned of wise men and after forgotten of all men, be so
> consumed by times as they be now not only out of use but also
> out of memory of man; which thing, I surely think, will shortly
> chance to the whole doctrine and all the books of phantastical
> Anabaptists and Friars and of the beastly Libertines and Monks.
>
> Again behold on the other side how God's wisdom hath
> wrought, that of the Academici and Peripatetici, those that
> were wisest in judgment of matters and purest in uttering their
> minds, the first and chiefest that wrote most and best in either
> tongue, as Plato and Aristotle in Greek, Tully in Latin, be so
> either wholly or sufficiently left unto us as I never knew yet
> scholar that gave himself to like and love and follow chiefly
> those three authors, but he proved both learned, wise and also
> an honest man, if he joined withal the true doctrine of God's

> holy Bible, without the which the other three be but fine-edge
> tools in a fool or madman's hand.   (Ascham, *The Schoolmaster*
> [ed. Arber], p. 118 f.)

The Humanist schoolmasters were relying rather heavily, we may
suppose, on God's providence for learning,[35] but it was this supposition indeed that gave their educational programme its drive and
dynamic: the "bloterature" of the Middle Ages, the product of minds
divorced from secular reality and caught in the tenuous web of their
own cunning, was at a furthest remove from the luminous certainty
and order of Christ's life upon earth dwelt on so heavily in its literal
meaning in Colet's epoch-making lectures on St Paul;[36] to recover
the primitive harmony between wit and wisdom, word and truth,
seen in the early Fathers as in Christ, was a work of piety indeed, a
true *Imitatio Christi*.

It was in this spirit that Colet's school was dedicated to the boy
Jesus; Erasmus describes[37] how there was "an excellent picture of the
boy Jesus, seated in the attitude of one teaching, over the headmaster's chair, to which all the boys sing a (Latin) hymn as they enter
and leave the school":

> Sweet Jesus, my Lord, who as a boy in the twelfth year of
> thine age didst dispute in the temple at Jerusalem among the
> doctors so that they all marvelled and were amazed at thy most
> excellent wisdom, I beg thee that in this thy school, of which
> thou art governor and patron, in which I daily learn letters and
> wisdom, I may chiefly come to know thee, Jesus, who art thy-
> self the true wisdom, and then through that knowledge come to
> worship and imitate thee . . .[38]

It may seem a long way from irregular verbs to our heavenly home,
but to these Humanist educators the distance could be expressed simply as the distance from the bottom rung of a ladder to the top. The
ladder itself bore the name of Imitation, and the stages by which the
scholar mounted from grammar and rhetoric to rectitude and Grace is
expressed with logal clarity by the schoolmaster, William Kempe:

> all knowledge is taught generally both by precepts of art and
> also by practice of the same precepts. They are practised partly
> by observing examples of them in other men's works, and partly
> by making somewhat of our own, and that first by imitation,

> and at length without imitation; so that the perfection of the
> art is not gotten at the first, but *Per numeros veniunt ista gradus-*
> *que suos.* Wherefore first the scholar shall learn the precepts;
> secondly he shall learn to note the examples of the precepts in
> unfolding other men's works; thirdly, to imitate the examples
> in some work of his own; fourthly and lastly, to make some-
> what alone without an example. Now, all these kinds of teaching
> are seen in every special sort of the things taught, be it Grammar,
> Logic, Rhetoric, Arithmetic, Geometry, or any other art.   (*The*
> *Education of Children* (1588), sig. F2)

The pious aims of the founder of St Paul's and the pious nature of
the first headmaster could not have allowed the ladder of Imitation
to have stopped at this point. For them, as for Erasmus, the end of
education is *sapiens et eloquens pietas*,[39] active Christian virtue rendered effective in the service of the community by the power to
write and to speak. *Propositum a nobis est sapientem atque eloquen-*
tem pietatem finem esse studiorum, is the definition that Johannes
Sturm, the German pedagogue so much respected in England, gives
of his aims (*De literarum ludis* (1538), p. 104). More himself uses
the traditional defence of secular study when he writes his letter to
the University of Oxford, putting down the "Trojan" or anti-Greek
movement there.[40] He points out how secular learning can be justified because it prepares the mind for virtue, and can be used as a
road towards the awareness of things supernatural; moreover it enables the theologian to reach into and control the minds of other
people, by giving into his hands the techniques of the poets and
orators of antiquity. From this point of view the secular content of
the authors used to teach eloquence hardly mattered, given the methods by which they were taught. As one advanced up the ladder of
imitation, any grossness in Terence or Lucian could be purged away,
as in the ladder of Platonic love the grosser passions are lost in the
contemplation of the soul and the deity. Colet, it is true, does not
mention secular authors in his statutes quoted above, but he is specifically avoiding anything like a list of set books (which, he says,
"it passeth my wit to devise"). He writes to Erasmus in 1512 that "a
bishop . . . took our school to task, and said that I had founded
. . . a house of Idolatry. I believe that he said this, because the Poets
are read there."[41] As T. W. Baldwin remarks in quoting this passage,
"the objector was certainly not referring to the 'Christian Poets,'

which some have supposed were the only poets to be taught at Paul's" (*Small Latine*, I, 78). It was indeed inevitable that "the very Roman [or Greek] eloquence" would have to be taught out of unChristian (though not unethical) authors, but it could be taught in such a Christian perspective that all the major authors turned out to have had *mentes naturaliter Christianae*. If, as Ascham suggests (and he was reasonably typical), outward eloquence is a sign of inward grace, then the study and the acquisition of eloquence could hardly have a bad effect. The figure of Cicero—that archetypal *novus homo*—promoting public virtue and putting down public vice by the power of his philosophical eloquence, was one that remained central to the education of the whole period.

How far it could remain central to the lives of those who, like Cicero, had actual experience of politics, is another matter. If Colet's own experience is any indication, the relation between apostolic virtue and practical politics is apt to be a little strained. While Henry VIII was preparing for war in 1513, Colet was invited to preach the Good Friday sermon at court. Like Erasmus, Colet thought that the wars of kings were insane folly and in his sermon he praised the victory of Christ as the only victory worth winning; he pointed out the difficulty of Christian conduct in time of war, and spoke much to discourage the intending soldiers.

After an interview with Henry, however, it is said that the good Dean then preached another sermon, praising a defensive war such as the king was about to undertake. If this story is true, it is not surprising that Henry should have remarked, "Let every man have his own doctor, and everyone follow his liking; but this is the doctor for me."[42] All the flexibility of mind that Humanist training could impart was needed by those who came close to the centres of power.

William Lily died of plague in 1523 and was succeeded in his High Mastership by John Rightwise who succeeded also to his daughter Dionysia (Lily's will suggests that this was not achieved without compulsion). She, keeping the family and school traditions well aligned, subsequently married James Jacob, the school Usher, and so procured for John Lyly a set of uncles and aunts with names like Polydore and Scholastica. But though the family continued to be what Feuillerat has called it, *"une famille d'érudits,"* the heroic quality of *making* traditions disappears from the scholastic world. Rightwise, says Anthony à Wood, was the most distinguished grammarian of his day (he means in England). He revised Lily's poem on the gender of nouns, and added a vocabulary to it. He took a troop of children to present a Morality before Henry VIII, and he may have writen a play (*Dido*) which was performed at Cambridge.[43] He led a useful and distinguished life, but it was the life of a follower rather than a leader. The ladder of Imitation has been planted in the schools of the country; interest passes to the question of how it is to be used by those who have to implement the ideals of Humanism in life rather than in school. The pupils of Humanism look abroad for the power that has been promised to the eloquent man, and in looking are transformed.

The career of William Lily's eldest surviving son, George, illustrates neatly and conveniently the opportunities and problems that beset the next order of Humanists. George followed his father to Magdalen in 1528 but left the University without taking a degree; and he next appears at Padua in 1534 as a member of the learned household which was assembling round Reginald Pole, the young scholarly kinsman of Henry VIII; he studied law at Padua, having as his companions men whose future was to lie in state service, such as Richard Morison, Henry Cole (who preached the funeral sermon over the dying Latimer and Ridley), Thomas Starkey and Thomas Lupset.

Pole had been sent abroad with a very generous (indeed unheard of) allowance from the king, not only because he was of the blood royal but because the Humanistic disciplines were acquiring so much importance in politics that one might expect money spent in this way to repay interest in diplomatic advantages. Pole's clients can be seen no less, though less directly, as investments by the state. Padua was not only the home of Pietro Bembo and the high-polished Ciceronian style but also of the Civil Law and of the sceptical and libertine views of Pomponazzi and Zabarella.[44] Men educated there were in a strong position to view English customs and traditions with intellectual detachment, and so to understand the purposes of a minister like Thomas Cromwell with some sympathy. Thomas Starkey tells us of himself,

> because my purpose then was to live in a politic life, I set my-self now these last years past to the knowledge of the Civil Law, that I might thereby make a more stable and sure judgment of the politic order and customs used among us here in our country . . . ever having in mind this end and purpose at

the last in this commonalty, where I am brought forth and
born, to employ them to some use.[45]

Starkey matriculated into political service by writing for Cromwell
an exercise on "what is policy, after the sentence [*opinion*] of Aristotle." Humanist education begins to appear as if its function were to
liberate the mind from the traditional and instinctive morality of
Christian societies. One can see how this distortion of the original
impulse came about. It has been remarked that Erasmus' advice to
Princes suffers from "a detachment and lack of concreteness which
often stood in the way of a practical application of his ideas" (Caspari, p. 76), and this would seem to be true of the whole circle of
early Humanists. They formulated theories and principles of action
in this world, constructed Utopias of statecraft, but they sought to
avoid too close or precise a reference to the world of national action.
But the great debate on religion, sharpened in England by the king's
"great matter" of divorce, presented the problem in a way which
they could hardly evade. Faced by the necessity, More and Fisher
chose the road to martyrdom, but noble though their sacrifice was, it
was not in itself a Humanist act; it could provide no lessons in be-
haviour for the next generation—the generation of Starkey, Pole and
George Lily. It has been suggested[46] that there was no real continuity
in the principles of Humanism, that Henry's executions and depriva-
tions broke the tradition; but though the tradition only survived in an
altered and perhaps a diminished form, the movement from theory
to practice was implicit in the original impulse, and brought its tensions and potentialities to a sharper focus. Morison, Cheke, Smith,
Cole, Ponet, Ascham etc. not only survived themselves, but passed on
a living, flexible and relevant tradition to the Elizabethans, capable
of being applied to the great days of the Queen.

The debate whether or not learning should emerge from the cloister into the immediate political arena, which takes such a large part
of Starkey's *Dialogue between Pole and Lupset* and of the actual life
of Pole, had to be answered decisively when the monarch required it;
the nicely balanced ambiguities of Erasmus were almost possible in
a cosmopolitan and peripatetic scholar, but were not at all open to
patriotic Englishmen under the Tudors. William Lily and John Colet
died in time to avoid the question, but their gravity and sweet other-
worldliness could not have saved them from having to answer it.
Even exile, as the career of Pole (and of his secretary, George Lily)

shows, provided no shelter from the choice between the political life of schemes and shifts and the *vita contemplativa*, with its negation of Humanist involvement in *this* world. Those who persisted in the noble humanist aim "To make all the land know *quam sit humaniter vivendum*, help to take out all barbarous customs, and bring the realm to an antique form of good living"[47] had to push their effort through the narrowing alleyways of Reformation diplomacy, and were inevitably deprived of the wide and luminous views of More and Erasmus; but it might be argued that the necessity forced them to restate their humane view in terms which were more concrete, more real and hence more poetic.

The "refocussing" of Humanist idealism on national politics certainly meant some dislocation of the learned tradition. This was not because the Humanist dream of educating the nobility had failed but rather because it had succeeded. At Elizabeth's accession we find among the memoranda of parliament "that an ordinance be made to bind the nobility to bring up their children in learning at some university . . . the wanton bringing-up and ignorance of the nobility forces the Prince to advance new men" (H.M.C. Salisbury, I. 163). But the marriage of statecraft and learning was not one that was immediately fruitful of good. For one thing it meant a continual interference in the universities by royal favourites and interested politicians, and a loss of certainty about what learning was meant to do. This is the burden of Thomas Cooper's complaint, in the dedication of his great *Thesarus* (1565) to Leicester (Chancellor of Oxford University):

> For that kind of life which was formerly proposed, in its dignity and greatness, as a reward for the labours of the studious, is now either (as many people hope) being debased to ignominy, or else (as the impious expect) to imminent disaster. The result is that parents, seeking the advantage of their own, prescribe other disciplines for their children; and the children themselves judge rather by popular esteem than by the inherent dignity of the matter; and so they prefer to pursue whatever they find easy rather than endure the daily grind of studying, without any aim in sight. Hence it is that the Universities and public schools have been promptly abandoned by the best minds; and of those who were well educated as children but few are anxious to penetrate into the depth of things—except for those who go on to study law or medicine. The rest give up their studies

and betake themselves to the life of a courtier, or devote themselves to the law of the land [at the Inns of Court] or withdraw
to some other kind of pastime, which they think will prove
more profitable. For this reason, the priests of the Christian
religion and those very learned men in whose hands lies the
present administration of the church complain (it seems to me
with justice) that there is destitution everywhere in the
churches, causing incredible detriment to the flourishing of
the Gospel; and that poverty is the lot of those who take up the
preaching of the Divine Covenant, who fulfil the duties of the
church and who exercise the other functions of pious eloquence
[*literatae pietatis*]. For though certain honour and great reward
is promised to those who undertake functions in the state; the
lot of rectors in churches and masters in schools is contempt
rather than praise. No wonder if many are found seeking glory
and dignity, but few following virtue and learning when these
are joined with shame.

Cooper goes on to suppose that Leicester with Burghley (Chancellor
of Cambridge) and the Queen will shortly reform this state of affairs,
and his flattery was sufficiently persuasive to cause him to sprout into
a bishopric in a very short time; but the supposition that anyone
could understand the situation well enough to alter it fundamentally
is not justified. The Humanist assumption that learning could teach
a man how to live piously in the world of politics could not bring
with it the creation of a learned Civil Service, and nothing less than
this kind of Gladstonian Humanism could have cured the ills that
Cooper complains of.

What is clear, in Cooper as elsewhere, is that the Humanist dream
forced the learned into dependence on a court which did not really
need them. Elizabeth's court remained, throughout its history, a
largely medieval pageant of royal bounty and chivalric allegiance.
The progressive and intellectual elements in the country were gradually squeezed into Puritan opposition which had as little time for
eloquent classicizing as had the politicians. Yet the dream that the
centre of power was the natural home of learning and eloquence was
by now so ingrained that it was not to be denied; reluctance to enter
the Church, together with inability to find any other niche for learning was the common lot of those Elizabethans who made the "pilgrimage from Parnassus,"[48] John Lyly among them. Lyly was at least
able to indulge his dream in his writing:

In universities virtue and vices are but shadowed in colours,
white and black; in courts showed to life, good and bad. There,
times past are read of in old books, times present set down by
new devices, times to come conjectured at by aim, by prophecy
or chance. Here are times in perfection, not by device as fables,
but in execution as truths. Believe me, Pandion, in Athens you
have but tombs, we in court the bodies; you the pictures of
Venus and the wise Goddesses, we the persons and the virtues.
What hath a scholar found out by study that a courtier hath
not found out by practice? (*Sapho and Phao*, I. ii. 12-21)

The careers of William Lily and George Lily might seem to us
almost like object lessons in the futility of the Humanist dream of
learning as politically effective. But we cannot expect the process of
living to look like this from the inside. We can hardly doubt that the
pressure of family tradition on John Lyly was such that he was driven
along the same paths of expectation, regardless of the fact that the
situation about 1575, when he left Oxford, was radically different
from that about 1488, when William Lily went down, or from that
about 1533, when George Lily left. By 1575 the scholastic innovations of the first had become a matter of routine mediocrity, though
occasionally a schoolmaster (like Richard Mulcaster) could still make
a mark; by 1575, no less, the pressing cry for learning to aid the state
had died down. The court of Elizabeth had established a mode of
life which was able to use the Humanistic training without depending upon it.

Elizabeth was in many ways a Humanist herself, as her father had
been before her: she could translate from Greek and she could make
a speech in Ciceronian Latin. But with her, as with him, the gloss of
Humanist ideals accompanied other and probably more fundamental
interests, and other more empirical modes of judgment. Anyone who
approached the Tudor court supposing that it was another Florentine
Academy was liable to a series of rude shocks.

In fact, hardly anyone (except a constitutional eccentric like Gabriel Harvey) was foolish enough to apply to any Renaissance court
the full Ciceronian expectation of the *novus homo*. Long before
Elizabeth's reign the Humanist ideal had shrunk to that of "the
courtier"[49] who was required, within a certain elegant and disdainful
playfulness of manner (what Castiglione calls *sprezzatura*), to have
some knowledge of classical authors. But the courtier was to use his
learning as decoration, not as part of his belief; he was the servant of

his breeding and his sovereign, not of his understanding. And in the end, the Humanist's and the courtier's interests pointed in different directions. The Humanist admired peace, good government and the placid life of study; the courtier must praise war and honour. The Humanist inherited the learned tradition of misogyny, and the courtier the medieval conventions of Courtly Love. It was the Humanist's duty to remain detached and quizzical, the courtier's to lay down his life at his sovereign's feet. Thus the tradition of practical learning and ethical preoccupation which brought the Humanists to the court was met with a requirement that they use their literary gifts and forget their ideals, that they abandon their internationalist, pacific and misogynist impulses and become the encomiasts of tournaments, of hunting, and of amorous dalliance. The asceticism of the scholar was met by a demand that he praise license and display. Petrarch could complain, "Where do we read that Cicero or Scipio jousted?",[50] but this reaction was hardly open to the Tudor court entertainer. He could only achieve success by arranging a temporary union between the two traditions; and it was here that the "wit" of which I have spoken was so valuable to the writers. Looking at the courtly writings of John Lyly we can see how wit is used to keep the author detached from the courtly passions of his creatures. Euphues tastes the pleasures of the metropolis, but he soon returns to his university, able to see such a life for what it is, and so to advise Livia to abjure the court. His vision of courtly love is sympathetic, but again detached by wit. He balances misogyny against adoration, "places" his flattery by its exaggeration, and throughout remains witty enough to avoid being identified with any of the views he puts forward.

The difficulties that the Humanist attitude to life and letters produced in the late Renaissance period are writ large and documented fully in the life of Lyly's contemporary and enemy, Gabriel Harvey. Harvey was born of prosperous burgher stock and went to the local grammar school; from there, as a brilliant pupil, he was sent to Cambridge, where senior, politically oriented Humanists, Sir Thomas Smith and Sir Walter Mildmay, helped to pay his expenses. At Cambridge Harvey showed the combination of brilliance and truculency which is commonly a feature of the upstart scholar, pulled up by his brains from an obscure background; this unbalance of temperament serves to magnify for our inspection the tensions which were present in the Humanist outlook in any case.

Harvey took his education, with pathological singlemindedness, to be a means of getting nearer to the life of power and becoming what he calls a "curtisan politique" [a politically influential courtier]. Like Starkey and many another Humanist, his hopes of preferment made him transfer his career from theology to the civil law: "being willed by my friends and set on by others' example to determine with myself to what kind of study I were best to betake me to, and having a great good liking of the Civil Law, which I know to be so highly commended of the worthiest of men, and namely of Tully . . ." (*Letter Book*, p. 162).

But Harvey's contacts with the court, when he actually made them, were (like other poor scholars') a disappointment to him. Little (or at any rate, too little) attention was paid to his gifts of intellect; he had not the power of waiting till some great person deigned to notice him; he thrust himself forward in a series of much pondered-on, but ill-timed and tactless devices, and the court soon showed that it could do without his intellect more easily than he could do without its glamour: "He that most patronized him [*probably Leicester*], prying more searchingly into him and finding that he was more meet to make sport with than any way deeply to be employed, with fair words shook him off, and told him he was fitter for the University than for the court or his turn, and so bade God prosper his studies, and sent for another secretary to Oxford" (Nashe, III. 79). This is the portrait of an enemy and we need not take the details (especially the *Zuleika Dobson*-like conclusion) too seriously; but it is certain enough that Harvey failed in the very point that his doctrines told him was crucial:

il pensare non importa, ma il fare.   (*Marginalia*, p. 141)

His Humanist belief that the *vita activa* was the natural end of study deprived him even of the pleasures of contemplation which Spenser's sonnet imputes to him

> that sitting like a looker-on
> Of this world's stage, dost note with critique pen
> The sharpe dislikes of each condition
> . . .
> And the evil damning evermore to die.
> For Life and Death is in thy doomful writing;
> So thy renown lives ever by inditing.

Frustrated of the Humanist's chief end he was reduced to communicating furiously to the margins of his books those beliefs by whose
light he himself stood condemned: "Any serviceable point, either
civil, courtly or militar, is very soon learned by art and practice"
(*Marginalia,* p. 89). "Visible flattery is abject and unworthy of a
gentleman; invisible flattery a matter of skill and suited for men of
affairs" (ibid. p. 56). But even as he did so, the would-be man of
action slid from one college fellowship to another, and so out of fellowship, landing up eventually in medicine, which was of dubious
social status, and certainly well off the imaginary highway which led
from the University to the Privy Council.

The obsessive quality of Harvey's temperament makes the tensions
in the Humanist position especially obvious, but I think that the same
tensions existed for other men, and can be seen specifically in the life
of John Lyly. Lyly had poise enough to make literature out of his
situation between the court and the university; I shall argue below
that this provides a principal interest of *Euphues,* and it appears also
in *Campaspe* and *Sapho and Phao;* but the supposition that literature
is a kind of courtship display of general secular capacity[51] informs
and I think explains much of his life, and serves to cut him off
from such mere writers as Shakespeare. At the end of his life he
found that he had wasted his time (he had no post) and the beauty
of his literary productions (and even their fame) was no consolation
to him. The literature of the 'eighties and 'nineties is, in fact, largely
a product of frustration. As we see with the students of the Parnassus Plays, literature is only a stopgap, one stage better than divinity
perhaps, but not the real end of learning. As treatises on the (political) fruits of learning give way to defences of poetry, as the scope
open to eloquence shrinks from statecraft through polemic to mere
entertainment, so the "University Wits" of the period have to contain their sense of divine mission within the bounds of a poor pamphlet. The eventual result of this union of learning and the need for
popularity, of moral zeal and profane forms, is the greatest literature
our language has known; but it was a product that theory could
hardly account for, so opposed were the worlds it sprang from, the
worlds of Lyly and Shakespeare. For, as C. S. Lewis has pointed out,
Humanism "would have prevented, if it could"[52] the literary masterpieces at the end of the century.

The development I have been tracing can be seen also as involving the relations between wit and wisdom. Throughout the Human-

ist tradition "wit" (= cleverness) was treasured as an essential part of eloquence, always remembering what Fuller calls the "real distinction between facetiousness and nugacity" (see *D.N.B.* s.v. Toby Mathew). *Facetudo* indeed meant elegance as well as facetiousness, and was supposed to represent that courtly virtue which stands midway between flattery and aggressiveness, an essential virtue if learning was to survive in the dangerous context of power.[53] And the earliest Humanists possessed it in plenty. Before we suppose that these men were grave divines, insensible to the frivolities of art (see Feuillerat, pp. 46ff.) we should remember that the first piece of Greek translated by an Englishman was Synesius' "Praise of Baldness,"[54] and remember likewise the well documented fondness of More and Erasmus for Lucian. Erasmus defends Lucian, it is true, as the author of works *quae faciunt ad morum institutionem* (make for instruction in morals),[55] but this didactic approach is not narrow or restrictive in its effects. In fact, More and Erasmus are so sure of the place of wit in a context of learned piety that they went much further in boldness of wit than their successors dared to. When we find one of More's letters of theological controversy headed *Doctissima simul ac elegantissima. . . . Epistola in qua non minus pie quam facete . . .* [To John Bugenhagen] the combination of learning and elegance may strike us as strange, but it is not nearly as strange as the collocation of piety and facetiousness. Yet this is a combination which is displayed at large in More's life, even to his final joke on the scaffold: "I pray you, good Master Lieutenant, see me safe up; and for my coming down let me shift for myself."

So long as the study of rhetoric continued to have a central place in the learned tradition, so long did wit and didacticism continue to walk hand in hand. But the reign of Elizabeth was marked by the fact that the subject-matter that seemed proper to these Cicero-inspired Humanists—the moral condition of their own time—, and the proper audience—the executive authority of the land—were more and more denied to them. Their gift for wit finds itself isolated from their belief in wisdom; at least the wisdom that is available to them is the wisdom for private life and for individual cases. But it may be thought that the pressure to make universal statements through the evocation of precise particulars is the very soul of art.

Feuillerat's view of the scholarly gravity of William Lily and his circle yields a subsequent view that John Lyly betrayed his Humanist background by writing works which would "rather lie shut

in a lady's casket than open in a scholar's study"; *wit* which is the
subject of *Euphues* is supposed to have replaced the *wisdom* of the
early Humanists. It has been my aim to complicate this distinction to
the point of showing its insufficiency.[56] The earlier Humanists were
wits no less than the later ones; but their wit operated in a context
where it was the natural servant of wisdom aiming to be politically
effective. What the court of Elizabeth allowed was a brilliant scope
for wit coupled to a dislike of speechifying and a disdain for merely
intellectual formulations. It was not the private degeneracy of Lyly
that made a work like the *Utopia* impossible by 1575; *Euphues* did
not betray the tradition that began with the *Utopia*; but it revealed
what had happened to it. Its superficiality marks the drying up of a
tradition beneath whose notice there was developing, in the odd and
unregarded corners of the literary world, a new literary mode, which
was to supersede the old and obscure it from our gaze.

NOTES

1. I refer to the supposition that what is to be valued in the age is what
   points forward to the liberal civility of the late nineteenth century.
   See H. Butterfield, *The Whig view of history* (1931); cf. L. B.
   Smith, "The 'taste for the Tudors' since 1940," *Studies in the Renaissance* VII (1960), 167-83.

2. Thus when J. E. Neale says that "Elizabethan England should be
   regarded as a revolutionary age" (*Essays in Elizabethan history*
   (1958), p. 28) he speaks accurately enough of the *tendency*; but he
   does not describe at all (he is not seeking to) the self-consciousness
   of the period. But this can hardly be disregarded when we discuss
   writers and their relation to their background.

3. Perhaps the most uninhibited expression of what the late nineteenth
   century wanted to see in the Renaissance is given by Vernon Lee in
   her *Euphorion* (?1882) from which one may quote one sentence:
   "For the first time since Antiquity man walks free of all political and
   intellectual trammels, erect, conscious of his own thoughts, master of
   his own actions, ready to seek for truth across the ocean like Colum-
   bus, or across the heavens like Copernicus" (I. 46 f.). Against this one
   may set the fact that the Copernican hypothesis was a mathematical
   accommodation put forward by a pious monk in an effort to "save the
   appearances," or one could point to the common view that the discovery of America only revealed the baseness of man's nature. The
   widely used American college text-book, H. S. Lucas' *The Renaissance and the Reformation* (1934, 1960) is a good current example
   of these older views.

4. *Miscellaneous Works of Sir Philip Sidney,* ed. W. Gray (1860), p. 22. J. B. Black tells us how "Euphuism . . . spread like an epidemic" and how Robert Greene "broke new ground *in the right direction* with his coney-catching tracts" (second edn. p. 293 [my italics]). Legouis calls Euphuism "a disease of language" (p. 261).

5. See H. Weisinger, "The Renaissance theory of the reaction against the middle ages as a cause of the Renaissance," *Speculum* XX (1945), 461-7. The Humanist attitude is summed up in Richard Pace's comment that a monkish opponent is "non theologus sed Scotista" (*De Fructu,* p. 93). Erasmus in the Preface to his New Testament says, "Let those who like, follow the disputations of the schools, but let him who desires to be instructed rather in piety than in art of disputation first and above all apply himself to the fountain-head" [the Gospels]. In his Ratio verae theologiae (*Opera Omnia* (1703-06), V. 134) he gives a long list of the unfruitful speculations and needless subtleties of the schoolmen. This is not to deny, of course, the plain fact that most of the Renaissance attitudes are derived from the middle ages. The change was a change of emphasis. A Renaissance author writes, "If we enter into the consideration of the nature of bees, how well they are ordered in their hives; if we look into the spinning of the spider's web, if we note the members of a man's body, how well they are ordered, much more ought Reason to persuade and teach us . . . ," and so far he writes entirely in a medieval tradition, which might have gone on, ". . . teach us the Infinite Goodness and Wisdom of the Maker of all these." Actually the passage concludes, "teach us to range and bring the subjects of a good commonweal into a decent order"—which indicates clearly enough the different focus with which these same things are now seen. Cf. also E. L. Surtz, "Oxford reformers and scholasticism," S.P. XLVII (1950), 547-56.

6. Lyly speaks of "these abbey lubbers . . . which laboured till they were cold, ate till they sweat and lay in bed till their bones ached" (I. 250 f.). Abraham Fraunce speaks of ideas, "not lurking in the obscure headpieces of one or two loitering friars, but manifestly appearing in the monuments and disputations of excellent authors" (*Lawyer's Logic,* p. 2). Ascham speaks of "idle monks and wanton canons." For Idleness as the first of the Puritan sins see Louis B. Wright, *Middle class culture in Elizabethan England,* p. 256.

7. "Discourse on Sedition," printed in John Strype's *Sir John Cheke* (1705), pp. 245, 246.

8. So Erasmus instructs Charles V in his *Institution of a Christian Prince* that "there is no duty by the performance of which you can more secure the favour of God, than by making yourself a prince useful to the people" (quoted in Seebohm, *The Oxford reformers* [Everyman edn.] p. 233).

9. The locus classicus for this view is Pico della Mirandola's oration *De hominis dignitate*.

10. *Opera Omnia*, X. 1742, quoted in F. Caspari, *Humanism and social order in Tudor England* (1954), p. 39.

11. *English Literature in the Sixteenth Century* (1954), p. 53.

12. The single figure of Ralegh might serve by itself to scotch the idea that the energy of Elizabethan courtiers and seadogs operated so freely because they knew no law of constraint. Ralegh's poetry and still more obviously his *History of the World* show a mind racked by melancholy and a strong sense of the world's vanity.

13. Cf. Legouis, op. cit., p. 377: "The most direct and original expression of the national genius [is] dramatic. Elsewhere imitation and artifice play a part; aristocratic sentiment or an ephemeral fashion is a check on spontaneity, ruling out whatever is of the people, or colouring style or subject to make it archaic, euphuistic, Arcadian or pastoral." Cf. H. S. Lucas, op. cit., who tells us that Shakespeare "grew up without discipline, married at eighteen, . . . a self-made man . . . took an independent attitude toward tradition . . . relied almost entirely upon his own instincts" ([2nd ed., 1960], p. 439).

14. J. F. Danby, *Poets on Fortune's Hill* (1952), p. 71.

15. See Edgar Wind, "Art and Anarchy," *The Listener*, 1st Dec. 1960, p. 976.

16. This is especially obvious in Legouis' praise of the Elizabethans for their "rejection of strict rules," that is, because their syntax and their prosody was uncertain (pp. 255 ff.).

17. It is odd that C. S. Lewis, *Studies in Words* (1960), though he devotes a chapter to "wit," does not mention Lyly.

18. See J. E. Neale, *Elizabeth I and her Parliaments, 1584-1601*, pp. 278, 297.

19. E. A. Baker, *History of the Novel*, II. 14: "The other great obstacle to the advance in the art of fiction—the one indeed which was at the root of all the trouble—was the lack of any definite notion of what a story or novel should be."

20. Richard Pace, *De Fructu* (1517), p. 72.

21. Cf. Henry Peacham, *The Complete Gentleman* (1634): "For since all virtue consisteth in action, and no man is born for himself . . . hardly they are to be admitted for noble who (though of never so excellent parts) consume their light, as in a dark lanthorn, in contemplation and a Stoical retiredness." (1906 edn. p. 2)

22. See the excellent treatment of this point in W. G. Zeeveld, *Foundations of Tudor Policy* (1948).

23. In adopting this spelling of the grammarian's name I have followed the practice outlined in the preface, of choosing the accepted rather than the proper or consistent form. "Lily" is the form used in D.N.B. and the British Museum Catalogue, and would seem to be an Anglici-

zation of the Latin *Lilius*. From his will it would look as if *Lyly* was the English form used by the grammarian. Feuillerat has used this form consistently for the whole family, but I feel it is too late now to disagree with the accepted works of reference.

24. R. S. Stanier, *History of Magdalen College School* (1940), p. 19.

25. This information, like almost everything else we know about William Lily, comes from the "elogium" that George Lily, his eldest son, contributed to Paulus Jovius' *Chronicon*.

26. See José Ruysschaert, "Les manuels de grammaire Latin composés par Pomponio Leto," *Scriptorium* VIII (1954), 98-107.

27. G. B. Parks, *English Travellers to Italy* (1954).

28. See Seebohm, op. cit., pp. 53 f.

29. See L. Bradner and C. A. Lynch, *The Latin epigrams of Sir Thomas More* (1953).

30. Polydore Virgil, *History of England* [Camden Soc. LXXIV], p. 147.

31. On the tangle of parts which make up "Lily's Grammar" see V. J. Flynn, *Proceedings of the Bibliographical Society of America* XXXVII (1943), 85-113.

32. There is an edition of Stanbridge's and Horman's Vulgaria in E.E.T.S. o.s. 187 (1932).

33. See Ascham, *The Schoolmaster* (ed. Arber), p. 25 f.; cf. Douglas Bush, *The Renaissance and English Humanism* (1939), pp. 60 ff.

34. Quoted in J. H. Lupton's *Life of Colet* (1887), pp. 291 f.

35. A more powerful figure than Ascham expressed the same view: "There has never been a great revelation of the Word of God unless He has first prepared the way by the rise and prosperity of languages and letters, as though they were John the Baptists" (Letter of 29th March 1523, in Preserved Smith, *Luther's Correspondence*, II. 176 f.). Cf. More's letter to Bugenhagen, in E. F. Rogers, *Correspondence of Sir Thomas More* (1947), p. 142.

36. See Seebohm, op. cit.

37. Erasmus's description of St Paul's school is in his epistle to Justus (Jodocus) Jonas (*Opus Epistolarum*, ed. P. S. Allen, IV. 514-27).

38. Quoted in Lupton, op. cit., p. 290.

39. Woodward, op. cit., p. 73. cf. D. L. Clark, *John Milton at St. Paul's School* (1948), p. 45.

40. E. F. Rogers, *Correspondence of More*, pp. 111-20.

41. *Opus Epistolarum*, I. 508.

42. Lupton, op. cit., pp. 188 ff.

43. It has been suggested that Rightwise's *Dido* was in fact written by Dionysia Lily (see Feuillerat, p. 11).

44. On Paduan Aristotelianism see *Journal of the History of Ideas* I (1940), 131-206, and B. Nardi, *Saggi sull' aristotelismo padovano* (1958).

45. Herrtage, *England in the reign of Henry VIII*, E.E.T.S. e.s. 12

(1871), p. x. Cf. *Letters and Papers of Henry VIII,* VIII, item 581, in which George Lily replies to Starkey's advice that he should study "philosophy and the books of the old lawyers."

46. J. S. Phillimore, "Blessed Thomas More and the arrest of Humanism," *Dublin Review* CLIII (1913), 1-26; cf. Douglas Bush, "Tudor Humanism and Henry VIII," *University of Toronto Quarterly* VII (1937-38), 162-77.

47. The phrase comes from a letter written to Starkey by Edmund Harvel, dated 18th June 1531 (*Letters and Papers of Henry VIII,* V, item 301), quoted by Zeeveld, op. cit.

48. The three "Parnassus Plays" have been edited by J. B. Leishman (1949).

49. Cf. Caspari, op. cit., p. 81.

50. Quoted in Huizinga, *Waning of the Middle Ages* (English edn. 1924), p. 71.

51. Cf. R. M. Sargent, *At the court of Queen Elizabeth* (1935), p. 6; Eleanor Rosenberg, *Leicester, patron of letters* (1955), pp. 179, 323 f.

52. C. S. Lewis, *Sixteenth century,* p. 19.

53. See G. Luck, "*Vir facetus:* a Renaissance ideal," S.P. LV (1958), 107-21.

54. Roberto Wiess, *Humanism in England during the fifteenth century* (1941) [second edn. (1957), p. 109].

55. C. R. Thompson, *Translation of Lucian by Erasmus and More* (1940), p. 22.

56. The case of Edmund Spenser may well be cited to show the insufficiency of the generalizations here attempted, for he was not confined to a world of witty irresponsibility by the pressure of Elizabeth's court. On the other hand, Spenser seems to have chosen, deliberately, an old-fashioned mode of writing. His political and religious outlook is as much Edwardian as Elizabethan; and the immediate price he paid for this power to generalize the Tudors was an immediate neglect. It is worth remembering that in this period *The Shepheards Calendar* seems to have sold better than *The Faerie Queene*.

↙

"Imitation" and Images

I Imitation and Images as Artifice

On the level of formal excellence, images were expected to please readers looking specifically and with well-trained eyes for formal beauty rather than for a faithful description of a section, however small, of the world of fact. Formal beauty as far as images are concerned meant design given to the natural (otherwise inadequately expressive), through the admirable craftsmanship of the maker; and men of the Renaissance, like their predecessors, thought of the discipline of rhetoric as affording the poet necessary training in this respect. Every sixteenth- and seventeenth-century image quoted will exemplify this kind of formal beauty, for this primary expectation is basic to the other criteria for images, and it was as well met by the carefully paired terms of Donne's similitude of the compass as by the *carmen correlativum* of Spenser's island of Phaedria—"No tree, whose braunches did not bravely spring; / No braunch, whereon a fine bird did not sit: / No bird, but did. . . ." (etc., *FQ*, II, vi, 13). The most seemingly ingenuous of Renaissance images are not formally artless; the images which would fail to meet this first expectation would be some of Whitman's enumerations, or Sandburg's

Reprinted from *Elizabethan and Metaphysical Imagery*, pp. 27-49, by Rosemond Tuve by permission of The University of Chicago Press. Copyright 1947 by The University of Chicago. Several appendices, which expand points made in this chapter, have been omitted.

casually piled modifiers, or that hill of moss beside Wordsworth's *Thorn*, "Just half a foot in height."

Extreme pleasure in poetry as a craft probably closed Elizabethan eyes to kinds of poetic pleasure which the Romantics placed very high; it certainly operated to make this age impatient of artless reportage. As Gascoigne tells writers, "if you do . . . never studie for some depth of devise in the Invention, and some figures also in the handlyng thereof, it will appeare to the skilfull Reader but a tale of a tubbe." For the method of avoiding this insupportable result, he advises poets to make things-as-they-are more expressive by the use of some "covert meane," some rhetorical figure less obvious, more shadowed, than mere descriptive epithet:

> If I should undertake to wryte in prayse of a gentlewoman, I would neither praise hir christal eye, nor hir cherrie lippe, etc. For these things are *trita et obvia*. But I would either finde *some supernaturall cause* wherby my penne might walke in the superlative degree, or els I would undertake to aunswere for any imperfection that shee hath, and thereupon *rayse the prayse* of hir commendacion. Likewise, if I should disclose my pretence in love, I would eyther make a strange discourse of some intollerable passion, or *finde occasion to pleade* by the example of some historie, or discover my disquiet in shadowes *per Allegoriam*. . . .[1]

These are not so much remarks on style as on poetic subject, although they are sometimes quoted as illustrative of the "quaint" early Elizabethan affection for ornamental trimmings. The two intentions posited—a "praise" and a "persuasion"—are typical intentions for lyric in the Renaissance; of the two resulting poems, one would be an evaluation of the lady, and the other would be an argument with her. Only artificial heightening will successfully imitate the real subjects indicated by these intentions, for neither subject is simply a segment of actuality, either physical or psychological, and neither intention is merely descriptive, either of the lady or of the lover's feelings. Writers and readers who decline or suspect the pursuit of "supernaturall causes" in poems will find a sufficient and convincing image of the beauty of a loved girl in MacLeish's "And you stood in the door and the sun was a shadow of leaves on your shoulders / And a leaf on your hair" ("Not Marble nor the Gilded Monuments," p. 48). But one will find, rather, images like those I have quoted earlier (Campion's lute and heart, or Herrick's metaphor fetched from the dawn) in writers who pursue causes beyond the natural with that "curious Imitation" which Harvey says is learned only in the "apprentishood" of "Arte" (*Pierce's Supererogation* [1593], in Gregory Smith, II, 276).

Elements of formal beauty in images are not to be thought of as added on but as intrinsic. We may quarrel with some poets' interpretations of the requirement of formal excellence. But at least Puttenham is not talking about adding detachable "beauties" to a subject when he says that the writer must make use of "figurative speaches the instrument wherewith we burnish our language fashioning it to this or that *measure and proportion*" (III, iii, pp. 142-43 [1589]). Thus poems come to possess that quality "the Greeks called *Enargia*[2] . . . because it geveth *a glorious lustre and light*." This resultant "light" is simply that "illumination"—revealing harmony, order, proportion—which had been indicated time out of mind as an attribute of works of art achieving formal excellence, by Cicero, by Augustine, by Aquinas.[3] The metaphor was constantly and unself-consciously used by all manner of writers on poetry in the early Renaissance and seventeenth century, and it was used to indicate the desirability—simultaneously—of qualities of imagery frequently set in opposition by modern critics of the two periods.

For example, "illumination" is connected simultaneously with splendor, majesty, and with perspicuity, *clarté, chiarezza*. This has come to seem contradictory only as modern usage has stressed the relation of perspicuity to plainness, and omitted what Renaissance writers generally mention in the next breath: that this clearness is a matter of *fitness* in images and words, so that the manner of achieving it will vary as subjects vary. It is characteristic that Minturno's long discussion beginning "How can that be luminous which is hidden?" does not even warn against difficult conceits but simultaneously praises splendor and warns against crowding with ornaments, since a work cannot be illuminated if it is *less splendid by virtue of the number* of ornaments. Moreover, ornaments must be "members," not "pieces."

That is to say, "clearness" is set in opposition not to intellectual difficulty but to confusion, and lustrous splendor is not praised instead of, but as an accompaniment of, structural lucidity. We all remember that Jonson, in speaking of perspicuity as the "chiefe vertue of a style," translated Quintilian's "nothing so vitious in it, as to need an Interpreter" (*Discoveries*, p. 98; Quint. i. vi. 41). We should remem-

ber as well, however, that Sidney's famous sentence about the illuminating power of poetry is concerned with the power of images in all
arts to bring a man "to a iudicial *comprehending*" of matters; Sidney,
too, is concerned that the grounds of wisdom should not "lye darke
before the *imaginative and iudging powre*" (in Gregory Smith, I,
165). Both poets are talking about an effect of art directly upon the
"inward conceits" of those who see, hear, and read; both are interested
in "true lively knowledge" and the functional use of art-ful writing to
convey it with immediacy.

To ask for the aesthetic quality of *clarté*, then, is not to ask for a
special type of style. And although Jonson talks about "pure and neat
language," and Sidney about language not too abstract and generalized, and Minturno about language "non humilis, non abiecta,"[4] all
three seem to recommend a kind of luminous immediacy, a formal
clarté that was not called in question until long after the seventeenth
century. Such a poetic might see as a flaw Donne's crowding of his
tropes, but it would have to censure him for his failure to illuminate
the subject for his reader rather than for his lack of mere expository
lucidity. By the criterion of *clarté*, both early critics and late would
have to admit praiseworthiness alike in the "illustrious" majesty of
Spenser's fourth *Hymne* and in the fiery clarity of "Batter my heart,
three person'd God," with its three traditional "shadowes *per Alle-
goriam.*"

Attempts to achieve "clearness" so defined produced, in fact, both
openly resplendent and artificially shadowed images; their common
denominator was the art with which they were designed to convey a
poet's exact and whole meaning, with force, to a reader. Chapman
claimed "clearness" for his covert figures, on the usual ground of fit
and expressive clothing of high invention:

> That, *Enargia*, or *cleerenes of representation*, requird in
> absolute Poems is *not* the perspicuous delivery of a lowe inven-
> tion; but high, and harty invention exprest in most *significant*,
> and unaffected phrase; it serves not a skilfull Painters turne, to
> draw the figure of a face onely to make knowne who it repre-
> sents; but hee must lymn, give *luster, shaddow, and heightening*;
> which though ignorants will esteeme spic'd, and too curious, yet
> such as have the iudiciall perspective, will see it hath, *motion,
> spirit and life*. . . .
> Obscuritie in affection of words, & *indigested* concets, is

pedanticall and childish; but where it shroudeth it selfe in the
hart of his subiect, utterd with *fitnes* of figure, and *expressive*
Epethites; with that darknes wil I still labour to be shaddowed:
. . . . [p. 49; prefatory letter to *Ovids Banquet of Sence*
(1595)].

This understanding of the place and purpose of the shadowed image
is not at all unlike Gascoigne's. It covers the kind of obscurity we
looked at above in Yeats's "Sailing to Byzantium" (st. 1), in which
the poet's invention is high and complex but delivered in images
whose connection with his interpretation is not left vague or tenuous
to a careful reader. Chapman's defense of such darkness is as old as
the discipline of rhetoric; his shadowing is an art-ful means to *clear*
expression of the very life of a subject.

Chapman's connection between clearness or luster and painting a
subject with motion, spirit, and life is also traditional; Quintilian
discusses it at length.[5] And Minturno's and others' discussions lead
one to suspect that *chiarezza* has more to do with poetry's power to
realize clearly than with facile lucidity.[6]

I do not believe that there was any relaxation, in the early seventeenth century, in poets' sense of their responsibility for achieving
clarté by formal artifice. If the characteristics thought of as opposed
to *clarté* were those of inadequately perceivable *form*, and lifeless insipidity, surely the Metaphysicals neither desired nor exhibited them.
Their "obscure" images are as cunningly framed to achieve the eloquence that accompanied formal excellence as any in the period.
Through all these discussions of "illumination" and of the artistry
which assists it, the rhetorical ideal of eloquent communication per-
sists. The ingenious images of Metaphysical poets offer no evidence
that they disagreed with Quintilian's insistence on the need for art in
achieving what he defines, from the verb *eloqui*, as "the production
and communication to the audience of all that the speaker has conceived in his mind" (viii. Pref. 15). The typical modern objections to
clearness and eloquence had not yet arisen, and commands like that
of Verlaine's "Art poétique"—"Prends l'éloquence et tords lui son
cou!"—would have stifled the Metaphysicals' voices along with the rest.

Rhetorically figured language is not the sole instrument for achieving pure formal beauty, but it had the most immediately distinguishable effect upon images. This effect was not toward making them
"purely decorative." Modern misrepresentations of the Renaissance

writers' theory of the didactic usefulness of poetry have intervened to blind us to the extreme complexity and flexibility of their definitions of the functional image. That theory did not operate to divide images into the formally beautiful and the logically useful, with tolerance for the first and respect for the second. The whole vast store of figures classified in the rhetorics (some producing images and some modifying their character) was used with the subtlest possible understanding of their effectiveness upon a reader's sensibilities. The enhancement of eloquence through rhetorical skill did, however, make images "artificial" and carefully patterned:

> Call not these wrinkles, *graves*; If *graves* they were,
> They were *Loves graves*; for else he is no where.
> Yet lies not Love *dead* here, but here doth sit
> Vow'd to this trench, like an *Anachorit*.
>   (Donne, "Elegie IX," *The Autumnall*, p. 93)
>   (Author's italics)

Much of the vigor, clarity, and impressiveness *of the image in its functional relation to the whole* results from the use of the initial *catechresis*, a short *allegoria* needing a metaphor and a simile, with two more recherché types of figure, two common ones, and at least two or three schemes.[7] The Elizabethans were responsive to these delicacies of relationship between the eloquence and the poetic integrity of a poem, whether we are or not.

This is merely to say that part of the "harmony" which was enjoyed was the skilful fitness of the figures, their relation to a luminous whole design. The extent to which response to this was conscious must have varied greatly, as it does among readers of all eras. When E. K. remarks appreciatively of Spenser's January eclogue, line 61, "a prety Epanorthosis . . . and withall a Paronomasia," he is saying what any educated reader might say; part of his pleasure, as sentence after sentence in his Prefatory Epistle would show, is that aesthetic pleasure of marking the *fitness* with which formal beauty of design has been imposed upon the natural.[8] With the eye fixed upon this *relationship*, it is as inadmissible to neglect formal beauty for matter as the other way around. "Ye know not what hurt ye do to learning," says Ascham, that most moral of critics, "that care not for wordes but for matter, and so make a devorse betwixt the tong and the hart" (*Scholemaster* [1570], in Gregory Smith, I, 6). Neither are we told to care more for words; we are told not to make the separation.

Readers as well as poets are to attend to this warning. We forget it most easily if the subject has led the poet to heightening of an opulent rather than an ingenious kind. Modern readers are prone to think, for example, that either ineptitude in narrative or naïve pleasure in merely decorative ornament must have produced a long, slow, rhetorically ornate and sumptuous description like that of Mortimer's tower in Drayton's *Mortimeriados* (1596). But an artist's images are not likely to assist the aims we set for swift and faithful narrative of happenings if his intention is that his images should go far beyond naturalistic fidelity in expressiveness and should be part of a design which by its formal beauty heightened the significance of his matter. When Drayton re-wrote the piece six years later as *The Barons Warres,* he made change after change in the imagery. These changes show not a simple outgrowing of "rhetoric" but rather a maturer attention to the Decorum which governed the relation of ornament to subject.[9] In Donne's image above and in Drayton's tower, the artifices used differ as they properly should according to matter, genre, cause of poem. Donne's image is ingenious and Drayton's is florid, but either poet exemplifies the normal methods used to satisfy that primary requirement of formal design which is here discussed. The images quoted in other chapters will exemplify these methods dozens of times over, in endless variety, up and down the entire range of the period.

Another difference between Elizabethan notions and ours I may not omit from this section—the absence of opposition between the "artificial" and the "natural." The reasons for this carry us into Renaissance conceptions of the reality to be imitated through the help of images. One of Tasso's statements will explain very quickly why "art" in Renaissance images was formally rather than naturalistically conceived, and yet was not divorcible from subject, also conceived formally as idea (equated with *res,* in Scaliger's Book iii). The poet makes likenesses of "cose sussistenti": "But what sort of things shall we say subsist? Are they the intelligible or the visible? Certainly they are the intelligible."[10] This is the extreme of the position, but later citations will show how widely accepted was the general position, in various forms which all had the same effect upon imagery. To put it too bluntly, the poet who imitates not the visible world but the intelligible as manifested in the visible will not consider that the use of artifice to emphasize form makes imagery less "true to Nature."

Instead of thinking about differences between images in that they offer, respectively, "artificial" or "natural" likenesses of the visible

world, we must think about differences between images in that they
imitate the different aspects poets see of the intelligible world. The
following four images happen to deal with a similar phenomenon or
content—a flush brought to the cheek. This is unimportant; what
is important is the difference in the four poetic subjects (the "intelligible" things) illuminated by the images. Those differences were a
most potent factor in producing great differences in form, much as
the blushes must have resembled each other when they took place.

> As after pale-fac'd Night, the Morning fayre
> The burning Lampe of heaven doth once erect,
> With her sweet Crimson sanguining the ayre,
> On every side with streakie dappl's fleckt,
> The circled roofe in white and Azure deckt,
> Such colour to her cheekes these newes do bring. . . .
>> (the news brought to Queen Isabella, of Mortimer's join-
>> ing the faction against Edward II [Drayton's *Mortimeri-
>> ados*, vs. 141])

> And ever and anone the rosy red,
> Flasht through her face, as it had been a flake
> Of lightning, through bright heaven fulmined;
> At last the passion past she thus him answered.
>> (Britomart when describing Artegall to her companion
>> [*FQ*, III, ii, 5])

> wee understood
> Her by her sight; her pure, and eloquent blood
> Spoke in her cheekes, and so distinctly wrought,
> That one might almost say, her body thought. . . .
>> (Donne, *The second Anniversary*, 243, p. 258)

> And troubled bloud through his pale face was seene
> To come, and goe with tydings from the hart,
> As it a running messenger had beene.
> At last resolv'd to worke his finall smart,
> He lifted up his hand. . . .
>> (Red Crosse, in the Despair canto [*FQ*, I, ix, 51])

All these are "artificial," no one more than any other. Of the many
factors which have operated to make them differ as to formal qualities, none is more important than the widely differing purposes which

accompany the four *differing* choices of aspects of nature to be imitated (for "art" stands in the same relation to "nature" in all of them). Drayton magnifies the Queen's beauty and her guilty love, using an exalted simile that requires ornate sensuous elaboration; Donne clarifies the notion of the relation between a fair body and a fairer soul through the use of a combined synecdoche and metaphor, based on the rhetorical commonplace of the relation of eloquence to thought and drawn out to a logical conclusion; Spenser uses in the first case a simile based on common qualities to assist a dramatic but simple narrative purpose; and in the second, a comparison, based on common purpose, to assist the purposes of psychological narrative (the heart is the seat of the will, and the next lines indicate Red Crosse's decision to accept despair's subtly insinuated advice to self-destruction).

The four images assist the poets' attempts to trace out four different structures of meaning; of each meaning the outer appearances of things (though similar to the eye) are a true expression, but without the poet's art an insufficiently luminous or striking one. In this sense "le naturel" is not "suffisant," as Du Bellay says (ii, chap. 3) in a famous passage bewailing the fact that there is no sleep for poets. The task of imposing form was not assumed to be easy, but neither was it assumed to set the poet in opposition to "nature," the mother of forms within the poet's mind as without it. The qualities of all four passages quoted rest on a conception of naturalness in images which is far removed from any Romantic equation of the most natural with the most artless—as far removed as is Quintilian's definition: "No, that which is most natural is that which nature permits to be done to the greatest perfection."[11] Similarly, Tasso tells the poet to seek his subject among things disposed to receive form (p. 32). This is advice, of course, which no poet of any time can help trying to follow. In addition, however, definitions of nature at the time these poets wrote encouraged them to see no enmity between her and an order-imposing art.[12] For such reasons as these, then, the Renaissance image could be extremely and carefully artificial without being thought of as unreal, as not natural, or as mere decoration.

Although the opposition did not lie between artificiality and artless naturalness, there was, of course, a vicious opposite to true art. Renaissance emphasis on the difficulty of the art of poetry is commonplace, and it is frequently accompanied by an emphasis which is equally a commonplace—disdain of false art. Both emphases are as characteristic of Sidney as of Jonson, present equally in Du Bellay or in Carew's elegy on Donne. And none of them thinks true art need be confused with that "feigned art with pompous words" which Giraldi Cinthio says leads writers to "swelling words and strong epithets," to "bloody dead men in laments and nothing but flowers, caves, waves, soft breezes, if gladness is written of" ("An Address to the Reader by the Tragedy of *Orbecche*" [1541], in Gilbert, p. 245). The Muses' garden was not to be purged of such soft melting phrases and pedantic weeds by a return to Nature as the last century and a half has defined her. Not in Carew's eyes, at least; he does not praise Donne for a return to the natural, but for true and right artificiality. He is as scornful of mere ballad-rhyme, not "refined," as of the exiled trains of gods and goddesses. "Nature with *fit* ornament"—the phrase is Giraldi Cinthio's, but it indicates that which is set over against false art, throughout the period.[13]

Feigned or pedantic or lifeless art does not find its opposite, then, in the natural feeling of the heart, rebelliously bursting through the trammels of form. Sidney says "look in thy heart and write," but he is talking about "inventing" or finding matter; and, anyhow, no one gives as poetic advice the Elizabethan analogue to what this counsel means to most moderns—no one bids the poet look into his liver to find words. No school advocated as desirable poetic imagery "that naturall stile" for which Harvey taunts Nashe so unmercifully. Harvey's snorts of ironic scorn for him who calls carelessness "nature" show how far both he and his enemies were from a poetic in which "spontaneous" meant praise for an artist:

> It is for Cheeke or Ascham to stand levelling of Colons, or squaring of Periods, by measure and number: *his* [Nashe's] penne is like a spigot, and the Wine presse a dullard to *his* Inkpresse. There is a certaine lively and frisking thing . . . that scorneth to be a booke-woorme, or to imitate the excellentest artificiality of the most renowned worke-masters that antiquity affourdeth. The witt of this & that odd Modernist is their owne. . . . Whuist Art! And Nature advaunce thy precious Selfe in thy most gorgeous and magnificent robes![14]

Those who substituted vigor for art continued to be laughed at. The "terrible gunpowder" of the pamphlet style did not find adherents in any poetic school; and what is analogous, in imagery, to "squaring of Periods" in sentence structure continued to characterize all but mere ballad wits. Applications of the principle of Decorum were to vary, most with genres, less with date. But neither Spenserian nor lover of "strong lines" was to relinquish as a first requirement for images that proper artificiality which characterized the parts of a construct designed to satisfy laws of formal excellence.

This is only a first expectation for images. They may be either openly illustrious or ingeniously shadowed; they will always be eloquent. Although this eloquence is a function of form, the constant in all eloquent images is their expressiveness, that inescapable relation to the poet's subject by virtue of which they vary infinitely as poets' subjects vary.

II Imitation and Author's Ordering

The requirement of right artificiality, strictly defined, was not a sufficient criterion for images in so far as they assisted—on the second level of aesthetic intention—in expressing the author's interpretation of nature, the meaning to be conveyed by his reordering. This conception of what Imitation involved led to a careful selection of images on grounds of their decorous relation to the coherent pattern which is the author's subject.

This rigorous selectivity according to the concept of Decorum[15] has caused great difficulty to modern minds. Although we have balked most at the way it functions with respect to characterization in fiction or drama, it functions in a precisely similar way with respect to images. Hoskins commends Sidney's *Arcadia* because Philoclea shows always "mild discretion," and Mopsa, "proud ill-favored sluttish simplicity"—"wherever you find them,"[16] and Spenser introduces no lovely thing into his Bowre of Blisse that we can feel to be quite innocently lovely. The modern eye is quick to see in this an irresponsible disregard of the complexities of human character and experience. The Elizabethan answer to such a charge of irresponsibility is Donne's answer to Ben Jonson's complaints against his *Anniversary*: "that he described *the Idea of a Woman*" (see chap. vii, n. 4, below). This intention once accepted, Donne's "blasphemies" were entirely decorous, and decorous in the same sense and for the same reason as Sidney's "perfect expressing" of qualities and affections in his characters.

We do not find Renaissance writers offering either the defense "But I described *my* idea of a woman" or "But I described how *that* woman was." These phrases—they would be the modern answers to Jonson —do not seem to fit their intentions. Elizabethan poets were far more likely to be concerned with imitating Cicero's "intellectual ideal by reference to which the artist represents those objects which do not themselves appear to the eye" (*Orator* iii; a Ciceronian commonplace in the Renaissance, in various phrasings). Or, as a result of the pervasiveness of Platonic and Neo-Platonic conceptions of reality, they were more likely to be concerned with imitating Plotinus' ideal form and order, or the very pattern and concentrated essence of Love, or Anger (or Variety—see Donne's "Elegy XVII," p. 113). Or (if one prefers Aristotelian terms for a point of view which affected the practice of poetry similarly, however different its metaphysical implications) they were more likely to be concerned with what Fracastoro calls "imitat[ing] not the particular [that is, 'the object exactly as it is'] but the simple idea clothed in its own beauties, which Aristotle calls the universal" (*Naugerius* [1555], fol. 158ᵛ; trans., p. 60). The commonly held conception is phrased in dozens of ways, of which the most familiar to us perhaps is Sidney's discussion of embellished nature. Probably equally familiar to the Renaissance Englishman were Scaliger's many statements concerning the poet's imitation of the perfect pattern, not the imperfect particular object.[17]

As we shall see, imagery was bound to be affected when such ideas as these watched over poets' putting-in and their leaving-out. Elizabethan poets differ most from modern ones perhaps in what they thought it quite truthful to excise; but the range and treatment of what was put in were affected as well. Techniques vary extremely; what is shared is the common refusal to narrow the task of images to that of a truthful report of experience. Even when he writes on "Going to Bed," Donne is ready to desert the particular for the personified universal, and apostrophizes the idea of "Full nakedness!" for full fifteen lines, with three analogies to demonstrate why "bodies uncloth'd must be, / To taste whole joyes" ("Elegy XIX," p. 119). Instead of confining himself to the story of Malbecco's experience of jealousy, Spenser transcends the novelist's method with a piercing and sudden daring, and Malbecco "Yet can never dye, but dying lives,"

> woxen so deform'd that he has quight
> Forgot he was a man, and *Gealousie* is hight.
> (*FQ*, III, x, 60) (Author's italics)

The Elizabethan poet simply has no nervousness about dealing overtly with universals (perceptual, affective, and conceptual). By rare good luck, Fracastoro illustrates his statement of the theory with an image. A heightened visual image from Virgil serves as an example of how the poet writes when he "seeks all the adornments of speech, all the beauties" which can be given, not to some particular, but to this "different idea" he makes "for himself, of untrammeled and universal beauty." The "adornments" which Fracastoro isolates for comment do not chiefly individualize; they select such particulars as will best indicate the intended universal. Such is the common intention of Elizabethan and early seventeenth-century imagery.

This does not force the poet to omit apparently discordant elements of experience; it does force him to make up his mind, and subtly indicate, why he chose to admit them. The coherence is imposed by the author's meaning, by subject and not by stuff. Although such ideas have not ceased to affect poetic imagery, the writers of the Renaissance, as they were more comfortable in the acceptance, were more bold in the application of them.

This recognition of author's *interpretation* as controlling subject must be distinguished from the modern author's portrayal of his own *process* of interpreting or feeling, of "the very movement of thought in a living mind," the "interplay of perception and reflection" (these phrases come from F. O. Matthiessen's and Edmund Wilson's essays on Eliot).[18] The earlier author's subject was different, however similar his stuff; his subject was still "his meaning," not "himself-seeing-it." One finds the choice of the images made upon different grounds, and their structural function differently affecting their nature, if one reads first Eliot's "Prufrock" (p. 11) and then even a difficult border-line case like Donne's "Elegy XI, Upon the losse of his Mistresses Chaine, for which he made satisfaction" (p. 96). Eliot shows us a man having a thought. Donne arranges the thoughts a man had, upon losing his mistress' property, into a carefully logical and hence wantonly witty exposition of the "bitter" and disproportionate cost of ladies.

The measure of the difference is the strict logical coherence of Donne's images. This does not mean that the images are not sensuously vivid; only that they are not primarily so. Each is chosen and presented as a "significant" part of an ordered pattern, and every care is taken to make that order rationally apprehensible. The relation of each image to the point in hand is as clear, to us, as logical association can make it—the relation of circumcis'd French crowns and unlickt Spanish bear-whelps to bad money, the relation of martyred angels in the fire to wasted good money. Eliot's "lonely men in shirt-sleeves, leaning out of windows" are no less clearly seen than Donne's "lowd squeaking Cryer," but their attachment to their author's meaning is; for Donne's crier is a perspicuously logical part of his suggestion that the lady might save more than money by letting him out of the restitution.[19]

The fact that Donne's images and his logical pattern lead us to an unconventional and satirical conclusion (what lady is worth *good* money?) is neither here nor there. It would not operate in the least to make his subject or images indecorous either to his contemporaries or to his predecessors. The Elizabethan demand for a unified and coherent meaning does not confuse coherency with moral orthodoxy. The requirement that images be "significant" of a coherent meaning rationally imposed by the author and rationally apprehensible by the reader holds in Donne's poem, with just the same kind of effect upon images, as it holds in poems that state the more usual conclusions made about ladies during this period. Sensuous images, like others, were scrutinized for their decorum in this respect.

III   Imitation and Didactic Intention

At this level of intention, Imitation involves the presentation of valid concepts about the order and operation of nature in its most inclusive sense. This "useful" purpose of poetry receives attention not alone in discussion of aims but in one treatment of ornament after another. Renaissance poetic is so universally adamant on the question of the importance of Wisdom as well as Eloquence that I need only take up here certain possible misapplications of Renaissance didactic theory.

It leads to fatal misinterpretations of the didactic aim in Renaissance poetic to speak of it unconnected with that other universally accepted requirement, the decorous relation between subject and style. The preoccupation with this relationship shows that the theorists were more aware than were the poorer poets of the period that the didactic aim can be vicious *if* matter be considered a good separable from the expressing of it. Ascham saw this danger fully as clearly as those modern critics who fear the overdidactic reader. "They be not wise therefore that say, 'What care I for a mans wordes and utterance, if his matter and reasons be good'" (in Gregory Smith, I, 6). Such men generally have an ax to grind, some "private and parciall matter," some propaganda to spread. But Ascham does not therefore see "the didactic aim" as the enemy of poetry. He attacks instead such a reader's arbitrary division between matter and utterance. Obviously, the principle of Decorum rules out, as an understanding of the didactic aim, any idea that one should be able to reduce a poem to some paraphrasable message. Thus to restate "a poem's ideas" is simply to deny those ideas their fit and decent form. Above all the many disagreements on the exact definition of poetry's aims there runs this constant theme of pleasure in a fit relation, and critics are as quick to imply that mere enjoyment of a content is an enjoyment not possible in poetry as to assert that there must be sound matter to enjoy.

Of course, critics were at variance as to *what* constituted wise matter, what concepts were valid and valuable, what images demonstated imperfect integration of meaning and ornament. A rebel like Castelvetro states firmly that the end of poetry is to "delight and to recreate the minds of the crude multitude"; he objects to versified natural philosophy; his statement of the various conceptual universals which give pleasure to the spectator of a tragedy might not have satisfied an Ascham (*Poetica d'Arist.* [1576]; trans. in Gilbert, pp. 307, 351). But such disagreements do not mean that a Castelvetro is to be placed with modern antididactic critics who relinquish the criterion of an intended rationally coherent meaning to be examined for its validity.

Some types of disagreement conceivably draw in the question of imagery. Castelvetro scores Scaliger for the "absurdity" of seeing in Aeneas a constant moral perfection (*ibid.*, p. 317). But Scaliger does what the didactic theory does *not* ask a reader to do: praises a certain specific moral meaning which he is determined to find as a primary aim in the poem—and hence he mistakes his author's subject. This is easy to do. It occurs frequently, and irrespective of a reader's search for didactic meanings, since it is caused rather by insufficient attention to the decorum to which the poet has held his images.

Modern readers are more likely to mistake the author's meaning by forgetting that there may be a controlling didactic aim than by hunting for one, like Scaliger. For example, Spenser, in Una's lament for the supposed death of Red Crosse, chooses not poignantly simple or particularized images, but instead a high-flown and lengthy apostrophe to the sun:

> O lightsome day, the lampe of highest *Iove,*
>> First made by him, mens wandring wayes to guyde, . . .
>> Henceforth thy hated face for ever hyde,
>> And shut up heavens windowes shyning wyde:
>> For earthly sight can nought but sorrow breed. . . .[20]

This may seem to us, for one thing, a lamentable failure in the precise communication of emotional experience. But the poet's subject is not "how the girl Una felt at the loss of her lover"; it is the infinite sadness of the breach between right Truth and Red Crosse, the representative of human kind, and the image must hold all the heavy weight of all the ways and times that breach has been made. The heightening of the style is one with the conveying of the matter. Spenser makes here no division between style and matter, but we do—if we demand, much like Scaliger, our own preferred meaning.

The acceptance of conceptually definable aims for poetry meant stress on the ideational element even in sensuous images. This meant often the use of images with known significances, like those of myth. The image unsuited to didactic poetry is, however, not the image drawn from unconventional or "low" matters, but the malproportioned or the irrelevant image. The poet's images to be decorous must keep close to the heart of his subject. The precise local particulars so congenial to modern taste are absent from sixteenth- and seventeenth-century poems; nevertheless, any homely particular which could take on symbolic or ideational significance could be as decorously admitted to a poem as Una's lamb. Such reservations and discriminations in the use of images proceed from an acceptance of poetry's responsibility to convey the poet's ordering of the world of values and meanings.

Neither all poets nor all critics would have agreed with a Sidney's or a Lodge's statement of didactic aims. But I cannot find that early or late objectors to overnarrowly defined didacticism take any one of three characteristic modern ways out: the substitution of nonlogical ("imaginative") truth as poetic subject; or the substitution of naturalistic representation as a poetic aim; or the notion that one may look on and understand how a certain poet might believe what seem to him to be truths, withholding judgment the while on the truth or falsity of concepts conveyed. Eliot's discussion on "entering the world" of Dante, "suspending both belief and disbelief," states this last and common attitude of modern criticism with more delicacy than most. The whole vast body of Renaissance defense of the ancients shows how inconceivable such an attitude would have been to these men, with their very different conception of poetic belief. Their approaches to older poets show also how the habit of thinking in metaphor (partly inherited from the Middle Ages) operated to remove difficulties of "belief" that loom much larger to the more inflexible modern mind, primarily trained to be literal.[21]

These three commonest modern forms of revolt against didacticism do not find Elizabethan or seventeenth-century exponents. Nevertheless, abuses of didacticism could be fought on quite as firm a ground by the Renaissance judge of imagery as by any modern critic, for as the law of decorum was stern in ruling out beautiful non-sense, so was it equally stern in ruling out non-beautiful sense. The position where careful statement enables one to examine it to the bottom seems to be that neither of these is really possible in good poetry; it is everywhere accepted that neither is commendable.

Thus, on all three levels of poetic intention—of formal construct, of coherent ordering, of artistic statement of truth—divorce between poetic subject and image is inadmissible. This is recognized in the humblest corner of the first level; the vices of style as the rhetorical handbooks describe them are some form or other of such a divorce (tapinosis, bomphiologia, et al., if any reader wishes to pursue them). This is quite out of line with the currently received opinion, to which I cannot subscribe, that the Elizabethan stress on rhetoric normally produced such a divorce. Emphasis on technique does not produce "ornament for ornament's sake"; foolish technicians who have nothing to say by means of the technique produce it. The Elizabethan period exhibits the normal number of foolish writers.

It is quite possible that we add to the category some who do not belong there by misjudging the matter their images were meant to illuminate, or by disagreeing with its validity, arguing thence a disproportion between their heightened style and their matter (to us trivial or unprepossessing). For it is true that, outside the drama, that matter does not satisfy the peculiar modern humility (arrogant enough) which thirsts for presentation of the whole baffling, ironic, conflict-filled complex of life. In so far as this thirst is just the special modern form of avidity for the particular, we tend even to prefer reading around the resolutions of the ironies, giving our attention to that presentation of conflict which is often the first step in the dialectical method favored by later poets. Even our honest discontent with their concepts we do not like to call by just that name, the whole matter of the poetic statement of "truths" having got such a shady reputation by reason of its blander adherents.

If we cannot lend ourselves sympathetically to these understandings of imitation and of reality, however, we shall read sixteenth- and seventeenth-century images with a certain inner hostility.[22] Our suspicion is waked when we find that the Elizabethan was not generally writing (rarely even for the length of a single image) "here is the thing that happened, here the object, the landscape, the human being that was seen." It still more wakes our suspicions to notice that he was not generally writing "this is how *I* felt about the experience, how *I* saw the object, the landscape." A Renaissance poet's conception of the subject of poetry and of the nature of truth allowed him to seek to present true meanings of things without looking first to the local particularities they exhibited (which the Romantic and late Romantic did not dare to do); and his conception of poetry's aim and of the nature of truth led him to stress the "conceipt" without stressing the conceiver (which the modern does not care to do). This distribution of pressures removed the necessity for support in the shape of imagery with a sensuous function as we see it most commonly used in modern lyric, short narrative, or reflective poem.

NOTES

1. *Certayne Notes of Instruction* (1575), in Gregory Smith, I, 48. The Latin phrases are italicized in the text.
2. *Enargia* is not quite conveyed by "a style vivid with images." It was a favorite recommendation in the Renaissance, perhaps because of Quintilian's fairly full discussions in vi. ii. 32 and viii. iii. 61, where he equates it with Cicero's *illustratio et evidentia* and discusses its relation to the stirring of the emotions, and to mere lucidity, which does not "thrust itself upon our notice." It was sometimes confused with *energia;* see Chamard's note to Du Bellay's recommendation of *energies* (n. to i, chap. 5 [1549]). Sidney praises *energia,* that "forcibleness" which betrays the writer's own feeling (I, 201; Gregory Smith's note gives references to Aristotle and Scaliger, who equates it with *efficacia,* a criterion I discuss in chap. viii). Puttenham's distinction between these two is not usual; his close relating of both to figured language is. Mazzoni's discussion is perhaps more typical, e.g., *Della difesa,* iii, esp. p. 686 (1587); the warnings against *soprabbondanza* follow in the next chapter.
3. See K. E. Gilbert and H. Kuhn, *A History of Esthetics* (New York, 1939), pp. 135-44 and note. Thomas Aquinas' statement there quoted is as clear as any: the clarity of the beautiful is that property of beauty which is "the shining forth of the *form* of a thing, either of a work of art or nature . . . . in such a manner that it is presented to the mind with all the fullness and richness of its perfection and order." Through it the elements of beauty in things manifest themselves with clearness. Like Sidney, sixteenth-century writers

generally use some such locution as "figure forth," "make evident"; they were perfectly aware that the relation between what we call "aesthetic effect" and form and conceptual content was not a simple one, and their theories on the formal qualities of images exhibit that awareness. Here, as elsewhere, the Renaissance made fruitful use of ideas inherited from or through the Middle Ages; I could frequently take citations quite as well from medieval as from later poetic and rhetoric and could illustrate equally well with images from Chaucer or Machaut or the Gawain poet.

4. "De perspicuitate," *De poeta*, vi, p. 447; like Quintilian viii, ii. 2 (*sordida et humilia*). Or see Tomitano's three manners of writing a *narratio*: Brieve, Chiara, Verisimile, and his examples from Petrarch—differing in fulness of detail (*Ragionamenti della lingua Toscana* [Venice, 1546], Book ii, p. 156).

5. He adds that *perspicuitas* "results above all from *propriety* in the use of words"; one form of this, deserving highest praise, is "employment of words with the maximum of significance." In Sherry's handbook of 1550, perspicuity is expressly identified with clearly realized description: *"Enargia*, evidence or perspicuitie called also descripcion rethoricall, is when a thynge is so described that it semeth to the reader or hearer y^t he beholdeth it as it were in doyng" (sig. E i^v). We see that these meanings suit with those of Jonson and others (emphasizing intelligibility), when we remember that "light," not prosaic plainness, is in question. It is not possible to think Jonson so ignorant of rhetorical tradition that he would use this weighted word to mean merely what most moderns mean by "clearness."

6. See Minturno, *L'Arte poetica*, i, p. 22 (1564); see also *De poeta*, p. 118 (1559); Tasso, *Discorsi*, iv, p. 186 (1594) (treating of metaphor). Hoskins's (1599) list of figures used for "Illustration" shows that his understanding of this technical term was far from the flattened modern notion of mere exemplification. The requirement of *clarté* by Du Bellay, the Spenserians, and others must be interpreted against the background of these uses. Certain oppositions posed between the Spenserians' lucidity and the Metaphysicals' intensity, supposedly resulting from their "different" aesthetic, are accordingly suspect (see, e.g., R. L. Sharp, *From Donne to Dryden* [Chapel Hill, N.C., 1940], chap. i).

7. The figure *concessio* in the granting and remolding of the sense—inducing two *distinctio* or figures of difference, and epanalepsis in the second line; plus a mild apostrophe and a conventional personification, and several repetitive schemes which I shall not call by their complicated names.

8. I choose this well-worn example partly because H. D. Rix's analysis of the January eclogue enables a modern reader to see the kind of observant reading we would give to rhetorically patterned writing if

we were Elizabethans (*Rhetoric in Spenser's Poetry* ["Pennsylvania State College Studies," No. 7 (1940)], pp. 64 ff.). One of the most striking things about the very numerous notes by E. K. which presuppose rhetorical training is the evidence they give of a kind of reading pleasure which modern readers are not prepared to share easily and immediately.

9. A very few examples: Drayton cuts, later, the pun on Orwell (or ill), the apostrophe to Thames and Isis (*Mort.,* 1338, 1604; cf. *BW* iv; he is stern even with lovely images like "Nor let thy Ships lay forth their silken wings"). He cuts the *accumulatio* of apostrophes to the letter of Mortimer received by the Queen (2758; cf. *BW* vi, losing "pretty" and "radical" images alike, e.g., "Pully which draw'st the curtaine of the Day"). Compare the change of image from the soft wax kissing her fingers to red wax sticking to them like a portent of blood (*BW,* st. 90). On the other hand, there are consciously rhetorical additions to *BW*: an *icon* of Mischief, a *descriptio* of the potion, *sententia* deliberately set off, "A Metaphor from Timber" and other expanded analogies (*BW* ii, 5; iii, 7, 41). There is constant interplay between all Drayton's reasons for revisions—stylistic, politic, structural; see K. Tillotson's excellent notes in Vol. V of the Hebel edition, where variants in editions of *BW* may be found (1603 to 1619, too complicated to notice here).

10. *Discorsi,* Book ii, p. 50; in Gilbert, p. 477.

11. "Verum id est maxime naturale, quod fieri natura optime patitur" (ix. iv. 5). The discussion is a mine of Renaissance commonplaces (whether language in the rough is more manly—*virilem;* why train the vine, then? why not continue to live in huts? etc.). Spenser, in a famous passage in defense of the natural life (*FQ,* II, vii), has Guyon make pronouncements against adding "superfluities" to "Untroubled Nature," but he shows no sign of regarding this as including a condemnation of elaborate similes; the sacrilege of digging up gold and silver for Mammon's uses did not cover the mining of the jewels of rhetoric. There is no inconsistency here. Spenser is talking about intemperance and pride—falsity of ends, not elaborateness of means; licentious and pompous-proud language would come under the same ban, as an offense against Nature. But not artificial language.

12. Art is the "coadiutor to nature," "a surmounter of her skill" (her expressive skill, not her pleasing prettiness; Puttenham, III, xxv, p. 303). These two are inescapably co-operative "conjurateurs" (see Thomas Sebillet, *Art poétique françoys* [1548], ed. Félix Gaiffe [Paris, 1910], i, chap. 3, p. 25; *L'Art poëtique du Jacques Peletier* [1555], ed. André Boulanger [Paris, 1930], i, chap. 2, p. 73).

13. This does not quarrel with the evidence of widespread distrust of the vanities of rhetoric (adduced, e.g., by R. F. Jones in "The Moral Sense of Simplicity," *Studies in Honor of F. W. Shipley* [St. Louis,

1942], pp. 265-87). Current rhetorical theory recognized the plain style as proper to many purposes, certainly to those of theologians and scientists whose disclaimers of "eloquence" are so numerous; and vain eloquence was berated on all hands—while then, as now, men disagreed on the line dividing "true" from "false" elaboration. When these disclaimers occur in prefaces, the centuries-old epistolary convention of including them as part of a *captatio benevolentiae* must be remembered.

14. From *Pierce's Supererogation* (1593), in Gregory Smith, II, 277. Harvey's entire discussion is in the vein of ironic satire—including those references to the marvels of the new style, "the nippitaty of the nappiest grape" (p. 250), which R. L. Sharp interprets without this reservation (*op. cit.*, p. 37; in n. 6 above). We may find some of Harvey's applications pedantic, but the fundamental tenets in his theory continued to be accepted as sound—hence the power of his irony. In verse, the newer writers do not pour themselves out in artless images; they turn from some types of rhetorical art and choose others, equally orthodox. Their images do not show them as repudiating what Boccaccio calls *exquisita locutio* (*De geneal. d.*, XIV, vii; the whole chapter is congenial to Renaissance ideas).

15. Since fitness or Decorum was the basic literary desideratum during the Renaissance, it had manifold aspects which I must define gradually throughout Part I, and I shall treat it in a culminating chapter (ix) as a specific criterion for images. Here we are concerned with it only in that it was the regulative concept which held the writer's images (and his characters and his incidents) to his chosen subject or interpretation.

16. Hoskins's notion of how one goes about creating real character is quite the opposite of the naturalistic writer's: one first learns to "set down an humor" truly, then fixes names; each character "expresses" an affection throughout "with steadfast decency" (decorum, of course; *Directions for Speech and Style* [1599], pp. 41-2). This affected imagery especially in narrative poetry; it was, of course, a commonplace (see, e.g., Minturno, *L'Arte poetica*, i, 45 ff., on the dispositions of the mind). The Elizabethans were no more naïve than we are in their observation of human character; they regarded the whole piece as the unit, and we look at the single character.

17. Later objectors do not call these basic tenets in question, when the particular critics here cited ceased to be the fashionable authorities.

18. *The Achievement of T. S. Eliot* (Oxford, 1935), p. 13; *Axel's Castle* (New York, 1932), p. 107; these are modern critical commonplaces. One might use equally well phrases from C. Brooks's discussion objecting to Wilson, in which he stresses the similarities between Metaphysical and Symbolist poetry, denying the importance of logical unity in either, and comparing Donne's poetry to Yeats's,

whose symbols are "nothing but concrete and meaningful images in terms of which the play of the mind may exhibit itself" (*Modern Poetry and the Tradition* [Chapel Hill, N.C., 1939], pp. 59 ff.).

19. This is not an especially typical Donne poem, but, even so, it would seem to me that Allen Tate's phrase "the poet's dramatization of his own personality" indicates for it a modern subject-and-intention which will not account for what is left out, nor for the order of what is put in (*Reactionary Essays* [New York, 1936], p. 72). If we speak as psychologists of ultimate motivations, and thus weaken this statement into something that fits all expression in any medium in any era, then it will (if true) fit Donne also.

    For the differences we feel between this kind of poem and, e.g., the Drayton and Spenser passages quoted in sec. I, I should urge both more numerous and more complicated reasons, and the reader will find more of them perhaps in chap. ix than anywhere else.

20. Etc., *FQ*, I, vii, 23. (Author's italics.) The parallel with *I Tamb.*, V, 2, does not affect my remarks. Borrowings often (as here) demonstrate the extreme sensitivity of Renaissance poets to points of decorum; the astrological point of the image in Bajazeth's *curse*, and the relation between the obscuring of God's Light and man's severance of connections with Truth in Una's *lament*, are proper, respectively, to the differing purposes of the authors. W. B. C. Watkins, "The Plagiarist: Spenser or Marlow?" *ELH*, XI (1944), 249-65, gives citations to previous discussions.

21. The Eliot quotation is from *Selected Essays* (New York, 1932), p. 219.

22. Although my organization of Renaissance principles was made on the basis of their own theory and practice before the appearance of T. M. Greene's *The Arts and the Art of Criticism* (Princeton, 1940), the aesthetic orientation of these principles will be more clearly seen by reference to a modern restatement of the problems of aesthetics such as Professor Greene's. In response to his suggestion that critics deliberately seek more common ground by agreement as to categories discussable, I have occasionally substituted his terms for similar ones of my own or for Elizabethan ones.

Donne and the Rhetorical Tradition

I can't offer any new view of Donne, that is, my opinions however unacceptable have appeared in book form already; but I have been reading some of the recent learned works about the Elizabethan rhetoric teaching and its influence on the poets, and I feel something needs to be said about them. I shall mainly be concerned with Miss Rosamund Tuve's massive study *Elizabethan and Metaphysical Imagery*. I also read *Shakespeare's Small Latin and Less Greek* by T. W. Baldwin and *Shakespeare's Use of the Arts of Language* by Sister Miriam Joseph (comforting things to have in bed with one while the guns fired over Peking) and such is the extent of my erudition on the matter.

Of course, in a broad way, these authors are quite right; the rhetoric training did have a great effect on any poet who had been through it, and even the assertively unlearned Shakespeare (the case seems pretty well proved) had been through it all in his grammar school. All the same, the new research does not seem much use in detail. The only important Shakespeare crux I can find Mr. Baldwin trying to clear up is Hamlet's "Fix a comma twixt our amities." He speaks triumphantly about this, and really does I think explain how it came to be written; and yet the only moral seems to be that Shakespeare's training led him for once into writing a bad line—bad now and bad

From *The Kenyon Review*, XI (1949), pp. 571-87. Reprinted by permission of the publisher and author.

then (maybe as an attempt to make Hamlet a bit of a university pedant it went over with the first audiences tolerably). In general, I feel that the recent enthusiasts for the rhetoric training don't show enough respect for the united verdict of three centuries (with which Shakespeare concurred before his time—the main evidence that he had the training comes from his jokes against it) that the whole structure was footling, that "all a rhetorician's rules / Serve only but to name his tools." So far as it made the boy practise inventing tropes it did give a sort of professional ease in handling them, which no doubt improved both the poet and his audience. But the final use of the learned research, when Miss Tuve applies it to a man like Donne, turns out to be that he did not mean at all the kind of thing a modern critic admires him for, because Donne thought he was only applying the rules of rhetoric in a particularly vigorous and stringent manner. Of course I don't deny that some modern critics may have misread him. But it seems to me that she is cutting out one of the major themes of Donne's poems, and telling us that it was only put in by our own ignorance and self-indulgence.

The chief technical question raised by Miss Tuve, it seems to me, is how far the meanings of words in such poetry are meant to be narrowed. She sometimes goes very far, as when saying that in *catachresis* "only the prick of the point of connection is to be felt, whereas in synecdoche what is unmentioned is meant to be half-glimpsed . . . it is clear, when one reads whole poems, rather than culled images, that the poets expect the reader to sheer off irrelevant associations with a keenness approaching their own." *Irrelevant* begs the previous question, which is whether the prick of more than one point may be relevant, as surely it may. Thus, in Donne's comparison of the separating lovers to the pair of compasses, she says, some modern readers think there is a "self-protective irony" because compasses are low and inherently "unimaginative" objects employed by school children; but this is a misreading; Donne does not express a "tortured confusion." I am rather hampered by not having read any critic who takes this view of the compasses. But surely the reality, the solidity, the usefulness, and the intellectual uses of the compasses, their reliability in a situation where native intuition cannot guess the answer unaided, are all relevant to the comparison. The series of "pricks" from detailed points at which the comparison fits are a delightful grace, but they can be thrown aside in the last line, "And make me end where I begun"— the final point in drawing the circle is where the pencil began, but not also the centre, whereas Donne means he will return to his wife. What he chiefly wants to imply by the comparison is that his argument about true love is not a fanciful convention, such as he has laughed at in earlier poems, but something practical which he has proved in experience. No doubt Miss Tuve might answer that this is an *allegoria* not a *catachresis,* but it has always been considered a specially "violent" image, and that seems to be her criterion for *catachresis.* If you can switch round the technical terms however you like I do not see how they can ever decide anything.

Earlier in the book, however, she has emphasized very strongly the wealth of possible meanings in a metaphor. In a *translation* (such as "Another Antony / In her strong toil of grace") the figure furnishes many meanings, she says, not under the control of the poet "except as he reins them in with the tiny threads of the co-operating words. All tropes give the reader his head in this fashion." Thirty pages later she has managed to jerk back the reader's head in a savage bearing-rein or martingale, obviously weakening the powers of this poor horse, and I cannot see how she has done it. Nor indeed do I know why his head was ever loose. I think it is true to say that she can never quote her rhetoricians as specifically admitting that a metaphor may have more than one point of likeness; she is reduced to claiming that the Elizabethans "could hardly fail to know it." The Ramists, apparently, recognized that a metaphor could have more than one logical function, but that is not the same thing. If the rhetoricians did not even say this much it seems clear that the poets had to go beyond them even to do what Miss Tuve approves.

The license allowed to Cleopatra's "toil of grace" is not extended to Hamlet, and here I think Miss Tuve is overplaying her hand. Many people would be prepared to read Donne in a narrower manner, but when the same argument is used on Shakespeare they will have more of a shock. There is a footnote about

> Or to take arms against a sea of troubles
> And by opposing end them.

If you have been properly trained in rhetoric, she says in effect, and are thereby able to pick out the logical essential in a metaphor and drop the irrelevant, you will be spared from the romantic idea of fighting the waves and also from the absurdity of thinking you could win; that is, the *sea* here is a metaphor intended to be forgotten at once, which does not affect the phrases either before or after. I do not understand why she thinks this an attractive offer. The Arden edition, which happens to be the nearest, tells me of four authorities who report that "the Celts, Gauls, and Cimbri exhibited their intrepidity by armed combats with the sea," and says where Shakespeare could have read about them in English. (Anyway there is Xerxes as well as the northern legends.) However, it goes on, the word *sea* is anyway a stock metaphor for a battlefield, fitting *slings and arrows,* so on either count the 18th Century critics were wrong in wanting to emend it. Even the narrower half of this very sensible note, written by the despised Dowden, goes beyond Miss Tuve, who thinks that our only business with *sea* is "the logical task of abstracting 'vastness, recurrence of numberless units.'" No doubt few listeners in the theatre have much time for taking arms against the sea, as the speech is rattled off; but the overtone of this idea is just what is wanted. Hamlet already feels that it is hopeless to fight his situation, so the idea of a possible surprising success needs to be excluded from a phrase which otherwise sounds hopeful in a heroic manner; also he feels that to act as if fighting the waves (a traditional idea even if remote) would have a certain splendor and might therefore lead to peace—the idea of *ending* the waves of course is not absurd because it means they stop attacking you when you drown. In a case like this, surely, the ordinary reader is entitled to ask, like the Caliph in "Hassan," for "one reason, one small and subtle reason" *why* he must be ordered to regard this passage as so much duller than it appears. Miss Tuve is content to report the findings of taste; her phrase is "I cannot believe that Renaissance readers would be much troubled by. . . ." What she is really doing, I fancy, is going back to the 18th Century, not the 16th; she is trying to give Theobald what he wanted without the embarrassment of having to emend the text.

The argument is not really different, I think, when it is applied to more strained and less good authors. For example "Marston's first image below would be the opposite of efficacious if the *gulf* remained long enough to swallow the *cormorant*":

> TO EVERLASTING *OBLIVION*
> Thou mighty gulf, insatiate cormorant,
> Deride me not, though I seem petulant
> To fall into thy chops. . . .

"The vaguely sensuous epithet for *gulf* allows it, too, to have *chops.*" Actually *gulf* had a regular meaning "space into which prey is swal-

lowed," best recalled nowadays through "maw and gulf, / Of the ra-
vined salt-sea shark" in *Macbeth,* but not as strained as you might
think from that one use; the N. E. D. has quite flat uses like the
wicked wolf who had taken many sheep into his gulf (Spenser). Miss
Tuve seems to take for granted that the word means, as nowadays,
"great empty space below one, into which one might fall," but the
primary English use is about the sea, though the root is cognate with
"gulp"; various uses including the modern one arise toward the end
of the 16th Century, but I should fancy "whirlpool" or maelstrom (as
more directly connected with a bay of the sea) was what Marston
would take as the head meaning in this rather blank context. Anyway
the idea that the word has only one meaning, most of which must be
abandoned before you arrive at the cormorant, seems to me ill-
informed. Nor can I see that *mighty* as an epithet for a chasm has
the peculiar merit of being "vaguely sensuous" in so high a degree as
to let it have jaws; at least I suppose I can, but that would mean
reading it like Victorian poetry; what Miss Tuve is doing here is just
what she blames other people for. Surely the process is quite simple;
the word has two senses, of which the first is non-living to mark the
inhumanity of Oblivion (a whirlpool I think, but a chasm if you prefer); then the poet wants to personify this abstraction rather more, so
he moves over to the sense "gullet," and this is attached to the cormorant without any strain. The cormorant has the jaws; its gullet need
have no jaws; and its own gullet is not likely to swallow it. In general,
I think, what seems to us a strained metaphor in these authors was
supposed to be mediated by a double meaning (replaced in "the *sea
of troubles*" by a stock metaphor). I am rather surprised that Miss
Tuve never even envisages this possibility.

There is a similar puzzle when she sets out to illustrate the difference between 17th Century poets and modern ones. The first lines of
Yeats's "Byzantium" are quoted as a case where "we explore irrele-
vances and delight in ambiguous suggestions," a thing which the
reader of Donne should avoid doing.

> The *unpurged images of day* recede.
> The *Emperor's drunken soldiery* are abed.
> *Night's resonance* recedes, night-walker's song
> After great cathedral gong.

The italics are Miss Tuve's, and she says that Renaissance writers

might easily have used such details, but they would not have
been metaphorical; if part of an *allegoria,* either the similitudes
would have had the public character of symbol, or some indication would assist the reader to enjoy clearly perceived related-
ness and such suggestions as fell in therewith.

All this baffles me completely. Yeats has told us in "Sailing to Byzantium" that he is going there, and explains what he expects of it; the
second poem, written a few years later, describes (very properly) the
disillusion of the spiritual tourist when he has arrived. The lines are
simple description; part of an allegory of course, but not metaphor
at all. We do not need to hunt about in Yeats's prose writings to learn
what Byzantium "meant to" him; it can hardly help meaning what it
meant to Yeats. It survived the Dark Ages of Europe and maintained
a splendid otherworldly art throughout them; any mystical old poet
could have wanted to withdraw there from our coming troubles. But
when Yeats gets there he finds an ordinary Fascist type of state, gross,
brutal and violent. The memories of what he saw there during the
day in Byzantium have to fade before his vision of ghostly and eternal
perfection, the thing he came there to see can arise again in his mind.
Such is the meaning of the first two lines, wonderfully compact; then
"night's resonance recedes" is a direct sensuous description of the unexpected calm of the night, and how far an echo will carry in it; well
may a ghost appear. There is no question of metaphor in all this. I
have to suspect that Miss Tuve simply doesn't know what the lines
are about.

A good deal therefore seems to depend, in Miss Tuve's account of
the Metaphysicals, on her technical term *catachresis;* they often use
this figure, and in this figure it is assumed that extra meanings are
cut out. I am not sure that this is her line of argument, but at least it
would be a real one. The figure is said to be the same as *abusio,* is
described as "violent metaphor," and is claimed as "what modern
criticism calls the 'radical' or the 'dissonant' or the 'conical' metaphor,"
which do not sound identical in any case. Apparently one 17th Century rhetorician, Hoskins, actually did say that it was "more desperate
than a metaphor." I am quite ignorant about this, but Sister Miriam
Joseph's book is obviously a careful summary of the rather confused
uses of these technical terms, and her picture of *catachresis* is quite
different. There are three distinct accounts of the term, listed in her
index; the second specifically defines *catachresis* as "verbs and adjec-

tives employed in a transferred sense" (whereas ordinary metaphors are nouns); the third defines it exactly like metaphor and gives examples which are all verbs or adjectives; the first is Sister Miriam's attempt to reconcile the other two. I gather that some rhetoricians toyed with the idea of generalizing the term, but that the idea itself was a thoroughly tidy and pedantic one, making a distinction about grammar, not about whether you were "radical" or whether you had to cut out all but the prick of the point of connection. As to Hoskins, no doubt he thought it a bit "desperate" to use a verb as a metaphor at all. As to *abusio*, Sister Miriam does not list the term, and Miss Tuve does not quote anyone actually using it as a term of praise. I suspect that they did not. Except of course as one might say "one of the most brilliant things in the style of Henry James is his decisive use of *the vulgarism. How artificial*, to a truly refined reader, his use of *the vulgarism* will always appear." This critical remark strikes me as true and yet as a silly way to talk about the style of Henry James. In any case, it is far from what we were looking for, that is, that people were *taught* to cut out all the meaning except the prick of the point from the specific trope *catachresis.*

However the only possible objection to the exercise of analysing Donne's rhetoric is that it tends to "explain things away," and I must now try to show that that happens. As I understand her, she treats the Donne line of talk that the idealized woman is a world, or that the two happy lovers are a world, as a straightforward use of the trope *amplificatio.* That is, in effect, it is like Pope in the "Pastorals," saying "Where'er you walk, cool gales will fan the glade. / Trees, where you sit, will crowd into a shade." I do not mean that the Pope lines are flat; the nostalgia of their frank untruth is almost heartbreaking; but still the thing is meant to be untrue; it is a trope. I do not think you get anywhere with Donne unless you realize that he felt something different about his repeated metaphor of the separate world; it only stood for a subtle kind of truth, a metaphysical one if you like, and in a way it pretended to be only a trope; but it stood for something so real that he could brood over it again and again. The question is one of truth, or rather truth-feelings, and Miss Tuve ought not to be eager to disagree here, because one of her main points is that 17th Century poets believed it was their business as poets to display general truths. But she says that the astronomical images in Donne are "dialectical counters in a war of wits," and she has a firm footnote denying that "what we like to think of as the peculiar character of metaphysical imagery" has among its causes "the disturbed *welt-anschauung* which accompanied the acceptance of the Copernican world-picture." I agree that the poets who imitated Donne do not seem to have caught from him any of this line of interest, but in the young Donne I believe it was fundamental. I think it is obvious that his separate planet, which comes in one form or another into practically all his good poems, was connected with Copernicus; and I notice that Miss Tuve gives no reason for thinking otherwise. She merely finds it natural, as she is classifying tropes, to assume that they are fairly similar standard objects, rather like spare parts of machinery.

She seems a little embarrassed by Jonson's remark that the "Anniversaries" were blasphemous, and has to explain that educated readers knew they were only a standard trope. "Jonson mistook his amplification of a universal for a description of an exception. . . . Renaissance images of this sort . . . ask us to look, through particulars, at the blinding light of significances or essences." Donne is praised for answering that "he described the idea of a woman, and not as she was," and we are given other phrases such as "imitating not the particular but the simple idea clothed in its own beauties." But it doesn't seem likely that Jonson wouldn't know what every educated reader knew, and in any case I shouldn't have thought that it *is* part of the idea of a woman that her death is making the sun fall onto the earth, "being weary with his reeling thus." The only saving grace of the "Anniversaries," granting that poor Elizabeth Drury had nothing to do with it, and that the whole thing seems in rather bad taste however much he needed the money, was that Donne really did feel things were breaking up. Blasphemy was a serious accusation, and we need not suppose that he expressed his deepest feeling in defending himself against it. I feel the two poems really are a bit blasphemous, somehow; perhaps from assuming that anybody can be treated as the Logos, perhaps from feeling that things can break up so completely not through any act of God but through a failure of the spirit of man. In any case, it seems to me that Jonson's criticism was a penetrating one, and it is tedious to be assured that they were only talking about rhetorical rules.

Owing to Donne's complete control of the rhetorical instrument, says Miss Tuve, it is particularly "illegitimate" in his case "to fit out his poems with overtones which diverge ambiguously from his apparent meaning and which are only to be traced in the connotations of his image-terms." It seems to me, on the contrary, that much of the haunting quality of Donne comes from writing about a total situation, without realizing quite how much of it he was getting into his language or even what all his cross-currents of feeling about it were; he broods like a thundercloud, as well as flashing like one. I have tried to show this in detail in two previous books of mine, and will give page references in case anyone cares to look them up; assuming, you understand, that this is the kind of criticism of Donne that Miss Tuve disapproves. In "The Valediction, of Weeping" (my *Ambiguity* pp. 139-45) I think there is an idea that the lovers will be unfaithful when they are separated, an idea which adds to the extremity of grief but is much opposed to the absolutism of the kind of love which seems to be presented; and in the *Holy Sonnet* "I am a little world made cunningly" (my *Pastoral*, pp. 74-8) I think the remorseful hope of atonement with God is crossed with a shrinking hunger for annihilation and escape from God. Both of them are dominated by the image of the separate planet, and the point is not so much what "connotations" this "image-term" *might* have to a self-indulgent reader as what connotations it actually does have in its repeated uses by Donne. At least, I hope I made this clear about the religious poem, where a definite argument is needed. In the "Valediction" I think my approach to the poem is simply the natural one; after all it begins

> Let me pour forth
> My tears before my face, while I stay here

and the whole reason for this, unflinchingly elaborated, is that they will become "nothing" when they are apart. The planet metaphor is not needed at the start but serves to drive home the awful isolation of the human creature; he can't be blamed if he tries to get along with what his planet provides him; once the lovers are separated they are absolutely separated. Of course, a critic must then go on to argue that other metaphors in the poem fit in with what he puts forward as its central theme, but to do this is merely to show that they "observe decorum," in Miss Tuve's language. I am not sure whether she would consider this an adequate defence. If she objected that the emotion or attitude of the poet cannot be complex, merely because he argues so much, I think she would ignore the whole tone of his better poems:

> Till my tears mixed with thine do overflow
> This world, by waters sent from me, my heaven dissolved so.

"These broken pieces of grammar which may be fitted together in so many ways are lost phrases jerked out whilst sobbing," I said in my piece about it, and no doubt that way of putting the thing under-rates the control which the poet never loses, but it still seems to me more lifelike than the way Miss Tuve talks. No doubt she could turn round and say that my ignorant modernistic conception of rhetoric is a false one, and that a really well-trained Ramist would think of the conscious disorder in these cries of pain as a triumph of the true art. I should applaud her if she said that, but I do not see that it would leave anything surviving of her attacks on the critics who have tried to strike out phrases about the metaphysical style. Of course my par-ticular interpretations might still be wrong, but she would have lost her main line of defence.

Poor Mr. Eliot, not to mention minor figures, comes in for a good deal of teasing for having said that Donne felt his thoughts, or did not suffer from the peculiar separation between intellect and emotion which arose later. It was a time when "the intellect was at the tips of the senses" and so on. Admittedly these are literary phrases, therefore a kind of pot shot at the real point, but they seem to me good ones. As Miss Tuve spends a great many pages in claiming that the old rhetoricians firmly avoided ever making the separation in view, it seems clear that she agrees with the point Eliot was making. How-ever, I can understand that she might not feel quite easy about saying so. What she does succeed in showing about the dear old pedants whom she praises is that they rode serenely over a number of baffling gulfs lying in the path of a writer, which later thought has been forced to examine; she can never (so far as I can see) quote them as saying anything helpful about these gulfs—they seem sensible only because they seem like children, and any actual writer then as now had to jump over the gulfs by his own muscles. One can heartily agree with her that the innocence of the rhetorical training saved it from giving false answers to the problems facing a writer; but she cannot combine this with claiming that the rhetoricians gave definite an-swers which the writers must have acted on.

All the same, she offers two definite points of difference between 17th Century poets and Romantic or modern ones; the later ones be-lieved in Expressing their Personality and thereby Exploring the Un-conscious, and you misread the early ones if you suppose these ideas present. The second is different from the first, because your person-ality is expected to be worth attention but you are vaguely assumed to have the same unconscious as everybody else. The reason is a prac-tical one; if you can't explain what seems to you a good line, and still decide to print it, you are trusting that the reader has the same feelings as yourself. The two halves of the puzzle inherently go together; there would be no point in publishing lines which are *only* good because they express your (unique) personality unless the public had some (underground) means of knowing what they had expressed. The puzzle is real, but that is only to say that it had always existed; the Romantics only drew attention to it. (In the same way, if the Freudian theory is true, writers previous to Freud ought to illustrate it; the idea that it is unhistorical to suppose that Hamlet illustrates it merely takes for granted that it is not true.) I don't deny that there is a certain lack of self-consciousness about 17th Century writers even when they are writing about themselves, even when like George Herbert they treat the reader with a certain reserve. The reason why "Ah, my dear Lord, though I be clean forgot, / Let me not love thee if I love thee not" is not fussy in spite of its baffling ambiguity is that he thought of it as an effective appeal to the heart of God (as it might have been to a loved woman—"Give me more love or more disdain"); it is not primarily a display of his own complex state of mind to an interested reader. Cases where the difference is important are rather rare, but I should think this is one. While Miss Tuve is blaming the modern critics for ignoring the difference, it seems to me, she gets very near saying that a poet trained in rhetoric must be read only for his surface intention. These poets had also heard (if they needed to hear of it) of the ancient doctrine that a poet when inspired might say more than he knew. Her ideas about the simplicity of Donne's purpose in a love-poem sound to me hard to distinguish from the objections of Dryden, saying that Donne perplexed the minds of the fair sex when he would have been more sensibly employed in moving their passions.

In short, I think it has a steadying effect if you contrast Donne with Pope, instead of letting Miss Tuve drive home the contrast that she supposes between Donne and Yeats. Pope apparently did feel that he ought not to publish a line unless he could explain why it was good at every point. Miss Tuve in effect asks us to believe that Donne felt the same; a particularly odd idea about Donne, who took for granted that none of his good poems could be published in his lifetime at all, and was ashamed because he had to publish the "Anniversaries." The more usual view is that authors before and after the Dryden-Johnson period were alike in an important point of practice; they would stick to a line merely because it felt good, not necessarily because they were

equipped to defend it. This must be true in the main about the Elizabethans, or Shakespeare could not have happened. The unconscious
was therefore let in, though the unformulated rules about just where
it could be let in were very different from the Victorian ones. In comparison with this practical matter, the question about whether you
express your personality does not seem to me important. Any tolerable
author knows that the way to express your personality is in the course
of expressing something else, which you care about and want other
people to care about. Donne obviously does express a striking personality in a pungent and concentrated manner; T. S. Eliot indeed sus-
pected him of being too keen on it to write good sermons. It is hard
to believe that he was wholly unconscious of the process, merely because he had been taught rhetoric; and Miss Tuve herself insists that
the rhetoricians did not get in a writer's way. However I do not feel
that these questions, though they have to be recognized, are really the
important ones.

The important ones seem clear if you have to lecture about him to
students who find him a novelty (by the way, I get an impression that
the young feel him much more remote now than the young did
twenty years ago, and I wish they didn't). You get a series of assertions such as that the individual praised is the Logos of the virtues he
or she typifies, he or she *is* the abstract idea Beauty or Virtue itself,
and therefore constitutes the reality of those qualities in any person
who possesses them. The lovers who are a separate planet get part of
their dignity from this process, because they epitomize the actual
world and are partly its Logos; this is what equips them to be a complete planet. Now first, as Miss Tuve emphasizes, one has to recognize
the rhetorical method; the student has to agree that it is linguistically
tolerable for a poet to talk in this extraordinary way. But that is only
part of the necessary fuss of exegesis; the second stage is the important
one, when he has to decide "What is the point of it? Is it silly?" I do
not think it is much help, except as a kind of soother to a student, to
point out like Miss Tuve that the allegory of Spenser is at bottom
toying with the same fundamental ideas. The point about Donne is
that he makes the absurdity of the ideas hit the reader with such
force.

The contemporary Spaniards, I understand, were using these ideas
as starkly as Donne, who knew Spanish and was brought up as a
Catholic; he read Spanish mystics as a boy at Oxford. There seems no
doubt that he learned his main rhetorical trick from Spain. (The

motto on his youthful portrait is in Spanish, and Spain was still the great danger to England; it must have been rather like a modern Englishman or American displaying a motto in Russian.) But the Spaniards used these tropes, in a certain sense, like Pope; they did treat them as a device of rhetoric. True about Christ, this kind of assertion could be used by a Catholic poet in a Catholic country as a well-known and supremely magnificent formula of praise, and yet not be blasphemous because it was clearly recognized as a trope. However this account is too simple; the Catholics, as the Protestants put it, worshipped saints; that is, when they used the formula about a saint not a king (or when the English Crashaw used it about a saint) there was supposed to be a queer but not at all embarrasing kind of truth in it. Contrariwise the Protestants tended to feel that man should meet God unobstructed and were not keen to use the paradoxes of Godhead even on Christ himself when regarded as man. Miss Tuve I should expect is making an important point when she says that the Metaphysicals used Ramist rhetoric or logic, and that this was felt as interesting because it went with being Protestant (Ramus was a Protestant martyr). One can quite see Donne feeling that the Protestant treatment gave an extra gaiety to his defiantly Catholic but startlingly displaced trope. In any case, when his imported line of paradox first hit London, it meant something a great deal odder than it had done in Spain. I think it seemed nearly as strange as it does to a reader nowadays (and if so Miss Tuve's account is misleading). Donne too, of course, in spite of the Catholic upbringing, felt the strain of the thing, and made use of it. No doubt the trick satisfied the violence of his temperament; he really did feel that the rest of the world was dissolved by the passion of the moment. But the idea of generalizing the doctrine of the Logos also fascinated him because he had a deeply sceptical and inquisitive mind, even if one that felt the drama of scepticism rather than any rational necessity for it. Miss Tuve suggests that we read these ideas back into Donne; so far from that, I think that by sticking to the surviving texts we tend rather to underrate the scepticism of the 1590's, which could not get printed. The tavern talk, it seems probable, was full of brash atheism, suggested for one thing by the repeated changes of official religion; full of what comes down to us in the accusations claiming to report the talk of Marlowe. These are not particularly "like" Marlowe, but he probably said them as well as a lot of other people; the only point of reporting them was that they served to classify him as a well-known wicked type. It is odd to find, for instance, that the great work of Hooker, so much revered by later Anglicans, could be published only by Government influence; no publisher would take it on its merits because they knew nobody would buy it except the Government side. The first readers of Donne in manuscript, it seems clear, were quite ready to pick up the sceptical implications.

They were driven home by his other standard trope, indeed the two together are required if the new idea is to be given its full force and generality. Donne incessantly clashed the rhetorical claim that some individual or pair of individuals was the Logos against the new ideas of Copernicus, in the only form which made them a practical danger to theology—the idea that there is life on other planets, to which presumably Christ has not gone. We are often told that Galileo was condemned merely because he made man unimportant, no longer at the center of the universe; this is unfair to his accusers, and I suspect it has been a disingenuous way of avoiding the real difficulty he raised. Man could easily be made trivial as half of the paradox that he was also supreme. The career of Bruno makes the position clearer; one of the main points in his condemnation was that he believed in a plurality of worlds. If there are more worlds than one they cannot all be under the control of one Pope; if Copernicus says that the earth behaves like the planets we are faced with the problem of how the inhabitants of other planets can achieve salvation. Of course your own planet, in that age of discovery, raised the same problem very sharply; wherever one's ship beached one found innocent islanders or civilized Chinese or what not. But it could be said that they all might have heard of Christ, and ought to be under the Pope; about the inhabitants of Mars no such argument could be used. The separate planet stood for freedom. Milton, for example, was being particularly Protestant when he put in his epic, though he was shifty about astronomy, lines like "Stored in each orb perhaps with some that live." But he could not have gone on to discuss their relation to the Redeemer; the problem was a real one to both sects; the point was that it was sharper for the Catholics, since they were committed to a single living authority as well as a single Christ, and the Protestants tended to ride out of the difficulty (so far as they admitted it) by treating it as one that hurt the Catholics more.

I deny, then, that Donne is simply "using" a well-known trope, the standard howling hyperbole of the Counter-Reformation, when he identifies any person or pair of persons he chooses to praise with the

Logos; because he regularly throws in the idea forbidden to Catholics of a separate planet, out of reach of the Pope, and this inherently lifts the old trope into a new intellectual air. For one thing, on the new planet, having got there by recognizing a mystery, you can thumb your nose at the old earth and express your personality or your unconscious desires. You might even be thumbing your nose at industrious persons who can't understand what you mean because they know the rules of the rhetoricians.

I. A. RICHARDS

ⅇ

The Places and the Figures[1]

With a tradition we incur its wars along with the rest and one measure of our participation may be our readiness to suspect. Even a harmless-looking academic sentence may not be exempt: "In the renaissance, as in earlier times, educated men amplified a subject by drawing it as a matter of course through the topics of invention." Of these sixteen are intrinsic: definition, division, genus, species, contraries, contradictories, comparison, similarity, dissimilarity, adjuncts, cause, effect, antecedent, consequent, notation, and conjugates. These supply the *artificial* arguments, "so called because they are discoverable through the art of topical investigation." In addition there are the extrinsic, *inartificial* arguments, whose source is testimony. The Lucifer-like fall of this word *artificial* (along with *trivial*) is an indication of a shift in the intent of education since then. We are not so sure, now, that we should amplify subjects rather than contract them, and this not merely because, in contrast to the renaissance, we are short of time rather than of books. There is a hidden polemic behind the decline of these studies and another behind attempts to restore them. The handling of language comes so near us that we may with reason wonder whether such a thing as an impartial view of its aims is possible.

Reprinted from *Speculative Instruments*, pp. 155-69, by I. A. Richards by permission of Routledge & Kegan Paul Ltd. and The University of Chicago Press. Copyright 1955 under the International Copyright Union. To be reissued by Harcourt, Brace and World, Inc.

The occasion for these doubtings and deliberations is supplied by two books[2] which raise the question, without attempting explicit answer, how far Shakespeare and Milton owed their achievements to their school training.

Mr. Clark's book is a rich and very well documented contribution to the history of education, judicious, instructive, graceful, and well ballasted with humour and caution. Sister Miriam Joseph's work is more ambitious and conjectural. It relies largely on T. W. Baldwin's book, *William Shakspere's Small Latine and Lesse Greeke,* as to what the poet's schooling may have been and is chiefly concerned with establishing—through laborious and systematic collation—a close parallelism or equivalence between logical and rhetorical teaching and the work of the figurists of Shakespeare's time. These figurists, of whom Puttenham is the best known, stretched the notion of a figure as "a form of speech artfully varied from common usage" (Quintilian) to cover—with changed headings and nomenclature—the points handled by others under Logic and Rhetoric. By reclassifying the figures Sister Miriam Joseph succeeds in compiling "an eclectic handbook" in which each item is discussed in extracts from the Tudor author who in her judgment handles it best.

This was no light undertaking and the labour and skill it has required should be insisted upon. So should the utility of having a clear and well arranged compendium, in their own words, of what Shakespeare's contemporaries thought most worth while remarking about the art of composition. These observations and distinctions sum up a long tradition now abandoned. They are presented here in a form convenient for our reflection and we have an improved opportunity to consider what they were trying to do and how this differs from whatever current attempts we may be making toward the same general end —improvement of verbal conduct.

Before venturing into these very difficult considerations, there are some relatively minor matters I would like to touch upon and put aside. Sister Miriam Joseph set herself an additional task—the exemplification from Shakespeare of the whole body of these named and described devices of composition. Here occasionally she gives her thesis a shade too much benefit of the doubt, prepossessing a word with a meaning to suit her purpose in a fashion especially dangerous with Shakespeare. She equates *invention,* for example, over-simply with "finding matter for speech or writing," though its senses of devising, fabricating, discovering, and originating were all current in

Shakespeare's time. "To the Elizabethan, invention meant finding matter for composition" (p. 92) is an assertion which narrows interpretation unduly. It is a very frequent meaning, without doubt, but neither the only meaning nor the most active meaning in Tarquin's cry, "O what excuse can my invention make?" or in others among the passages she cites. To suppose that it is flattens them out somewhat comically. And in general, it is not, I think, unfair to say that this preoccupation with rhetorical usages has been an obstacle as often as it has been an aid to her comments, which rarely add to or light up the accepted meanings. This in its way is an outcome. These specimens from Shakespeare, arranged in an order strictly parallel to that of her eclectic textbook, do enable us to ask rather pointedly how far this sort of concern with composition is useful in reading. In the "eclectic handbook" we are identifying the figures through explanations and examples; returning thence to Shakespeare, we should be able to reverse the process and consider what help our now technicalized interest in the figures gives to each passage.

Here I think Sister Miriam Joseph has allowed herself to be distracted by a collational or biographical aim instructively typical of recent scholarship. The interesting question is surely NOT whether Shakespeare .uses a given figure, but what *that* variation from flat writing does for him and for us just there. Sister Miriam Joseph does indeed demonstrate that all the named devices of the arts of language "with two or three negligible exceptions" are employed by Shakespeare. It is not so clear that the trick of identifying the figure is an aid to the reader; still less that any *conscious* employment of it was part of Shakespeare's method. This whole study seems in fact still to be in danger of forgetting one of the morals which animate and add its undertone of grave concern to *Love's Labour's Lost*.

On the more specific question, "How far does Shakespeare's use of the devices of language traditionally described in Rhetoric tell us anything about his schooling?" it behooves us, surely, to be extremely wary. Shakespeare, notoriously, will not abide our question. It looks as if he could have picked up almost any lore from anywhere. He, who illustrates so much, could illustrate "rhetorical theory in its entire scope," if any man ever could, without any need for formal instruction. "Rhetorical theory in its entire scope" is after all no more than a somewhat chaotic collection of observations made on the ways of lively, venturesome speech and writing. It would be very strange if the liveliest and most venturesome writer did *not* fully illustrate these observed ways. It is a long and hazardous hop from this to the position that "He shows a grasp of the theory as presented by the various texts through Quintilian."[3] There are ambiguities of "grasp" and "theory" to watch here. No doubt Shakespeare does frequently show acquaintance with the formal discussion of rhetoric, as with how much else in contemporary studies; but we do not suppose him to have had legal or medical training. It is very likely that he would be curious about the arts of language (in the medieval sense of "art"), but in so far as he was an artist in the contrasting modern sense, it would be over-simple to conclude that his practical skill *need* have owed anything substantial to school studies.

Behind this problem of biography several more important questions lurk: to mention two, as to the kind of proof such points may admit and as to the pedagogic relations between precept and example. Sister Miriam Joseph does not enter upon their discussion. A modern student of the *Topica* ("Dialectic is a process of criticism wherein lies the path to the principles of all inquiries," 101*b*; "Moreover, it is well to expand the argument and insert things that it does not require at all . . . for in the multitude of the details the whereabouts of the fallacy is obscured," 157*a*) ought, I think, to be deeply troubled, though to be tolerant toward Aristotle's treatment of dialectic has been the tradition. The fundamental and double-edged old question which that treatment clouds and slights is as curative today as ever: What sorts of persuasion are there? and to what ends may we reasonably employ them? This is a question we all hope to dodge. To be local and specific in this matter: which sorts of points in literary history are capable of being established with what sorts of security? When a highly conjectural "Maybe so!" is the best we can hope for in a given case, how much collective toil and elaboration of detail is justified in its pursuit? Academic tradition (which may doom itself so) is apt to regard such queries as no more than graduate growing pains. The purity of the scholar's quest for knowledge is often supposed to sanction no matter what waste of time and talents, and in many quarters there is genuine ignorance as to what else a student of literature could be doing. It is well to remember that more than a little unemployment for academics is one of the more persistent of the economists' prophecies. In a time of high competition for needed endowment not many modern literary inquiries are going to be easy to justify.

Two answers are usually given to such gloomy reflections. One is that the inquiry may be of value—however unprofitable in itself—

through things encountered on the way. The bootless journey may be through fine scenery. Here there were many short passages of Shakespeare—but these are otherwise available; much lively, if ramshackle, sixteenth-century prose, not easily come at, and the spectacle of a great and derelict endeavour spanning 2000 years. The other answer is that the inquiry may be of value as suggesting other problems, which may be tackled with better hope of outcome. To me this second answer offers comfort and I would help if I could to prepare some of these other problems, among them the ordering of the intellectual ends. But let me turn first to the pedagogic question of precept and example.

We are at present risking the futures of all those to whom we give any sort of teaching that does not shame us upon practices highly contrary to those which Mr. Baldwin and Sister Miriam Joseph believe that Shakespeare underwent, and Mr. Clark describes so carefully in his account of Milton's schooling. If those practices were wise then it is hardly possible that ours are not extremely unwise, and *vice versa*. These schoolrooms present a grim picture indeed to modern eyes—"heroic" is Mr. Baldwin's word for it, and certainly it was not bloodless, the rod was an ever-present threat. "If the foregrounds be well and thoroughly beaten in"—it has been endlessly remarked before that too many schoolmasters seem to have taken literally this phrase from the directions for teaching the Lily *Grammar*. The children—absurdly young for such work as we think—rose at five; "class from six to nine; breakfast; class from nine-fifteen to eleven; dinner; class from one to five; supper. After supper, from six to seven, the pupils recited to their fellows what they had learned during the day." The materials on which all this time was spent were rules from the Lily *Latin Grammar* to be memorized, and *Sententiae pueriles* or *Catonis disticha moralia* to be construed. Later on, there were English sentences from *Sententiae Ciceronis* to be translated and compared with the original and passages from the Psalms, Proverbs, Ecclesiasticus or Ecclesiastes to be rendered in Latin. Erasmus and Terence and perhaps Plautus would supply the lighter fare. At a certain stage a grounding in Cicero's *Topica* prepared the boys to study the one hundred and thirty-two figures of speech of Susenbrotus. "The method prescribed unremitting exercise in grammar, rhetoric, and logic. Grammar dominated the lower forms, logic and rhetoric the upper. In all forms the order was first to learn precepts, then to employ them as a tool of analysis in reading, and finally to use them as a guide in composition."

We had better, I think, clearly face any suggestion that this procedure was *responsible* for the excellence in literature of Shakespeare and Milton. Sister Miriam Joseph does not, I think, anywhere state such a view. The nearest she comes to suggesting it is perhaps in the following (p. 10): after memorizing Ovid, "A form would recite to the one next above it, which in turn would recite to the one higher." (I can just hear them.) "Thus were poetic rhythms, as distinguished from mere metre, fixed in the ears of the students as an aid in writing verse. Elizabethan poetry illustrates the results of this method."

I hardly know to what place or figure Fraunce or Puttenham would have assigned this use of "illustrates." Possibly it is best considered under "Notation." In Sister Miriam Joseph's summary (p. 339), "When a word is regarded as a word, it is called a notation, that is, a mark representing a sound. As such it may shed light on the thing it names through its etymology, or it may occasion ambiguity or obscurity. . . . From the fact that a word or notation may have a number of different meanings arises ambiguity, sometimes inadvertent, sometimes deliberate." Fraunce, however, like logicians in many ages, prefers to hand a prime problem here to others: "So in Notation, the interpretation of the name, seemeth rather the dutie of a dictionary, then of any Logicall institution . . . it seemeth also a Rhetoricall agnomination." "Agnomination" here is Fraunce's way of saying "pun," fifty-five years before the first appearance of that handy word. (Incidentally, Fraunce's reference to a dictionary makes better sense today than in terms of any dictionary existing in 1588). It is not clear, however, how far the figures of ambiguity can help us with what "illustrates" may be doing here. It might be *syllepsis of the sense*— the senses combined being "to set in a good light" and "to confer honour on" as well as, perhaps, "to exemplify." We may hope the figure is not *schematismus*: "when the Orator propoundeth his meaning by a circuite of speech, wherein he would have that understoode by a certaine suspicion which he doth not speake" (Peacham's definition). We may be wrong, however, in supposing any figure to be present. Quintilian's definition reads: "a form of language *artfully varied* from *common usage*." We may take "Elizabethan poetry illustrates the results of this method" as an instance of a type of statement which is common usage, routine rather than artful, standard practice rather than a variation. But then Quintilian's definition itself, if we look at it hard, seems very odd. Are there not plenty of things we would wish to call figures which are in conformity with, indeed prescribed by, common usage—from "My dear Sir" onwards? "Usage," too, if we will consider it, will appear to be a very shifty word to be given such responsibilities.[4]

Sentences like "Elizabethan poetry illustrates the results of such methods" merit and will repay more attention than they commonly get. It would help a lot if they were generally recognized for what they are—necessarily void, inevitably misleading, formally incompetent. They do not have the structure needed to do what they profess to be doing. They assume a view of causality which is altogether over-simple. Educators have been patiently trying for some fifty years—with only slight success so far, it is true—to discover something reliable about the causal connections between teaching procedures and outcomes. This sort of confident blindness to the complexities is among the chief obstacles. In this instance common sense can detect the absurdity; not so in all cases. And I do not think the logical and rhetorical tools presented in this volume are a sufficient supplement to common sense in the undertaking. We must conclude, I believe, that even were it established that Shakespeare had received the most thorough school grounding in the figures through precept and practice, nothing would be proved either as to his debt to it or as to any general desirability of such modes of teaching.

All this, however, leaves many possibilities open. Some sort of systematic study of some at least of the devices of language so painstakingly labelled and arranged by these logicians, rhetoricians, and figurists may still be what education chiefly lacks. We may decide that the treatment reported and summarized by Sister Miriam Joseph is not the right treatment (and for more than a century few teachers have had any doubts upon this) without denying the need for treatment. Behind the proliferations of nomenclature and the upside-down practices of these old-time pedagogues, there was an aim which we have often lost sight of. They did at least direct their pupils' attention upon the *means* employed in language—if they came short in consideration of ends. By contrast, without much improving our understanding of these ends, we have in our schools almost entirely left out concern for the means. I am exaggerating here. We have, it is true, made a glorious advance in our regard for regularity in spelling. We have done away—in the schools—with our liberty to spell words to suit our pleasure and our purpose. And since the Dictionary assumed Divine Right, our freedom to trim and embellish our words departed with our freedom in spelling. Prosthesis, epenthesis, proparalepsis (or paragoge), not to mention metathesis and antisthecon, have been banished along with aphaeresis, syncope, synaloepha, and apocope[5] as means of rhythming our discourse, varying our orthography (and teasing the printer). We have set up a cult of uniformity here which has sensibly diminished the power of the pen. We have preferred rigidity (with some gain in mechanical convenience) to flexibility and resource and their attendant risks. And this regrettable interference, which has standardized us where we least needed ruling, has barred the natural way toward the improved spelling which English has needed so badly. A sad example this of the dangers of reform on the wrong level.

Probably we should be glad that the influences which were ready to standardize such an inconvenient and senseless spelling did not make any comparable attempt to freeze composition. Grammar suffered a little, as with the legendary rule against the split infinitive, but the itch to regularize did not reach the places and the figures. This whole world of effort—so long a prime focus for the teacher—enjoyed instead an increasing and protective neglect. So much so that when not long ago some of the very same concerns revived which had originally prompted the *Topica* and the *Rhetoric*, not many of those who set out, behind "anti-metaphysical" or "non-Aristotelian" banners, to teach us all how we should talk, evinced much curiosity about the ancient highways heading into their well-advertised new territory.

Doubtless they were justified. Few things are harder than to use, in the interests of one sort of metaphysics, work fed from and guided by another. Semantics had too much to do in making some observations on a few choice vices of language and contriving some corrective exercises, to bother with ancient remedies which might even seem to exploit and encourage these vices. It is more surprising that our modern theorists in Rhetoric, though they have described types of ambiguity, obliquities, transferences . . . which extend and deepen the catalogued varieties of interactions between meanings, have been nearly as slow to use the work of their forerunners. The dusty state of the materials may in part explain this and Sister Miriam Joseph's book will help here. The antic nomenclature of the figures and our not unfounded distrust of old-fashioned terms in Logic are added grounds. Still more dissuasive perhaps has been the feeling that the old treatment was encumbered with an over-elaborated, elsewhere directed methodology which would distract imaginative insight rather than stir it. In brief, we fear codification in these matters and with good reason.

Against the old treatment a number of charges, of varying gravity,

may be brought. The least might be a certain recklessness or frivolity
of purpose. It is amusing but not reassuring to notice how often the
inducement offered is that this study "helpeth to amplify any kind of
speech and make it more copious," or "copiously to dilate any matter
or sentence." An automatic aid to long-windedness, we may exclaim,
perhaps unfairly. We are not schoolboys short of matter. It is worse
when we are told that we will be enabled "to fortifie and make
stronge our assercion or sentence, to prove and defende, by the force
and power of art, things passyng the compasse and reach of our capac-
itie and witte." These, we may nowadays think, are the very things
we should be taught NOT to be assertive or persuasive about. Witt-
genstein's "Whereof we may not speak, thereof we must be silent,"
despite its equivocation, may well seem to us safer doctrine. From
Gorgias onwards too much in the literature of rhetoric has been sales-
talk selling sales-talk; and for very good reasons we are more interested
today in defensives against than in aids to eloquent persuasion.
Though often remarked, this fear and its implications have been little
studied. It contrasts strongly with the attitude of a Milton, conscious
champion among tongue-fighters and pen-wielders. Perhaps the ideal
is changing, at long last. The orator-statesman (along with the war-
rior-king) may be giving place to another model in the educator's
eye. Of course, there have always been those who distrusted eloquence
(as there have always been pacifists); but recently perhaps the
grounds of the distrust may have widened and improved. We may be
adding to our conscious weakness an awareness that in this verbal
warfare it is not the opponent's views which get demolished so much
as other things of more importance to mankind.

But before we pat ourselves on the back for some new sort of
honesty and care for truth, it may be well to go nearer to the sources.
Here is a renaissance translation of Isocrates' prose hymn to—Rhetoric,
shall we call it? But what we understand by Rhetoric is, of course,
just the question:

> To speak effectually of the full force of this science, we
> shall finde nothing done with reason which hath not been
> brought about by the helpe of Eloquence, so that she re-
> maineth the chiefest guide of all our thoughts and deed, being
> the only instrument of the wise and learned.[6]

Without supposing her to be the peculiar mistress of the ambitious
and the facile, we are likely to think that the early definition, "so to

speak as to gain the assent of the audience as far as possible,"[7] ought
to be a clear warning. The assent of the audience may have every sort
of motives, and our judgment of audiences may incline us to doubt
whether success with them is any good evidence of the soundness of
what has been said.[8] If so we are back clearly, in the earlier pages of
Gorgias, siding with Socrates on the important difference between in-
ducements to belief and instruments of instruction.

Perhaps this return to the sources may be our best way to search
our own minds on what is still a frontier problem—discussed today most
often as the place of emotive components in discourse. Isocrates, as
defender of Gorgias, may help us to remember that the conduct of
this search of the mind is itself the prize for which the opposing forces
endlessly struggle and intrigue. What I have just quoted from him is
a renaissance interpretation. A modern translation reads:

> If we sum up the character of this power, we shall find that
> no reasonable thing is done anywhere in the world without
> logos, that logos is the leader of all actions and thoughts, and
> that those who make most use of it are the wisest of mankind.[9]

There seems to be a world of difference between these versions.
"What is speaking here for what?" seeks precedence over the apparently more manageable question: "What is being said?" Isocrates was
at nearly if not quite as much pains as Plato himself to claim superior
integrity, a more perfect inner order, as the source and aim of the
education he offered. To him the Socratics were disputants and their
dialectic (eristic, he prefers to call it) little better than a training in
trickery, a corruption of lively-witted youth. As to what Plato might
have thought of the passage I have quoted, we may remember that
at the end of *Phaedrus* he makes Socrates say of Isocrates: "Nature,
my friend, has implanted a love of wisdom in the mind of the man."
A noble compliment to pay a great, lifelong opponent, the head of
your rival school!

The masters perhaps could have understood one another enough
to come to some accord. It was another matter with their followers—
especially when one of these was of the stature of Aristotle. It is argu-
able that both rhetoric—as "that which enabled us to perfect almost
everything we have achieved in the way of civilization"—and dialectic—as the audit of meaning—fell away within their authors' lifetimes,
that the first became a study of suasive tricks separable from the
criticism of the springs of the suasion, and the other an intellectual

pingpong unconcerned with understanding. But such an argument would perhaps exemplify both degenerations. What matters, in any case, is that modern attempts to improve the conduct of language should recognize how deep the undertaking must go. It is not enough to be "non-Aristotelian" while employing the least acceptable tricks of Aristotelian rhetoric, or to pursue propaganda-analysis propagandistically. Nor will it do to disparage renaissance rhetoric without deeper examination of its aims and nature than Puttenham, for example, gave them, or indeed without as deep a self-search into the grounds for the disparagement as a critic can compass. Doubtless the supreme balance, *phronesis*, and justice which any inquiry into language theory, language teaching, language control demand, are far away. Still this demand, which any interest in these matters must, however shyly and remotely, posit, does—whether we like it or not— rule all our efforts, if only as the latest, most encompassing, and synoptic principles of the physicist rule his. The strange thing is that of late his principles grow ever wider and deeper, whereas ours . . .

Perhaps I have only been echoing, darkly and yearningly, Richard Sherry in the "Epystle" to his *A Treatise of Schemes and Tropes* (1550): "The common scholemasters be wont in reading to saye unto their scholers: *Hic est figura:* and sometime to axe them, *Per quam figuram?* But what profit is herein if they go no further?" [10]

My doubt, though, is whether there ever has been any "further" in these directions and by these ways. Not because no more of the same sort can be done. It would be possible to double the two hundred or so Tudor figures by magnifying distinctions, but the upshot would be the same. As with other ancillary studies—grammar, prosody, phonetics among them—what was intended to be a help became a hindrance, preventing the student from remembering the true subject of all his study. Rhetoric and Dialectic, quarrelling with one another, jointly forgot their common aim. And now it is not easy to see in these products of scholastic drudgery the issue of an original concern with the salvation of man.

NOTES

1. A review article published in *The Kenyon Review*, January, 1949.
2. *John Milton at St. Paul's School:* A study of ancient rhetoric in English renaissance education, by Donald Lemen Clark (Columbia University Press, 1948). *Shakespeare's Use of the Arts of Language,* by Sister Miriam Joseph, C.S.C. (Columbia University Press, 1947).

3. T. W. Baldwin, *William Shakspere's Small Latine and Lesse Greeke*, II, 378, quoted by Sister Miriam Joseph, p. 12.

4. I have examined this treacherous custom at some length in *Interpretation in Teaching*, ch. xv and xvi, in the hope of persuading the careful that it is unwise to found our attempts to guide language on words which themselves so much need control. No wonder the attempts founder (if so limping a specimen of paronomasia may be pardoned).

5. See *Shakespeare's Use of the Arts of Language*, pp. 51-4.

6. *Nicocles*, 9, Thomas Forrest's translation, quoted by Clark, p. 9.

7. *Ad Herennium*, I, 2.

8. It is interesting to recall the connection between the new rhetoric and the Panhellenic ideal. To Isocrates, father of humanistic culture, "the new dream of national achievement appeared to be a mighty inspiration" (Werner Jaeger, *Paideia*, Vol. III, p. 53).

9. *Paideia*, Vol. III, p. 89.

10. Quoted by Clark, p. 168. What do we gain by being able to name an instance of aposiopesis?

PART II

Individual Poets and Modes of Poetry

YVOR WINTERS

The 16th Century Lyric in England
A Critical and Historical Reinterpretation

And it is not always face,
Clothes or Fortune gives the grace;
Or the feature, or the youth;
But the Language and the Truth.
Ben Jonson

I

Anyone who has read large amounts of the lyric poetry of the sixteenth century will realize that most of it is poor, much of it astonishingly poor. I believe that the lack of critical discrimination and interest on the part of such textual and other historical scholars as have worked in the field has led to serious misconceptions. We are creatures in a considerable measure of habit, and we tend in the main to be uncritical of our habits. It has come to be axiomatic that the Petrarchan movement of the late sixteenth century, especially as represented by Sidney and Spenser, is the most characteristic movement of the century and that it contains the best poetry of the century if we except certain work by Shakespeare, Donne, and perhaps (this depends on the critic) Ben Jonson. We tend to find in poetry about what we are looking for, and in the early sixteenth century most of us look, perhaps not altogether consciously, for imperfect Sidneys; but the poets preceding Sidney and Spenser, though they produced a good deal of imperfect Petrarchism, are not essentially Petrarchists. They constitute a school as definite as the Metaphysical, Petrarchist, or Cavalier, and a school fully as impressive as any of these, at least as to quality.

A literary fashion of a period may easily become fossilized in liter-

Reprinted from *Poetry,* LIII (1939), pp. 258-72, 320-35; LIV (1939), pp. 35-51, by permission of the editors and of the author. Copyright 1939 by Yvor Winters.

ary history in such a way as to obscure important values and great writers. This occurred at the close of the eighteenth century, when the rising romantic school, as represented chiefly by Gray and Collins, obscured the two greatest poetic talents of the period, those of Samuel Johnson and of Charles Churchill: Johnson and Churchill belonged to the party going out of power; in the subsequent generations they had few if any sympathizers, and their poetry had no opportunity to become embalmed in any authoritative body of criticism; their great poems, Johnson's two prologues to *Comus* and to *A Word to the Wise,* and Churchill's *Dedication to Warburton,* have been little read and less understood. So in the sixteenth century: the graces of Sidney and Spenser, graces which are often superficial but which are always obvious and frequently charming, and the legend of Sidney's character, have tended to obscure another school of poets greater as poets and more important if one is to have a clear idea of the history of poetic development in the century. It is curious to note that the one man whose critical writing did more, perhaps, than that of any other to establish the legend of Sidney's personality and hence to achieve the end described, was Sir Fulke Greville, one of the greatest of the poets in consequence obscured.

I shall attempt in this essay to define certain major talents of the century who have been neglected, along with certain related minor talents equally neglected; to revaluate certain established reputations; to offer a new historical outline and a new set of critical emphases for the century; and to base my conclusions in every case on poems specifically named. I shall be laboring under two difficulties: I shall be endeavoring in nearly every reader to shake an habitual approach to the century and to stimulate to new perceptions; and I shall of necessity have to be sparing of quotations. The reader of good will who has any deep interest in the subject will in all fairness read carefully the poems on which I base my conclusions, will read them after having read my analyses and with my analyses in mind. Even then, a fair judgment of my conclusions will scarcely be possible till the reader has through rereading and the lapse of time absorbed the poems and the critical ideas at his leisure. I do not wish to sound unduly pretentious in my warning. Much of what I say will of necessity be commonplace or only a little out of the run of ordinary opinion; but my position is essentially new, and I believe that I have made certain critical discoveries of the first importance. The belief is an accretion of about fifteen years of fairly constant immersion in the poetry under consideration.[1]

If we can disengage ourselves sufficiently, then, from the preconception that 16th century poetry is essentially Petrarchist, to sift the good poems, regardless of school or of method, from the bad, we shall find that the Petrarchist movement produced nothing worth remembering between Skelton and Sidney, in spite of a tremendous amount of Petrarchan experimentation during this period, if we except certain partially Petrarchan poems by Surrey and by Wyatt, and that the poetry written during this interim which is worth remembering belongs to a school in every respect antithetical to the Petrarchist school, a school to which Wyatt and Surrey contributed important efforts, perhaps their best, but which flourished mainly between Surrey and Sidney and in a few men who survived or came to maturity somewhat later, a school which laid the groundwork for the greatest achievements in the entire history of the English lyric, which itself left us some of those greatest achievements, and which is almost wholly neglected and forgotten by the anthologists and by the historians of the period, even by the editors, for the greater part, of the individual contributors to the school.[2]

The characteristics of the typical poem of the school are these: a theme usually broad, simple, and obvious, even tending toward the proverbial, but usually a theme of some importance, humanly speaking; a feeling restrained to the minimum required by the subject; a rhetoric restrained to a similar minimum, the poet being interested in his rhetoric as a means of stating his matter as economically as possible, and not, as are the Petrarchans, in the pleasures of rhetoric for its own sake. There is also in the school a strong tendency towards aphoristic statement, many of the best poems being composed wholly of aphorisms, in the medieval manner exemplified by Chaucer's great ballade *Flee from the press*, or, if short, being composed as single aphorisms. If we except Chaucer's ballade, we have no high development of the aphoristic lyric in England or in Scotland before the 16th century, and the great aphoristic lyrics of Gascoigne and of Raleigh probably represent the highest level to which the mode has ever been brought. Further, the aphoristic lyrics of the early sixteenth century represent only one aspect of the school I have in mind; Gascoigne, for example, cast his greatest poem, *Gascoigne's Woodmanship*, in the form of a consecutive and elaborate piece of exposition, and several other poems near his highest level are expository rather than aphoristic in outline.

The wisdom of poetry of this kind lies not in the acceptance of a truism, for anyone can accept a truism, at least formally, but in the realization of the truth of the truism: the realization resides in the feeling, the style. Only a master of style can deal successfully in a plain manner with obvious matter: we are concerned with the type of poetry which is perhaps the hardest to compose and the last to be recognized, a poetry not striking nor original as to subject, but merely true and universal, that is, in a sense commonplace, not striking nor original in rhetorical procedure, but direct and economical, a poetry which permits itself originality, that is the breath of life, only in the most restrained and refined of subtleties in diction and in cadence, but which by virtue of those subtleties inspires its universals with their full value as experience. The best poems in the early school are among the most perfect examples of the classical virtues to be found in English poetry. I am aware that Gascoigne as a critic recommended the choice of original subject matter, but his concept of originality in this respect was naïve if regarded in the light of later practice, and his own practice must be judged in relation to later practice.

The best poems of Barnabe Googe[3] are the following: *Of Nicholas Grimald, To Dr. Balle, To Mistress A., To the Translation of Pallingenius, Of Mistress D.S., Of Money,* and *Coming Homeward Out of Spain. Of Money* I quote entire:

> Give money me, take friendship he who list,
> For friends are gone, come once adversity,
> When money yet remaineth safe in chest,
> That quickly can thee bring from misery.
> Fair face show friends when riches do abound,
> Come time of proof, farewell they must away.
> Believe me well, they are not to be found
> If God but send thee once a lowering day.
> Gold never starts aside, but in distress
> Finds ways enough to ease thine heaviness.

The poem illustrates the qualities which I have enumerated. The sprung rhythm of this poem, which is most noticeable in the fifth line, is, while not essential to the school, very common in a few poets, especially in Googe and in Nashe, and is peculiarly expressive of their mood, in its combination of matter-of-factness with passion. By sprung rhythm, I mean the juxtaposition of accented syllables by either of two methods: by the dropping of an unaccented syllable from between two accented, as in the seven-syllable couplets of Robert Greene and in the sonnets of Wyatt; or by the raising of the accentual value of a syllable that should normally be unaccented till it is accented equally with the syllables on either side of it as in the poem just quoted. In the former type of sprung rhythm, the norm which maintains the identity of the line is accentual; in the latter it is syllabic.

George Turbervile is one of the most minute of the finished stylists of the century[4]: perhaps only Thomas Morley, the madrigalist, is more nearly infinitesimal, as he is likewise more polished. The important poems by Turbervile are: *To the Roving Pirate, To One that Had Little Wit, To an Old Gentlewoman Who Painted Her Face, Of the Clock and the Cock,* and *That All Things Are as They Are Used.* There are charming odds and ends of phrasing scattered through a good many additional poems. In *To One That Had Little Wit,* Turbervile raises pertness to artistry:

> I thee advise
> If thou be wise
> To keep thy wit
> Though it be small.
> 'Tis hard to get
> And far to fet—
> 'Twas ever yet
> Dear'st ware of all.

In the poem *To an Old Gentlewoman* he combines pertness with pathos:

> Leave off, good Beroe, now
>   To sleek thy shriveled skin,
> For Hecuba's face will never be
>   As Helen's hue hath been.
>
> Let Beauty go with youth,
>   Renounce the glozing glass,
> Take book in hand: that seemly rose
>   Is woxen withred grass.
>
> Remove thy Peacock's plumes
>   Thou crank and curious dame:
> To other trulls of tender years
>   Resign the flag of fame.

In *The Clock and the Cock* he defines the trivial and suggests the mysterious. In *That All Things Are as They Are Used* and in *To the Roving Pirate,* he attains a kind of forthright moral dignity.

The greatest poet of the school is George Gascoigne, a poet unfortunate in that he has been all but irrecoverably pigeon-holed as a dull
precursor in the history of certain major forms, but who deserves to
be ranked, I believe, among the six or seven greatest lyric poets of the
century, and perhaps higher. I base this opinion on the following
poems: *Gascoigne's De Profundis,* the second and third of *Gascoigne's
Memories, The Constancy of a Lover, Dan Bartholmew's Dolorous
Discourses* (from *Dan Bartholmew of Bath*), *Gascoigne's Woodmanship,* and *In Praise of a Gentlewoman Who though She Was not
very Fair Yet Was She as Hard-Favored as Might Be.* There are a good
many other poems of charm but of less power and scope.[5]

The third of the *Memories,* a poem on the subject of the spend-
thrift, and bearing certain resemblances to Wyatt's poem addressed to
Sir Francis Bryan, but more pointed, compact, and moving, is one of
the finest, and displays on a large scale the mastered hardness, the
aphoristic analysis, which we have already encountered in Googe.
The tone is set in the opening and never falters:

> The common speech is, spend and God will send;
> But what sends he? a bottle and a bag,
> A staff, a wallet, and a woeful end,
> For such as list in bravery to brag.
> Then if thou covet coin enough to spend,
> Learn first to spend thy budget at the brink,
> So shall the bottom be the faster bound:
> But he that list with lavish hand to link,
> In like expense, a penny with a pound,
> May chance at last to sit aside and shrink
> His hare-brained head without Dame Dainty's Door.

The most striking lines in the poem are probably those embodying
the colloquial personification toward the middle:

> Yet he that yerks old angels out apace,
> And hath no new to purchase dignity,
> When orders fall may chance to lack his grace,
> For haggard hawks mislike an empty hand:
> So stiffly some stick to the mercer's stall,
> Till suits of silk have sweat out all their land,
> So oft thy neighbors banquet in thy hall,
> Till Davy Debet in thy parlor stand,
> And bid thee welcome to thine own decay.

In Gascoigne's society, the destruction of the patrimony was a major catastrophe, and might well be irreparable; it was almost as serious a matter as death or moral disintegration, both of which it might easily involve. Considered in this light, the poem becomes something more than practical didacticism; it becomes a piece of moral analysis, nourished with moral perception. Davy Debet is not only debt, he is the bailiff, the new host, decay itself, and the moral judgment: he is pure terror. The poem displays a measure of the only kind of rhetorical affectation to be found in the school, the affectation of hard directness, supported in part by the traditional alliteration which later poets were to abandon.

There are perfect control and perfect directness in Gascoigne's love poetry:

> That happy hand which hardily did touch
> Thy tender body to my deep delight—

and yet again, from the poem entitled *In Praise of a Gentlewoman*:

> And could Antonius forsake the fair in Rome?
> To love his nutbrown lady best, was this an equal doom?
> I dare well say dames there did bear him deadly grudge,
> His sentence had been shortly said if Faustine had been judge,
> For this I dare avow (without vaunt be it spoke)
> So brave a knight as Anthony held all their necks in yoke:
> I leave not Lucrece out, believe in her who list,
> I think she would have liked his lure, and stooped to his fist.
>
> What mov'd the chieftain, then, to link his liking thus?
> I would some Roman dame were here the question to discuss.
> But I that read her life, do find therein by fame,
> How clear her courtesy did shine, in honor of her name.
> Her bounty did excel, her truth had never peer,
> Her lovely looks, her pleasant speech, her lusty loving cheer.
> And all the worthy gifts, that ever yet were found,
> Within this good Egyptian Queen, did seem for to abound.
> Wherefore he worthy was, to win the golden fleece,
> Which scorned the blazing stars in Rome, to conquer such a piece.
> And she to quite his love, in spite of dreadful death,
> Enshrined with snakes within his tomb, did yield her parting breath.
>
> If fortune favored him, then may that man rejoice,
> And think himself a happy man by hap of happy choice,
> Who loves and is believed of one as good as true,

As kind as Cleopatra was, and yet more bright of hue,
Her eyes as gray as glass, her teeth as white as milk,
A ruddy lip, a dimpled chin, a skin as smooth as silk,
A wight what could you more, that may content man's mind,
And hath supplies for every want, that any man can find,
And may himself assure, when hence his life shall pass,
She will be stung to death with snakes, as Cleopatra was.

In *Gascoigne's De Profundis* the same qualities of style and the
same rich humanity of feeling are heightened to devotional ecstasy:

Before the break of dawning of the day,
Before the light be seen in lofty skies,
Before the sun appear in pleasant wise,
Before the watch (before the watch, I say)
Before the ward that waits therefore alway:
My soul, my sense, my secret thought, my sprite,
My will, my wish, my joy, and my delight:
Unto the Lord that sits in heaven on high,
With hasty wing,
From me doth fling,
And striveth still, unto the Lord to fly.

The greatest poem of the author and of the school, a poem unsur-
passed in the century except by a few of the sonnets of Shakespeare,
is *Gascoigne's Woodmanship*. It is addressed to Lord Grey of Wilton,
and the allegory takes the form of an apology for the author's bad
marksmanship as a huntsman: it appears that he usually misses his
deer, or else kills by accident a doe carrying or nursing young, and
so unfit for food:

My worthy Lord, I pray you wonder not,
To see your woodsman shoot so oft awry,
Nor that he stands amazed like a sot,
And lets the harmless deer unhurt go by.
Or if he strike a doe which is but carrion,
Laugh not good Lord, but favor such a fault,
Take will in worth, he fain would hit the barren,
But though his heart be good, his hap is naught.

He explains this weakness, as one aspect merely of his fatal tendency
to failure; he has likewise shot at law, philosophy, and success as a

courtier, and in every case has failed—in the case of philosophy, he admits his own weakness as the sole cause of failure:

> For proof he bears the note of folly now,
> Who shot sometimes to hit philosophy . . .

In the case of the law and in that of the court, he complains further of his incapacity in the baser arts of succeeding, and these passages have remarkable force. Then follows the sombre and powerful passage in which he introduces his next failure:

> But now behold what mark the man doth find,
> He shoots to be a soldier in his age,
> Mistrusting all the virtues of his mind,
> He trusts the power of his personage.

But he finds that he cannot free himself into the exercise of unalloyed physical strength; he has no taste for putting the innocent villager to the sword:

> He cannot spoil the simple sakeless man,
> Which is content to feed him with his bread;

and neither has he a taste for the type of corruption within the army by which officers are able to acquire wealth. There follows a general meditation upon all of his failures; it concludes with a brilliant passage in which the poem is returned to the allegory:

> Now when my mind doth mumble upon this,
> No wonder then although I pine for pain:
> And whiles mine eyes behold this mirror thus,
> The herd goeth by, and farewell gentle does.

Then follows the conclusion, the greatest passage in the poem, and one of the greatest passages in English lyrical poetry, in which the subject is rehearsed and explained in terms of the allegory; in which the subject is explained in terms of Christian morality; in which the author is justified in so far as it comports with Christian humility that he should justify himself. I wish in particular to call attention to the rhetorical grandeur of this passage, the terseness, the subtlety of subdued but powerful feeling:

> But since my Muse can to my Lord rehearse
> What makes me miss, and why I do not shoot,

Let me imagine in this worthless verse,
If right before me, at my standing's foot,
There stood a doe, and I shall strike her dead,
And then she prove a carrion carcase too,
What figure might I find within my head,
To scuse the rage which ruled me so to do?
Some might interpret my plain paraphrase,
That lack of skill or fortune led the chance,
But I must otherwise expound the case.
I say Jehovah did this doe advance,
And made her bold to stand before me so,
Till I had thrust mine arrow to her heart,
That by the sudden of her overthrow,
I might endeavor to amend my part,
And turn my eyes that they no more behold
Such guileful marks that seem more than they be:
And though they glister outwardly like gold,
Are inwardly but brass, as men may see:
And when I see the milk hang in her teat,
Methinks it saith, old babe learn now to suck,
Who in thy youth couldst never learn the feat
To hit the whites which live with all good luck.
Thus have I told my Lord (God grant in season)
A tedious tale in rhyme, but little reason.

Schelling states that "George Gascoigne was held in high contemporary estimation."[6] He cites numerous passages in support of the assertion, which is worth remembering when we come to the examination of later poetry.

The mature and laconic bitterness of Raleigh, and the bitter terror of Nashe, both found their best expression in the mode established by the poets whom I have been discussing, and continued the mode well into the Petrarchan, and perhaps beyond the Petrarchan, era. Their best poems are *The Lie, What is our life,* and *Even such is time,* by Raleigh; and *In Time of Pestilence* and *Autumn hath all the fruitful summer's treasure,* by Nashe; *The Lie* and *In Time of Pestilence* employ the sequence of aphorisms in a rapid movement and at a high pitch of feeling; all five poems are too well known to require quotation.

II

I have described briefly the chief masters of the school when at its height, but there is much related and earlier poetry in the 16th century which possesses similar qualities and remarkable merit. The procedure of Wyatt resembles that of Gascoigne more closely than it resembles the procedure of Sidney, and if we consider him a member of the school and except Raleigh, he is Gascoigne's most formidable rival. His epigram, *Tagus Farewell*, bears a close resemblance to Googe's poem *On Coming Homeward out of Spain*, probably suggested it, and certainly surpasses it. Wyatt's poem on mutability, beginning *Is it possible*, is one of the finest poems of the century. One should mention as excellent examples of this aspect of Wyatt at least the following poems: *I abide and abide, They flee from me, It may be good, Your looks so often cast, Disdain me not, Perdie I said it not, If thou wilt mighty be, I have sought long, And wilt thou leave me thus, It was my choice, Forget not yet, What should I say, Hate whom ye list, Sighs are my food, Madam withouten many words, Within my breast I never thought it gain, It burneth yet, alas!, Speak thou and speed,* and *Under this stone.* Most of these lyrics are minor; none is as great as the best of Gascoigne or Raleigh; yet nearly all are masterly. The reader coming upon them directly from Gascoigne may be reminded of Sidney, for it is certain that Wyatt had effectively assimilated more of the Italian influence than Gascoigne was able to assimilate; yet if the reader will come to them from Sidney, he is likely to be more strongly reminded of Gascoigne. The resemblance to Gascoigne, which resides in a certain directness of diction and in a rich but matter-of-fact humanity, is the measure of Wyatt's superiority to Sidney. There are a few poems in which the resemblance to Gascoigne is more noticeable, especially, *A spending hand;* and there are some thoroughly fine poems that bear a greater resemblance to Sidney, especially, *My lute awake, All heavy minds, Comfort thyself, Lo what it is to love, Leave then to slander love, Ah, my heart, what aileth thee.* The sonnets, of course, like certain other poems are Petrarchan in intention as well as in derivation; but of the entire group, only one, *Whoso list to hunt,* has any notable interest as poetry. In making these comparisons, I am concerned with qualities of style and not with the derivations of individual poems, passages, or lines. Wyatt, in a few of his more polished lyrics, and within a limited range of subject, came nearer to effecting a fusion of these two tendencies—before, properly speaking, the advent of either of the two schools best representing them—than anyone else was to come until the period of Jonson and Donne.

Surrey has moved closer to Sidney, but in part because of the language inherited from Wyatt, in part because of the relative stiffness of his meters, lines emerge suggestive of the plainer school:

> The secret thoughts imparted with such trust,
> The wanton talk, the divers change of play,
> The friendship sworn, each promise kept so just,
> Wherewith we passed the winter nights away.

And again:

> Calm is the sea; the waves work less and less.

In general, we may say of Surrey that he exemplifies in some measure a struggle between the two tendencies: he is striving to come closer to what Sidney later achieved than his language permits; whereas in Wyatt there was, at the best, a kind of reconciliation. There is a similar struggle later and on a larger scale in Drayton and in Greville, and a similar reconciliation in Jonson. When I use the term struggle, I mean that there is a tendency for certain lines to stand out sharply from the more or less Petrarchan frame-work as reversions to the earlier type; the struggle is not, ordinarily, destructive of poetic style, but it is sometimes very obvious notwithstanding. Nicholas Grimald, ordinarily one of the worst of poets, contributed one fine poem to Tottel's miscellany, a poem purely in the older manner, beginning: *Mirror of matrons.* Thomas Lord Vaux, who appeared in Tottel and in *The Paradise of Dainty Devices,* is one of the finest representatives of the school; except for the small number of his poems, he is nearly as impressive as Wyatt. His best poems are: *I loath that I did love,* in Tottel, and in the later collection, *When I look back,* and *When all is done and said,* the last in particular being one of the most suave and urbane fusions of wit, wisdom, and sincere feeling to be found in the miscellanies. One should mention also Jasper Heywood, the son of Heywood the epigrammatist, and the maternal uncle of John Donne, who contributed a few poems to *The Paradise of Dainty Devices.* Heywood was a Jesuit and for much of his life an exile. His poetry is competent in execution; his moral penetration is sometimes impressive. As a poet, he suffers from the fact that his morality is purely a morality of expediency—he expresses a grief motivated mainly by the realization that the best laid plans go wrong; though a priest, he is worldly, yet within narrow limits his poetry is moving. His best poem is that beginning, *My friend if thou wilt credit me in ought*, an analytical poem strongly suggesting Gascoigne but looser in texture.

The technical range of this school, as compared with the range of the greater Petrarchans, is narrow, but this is not in itself a defect. Morally these poets display a great range and acute perceptions. A limited technique, if it is mastered, may be capable of perception as fine and as varied as a more elaborate one. In fact, the elaboration of technique may be carried considerably beyond the point at which the elaboration has any immediate usefulness, and that is more or less the service which Sidney and Spenser performed for English letters and the disservice which they performed for themselves. They are concerned largely with the pleasures of rhetoric for its own sake, though this is more true of Spenser than of Sidney, and is more true of Sidney's sonnets than of his songs, or at least than of the best of them. As a result, these poets communicate in a remarkable way the joy of purely rhetorical invention, but they spin out small themes to extreme tenuity as a result of their inventiveness, for their sensitivity to language is far in excess of their moral intelligence. Spenser developed the main outlines of a discursive and decorative rhetoric, and so taught much to the dramatists and to Milton, who commonly used the instrument with more discretion than did Spenser. Sidney perfected most of the lyrical graces, and worked out in detail the relationships between elaborate syntax (that is, the forms of logic) and a variety of beautiful stanzaic and linear structure: he thus became the schoolmaster of more than a century of lyric poets. He introduced a mode of perception too complex for his own poetic powers, which were frequently forced to seek matter in the precious and the trivial; a mode of perception too complex, indeed, for any save the greatest lyrical masters of the Renaissance, Shakespeare, Jonson, Donne, and Milton, and which was not incapable of leading even those masters frequently astray. In such poems as Milton's sonnets *On His Blindness* and *To Cyriack Skinner*, as the first of Donne's *Holy Sonnets* (*Thou hast made me*), as Shakespeare's *Tired with all these*, we have a directness, a freedom from superfluity, equal to anything in Gascoigne or in Raleigh, coupled, probably, with greater scope and greater flexibility of perception than can be found among the early Tudor poets. Or at least we can say this: that the later poets were enabled to achieve a more finished and sensitive surface through re-treating from excesses which they fully understood, through suggesting by fine modulation qualities which they preferred not to pursue, than were the earlier poets who wrote relatively in ignorance of these excesses; the situation is analogous to that of human virtue, which can scarcely be said to exist in the absence of a knowledge of sin, since without such knowledge choice is impossible.

Between the extremes of Gascoigne and of Shakespeare, throughout the sixteenth and seventeenth centuries alike, we have the taint of decadence, of decoration, of means in excess of matter, usually charming, frequently beguiling in the extreme, sometimes appropriating most of the poem, sometimes scarcely discernible, but likely always to appear a little trivial if suddenly faced with one of the more classical masterpieces.

In relation to the poets who preceded them, then, Sidney and Spenser, and their fellow Petrarchans, are decadents, in the sense that their ingenuity exceeds their intelligence; they are concerned in some measure with the meaningless fabrication of procedure, and only imperfectly with moral perception. In relation to the poets who suc-ceeded them, they are "experimenters" and prophets, for the measure by which Shakespeare and Milton surpass Gascoigne and Raleigh is at least in part their work. This indicates that Sidney and Spenser are poets of transition, linking two periods of mastery, and are not the first flowers of Elizabethan poetry, sprung from the desert, which they are commonly reputed to be.

Let us consider briefly the period of transition. The principal mas-ters of the Petrarchan movement of the close of the century, if we exclude for the moment the poets of the song-books, are Sir Philip Sidney, Edmund Spenser, Samuel Daniel, Michael Drayton, Sir Fulke Greville, and, in whatever degree and at whatever times he is to be considered a Petrarchan, William Shakespeare. Greene, Peele, Lodge, Lily, and other lesser figures show the same influence, and there are many extremely bad Petrarchan sonneteers who are of historical rather than of critical interest, and whom we need not mention.

The Petrarchan movement may be said to have gained its first great impetus in the eighties with Sidney and Spenser and Greville, and to have continued in part unaltered, in part somewhat altered, beyond the end of the century. The number of sonnets produced in the last decade of the century is well known to have been enormous. For reasons that will presently appear, we may say that the Petrarchan movement, in so far as it may be said to exist in a fairly pure form, reaches its highest development in its first two masters, Sidney and Spenser. Samuel Daniel, a slighter poet, is also a fairly pure representative. Drayton and Greville, on the other hand, show the Petrarchist tendency in conflict with the earlier tendency. Spenser's greatest contribution to the movement is his *Epithalamion,* a poem too familiar to need quoting: the poem is long and is discursive to the point of diffuseness, but the diffuseness is fresh, enthusiastic, and lovely; the poem is ornate, but the ornament has splendor; the poem lacks weight and concentration, and has little of the moral grandeur, the grandeur of personal character, to be discerned in Gascoigne and in Raleigh; however, the subject—love—is heightened by the Platonism of the Petrarchist movement, a Platonism in accordance with which the poet tended to see the physical beauty of his mistress as the representation of her moral and intellectual beauty, and the latter beauty in turn as the representation or symbol of ideal beauty, and thus a guide to perfection and an object worthy of worship. Though far from being a mere lyric, *The Faerie Queen* itself is a monument to the Petrarchist ideal of poetry, and whether or not the greatest monument, certainly the most ambitious. Other long poems which bear a close relationship to the movement are Marlowe's *Hero and Leander,* and Shakespeare's *Venus and Adonis.*

The form that we commonly regard as most characteristic of the school is the sonnet; and we may easily indicate the common Petrarchan qualities of style by quoting a sonnet of Sir Philip Sidney:

> Highway, since you my chief Parnassus be,
> And that my Muse, to some ears not unsweet,
> Tempers her words to trampling horses' feet
> More oft than to a chamber melody,
> Now blessed you, bear onward blessed me
> To her, where I my heart, safe left, shall meet;
> My Muse and I must you of duty greet
> With thanks and wishes, wishing thankfully.
> Be you still fair, honored by public heed;
> By no encroachment wronged, nor time forgot;
> Nor blamed for blood, nor shamed for sinful deed;

> And, that you know I envy you no lot
>   Of highest wish, I wish you so much bliss,
>   Hundreds of years you Stella's feet may kiss!

The opening quatrain is not only graceful, but direct and forceful; the second quatrain becomes progressively more whimsical and precious, till it culminates in a trivial and stereotyped play upon words, introduced no doubt in the interests of elegance and perhaps in part for lack of something better to say; the quatrain of the sestet is a slightly precious prayer on behalf of the highway, the assumption that the highway is an interested listener and actor being purely decorative, and the couplet with which the sestet ends, a continuation of the prayer, enabling the poet to pay to his lady the formulary compliments of so many Petrarchan conclusions.

The poem might be paraphrased thus: Highway, since I write most often under your influence (it is to be hoped that this nearly unparalleled falsehood troubled the highway no more than it appears to have troubled Sidney), I beg you to bear me to my lady; and, since you appear to be doing so, my Muse and I will thank you. May you never suffer infamy, and—as a final proof of my sincerity—may you kiss Stella's feet for hundreds of years.

I do not offer this paraphrase as an equivalent of the poem; nor do I offer it in levity. The rational framework of a good poem should bear inspection, and the framework of this poem is trivial and inconsecutive. The feeling achieves dignity mainly in the first quatrain, which, if it states a falsehood regarding Sidney's poetry, implies a truth regarding his life, but of which the subject matter is irrelevant to the poem as a whole. The incoherence of thought and feeling alike are smoothed over by conventional technical procedure.

Some of Sidney's sonnets are better than this; yet this is generally—and fairly—regarded as one of the best. In spite of gross faults, it has vitality and is still charming to most of us. It should be observed, however, that Sidney is concerned here primarily with obtaining what he regards as a graceful manner, a polished surface; that his theme is trivial; and that his best poetry is irrelevant to his theme and a casual accident.

I should select as the best sonnets in *Astrophel and Stella* the following: *With how sad steps* (XXXI), *Come, Sleep! O Sleep!* (XXXIX), *Having this day my love, my hand, my lance* (XLI), *I never drank of Aganippe well* (LXXIV), *Highway, since you*

(LXXXIV), *Ah bed! the field* (XCVIII), *When far-spent night persuades each mortal eye* (XCIX), *Unhappy sight* (CV), *The blind man's mark* (CIX), *Leave me, O Love* (CX). Of this group a few approach the economy and seriousness, though scarcely the profundity, of such a poet as Jonson or the later Greville: I refer especially to *The blind man's mark, Leave me, O love, With how sad steps,* and in particular the sonnet, in some ways the most effective of the group, beginning *Unhappy sight.* One can discern his weakness in all of these poems, however, and it is extremely evident in the remainder. One should mention also the sonnet beginning *Oft have I mused,* from the *Arcadia,* as one of the best and as characteristic: in this poem, as in some of Shakespeare's sonnets, the play upon words, superficially as trivial as in the poem quoted, becomes in some manner more serious, and involves important perception; it is not the most dignified or efficient of methods, perhaps, but the poem has substance and beauty. Sidney's songs I shall discuss in another connection.

Michael Drayton is a Petrarchist who does not take naturally to the method. His rhythms, as compared to the graceful movements of Sidney, are stiff and plain. In his search for decoration, he often becomes grotesque and violent, for he lacks Sidney's talent for charming triviality. In estimating these qualities, we should remember that Drayton wrote, in his two great patriotic odes, on the Virginia voyage, and on the battle of Agincourt, poetry as forthright as any of Gascoigne, and that nearly (though not quite) all of his greatest lines have the same forthrightness, though they often appear in ornately Petrarchan settings. Consider the following passages by way of examples:

> How happy are all other living things,
> Which though the day disjoin by several flight,
> The quiet evening yet together brings,
> And each returns unto his love at night.
>
> . . . . . .
>
> Since there's no help, come let us kiss and part.
> Nay I have done; you get no more of me.
>
> . . . . . .
>
> Three sorts of serpents do resemble thee.

On the other hand, the conflict between the two qualities in Drayton sometimes produces a new quality. The laborious effort which Drayton expended to achieve the ornate sometimes resulted in great magnificence of feeling: one has not only splendor of language but an

heroic feeling, a feeling of great difficulties overcome, and, within
certain passages, at least, the economy born of difficulty. For an example, we may consider two lines from the sonnet beginning, *Cupid,
dumb idol, peevish saint of love,* a poem in dispraise of Cupid, and in
its main outlines perfectly formulary:

> Thy bow, half-broke, is pieced with old desire;
> Her bow is Beauty with ten thousand strings . . .

Having achieved such lines, however, Drayton characteristically mars
them somewhat, for the second sentence continues to the end of the
quatrain:

> Of purest gold, tempered with virtue's fire,
> The least able to kill an host of kings.

The third and fourth lines are good enough in themselves, but, following the first and second are an anti-climax and unnecessary. The
poem gives us, perhaps, the measure of Drayton's genius, as well as
the difference between Sidney and Drayton: Drayton has greater
toughness and directness than Sidney, and an heroic cast of feeling,
which, as I have said, appears to inhere in the rhetoric itself, and in
the victorious struggle with difficulties; he has, however, less subtlety
of perception and of subject than has Sidney at his best and is a less
considerable poet.[7]

Fulke Greville, Lord Brooke, the friend and biographer of Sir
Philip Sidney, is essentially similar to Drayton in respect to Drayton's
virtues, but is a man of far greater intellectual power and is an abler
and more consistent stylist. It is my own opinion that he should be
ranked along with Gascoigne, Raleigh, Shakespeare, Jonson, and
Donne as one of the most considerable lyric poets of the century.
Further, he not only bridges the gap between the school of Gascoigne
and the school of Sidney, but he bridges the gap between the school
of Sidney and the school of Donne, so that he is a figure of considerable interest to the student of alterations in method.

His epitaph on Sidney is written in a measure common to the early
school, and in a style plain enough and forceful enough for Gascoigne. The poem is well known, but it may aid the reader to see
more clearly the qualities of the early school if I quote from it:

> Heart's ease and only I, like parallels run on,
> Whose equal length keep equal breadth, and never meet in one;

Yet for not wronging him, my thoughts, my sorrow's cell,
Shall not run out, though leak they will, for liking him so well.

Farewell to you, my hopes, my wonted waking dreams,
Farewell sometimes enjoyed joy; eclipsed are thy beams.
Farewell self-pleasing thoughts, which quietness brings forth:
And farewell friendship's sacred league, uniting minds of worth.

And farewell, merry heart, the gift of guiltless minds,
And all sports which for life's restore variety assigns;
Let all that sweet is void; in me no mirth may dwell.
Philip, the cause of all this woe, my life's content, farewell!

Now rhyme, the son of rage, which art no kin to skill,
And endless grief, which deads my life, yet knows not how to kill,
Go seek that hapless tomb, which if ye hap to find,
Salute the stones, that keep the limbs, that held so good a mind.

Greville is able to combine the Petrarchan polish and bucolic wit of his friend, with the direct realism of the earlier period:

> I, with whose colors Myra dressed her head,
> I, that ware posies of her own hand-making,
> I, that mine own name in the chimneys read
> By Myra finely wrought ere I was waking,
> > Must I look on, in hope time coming may
> > With change bring back my turn again to play?
>
> I, that on Sunday at the church-stile found
> A garland sweet, with true-love knots in flowers,
> Which I to wear about mine arm was bound,
> That each of us might know that all was ours;
> > Must I now lead an idle life in wishes,
> > And follow Cupid for his loaves and fishes? . . .

The best of his poems in more or less the Petrarchan manner are probably the following: *Love the delight of all well thinking minds* (*Caelica* I), *The world that all contains is ever moving* (VII), *Cupid thou naughty boy* (XII), *I with whose colors* (XXII), *Absence the noble truce* (XLIV), *Away with these self-loving lads* (LII), and—if it is fairly to be classified in this group—the obscure but thoroughly extraordinary lyric beginning *All my senses like beacon's flame* (LVI). It appears to me that these poems are fully equal to anything in Sidney, in spite of their not displaying comparable technical invention. When we add to them the great elegy on Sidney and the later devotional and theological pieces we have a very great poet indeed.[8]

These later poems are written with a polish equal, in its way, to that of Sidney at his best; they are replete with thought; and they are profound in feeling. Greville was one of the first poets to endeavor with some consistency to employ the elaborate Petrarchan machinery of style on subject matter worthy of it; yet in some measure he simplified that machinery, or at least in reading him, one seldom feels that he displays means in excess of matter. Of himself he wrote, in his life of Sidney: "For my own part I found my creeping genius more fixed upon the images of life, than the images of wit, and therefore chose not to write to them on whose foot the black ox had not already trod, as the proverb is, but to those only that are weather-beaten in the sea of this world, such as having lost the sight of their gardens and groves, study to sail on a right course among rocks and quicksands." M. W. Croll in quoting this passage points to the difference between Sidney and Greville; among other things, he says: "By trying to make his words tally exactly with actual experience he succeeded in giving to simple lines, and sometimes to longer passages, in absolutely simple words, a peculiar power which is unlike anything in the poets with whom he was personally associated. It is different in kind rather than in degree from the fanciful eloquence of Sidney. . . . The best parallel . . . is to be found in the works of John Donne." He might have added the equally striking parallel of Gascoigne.

III

Of Samuel Daniel little need be said. His best single poem is the sonnet beginning *Beauty, sweet love*; his best poems are all available in the standard anthologies and are well known. Like Sidney, he aims primarily at grace of expression; his tone is less exuberant than that of Sidney; his style is more consistently pure; his inspiration is less rich. His tone is one of polished melancholy.

A form nearly as popular with the Petrarchan poets as was the sonnet, we shall find in the song; that is, in the lyric written expressly to be set to music. England possessed great musical composers before the age of Elizabeth, and their lyrics were naturally fairly typical of their ages. But most of the great English music was written during the twenty-five years or so which saw the rise and decline of Petrarchan poetry in England, and it is not surprising that most of the lyrics set to music in this period should be the products of the Petrarchan movement. Most of the songs of Sir Philip Sidney were obviously written to be sung, and many found their way into the song-books. Of those composers who appear in the main to have set the lyrics of other men, John Dowland, the lutanist, is perhaps the most valuable collector of poems, as he is one of the greatest of composers, but many beautiful poems, most of them of unknown authorship, are to be found in the collections of other men. Of the composers who regularly wrote, or appear to have written, their own lyrics, the best poets are Campion and Morley. Of the writers, not composers, who wrote many lyrics to be set, the greatest are Sidney and Shakespeare.

Thomas Morley, the gayest and one of the finest composers of madrigal music, and the most minute of all the masters of the English lyric, as well as one of the most polished, may be used to illustrate the song:

> Ladies, you see time flieth,
> And beauty, too, it dieth,
> Then take your pleasure,
> While you have leisure,
> Nor be so dainty
> Of that which you have plenty.

Or again:

> No, no, Nigella!
> Let who list prove thee,
> I cannot love thee.
> Have I deserved
> Thus to be served?
> Well then content thee,
> If thou repent thee.
>
> No, no, Nigella!
> In sign I spite thee,
> Lo, I requite thee.
> Henceforth complaining
> Thy love's disdaining,
> Sit, thy hands wringing,
> Whilst I go singing.

The songs of Campion have greater scope, equal polish, and a sombre and profound feeling. The two best, perhaps, are the famous lyrics beginning, *Now winter nights enlarge,* and *When thou must home to shades of underground,* poems that probably surpass anything in Sidney, both in scope and in execution, in spite of the fact that Sidney is commonly ranked among the greater poets and Campion among the minor. The first of these two is particularly rich and beautiful, not only in the sensuous imagery of the first stanza, but in the humanity and wise disillusionment of the second; one should note the vastness of night suggested in the first four lines, the fusion in images of light of the fire, wine, and wax, the continuation of this suggestion in the word "honey" used, however, metaphorically, and the way the spirits of the convivialists leap in the line subsequent to that in which the cups overflow. Among the best of his poems are the following: *Shall I come, sweet love, to thee* (perhaps the inspiration of the *Indian Serenade,* by Shelley), *Sleep, angry beauty, There is a garden in her face, Thou art not fair for all thy red and white, What then is love but morning,* and, especially, *Whether men do laugh or weep.*[10]

The songs of Shakespeare are roughly similar to those already discussed: they show the combination of gaiety and pathos normal to the Elizabethan song; they often combine realistic detail, of more or less popular antecedents, with Petrarchan ornament and elaborate meter; they display, in fact, greater metrical virtuosity even than the lyrics of Campion; but in spite of their great beauty and in spite of the glory reflected upon them from Shakespeare's greater work, it would be unfair to say that they were more moving than the best of Campion.

Sidney's best songs are probably the following: *Doubt you to whom my Muse these notes entendeth, Only joy, now here you are, O you that hear this voice, Who is it that this dark night, The nightingale as soon as April bringeth, Ring out your bells, Who hath his fancy pleased, What tongue can her perfection tell.* Sidney's best work was done in the form of songs; his songs are nearly all perfect in execution; the slighter songs display extraordinary wit and polish, and some of the most ambitious have considerable depth. But whereas the songs of Campion and of Shakespeare and of the lesser writers tend to be simple in construction (I am alluding now to plan, not to meter), Sidney often employs elaborate expository frames, and he makes no discernible sacrifice of elegance in employing them. These frames are often expended on very slight subjects, but sometimes are dignified by serious subjects. In addition to writing certain fine poems of his own, he brought the technique of the expository lyric to a state of refinement and of variety which it had not before enjoyed. Ben Jonson's debt to Sidney is very great; so is that of Donne, whose lyrical genius amounted to a kind of grim parody of Sidney; so is that of most of the 17th century. As late as the 19th century, we find Swinburne trying to imitate Sidney's rhyme schemes and Browning modeling one of his best poems—his *Serenade at the Villa*—very closely upon Sidney's lyric beginning, *Why is it that this dark night*. Sidney is probably at his best in the lyric beginning *Who hath his fancy pleased*, a poem which develops one of the two most serious themes of which he is capable (namely, Platonic love, and, as in the closing sonnets of *Astrophel and Stella*, the Christian renunciation of love) in the finest style of which he is capable. I wish to reiterate, however, that in spite of the historical importance of this and other songs of a similar nature, Campion's two best poems seem to me essentially richer and more moving poetry.

The all but innumerable anonymous songs of the period likewise played an important part in refining English style, more than one song being notable for a single phrase or cadence but so notable for that alone as to be unforgettable. The influence of the song-books and miscellanies on such poets as Herrick and as Crashaw is very extensive, but the subject would take us out of our century. We may fairly conclude the subject of the songs by quoting one of the best of the anonymous specimens. It is to be found in John Dowland's second book of airs (Dr. Fellowes, in reprinting it, has damaged it very seriously by giving it a lineation which is obviously incorrect) and in *England's Helicon* (where the correct form may be found):

> Come away, come, sweet love,
> The golden morning breaks;
> All the earth, all the air,
> Of love and pleasure speaks.
> Teach thine arms then to embrace,
> And sweet rosy lips to kiss:
> And mix our souls in mutual bliss.
> Eyes were made for beauty's grace,
> Viewing, ruing, love's long pain:
> Procured by beauty's rude disdain.
>
> Come away, come, sweet love,
> The golden morning wastes:
> While the Sun from his sphere

His fiery arrows casts,
Making all the shadows fly,
Playing, staying, in the grove;
To entertain the stealth of love.
Thither, sweet love, let us hie
Flying, dying in desire:
Winged with sweet hopes and heavenly fire.

Come away, come, sweet love,
Do not in vain adorn
Beauty's grace that should rise
Like to the naked morn.
Lilies on the river side
And fair Cyprian flowers new blown,
Desire no beauties but their own.
Ornament is nurse of pride,
Pleasure, measure, love's delight:
Haste, then, sweet love, our wished flight.

It will be seen that poetry of this type introduced into England a quality of style wanting in such writers as Gascoigne and Raleigh—a quality not only of technical grace but of refined sensuous perception —at the same time that it very largely neglected their virtues.

We will turn now and briefly to the poets who combined the essential qualities of both schools, and who brought the fusion of these qualities to a high level of accomplishment. I shall confine myself to three of these: Ben Jonson, John Donne, and William Shakespeare. My treatment must necessarily be suggestive rather than exhaustive, and will relate wholly to the subjects which I have been discussing.

Considering these poets purely as lyrical writers, we should probably find Ben Jonson the easiest to define. His style is on the whole plain and direct, but it is likewise polished and urbane. It shows the solid substructure of Gascoigne and of Raleigh, with at least evidence of a knowledge of the flexibility of Sidney. Jonson is no such enraptured rhetorician as Sidney, but on the other hand his knowledge of Sidney's rhetoric prevents his indulging in any such affectation of roughness as we find to some extent in Gascoigne: he is, in a sense, freer from mannerism and more direct than either.

Jonson is a classicist in the best sense, and though his classicism is no doubt in part the result of his study of the Greek and Latin poets, as it was probably in greater part the result of his natural bent and genius, it is reasonable to see in his work a resolution of the best qualities to be found in Sidney and in the earlier poets. One does not learn to write English verse from studying Latin, though one may thus acquire valuable training; Jonson must have been familiar with the poets in question; and the poets in question *were the English language,* so far as poetic style was concerned, at the time when Jonson was mastering the language, and there was very little to distract the attention from them. There is in Jonson no conflict of the two tendencies, as in Drayton, but there is distinctly a resolution of the two.

Jonson's lyrics are expository in structure and need to be read very closely if one is not to lose the continuity of the argument. He wrote a little devotional poetry of a high order, but his subject matter is chiefly ethical in the narrowest sense of the term: that is, he deals with problems of conduct arising from relationships between one human being and another, or between one human being and certain tragic or other difficulties; indeed, his devotional poetry concerns itself explicitly with man's moral relationship to God. His view of life is thus both dramatic and heroic; it is seldom devout; it excludes the mysterious. His poems have not only directness, but poise and nobility. The language is accurate not only in the statement of feeling, but in the statement of idea; there is an exact correlation between motive and feeling that may easily be mistaken for coldness and mechanical indifference by the reader accustomed to more florid enticements. The feeling of his poems resides commonly in the very language in which the idea is defined; the idea is a conceptual statement of the motive of the feeling. Among the greatest poems illustrating these qualities are the following: *Though beauty be the mark of praise, Where dost thou careless lie, High-spirited friend, From death and dark oblivion, near the same, False world, good night* (I refer to the complete poem, not to the bleeding remnant in the *Oxford Book of English Verse*), *Good and Great God, can I not think of Thee,* and *To draw no envy, Shakespeare, on thy name.* The qualities of this group of poems may be indicated by the quotation of the latter half of *False World, good night* (*To the World, A Farewell, for a Gentlewoman Virtuous and Noble*):

> Yes, threaten, do. Alas, I fear
> As little as I hope from thee:

I know thou canst not show nor bear
    More hatred than thou hast to me.
My tender, first, and simple years
    Thou didst abuse, and then betray;
Since stirdst up jealousies and fears,
    When all the causes were away.
Then in a soil hast planted me
    Where breathe the basest of thy fools;
Where envious arts professed be,
    And pride and ignorance the schools;
Where nothing is examined, weighed,
    But as 'tis rumored, so believed:
Where every freedom is betrayed,
    And every goodness taxed or grieved.
But what we're born for we must bear:
    Our frail condition it is such,
That, what to all may happen here,
    If't chance to me, I must not grutch.
Else, I my state should much mistake,
    To harbor a divided thought
From all my kind: that for my sake,
    There should a miracle be wrought.
No, I do know, that I was born
    To age, misfortune, sickness, grief:
But I will bear these with that scorn,
    As shall not need thy false relief.
Nor for my peace will I go far,
    As wandrers do, that still do roam;
But make my strengths, such as they are,
    Here in my bosom and at home.

The passage illustrates perfectly the qualities which I have described;
it illustrates further a plainness and directness far more akin to Gascoigne and to Greville than to Sidney; Jonson is another who writes
for those on whom the black ox has trod. But above all, it illustrates
that fine perception and control of nuances of feeling which are possible only to the stylist who deliberately abandons the obvious graces;
such writing is not only more weighty than that of Sidney, but is by
the same token more sensitive and more skillful.

Jonson's major lyrics have been neglected, in favor of his minor lyrics, masterly performances in themselves, but less illustrative both of Jonson's genius and of the age. The minor lyrics, however, with the aid of his plays, miscellaneous writing, and legendary personality, have been able to keep him in some measure before the student's eye as a lyrical poet; he has never, in this capacity, lapsed into the obscurity in which Raleigh was long permitted to rest and in which Gascoigne and Greville (in spite of a few attempts to revive an interest in the latter) rest to this day. If the reader with fixed habits could wrench his attention to the major lyrics long enough to appreciate them, it would aid him to appreciate Gascoigne and Greville as well. There are many valuable secondary lyrics of a quality similar to that of the great lyrics which I have listed, and most of them but little read: the epitaphs on his children, especially that on his son, the epitaphs on the Countess of Pembroke and on Salathiel Pavy, the lines to the Countess of Bedford beginning: *This morning, timely rapt with holy fire, A Hymn to God the Father,* the first and second poems to Charis, *The Hour-Glass, My Picture Left in Scotland,* and the song in *Love's Triumph through Callipolis* beginning: *Joy, joy to mortals the rejoicing fires.*

There are, in addition, the justly popular minor masterpieces, like *Drink to me only with thine eyes, Come, my Celia,* and *Queen and huntress chaste and fair,* poems which discipline the heritage of the song-books and bequeath it to the seventeenth century.

John Donne differs from Jonson in ways that are obvious though perhaps easier to see than to define. His meters are sometimes grossly incorrect, the chief difficulty arising from the perverse misplacement of accents. Though he owes much to Sidney, his debt differs from that of Jonson: Donne utilizes the procedure of Sidney, but appears less a disciple than a serious parodist. If there is an affectation of directness in Gascoigne, there is a greater affectation of directness in much of Donne: in fact, in temperament and in achievement Gascoigne probably resembles Donne more than does any of Donne's disciples. Jonson's employment of abstractions shows the easiness that comes of use; Donne, though genuinely profound, affects profundity, sometimes with grotesque results. These defects sometimes over-ride his genius wholly and produce bad poetry. On the other hand, they are sometimes restrained sufficiently for the corresponding virtues to emerge, and we then have one of the greatest English poets. His greatest poems deal with love, human and divine. His greatest single poem, perhaps, on the happy fruition of human love is the well-

known *Valediction Forbidding Mourning;* on the unhappy outcome
of human love, the greater but less known *Valediction of His Name
in a Window.* Both poems display most of the defects which I have
mentioned, though not in an aggravated form; they represent an extreme use of the Petrarchan machinery, as exemplified in Sidney's
songs, by a poet with a metaphysical view of life, with a talent for
realistic detail, and with no love for ornament that is sensuous rather
than intellectual. Some of the divine poems display equal force and
a purer style. One may cite as a particularly great example the first
of the Holy Sonnets, beginning: *Thou hast made me, and shall thy
work decay.* Donne's characteristic defects are absent from such a
poem as this; the virtues are comparable to the virtues of Jonson.

It is interesting to compare the Shakespeare of the sonnets to both
of these writers, though my present comparison must be brief and
superficial. Some of the greatest sonnets come to mind as resembling
very closely Jonson and the Donne of the purer poems: *Tired with
all these, Let me not to the marriage of true minds, The expense of
spirit in a waste of shame, Poor soul, the center of my sinful earth,*
are among the more obvious. In many poems, however, he seems
closer to Sidney, or is at least employing devices which are more comprehensible in terms of Sidneyan practice than of the earlier. Shakespeare treats material of more or less the same ethical range as does Jonson; but unlike Jonson, he displays in certain poems an obsession with
certain metaphysical notions of time and destruction, particularly in
their subtle and imperceptible impingement upon the human consciousness. Shakespeare is minutely aware—almost sensuously aware
—of the invading chaos, the unmanageable and absorptive continuum,
amid which the ethical man, the man of free choice and of usable
distinctions, exists.

Unlike Donne, Shakespeare does not write devotional poetry; there
is only one more or less devotional poem among the sonnets. Shakespeare's difficulties are pre-Christian; his sensibility is metaphysical
at times but not theological; his mood is perplexed, awed, and at
times astounded, but it is practically never devout.

We can make another distinction between Shakespeare and Donne,
a dangerous distinction, perhaps, but one which I feel would be justified by fuller analysis. Donne also deals with the metaphysical, but
his poetry deals with a kind of experience profoundly different from
that of Shakespeare. Donne tends to deal with the recognition of definitions. His best poetry is composed mainly of explicit definitions, or

of explicit and definite figurative excursions from definitions; the passion with which the human significance of these definitions is felt by him, he communicates in the quality of the language with which he states them. This is true of Jonson as well. Still speaking as cautiously and as relatively as possible, I should say that Shakespeare tends to approach the metaphysical in a more direct and immediate fashion, as regards the experience, an approach which, paradoxically, leads to a more evasive, or at least elusive, expression. That is, he constantly sees the matter that haunts him, as a quality, and frequently as an almost sensuous quality, of something else, and so treats it indirectly. He does not, as does Donne, isolate the quality in a definition and then treat the definition directly or in a clearly illustrative figure. Shakespeare's method makes for a richer sensuous texture, for greater and more elusive suggestion. Donne's makes for greater certainty and for greater concentration and completeness. Of the two methods, Donne's appears to me, abstractly considered, the sounder, or at least the safer: Shakespeare's method is the first step in the dislocation of feeling from motive which has been carried to its logical conclusions in the 19th and 20th centuries. But Shakespeare's discretion is proof against most dangers, and his genius is far greater than Donne's. I shall attempt to illustrate what I mean before proceeding. Allow me to quote Sonnet 77, which appears to have been written to accompany the gift of a blank book:

> Thy glass will show thee how thy beauties wear;
> Thy dial how thy precious minutes waste;
> The vacant leaves thy mind's imprint will bear,
> And of this book this learning may'st thou taste.
> The wrinkles which thy glass will truly show
> Of mouthed graves will give thee memory;
> Thou by thy dial's shady stealth may know
> Time's thievish progress to eternity.
> Look! what thy memory cannot contain
> Commit to these waste blanks, and thou shalt find
> Those children nursed, delivered from thy brain,
> To take a new acquaintance of thy mind,
> These offices, so oft as thou wilt look,
> Shall profit thee and much enrich thy book.

The imperceptible coming of wrinkles displays the physical invasion of the enemy, just as the imperceptible changing of the dial's shadow displays the passing of the enemy. The comparison is a common one in the 16th century, though not elsewhere so beautifully stated except in Shakespeare's own sonnet 104. Shakespeare can apprehend a common figure in a profoundly original manner, just as we observed that Gascoigne could apprehend a moral truism in an original manner. In the ninth line, the enemy invades the mind, the center of being; it was the conceit of the blank book that enabled the poet to extend the familiar figure to this brilliant and terrifying conclusion. This terrifying subject, the loss of the identity before the uncontrollable invasion of the impersonal, is no sooner suggested than it is dropped; and the poem ends with a sound and beautiful moral statement regarding the advantages of writing.

There is in such a poem a very guarded employment of the type of irrelevant excursion to be found in a very unguarded form in many of the sonnets of Sidney. In this connection, we may consider especially the adjective *waste,* in the phrase, *Commit to these waste blanks.* The word is obviously a pun, with the emphasis on the secondary meaning. It means not only *unused,* or *blank,* but it means *desert,* or *uninhabited,* or *uninhabitable,* a sense reinforced by the verb *waste* in the second line. It carries over the feeling of the invading chaos from the preceding line; but rationally considered, the pages are not waste in this sense, but are the instruments offered for actually checking the invasion of the waste. A feeling, in other words, is carried over from its proper motive to a motive irrelevant to it, and the dominant feeling is thus reinforced at the expense of the other. This procedure is foreign to Jonson and to Donne alike; carried a step or two further, it would lead to aesthetic chaos. In Shakespeare it contributes in part to the aura of suggestion which we are likely to feel about his statements; of suggested terror in some of the metaphysical sonnets and of suggested sweetness in some of the more human. In such a poem as this we have a discreet example of the most perilous of all procedures, the use of expressive, or imitative, form; in order to express the invasion of confusion the poet for a moment actually enters the realm of confusion instead of describing it.

It is in such poetry as this that one can best appreciate the benefit conferred by the Petrarchists. In spite of their limitations and errors, they enriched the sensuous texture of the language; they made possible the metaphysical sensuousness—and we have seen that the expression is not wholly obscure—of such writing as this, or they appear to have made it possible. The flexibility and sinuosity of such poetry are at least in part their gift, as is the classical precision of Jonson. They completed the poetic vocabulary, although their own vocabulary was incomplete, and they appear to have rendered possible, or at least greatly to have facilitated certain poems that have never been surpassed.

Yet in conclusion I wish to reiterate that the Petrarchans represent a tendency of secondary importance in the century, not of primary. The great lyrics of the 16th century are intellectually both profound and complex, are with few exceptions restrained and direct in style, and are sombre and disillusioned in tone. If we regard as the major tradition of the century the great poems of Gascoigne and Raleigh, and those most closely resembling them by Greville, Jonson, Donne, and Shakespeare, we shall obtain a very different view of the century from that which we shall obtain by regarding as primary Sidney, Spenser and the song-books; we shall bring much great poetry to light; and we shall find the transition to the next century far less obscure.

NOTES

1. Our chief sources of lyric poetry for the 16th century in England, in addition to published collections of poems by various poets, are the poetic miscellanies, the song-books, the plays, and unpublished manuscript collections. The first miscellany, popularly known as *Tottel's Miscellany*, appeared in 1557; the last important collection of 16th century lyrics appeared in 1602, under the title of *A Poetical Rhapsody*. The most important miscellanies ranging between are *A Handful of Pleasant Delights*, *A Paradise of Dainty Devices*, *A Gorgeous Gallery of Gallant Inventions*, *The Phoenix Nest*, *The Passionate Pilgrim*, and *England's Helicon*. These volumes cover a long period and a wide variety of kinds of poetry; it is therefore not profitable to attempt to treat them individually or together as representative of any particular tendency or tendencies, or not, at least, from my present point of view. The poetry contained in them is mainly rather poor, yet a large amount of very good poetry can be culled from them. *Tottel's Miscellany* contains the greatest amount of fine poetry, thanks largely to the presence of a very large amount of Wyatt; the next best is *England's Helicon*, which appeared in 1600, a collection of more or less pastoral lyrics. There is much greater uniformity in the Elizabethan song-books. Dr. Fellowes has reprinted in a single volume (*English Madrigal Verse*, The Oxford Press) the lyrics of most of the great Elizabethan madrigalists and lutanists. There is a

good deal of variation of type in this volume, but most of the pieces by far are love-songs, more or less influenced by Italian models, and often translated from the Italian. The poems to be found in the plays are roughly of a kind; the poems to be found in the other deposits mentioned vary widely.

2. The school reached its chronological and poetical culmination in the work of George Gascoigne (1525-77) and in Sir Walter Raleigh (1552-1618), more particularly in Gascoigne. Thomas Nashe (1567-1601) made a few of the best contributions, and certain others were made by Barnabe Googe (1540-94), whose only volume appeared in 1563, and by George Turbervile (1540-1610), men who came between Gascoigne and Raleigh. There are other representatives of the school, more or less imperfect as representatives, whom I shall mention later.

3. Published among Arber's English Reprints.

4. Chalmers' *English Poets*: Vol. 2.

5. *The Complete Works of George Gascoigne*, edited by John W. Cunliffe. Cambridge University Press, 1907.

6. Felix E. Schelling: *The Life and Writings of George Gascoigne*. Publication of the University of Pennsylvania: Series in Literature and Archeology, II-4.

7. His best poems in the shorter forms I take to be the following: The sonnets beginning, *The glorious sun went blushing to his bed, Cupid dumb idol, Three sorts of serpent do resemble thee, Sweet, sleep so armed, To nothing fitter can I thee compare, You not alone, Dear, why should you command me to my rest, How many paltry, foolish, painted things, Since there's no help, Stay, speedy Time, Calling to mind since first my love began*; the two great patriotic odes; and *The Shepherd's Sirena*. These poems at least will illustrate the qualities which I have defined, and I believe that none will be found greatly to impeach my definition.

8. One should mention especially among the later poems: *You that seek what life is in death* (Caelica LXXXIII), *The earth with thunder torn, with fire blasted* (LXXXVII), *Man dream no more of curious mysteries* (LXXXIX), *The Manicheans did no idols make* (XC), *Eternal Truth, almighty infinite* (XCVIII), *Wrapt up O Lord in man's degeneration* (XCIX), *In night when colors all to black are cast* (CI), *How falls it out, the sincere magistrate* (CVII), *Syon lies waste, and Thy Jerusalem* (CX), *Down in the depth of mine iniquity* (C), *Man's youth, it is a field of large desires* (CII), *The Serpent Sin, by showing human lust* (CIII).

9. M. W. Croll: *The Works of Fulke Greville, A Thesis*. University of Pennsylvania, 1901.

10. Among the best poems in Dr. Fellowes' English Madrigal Verse (Ox-

ford, 1920), exclusive of poems by Campion, or usually attributed to him, are the following: Alison: *What if a day;* Bateson: *I heard a noise;* Byrd: *I joy not, My mind to me, Where fancy fond, O You that hear this voice, When younglings first, Is Love a boy;* Gibbons: *The silver swan, Laïs now old;* Morley: *Now is the gentle season, Round, around, In nets of golden wires, Now is the month of maying, Sing we and chant it, No no Nigella, Thus saith my Galatea, Fire! fire! my heart, Damon and Phyllis squared, Ladies you see time flieth;* Mundy: *Were I a king;* Peerson: *Can a maid that is well-bred, The spring of joy is dry;* Pilkington: *Pour forth, mine eyes, Stay nymph, the ground, Have I found her;* Vautor: *Sweet Suffolk owl, Weep, weep mine eyes, Dainty sweet bird;* Ward: *Sweet pity, wake;* Weelkes: *Welcome sweet pleasure, Death hath deprived me;* Attey: *Vain hope, adieu!* Barley: *Short is my rest;* Cooper: *Oft thou hast;* Corbine: *Some can flatter, Sweet Cupid;* John Dowland: *Dear if you change, Sleep, wayward thoughts, His golden locks, Fine knacks for ladies, Behold a wonder here, Flow not so fast, ye fountains, Stay time awhile thy flying, Go nightly cares;* Jones: *Once did I love, Shall I look, O thread of life, How many new years;* Pilkington: *Whither so fast;* Porter: *Love in thy youth.*

HOWARD BAKER

The Formation of the Heroic Medium

PART I

I

Whenever a period has produced a fine and characteristic literature,
it has used a fine and characteristic medium of expression. Aristotle
is painstaking in describing the connections between the substance
of tragedy, comedy, and the epic, and the poetic forms which they
employ. We, in our day, are usually no less diligent. We say that
the heroic couplet—the regular, antithetic closed couplet—is the embodiment of wit; and, if we are orthodox, we say that before Pope
was born the heroic couplet was taking shape in the hands of Waller.
We look at Corneille, and behind Corneille, in the same fashion.
Such inquiry is not limited to the forms of classical poetry; it is perhaps most complete in connection with the work of the English
romantic poets.

But in connection with the Elizabethan drama it has only been
begun. There are, it is true, studies which deal more or less narrowly with the prosody of blank verse;[1] what is needed, however, is
an account of the more-than-mechanical qualities of early unrhymed
poetry—its relations to still earlier poetry, its rhetorical peculiarities,
its affinity with certain subjects and with certain attitudes towards

From *Induction to Tragedy* (Baton Rouge: Louisiana State University Press,
1939), pp. 49-105. Reprinted by permission of the publisher.

life; an account, in fine, of the complex qualities comparable with those which we recognize in the heroic couplet. This is the need which the present chapter will attempt to fulfill.[2]

It is intended to have a twofold relation to the other chapters. On the theoretic side, in trying to isolate one of the formal elements of Elizabethan tragedy, I suppose that the principles underlying the formation of the medium of expression will apply to the general formation of tragedy: a history of heroic blank verse should be essentially a first sketch of the rise of English tragedy; for the tragic hero will be roughly what he is able to express in words. On the practical side I hope to contribute a clearer description of early poetic style and of its remarkable uniformity, to bring some small support to Sir Edmund Chambers' very important theory of a uniform "school of the 'eighties,"[3] and consequently to indicate a few of the hazards, already alluded to, of pronouncing a doubtful play, on the basis of style alone, this man's work or that man's work.

Poetical rhetoric does not lend itself easily to an obviously systematic analysis. I have thought it best to adopt a plan of this sort: to present first, as a point of reference for later discussion, a characterization of immediately pre-Shakespearean blank verse; to turn then to a chronological survey of the rise of the medium, and to inject into this survey some rather free comparisons of early and late examples; and finally, to give a more substantial account of the later practices.

2

Professor Tucker Brooke, writing on "Marlowe's Versification and Style,"[4] has contributed a valuable and culminant essay to the numerous studies of Marlovian rhetoric. With some shifting of emphasis, Professor Brooke's paper will remain, I think, an important description of blank verse in a crucial stage of development. Its brief account of the pre-Marlovian stages, however, seems to me to be unsatisfactory.

The general feeling, in which Professor Brooke shares, is that before *Tamburlaine* blank verse was not native to the genius of the English language, that it was employed only when Englishmen were affecting to write like Romans, and that in Marlowe's hands it became instantly, as Hallam said,[5] the finest instrument that a tragic poet has ever employed.

Without denying Marlowe's genius for the medium, we may resist this tide of general feelings and sweeping claims. It is difficult

to say how and when any verse form becomes native to the English
language. I believe, and I think the following pages will show, that
Marlowe did not change blank verse so much as he exploited to the
limit a newly developed taste for it: the "mighty line" was born
early; if it was hidden, as it often was, in a context of brittle, non-
flowing lines,—that was what native English taste in the mid-sixteenth
century demanded of verse in general. There are probably as good
heroic couplets in Shakespeare as in Waller;[6] they are not conspicuous, are not used extensively, because taste had formed no predominant bent towards the intellectualizing and ironic effects of the closed
couplet. When we talk about such elusive matters as the native genius
of English, the only relevant question is whether the verse of *Gorboduc* was less effective than the best contemporaneous examples of
tumbling verse or poulter's meter. I think it was not; this statement
will come as no surprise to the readers of the first chapter of this
study. I also think it possessed a few virtues of its own as well as the
resources and defects of contemporaneous forms.

Later on we shall glance at the detail of the connections between
English blank verse and Latin quantitative verse. But, as a matter of
fact, all that should need to be said can be said in two sentences:
Those poets, led by Gabriel Harvey, who consciously attempted to
simulate the effects of the Romans did not regard blank verse, any
more than rhymed verse, as a means to their ends. And the translators
of Seneca, in their deliberate efforts "to keepe that Grace and majestye of stile, that Seneca doth,"[7] employed, in a project running from
1559 to 1581, every common meter except blank verse. The absence
of rhyme is by no means a mark of the imitation of classical poetry;
and conversely, blank verse was regarded no more than any other
form as an equivalent to classical Latin verse.

Nor is it reasonable to suppose that blank verse in Marlowe's hands
became instantly the finest instrument that the tragic poet has ever
employed. Such things do not happen instantly. So extreme a view
ignores the changes which Marlowe himself imposed, in his more
mature years, upon the medium, not to mention the changes which
Shakespeare imposed upon it. So sweeping a view tosses *The Spanish
Tragedy* completely aside; and Thomas Kyd's contribution to early dramatic blank verse, though it may not be earlier than Marlowe's, is
certainly an independent contribution and one that proved to be
scarcely of less value to the maturing Shakespeare.

The history of the formation of blank verse is inevitably complicated. A medium which can give utterance to feelings of all shades and can sustain them, which can pursue complicated thought in all its delicate ramifications—such a medium must have roots which go deep and wide. It is the same with verse form as with dramatic form: there may be an occasional creaking and superficial imitation of Ovid or Seneca, but all that is essential to a line of poetry or to a drama will go so much deeper that the importance of the imitation is negligible. Blank verse, I am convinced, has its roots in medieval poetry. The evidence for this conviction will appear in a moment; meanwhile, I stress it on the grounds that it is probably the only reasonable view to take.

3

But Christopher Marlowe brought unrhymed poetry suddenly to a state of crystallization. This is axiomatic. To do so, he limited blank verse practically to a single effect: poetic oratory. And in singling out this one effect from the many which had formerly accompanied it, he was compelled to subject drama itself to amazing limitations: he forced *Tamburlaine* into the narrow structure of a vehicle for declamation, and, to motivate so much declamation, he relied only on the spectacular device of giving limitless heroic grandeur to pride, the first of the deadly sins. *Tamburlaine*, in simplest terms, is pride-oratory.

Marlowe's achievement overwhelmed his contemporaries quite as much as it overwhelms students of the Elizabethan drama. Allusions to Tamburlaine's conquest of the stage are extraordinarily frequent between 1587 and 1592; though they are familiar, we shall glance at a few of them, for they serve admirably to characterize blank verse at a significant time and also to indicate the importance which dramatists placed upon the medium of expression.

The medium of expression, the blank verse of *Tamburlaine*, is what Marlowe himself emphasizes above all else.

> From iygging vaines of riming mother wits,
> And such conceits as clownage keepes in pay,
> Weele lead you to the stately tent of War,
> Where you shall heare the Scythian Tamburlaine
> Threatning the world with high astounding terms
> And scourging kingdoms with his conquering sword . . .[8]

We shall hear Tamburlaine threatening the world; we shall *hear* him scourging kingdoms. Elizabethan audiences heard him, and were content for awhile only to hear more. Dramatist Robert Greene, finding himself forced to earn his livelihood by writing a prose romance, protests against those who "had it in derision for me that I could not make my verses jet out upon the stage," and who "set an end of scollarisme in an English blanck verse."[9] This was in 1588.

The next year Greene's friend Thomas Nashe appealed to their university friends, Spenser, Peele, Watson, and others, to assist Greene in reforming this new and extravagant taste for rhetorical drama. After praising the "scoller-like shepheard" Greene, Nashe proceeds to lay his contempt on the writers of plays, who, he says, "intrude themselves to our eares as the alcumists of eloquence, who, mounted on the stage of arrogance, think to out-brave better pens with the swelling bumbast of a bragging blanke verse." He goes on to sneer at their "kill-cow conceits and the spacious volubilities of a drumming decasyllabon."[10] On the same occasion, the appearance of Greene's *Menaphon,* another of Greene's friends, in condemning the fashionable drama, sees fit to criticize it from the point of view of its verse:

> Come forth, you witts that vaunt the pompe of speeche
> And strive to thunder from a Stageman's throat;
> View Menaphon, a note beyond your reach,
> Whose sight will make your drumming descant doate . . .[11]

But Greene and Nashe and Lodge, in spite of early antagonism and humiliating failures, soon achieved their own successes in drama. They even came later to regard themselves along with Marlowe as the special masters of declamatory verse. So it happened that, in 1592, Greene could turn his fire against Shakespeare, the newcomer, the "upstart crow," who, Greene says wrathfully, "with his *Tyger's heart wrapt in a Player's hide* supposes he is as well able to bumbast out a blank verse" as the best of them.[12]

These contemporary remarks indicate that for a short period a definite style of verse was the greater part of drama. And it was—but with limits which can readily be defined. The generalization applies, of course, only to the popular stage; the style of Lyly, which was doubtless the predominant style in comedy, was fundamentally that preferred by the court. But in the favorite popular forms, tragedy and chronicle-history, rhetoric must have been especially important because other things were not important: plots were anybody's property, and plays rewritten for rhetorical ends were as much in demand as new plays;[13] the lack of complicated stage equipment must have caused the dramatists to be but little concerned with stage effects; and since the actors themselves attended to stage business and even improvised extensively, the dramatist's occupation was essentially a literary occupation. It was, it seems, Shakespeare's ability to bombast out a blank verse that got him his fellowship in a cry of players.

Blank verse, in this period, is consistently described as *bombastic*. This is essentially good description, except that actual bombast (cotton padding), since it was an accepted aid to tailoring, probably was not so derogatory a term as it is now. Gascoigne uses it as a figurative equivalent to flesh: "It hath no bumbast now, but skin and bones . . ."[14] Perhaps the overtones in the phrase "to bombast out a blank verse line" were something like this: "to tailor out a line." The intention, however, to suggest an inflated, if not padded line, comes out in the expressions *bragging, swelling, jetting, drumming*.

The structure of the blank verse line, which is really Marlowe's "mighty line," is also indicated rather strikingly, I think, in the dramatists' own references to their verse. The mighty line is, I believe, in its narrowest form a balanced line in which the first part plays against the last part either verbally or alliteratively and often in both ways; it is structurally the type of line which we noticed in the account of *Gorboduc*. Its features are conspicuous in the first lines of the prologue to *Tamburlaine*:

> From *iygging* vaines of *riming* mother wits.
> And such conceits as *clownage keepes* in pay.
> And *scourging* kingdoms with his *conquering* sword.

It appears again in the verse which Greene flings back at Shakespeare,

> his *Tyger's* *h*eart wrapt in a *Player's* *h*ide;

and the verbal balance is worked out perfectly in Shakespeare's original line:

> O *tiger's* *h*eart wrapt in a *woman's* *h*ide.

The dramatists seem even to be imitating this balanced line in their prose references to blank verse. They drop into alliteration and play noun and adjective against noun and adjective to the extent that, if it were not for the extra syllable, Nashe's the *swelling* *b*umbast of a *bragging* *b*lanke verse

would be, itself, a fine example of the mighty line.

Blank verse, then, in the year 1592—the year which marks the
effectual end of the careers of Marlowe, Greene, and Kyd, and the
beginning of the career of Shakespeare—blank verse is characterized
by its deliberate cultivation of swelling rhetoric. It uses a strict decasyllabic line;[15] Marlowe's fairly frequent use of a final light eleventh
syllable is practically limited to his practice of winding up a line with
a resounding proper name. The stresses alternate regularly in the
iambic fashion, with reversals in stress usually excluded from the
body of the syntactically tight line. End-stopping is the rule; it is
indeed the most notable principle of heroic verse at this time and perhaps the chief source of its strength. For effective run-on structure is a
refinement and a subtilizing which was totally unsuited to the drama
of Marlowe and most of his contemporaries.

These are fundamental specifications. There will be numerous
irregularities, of course; but they are probably due merely to the over-
sights and compromises which accompany hasty writing.

4

The mighty line of Marlowe is signalized, I think, by rhetorical
balance. But I do not mean at all that every line in Marlowe, or that
even a large proportion of lines, will conform to the type which I
have described. In *Tamburlaine I* Professor Hubbard counts forty-
four lines that have strict grammatical balance;[16] if we count those in
which balance also results from alliteration or plays on words, the
number will not be much more than doubled, will not be more than
five per cent. But the number of these lines is not so important as
their position: in position they stand like keystones and cornerstones
in Marlowe's rhetoric. They may come as a climax to one of Tamburlaine's lofty periods:

> That perfect blisse and sole felicitie,
> That sweet fruition of an earthly crowne.   (879-80)

Or more often they comprise the introductory steps, the exclamatory
entrance to a lofty passage; this is the way in which Tamburlaine begins his speech at Zenocrate's deathbed:

> Proud furie and intollorable fit,
> That dares torment the body of my Loue,
> And scourge the Scourge of the immortall God . . .   (3046-9)

The formula of the balanced line is, for Marlowe, a point of departure and a point of return. It seems consequently to be the norm in his rhetoric.

This brings up a question of method. It appears to me that in order to give an effective account of blank verse rhetoric, we are obliged continually to extract a series of norms from our specimens: we must find foundational lines and passages, foundational modes of articulating the passions. These will not necessarily represent an author at his best; indeed an author like Shakespeare may be most interesting when he departs from the norm. But we are interested in the formation of Elizabethan blank verse, rather than in the special excellences of a Shakespeare.

The problem is serious enough to justify an illustration.

In Shakespeare's *Richard III*, the scene in which Clarence is murdered is constructed in this fashion: Clarence, imprisoned in the tower, has had a marvelous dream which he recounts in great detail. The dream prognosticates his death; he prays that God, in punishing him, may spare his innocent family. Then he falls asleep, and the murderers enter. In semi-humorous terms they also speak of divine punishment. Awakening, Clarence pleads for his life on the grounds that vengeance belongs to God alone. He dies, though one of the murderers has relented.

Now this scene is a series of manipulations of the theme of divine vengeance. Clarence's prayer is the foundational passage in it, the norm for the rhetoric. For the dream leads up to the prayer, and after the prayer follow rhetorical variations on it, including the prose variations of the murderers. The lines that compose the prayer are these:

> O God! if my deep prayers cannot appease thee,
> But thou wilt be aveng'd on my misdeeds,
> Yet execute thy wrath on me alone:
> O! spare my guiltless wife and my poor children.
>
> (I, 4, 68 ff.)

The lines preceding the prayer are richer poetry, but until they have been given a firm direction by the prayer, they must appear to be but a fine example of the tendency in the sixteenth century to exploit a common and beautiful and probably Virgilian theme; they have an evasive quality, as if the nervousness of Clarence is recapitulated in the form assumed by the lines themselves:

> I pass'd, methought, the melancholy flood,
> With that grim ferryman which poets write of,
> Unto the kingdom of perpetual night.
>
> . . . a legion of foul fiends
> Environ'd me, and howled in mine ears
> Such hideous cries, that, with the very noise
> I trembling wak'd, and, for a season after
> Could not believe but that I was in hell
> Such terrible impression made my dream.
>   (I, 4, 45-7; 58-64)

And then, in the speeches of the murderers which come soon after the prayer, we find an excellent illustration of Shakespeare's ability to vary a theme and to fit it to vastly different personages. When the clownish murderer takes up the theme of divine punishment, Shakespeare shifts from the serious, formal blank verse of Clarence clear over into prose:

> *Sec. Murd.* The urging of that word "judgment" hath bred a kind of remorse in me.
> *First Murd.* What! art thou afraid?
> *Sec. Murd.* Not to kill him, having a warrant for it; but to be damn'd for killing him, from the which no warrant can defend me.   (I, 4, 108-14)

Clarence's prayer, obviously, is not in itself a purple patch; but it is a perfectly good example of early Elizabethan blank verse, of the norm in phrasing and in feeling. The old king Gorboduc speaks of divine vengeance in quite the same voice:

> Yet, O ye goddes, if euer wofull kyng
> Might moue ye, king of kinges, wreke it on me
> And on my sonnes, not on this giltlesse realme!
>   (III, 1, 22)

And generally similar passages, in idea or in phrasing, are to be found in sixteenth-century literature wherever one starts turning pages.[17] Indeed, Tamburlaine's notorious challenge in which he "dares God out of his heaven" is, as it were, only the obverse of the conventional.[18]

Study of this sort of foundational and conventional rhetoric should provide us with a means, as limited as it may be, for generalizing about the unrhymed heroic medium.

5

The preceding pages may serve as an elementary sketch of blank verse as it was when Shakespeare first began to use it. There must follow now some account of its formative stages; later on the sketch of it in its approach to maturity can be taken up again.

The value of a chronological study is increased enormously, however, if there is evidence of a definite continuity in the subject. Before *Tamburlaine*, blank verse, so far as we know, had made only a dozen appearances. How safe is it to assume that the later poets profited by the examples of the earlier poets? Does each new endeavor in blank verse become an influence on succeeding endeavors? I am convinced that the work of the poets of the sixteenth century shows an extraordinary continuity. This belief, I think, is generally accepted. There is also, it happens, concrete evidence to support it which is pertinent to the subject at hand. One bit of evidence is the use of the rare, and of course in itself unimportant, adjective *hugie* in special contexts. The strange word and its context appear in the poems of most of the authors with whom we are concerned. This could not happen by accident; it must be an indication of definite influences. Moreover, to glance at the appearances of the word is practically to epitomize the history of poetics and poetic relationships in the century.

Probably the first problem in early sixteenth century poetics is the question of the arrangement of stresses in the decasyllabic line. Wyatt seems to have had his ear, especially in his early work, attuned to a cadence which was radically different from the iambic movement;[19] Tottel had an ear only for the iambic movement, and, by his vigorous editing of the manuscripts which he published, he appears to have forced our present principles of metrics upon his contemporaries. Surrey counted syllables; but though he was often negligent or at least not rigorous, he does move towards a line which has a smooth flow of alternate stresses. His efforts in this direction are apparent in the lines in his translation of the *Aeneid* which have to do with the wooden horse of Troy. At first he writes:

A huge horse made, hye raised like a hill.[20]

This awkward clutter of syllables—"a huge horse made"—results from his taking the phrase over bodily from Gavin Douglas' translation of the *Aeneid* into Scottish dialect:

Ane huige hors, like ane greit hill, in hy.[21]

When Surrey encounters the phrase again he has more or less difficulty with it:

Whereto was wrought the masse of this huge hors.   (188)

(Douglas: Onto quhat fyne this huge hors was heir.)   (p. 76, 14)

Yonder huge horse that stands amid our walls.   (420)

(Douglas: Within the wallis, yone mekle standand hors.)   (p. 88, 8)

Then suddenly Surrey overcomes all his difficulties by adopting the rare form *hugie*:

Clambe vp againe vnto the hugie horse.   (512)

(Douglas: Clam wp agane in the greit hors maw.)   (92, 11)

And thus a Gordian knot in metrics was cut.

Other poets followed Surrey's example. Jasper Heywood, when he had occasion to mention the horse of Troy in his introduction to his translation of Seneca's *Troas* (1559), fashions this line:

A hugie horse where many a warlike Knight
Enclosed was . . .[22]

Here implications abound. Heywood was an unusual translator of Seneca in that, besides sharing in the universal interest in the medieval aspects of Seneca's morality, he also aspired most seriously to reproduce Seneca's "Grace and majestye of stile."[23] From all of Seneca's plays he selected the one that had to do with Troy; he was versatile in metrics and apparently familiar with Surrey's blank verse.[24] Yet he renders Seneca in nearly every form—fourteeners, rhyme royal, decasyllabic quatrains—but not in blank verse. Two years later *Gorboduc*, a play based on English history and occupied with a problem in immediate national politics, is written in blank verse. The inference is that unrhymed poetry had no associations in the minds of the poets with Latin quantitative verse.

Thomas Sackville, in his medieval and Virgilian marvelous journey, *The Induction*, sees the fall of Troy painted in the shield of the personification War; he exclaims:

> The hugie horse within thy walls is brought.[25]

Farther along in the same poem he writes:

> The wide waste places, and the hugie playne.   (St. 73)

And this line reappears with but slight changes in *Gorboduc*:

> Let them beholde the wide and hugie fieldes.   (V, 2, 61)

The context for the adjective *hugie* has now broadened out. But that it remains an artificial literary word, a convenient poetic dissyllable, is indicated perhaps by its appearance in an alliterative, euphuistic, and ineffectual line, in its final occurrence in *Gorboduc*:

> To see the hugie heapes of these vnhappes.   (V, 2, 109)

This is the phrase which Turberville retains in his translation of Ovid's *Heroides*:

> And be enricht with hugie heapes of massy gold so brave.[26]

Finally the word makes some notable appearances in the later drama. Marlowe, in writing

> Your threefold armie and my hugie hoste,   (*Tam.*, 1192)

has retained the traditional alliterative context, and Sackville, moreover, had used precisely the same phrase in the *Induction*:

> The hugie hostes, Darius and his power.   (St. 58)

The phrase reappears in *The Misfortunes of Arthur*:

> With hugie hoast withstoode him at the shoare.   (II, 1, 58)

And Kyd, in a Virgilian description of hell which was doubtless influenced by Sackville's *Induction*, seems to paraphrase Sackville's line,

> The wide waste places, and the hugie playne,

with this line:

> Within a hugie dale of lasting night.   (*S.T.*, III, 11, 21)

And a little later *Selimus* has, "Like hugie mountains do your waters rear" (1765); and *Locrine,* "Hercules that tamed the hugy monsters" (260).

The intention in writing at this length about an inconsequential little word was primarily to indicate how closely interrelated are the works of sixteenth-century poets. The theory of a "school of the 'eighties" seems to be sound enough indeed, but the school probably runs over the boundaries of the decade. Several things in addition are suggested too. One is that the moment Surrey got hold of his decasyllabic line it became in his hands and then in the hands of Sackville as good a line as the very good lines of Marlowe and Kyd, and in no way different from theirs. This observation excludes the matter of the total effects of passages, but it is none the less, from a rhetorical point of view, an important truth. Another implication is that the Virgilian tradition, especially in regard to the fighting in Troy and Aeneas' descent into hell, is an influence of enormous vitality. And this, too, is an observation which should bear fruit later on.

PART II

I

It is generally accepted now that Surrey found suggestion for an English blank verse in an unrhymed Italian version of the *Aeneid,* perhaps in that of Cardinal Ippolito de' Medici or his secretary, perhaps in that of Nicolo Liburnio. It is also accepted that the date of the experiment would lie between the years 1539 and 1547.[27]

To belabor the question where blank verse came from is unprofitable. The urge to write a rhymeless verse was a general Renaissance phenomenon, behind which lay, no doubt, the example of the ancients. It was an urge towards a refinement in poetics, not a revision of poetic principles. Thus Surrey's blank verse cannot be considered an imitation of classical measures; for the revision in poetics, to which Surrey like Wyatt was devoted, was the syllable-counting principle, and nothing could be more contrary to classical prosody. Surrey simply wrote his decasyllabics without rhyme. The influence of the Italians could have made crucial the question of rhyming or not rhyming; but the question itself is inconsiderable.

What is considerable is the diction, the phrasing, the organization of the verses. And in these regards, just as Surrey's poetry as a whole is as native as Chaucer's, his blank verse is cut from the best of traditional patterns. For at bottom it is Gavin Douglas' version of the *Aeneid* transformed into unrhymed heroics. Now Surrey was a capable scholar and a fine poet: he departs from Douglas when he sees fit, though with notable infrequency at first; and he does, as we shall see, make his own essential contribution.

But discussion of Surrey's verse ought to be grounded on some lines. Those that follow, as editors have noted, represent Surrey in a fairly dependent passage:

> Here Hecuba, with her yong daughters all,
> About the altar swarmed were in vaine,
> Like doues that flock together in the storme;
> The statues of the gods embracing fast.
> But when she saw Priam had taken there
> His armure, like as though he had ben yong,
> "What furious thought, my wretched spouse," quod she,
> "Did moue thee now such wepons for to weld?"
>
> (II, 666-73)

Douglas had written:

> Hecuba thidder, with hir childer, for beild
> Ran all in vane, and about the altair swarmis,
> Brasand the godlik ymage in thair armis,
> As for the storme dowis flockis togidder ilkane.
> Bot quhen scho saw how Priamus hes tane
> His armour, so as thoch he had bene ying:
> Quhat fulich thocht, my wrechit spous and king,
> Movis ye now sic wapnis for to weild?
>
> (p. 99, 6-13)

And Virgil:

> Hic Hecuba et natae nequiquam altaria circum,
> praecipites atra ceu tempestate columbae,
> condensae et divom amplexae simulacra sedebant.
> Ipsum autem sumptis Priamum iuvenalibus armis
> ut vidit, 'Quae mens tam dira, miserrime coniunx,
> impulit his congi telis? Aut quo ruis?' inquit.
>
> (II, 515)

Perhaps the first remark should be that both the Englishman and the Scotsman do a creditable job of translating the Roman. Both retain something of the compactness of the Latin. Douglas' *swarmis* and *flockis* are happy condensings of implications; these Surrey has wisely retained. On the other hand there is loss in the omission of *atra*. The uneconomical locution *like as though he had been* is more troublesome in Surrey's English than in Douglas' dialect.

The second point must be that each of Surrey's lines is a version of a line in Douglas: the mere intention of translating the Scottish dialect into English iambic decasyllabics could scarcely have produced a closer version. It is also true, I believe, that if Surrey had used rhyme, he would have been forced to depart farther from his model, and the problem of writing his *Aeneid* would have been a different problem. This may have urged him in the direction of rhymeless verse.

In any event it was fortunate for Surrey that Douglas wrote a good strong line. For it must be apparent in the specimen above that the key-words, the impelling diction, as well as the syntactical structures are fundamentally Douglas'. Even Surrey's one run-on line comes from Douglas. Consequently I think there is no especial value in analyzing matters like *enjambement* and the *caesura* in Surrey's blank verse: these things will be the same (as indeed the findings of the prosodists have shown them to be) in all comparable verse of the period.

But there is also evidence here that Surrey has attained a mastery of the iambic decasyllabic period. He makes, for instance, an excellent line,

> Like doues that flock together in the storm,

out of one of Douglas' especially difficult tumbling-rhythmic structures.

Since this study is after all a sketch of sixteenth-century verse rhetoric, a comparison of Surrey's work with that of the much more popular Phaer is not out of place. The parallel passage is this:

> There Hecuba and her doughte[r]s all
> (pore soules) at the altars side
> In heapes together affrayd the*m* drew,
> like doues wha*n* doth betide
> Some storme the*m* headlo*ng* driue,
> & clippi*ng* fast their gods thei hold.

> But whan she Priam thus beclad
> in armes of youth so bold
> Espied: what minde alas (quoth she)
> o wofull husband you
> In harneis dight: and whither away
> with wepons run ye now?[28]

Phaer is the translator of Virgil who received the laudations of his century; even George Peele calls him "the fairest Phaer that ever ventured on great Virgil's works."[29] It is perhaps only right for us to cry doggerel, as everyone does, and have done with this fourteener version. Yet there was a time when these lines were sincerely admired: I think it is possible to see that they are fuller, are more leisurely, more affecting, more mournful than those of Douglas or Surrey, and are not without their appeal. They are not bare and bold, they are not declamatory, not heroic. But the sixteenth century liked them, and that is one reason why blank verse came only slowly into prominence.

Translations of Virgil are especially important to us in that a preponderantly rhetorical drama like the early English tragedy makes extensive use of epic fragments and epic technique. An illustration will conclude our remarks on Surrey's verse and begin the transition to dramatic verse.

The splendid and influential passage which tells of the fall of Priam is turned by Surrey into these lines:

> Of Priamus this was the fatal fine,
> The wofull end that was alotted him,
> When he had seen his palace all on flame,
> With ruine of his Troyan turrets eke.
> That royal prince of Asie, which of late
> Reignd ouer so many peoples and realmes,
> Like a great stock now lieth on the shore;
> His hed and shoulders parted ben in twaine,
> A body now without renome and fame.
>
> (721-29)

The relationship to Douglas can now be made perfectly clear; for Surrey is following Douglas here with what appears to be, in Book II, neither more nor less than his usual closeness. Douglas wrote:

> Of Priamus thus was the finale fait;
> Fortune heir endit his glorius estait

> Seand Ilion all birning in firis broun,
> And Troyis wallis fall and tumblit doun;
> That riall prince, wmquhill, our Asia,
> Apone sa fell pepill and realmis alsua
> Ringit in weltht, now by the coist lyis deid
> Bot as ane stok, and of hakkit his heid;
> A corps, but life, renowne, or wthir fame,
> Vnknawin of ony wycht quhat was his name.
>
> (101, 5-14)

Most of the essentials, I think, go back to Douglas, but this difference becomes apparent now: Surrey is studiously condensing the Douglas text. It is not that Douglas is prolix; the little elaboration on Virgil which occurs in the last lines is the really guiltless mark of the medieval moralist, and quite in keeping with the marginal note that Priam's fall is an "Exempyll of the infellicitye and inconstant fortune of the kingdomis of this world." But Surrey in his last lines gives utterance to the pure classic spirit, and in clear heroic lines. This is Surrey's greatness.

Technically he is as we have described him. The impelling diction is Douglas' and so is the general movement. Even details like alliteration and the very successful run-on structure going into "Reignd ouer . . ." come from Douglas. So it is back in Gavin Douglas and the felicitous Scottish traditions that English blank verse takes its source.

One aspect of the epic technique comes out in the recital of Priam's fall: the device of combining in one sentence the glories of the past and the woes of the present, the royal prince and the dead stock. Now in one of the most famous pages of *Gorboduc,* Marcella's report of Porrex's death, the foundational rhetoric is built upon precisely this same combination of glory and wretchedness. These are Marcella's central lines:

> Alas, he liueth not! It is to true
> That, with these eyes, of him, a perelesse prince,
> Sonne to a king, and in the flower of youth,
> Euen with a twinke a senselesse stocke I saw.
>
> (IV, 2, 199-202)

The diction here, it will be noted, contains interesting reproductions of Surrey's diction in the passage above. The contrast of Porrex's brilliant youth and his miserable end, which is developed throughout Marcella's long recital, is remarkably parallel with that which forms the structure of Surrey's lines written about his imprisonment in Windsor ("So crewell prison . . ."). Surrey, after comparing his childish years to those of "Priams sonnes of Troye," composed several lines like those given to Marcella—e.g.:

> . . . with sleves tyed on the helme.   (Surrey, p. 84)

> . . . thy mistresse sleue tied on thy helme.   (*Gor.*, IV, 2, 251)

The language of Marcella's narrative is sensational, and has been called Senecan; but Seneca's way of handling similar recitals, as for instance the report of Hippolytus' death, is to pile horror on horror with no contrasting elements; for, since his aim is to show that life is utterly ruinous and despicable, misfortune cannot come as a contrast to past glory—there is no glory. On the other hand there were enough sensations in Virgil's account of the fighting in Troy—which Douglas calls a "deidlie Tragedy"[30]—to satisfy even the avidity of the sixteenth century for horror; and there were these other things besides.

2

Four years before *Gorboduc* was written, Nicholas Grimald also had occasion to tell of the fall of a heroic character, Marcus Tullius Cicero, "of royall robe, and sacred Senate prince." Cicero, like Porrex, becomes a "senslesse stock."

> Popilius flyeth, therwhyle: and, leauyng there
> The senslesse stock, a gryzely sight doth bear
> Vnto Antonius boord, with mischief fed.[31]

Grimald used blank verse for his epic fragment.

Grimald contributed this piece, "Marcus Tullius Ciceroes Death" (88 lines), and another blank verse piece, "The Death of Zoroas" (115 lines), to Tottel's *Miscellany;* he translated the former from Theodore Beza's *De Morte Ciceronis,* and the latter from Gautier de Chatillon's *Alexandreis,* which, in turn, seems to have been influenced by Lucan. And Lucan, as is well known, is one of the chief patrons of epical expression in the sixteenth century.

The blank verse of "The Death of Zoroas" is jagged and ejaculatory. It does contain a few resounding balanced lines like those which, under the influence of *Piers Plowman,* were soon to make their way into *Gorboduc;* this one, for instance, occupies a telling position as the concluding line of the poem:

> From derk obliuion of deuouryng death.

But the exclamatory descriptive passages are remarkable and puzzling. For, on the one hand, Grimald's jaggedness results apparently from a direct transposition of Gautier's medieval Latin into English. And on the other hand, a swift, rough narrative seems to have been traditional in accounts of battles: Grimald's technique resembles Chaucer's in *The Knight's Tale,* and Chaucer's extraordinary manner here is thought to go back to the alliterative romances.[32]

Whatever may have gone before Grimald's lurid and explosive lines, a great deal of important poetry comes after them. I am about to suggest that the epical description of the battle, with which Kyd opens the action of *The Spanish Tragedy,* is modeled on them; I am persuaded in part to do this because Tottel's *Miscellany* was probably the most important of literary works in its times, certainly the most popular of the books containing blank verse: it went through seven or possibly eight editions in the thirty or so years preceding *The Spanish Tragedy.* Grimald wrote in part as follows:

> Now clattering arms, now ragyng broyls of warr
> Gan passe the noyes of dredfull trompets clang:
> Shrowded with shafts, the heuen: with clowd of darts,
> Couered, the ayre . . .
>
> Now corpses hide the purpurde soyl with blood.
>
> Shaking her bloody hands, Bellone, among
> The Perses, soweth all kindes of cruel death.
> With throte ycutt, hee roores: hee lyeth along,
> His entrails with a launce through girded quite:
> Him smites the club, him wounds farstryking bowe . . .[33]

Kyd:

> Both cheerly sounding trumpets, drums, and fifes,
> Both raising dreadfull clamors to the skie . . .
>
> Now while *Bellona* rageth heere and there,
> Thicke stormes of bullets ran like winters haile,
> And shiuered Launces darke the troubled aire . . .

> Heere falles a body scindred from his head,
> There legs and armes lye bleeding on the grasse,
> Mingled with weapons and vnboweld steedes,
> That scattering ouer spread the purple plaine.[34]
>
> (I, 2, 28-9; 52-4; 59-62)

I shall not pause to point out the reproduction here of arrangement, words and images, except to note that Kyd's obscure phrase "purple plaine" is clarified by Grimald's additional "with blood." Very probably Kyd's abrupt "here—there" construction is a holdover from Grimald's (and Chaucer's) inordinately abrupt "he—he" constructions. On the other hand Kyd has obviously succeeded in straightening out Grimald's contorted lines.

Marlowe was devoted to variations on these themes. For him they provided substance for Tamburlaine's most extravagant threats:

> Our quiuering Lances shaking in the aire,
> And bullets like Ioues dreadfull Thunderbolts,
> Enrolde in flames and fiery smoldering mistes,
> Shall threat the Gods. . . .
>
> (616-9)

> So shall our swords, our lances and our shot
> Fill all the aire with fiery meteors.
>
> (1495-6)

In another similar context (1246-56) Marlowe makes a direct reference to Pharsalia; this is only a slightly less direct reference to Lucan, and, since we are dealing here with the epical element in dramatic poetry, it has its importance to us. At two other places (1474 ff.; 3192 ff.) Marlowe combines imagery of the troubled air with elaborate astrological material; this has a possible significance too, for in Grimald's poem, immediately after the descriptive lines quoted above, twenty-four consecutive lines are devoted to astrology, to the erring stars and the fates. Marlowe, in his usual fashion, motivates his rhetoric with a simple reversal of precedents: Tamburlaine holds the fates bound fast in iron chains.

The conspicuous epic strain in the relatively early drama has, I think, the immediate ancestry which I indicate above—a Douglas-Surrey-Grimald ancestry. This is at variance with accepted theory. According to Dr. Boas, for instance, Kyd's description of the battle is derived from Garnier.[35] Now it is true that Garnier wrote a very similar narrative in Act V of *Cornelie*;[36] the similarity, however, is probably due to Garnier's own cultivation of Latin epical traditions. And a more serious difficulty follows upon the theory of Garnier's influence: the association of Kyd and Garnier brings up the connection of Garnier with Seneca (which in itself is by no means so close as is generally thought[37]), and by virtue of a hasty syllogism *The Spanish Tragedy* becomes a Senecan drama and this particular scene a Senecan scene with the report of a messenger. Over against this artificial construction, these are the important facts, I think: (1) since Kyd does not preserve the unities, a messenger's report is not an organic necessity to his play; (2) epical battle passages are common to both Marlowe and Kyd; (3) as will be shown later, Kyd utilized a number of poetic traditions, all of which are strictly literary and not dramatic; (4) Kyd, in adopting the unrhymed medium, directs it towards the same effects and the same ends as do the most available of his predecessors; (5) the influence of the classics on Kyd, as indeed on all of his contemporaries, is complex: ultimate sources for a passage like that in question are more likely to be found in Lucan or Virgil than in Seneca.

3

After Surrey's accomplishment and Grimald's laborious contribution, it is of some interest to find that blank verse was next exercised—so far as is known—by one of the authors of *Gorboduc* shortly before *Gorboduc* itself was written.[38] For Thomas Norton, in translating Calvin's *Institutes of the Christian Religion,* adopted blank verse as a means of rendering into English the portions of Virgil which had been quoted by Calvin. Norton's translation of Calvin's work was first published on May 6, 1561; *Gorboduc* was presented for the first time at Christmas in 1561. It is fairly certain that Norton had completed his translation before *Gorboduc* was written: this is commonly accepted as a fact on the basis of the difference between the above dates; and since *Gorboduc* was composed to provide "furniture of part of the grand Christmasses in the Inner Temple,"[39] it seems that Sackville and Norton must have written the play fairly late in 1561.

In the fifth chapter of Book I of the *Institutes* Calvin quotes from Virgil's *Aeneid,* Book VI, lines 724-731. Norton translates this passage as follows:

> Fyrst heauen, and earth, and flovvyng fieldes of seas,
> The shinyng globe of Moone, and Titans starres,
> Sprite fedes vvithin, and throughout all the lymmes
> Infused mynde the vvhole huge masse dooth moue,
> And vvith the large bigge body mixe it selfe.
> Thense come the kyndes of men and eke of beastes,
> And lyues of fliyng foules, and monsters straunge,
> That vvater beares vvithin the marble sea.
> A fyry lyuelynesse and heauenly race there is
> VVithin those seedes. &c.

And Calvin quotes immediately after this from the *Georgics,* Book IV, lines 219-227, which are translated by Norton:

> Some say that bees haue part of mynde diuine,
> And heauenly draughtes. For eke they say, that God
> Gothe through the coastes of lande, and crekes of sea,
> And through depe skye. And hense the flockes and heardes:
> And men, and all the kyndes of sauage beastes,
> Eche at their byrthe receyue theyr suttle lyues.
> And therto are they rendred all at laste,
> And all resolued are retournde agayne.
> Ne place there is for dcathe: but lyuely they
> Flye into nombre of the Starres aboue,
> And take their place vvithin the lofty skye.

These lines in themselves contain few points of especial interest. Like Grimald's, they are stiff decasyllabics. They employ, however, a fairly successful variation on the end-stopping principle in that the *enjambements* are marked sometimes by a heavy stress on the first syllable of the second line; this device serves to preserve the integrity of the individual lines, to prevent the blurring which results from careless *enjambement.* The two extra syllables in the next to the last verse from the *Aeneid* are probably a printer's error, which also went uncorrected in the revised edition of 1562.

Since it has always been assumed—and most reasonably, I think—that rhymeless verse was suggested to the authors of *Gorboduc* by the example of Surrey, these twenty-one lines may be regarded as the positive link between Surrey's blank verse and the blank verse of *Gorboduc:* these lines seem indeed to be a perfect proof of continuity.

4

Certain prominent rhetorical features of *Gorboduc* seem to have sprung directly from Sackville's *Induction,* and that is to say, from the vast and highly ornamented "vision" literature of the Middle Ages. These features may be gathered under two convenient heads—the symbolic landscape and the elaborately visualized personification. They are often intermingled.

What I mean by the symbolic landscape and the elaborately visualized personification, as well as the mode of treatment to which they are subjected, can be illustrated by these splendid lines of Sir David Lyndsay, which appear in the Prologue to the *Dreme:*[40]

> I met dame Flora, in dule weid dissagysit,
> Quhilk into May wes dulce, and delectabyll;
> With stalwart stormis, hir sweitnes wes surprisit;
> Hir hevynlie hewis war turnit into sabyll,
> Quhilkis umquhile war to luffaris amiabyll.
> Fled frome the froste, the tender flouris I saw,
> Under dame Naturis mantyll, lurking law.

Here Lyndsay is establishing a setting for a poem which is remarkably parallel with Sackville's *Induction.* Both poets find themselves in a sad winter scene; both poets, conducted by a personification-guide, go on a marvelous journey into hell; and both utilize the marvelous journey as a means for dramatizing the vices of their native lands.

Sackville begins by describing the sorrowful winter landscape:

> The wrathfull winter proching on apace,
> With blustering blastes had all ybarde the treene,
> And olde *Saturnus* with his frosty face
> With chilling cold had pearst the tender greene:
> The mantels rent, wherein enwrapped beene
> The gladsom groues that now lay ouerthrowne,
> The tapets torne, and euery blome downe blowne.

Sackville here and in the next few stanzas seems to be borrowing from one of Gavin Douglas' characteristically medieval prologues to the books of the *Aeneid;* he transposes Douglas' dialect into his own smooth, slightly archaic English in much the way that Surrey had done before him. The third line, for instance, seems to be condensed from these lines of Douglas:[41]

> Rany Orioune wyth his stormy face . . .
> Frawart Saturne, chill of complexioune . . .

Sackville's debt is known to all students of his work. But I think it has never been noticed that his rhyme royal stanzas have an intricate movement which is also, in all likelihood, derived from the Scottish poets. A comparison of the passages from Sackville and Lyndsay above shows that the end-stopped lines of both poets are modified in that they are parts of larger syntactic structures, which are marked by a harmonious interweaving of phrases and relative clauses.

The verse of *Gorboduc* in some scenes—in those scenes especially which seem to be Sackville's—reproduces not infrequently the harmonies of the rhyme royal stanza. The best illustration is doubtless to be found in the opening lines of the play.

> The silent night, that brings the quiet pawse
> From painefull trauailes of the wearie day,
> Prolonges my carefull thoughtes, and makes me blame
> The slowe Aurore, that so for loue or shame
> Doth long delay to shewe her blushing face;
> And now the day renewes my griefull plaint.

Thus *Gorboduc* opens with a continuation of the verbal, grammatical, and metrical practices of the *Induction* and the great Scottish works; and to the same end: the first lines of *Gorboduc*, in their reference to natural phenomena, are setting the tone, the *mood* of what is to follow.[42]

But such writing does not come to very much in the first regular tragedy. It lay fallow for another quarter century, and then, for Thomas Kyd, it yielded magnificently. For Kyd, realizing fully what was natural all along to the medieval "vision" literature, the expression, namely, of emotion in terms of a symbolic landscape or symbolic journey—Kyd took these materials and made of them the metaphors in which his characters express their feelings. To describe how he did this will be an objective of the final pages of this chapter.

Some of the most striking pages in Sackville's *Induction* are devoted to highly visualized portraits of abstract vices—Remorse, Dread, Revenge, Misery, Care. . . . Pure personifications, of course, are of

ancient lineage—one thinks of Fame in Book IV of the *Aeneid* and
Philosophy in *The Consolation of Philosophy*—and Sackville's personifications are suggested by Virgil's account of the descent into hell.
But the English poet has developed his figures along strictly medieval
lines; Remorse, Dread, Revenge, and the rest are closely related to the
Seven Deadly Sins as the sins are treated by Dunbar and the author
of *Piers Plowman*. Now, in *Gorboduc*, in the dumb show and the
chorus attached to Act IV, there is a description of the furies—

> The dreadfull Furies, daughters of the night,
> With serpentes girt, carrying the whip of ire,
> With heare of stinging snakes, and shining bright
> With flames and bloud, and with a brand of fire.
>   (IV, Ch. 11-14)

—which seems to reproduce the portrait of Debate, painted on the
shield of War, in the *Induction*:

> Deadly *Debate*, all full of snaky heare,
> That with a bloudy fillet was ybound . . .
>   (St. 58)

This suggests that the "Senecan" furies in *Gorboduc* are of complex
origin; and if we consider other descriptive passages in the *Induction*,
such as this of the "fat weeds" that rot on Lethe wharf—

> A deadly gulfe: where nought but rubbish grows,
> With fowle blacke swelth in thickned lumpes that lies,
> Which vp in the ayre such stinking vapors throws
> That ouer there, may flie no fowle but dyes . . .
>   (St. 31)

—or if we examine the sensationalism and the blood in the many passages like these in the *Complaint*—

> His head dismembred from his mangled corps,
> Her selfe she cast into a vessel fraught
> With clottered bloud of them that felt her force.
>   (St. 14)

> The launsed spear hee wrythes out of the wound,
> From which the purple bloud spins on his face . . .
>   (St. 21)

—we must conclude, I think, that the vast body of sensational Elizabethan rhetoric is not of specifically Senecan origin.[43]

The chief rhetorical accomplishment of *Gorboduc,* however, is the
declamatory, balanced alliterative line to which we have already
given much attention. Since the description of the way in which
Norton developed this line out of alliterative tumbling verse, has already been presented,[44] it will suffice here simply to compare a few
typical lines from *Gorboduc* with later examples of the line. The line
which we used in our earlier comments on *Gorboduc,*

> But *l*onge may they *l*earne, ere they begyn to rule,
>
> (I, 2, 232)

may be compared with *Tamburlaine,* 734:

> And *gl*adly yeeld them to my *gr*acious rule;

And *Gorboduc,* I, 2, 104,

> With *furrowed face* and with *enfeebled* lymmes,

with *Tamburlaine,* 660:

> The *fainting* army of that *foolish* king.

Kyd follows the same rhetorical principle:

> Where *wounded* Hector liues in *lasting* paine.
>
> (S.T., Ind. 48)

The rhetorical principle is applied here, moreover, to a line which
Kyd seems to have imitated from Sackville's *Induction,*

> Not wurthy Hector wurthycst of them all,
>
> (St. 65)

and Sackville's line itself is an illustration of another principle of alliteration, that is, one which does not result in a balanced structure.

In fact, after *Gorboduc,* lines of this kind began appearing everywhere. It is significant, for instance, that an able editor of Samuel
Daniel's poetry, Arthur Colby Sprague, in two out of three examples
of Daniel at his best, selects lines which follow the same rhetorical
pattern:

> O cleer-eyde Rector of the holie Hill.
> Thys sorrowing farewell of a dying kisse.[45]

Professor Sprague points out the perfection of these lines, and compares the last with Marlowe and the Ovidians. This suggests some generalizations: The later sixteenth century sought for and attained a mastery of the single line. In it polish and balance are exceptionally noticeable; consequently, though it appears to have sprung from *Piers Plowman*, it is also suitable to the sophisticated purposes of the Ovidians, and has an intrinsic character not unlike that of the eighteenth century couplet. But it comes to another peak in the broad declamatory heroics of Marlowe.

5

Balanced rhetorical lines are especially conspicuous in *Jocasta*. And this is no great wonder, for *Jocasta* in all essential respects seems to be a reflection of *Gorboduc*. Actually, of course, George Gascoigne and Francis Kinwelmarshe translated their tragedy from the Italian of Lodovico Dolce, who in turn had followed a Latin version of Euripides' *Phoenissae*. Thus only very indirectly was it a Senecan play; for the sixteenth century it was a Greek play notable for its morality.[46] But the translators worked with a certain freedom, and herein they showed not so much originality as dependence on *Gorboduc* their heightening of effects seems to be inspired by that play.

Jocasta was written during the year following the first publication of *Gorboduc*. It resembles the earlier play in the following respects: it uses the same theme (a reason for its selection for translation?)—civil war between two brothers; it was also presented to an Inns of Court audience; it moralizes further than the Italian version on the same commonplace sources of worry—monarchic ambition, the rashness of youth, the pains of civil war; it adopts blank verse and along with blank verse the dumb show for the second time in the regular drama; and it employs consistently the highly stylized rhetoric of the earlier play, e.g.:

Joc.:
    With stretching string, or else with bloudie knyfe.
                                                    (II, 1, 71)
Gorb.:
    By strangling cord and slaughter of the sword.
                                                    (V, 2, 9)

Joc.:
> Alas, alas, how wrekeful wrath of Gods.
> > (II, 1, 131)

Gorb.:
> That,—if the mindfull wrath of wrekeful gods.
> > (II, 2, 75)

Joc.:
> For crooked age and hory siluer heares
> Still craueth helpe of lustie youthful yeares . . .
> But rest a whyle thy weake and weary limmes.
> > (III, 1, 23-4; 28)

Gorb.:
> For cares of kynges that rule—as you haue ruled—
> Do wast mannes lyfe, and hasten crooked age
> With furrowed face and with enfeebled lymmes.
> > (I, 2, 101; 103-4)

Joc.:
> Euen so amidde the huge heape of my woes.
> > (II, 1, 116)
> Heape one mishap upon anothers head.
> > (V, 3, 37)

Gorb.:
> To see the hugie heapes of these vnhappes.
> > (V, 2, 109)

These lines are meant to illustrate the unvarying resemblance of *Jocasta* to *Gorboduc* in regard to alliteration, euphuism, vocabulary, and sensational phraseology. The examples above are by no means exhaustive; I have merely noticed the parallels for lines from *Gorboduc* which, for one reason or another, we have referred to earlier in this study.

The rhetoric of *Jocasta* is that of *Gorboduc* extended and elaborated, forced not too impressively to a higher pitch. *Jocasta*, as indeed *Gorboduc* too, exploits the clichés of the sixteenth century—clichés which are common to the metrical psalms, the authorized homilies, the Senecan plays, Surrey's Virgil, the miscellanies, and also Dolce's play; typical examples of them are expressions like "just revenge," "guiltless blood," "dreadful death," "slaughtering sword," etc.[47] Expressions of this kind are in themselves bombastic; they doubtless provided a stimulus to the formation of the bombastic heroics of the later dramatists. As an illustration of this we might consider the famous lines of Tamburlaine in which he commands the burning of the town in which Zenocrate died. In part they are the following:

> So, burne the turrets of this cursed towne,
> Flame to the highest region of the aire . . .
> Threatning a death and famine to this land,
> Flieng Dragons, lightning, fearfull thunderclaps,
> Sindge these fair plaines . . .
>
> (3191 ff.)

Behind these lines there seems most certainly to lie a complicated tradition of rhetoric. It is probably founded in part on the Biblical plagues; at least in *Gorboduc* this version of the curse sounds very much like the Bible:

> Thus shall the wasted soile yelde forth no fruite,
> But dearth and famine shall possesse the land!
> The townes shall be consumed and burnt with fire,
> The peopled cities shall waxe desolate.
>
> (V, 2, 225-8)

But it is also classical, as in *Jocasta*:

> And angry *Mars* shall ouercome it all
> With famine, flame, rape, murther, dole and death:
> These lustie towres shall haue a headlong fall,
> These houses burnde, and all the rest be razde.
>
> (III, 1, 137-40)

6

We come now to a series of examples of early blank verse which I believe did not have any very direct influence on the rhetoric of tragedy, but which are relevant here because they help, by antithesis, to define the heroic style.

Turberville's selection of blank verse in 1567 as a medium in which to render six of Ovid's *Heroides* was probably inspired by the fact that he was dedicating his work to Lord Thomas Howard, the younger brother of the Earl of Surrey. Turberville is a most interesting and admirable poet in his way: he is a precisionist, a meticulous filer of phrases, sophisticated and practically precious in his devotion to

Anglo-Saxon monosyllables. A moment's reflection on the part played by full, round multisyllable words in Marlowe's line, or for that matter in Shakespeare's or Milton's, will show why Turberville is at his best in his favorite meters—fourteeners and poulter's meter—rather than in blank verse. His lines tend to break up in small fragments:

> At length, of Sire, his servants, and the day
> Dreading: these words to break thy sleepe, I spake.[48]
>
> (p. 176)

His studious intellectuality is perhaps best exhibited in the singular poem, "The Translator to the Captious Sort of Sycophantes," which he appended to his *Heroycall Epistles*, of which this is a significant stanza:

> Devises of the language divers are
> Well couched words and feately forged phrase,
> Eche string in tune, no ragged rime doth jarre,
> With figures fraught their bookes in every place:
> So that it is a worke of prayse to cause
> A romaine born to speake with English jawes.
>
> (p. 342)

Dramatic blank verse, of course, demanded something larger, and at first something looser and plainer, than Turberville's featly forged phrases. His poetry, though it frequently glitters like barbaric jewelry, does not become the stageman.

George Gascoigne, in his blank-verse poem, *The Steel Glas* (1576), is a precisionist of a different stripe. He shares his contemporaries' propensities to alliteration, balanced lines, quibbles, euphuism; but he makes two individual departures from their practices: he is a stern advocate of parallel structure and a *caesura* after the fourth syllable. Neither of these principles, if it is held to as rigidly as Gascoigne holds to it, is congenial to dramatic heroics.

Yet Gascoigne has notable convictions as to the special properties of the unrhymed medium. In his prefatory poem, which I think has never been discussed in this connection, he says he aspires, with all due modesty, to lasting fame as a poet; but the tower of fame, on which he has his eye, is much too tall "for ladders made of ryme." Therefore he will try to batter it down:

> Such battering tyre, this pamphlet here bewraies,
> In rymelesse verse, which thundreth mighty threates,

> And where it findes that vice the wall decayes,
> Even there (amaine) with sharpe rebukes it beates.
> The worke (thinke I) deserves an honest name,
> If not: I fayle to win this forte of fame.
>
> (II, 140)

The metaphor is mixed. But it is clear that Gascoigne has realized, possibly because of his experience with *Jocasta,* that blank verse is a suitable medium in which *to thunder mighty threats;* and this characterization, coming as it does at least ten years before the prologue to *Tamburlaine,* makes the whole picture-puzzle of early blank verse history fall into shape: *Tamburlaine* is not the bolt out of the blue that it has been thought to be.

There still remains the question why Gascoigne wrote *The Steel Glas* in its peculiar kind of blank verse. The prefatory poem suggests Horace perhaps, and Professor Brooke has written that Gascoigne "appears to be aiming at the ostentatiously pedestrian elegance of Horace's *Sermones.*"[49] On the other hand the metrical features of the poem and conspicuous allusions in it indicate that it is much influenced by *Piers Plowman;* it is also very strikingly the same kind of poetry, both in point of satiric-moral purpose and parallel structures, as that which Gavin Douglas wrote in several prologues in the *Aeneid,* especially in the one before Book VIII. But this prologue was strongly influenced by alliterative poetry, and it itself is paralleled by much more medieval poetry. Certainly to find Horace in the bulk of *The Steel Glas* is to run far afield.

The question of relations between the English sixteenth century poets and the Latin poets demands another word. Professor Brooke finds that each important early example of unrhymed verse is an imitation of a Latin measure: Gascoigne is imitating Horace; the authors of *Gorboduc* and of *Jocasta* "are apparently seeking to give the impression of the Senecan senarius";[50] most of the other examples speak for themselves since they are translations; in fact "the un-English character" of Surrey's versification "is noted on the title-page of the second edition of Surrey's work (book iv), which calls it a 'straunge meter.' "[51] The last statement must be an error; the 'straunge meter' is from the first edition of the translation (1554), at which time the meter was indeed strange.[52] The other points come essentially to this: *Gorboduc* is motivated essentially by a passionate interest in English political morality; the most careful and literary of the translators, Turberville, favors the older meters rather than blank verse.

These men were all experienced and gifted poets. This means that to write with or without rhyme would involve them in no creative difficulties: they would choose one form or another at will; all depended on the effects they wished to produce, and for the studied, ink-horn poetry of the sixteenth century, rhyme was most suitable. Heroics had to wait for a stage on which to be declaimed. Allusions to the classics do not mean direct imitation; comparisons with the Latins, as Francis Meres amply proves, do not mean imitation either. Every poet hopes that his work will compare with that of the Ancients. But no poet who aspires to such comparison will want, or will be able, to divorce himself from the poetic disciplines which have been handed down to him.

7

For the sake of completeness I enter here a list, which I copy largely from Professor Brooke's article, of the remaining minor examples of blank verse that can be said positively to antedate *Tamburlaine*:

Spenser (?): Fifteen "sonnets" in Van der Noodt's Theatre, 1569.
Barnabe Riche: A poem (170 lines) in *Don Simonides*, 1584.
Peele: *The Arraignment of Paris* (parts only), 1584.
    "Lines to Th. Watson" (11 lines), prefatory to Watson's *Hekatompathia*, 1582.
    "The Device of the Pageant before Wolstan Dixi" (the opening speech only: 53 lines), 1585.

Of these only one item is of significance, and it, I am sure, is of the highest significance. It is the blank verse in Peele's *Arraignment of Paris*, especially Paris' "Oration to the Council of the Gods." The oration begins:

> Sacred and just, thou great and dreadful Jove,
> And you thrice-reverend powers, whom love nor hate
> May wrest awry; if this, to me a man,
> This fortune fatal be, that I must plead
> For safe excusal of my guiltless thought,
> The honour more makes my mishap the less,

That I a man must plead before the gods,
Gracious forbearers of the world's amiss,
For her, whose beauty how it hath enticed,
This heavenly senate may with me aver.
But sith nor that nor this may do me boot,
And for myself myself must speaker be,
A mortal man amidst this heavenly presence;
Let me not shape a long defence to them
That ben beholders of my guiltless thoughts.
                                    (IV, 1, 66 ff.)

Here the oratorical manner of *Gorboduc* has swung back fully into the drama. In these fifteen lines one-third are marked by the balanced structure which has been practically the theme of this chapter, and along with the balanced structures are traces of the familiar clichés and quibbles. The decasyllabics are of full heroic length, ringing, polished, yet suitable to the stageman's throat. Paris' words express a decorum proper to a mortal man defending himself before the gods; but it is a verbal decorum: the tone is Tamburlaine's.

The tone and the manner are more than that; they are the tone and manner of the tragic hero defending himself before a hostile or somehow remote audience.

Then for the deed,—that I may not deny,
Wherein consists the full of mine offence,—
I did upon command; if then I erred,
I did no more than to a man belonged.

Peele has brought the rhetoric of the "one-man play" to its full stature. For blank-verse rhetoric, in being essentially oratorical-declamatory, predicates a peculiar relationship between the speaker and the listeners; the listeners must be placated and won over, or scourged with threats. The speaker stands alone; the hero tries to enforce or to clarify and to reconcile his relationship to a contrary world. This is one good reason why there was a one-man drama, and a good reason for at least one aspect of Othello's rôle:

Most potent, grave, and reverend signiors,
My very noble and approv'd good masters,
That I have ta'en away this old man's daughter,
It is most true . . .

There is very little to add now to the foregoing remarks on Marlowe, the Marlowe at least of *Tamburlaine*. One point of interest, however, is that the direction taken by some of the most extravagant rant points back to the old popular drama. Oaths like this of Baiazeth,

> By *Mahomet*, my Kinsmans sepulcher,
> And by the holy *Alcaron* I sweare,
> He shall be made a chast and lustlesse Eunuke . . .
>
> (1173-5)

probably have behind them as a stimulus the ravings of Herod, although the lines themselves are clearly formed according to the heroic pattern. Similarly it is doubtless true that the bombastic Oriental drama of Greene and Peele drew some of its verve from the religious pageants.

The method used in these pages has neglected, of course, a consideration of the possibilities of general, extended effect; and Marlowe, it is perfectly evident, by turning upside-down the sin of pride and the overawing influence of fate, achieved a motivation for sustained effects of startling power and beauty. This is not to insinuate anything about the morality of *Tamburlaine*: we could call it an amoral rhetorical drama, but there is also some certainty in the proposition that *Tamburlaine* is a moral drama in that it opposes licentiousness, effeminacy, "Italian pleasures"—that is to say, the vices embraced by Tamburlaine's opponents and by Gaveston.

Marlowe also made positive strides in the development of eloquent and articulate metaphors. But a discussion of this aspect of blank-verse rhetoric will come out best in connection with the work of Thomas Kyd.

PART III

A good deal of the rhetoric of *The Spanish Tragedy*, it would appear, is derived from the metrical tragedy embellished with the marvelous journey and the graphically described, complaining ghost. And this rhetoric is not always ignoble: I hope that the following paragraphs will show that Kyd, despite possible intentions to write only sensationally, tapped one of the purest streams of English poetry, and at times, at crucial times, turned its current to what modern readers are obliged to call the most worthy of purposes.

For Kyd took materials like those which appear in Sackville's *In-*

duction, a marvelous journey, and *Buckingham,* a tragical complaint
of a ghost, and made of them the language of his characters' mental
anguish. This is to say, he reduced these traditional materials to figures of speech which could convey the personal emotions of a Hieronimo or an Isabella; and to credit him with this, is practically, in
view of chronology, to credit him with an important contribution to
the development of the great Elizabethan language of metaphors.[53]

This process of forming figurative language is particularly clear in
the passages in which Hieronimo mistakes the Old Man for the ghost
of Horatio. At first Hieronimo accepts the Old Man as a ghost as real
as any who visited the bedchambers of the writers of metrical tragedies:

> And art thou come, *Horatio,* from the deapth,
> To aske for iustice in this vpper earth . . . ?
> Sweet boy, how art thou chang'd in deaths black shade . . .
> *Horatio,* thou are older than thy father . . .
> (III, 13, 132 ff.)

But when the Old Man refuses to admit that he is either the ghost of
Horatio or a Fury sent to guide Hieronimo into the infernal regions,
Hieronimo makes this most interesting speech:

> Thou art the liuely image of my griefe;
> Within thy face my sorrowes I may see.
> Thy eies are gum'd with teares, thy cheekes are wan,
> Thy forehead troubled, and thy muttring lips
> Murmure sad words abruptly broken off
> By force of windie sighes thy spirit breathes . . .
> (III, 13, 161 ff.)

Hieronimo still seems to be taking the Old Man for an apparition; an
apparition in fact which bears a close resemblance to Sackville's
ghost of Buckingham, who with "vapored eyes upcast" thrice "began
his doleful tale, and thrice the sighs did swollow up his voice." But
for Hieronimo this is no longer a good solid ghost; it is a *lively image
of grief.*

Thus it was Kyd, it would appear, who made the transition from
the "filthy whining ghost" of the metrical tragedies to the Shakespearean ghost, to whom such words as these are addressed:

> Thou canst not say I did it: never shake
> Thy gory locks at me.

For what is this but a lively image of Macbeth's guilt? Or when Brutus, troubled in thought and bent over his book late in the night (familiar prelude to a ghost!), discovers the dead Caesar standing before him, and says,

> I think it is the weakness of mine eyes
> That shapes this monstrous apparition,

what the audience really sees is not the Ghost of Caesar but an outward manifestation of Brutus' state of mind.

Hieronimo also expresses his great sorrow by imagining that he will go on a marvelous journey down into hell where he will plead for justice and revenge. Sometimes he thinks a Fury or a Personification will act as guide for him, and sometimes, seeming at a loss to know what to do for a guide, he calls upon such a person as the Old Man to play Orpheus. Needless to say this is an adaptation of the regular business of the medieval poems. The following passage is one of many:

> *Hieronimo,* tis time for thee to trudge:
> Downe by the dale that flowes with purple gore,
> Standeth a firie Tower; there sits a iudge
> Vpon a seat of steele and molten brasse,
> And twixt his teeth he holdes a fire-brand,
> That leades vnto the lake where hell doth stand.
> Away, *Hieronimo;* to him be gone:
> Heele doe thee iustice for *Horatios* death.
> (III, 12, 6 ff.)

This should be entirely recognizable despite its somewhat fantastic imagery. It and the other passages like it are basically the Virgilian descent into hell. It might be added that in these passages the phrases descriptive of hell are frequently very close to those in Sackville's *Induction*.

Along with the figurative journey, Hieronimo, in similar passages, may draw in other details from the medieval poems; and the journey itself may become highly disguised:

> Where shall I run to breath abroad my woes . . . ?
> The blustring winds, conspiring with my words,
> At my lament haue moued the leaueles trees,
> Disroabde the medowes of their flowred greene . . .

Yet still tormented is my tortured soule
With broken sighes and restles passions,
That winged mount, and, houering in the aire,
Beat at the windowes of the brightest heauens,
Solliciting for iustice and reuenge.
But they are plac't in those empyreal heights,
Where, countermurde with walles of diamond,
I find the place impregnable, and they
Resist my woes, and giue my words no way.
                              (III, 7, 1 ff.)

For this complaint Kyd seems to have picked up phrases and images from the Virgil-Sackville stream of literature. He uses the connection of a natural aspect with a state of mind, repeating the diction of Sackville: *blustering winds, leafless trees, disrobed meadows, flowered green*—no collection of words could do more to reproduce the tone of the beginning of Sackville's *Induction,* and this is also to echo the beginnings of many medieval allegorical poems, including Gavin Douglas' Prologue to Book VII of the *Aeneid,* the immediate source of Sackville's lines. The latter part of the passage is plainly a variation on the Virgilian descent into hell, for the central description that the place is "countermurde with walles of diamond" and impregnable is practically borrowed from Kyd's own description of hell (". . . the faire Elizian greene, In midst whereof there stands a stately Towre, The walles of brasse, the gates of adamant." Induction to the *S.T.*) and is extremely close to Virgil's Tartarus. We know too that it is to hell that Hieronimo habitually promises to go in search of justice and revenge. And the sighs and passions which mount, winged, hovering in the air, have a resemblance to Virgil's unborn spirits. It is the imagery of the Virgilian and medieval hell which Kyd applies to heaven. In more than one way, Kyd deserved the jibe of Nashe for the liberties he took with the location of Elysium.

The use of the materials of the tragedies and the journeys for the metaphorical language in which Horatio's parents express their grief, provided, thus, the necessary imagery upon which effective expression of such feelings depends, and it also provided the perhaps even more valuable movement, the longer harmonies, which are essential to the best dramatic blank verse. Each of the speeches in which Hieronimo swears that he will go down into hell in search of justice and revenge develops an intensity which mounts from line to line.

Or some lines of Isabella—no doubt a further variation on the meta-phorical journey into hell—will illustrate what I mean:

> My soule—poore soule, thou talkes of things
> Thou knowst not what—my soule hath siluer wings,
> That mounts me vp vnto the highest heauens—
> To heauen: I, there sits my *Horatio,*
> Backt with a troup of fiery Cherubins
> Dauncing about his newly healed wounds,
> Singing sweet hymnes and chanting heauenly notes . . .
>
> (III, 8, 14 ff.)

Intensity, vigor, and movement are apparent here. In comparison with the studied, witty, euphuistic lines of earlier poets, these lines are simple and ringing; in comparison with the broad ringing heroics of the earlier Marlowe, they are sensitive, complex, and deeply moti-vated. In mechanics, so far as analysis can show, they are much the same as similar lines of Shakespeare.

Indeed it seems that Kyd, in these passages, is laying the founda-tion for Shakespeare's energetic, figurative poetry, the poetry in which joy or anguish of spirit expresses itself. On the side of mental anguish we might look at such lines as these of Macbeth:

> —Now o'er the one half-world
> Nature seems dead, and wicked dreams abuse
> The curtain'd sleep; witchcraft celebrates
> Pale Hecate's offerings; and wither'd murder,
> Alarum'd by his sentinel, the wolf,
> Whose howl's his watch, thus with his stealthy pace,
> With Tarquin's ravishing strides, toward his design
> Moves like a ghost.

Shakespeare, in making Macbeth speak thus in hysterical tones, gath-ers together in a single collection most of the images to which our attention has been directed. There are the semi-personifications *dreams* and *sleep*—*dreams* are regularly personified in medieval liter-ature, and *sleep* is one of Sackville's allegorical figures at the mouth of hell. There is mention of Hecate, who, as other parts of the play show, comes from an infernal region exactly like the one Kyd de-scribes. The complete personification *withered murder* suggests the portraits done by Sackville and the allegorists. Tarquin has come probably from Shakespeare's own modified metrical tragedy, *Lu-*

crece, to do metaphorical duty here. In close conjunction with the references to dreams, to an infernal creature, and to a typically medieval personification, there is the image of the ghost. Such fusion of material and such adapting of material to the purposes of drama constitute in all likelihood a debt which English dramatists owe to Thomas Kyd.

For Kyd took features of the Virgilian descent into hell and made of them the language of Hieronimo's suffering. An important step in this direction had already been made by Sackville in his *Induction,* for Sackville linked the descent into hell with a vision growing out of extreme sorrow, and even earlier poets did almost the same thing. But Kyd changed this from a narrative to a vehicle for expressing emotion; he provided the imagery necessary for a metaphorical journey of the troubled spirit. Hieronimo's agony is the core of *The Spanish Tragedy;* it is expressed almost entirely in the terms we have examined. Those same terms very soon became the language of the most intense parts of new and greater plays.

And to say that at last there is perfected here the language of suffering is to say that suffering has become articulate. Articulation goes hand in hand with ultimate understanding and adjustment; and understanding and adjustment, though they do not prevent the fates, though they see only death before them, are nevertheless the soul of tragedy.

NOTES

1. E.g.; Arnold Schröer, "Uber die Anfänge des Blankverses in England," *Anglia,* IV (1881), 1-72; Joseph B. Mayor, *Chapters on English Meter* (London, 1901); J. Schipper, *Englische Metrik* (Bonn, 1888); George Saintsbury, *A History of English Prosody* (London, 1906); Paul Verrier, *Les Principes de la Métrique Anglaise* (Paris, 1909); C. E. Andrews, *The Writing and Reading of Verse* (New York, 1918).

2. I am convinced of the especial value of a general work on the poetry of this period: W. J. Courthope, *A History of English Poetry* (London, 1897), vol. II.

3. "It is I think justifiable to speak of these poets—Marlowe, Peele, Greene, Lodge, Nashe, Kyd, and others more dimly discerned—as a school. They worked in collaboration and interchanged their praises. They have a common bond in classical knowledge and the attempt to conquer the popular stage for literature. . . . The analysis of style

must go a good deal further before it is possible to lay a finger on any passage of a play of the early 'nineties and say with confidence, 'This is Marlowe,' or 'This is Greene,' or 'This is the young Shakespeare.'" E. K. Chambers, "The Unrest in Shakespeare Studies," *The Nineteenth Century*, 101 (1927), 255-60.

4. *Studies in Philology*, XIX (1922), 186-205.

5. Professor Brooke reprints the relevant passage.

6. Cf. Lytton Strachey, *Pope* (New York, 1936), p. 22 ff. But in this regard the lines of the player-king in *Hamlet* are not without interest; e.g.:

> Most necessary 'tis that we forget
> To pay ourselves what to ourselves is debt;
> What to ourselves in passion we propose,
> The passion ending, doth the purpose lose.

—etc.

7. Jasper Heywood, "To the Reader," *Troas*, in *Newton's Seneca*, ed. T. S. Eliot (New York, 1927), II, 4.

8. All quotations from Marlowe are from *The Works of Christopher Marlowe*, ed. C. F. Tucker Brooke (Oxford, 1910).

9. Prefatory to *Perimedes the Blacksmith* (1588).

10. Prefatory to *Menaphon* (1589).

11. *Idem*.

12. Prefatory to *The Groat's Worth of Wit* (1592).

13. In this connection the title page of the new, blank verse version of *Tancred and Gismund* (1591) is significant: "Newly revised and polished according to the decorum of these days."

14. Cf. *NED*.

15. Van Dam and Stoffel hold doubtless too closely to the principle of the strictly decasyllabic line; they are led to maintain that variations are corruptions. Cf. e.g., *Chapters on English Printing, Prosody, and Pronunciation* (Heidelberg, 1902). But both the general principle and the works of these critics are important; cf. also B. A. P. Van Dam, "Marlowe's *Tamburlaine*," *English Studies*, Feb. and Apr., 1934.

16. See pp. 41-4 *supra* and Chapter I, note 55.

17. See p. 34 *supra*.

18. These remarks have implications. If we accept Clarence's prayer as an expression of literary convention, then we can overcome several perplexing problems. The question why this scene is, in Shakespeare, so unusually heavy in Christian theology, and how it can shift so lightly from serious to frivolous theology, becomes a question of little moment. (Similarly, if Tamburlaine is a variation on convention, then he is not very good evidence of Marlowe's atheism.) I do not

mean wholly to subscribe to Professor E. E. Stoll's theories: a poet's morality is to be found in wholes, not in lines and passages, and discussion of wholes cannot be attempted here.

19. Cf. A. K. Foxwell, *A Study of Sir T. Wyatt's Poems* (London, 1911).

20. *The Poems of Henry Howard, Earl of Surrey,* ed. F. M. Padelford (Seattle, 1928), Bk. II, 21.

21. *The Poetical Works of Gavin Douglas,* ed. John Small (Edinburgh, 1874), vol. II, Bk. II, 4.

22. *Newton's Seneca,* II, 6.

23. *Ibid.,* p. 4.

24. It is possible that Heywood is following Sackville's *Induction,* and that Sackville was following Surrey. If so, the *Induction* was then available in manuscript form earlier than 1559.

25. *The Mirror for Magistrates,* ed. Haslewood, II, 327.

26. *The Heroycall Epistles,* ed. F. S. Boas (London, 1928), p. 226.

27. Cf. F. M. Padelford (ed.), *The Poems of Henry Howard* . . .

28. Thomas Phaer, *The Nyne fyrst Bookes of The Eneidos.* . . . (London, 1562).

29. *The Complete Works of George Peele,* ed. A. H. Bullen (London, 1888); "The Honour of the Garter," l. 55 (II, 319).

30. The Prologue to Book IV.

31. *Tottel's Miscellany* (1557-1587), ed. Hyder Edward Rollins (Cambridge, Mass., 1928), I, 120.

32. Cf. *The Complete Works of Geoffrey Chaucer,* ed. F. N. Robinson (Boston, 1933), p. 783; l. 2601 ff. Some of the lines in the comparable passages are these:

Gautier (Migne's *Patrologia Latina,* vol. 209; Bk. III, l. 1263 ff.):

Seminat in Persas lethi genus omne, cruentas
Excutuens Bellona manus; gemit ille recluso
Gutture, trajecto jacet ille per ilia ferro:
Hunc sparus exanimat, hunc tundit funda . . .

Grimald follows Gautier's syntax:

Shaking her bloody hands, Bellone, among
The Perses, soweth all kindes of cruel death.
With throte ycutt, hee roores: hee lyeth along,
His entrails with a launce through girded quite:
Him smites the club, him wounds farstryking bowe . . .

But Chaucer had used similar syntax (*The Knight's Tale,* l. 2612 ff.):

He thurgh the thikkeste of the throng gan threste;
Ther stomblen steedes stronge, and doun gooth al;
He rolleth under foot as dooth a bal;
He foyneth on his feet with his tronchoun,
And he hym hurtleth with his hors adoun;
He thurgh the body is hurt and sithen take . . .

And compare *The Legend of Good Women*, 635 ff.

33. *Tottel's Miscellany*, I, 115. I use in part the readings of the second edition, also of 1557.

34. *The Works of Thomas Kyd*, ed. F. S. Boas (Oxford, 1901).

35. *Ibid.*, Introduction.

36. *Oeuvres Complètes de Robert Garnier*, ed. L. Pinvert (Paris, 1923), I, 157:

Bellonne, ardant de rage, au plus fort de la presse
Couroit qui ça qui là, d'une prompte allégresse,
Détranchoit, terrassoit, faisoit sourdre un estang
Ou passoit son espée ointe de nostre sang.

37. Cf. A. McL. Witherspoon, *The Influence of Robert Garnier on Elizabethan Drama* (Yale Studies, LXV [1924]). This work includes an excellent survey of the background of Garnier and of the relevant scholarship.

38. This and the paragraphs immediately following are rewritten from my note, "Some Blank Verse Written by Thomas Norton Before *Gorboduc*," *Modern Language Notes*, Dec., 1933.

39. The P[rinter] to the Reader, John Day's edition of *Gorboduc*, 1570.

40. *The Poetical Works of Sir David Lyndsay*, ed. David Laing (Edinburgh, 1879).

41. The Prologue to Book VII; Douglas' *Works*, III, 75. Sackville's introductory stanzas also resemble other medieval poems. Cf. Marguerite Hearsey's edition of the poem (*op. cit.*, pp. 93-4).

42. The opening speech of Videna has been compared with *Hercules Furens* 125-40, *Oedipus* 1-5, *Agamemnon* 53-6, and *Octavia* 1-6. Why I think that Videna's lines are not "distinctly Senecan in style" (H. E. Watt), the reader has seen; that they reproduce some Senecan imagery is clear, but that it is distinctly and exclusively Senecan imagery is very doubtful.

43. In this connection we might notice some of Gavin Douglas' rhetoric:

Pluto, thow patron of the deip Acheron,
Fadir of turmentis in thine infernale see,
Amid the fludis Stix and Flegiton,

> Lethe, Cochite, the wateris of oblivie,
> With dolorus quhirling of furious sisteris thre,
> Thyne now sal be my muse and drery sang;
> To follow Virgile in this dirk poese,
> Convey me, Sibill, that I ga nocht wrang.
>
> (Prologue to Bk. VI of the *Aeneid*)

Miss Hearsey also compares the passages in question with Douglas, and with Lydgate as well (*op. cit.*, pp. 98 and 108).

44. See pp. 41 ff. *supra.*
45. A. C. Sprague (ed.), *Samuel Daniel/Poems and A Defence of Ryme* (Cambridge, Mass., 1930), pp. xvi and xviii.
46. *The Complete Works of George Gascoigne,* ed. J. W. Cunliffe (Cambridge, 1907 and 1910). The play is called a "moral discourse" by Gascoigne in his prefatory epistle (I, 13); and both morality and Euripides are insisted on by the printer (Quarto 1, 1573: Cunliffe, I, 476).
47. A useful analysis of Gascoigne's rhetoric in *Jocasta* is contained in Richard Henning's *George Gascoigne als Übersetzer italienischer Dichtungen* (Königsberg, 1913); Henning calls the sensational clichés "Surreyisms," but I doubt that they can be ascribed so directly to a single literary influence.
48. *The Heroycall Epistles,* ed. F. S. Boas.
49. Brooke, "Marlowe's Versification and Style," *Studies in Philology,* XIX (1922), p. 188.
50. *Idem.*
51. *Ibid.,* p. 187.
52. I draw this conclusion from Padelford's bibliography, and from A. W. Pollard and G. R. Redgrave, *A Short-Title Catalogue* (London, 1926). The matter is worth mentioning because Professor Brooke's remark has misleading implications.
53. In a less extensive way, Marlowe did something similar. It is notable, too, that he uses the Troy story as a metaphor to describe Zenocrate's beauty:

> And had she liu'd before the siege of *Troy,*
> *Hellen,* whose beauty sommond Greece to armes,
> And drew a thousand ships to Tenedos,
> Had not bene man'd in *Homers* Iliads . . .
>
> (*Tamb.* 3055 ff.)

HALLETT SMITH

The Shepheardes Calender and Pastoral Poetry

The pastoral lyric distills emotion from an ideal of content and the good life. It is the purest of the pastoral forms and the one in which Elizabethan style and manner are most clearly evident. But the pastoral eclogue is more typical and more conventional; it is more important historically, because Spenser used the form to usher in a great new age of English poetry. A critical appreciation of the Elizabethan eclogue is not easy for a modern reader, because he does not discriminate as the Elizabethans did and because the commonplaces upon which pastoral is built have now lost some of their vitality.

The models for pastoral eclogue available to the Elizabethans were both classical and modern, Latin and vernacular, great and mediocre. The tradition is one which has often been traced from Theocritus to Virgil to the humanists of the Renaissance to Marot and Spenser. It now seems clear that Spenser's sources, or perhaps inspirations would be a better word, were largely Renaissance rather than ancient.[1] Of special interest among the neo-Latin eclogues are those of Baptista Spagnuoli, called Mantuan. They were used in Elizabethan school textbooks and became a part of the knowledge of anyone who learned Latin in the period. Mantuan was a Carmelite monk, and his eclogues contain satire on the Roman church which naturally pleased the taste

From *Elizabethan Poetry* (Cambridge, Mass.: Harvard University Press, 1952), pp. 31-51. Reprinted by permission of the publishers. Copyright, 1952, by the President and Fellows of Harvard College.

of Protestant Englishmen. Moreover, his Latin was of about the right degree of difficulty for schoolboys, the content was one which schoolmasters would believe healthy for their charges, and there is the illusion of pleasantness about the eclogues which is always a consideration in a textbook.[2]

Alexander Barclay's eclogues of 1515 contain imitations of Mantuan and of Aeneas Sylvius; Barnabe Googe's *Eglogs Epitaphs and Sonnets* in 1563 includes translations from eclogues in Montemayor; and George Turbervile translated into English verse the whole of Mantuan's eclogues in 1567. This is the extent of the pastoral eclogue in English before the appearance of Spenser's *The Shepheardes Calender* in 1579.

Spenser's sources have been elaborately worked out; his covert allusions to contemporary persons and events have been so laboriously and painfully investigated that it is with some difficulty that a modern reader threads his way through all the apparatus that has been provided for the poetry to the poetry itself. Yet the very commentators who have erected such a mountain of lumber around *The Shepheardes Calender* justify themselves by pointing, quite rightly, to the quality and significance of the twelve eclogues contained in it. It was the publication of these poems, everybody agrees, which ushered in the New Poetry of the Elizabethan age. Spenser's metrical experiments were bold and, for the most part, effective. His language, although serious critics like Sidney might be doubtful about it, utilized archaic and provincial words in such a way as to provide a diction suitable to the characters who are speaking. Most of all, he demonstrated with amazing confidence and flair that English verse was capable of the most varied and complex effects, all within a traditional mode which had a general European acceptance.

The Shepheardes Calender appeared anonymously, with a dedication to Sir Philip Sidney; its authorship could hardly have been a secret long, but whether the success of the poem made the poet or only the poem famous is not a matter of much concern to us. The volume did appear, however, with the annotations of one E. K., whose identity has fascinated many antiquarians but has never been perfectly established. E. K., whoever he was, was a mixed blessing. His confusions and his errors have been straightened out by modern scholarship, but one of his contributions, a classification of the eclogues, seems to have been very little utilized.[3]

These xij. Aeclogues euery where answering to the seasons of
the twelue monthes may be well deuided into three formes or
ranckes. For eyther they be Plaintiue, as the first, the sixt, the
eleuenth, and the twelfth, or recreatiue, such as al those be,
which conceiue matter of loue, or commendation of special personages, or Moral: which for the most part be mixed with some
Satyrical bitternesse, namely the second of reuerence dewe to old
age, the fift of coloured deceipt, the seuenth and ninth of dis-
solute shepheards and pastours, the tenth of contempt of Poetrie
and pleasaunt wits. And to this diuision may euery thing herein
be reasonably applyed: a few onely except, whose speciall purpose and meaning I am not priuie to.[4]

This classification would read as follows:
Plaintive: 1st (January), 6th (June), 11th (November), 12th (De-
  cember)
Moral: 2nd (February), 5th (May), 7th (July), 9th (September),
  10th (October)
Recreative: 3rd (March), 4th (April), 8th (August)

A glance at this list will show that the three kinds, if the distinction
between them is valid, are quite skillfully scattered through the pattern of the whole. There are five moral eclogues, four plaintive, and
three recreative. The division into kinds, even though it is of course
not absolute, serves as a means to achieve variety, and it bears some
relationship to the adherence of some of the eclogues to the atmosphere of the season concerned. The variety of verse forms is another
means by which the *Calender* distinguishes itself. But with all this
care to achieve variety, there is also a principle of continuity stronger
than the mere sequence of the months. In each of the three "forms
or ranks," as E. K. calls them, two of the examples occur consecu-
tively: the third and fourth eclogues are recreative, the ninth and
tenth are moral, and the eleventh and twelfth are plaintive. The
over-all structure of the *Calender*, then, is one which combines similarity and contrasts, variety and continuity. The complex relationships
of theme, of style, and of "rank or form" give *The Shepheardes Calender* a vitality and interest which no other collection of pastoral eclogues in English can boast.

The *Calender* begins and ends with plaintive eclogues. This is appropriate to the winter season of January and December, and it also

sets the over-all tone for the series. The total effect must not be harsh and satirical, as the moral eclogues tend to make it, not gay and care-free, as the recreative eclogues would suggest. The poet is our sage and serious Spenser, but his seriousness must be conveyed in tone and mood; doctrine and belief must be expressed primarily as poetry, and for this purpose the tone of the complaint will best serve.

"January" is simple in style. The plaintive eclogues increase in complexity up through "November" (a piece which E. K. says he prefers to all the rest), and then the style is somewhat simpler again for the final "December." "January" mainly equates the lovelorn shepherd's state of mind with nature around him. The poem might be called an extended simile:

> Thou barrein ground, whome winters wrath hath wasted,
> Art made a myrrhour, to behold my plight.

Rather than a simile, it is a mirror situation; the comparison between object and image extends both ways, and each has its validity. For example, stanza 5 describes the shepherd's heart, blood, and pain in terms of winter weather. The sixth stanza does the reverse: it turns the woodland into an abandoned and disconsolate lover of birds and flowers. What does this leave for the spectator as a point of view? It is impossible to keep the position of the shepherd, for he is sometimes only a reflection of nature; it is impossible to keep the point of view of nature, for it is often only a reflection of the moods and feelings of the shepherd. The result is a kind of "distance" or objectivity, which gives us both shepherd and nature in perspective, in the round. We are not sure which is object and which is reflection because they reverse roles. Sometimes this is made explicit by means of rhetorical figures, which commentators who belong to the tribe of E. K. have noticed:

> With mourning pyne I, you with pyning mourne.

This, addressed to the sheep, seems stilted and frigid under the comment of those who merely give the name for the rhetorical figure; seen as a detail which reinforces the whole mirror device of the eclogue, it acquires some artistic significance.

The device of lovers in series, or the fragmentary cross-eyed Cupid situation, is also used here. As Hobbinol is to Colin ("His clownish gifts and curtsies I disdaine," line 57), so Colin is to Rosalind ("And of my rurall musick holdeth scorne," line 64). This device also provides scale and "distance." Finally, it leads up to the resolution, in which Colin breaks his pipe (the symbolic significance of poetry as such is very great in the *Calender,* and this is an unobtrusive and yet powerful way of opening the theme) and concludes his outburst. The final stanza shows how delicately the point of view of the spectator has been adjusted:

> By that, the welked Phoebus gan availe
> His weary waine, and now the frosty Night
> Her mantle black through heauen gan ouerhaile,
> Which seene the pensife boy halfe in despight
> > Arose, and homeward droue his sonned sheepe,
> > Whose hanging heads did seeme his carefull case to weepe.

The effect here should be compared with that achieved by Milton in *Lycidas,* when he shifts from a tone of austere rejoicing at the picture of Lycidas being entertained by all the Saints above

> In solemn troops and sweet societies
> That sing, and singing in their glory move
> And wipe the tears for ever from his eyes

to a return to the pastoral environment and level of feeling:

> Thus sang the uncouth swain to oaks and rills,
> While the still morn went out with sandals grey:
> > .   .   .   .   .
> At last he rose, and twitched his mantle blue:
> Tomorrow to fresh woods, and pastures new.

There is something more here than the mere formal close to pastoral elegy; there is the sudden involvement of the reader himself in the attitude and position of the shepherd. The same kind of shift occurs at the end of Gray's *Elegy* when the meditations on the reluctance of the dying culminate in "Ev'n in our Ashes live their wonted Fires" and give way to the placing of the melancholy youth among his subjects, and the reader of the poem is directed by "some hoary-headed Swain" to the youth's epitaph. In comparison with these two famous examples, Spenser's art seems more delicate and particular. He involves the reader in the fortunes and feelings of Colin less sentimentally, with more reserve.[5]

"June," the second of the plaintive eclogues, is a dialogue in form;

the complaint here derives its strength from the conflict of two situations and points of view and finally proceeds to paradox. The contrast
is between Hobbinol and Colin. Hobbinol represents the standard,
happy pastoral existence. He has found, according to Colin, that
Paradise which Adam lost. This is one way of making the equation
between mind and nature, content and Arcadia. But Colin is not so
fortunate; he has grown older, sadder, and wiser. His youth was
marked by love and poetry, "But ryper age such pleasures doth re-
proue"; sad experience has turned him away from vain love and
"those weary wanton toyes" of poetry.

The paradox develops when Hobbinol praises his poetry: Colin
was able to teach the birds themselves how to sing, and when the
Muses heard him, even they had to confess themselves outdone in
their art. Colin replies by denying all the ambitious implications of
this praise and asserts that his aims are very modest:

> But pyping lowe in shade of lowly groue,
> I play to please my selfe, all be it ill.

> Nought weigh I, who my song doth prayse or blame,
> Ne striue to winne renowne, or passe the rest:
> With shepheard sittes not, followe flying fame:
> But feede his flocke in fields, where falls hem best.

This is, of course, the shepherd's denial of ambition, the literary form
of the central pastoral philosophy of life. And Spenser uses this
poetic equivalent of "the quiet mind" as a background for Colin's
proudest boast:

> The God of shepheards Tityrus is dead,
> Who taught me homely, as I can, to make.
> He, whilst he liued, was the soueraigne head
> Of shepheards all, that bene with loue ytake.

Colin, although he protests his verses are rough and rude, is still the
true heir of Chaucer. Here is the paradox: he is both uncouth and
unambitious, yet he is the pupil of great artists and proud to be in
their tradition. There is a contrast of mood, too. Chaucer, as Tityrus,
was able to dampen the flames that love bred in him and to entertain
the shepherds with merry tales to keep them awake, but Colin cannot
achieve this gaiety. Therefore, in the act of bewailing his sad state,
he says he is not able to continue, and instructs the other shepherds

(inferior to him in ability at complaints) to tell Rosalind what she has done.

The involutions of the complaint are quite elaborately exploited in this eclogue, and the contrasts and paradoxes might absorb all of our attention. It is worth noticing, however, that Spenser has really shifted the grounds for the pastoral complaint. There is a good deal more about poetry here than about love. The unhappy love situation is felt to be important chiefly because it is said to affect Colin's poetry. The shift has been subtly managed, and no doubt those gullible readers who follow E. K.'s challenge and speculate on the identity of Rosalind miss it; but they are hardly reading the poem anyway; they are playing with biographical puzzles. E. K. in the argument to the eclogue says nothing about poetry, but of course poetry is the main theme of "June"; there is a link here with the next plaintive eclogue, "November," and with "October," its predecessor, also.

"November," like "December," follows the model set by Marot in pastoral. The November poem is a dialogue between Thenot and Colin, leading up to the elaborate pastoral elegy which Colin composed to celebrate the death of Dido, the great shepherd's daughter. The most interesting thing about "November" is not the identity of Dido, whatever the commentators say; it is the elaborateness of the elegy, at the most formal and most elevated level of the complaint. E. K. did not know the identity of Dido, but he declared this eclogue his favorite, "farre passing his [Marot's] reache, and in myne opinion all other the Eglogues of this booke." Plaintive poetry starts with the complaining lover, then has to refine him out of it for the sake of the form and objectivity of the work of art; finally, it discovers in the formal pastoral elegy a vehicle which permits elaborate verse technique together with heightened rhetorical style and a subject which is large enough to permit the expression of deeply felt personal sorrow within the limits of decorum. It is the emancipation of the lover's complaint.

Formally, "November" contains the invocation to the Muse (line 53), the calling on others to wail (lines 63ff.), the description of the effects of her death on Nature (line 83ff. and 123ff.), the parade of the nymphs (lines 143ff.), and the change from grief to joy (lines 163ff.), which characterize the conventional pastoral elegy. From these conventional features of the elegy the poet has his opportunity in varying and increasing the emotion. The combination of grief and joy makes a "doleful pleasaunce," as Thenot calls it; he hesitates whether to rejoice or weep. This fine balance is what the pastoral elegy tries to achieve.

Spenser's metrical form in this poem is very remarkable. He varies line length, adds a fifth line to his modified quatrain, and finishes the stanza with a lyrical chorus section which links the stanzas together and provides a continuity of emotion. The flexibility and fluidity of the versification do much to keep the formal elements from seeming stiff and rigid.

"November" is connected rather more definitely with the season than some of the other eclogues.[7] The mood of the elegy is prepared for by the explanation of Colin that other types of poetry are unsuitable for this time of year. This contrast calls to mind another, that between the elaborate elegy for Dido in "November" and the elaborate praise of Eliza in "April." The two are in a sense complementary, and their importance is clearly marked for us by the wealth of metrical invention Spenser lavished upon them.

"December," the final eclogue, returns to monologue and rounds out the tonal pattern "even as the first beganne," as E. K. says. This poem, too, is dependent on Marot, but a more important influence is that of the calendars, with their symbolic representations of the four seasons as representing the stages of a man's life.[8] The career of Colin, which I take to be somewhat more fictional than the commentators do, is here summed up. In spring he experienced exuberance and freedom, felt pride in his songs. In summer he learned his craft, but was smitten with love. In harvest he reaped only a weedy crop of care. And now winter comes:

> Winter is come, that blowes the balefull breath.
> And after Winter commeth timely death.

The paradox here depends upon the idea of a calendar: it runs out as time runs out; and yet the calendar of months is still good, it records something which is permanent. Just so the poet, saying adieu to his delights, to his love, to his sheep and his woods, to his friend, as Colin does in the last stanza, is by the very form in which he says it achieving something that stops time, that contradicts and denies the Death which is the subject. The detachment or the "distance" between the content or argument and the poetry itself produces a paradoxical relationship between them. That Spenser's use of the calendar device was useful for "scale" was first pointed out, I think, by Pope: "The addition he has made of a Calendar to his Eclogues, is very beautiful: since by this, besides that general moral of inno-cence and simplicity, which is common to other authors of pastoral, he has one peculiar to himself; he compares human Life to the several Seasons, and at once exposes to his readers a view of the great and little worlds, in their various changes and aspects."⁹ The missing emblem for Colin is explained by E. K.: "The meaning wherof is that all thinges perish and come to theyr last end, but workes of learned wits and monuments of Poetry abide for euer."¹⁰ This is clearly the implication of the whole eclogue and, as summary, of the whole *Shepheardes Calender*. Shakespeare found in Ovid the same commonplace and developed it in a non-pastoral setting in his sonnets. The pastoral handling of the theme enjoys an added richness, for, as the reply to Marlowe's "Passionate Shepherd" shows, time is the an-swer to the pastoral ideal. But what if, in poetry, there is an answer to the answer?

The five "moral" eclogues, "February," "May," "July," "Septem-ber," and "October," are arranged in such a way as to develop a cli-max, just as the plaintive eclogues were. In this series the climax comes in the September eclogue, and the succeeding and final one, "October," turns as the plaintive series did, specifically to the subject of poetry. If in the plaintive series the difficulty was to build out of the given state of mind of the lovesick shepherd an expression which would do justice to the emotion itself and yet reconcile with it the verve of the poetry, the problem in the moral eclogues is to find a function for poetry in the social, political, and cultural environment.

Far from being escapist, pastoral poetry was the most apt of all the kinds for serious humanistic purposes. Because of the central concern with the relative value of wealth, power, riches, and the "contented mind," and because of its conventional machinery of shepherds, with their singing contests, debates, and complaints, the eclogue lent itself readily to indirect or slightly masked criticism of contemporary affairs. It had been so used by Virgil, and the Renaissance imitators of the greatest of Roman poets had developed the satirical, critical strain still further. Spenser's chief model in this series is Mantuan, espe-cially his eclogues 7, 8, and 9. But he fuses with Mantuan's serious, satirical manner something from his own English Tityrus, Chaucer. It is not so apparent to us as it was to the sixteenth century that Chaucer is a very moral poet; Spenser was chiefly impressed with his use of fables. So "February," "May," and "September" utilize Aesopic or pseudo-Aesopic material, told in the manner of Chaucer. The fable gives a narrative interest to these eclogues; there is something more primitive and perhaps more solid in their stories than there is in the extended emotion of the plaintive series. For this reason, perhaps, as well as to produce further variety, Spenser has devised a characteristic style for these eclogues—rough, uncouth, non-lyrical, and full of dialect words. The matter is harsh, the meter is old-fashioned, suggesting the alliterative accentual verse of an earlier age in "February," the stolid fourteeners of the 1560's and 1570's in "July."

"February" tells the fable of the oak and the briar, after a dramatic introduction in the form of a quarrel between the young shepherd Cuddie and the old shepherd Thenot. There is a connection here with the time of year, for old age and winter are explicitly identified:

> For Age and Winter accord full nie,
> This chill, that cold, this crooked, that wrye.

The conflict of age and youth is very common in the pastoral mode.[11] It is simply another form of the central problem which makes pastoral —the problem of the values inherent in the good life. Here the quarrel is resolved by a story, the briar finding out when winter comes that it has been dependent upon the old oak. So the threat of winter and rough weather or old age, when time drives the flocks from field to fold, is the basic challenge to the pastoral ideal and must be faced. The fable in the February eclogue is simple, but its theme is central.[12]

The May eclogue first introduces what E. K. calls "some Satyrical bitternesse"; it is an attack on Catholic pastors, who are not true shepherds but deceitful and malicious, like the fox that devoured the kid. This involves of course the equation of shepherds—pastors— priests; more significantly, it poses the question of the relative value of the gay, irresponsible pastoral life and the conscientious tending of sheep. The month of May is utilized to give the shepherd Palinode an opportunity to urge participation in the pagan revelries of May Day and to have Piers, the spokesman for the serious, Protestant, point of view, reprove these sports as follies, fit for "Younkers" but reprehensible in men of elder wit. The connection between this subject of true and false pastors (a theme which Milton later developed, with even more satirical bitterness, in *Lycidas*) and the personal, direct, moral effect of these eclogues lies in the subject of friendship and trust. Palinode believes that tolerance and resignation are the only ways to deal with differences between shepherds:

> Let none mislike of that may not be mended:
> So conteck soone by concord mought be ended.

But Piers, who is given the advantage of being the teller of the fable, says that no peace or compromise is possible with that shepherd "that does the right way forsake." The story is told with more art and elaboration than the story of the oak and briar; besides, in accordance with the climactic scheme of the series, the whole eclogue is more vigorous and outspoken. A link with a later moral eclogue, "September," is prepared in the lines (126-9) about the wolves in sheep's clothing. In the lines just preceding these, Spenser prepares for the theme of "July." By the time "July" is reached, the basic theme has been so clearly introduced, through the narratives of the preceding moral eclogues, that now it can be debated directly, taken out of the fable framework, and presented dramatically. Spenser chooses the old familiar 4-3-4-3 ballad measure, that of the versified psalms and of all matter to be committed to memory, the most familiar of Elizabethan verse forms.[13]

Thomalin, in a long speech, gives the conventional praise of shepherds derived from Mantuan, which we have already noticed. His emphasis is that the true shepherds are not ambitious, not aspiring, but humble and low. This serves as an image which works in several ways: Thomalin and Morrell represent, respectively, the valley and the hill, and the woodcut at the head of the eclogue naïvely shows them stationed at these two points while they hold their debate: Thomalin represents the Puritan ideal of a clergy unelevated, humble, and devoted to pastoral care, while Morrell represents the Catholic or Anglican clergy gloating in worldly pomp; most general and most significant of all, Thomalin represents the mean estate, the central theme of pastoralism, and Morrell embodies the aspiring mind. Their emblems summarize this contrast:

> Thomalins Embleme.
> *In medio virtus.*
> Morrells Embleme.
> *In summo foelicitas.*

So rich is the central doctrine of pastoral that the poet can find application for it pictorially, topically, and gnomically. The ethical imagination of the Elizabethans was not narrow and compartmentalized but broad and versatile in scope. Feeling about a great moral commonplace could find its expression in picture, topical narrative, or satire, or in the posy of a ring.

"September," though it has been called "the least interesting and most difficult" (Herford) of the eclogues in *The Shepheardes Calender*, and even more harshly "a tedious though fluent stream of commonplace complaint" (Palgrave), is really the climax of the moral series.[14] Here the bitterness about bad shepherds is stronger than in any of the other eclogues; here the verse form is a hard, punching couplet. Hobbinol and Diggon Davy do not argue, but Diggon reports to Hobbinol the sad state of things in the country he has just visited, and Hobbinol provides the choral comment. It is again the pastoral assertion:

> Content who liues with tryed state,
> Neede feare no chaunge of frowning fate.

In this eclogue, as Friedland points out,[15] the technique of the fable is brought to its climax; here the fable is an integral part of the eclogue, not just appended for illustrative interest as in "February" and "May." The fable this time is a genuinely poetic idea. Spenser's source was Mantuan, as usual in the moral eclogues, but the idea, concisely expressed in Matthew 7:15, "Beware of false prophets, which come to you in sheep's clothing, but inwardly they are ravening wolves," appears often in the sermons of the time,[16] and its suggestions are so wide that it provides the satisfactory image for the unification of the pastoral, religious, and social ideas in this whole group of poems. The shepherd's life is always stressed as one in which the characteristics of the mind and will are important; the conditions for human existence are most favorable, and there are few dangers from pride or ambition, but the goddesses still appear before a shepherd and demand that he choose between them. A wrong choice is always possible. The shepherd is still man seen simply, but his idyllic life is now put upon a basis of moral responsibility, and the existence of evil is recognized.

Hobbinol's statement presents an awareness of human limitations and an acceptance of them, within the pastoral framework, as sad but valuable. Here is a link, in mood, with the encompassing tone of the plaintive eclogues, and the moral poems are finding their place in the unity of the whole.

The October eclogue, which E. K. placed among the moral eclogues, has seemed to some students to belong by itself because it treats the subject of poets and their low state at the present time instead of the problem of the good pastor. But as I have shown, the plaintive series developed toward a self-conscious emphasis on poetry, and it is only according to the pattern that the moral eclogues should do so too. Herford, who separates "October" from its group, says that "this noble and pregnant piece is the very core of *The Shepheard's Calender*."[17] It is interesting, by the way, to see how the critics decide what is central in the book. Greenlaw, partly because he reads the poems so heavily as historical allegory and propaganda, sees the moral eclogues together as "the core and heart" of the *Calender*.[18] R. E. N. Dodge calls the Rosalind story "the central theme of S. C."[19] I have been trying to show that there is not a core of something wrapped up in a covering of pastoral, but that the pastoral idea, in its various ramifications, *is* the *Calender*. H. S. V. Jones regards "October" as the keystone of the arch structurally because he recognizes only two kinds of eclogues, the plaintive-recreative and the moral.

The shepherd as pastor is responsible for caring for his flock; he has his reward in protecting them from the wolves. What, then, are the responsibilities of the shepherd as poet? Shall he be content "to feede youthes fancie, and the flocking fry" with his dapper ditties? Is he a mere entertainer? No, Piers replies, he can influence them morally. Here Piers is giving voice to the justification for poetry that runs through Elizabethan criticism from Sir Philip Sidney to Milton:

> O what an honor is it, to restraine
> The lust of lawlesse youth with good aduice:
> Or pricke them forth with pleasaunce of thy vaine,
> Whereto thou list their trayned willes entice.

But if the lowly are not grateful for instruction, then the poet should turn to heroic poetry, celebrating deeds of greatness and becoming the spokesman for the national spirit. This was the pattern followed by Virgil, who, being favored by Maecenas, was enabled to rise above the humble style of the pastoral and write the epic of Rome. Yet as Cuddie recalls this, he says that in these degenerate days the poet has no such prospect; he must make "rymes of rybaudrye" or resign in favor of the doggerel-monger Tom Piper.

This concern over the place of poetry is not so much professional as it is moral. True, some glances at the niggardly ways of patrons are taken over from Mantuan, but the primary concern is for the use and value of poetry, and the final conclusion is that it is holy. The Platonism which here enters the *Calender*[20] serves this purpose. It gives a theory of poetic inspiration which allies the poet with the priest. Their work is in essence divine. Love is a source of such divine inspiration, and even love poetry may provide it, as is the case with Colin. Cuddie, however, can approximate the high elevated style of truly inspired poetry only by imagining himself aroused by wine, and when he does we have, for a moment, heroic poetry. But the feeling must soon subside and return within the scope of pastoral:

> But ah my corage cooles ere it be warme,
> For thy, content vs in thys humble shade:
> Where no such troublous tydes han vs assayde,
> Here we our slender pipes may safely charme.

The contrast between the style of this eclogue and that of the other moral eclogues is very striking. It is as if Spenser deliberately made the satirical eclogues rough and uncouth for reasons of decorum and effectiveness of the moral ideas, but culminated his series in an eclogue which not only showed that the poet is as directly connected with the divine in his business as the pastor is, but that his sounds, too, are closer to heavenly music than to the sounds of Tom Piper.

The three remaining eclogues, "March," "April," and "August," have not been taken seriously as a group by themselves, presumably because E. K. does not specify the members of his "recreative" category, "such as al those be, which conceiue matter of loue, or commendation of special personages." As Jones observes,[21] some of the plaintive eclogues come within this definition. But the three poems under consideration are not plaintive, and in examining the structure of the whole series they may well be considered separately. "March" is the most clearly recreative of all. It comes after the plaintive "January" and the moral-fabulist "February"; it is high time for some relief. Specifically, "March" is a comic eclogue. The tone is set by the loutish Thomalin, who is annoyed at his sheep for getting lost, fearful that something will happen to them if he even turns his attention long enough to tell a story, petulant about his pastoral duties. He has gone hunting on a shepherd's holiday and hears something stirring in a bush. Without knowing what it is, he shoots at it. Thomalin here is some sort of cousin of Lyly's Sir Thopas, the braggart hunter and fisherman. His quarry is the nimble laughing god, and Thomalin relates how with heavy earnestness he shoots all his bolts at Cupid and then falls to throwing "pumie stones" which Cupid easily and lightly catches. The point here is the contrast between the lubberly shepherd and the fleet god of love; the effect is remotely like that of Bottom and Titania. When Thomalin is wounded in the heel, and he is no Achilles nor was meant to be, a mock-heroic touch is added to the comedy of simple contrast. E. K.'s elaborate nonsense about the Achilles' heel is, I suppose, further pedantic contribution to the joke.

The sage and serious Spenser was no great humorist, to be sure; the comedy is feeble enough. But perhaps the commentators have been so intent upon connecting Spenser with Bion and Ronsard that they have missed the point. The verse form, which is that of Chaucer's *Sir Thopas,* should have given the clue. Are we to suppose that Spenser with all his worship of Chaucer never once saw the comic element in his master or tried to imitate it?[22]

The following eclogue, which has already received some attention in the discussion of the pastoral lyric, has been much admired. It is "the gem of the whole *Calender,*" according to B. E. C. Davis,[23] and it surpasses its only competitor, "November," in subtlety of versification and freshness of atmosphere. Structurally, it provides a transition to the moral eclogue of "May." The serious Protestant subject matter of "May" cannot be approached directly from the absurdity of "March," and the lyrical, religious-patriotic quality of the blazon for Eliza, queen of shepherds all, is the natural modulation. The adulation of Elizabeth is tactful and politic coming where it does, just before Spenser opens his case against deceptive Catholic pastors. Moreover, the dryness of pastoral doctrine is justified artistically only when it can be used as the foil for lyric expression, just as the humble occupation of shepherds is felt to be saved by the fact that they have freedom and time to play upon their oaten pipes.

"August," which comes between two moral eclogues, the seventh and ninth, where the climax of the satirical bitterness is reached, also offers primarily a lyric interlude. The framework of the eclogue is the singing match, a conventional and traditional pastoral device which Hughes has shown Spenser derived not from the classics but from the Pléiade.[24] Whether the elements of this device, the challenge, the pledges, the election of the judge, and his decision, were "ripe for parody" or not, they serve Spenser adequately for the purpose of his poem—to introduce the roundelay, with its gay, popular rhythm and its well-known tune, and an art work of the opposite kind, a sestina.[25] The subject matter of both the roundelay and the sestina is painful love, so we have here a pair of miniature plaintive pieces, reflecting the mood of the first series and preparing for the reappearance in "November" and "December" of this motif. The scale or "distance" which I have pointed out so frequently in this discussion comes from the framing of complaint in the singing-match convention and, stylistically, from the contrast of two extremes, the roundelay and the more formal and lugubrious sestina. Again we can observe the subject matter and the technique turning together toward a focus on poetry.

It is not difficult to see, then, why *The Shepheardes Calender* occupies a most important place at the beginning of a great age of English poetry. Spenser's achievement must be evaluated in artistic terms; its magnitude can be understood only when justice is done to the shape and design of the *Calender,* to its realization and exploitation of the possibilities in the commonplace of pastoral, and to the concrete details of its marvelous experiments in style. Like the *Lyrical Ballads* in 1798 and *Prufrock and Other Observations* in 1917, it is a book which changes the course of English poetry, but like them also its importance lies not in what it does but in what it is.

NOTES

1. M. Y. Hughes, *Virgil and Spenser* (Berkeley, Calif., 1929), Part I.
2. See the edition by W. P. Mustard for text, comment, and notes on Mantuan's literary influence.
3. There is no comment on the classification in the Spenser Variorum (9 vols.; Baltimore, 1932-1949). O. Reissert, in "Bemerkungen über Spensers *Shepheards Calender* und die frühere Bukolik," *Anglia,* IX (1886), 205-24, takes up the eclogues according to E. K.'s classification but only for purposes of source study.
4. "The Generall argument of the whole booke," Variorum *Minor Poems,* ed. C. G. Osgood and H. G. Lotspeich, 2 vols. (Baltimore, 1943, 1947), I, 12.
5. Whether this emotional treatment of the shepherd and the "distance" achieved by Spenser owe anything to pictorial art is an interesting question. The investigators of Spenser's relationship to the fine arts have so far considered mostly color and illustrative details. See Rosemond Tuve, "Spenser and Some Pictorial Conventions," *SP,* XXXVII (1940), 149-76; Frederick Hard, "Clothes of Arras and of Toure," *SP,* XXVII (1930), 162-85; J. B. Fletcher, "The Painter of the Poets," *SP,* XIV (1917), 153-66.
6. See George Norlin, "The Conventions of the Pastoral Elegy," *AJP,*

XXXII (1911), 294-312, and T. P. Harrison, Jr., "Spenser and the Earlier Pastoral Elegy," *Texas Studies in English,* XIII (1933), 36-53. The relationship between Spenser's "November" and Marot's *Loyse de Savoye* can be studied conveniently in *The Pastoral Elegy,* ed. T. P. Harrison, Jr., and H. J. Leon (Austin, Texas, 1939).

7. See Mary Parmenter, "Spenser's *Twelve Aeglogues Proportionable to the Twelve Monethes,*" ELH, III (1936), 190-217, for an exposition of the background of calendar and season; the author's suggestion of Queen Elizabeth as Dido is less useful.

8. See Parmenter, p. 191.

9. "A Discourse on Pastoral Poetry," *The Prose Works of Alexander Pope,* ed. Norman Ault (Oxford, 1936), pp. 301-2.

10. A. H. Gilbert, "The Embleme for December in the *Shepheardes Calender,*" MLN, LXIII (1948), 181-2, gives reasons for thinking that *Merce non mercede,* at the end of the book, is the misplaced December emblem. Whatever the case, we have the meaning of the December emblem preserved for us in the Glosse, and it is the meaning that is here important.

11. The reason is sometimes the differing attitudes of young and old toward love. See, for example, the conflict between Geron and Philisides in the old *Arcadia* (*Works,* ed. Feuillerat, pp. 68-72).

12. The sources and significance of the fables in the moral eclogues are discussed by L. S. Friedland, "Spenser as a Fabulist," SAB, XII (1937), 85-108, 133-54, 197-207. I agree with Renwick, Parmenter, and Friedland (and E. K.) that the February eclogue is merely moral and general, on the subject of youth and age, not specifically allegorical, as Greenlaw and others would have it.

13. Sixteenth-century attitudes toward this verse form are discussed in my article, "English Metrical Psalms in the Sixteenth Century and Their Literary Significance," HLQ, IX (1946), 249-71.

14. Variorum *Minor Poems,* I, 350-51. H. S. V. Jones, *A Spenser Handbook* (New York, 1930), p. 51, places "September" more accurately when he says it is the most persuasive statement of the philosophy of moderation and that " 'September' points the moral to be drawn from the whole series." But he curiously finds this philosophy and moral to be the distinctive property of Gabriel Harvey. Harvey no doubt approved of it, but the significant point is that it is the central doctrine of pastoral. The *Calender* is organized as pastoral; a realization of this fact is different from saying, "We may conclude, then, that in the opinions of Harvey we find a principle of unity for the *Shepheardes Calender* as a whole" (Jones, p. 52).

15. "Spenser as a Fabulist," p. 147.

16. W. L. Renwick (ed.) *The Shepherd's Calendar* [London, 1930], p. 213) quotes usefully from Thomas Cartwright.

17. C. H. Herford, ed., *Shepheards Calendar* (London, 1907), p. xlv.
18. Variorum *Minor Poems,* I, 603.
19. *Ibid.,* p. 602.
20. See Osgood in Variorum *Minor Poems,* I, 371.
21. *A Spenser Handbook,* p. 43.
22. Drayton apparently saw Spenser's intention here and used the same verse form for his poem of "Dowsabell" in the eighth eclogue of *Idea The Shepheards Garland* (1593). Mrs. Tillotson speaks of "a factitious and charming air of archaism" achieved by Drayton in using this meter, and her comments on the manner of Drayton's poem are excellent criticism (see *Works,* ed. Hebel, V, 11-12). The most useful examination of Spenser's relation to Bion and Ronsard is Leo Spitzer's "Spenser, *Shepheardes Calendar, March,*" SP, XLVII (1950), 494-505.
23. *Edmund Spenser* (Cambridge, England, 1933), p. 198.
24. *Virgil and Spenser,* pp. 271-286.
25. Herford's idea that the second part may be an afterthought (ed. *Shepheards Calendar,* p. xl), because E. K. confines his glosses to the first part, does not carry much weight against the general considerations of the structure of this part of the *Calender.* Even if it should be true, the question of why Spenser thought the addition necessary might be answered on the basis I have just suggested.

DAVID KALSTONE

Sir Philip Sidney: The Petrarchan Vision

> Love's not so pure, and abstract, as they use
> To say, which have no Mistresse but their Muse,
> But as all else, being elemented too,
> Love sometimes would contemplate, sometimes do.
>
> JOHN DONNE, "Loves Growth"

Tempus adest plausus aurea pompa venit. So Nashe heralded *Astrophel and Stella* upon its first edition, an unauthorized publication of 1591.[1] The golden procession proves to be a somewhat angular and witty set of one hundred and eight sonnets and eleven songs, and its richness lies not in the brocaded texture of particular poems, but in the fertility of invention that Sidney sustains over the entire set. Here, for the first time in English poetry, an engaging persona governs a whole sequence in the way that the lover of Laura controls with recognizable voice and attitudes the *Rime* of Petrarch. Whatever the biographical significance of *Astrophel and Stella*, it holds its rewards for the reader as a poetic sequence. Enough attention has been paid to the deduced narrative of Sir Philip Sidney's love for Penelope Rich,[2] but nor nearly enough to the poetic enrichment given the simple ground bass of event.[3] Though a narrative is closer to the surface of Sidney's sequence than it is in most others, this narrative is composed of familiar elements: the knight taken by love, kept at a distance by his lady, allowed a kiss, finally separated from her and left complaining fiercely of love. It is the passions engaged by this narrative, the lover's reaction to it, that mark these sonnets as unique. Here, as in the *Arcadia*, we find a sharply defined concern for the

Reprinted by permission of the publishers from David Kalstone, *Sidney's Poetry*, Cambridge, Mass.: Harvard University Press, pp. 105-32, Copyright, 1965, by the President and Fellows of Harvard College.

corrosive effects of love upon the heroic life and the education of a
Renaissance hero. The sonnet sequence allows Sidney to dramatize
from yet another point of view the lofty aims of the lover and the
defeats imposed by desire.

In the *Arcadia* the havoc of desire led to the comic game of dis-
guises, to the ridiculous postures of the irresponsible Basilius, as well
as to the nightmares of Strephon and Klaius. These comic and tragic
insights are combined in the dramatic reactions of Astrophel. He
stands apart as one of the most self-conscious of Elizabethan poet-
lovers—a Protean figure by comparison with the heroes of the *Arcadia*. He is nothing if not critical of the way in which others have
expressed their experience of love, of poets who trade in "poore Petrarch's long deceased woes."[4] Yet our ordinary terms, Petrarchan and
anti-Petrarchan, are too crude to describe the nimble movements of
Astrophel's mind. It is easy enough to see what is anti-Petrarchan in
Shakespeare's "My mistress' eyes are nothing like the sun" or Sidney's
own mockery of the Petrarchan in phrases like "living deaths, deare
wounds, faire stormes, and freesing fires" (*AS*, 6). In each case the
writer of the sonnet finds conventional hyperboles or Petrarchan oxymorons inadequate to the true voice of feeling. But Astrophel, in a
more harmonious mood, invokes the Petrarchan contraries himself:

> Soule's joy, bend not those morning starres from me,
> Where Vertue is made strong by Beautie's might,
> Where *Love* is chastnesse, Paine doth learne delight,
> And Humblenesse growes one with Majestie.
>
> (*AS*, 48)

Astrophel's opposing attitudes—his alternate mockery and acceptance of Petrarchan rhetoric—prevent us from making any simple de-
cisions about his role in the sonnet cycle of which he is the protagonist. He seems to be calling attention to his own shifting attitudes
more explicitly than one expects in a conventional Petrarchan cycle.
He belongs among those lovers who not only suffer but, apprenticed
in the rhetoric of love, are also acutely conscious of the role a lover is
expected to play. When reading *Astrophel and Stella*, it is well to
keep in mind the tragicomic experience of a later young Elizabethan
hero:

> *Troilus:* O, let my lady apprehend no fear. In all Cupid's
> pageant there is presented no monster.

> *Cressida:* Nor nothing monstrous neither?
>
> *Troilus:* Nothing but our undertakings when we vow to weep seas, live in fire, eat rocks, tame tigers, thinking it harder for our mistress to devise imposition enough than for us to undergo any difficulty imposed. This is the monstruosity in love, lady, that the will is infinite and the execution confin'd, that the desire is boundless and the act a slave to limit.   (III. ii. 68-77)

The boundless desires and expectations of wonder embodied in Petrarchan rhetoric help to define the speech and character of both Troilus and Astrophel. Troilus accepts their promise naively. For him the marvels of love create a confusion of spirit and sense: "I am giddy; expectation whirls me round. / Th' imaginary relish is so sweet / That it enchants my sense." For Astrophel the promised refinements of love remain clear as a background against which he can test his own experience—his responsibilities to the heroic life or the strength of sexual desire. Often things are quite different from what he has been led to expect: he does not love at first sight (sonnet 2); he is impatient with attitudes his role imposes (sonnet 56: "Fy schoole of Patience, Fy, your lesson is / Far far too long to learne it without booke"). Petrarchan language comes to these young heroes as might the Ciceronian style,[5] as part of an inherited way of dealing with or projecting experience. Their characters are created for us in terms of their reactions to the language of the conventional lover, the degree to which they accept or resist it as a way of describing experience, the degree to which they exaggerate certain features of conventional language at the expense of others.

Petrarch again provides a beginning for our study. In what way do his sonnets furnish a meaningful framework for the discussion of Sidney's poems? What are some of the assumptions that lie behind the Petrarchan style? There is more to it than hyperbole and oxymoron, its most obvious and easily imitated features. With more precise knowledge about the resources of the convention, it will be possible to understand the special demands placed upon it by the protagonist of *Astrophel and Stella*.

I

Petrarch's songs and sonnets are designed to represent a lifetime of passionate attention to one mistress, to Laura. Their qualities of sustained devotion and acceptance of pain are truly remarkable, especially when we place them beside the energetic and impatient utterances of Astrophel. Never is there a question of the promise of Laura's favors,[6] as there is of Stella's in Sidney's sequence. An Italian critic has pointed out—without deprecation—that the strength of the *Rime* lies in their quality of *monotonia*; they strike a single note and focus with variations on a single emotional experience.[7] The satisfactory activity in Petrarch's poems is memory; pleasure lies in recalling the sudden illumination of his first sight of Laura. To that experience he returns again and again, and he pays tribute to its informing power by marking, year by year, the anniversary of the day on which it occurred. The poet's first vision of Laura (a point observed in Chapter One in another connection) becomes for him a type of the imagination of earthly beauty and an unfailing source of poetic invention. He willingly takes on symbolic exile ("In una valle chiusa d'ogn'intorno") and a painful separation from Laura, attempting to preserve in the mind's eye the wonder and fear of these first moments:

> Ivi non donne, ma fontane e sassi,
> e l'imagine trovo di quel giorno
> che'l pensier mio figura, ovunque io sguardo.
>   (*Rime*, 116)

When it is accepted, such exile is quite literally the death of the lover, although it may be the birth of the poet. The *Rime* refract the poet's viewpoint from many angles; the balance of poetic emphasis constantly shifts back and forth, now stressing the fearful exhaustion, the painful frustration of separation from Laura, now responding to the enrichment of imagination in meeting her again or remembering the first encounter. But, in any case, recollection is at the center of these poems.

It is most important to emphasize the dramatic ground of the lover's trials: the series of dazzling presentations of Laura that recur frequently and justify the poet's sustained passion. Perhaps the most famous of these scenes is one based upon the appearance of Venus in Book One of the *Aeneid*:

> Erano i capei d'oro a l'aura sparsi
> che'n mille dolci nodi gli avolgea,
> e'l vago lume oltra misura ardea
> di quei begli occhi, ch'or ne son sì scarsi.

e'l viso di pietosi color farsi,
 non so se vero o falso, mi parea:
 i' che l'ésca amorosa al petto avea,
 qual meraviglia se di subito arsi?
Non era l'andar suo cosa mortale,
 ma d'angelica forma, e le parole
 sonavan altro che pur voce umana;
uno spirto celeste, un vivo sole
 fu quel ch'i' vidi; e se non fosse or tale,
 piaga per allentar d'arco non sana.*

        (*Rime,* 90)

After a simple heralding *erano*, the initial impression of the sonnet is that of brilliance: a figure suddenly appears, golden hair loosened in the wind, eyes shining. The poem gathers its first effects from these few striking details and from the felicitous recall of Venus appearing, dressed as a huntress, before Aeneas: "dederatque comam diffundere ventis, / nuda genu nodoque sinus collecta fluentis" (and she had given her hair to the winds to scatter; her knees bare, and her flowing robes gathered in a knot.)[8] The notion of a miracle is introduced quietly and almost ironically in the second quatrain when the poet describes the effect of the vision; it is *no* miracle, he says, that one should be fired by such a sight, by the look of pity he reads into her expression. In the sestet the poem moves away from particulars to dramatize the fullness of his reaction. He shares some of the wonder of Aeneas' response to Venus, "o dea certe!" and closely echoes the Latin ("nec vox hominem sonat," line 328) in "le parole / sonavan altro che pur voce umana." To that vision of a pagan goddess, he adds the splendor of "angelica forma." The sestet is indeed a marvelously managed transformation building through negatives—what Laura was not ("Non era l'andar suo cosa mortale"; "altro che pur voce umana")—to the simple climax, what she was, achieved in a line of lovely balance: "uno spirto celeste, un vivo sole."

---

* Her golden hair was loosened to the breeze, which tangled it into a thousand sweet knots; and the fine light burned beyond measure in those beautiful eyes, where now it seldom shows. And her face took on pitying colors, it seemed to me; I do not know whether true or false. I—who had love's tinder in my breast—what wonder if it flared at once? Her movement was not a mortal thing, but that of an angelic form; and her words sounded different from a mere human voice. A divine spirit, a living sun, was what I saw, and if it is not so now, the wound does not heal though the bow is slackened.

Only when we reach the last lines of the poem do we become fully aware that the narrative has been conveyed in past tenses. With a subtle modulation we move from the climax of "vivo sole" to the past definite, "fu quel ch'i' vidi," and a moment that we have been experiencing in the continuous past ("era," "sonavan") recedes before our eyes into the remote, the historical, the not-to-be-repeated. We have been blinded to the progress of time by the immediacy of Petrarch's vision. The poem is deftly arranged so that we should not be reminded until the end, though it prepares for the possibility that Laura may not be now as she was then ("se non fosse or tale") in a modifying phrase easily passed over in the first reading: in the opening quatrain, with an intrusion in the present tense, he remarks on the diminished brilliance of her eyes ("ch'or ne son sì scarsi"). The last lines of the sonnet bring together the present, with the possibility of a Laura touched by age, and the past with its fierce and lasting illumination. Laura may no longer be beautiful; but the wound does not heal though the bow is slackened. For a moment the lover's suffering, prominent in most of the poems but subdued here, comes to the surface with a reminder of the wound and the huntress. Yet the subject of the sonnet is really the vividness of memory and imagination.[9] The sonnet holds a number of contrary emotions in equilibrium: desire, at once painful and enchanting; the sense that beauty fades; and a feeling for the enduring mythical qualities of beauty. It is memory that resolves the conflicting elements; with its retrospective point of view, imagination is capable of restoring a moment of ideal beauty otherwise threatened by time and desire.

"Erano i capei" reveals an aspect of Petrarch's style more difficult to imitate than the oxymorons, the contraries of "dear wounds" and "living deaths" that became common currency for those who took the *Rime* as their model. In some of his best sonnets, Petrarch presents harmonious visions of Laura that yoke oppositions of feeling irrevocably and without violence. Such power is at work in a poem more "conventionally" Petrarchan than sonnet 90:

> In qual parte del ciel, in quale idea
> era l'esempio, onde Natura tolse
> quel bel viso leggiadro, in ch'ella volse
> mostrar qua giù quanto lassù potea?
> Qual ninfa in fonti, in selve mai qual dea,
> chiome d'oro sì fino a l'aura sciolse?

> quando un cor tante in sé vertuti accolse?
> benché la somma è di mia morte rea.
> Per divina bellezza indarno mira
> chi gli occhi de costei già mai non vide
> come soavemente ella gli gira;
> non sa come Amor sana, e come ancide,
> chi non sa come dolce ella sospira,
> e come dolce parla, e dolce ride.*
>
> (Rime, 159)

This sonnet exemplifies a poise and maturity in the Rime, an acceptance of the lover's plight for the sake of the few moments of illumination and felicitous memory that form part of his experience. The poem reconciles opposing effects of love: its power to wound and to heal (lines 8 and 12). But what is uniquely Petrarchan about it is the resolving agent, the tone of wonder captured in the three rhetorical questions of the octet. These questions serve as hyperbolical praise of Laura: in what part of heaven, in what "idea" could Nature have found a model for Laura? What nymph, what goddess loosens to the breeze such fine golden hair? When did a heart hold so many virtues? She gathers to herself the brilliance of a nymph, a pagan goddess, and a divine beauty whose divinity (the poem leaves it unspecified) may derive from the realm of Platonic ideas or Christian virtue or some fusion of both. The transfiguring process is assisted by a pattern of repetitions, phrases echoing and reinforcing the questions asked: "in qual parte . . . in quale idea"; "Qual ninfa . . . qual dea." The poet's "death" is reserved for a qualifying clause ("benché la somma è di mia morte rea"), and the poem slips immediately into the tone of renewed admiration in the sestet. Discord reappears, reminding us of line 8, with "non sa come Amor sana, e come ancide." Then conflict is muted once more; for it is a privilege to know how Love wounds, a special knowledge conveyed by Laura's sweet speech and laughter. Any paraphrase obscures the rhetorical effectiveness of the

* In what part of heaven, in what idea was the model from which Nature took that lovely glad face, in which it wanted to show, here below, how much it could do above? What nymph in a fountain, in the woods what goddess, ever loosened to the breeze such fine golden hair? When did a heart gather so many virtues into itself? although their sum is guilty of my death. He looks in vain for divine beauty who never saw the eyes of this lady as she gently turns them; he does not know how Love heals, and how it kills, who does not know how sweetly she sighs, and how sweetly talks, and sweetly laughs.

three "dolce"s and the repeated "non sa come . . . e come . . . /
chi non sa come dolce . . . / e come dolce." The rhetorical pattern and the unusually close rhyme of the sestet (CDCDCD) emphasize
a bit of grammatical sorcery: *come* in line 12 connotes the "manner
in which"—the manner in which love heals, the manner in which it
kills; but in lines 13 and 14 *come* is an adverb intensifying *dolce*. It
is a subtle shift, but of course all the sting of "come ancide" disappears when the adverb is subsumed in the echoing rhythms of "come
dolce ella sospira, / e come dolce parla, e dolce ride." The human
details of these last lines are given, by the pattern of the verse, something like the transcendent qualities of the vision in the octet; we
feel this even before we recognize the special classical resonance of
the last line, an echo, in the manner of the allusion to Virgil in
"Erano i capei," of the Horatian "dulce ridentem Lalagen amabo, /
dulce loquentem."[10]

Like "Erano i capei," this sonnet presents Laura in resplendent
fashion. It illustrates another quality of Petrarch's style that goes
along with such a presentation: his majestic public manner. The invitation to public admiration of Laura is a corollary of her uniqueness;
she embodies a general truth that all should join the poet in recognizing. From the poet's recognition springs the grandeur and generosity of the rhetorical questions in the octet and the general claims in
the sestet ("he who . . ."). The certainty and conviction that lie behind this sort of utterance should be remembered when we compare
the *Rime* with some of the sonnets in *Astrophel and Stella*.

It would be a misrepresentation of the *Rime* to give the impression
that all the poems convey brilliant visions of Laura, or indeed that
all the poems so successfully harmonize pain and delight. But there
are enough such presentations of her throughout Petrarch's collection
to lend credibility and unity to the poet's rendering of experience:
the long passion, the endless complaints, the yearly celebrations of
their first meeting, the repeated enshrinement of places Laura has
visited. The sonnets and canzoni evidence a continuing nourishment
of the imagination, "emotion recollected in tranquility," and the
source of such nourishment lies finally in the image, the heightened
intuition of Laura's beauty, rather than in the changing, aging
woman. Part of the assurance that lies behind the poems of wonder
and public praise grows from Petrarch's insight into the nature of
love poetry. He perceives that the apparently static relation between

poet-lover and mistress is really a product of tension and poise. There are repeated dangers: chief among them, the ferocity of desire and the depredations of time. Only by re-creating his vision in the poems themselves is he able to preserve its initial fullness, its informing power. Petrarch's insight has its mythological buttress in the tale of Apollo and Daphne that threads through the *Rime*. His puns on the laurel and Laura justify themselves when he recognizes, in the sonnets, that only the poetic metamorphosis can preserve the beauty he has seen in the meetings that have roused his desire.

Such knowledge, hard-won, can be held in verse. Petrarch maintains a delicate balance between day-to-day passions and an evaluation that we might call, too simply, philosophical. The vitality of love poetry depends upon its power to mediate between, and in some cases fuse, momentary passionate attention and ideas, perhaps illusory, of permanence and value. It is well to remember Petrarch's own response to a charge made by his friend Colonna that Laura was *literally* a poetic fiction and a symbol for the Muse:

> You actually say that I have invented the name of "Laura" in order to have some one to talk about, and in order to set people talking about me, but that, in reality, I have no "Laura" in mind, except that poetical laurel to which I have aspired, as my long and unwearied toil bears witness; . . . On this point would that your jests were true; O that it were dissimulation and not madness.[11]

Presumably there are other—and less harmonious—relationships between the poetical passion and the human one than that finally achieved by Petrarch in the *Rime*.

II

By emphasizing the dramatic function of the presentations of Laura in Petrarch's sequence, I have wanted to call attention to some of the special qualities of Petrarch's style and to some of the assumptions behind it. It is misleading to claim, as Richard B. Young does, that by the end of Sidney's sequence "Astrophel has been made aware of the nature of Love as the Petrarchan universal."[12] Such a statement turns Petrarchanism into a formula and ignores it as the product of a highly individual poetic sensibility. Young is making a valuable point about

Sidney, however: that he uses elements of Petrarch's style more frequently than his opening protestations of independence might suggest. But there are as many varieties of Petrarchan style as there are
good poets who have found some meaning in the dramatic situations
and language of the Petrarchan tradition. Sidney stands close to the
end of that tradition. It is only natural that we should be able to
mark in his work differences of sensibility that grew out of the time
and place in which he wrote. Then there are the subtler differences
that, in any exercise of the "individual talent," transform and criticize,
implicitly or explicitly, the material with which the poet works.

These remarks are by way of prologue to some more specific observations about *Astrophel and Stella*. Whatever familiar figures and
dramatic situations Sidney's sonnets employ, they devote less attention to the continuing and brilliant presentations of the poet's mistress
than Petrarch gives to his visions of Laura. It is not that Sidney has
drastically altered the roles of lover and lady. The mistress keeps her
unattainable state, a fixed star; but there is less wonder in the poet's
response, and his admiration has less power to reconcile him to his
suffering. A reading of *Astrophel and Stella* must take into consideration this observable shift in the poet's attention; Stella's position is
often taken for granted, and a great deal of poetic vitality is absorbed
in Astrophel's impatience, in his energetic attempt to disentangle
what is and what is not satisfactory in Petrarchan love.

In one of Sidney's best sonnets (number 71), we have a rare example of what appears to be a direct response to a poem by Petrarch.[13]
Juxtaposing the sonnets will provide some indication of the direction
Sidney takes:

> Chi vuol veder quantunque pò Natura
>   e'l Ciel tra noi, venga a mirar costei,
>   ch'è sola un sol, non pur a li occhi mei,
>   ma al mondo cieco, che vertù non cura;
> e venga tosto, perché Morte fura
>   prima i migliori, e lascia star i rei;
>   questa, aspettata al regno delli dei,
>   cosa bella mortal, passa, e non dura.
> Vedrà, s'arriva a tempo, ogni vertute,
>   ogni bellezza, ogni real costume,
>   giunti in un corpo con mirabil tempre:
> allor dirà che mie rime son mute,

l'ingegno offeso dal soverchio lume:
ma se più tarda, avrà da pianger sempre.*
(*Rime*, 248)

Who will in fairest booke of Nature know,
    How Vertue may best lodg'd in beautie be,
    Let him but learne of *Love* to reade in thee,
    Stella, those faire lines, which true goodnesse show.
There shall he find all vices' overthrow,
    Not by rude force, but sweetest soveraigntie
    Of reason, from whose light those night-birds flie;
    That inward sunne in thine eyes shineth so.
And not content to be Perfection's heire
    Thy selfe, doest strive all minds that way to move,
    Who marke in thee what is in thee most faire.
So while thy beautie drawes the heart to love,
    As fast thy Vertue bends that love to good:
    "But ah," Desire still cries, "give me some food."
(*AS*, 71)

These sonnets, each a fine and characteristic achievement, reflect profound differences in attitude. Petrarch's poem belongs, in his sequence, among those meant to prepare the reader for Laura's death. It has the poetic qualities we have noted before, exaggerated by the presence and pressure of mortality. The first quatrain claims immense significance for Laura: she is the chief handiwork of Nature and Heaven together; she alone is a sun, illuminating not only the poet's life, but also a blind world that does not care for virtue. Petrarch uses his majestic public manner, opening with hyperbolic praise and a resonant invitation ("chi vuol veder . . .") to join him in admiring this rarity of nature. That compliment is intensified by the next quatrain, which urges us to hurry; death steals away the best first. The effect of the lines is simultaneously to heighten the tone of won-

* Whoever wishes to see what Nature and Heaven can do among us, come to gaze at her, who alone is a sun, not only to my eyes, but to the blind world which does not care for virtue. And let him come soon, because Death steals away the best first, and leaves the bad behind. She, awaited in the kingdom of the gods, a beautiful mortal thing, passes and does not remain. He will see, if he arrives in time, every virtue, every beauty, every regal quality, joined in one body with admirable temper. Then he will say that my verses are mute, my talent overwhelmed by excess of light. But if he delays too long, he will have to weep forever.

der by emphasizing Laura's fleeting brilliance and to reinforce the note of philosophical gravity ("cosa bella mortal, passa, e non dura") struck earlier by "mondo cieco, che vertù non cura." Tempered by time, desire has disappeared, and the poem gives less sense of Laura's physical presence than sonnet 90 ("Erano i capei") does. Rather, in the sestet, Petrarch stresses general characteristics: a harmony of virtue, beauty, and regal bearing. The poem makes no explicit philosophical statements, but it does, by placing Laura against the background of death and time, make clear the role of the visions of Laura in the sequence. She embodies the refining power of earthly beauty; one suffers if one has not seen her. This sonnet dramatizes in its tone of dazzled admiration the kind of life-giving effect she has upon the poet and upon a world faced with the prospect of her absence.

Sidney's sonnet opens with a promise of the same majestic harmony and ends with a devastating comment on the whole Petrarchan vision. It is a troubled poem, inviting multiple interpretations. For the first thirteen lines Sidney's poem appears to be a version of Petrarch's praise of Laura; then in the last line the poem departs completely from its model and our attention is pivoted to Astrophel, forcing a re-evaluation of all the lines that have come before. Two different views of love are balanced against one another: one, noble and assured; the other, impetuous and unanswerable. It is a curious kind of balancing and testing, thirteen lines against one; but the point of the poem is to show the power of desire to bring a carefully created structure toppling to the ground. There is no danger here that the mistress will die, that the vision will disappear (the cause of anguish in the last line of Petrarch's poem). Astrophel, no matter how much he is exposed to Stella's purifying power, still suffers from unsatisfied desire.

The first thirteen lines of Sidney's sonnet are public praise, impressive and formal, an account of the conventionally accepted power of beauty; the tension of the sonnet depends upon the speaker's involvement, his willing response to beauty's refining power. Sidney echoes Petrarch's opening proclamation: "Who will in fairest booke of Nature know." For the most part, the language of the poem is more abstract than Petrarch's, more explicitly "Platonized." The meaning of "booke of Nature" is not substantially different from that of "quantunque pò Natura / e'l Ciel tra noi," but Sidney's poem develops the metaphor of the book and concerns itself, almost systematically, with the process of learning from Stella. The observer will "know," will "read." Petrarch asks us to see and admire; and he gives us more of a sense of Laura as a woman who *embodies* virtue ("ogni real costume, / giunti in un corpo con mirabil tempre"). A sense of illumination is implicit in the tone and dramatic situation, but is not conveyed as explicitly as it is in Sidney's sonnet. Reason appears on the surface of the latter poem; the symbolic identification of the sun with the inward light of reason is drawn for us.

Sidney disposes his materials to emphasize an almost formalized ladder of virtue, the self-conscious lover initially feeling the way Neoplatonic doctrine says he should feel. He learns to read in Stella "those faire lines, which true goodnesse show." It is a vision made concrete mainly by the direct address to Stella, using her name, and by the delicacy of diction in "sweetest soveraigntie," the effect of which is transmitted by a skillful enjambment to the otherwise colorless "reason" of line 7. The octet gains life most strikingly from the one foreign element, its most concrete detail, the disturbing nightbirds. These are presumably vices, whose flight from the light shining in Stella's eyes serves to particularize the power of reason that, up to this point, has been presented abstractly.

The sonnet, with a linking "and," moves into the sestet, which is designed to continue in long smooth clauses the description of Stella's effect upon onlookers. The whole sonnet is pitched toward a climax of activity: "So while thy beautie drawes the heart to love, / As fast thy Vertue bends that love to good." After these lines, which gather up the movement of the entire poem, the sonnet shifts from Astrophel's experiencing the public evaluation of beauty and virtue to a private reaction: "'But ah,' Desire still cries, 'give me some food.'" It is a telling thrust, defeating all expectation of a harmonious ending for the sonnet and a smooth close to the final couplet. "Still" carries its Elizabethan force of "always" and accents the urgency of Desire's crude and direct imperative; the rhetorical control and promise of lines 12 and 13 ("while . . . beautie drawes . . . heart to love, / As fast . . . Vertue bends . . . love to good") is dissipated by the contrast.

The feelings asserted by the line are of necessity complicated. Astrophel seems to regret his position. In Petrarch's sonnet the poet and the public join in admiring Laura from a distance; Astrophel has been set apart, unable to join the community of those "who marke in thee what is in thee most faire." His position parallels that of the night-birds, forced to fly from the light of reason. The shift of attention from the mistress' perfection to the lover's imperfection is an important one; if it stresses his guilt, it also stresses his vitality. In Astrophel's praise of Stella, we detect a note of strain, particularly in a second reading when we are conscious of the ending to come. He describes his mistress' power more abstractly than Petrarch does, treating love as doctrine to be learned and emphasizing less its grounding in feeling. The phrase of regret, " 'But ah,' Desire still cries," also expresses release from the effort implied in "striving" to move all minds toward perfection and in "as fast" bending love to good. Astrophel's is the kind of human response, stressed by the bluntness of his speech, that is felt by Signora Emilia after Pietro Bembo's rapt discourse on Platonic love at the end of *The Courtier*. She "tooke him by the plaite of hys garment and pluckinge him a little, said: 'Take heede, Master Peter, that these thoughtes make not your soule also to forsake the bodye.' "[14]

Astrophel cannot resolve the opposing perceptions of the sonnet, though he gives full value both to the claims of ideal beauty and to the energetic promptings of desire. In Sidney's sequence the burden of interest falls upon unreconciled conflict in a way that it does not in the more harmonious sonnets of Petrarch. By presenting love against an extended backdrop of time, Petrarch can convince us of its refining power and its stimulus to the imagination; he can make evaluations that convey some air of order and certainty. Sidney's sonnets noticeably lack a sense of time and the bearing of time upon love, a characteristic that distinguishes them from the sonnets of Shakespeare and other Elizabethans. He chooses to ride on the dial's point of the moment and to dramatize the demands of appetite on the world of the ideal. When we think of Sidney as writing in the Petrarchan tradition, then, we should allow for his special version. His mind is well tuned to the conventional responses to love, of course; they have shaped his expectations and he feels them fully enough to find drama in the defeat of expectation. As in the *Arcadia*, the relation of lofty aims to the immediately destructive nature of love is a subject to engage the imagination.

The sonnet as Sidney uses it in *Astrophel and Stella* proves to be a form supple enough for his drama. He has moved away from the static repetitions and parallel structure that lend strength to the laments in the *Arcadia*. He has also abandoned the open rhyme scheme of Surrey for a version of the tighter Italian sonnet. The most common form used in *Astrophel and Stella* is ABBA/ABBA/CDC/DEE.[15]

Sidney retains the final couplet of the Surrey scheme, but seldom uses it for purposes of witty summary as he did in the *Arcadia*. In fact, the formalities of the rhyme scheme conceal rather than reveal the movement of a sonnet like "Who will in fairest booke of Nature know." Sidney fills out his sonnets completely and very often works from a generally held view of love to the private reaction of Astrophel, which he reserves as a surprising or qualifying comment in the last line. The sonnet in these cases builds toward a climax in line 13 and defeats our expectations in form as well as content by using the last line of the couplet as contrast, not to complete an epigram. The subtle movement of the sestet of sonnet 71 should illustrate the point. Three kinds of articulation are at work there. The organization by rhyme, CDCD/EE, is countered by the grammatical arrangement; the six lines fall into three sentences CDC/DE/E. The linking rhyme "love" (D) mutes the first grammatical separation and continues the important movement of meaning that divides the first five lines of the sestet from line 14, the urgent " 'But ah,' Desire still cries, 'give me some food.' " This last articulation, CDCDE/E, is the one that the reader notices first, but his experience of the sestet is richer because of the interlocking of divisions by grammar and by rhyme. For none of the usual or expected separations—a sentence ending or a completed rhyme—is allowed to stop us in our reading; this reinforces the effect of "strive" and "drawes." But where one expects continuity—a completion of the final couplet—just there the guillotine falls.

Sidney's main adaptation or innovation in the sonnet form lies in his handling of the sestet. He seems to prefer the Petrarchan octet; with its two rhymes (in contrast to Surrey's four) and its closed pattern (ABBA/ABBA rather than ABAB/CDCD), it buttresses the single well-knit statement. Sonnet 71 is an excellent example of such harmonies. For the sestet, and particularly for the last line of the poem, he reserves the ironic comment, the sudden agile criticism of harmonies that have been weighed and appreciated before.

III

The comparison of "Who will in fairest booke of Nature know" with its Petrarchan model takes us now to the center of poetic interest in *Astrophel and Stella*. Astrophel can entertain only momentarily the Petrarchan vision of earthly beauty that restores the lover to grace or wisdom. His significant activity is the discovery of conflict, and he delights in it. Astrophel moves freely back and forth between poles marked, on the one hand, by the conventionally defined roles of lover and lady and, on the other, by the attitude expressed with more certainty at a later time by Donne: "Love's not so pure, and abstract, as they use / To say, which have no Mistresse but their Muse." He participates in and then questions traditional attitudes. As in sonnet 71, Astrophel's role in this sequence is that of critic—he tests conventions without necessarily transforming them.

Sidney announces his restiveness and his questioning of conventional attitudes toward love at the very opening of *Astrophel and Stella*. Sonnet 1 is well known:

> Loving in truth, and faine in verse my love to show,
>   That the deare She might take some pleasure of my paine:
>   Pleasure might cause her reade, reading might make her know,
>   Knowledge might pitie winne, and pitie grace obtaine,
> I sought fit words to paint the blackest face of woe,
>   Studying inventions fine, her wits to entertaine:
>   Oft turning others' leaves, to see if thence would flow
>   Some fresh and fruitfull showers upon my sunne-burn'd braine.
> But words came halting forth, wanting Invention's stay,
>   Invention, Nature's child, fled step-dame Studie's blowes,
>   And others' feete still seem'd but strangers in my way.
> Thus great with childe to speake, and helplesse in my throwes,
>   Biting my trewand pen, beating my selfe for spite,
>   "Foole," said my Muse to me, "looke in thy heart and write."
>   (AS, 1)

The sonnet opens *Astrophel and Stella* with a fanfare justifying Nashe's exuberant preface to the 1591 edition. It is a sonnet about style, the relation of style to matter, and it makes its declaration in splendid, controlled alexandrines, drawing the reader's attention immediately to the boldness of the sequence and to its capacity, at will, to vary from the accepted pentameter line. Most of the poems in fact utilize a five-foot line, and most of them follow a common rhyme scheme. But it is not until sonnet 7 that Sidney first repeats a form exactly, as if to remind us through the variety of the first sonnets of a latent versatility, a sleeping strength, in what we are to read. Such maneuvers are playful and self-conscious, characteristic of *Astrophel and Stella*. For Sidney's sequence asks wakefulness of its readers and raises doubts that, as sonnet 71 illustrates, it does not always attempt to resolve.

What kind of alertness do the poems demand? As Rosemond Tuve has pointed out, the surprises are not those a modern reader might expect. The last line of sonnet 1 does not register a broad claim for "the natural feeling of the heart, rebelliously bursting through the trammels of form. Sidney says 'look in thy heart and write,' but he is talking about 'inventing' or finding matter."[16] The complaint is not against art, but against false art. The poet is asked to devise, to find conceits that make fully articulate the strength and particularity of his love: in Gascoigne's words, "what Theame soever you do take in hande, if you do handle it but *tamquam in oratione perpetua*, and never studie for some depth of devise in the Invention, and some figures also in the handlyng thereof, it will appeare to the skilfull Reader but a tale of a tubbe."[17] The occasions for invention, he goes on to say, are infinite; there are no firm rules, but the poet can at least begin by avoiding the trite and the obvious: "If I should undertake to wryte in prayse of a gentlewoman, I would neither praise hir christal eye, nor hir cherrie lippe, etc."

To be told then, as Astrophel is told at the end of sonnet 1, to look into one's heart and write is to be reminded of the *source* of eloquence in love poetry. There are several traditions that account for what Astrophel finds when he "looks." For one thing, the heart is the traditional dwelling place of Cupid or Love.[18] But a more relevant strength of the heart in Renaissance poetry is that it holds the image of the poet's mistress. Sidney accepts this as a commonplace in a later sonnet:

> Whence hast thou Ivorie, Rubies, pearle and gold,
> To shew her skin, lips, teeth and head so well?
> "Foole," answers he, "no *Indes* such treasures hold,
> But from thy heart, while my sire charmeth thee,
> Sweet *Stella's* image I do steale to mee."
>
> (AS, 32)

"Looke in thy heart and write" may be read as a call to order, pointing out to Astrophel that Stella's image is the source of his powers of invention. The substance of the line is entirely conventional. But the manner of its presentation is not: the violence and release of tension with which the poet is advised to look at Stella's image marks Sidney's version as quite special. He presents this conclusion as a per-

sonal discovery, marking it with a burst of direct speech and colloquial reproof ("Foole") that hardly befits the dignity of the supposed
Muse who warns him.

In its manner the poem both shares in and calls into question a
merely public courtly mode. Astrophel opens with a recognition that
"loving in truth" requires with it participation in a world of courtly
gesture, "her wits to entertaine." If any tension exists between the
poet and that world, it is certainly not evident in the elegant balance
and rhetorical polish of the opening lines. The octet consists of one
sentence whose subject, "I," does not appear until line 5 and whose
movement is sustained by strongly accented participles ("loving,"
"studying," "turning") and the elaborate rhetorical flourish of the
opening ("pleasure . . . / Pleasure . . . reade, reading . . . know,
/ Knowledge . . . pitie . . . pitie grace").[19] The smoothness and
facility of these lines help to characterize the world of "inventions
fine" and the civilized pleasures of expressive love poetry.

Yet the activity of the octet seems to be in vain. Quite systematically, the sestet denies the efforts of lines 5-8 and sets out Astrophel's
frustrations in lines 9-11: the "fit words" he seeks "came halting
forth"; in "Studying inventions fine," he succeeds in frightening Invention away; and "turning others' leaves" he finds them "strangers in
my way."[20] A study of courtly verse, instead of helping him, accounts
for his "sunne-burn'd braine." This striking phrase refers to an accepted Elizabethan figure for poetic imitation. Thomas Wilson, rec-
ommending imitation of the ancients, used it in a simile: "For if they
that walke much in the Sunne and thinke not of it, are yet for the
most part Sunne burnt, it can not be but that they which wittingly
and willingly travayle to counterfect each other, must needes take
some colour of them."[21] But where Wilson and other rhetoricians
urge imitation, Sidney distrusts its ease and sees some danger in it.
He draws out what is implicit in the metaphor, the parched sense of
the man who has walked too long in the sun of the ancients.

The poem also plays quite deliberately with the word "invention,"
which contains in Renaissance rhetoric and poetic theory an implicit
complication of meaning.[22] It must be both a "stay" and "Nature's
child"; it must provide formal excellence and be fully eloquent in
representing the feelings from which the poem springs. In sonnet 1
Astrophel first refers to the "inventions fine" of others, poems that define the convention in which he is trying to write. Then it becomes
the "stay," the prop that he gropes for as a support or buttress for his

own poetic ideas. By an extension of meaning, it becomes the elusive child of Nature, fleeing "step-dame Studie's blowes." Here it gains animation, a homeliness and vitality of its own, to which the fine inventions are hostile. The growing vividness in characterizing invention is part of the movement of the poem away from "studying" conventional sonnets (with the punning "And others' feete still seem'd but strangers in my way") toward the activity hoped for, the "fresh and fruitfull showers" of line 8. In the final tercet, Sidney prepares a climax remarkably like that of sonnet 71: two lines of summary that bring the poem to a point are followed by a surprising completion in the final couplet. Here (lines 12 and 13) the sharply accented lines each fall into two sections of equal length; the tension of "great with childe" and "helplesse in my throwes" is reinforced and heightened by the alliterative participles, "Biting my trewand pen, beating my selfe for spite." All the frustrations of the poem are finally dispelled by the energetic outburst associated with the discovery of Stella's image in the heart. The effect of the poem depends upon contrasting the tightly controlled rhetorical pattern of the first thirteen lines with the monosyllabic directness, the imperatives, the surprising colloquialism, of the last line (which breaks into the poem with only a tenuous syntactical connection to what precedes it).

The interesting point about this sonnet is the self-conscious necessity that Sidney feels to act out, here at the very beginning of the sequence, the process of true invention and to portray it in part as youthful (a victim of step-dame Study), plain-talking, and explosive. But it is equally interesting that the sonnet does not disclaim artifice and convention. With its elaborate rhetorical figures and its attention to Stella's image, it uses a formal literary manner and sonnet conventions quite ostentatiously. Still, it proceeds toward an ironic reminder of the energy that lies behind artifice, and it associates the conventionally hallowed image of the mistress with that reminder.

Astrophel is hostile throughout the sequence toward those who seem to be indulging a merely literary fancy.[23] This distrust makes itself felt in the numerous poems about style, whose presence in *Astrophel and Stella* is one of the marks distinguishing it from other Elizabethan sequences. These poems continue the gesture of the opening sonnet, the professions of independence from courtly wits, and they specify some of the affectations of contemporary love poetry: in sonnet 6, the Petrarchan oxymorons ("living deaths, deare wounds, faire stormes, and freesing fires"), mythological poems, pastoral tales;

in sonnet 15, excessive alliteration and "poore Petrarch's long deceased woes"; in sonnet 28, "allegorie's curious frame." Like sonnet 1, though without its comic energy, each of these sonnets returns to Stella, in order to stress the particularity and directness of the poet's love for her: "*Stella* behold, and then begin to endite" (sonnet 15); or "I in pure simplicitie, / Breathe out the flames which burne within my heart, / *Love* onely reading unto me this arte" (sonnet 28).

Critics have been disturbed by the seeming contradiction between the speaker's professions of simplicity and the poems that use the very modes Astrophel distrusts.[24] Sidney does use mythology (five of the first fifteen poems are fables involving Cupid), and he frequently invokes the Petrarchan contraries. We are bound to be puzzled if we take Astrophel's poems on style as a program of reform rather than as a series of rather troubled and self-conscious gestures. His straining after sincerity suggests an uncertainty about the inherited vocabulary of love poetry. His sonnets, at some points, attempt to recover the energy in that tradition and, at other points, to chafe at its limitations and the distorted uses to which it had been put.

IV

I began these preliminary remarks on *Astrophel and Stella* by saying that the sequence noticeably lacked the sustained and sustaining visions of the poet's lady that made Petrarch's cycle one of meditation on earthly beauty and its continuing effect on the imagination. Without dethroning Stella, Sidney's sonnets shift a great deal of the energy and poetic attention to Astrophel. The two major sonnets we have been considering, 1 and 71, suggest that inherited attitudes cannot fully express Astrophel's feelings. The dialogue form in which both poems are cast (with line 14 countering the rest of the sonnet) is for that reason important to Sidney; in the final line of both sonnets he presses Astrophel's claims of singularity against an accepted public manner. Once we have understood the demands of desire upon virtue in a sonnet like 71, we are in an even better position to appreciate in sonnet 1 the mocking discomfort of Astrophel in the presence of conventional courtly poetry. Conflict, as expressed in the two poems, exists at different levels of intensity. Sonnet 1 springs from a satirical impulse directed against affectations in literary manner, against love poetry as a court game, concealing the emotions it was intended to convey. The poet appeals to Invention, as he later appeals to the "booke of Nature" written in Stella's features. Sonnet 71 shows, further, how complicated the book of Nature can be for him, when the wonder and dignity of Stella come into abrupt conflict with the urgencies of desire. Renaissance love poetry, of course, thrives on conflict. What sets Sidney's apart is the continued pointing of the poems toward the *discovery* of conflict, the frequent emphasis on disruption itself.

Astrophel's definition of "loving in truth" is a complicated matter, as one might gather from his claims to particularity. As Hallett Smith puts it: "He constantly mentions the difference between himself and others. Distinctiveness, not variety of feeling, is thus important."[25] There is more variety than Smith suggests—we have already noted the shift in feeling between sonnet 1 and sonnet 71, between the satirical criticism of affectation and a poem that passionately specifies the dilemma of the critic. These are poems of definition. We do not depend upon the certain grounds for love that provide the base of Petrarch's sonnets, but upon the sonnet-by-sonnet distinctions made by Astrophel. Astrophel's role is one of sustained alertness and questioning in exercises of a varied sensibility. We never are allowed to rest with an attitude, a gesture; for the next sonnet may exactly contradict an expressed view or remind us that a particular experience is momentary or that a newly discovered truth leads only to further complexities. Our delight depends more firmly upon the persona the poet creates for us—that of the questioning critic—than it does in the more impersonal sonnets of Petrarch. A closer look at Astrophel's progress through the Sidney sequence should bear this out.

NOTES

1. There were three unauthorized quartos of the sequence (two in 1591, printed by Thomas Newman, and one printed by Matthew Lownes, probably 1597-1600), in addition to the canonical version of the sonnets included by the Countess of Pembroke in her folio edition of the *Arcadia,* 1598. See Ringler's description of manuscripts and early editions in *Poems,* pp. 538-46.

2. The most recent and most intelligent discussion of this problem is that of Jack Stillinger, "The Biographical Problem of *Astrophel and Stella,*" *Journal of English and Germanic Philology,* LIX (1960), 617-39.

3. Critical attention to the poetic problems in *Astrophel and Stella* has increased since Theodore Spencer's 1945 article on Sidney's poetry.

See also Ringler's introduction and notes in *Poems*; Robert L. Montgomery, *Symmetry and Sense* (Austin, 1961); and Hallett Smith, *Elizabethan Poetry* (Cambridge, Mass., 1952), pp. 142-58. Also J. W. Lever, *The Elizabethan Love Sonnet* (London, 1956), pp. 51-91, and Richard B. Young, "English Petrarke: A Study of Sidney's *Astrophel and Stella*," in *Three Studies in the Renaissance: Sidney, Jonson, Milton* (New Haven, 1958), pp. 1-88.

4. *Astrophel and Stella,* No. 15. All quotations are from Ringler, *Poems,* hereafter cited *AS* followed by the number of the sonnet in Ringler's edition.

5. Sidney's own reaction to Ciceronianism is interesting in the light of the critique of Petrarch's unquestioning imitators implied in *Astrophel and Stella.* He wrote to his brother Robert: "So you can speak and write Latin, not barbarously, I never require great study in Ciceronianism, the chief abuse of Oxford, *Qui dum verba sectantur, res ipsas negligunt.*" The letter is dated 18 October 1580 and is quoted in M. W. Wallace, *The Life of Sir Philip Sidney* (Cambridge, Eng., 1915), p. 225.

6. A notable and surprising exception is the sestina, "A qualunque animale alberga in terra," *Rime,* No. 22.

7. Adelia Noferi, "Per una storia dello stile Petrarchesco," *Poesia,* V (1946), 10.

8. Virgil, *Aeneid,* I.319-20. An interesting poetic transfer, conscious or unconscious, has taken place. The Latin *nodo,* which refers to Venus' garment, becomes the Italian *nodi,* used to describe Laura's hair twisted by the wind.

9. For a discussion of the power of *memoria* in the *Rime,* see Noferi, pp. 15ff.

10. Horace, *Odes,* I.xxii.23-4.

11. Petrarch, *Familiari,* II.ix. Translation by Theodor Mommsen in Petrarch, *Songs and Sonnets* (New York, 1946), p. xxxiii.

12. Young, p. 88.

13. Janet G. Scott, *Les Sonnets elisabéthains* (Paris, 1929), p. 306, points out this connection. See also Lever, pp. 58-62.

14. Baldessare Castiglione, *The Book of the Courtier,* tr. Hoby, The Tudor Translation (London, 1900), p. 363.

15. Sixty sonnets in *Astrophel and Stella* follow this form exactly. The octave ABBA/ABBA, in combination with the regular sestet or some other arrangement, is used seventy-five times. Sidney's regular sestet CDC/DEE, combined with the octave ABBA/ABBA or in some other arrangement, appears in eighty-five sonnets.

16. Rosemond Tuve, *Elizabethan and Metaphysical Imagery* (Chicago, 1947), p. 39.

17. *Elizabethan Critical Essays,* ed. G. Gregory Smith (Oxford, 1904), I, 48.

18. For an extended discussion, see Lisle C. John, *The Elizabethan Sonnet Sequences* (New York, 1938), pp. 56ff.

19. Lines 1-4 appear as an example of the rhetorical figure "climax" in Fraunce's *The Arcadian Rhetorike*. "*Climax,* gradation, is a reduplication continued by divers degrees and steps, as it were, of the same word or sound." See *The Arcadian Rhetorike,* ed. Ethel Seaton (Oxford, 1950), pp. 38-39.

20. See Arthur Dickson, "Sidney's *Astrophel and Stella,* Sonnet I," *The Explicator,* III, no. 1 (1944).

21. Thomas Wilson, *The Arte of Rhetorique* (1560), ed. G. H. Mair (Oxford, 1909), p. 5. One finds the figure also in E. K.'s prefatory remarks to *The Shepheardes Calendar.* The original source appears to be Cicero, *De oratore,* II.xiv.60. It is of course part of the wit of the poem that Sidney should use the learned reference against the excesses of learning.

22. For a discussion of Renaissance uses of "invention," see Tuve, pp. 310ff.

23. For an interesting discussion of this point from another angle, see Young, p. 8.

24. See Smith pp. 142-57, which discusses the contradiction in terms of the two audiences, the lady and the reader, to whom the sequence is directed.

25. *Ibid.,* p. 149.

NEIL RUDENSTINE

Sidney and Energia

Sidney criticism has been plagued since the nineteenth century by a form of dualism which has seriously hindered the understanding, not only of particular works by Sidney, but of his poetic development as a whole. The verse of the Arcadia has been almost invariably described as ornate, decorative, or conventional in the pejorative sense of those terms. Hazlitt insisted that the "Sonnets, inlaid in the Arcadia, are jejune, far-fetched and frigid"[1]; as for the book as a whole, it was "not romantic, but scholastic; not nature, but art, . . . Out of five hundred folio pages, there are hardly, I conceive, half a dozen sentences expressed simply and directly, . . . Every page is 'with centric and eccentric scribbled o'er'; his Muse is tattooed and tricked out like an Indian goddess."[2] While Hazlitt was attacking the *Arcadia*'s verbal artifice, however, Lamb was declaring that the sonnets of *Astrophel and Stella* presented "not a fever of passion wasting itself upon a thin diet of dainty words, but a transcendent passion pervading and illuminating action, pursuits, studies, . . ."[3] If Hazlitt was certain that Sidney's earliest verse was verbal "art" of the worst sort, Lamb was equally sure that the later poetry was anything but mere "dainty words." On the whole, both judgements have persisted to the present time, and they have—between them—made the question of Sidney's development something of a puzzle. How can we explain

From *Sidney's Poetic Development* (Cambridge, Mass.: Harvard University Press, 1967), with permission of the publishers. Copyright, 1967, by the President and Fellows of Harvard College.

Sidney's early devotion to rhetorical ornament and pattern, and what influences can help us to account for the plainer, more dramatic poetry of feeling that we find in *Astrophel?*

Critics have answered these questions in essentially two ways. Theodore Spencer, for example, suggested that the *Arcadia* verse revealed Sidney's initial bondage to the literary conventions of his time. *Astrophel,* by contrast, exhibited a new freedom of expression—it represented a triumph of "personal feeling" and "sincerity" over the inhibiting, restrictive force of mere convention.[4] Other critics have altered Spencer's terms, but have preserved the fundamental dichotomy which he (as well as Lamb and Hazlitt) discovered in Sidney's work. Kenneth Myrick suggested that the young Sidney was a victim of sixteenth-century Ciceronianism: "To use Sidney's own language, he has (in the *Arcadia*) 'cast suger and spice uppon everie dish.'"[5] Yet, although "Sidney, in school and university, could not have escaped . . . Ciceronianism," he was at least discerning enough to begin to distrust it.[6] The plainer language of *Astrophel* was a step in the right direction, and it linked Sidney with later plain stylists like Bacon, Donne, and Jonson. To Myrick, all Elizabethans

> in their enthusiasm for choice language, too often conceived style as an end in itself, the ornament, not the inevitable expression, of thought . . . But among English writers Bacon is only one of those who, toward the end of the sixteenth century, were beginning to grasp more clearly than the Ciceronians the meaning of artistic form. . . . In this maturing of English taste, Sir Philip Sidney, had he lived, would doubtless have had an important part . . .[7]

A more recent critic, Robert Montgomery, has extended this line of argument. Sidney began his career concerned with "manner" rather than "matter," and the *Arcadia* shows clearly this youthful "tendency to hunt verbal ornament at the expense of other goals."[8] Later, dissatisfied with his work, he created a plainer and more dramatic idiom in *Astrophel.* Like Gabriel Harvey, Sidney rebelled against Ciceronian artifice, and the *Apologie for Poetrie,* with its cautionary remarks on the subject of poetic ornament, announces his new principles of style:

> Sidney's critical statements about lyric point in two directions. On the one hand, they seem to betray an intention to dismantle the principles of style implicit in the *Arcadia* poems. . . . *The*

Defence of Poesie was probably composed after most, if not all, of the *Arcadia* verse was completed. As he lists his objections to over-decorative lyric, Sidney confesses himself "sicke among the rest." On the other hand, the *Defence* is echoed in a number of sonnets in *Astrophel and Stella* which argue against conventional devices in lyric ornament, and urge a plainer, more direct style, and had the sequence carried out this program with utter and obvious fidelity to its new principles, the work of the critic would be simpler than it is.[9]

Montgomery's own remarks hint at the difficulty which his interpretation raises: for Sidney failed to carry out his "new program" faithfully, and this failure does indeed complicate the work of the critic. As nearly everyone has noticed, *Astrophel* contains a great deal of verbal ornament. If Sidney was rebelling against rhetorical artifice, he did so extremely ineffectively—so ineffectively, that we must wonder whether the general theory of his stylistic development as outlined by Montgomery, Myrick, and others is in fact an adequate one.

This essay will suggest, briefly, that the effort to describe Sidney's development in terms of sharply opposed tendencies is a misleading one. If we view him as changing from ornate to plain, conventional to personal, or Ciceronian to Baconian, we will be forced to charge him with curious inconsistencies at any number of points in his career. His last substantial work, for example, was almost certainly his revision of the *Arcadia*'s prose, and yet—as Praz and Zandvoort noticed —he went out of his way to make that prose much more, not less, ornate than the original. Myrick attempted to explain this discrepancy by declaring that Sidney was, in effect, too strongly bound by old habits of style to break free: "The bad tendencies of the first version, to be sure, he did not correct in the revision. . . . Yet however firmly the mannerisms may have been fixed in Sidney's style, the path toward improvement could be found only by experience."[10] It seems odd that so self-conscious and accomplished a stylist as Sidney could not have written more plainly if he had chosen, particularly after he had demonstrated his ability to do so in *Astrophel*. The fact suggests that plainness was really not his goal in the New *Arcadia*; and if we remember that he was in his revision giving the *Arcadia* something like epic proportions, adding nearly all of its heroic materials, the increased ornateness of his style becomes perfectly explicable. Sidney was essentially writing in accordance with Renaissance ideas of decorum, giving his New *Arcadia* a more elevated "high" style to suit its epic subject. Similar ideas of decorum, I would suggest, can account for Sidney's choices of style in his earlier work. He was never committed to any single style—neither Ciceronian ornateness nor Baconian plainness—and it is impossible to present a coherent picture of his development in such terms. Rather, he used a number of different styles from the very beginning of his career, and he continually varied his style from work to work, from genre to genre, in order to suit the decorum of each. Far from ever preferring "manner" to "matter," his main effort was devoted to achieving—in even his earliest work—a union of the two.

A few remarks from Sidney's correspondence may help to demonstrate these points. It seems certain, for instance, that Sidney was never a Ciceronian in any sense. As early as 1574, some years before he began the original *Arcadia*, Sidney wrote to Hubert Languet asking advice about Latin composition. Languet replied:

> You ask me to tell you how you ought to form your style of writing. I think you will do well to read both volumes of Cicero's letters, not only for the beauty of the Latin, but also for the very important matter they contain. . . . But beware of falling into the heresy of those who think that the height of excellence consists in the imitation of Cicero, and pass their lives in labouring at it.[11]

Languet stresses the importance of Cicero's matter, and urges the young Sidney to avoid the Ciceronian excesses of the time. Sidney's reply intimates that he intends to follow Languet's advice,[12] and a later letter (October 1580) from Sidney to his brother Robert makes his point of view thoroughly clear:

> So you can speak and write Latin, not barbarously, I never require great study of Ciceronianism, the chief abuse of Oxford, 'qui dum verba sectantur, res ipsas negligunt.' My toyfull books I will send, with God's help, by February, . . .[13]

The passage is particularly interesting because it combines an expression of anti-Ciceronianism with a reference to the original *Arcadia* ("my toyfull books") which Sidney was just bringing to conclusion.[14] It dramatizes, in other words, not only that Sidney was anti-Ciceronian, but also that his anti-Ciceronianism was altogether compatible with the ornament and high rhetoric he was at the moment lavishing upon his pastoral romance. Ciceronians followed "words" and neglected things themselves ("res ipsas"). Sidney, meanwhile, gives every indication that he considers neither himself nor his work—including specifically the *Arcadia*—to be guilty of such a charge. He "never" requires great study of Ciceronianism, and the "never" suggests a long-standing, well-formulated attitude on the subject. It suggests that his principles of style were settled long before he had undertaken the *Arcadia,* that they would not have tolerated a decorative preference for manner over matter, and that the *Arcadia* (indeed, all of Sidney's work) was very much the creation of a man who cared pre-eminently for the substantiality of "things" themselves.

Not only Sidney's correspondence, but his actual poetic practice in the *Arcadia* tends to support such a view. The Arcadian poetry is anything but uniformly ornate in style; Sidney has in fact maintained throughout the work a general distinction between the verse of his shepherds and that of his courtiers:

> O stealing time the subject of delaie,
> (Delay, the racke of unrefrain'd desire)
> What strange dessein hast thou my hopes to staie,
> My hopes which do but to mine owne aspire?
>
> Mine owne? ô word on whose sweete sound doth pray
> My greedy soule, with gripe of inward fire: . . .
> (OA 53)[15]

> O gods, how long this old foole hath annoi'd
> My wearied eares! O gods yet graunt me this,
> That soone the world of his false tong be void. . . .
> Then who will heare a well autoris'd lye,
> (And pacience hath) let him goe learne of him
> What swarmes of vertues did in his youth flye
> Such hartes of brasse, wise heads, and garments trim
> Were in his dayes: . . .
> (OA 9)

> Downe, downe *Melampus;* what? your fellow bite?
> I set you ore the flock I dearly love,
> Them to defend, not with your selves to fight . . .
> (OA 10)

The first passage, spoken by the Princess Philoclea, is in an elevated, self-consciously rhetorical style; parallel apostrophes, intentionally obtrusive *anadiplosis*, carefully balanced alliteration, and correct diction all give the lines an air of calculated artificiality and formality. The next two passages, by contrast, belong respectively to the courtier-shepherd Philisides, and the shepherd Geron. Despite their awkwardness, they are clearly informal and conversational, with their vigorous exclamations and questions, their colloquial phrases ("this old foole"; "swarmes of vertues"), and their general lack of rhetorical heightening. Sidney could write "plain" poetry when he wanted, but he decided (not surprisingly) to distinguish the verse of his courtiers from that of his shepherds, in order to suggest the greater sophistication, the grace and wit, and the more refined feelings and nobler passions of his princes and princesses.

Despite the undoubted preponderance of ornate verse in the original *Arcadia*, then, the work also contains a great deal of poetry that is in no sense "decorative." Considerations of decorum, not any youthful devotion on Sidney's part to ornament and high rhetoric, were the main determinants of the book's different styles. Once we have recognized this, moreover, we are in a position to see that even the verbal artifice of Sidney's courtiers is in fact highly "functional" and essentially undecorative, for it is one of the primary means by which Sidney creates the romantic and refined atmosphere of his idealized, remote Arcadian world. Most comments on the *Arcadia*'s verse tend to imply that it should be viewed in the same light, and judged by the same standards as *Astrophel*: that we should approach it, in other words, as if it were the intimate, rather private poetry of a courtier, written *in persona propria*. But Sidney was not simply trying to write verse like *Astrophel*'s and doing a bad job of it. He was framing a style that would relate plausibly to the fictional world he had created in the *Arcadia*'s prose, and the mannered, rhetorical mode he fashioned for his courtly characters was the perfect medium for his purposes. It is capable of extraordinarily powerful and yet highly formal expressions of emotion (as in the famous double sestina); and it can suggest, equally, the youthful, naive, exaggerated feelings and gestures of romantic young lovers. Reading the poetry in context serves to underline its affinities to the *Arcadia*'s prose, and to stress the extent to which it participates in the book's delicate, artificial, witty spirit. For example, when Pamela and Musidorus are fleeing from Arcadia, they rest momentarily in a lovely forest:

. . . *Pamela* had much more pleasure to walke under those Trees, making in theyre Barckes prity knottes wch tyed together the names of *Musidorus* and *Pamela*, sometymes intermixedly chaungyng them to *Pamedorus* and *Musimela*, with xxti other Flowers of her traveling fancyes wch had bounde them selves to a greater Restraynt, then they coulde withoute muche payne well endure: And to one Tree more beholding to her then the Rest, shee entrusted the Treasure of her thoughtes in these verses.

> *Doo not Disdayne O streighte upraysed Pyne?*
>   *That, wounding thee, my Thoughtes in thee I grave,*
> *Synce that my thoughtes as Streighte as streightnes thyne,*
>   *No smaller wounde, (Alas) furr deeper have?*
>
> *Deeper engraved which salve nor Tyme can save,*
>   *Given to my harte by my fore wounded eyen. . . .*[16]

Pamela is here seen as charming and naive, making love-knots and indulging fancies in a scene suffused with the particular blend of grace, delicacy, and irony which Sidney manages so well. Her song, which seems so stiff when it is read in isolation, rises very naturally from the context created for it. A poetry of sincere personal feeling, full of tension and drama, in a plain or conversational idiom, is precisely what the situation will *not* bear. That the *Arcadia* poetry is often strange and sometimes mediocre, no one need deny; but the fact should not be allowed to obscure the success of several individual lyrics nor (even more important) should it hinder our understanding of the rationale behind the *Arcadia*'s ornate style as a whole.

The evidence of both Sidney's correspondence and of the *Arcadia*'s verse itself thus suggests that traditional theories of his poetic development are, for various reasons, inadequate. It may be worthwhile, therefore, to re-examine Montgomery's contention that the *Apologie for Poetrie* betrays an "intention to dismantle the principles of style implicit in the *Arcadia* poems." Does Sidney's essay argue against various kinds of "lyric ornament" in the interest of plainness? There is hardly space for a full discussion of the question within the confines of a brief essay, but an answer can at least be suggested. Few if any of the charges Sidney brings against English poets in the *Apologie* (or in the *Astrophel* sonnets associated with the *Apologie*) apply to his own writing, either in the *Arcadia* or elsewhere. He complains of far-fetched words, of slavish imitators of Tully and Demosthenes who keep "Nizolian paper-books," or "Herbarists" and those who search out endless similes from "stories of beasts, fowls, and fishes," of those who plagiarize Pindar, who use the worn-out oxymorons of Petrarchan poetry, who draw on Ovid for "*Jove's* strange tales," who generally search out other writers for the materials with which to fill out their own poor verses![17] The fundamental charge underlying these individual complaints is that English poets lack originality and imagination. They mistrust the validity of their own lights. They begin with other writers, and import similes, "flowers" of rhetoric, phrases and "strange tales" as a compensation for their own poverty. Throughout the *Arcadia*, however, we shall find scarcely a fowl or a fish or an Ovidian tale; and Sidney's editor attests very firmly to the poet's ability to resist any Nizolian inclinations he may have had.

> The tracing of sources is more difficult in Sidney than in almost any other Elizabethan poet, because he did not write, as did so many of his contemporaries, with source books open before him, but from a mind well stored with reading that he had thoroughly assimilated and made his own. He prided himself on being "no pick-purse of another's wit" (AS 74) and, except for his avowed translations, he only once in all his verse directly repeated the words of another poet . . .[18]

In addition to the general charges which the *Apologie* brings against English poets, the essay also lodges more specific complaints which do at first seem aimed at poetic "devices" and ornaments. Sidney's remarks in these passages, however, are extremely carefully qualified. He never in fact complains about ornament *per se*, but only about the abuse of ornament. For instance, he regrets the use of "figures and flowers, extreamelie winter-starved," and the qualifying phrase in apposition is crucial to his meaning.[19] Similarly, he objects to writers who delight in the "coursing of a Letter, as if they were bound to followe the method of a Dictionary": methodology—any "mechanical" approach to composition—is his target, not alliteration itself.[20] Sidney only requires that ornaments be used creatively (one should avoid whatever is "winter-starved") and that they should suit their context. This is quite clear from an important passage near the end of the *Apologie*:

> For nowe they cast Sugar and Spice upon every dish that is served to the table; like those Indians, not content to weare eare-rings at the fit and naturall place of the eares, but they

will thrust Iewels through their nose and lippes, because they
will be sure to be fine. *Tullie*, when he was to drive out *Cate-
line*, as it were with a Thunder-bolt of eloquence, often used
that figure of repitition, *Vivit, vivit? imo in Senatum venit & c.*
Indeed, inflamed with a well-grounded rage, hee would have
his words (as it were) double out of his mouth; and so doe that
artificially, which we see men doe in choller naturally. And
wee, having noted the grace of those words, hale them in sometime to a familier Epistle, when it were too much choller to be
chollerick.[21]

"Sugar and Spice" are perfectly acceptable in their "fit and naturall"
place, and decorum determines what is natural. Cicero's repetitions
are proper for forensic oratory. It is when they are thrust into "a
familier Epistle" that they become objectionable. It is the striving to
be "fine" that Sidney here objects to—the striving without any real
sense of what is appropriate for a given occasion. To decry the abuse
of ornament, however, is very different from decrying ornament itself, and Sidney never confuses the two. At bottom, the *Apologie* reveals the same sensitivity to questions of decorum, and the same concern for "functional" ornament, that we have found in Sidney's letters
and in the poetry of the *Arcadia* itself.

If traditional theories of Sidney's development seem inadequate
because they have failed to take into account either the diversity of
the *Arcadia*'s poetry or the ideas of decorum which underlie that
poetry, it is worthwhile inquiring whether any alternative approach
to the subject seems more satisfactory. The crucial point, of course, is
to discover early verse by Sidney which is strictly comparable to the
later, mature poetry of *Astrophel and Stella*. Fortunately, the collection of lyrics known as the *Certain Sonnets* provides us with just such
verse. It was composed over a period of years (ca.1577-81) and represents an apparently personal selection of miscellaneous pieces which
Sidney wished to preserve.[22] Since it was composed while Sidney was
also at work on the *Arcadia* verse, it gives a clear and important indication of the kind of poetry he was inclined to write informally or
privately—outside the strict confines of pastoral romance. A few of
the *Certain Sonnets*, particularly the songs, are unquestionably in a
formal style that resembles some *Arcadia* lyrics. But most of the
poems are very different from either the highly patterned lines of
Pamela and Philoclea, or the unabashed plain talk of shepherds like
Geron:

Oft have I musde, but now at length I finde,
  Why those that die, men say they do depart:
Depart, a word so gentle to my minde,
  Weakely did seeme to paint death's ougly dart.

But now the starres with their strange course do binde
  Me one to leave, with whome I leave my hart.
I heare a crye of spirits faint and blinde,
  That parting thus my chiefest part I part. . . .
                                                (CS 20)

. . . Are *Poets* then the onely lovers true,
  Whose hearts are set on measuring a verse:
Who think themselves well blest, if they renew
Some good old dumpe, that *Chaucer's* mistresse knew,
And use but you for matters to rehearse?

Then good *Apollo* do away thy bowe:
  Take harp and sing in this our versing time:
And in my braine some sacred humour flowe:
That all the earth my woes, sighes, teares may know,
And see you not that I fall now to ryme? . . .
                                                (CS 17)

Wo, wo to me, on me returne the smart:
  My burning tongue hath bred my mistresse paine,
For oft in paine to paine my painefull heart
  With her due praise did of my state complaine.
I praisde her eyes whom never chance doth move,
  Her breath which makes a sower answer sweete,
Her milken breasts the nurse of child-like love,
  Her legges (O legges) her ay well stepping feete.
Paine heard her praise, and full of inward fire,
  (First sealing up my heart as pray of his)
He flies to her, and boldned with desire,
  Her face (this age's praise) the thiefe doth kisse.
O paine I now recant the praise I gave,
And sweare she is not worthy thee to have.
                                                (CS 9)

The distinctive characteristic of such verse is its particular blend of
sophistication, wit, verbal polish, and conversational ease: it is, like
Astrophel, the poetry of a courtier written *in persona propria.* It

avoids both the elaborate ornateness of the *Arcadia*'s high style, and
the rather naive, exuberant plainness of its low style. It has artifice
("For oft in paine to paine my painefull heart . . ."), directness
("Take harp and sing . . ."), colloquial vigor ("Some good old
dump, . . ."), and the same self-consciousness and spirit of banter
which Astrophel later cultivates:

> O paine I now recant the praise I gave, . . .
>   (CS 9)
> O Doctor *Cupid,* thou for me reply, . . .
>   (AS 61)
>
> Then good *Apollo* do away thy bowe: . . .
>   (CS 17)
> Good brother *Philip,* I have borne you long, . . .
>   (AS 83)
>
> . . . . I now recant the praise I gave,
> And sweare she is not worthy thee to have.
>   (CS 9)
> And I do sweare even by the same delight, . . .
>   (AS 82)

Such quotations show clearly the intimate relationship between much
of the poetry of the *Certain Sonnets* and that of *Astrophel.* Indeed,
the whole of the sonnet quoted above (CS 9) is entirely in Astrophel's vein, with its mixture of courtly praise and strategy, and its
personified figure of Pain, so like Apostrophel's Cupid. Compare, for
example, the sestet of CS 9 with these lines from AS 8:

> But finding these North clymes do coldly him embrace,
>   Not usde to frozen clips, he strayd to find some part,
>   Where with most ease and warmth he might employ his art:
> At length he perch'd himself in *Stella*'s joyfull face . . .

Sidney was creating the *Astrophel* manner as early as 1577-81. The
style which characterizes a majority of the *Certain Sonnets* is one of
the middle range: it is responsive to the rhythms and pressures of a
speaking voice, and in this it differs radically from the high style of
the *Arcadia;* but it is also courtly in its balance, its verbal play, its
concern for the surface of the verse. Essentially, it unites elements of
both the high and low styles of the *Arcadia,* in the interest of creating a poetic version of courtly conversation: artificial and self-con-

scious, yet fluid and natural; witty, calculated, and strategical, yet also full of vigorous feeling. Thus while Sidney was writing the *Arcadia* and adjusting his style to meet that book's varied demands, he was equally able to write as "himself"—as a polished, urbane devotee of Petrarch and Castiglione, a man whose poetry (like his conversation) could be both formal and colloquial, ornate and plain, witty and passionate. The *Certain Sonnets* exhibit precisely that fusion of the natural and the artful—that art concealing art—which Sidney, Castiglione, and others defined as the courtier's ideal style. The decorum of the *Certain Sonnets* is fundamentally different from that of the *Arcadia,* but identical to that of *Astrophel.*

Despite the importance of the *Certain Sonnets,* however, the greatest portion of the collection's verse is relatively undistinguished. The sonnet quoted above (CS 9) is one of the most accomplished of all the lyrics in the group; yet even this poem is rather stiff, and the collection as a whole betrays a general lack of tension and vitality. Some of the lyrics (particularly CS 9-11 and CS 31-2) have a degree of feeling and drama, but the majority are essentially tepid:

> Finding those beams, which I must ever love,
>> To marre my minde, and with my hurt to please,
>> I deemd it best some absence for to prove,
>> If further place might further me to ease. . . .
>> (CS 21)

> My mistresse lowers and saith I do not love:
>> I do protest and seeke with service due,
>> In humble mind a constant faith to prove,
>> But for all this I cannot her remove
>> From deepe vaine thought that I may not be true. . . .
>> (CS 17)

The difficulty with such verse is its lack of animus. It is "plain" and natural enough, and it suits the courtliness of its speaker, but it wants inner warmth and light. The stiff metrics are a major problem—the rhythms are insufficiently supple for either the poetry's conversational manner or its range of feeling. Beyond this, however, there is a more general lack of force, of compelling quality, of that Energia which Sidney valued so highly:

> But truely many of such writings, as come under the banner of unresistable love, if I were a Mistres, would never perswade

mee they were in love: so coldely they apply fiery speeches, as
men that had rather red Lovers writings, and so caught up certaine swelling phrases, which hang together, like a man which
once told mee, the winde was at North West, and by South,
because he would be sure to name windes enowe,—then that
in truth they feele those passions: which easily (as I think)
may be bewrayed by that same forciblenes or *Energia* (as the
Greekes cal it) of the writer.[23]

Sidney's verses from the *Certain Sonnets* are not a patchwork of
swelling phrases borrowed from other poets, but they do have all too
little of that "forciblenes" which makes love poetry convincing and
persuasive. Such forcibleness or Energia cannot, of course, be simply
learned. It derives as much from the poet's intense and imaginative
involvement with his subject as it does from his skill in handling
words and rhythms. But neither can it exist apart from specific skills
and techniques—from "devices" and practiced habits of phrasing and
structuring which must first be discovered and then developed by
training. No such training can endow a writer with the passion to
write verse like that of *Astrophel*, but Renaissance rhetoric books
could and did set out all the technical means necessary to help give
passion effective and beautiful form. Aristotle, Quintilian, Scaliger
and others all discussed the importance of Energia in this regard, and
outlined the means of achieving it. Sidney was of course a student
of their work. What the following pages suggest is that Sidney's
development between the years ca. 1580 and 1582 (when *Astrophel*
was written) can be described mainly in terms of his effort to achieve
Energia within the decorum of the "private" courtly love lyric. The
style of *Astrophel* is essentially the style which Sidney first began to
develop in a number of the *Certain Sonnets*; but *Astrophel* possesses
the vitality and persuasive power which the *Certain Sonnets* all too
rarely display.

Sidney's brief discussion of Energia suggests both its richness and
its elusiveness. He glosses it as "forciblenes" and sees it as a kind of
proof of passion: it convinces or persuades us that poets "in truth
. . . feele those passions" which they purport to feel. Since persuasion lies at the heart of Sidney's entire theory of poetry, Energia
emerges as the most crucial of poetic qualities. Without it, poetry is
superior to neither history nor philosophy; lacking it, the love verses
of courtiers are certain to languish unacknowledged. Effective expressions of passion, on the other hand, produce immediate, powerful

responses: young men are driven to emulate Ulysses and Aeneas, and young ladies believe (and finally show mercy to) their lovers. It is no accident, therefore, that Astrophel begins his sequence by searching (not always successfully) for a "feeling skill" (AS 2) to paint his passions. Stella will read his verse, and

> reading might make her know,
> Knowledge might pitie winne, and pitie grace obtaine.
>
> (AS 1)

The "knowledge" of the poet's love which the lady is to gain will not simply be told her by a plain-speaking man. It must be communicated through the total activity of the verse itself. She must be made to see her lover's plight, to feel what he feels, and to respond with sympathy. Energia, although Astrophel does not use the term, is the chief means to that end.

Once we begin to grasp the important role of Energia in Sidney's poetic theory and practice, noting particularly its connection with the passions and its consequent power as an instrument of persuasion, we can see more clearly how thoroughly this concept pervades the discussion of poetry in the *Apologie*. Sidney defined it loosely as "forciblenes," and the word (or its synonyms) occurs time and time again throughout the essay: "For the question is, whether the fayned image of Poesie, or the regular instruction of Philosophy, hath the more force in teaching." The *Apologie* decides that "a fayned example hath as much force to teach, as a true example (for as for to moove, it is cleare, sith the fayned image may bee tuned to the highest key of passion) . . ."[24] Poetry, "by the reason of his sweete charming force, . . . can doe more hurt then any other Armie of words";[25] if put to proper use, however, poetry's "image of each action stirreth and instructeth the mind."[26] Sidney was sensitive to a great many qualities in poetry, but he was most vitally interested in verse that "stirred" the mind, or that could "bee tuned to the highest key of passion." The persuasive forcibleness or Energia of such verse was for Sidney the very essence of great poetry. Other passages in the *Apologie*, moreover, give us a fuller sense of the precise ways in which Energia might be achieved. David's *Psalms*, for example, are declared to be "meerely (absolutely) poetical" in their handling:

> For what els is the awaking his musicall instruments; the often
> and free changing of persons; his notable *Prosopopeias,* when
> he maketh you as it were, see God comming in his Maiestie;

his telling of the Beastes ioyfulnes, and hills leaping, but a heavenlie poesie, wherein almost hee sheweth himselfe a passionate lover of that unspeakable and everlasting beautie to be seene by the eyes of the minde, onely cleered by fayth?[27]

David is seen as a passionate lover whose powerful feelings reveal themselves in forcible verse, and Sidney has elaborated interestingly on the rhetorical details of that revelation. Some of the devices, at least, which exhibit Energia are apostrophe ("changing of persons"[28]), *prosopopoeia,* and more general visual effects which make one "see" God coming or the hills leaping. In addition, there is simply the obvious vitality of the actions mentioned—the animated joyfulness of the whole landscape scene. Nearly all of these elements were mentioned by Aristotle in his discussion of Energia in the *Rhetoric:*

> . . . the thing should be set "before the eyes," for the hearer should see the action as present, not as future. . . . those words "set a thing before the eyes" which describe it in an active state. . . . This phrase, . . . "in the flower of his vigor," or this one: "at large like a sacred animal," are images of an active state. And in the verse "from there the Greekes, then *darting* with their feet," the word "darting" gives both actuality and metaphor. . . . Or we may use the device, often employed by Homer, of giving life to lifeless things by means of metaphor [*prosopopoeia*]. In all such cases he gets successful effects by describing an active state: as in these words:
> . . . "The arrow *flew*"
> "The arrow, *eager* to fly on"
> "The spear stuck in the ground, quivering."[29]

Sidney translated at least two books, if not all, of the *Rhetoric,* and he must have known this passage well.[30] It emphasizes "activity" and the sense of things being present before one's eyes, as well as more general visual effects and prosopopoeias ("giving life to lifeless things"). Words like "darting" or "quivering" have the same animated "present" sense as King David's "leaping" hills. Energia may be in some ways elusive, but there are in fact techniques for its expression, and Sidney clearly knew of them. Moreover, Scaliger—whom Sidney mentions several times in the *Apologie*—enlarges considerably upon Aristotle's discussion, and his comments are very illuminating. He defines Energia (Latin: *efficacia*) as "vigor of speech" and mentions, in addition to Aristotle's points, that exclamations, cries, direct addresses, and apostrophes are all effective means of achieving Energia.[31] "There is also such *efficacia* in apostrophe and interrogation, that it makes the spirit of the listener leap up. When these are joined the highest vigor is produced. . . . And with greater effect, direction of speech to inanimate objects: 'O spear, that has never frustrated my efforts!' And in the Twelfth Book, 'Good earth, hold my sword.'"[32] Nearly all of the devices which Scaliger mentions create a sense of vivid dramatic action, and Scaliger expands upon this aspect of Energia in his long discussion of the *Aeneid*. Particular actions, situations, or whole scenes can have the quality of Energia for him, and he mentions "Turnus shut up within the camp of the Trojans . . . The helmet of Turnus. His sword broken."[33] He continues, retelling the flight of Aeneas, Anchises, and Iulus, and adding his own responses to the developing actions:

> "I go under my burden" (i.e. "I take up my burden.") Indeed
> I seem to carry my own father, a man most brave. "Little Iulus
> entwined his hand in his father's and follows his father with
> unequal steps." Here I seem to be dragged along. For whatever
> "implicuit" means, the passage surely arouses pity in me. . . .
> Who would not accompany Aeneas in spirit there?[34]

Scaliger's asides are an interesting testimony to the moving powers of Energia, and his discussion of Turnus and Aeneas almost certainly influenced Sidney's in the *Apologie*:

> Who readeth *Aeneas* carrying old *Anchises* on his back, that
> wisheth not it were his fortune to perfourme so excellent an
> acte? Whom doe not the words of Turnus moove? (The tale of
> *Turnus* having planted his image in the imagination.) . . .[35]

Sidney's discussion of Aeneas and Turnus reveals the same kind of response as Scaliger's to vivid scenes and compelling actions, although it goes a step further in showing how "moving" leads to emulation. Both writers extend the concept of Energia beyond the province of rhetoric (apostrophe, *prosopopoeia*, etc.) to that of narrative and dramatic situations. They generalize Aristotle's dictum about setting things before the eyes. "When I hear," writes Scaliger, "of Venulus in the arms of Tarchon, I see it too: 'Fiery Tarchon flies over the plain, carrying the man and his weapons.'" And he jots down a series of vivid scenes and actions: "Shame in the case of Deiphobus, 'trembling and covering his horrid torments.' Wrath in the case of Turnus: 'Sparks come forth from all about his mouth as he speaks; fire gleams from his piercing eyes.' "[36] Sidney, too, offers a series of such vignettes, and discusses their significance:

> Let us but heare old *Anchises* speaking in the middest of Troyes flames, or see *Ulisses,* in the fulnes of all *Calipso*'s delights, bewayle his absence from barraine and beggerly *Ithaca.* Anger the *Stoicks* say, was a short maddnes: let but *Sophocles* bring you *Aiax* on a stage, killing and whipping Sheepe and Oxen, . . . and tell mee if you have not a more familiar insight into anger then finding in the Schoolemen his *Genus* and *difference?* See . . . the sowre-sweetnes of revenge in *Medoea;* and, to fall lower, the *Terentian Gnato,* and our *Chaucers* Pandar, so exprest, that we nowe use their names to signifie their trades. And finally, all vertues, vices, and passions, so in their own naturall seates layd to the viewe, that wee seeme not to heare of them, but cleerely to see through them.[37]

Energia is above all a means of giving feeling some tangible form, and Sidney suggests in this passage how poetry makes us see revenge, anger—indeed all passions—expressed in such a way that we understand them for what they are. The result is that "true lively knowledge" or "hart-ravishing knowledge" which only poetry can render: "an image of that whereof the Philosopher bestoweth but a woordish description: which dooth neyther strike, pierce, nor possesse the sight of the soule so much as that other dooth."[38] Knowledge and persuasiveness are here synonymous. If the image is forceful enough, we will both understand and be moved. Finally, we should note that Sidney returns several times in the *Apologie* to the importance of dramatic situation or plot ("tales") as a source of such persuasive images. The poet comes "with a tale which holdeth children from play, and old men from the chimney corner";[39] the "tale of *Turnus*" similarly holds the imagination; and Menenius Agrippa, when he went to quiet the Roman mob, "came not among them upon trust of figurative speeches, or cunning insinuations; . . . but forsooth he behaves himselfe, like a homely, and familiar Poet. He telleth them a tale, . . ."[40] Poetry is, in effect, identified with what we would normally think of as drama or fiction. It is, for Sidney, not essentially rhyme or meter, but "that fayning notable images of vertues, vices, or what els"—and these are presented with such vigor, with such a "feeling skill," that we are drawn irresistibly into their life and world.

One last aspect of Energia deserves at least brief mention before we turn to Sidney's actual poetic practice. Sidney, like so many of his contemporaries, was deeply interested in problems of English prosody, and it is worth noticing that he was particularly intrigued by the expressive powers of rhythms and meters:

> Now, of versifying there are two sorts, the one Auncient, the other Moderne . . . Whether of these be the most excellent, would beare many speeches. The Auncient (no doubt) more fit for Musick, . . .and more fit lively to expresse divers passions, by the low and lofty sounde of the well-weyed silable. The latter likewise, with hys Ryme, striketh a certaine musick to the eare: and in fine, sith it dooth delight, though by another way, it obtaines the same purpose: there beeing in eyther sweetnes, and wanting in neither maiestie.[11]

Sidney makes it clear that he admires meters which, through their variety and flexibility, can "lively" or vividly "expresse divers passions," and he regrets the inferiority of English prosody in this regard. The essentially regular, monotonous iambics which Sidney himself had used in the *Arcadia,* and which every poet since the time of Surrey had been bound by, clearly offered very little to interest the ear of a poet who had been schooled in the complex harmonies of Virgil. "Ryme" can perhaps achieve for English verse some of the same effects which the "well-weyed" syllables of classical poetry had created; but Sidney's way of putting the matter suggests that he accepts the limitations imposed by fundamentally inflexible iambics with considerable reluctance.[42] Ideally, he would relish meters that could indeed "expresse divers passions"—meters capable of communicating strong feeling in a way that is analogous to the action of devices like apostrophe and *prosopopoeia,* or the forms of narrative and drama. Such meters would be another important means of achieving Energia, that general vigor of language which reveals the genuinely engaged passions of a writer.

Once we have a clear idea of Energia, and of the important role it plays in Sidney's conception of poetry, we can begin to observe some of the ways in which it bears upon his actual writing. We should

notice, first, that Energia makes its appearance in Sidney's work long
before he discussed it in the *Apologie*:

> And Lorde, deare Cossyn (sayde hee) dothe not the pleasant-
> nes of this place, carry in yt self sufficyent Rewarde, for any
> tyme lost in yt. . . ? Doo yow not see the grasse, howe in
> Coloure they excell the Emeraudes every one stryving to passe
> his fellowe, and yet they are all kept in an equall heighte? . . .
> Ys not every Eccho here a perfect Musick? and these fressh and
> delightfull brookes, how slowly they slyde away, as, lothe to
> leave the Company of so many thinges united in perfection,
> and with how sweete a Murmer they lament theyre forced de-
> parture: Certeynly, certeynly Cossyn yt must needes bee, that
> some Goddess this Dezert belonges unto, who ys the sowle of
> this soile. . . .[43]

> Shall I that saw Eronae's shining haire
>   Torne with her hands, and those same hands of snow
>   With losse of purest blood themselves to teare,
> Shall I that saw those brests, where beauties flow,
>   Swelling with sighes, made pale with minde's disease,
>   And saw those eyes (those Sonnes) such shoures to shew,
> Shall I, whose eares her mournefull words did seaze,
>   Her words in syrup laid of sweetest breath,
>   Relent those thoughts, which then did so displease? . . .
>   (OA 30)

In the first of these passages, Prince Pyrocles celebrates the beauties
of Arcadia in prose that is characterized chiefly by its Energia. Nearly
all the devices which Aristotle and Scaliger mention are present: the
apostrophes, the strong sense of dialogue, the exclamations and emphatic repetitions, the direct addresses, the "interrogations," and *prosopopoeias* (of the grass, the brooks), the "direction of speech to inanimate objects," and the eloquent rhythms of the whole. Pyrocles,
like King David in the *Psalms*, "sheweth himselfe a passionate lover"
of a landscape that recalls both David's "leaping" hills and Sidney's
Apologie description of that golden world which poetry "delivers" to
men. In the second passage quoted above, Sidney's formal rhetoric,
with its powerful repetitions and forceful rhythms, creates a vigor-
ously expressive poetry of passion which continually sets objects
before our eyes; we "see" Erona's plight, and we are made to concur
in the shepherd Boulon's reply:

> Thy wailing words do much my spirits move,
> They uttred are in such a feeling fashion,
> That sorrowe's worke against my will I prove.
>
> (OA 30)

The *Arcadia*, then, possesses Energia, but it is Energia of a rather special sort. Emotion is primarily expressed in the elaborately ornate, formal ways which suited the demands of Sidney's pastoral romance, but which were not directly transferable to other contexts. The stylized gestures of high rhetoric, the diffuse and incantatory technique employed in the sestinas and other poems, worked well enough in the remote, idealized realm of Arcadia. A quite different tone and manner were necessary, however, when Sidney chose to write *in persona propria*, as a member of Elizabeth's court. Moreover, all the sources of Energia which the Arcadia's prose narrative supplied—the "tale," the clash of characters in argument, the vivid descriptions and actions—would no longer be immediately available. Sidney's problem, in effect, was to discover ways in which the courtly love lyric could be shaped to express something of the passion and drama which animated the *Arcadia*, and yet to do so with all the polish, ease, and wit required of a courtier among his familiars.

Sidney took the most natural way he knew. He simply began to create in verse that ironic, intimate tone and manner which we can discover in the prose of the narrator's portions of the *Arcadia*, as well as in the *Apologie for Poetry*. In addition, he imported into the sonnet and related lyric forms the dramatic energy typical of so many Arcadia eclogues.[44] The achievement of the *Certain Sonnets* is that they come very close to fusing these diverse elements—to establishing a dramatic, poetic voice which takes courtly conversation for its norm, but which can rise easily to higher strains of praise and grief, or fall to more colloquial outbursts of anger and sarcasm:

> Sweet Ladie, as for those whose sullen cheare,
>   Compar'd to me, made me in lightnesse found:
>   Who Stoick-like in clowdie hew appeare: . . .
>
> But now the starres with their strange course do binde
>   Me one to leave, with whome I leave my hart.
> I heare a crye of spirits faint and blinde, . . .
> Wo, wo to me, on me returne the smart: . . .
> Ah saucy paine let not thy errour last, . . .
> O faire, O sweete, when I do looke on thee,

> In whom all joyes so well agree,
> Heart and soule do sing in me.

The voice is still unperfected, but it is Sidney's, and it manages transitions from familiar tones of address ("Sweet Ladie") to more formal ones ("O faire, O sweete") to abrupt exclamations and imperatives ("Wo, wo to me, . . .") with no great strain. The accomplishment was an important one. It gave to the speaker of a group of lyrics a poetry both supple and various enough to express the conflicting feelings of a courtier in love. It intimated that Sidney might well search for his chief sources of Energia in the situations, moods, and emotions of a single, fully articulated love story and, ultimately, in the conversational, dramatic speech of that story's hero. Sidney's first steps in the new mode were tentative, and we need not exaggerate the quality of the verse in the *Certain Sonnets* to understand its importance. Despite the collection's considerable variety, most of the lyrics are undeniably pedestrian. Sidney had adopted the principle of using a dramatic voice—of approximating courtly conversation—as his main source of poetic energy, but he was still far from working out the full implications of that choice in terms of style.

The change from the *Certain Sonnets* to *Astrophel* was promoted by his further reflection on the possibilities of the lyric as a form for the expression of those powerful and conflicting feelings which lay at the heart of all his writings on love. The commitment to a norm of courtly conversation led him necessarily to seek a greater fluency in his verse, a greater approximation to the phrasing patterns of actual speech. It was this search which must have forced his invention of the new, irregular iambic line. If G. L. Hendrickson and John Thompson are correct, Sidney understood the subtle technique of counterpoint between accent and metrical *ictus* in Latin dactylic hexameters, and he successfully imitated the effect in his own experiments with that meter in English.[45] When his early attempt to domesticate Latin quantitative measures was finally abandoned, he managed to create a similar form of counterpoint in native iambics—the system of stress-variation as we know it in late Elizabethan and post-Elizabethan poetry: a constant interplay between speech accent and the established metrical norm, giving the iambic line an internal dynamics it had never before possessed. Sidney's determination to discover forms which could "expresse divers passions" for persuasive purposes thus led finally to the invention of a prosody which could communicate subtler shades of feeling with different kinds of power than the essentially regular meters he had used in the *Arcadia* and the *Certain Sonnets*. His lines could now accommodate the irregularities of ordinary speech rhythms, thereby adding variety to the music of his verse, and yet they might still retain (when desired) a high degree of courtly formality and stateliness. Finally, a general freedom of syntax, a broadening of the usable range of vocabulary, and a bolder use of the sonnet were equally natural consequences once Sidney had decided to let his speaker's changing moods and feelings direct the flow of essentially dramatic verse.

If dramatic speech or conversation was to be the new poetry's main source of Energia, however, Sidney did not at all want to forgo the other sources of Energia mentioned in our analysis of the *Apologie*. The emphasis there was on the importance of dramatic situation, on tales, on what Aristotle called "setting the object before the eyes," on the sense of activity and of things being "present," on characters like Medea and Ajax who act out their feelings of revenge or anger with such vividness that "wee seeme not to heare of them, but cleerely to see through them." The new poetry was to retain, if possible, all these other senses of dramatic as well, and Sidney's desire to do so led to his invention of what was really a new form in English—the so-called dramatic lyric and its sequence. It is no accident that *Astrophel* is the most carefully plotted and the most overtly dramatized of all the English sonnet sequences. Sidney wanted a hero whose tale would be played out before us, whose love would be rendered with such immediacy that it could not help but move and persuade:

> Flie, fly, my friends, I have my death wound; fly,
> See there that boy, that murthring boy I say,
> Who like a theefe, hid in darke bush doth ly, . . .

> Alas have I not paine enough my friend,
>   Upon whose breast a fiercer Gripe doth tire
>   Then did on him who first stale down the fire, . . .

> Vertue alas, now let me take some rest,
> Thou setst a bate betweene my will and wit, . . .

> O how for joy he leapes, ô how he crowes, . . .

> Stella, whence doth this new assault arise,
> A conquerd, yelden, ransackt heart to win?

> With how sad steps, ô Moone, thou climb'st the skies,
> How silently, and with how wanne a face, . . .

> Be your words made (good Sir) of Indian ware,
> That you allow me them by so small rate?

> This night while sleepe begins with heavy wings
> To hatch mine eyes, and that unbitted thought . . .

> Out traytour absence, darest thou counsell me,
> From my deare Captainnesse to run away?

We know enough of Energia now to feel its presence immediately in Sidney's lines. In *Astrophel*, the action is always present and the objects continually set before our eyes. The exclamations, sharp questions, apostrophes, abrupt openings, the "direction of speech to inanimate objects" ("ô Moone"), the sense of particular places and times ("This night while sleepe")—all of these have found their way into a lyric poetry which is fully dramatic. The whole is endowed with a lively "demonstrative" quality: the activity of Astrophel arguing, pointing, praising, gesticulating, and pleading. We know his voice, witness his tale, and accept the Energia of his verse as the sign of his passion. As Lamb said long ago:

> (Sidney's sonnets) are not rich in words only, in vague and unlocalised feelings—the failing too much of some poetry of the present day—they are full, material, and circumstantiated. Time and place appropriates every one of them. It is not a fever of passion wasting itself upon a thin diet of dainty words, but a transcendent passion pervading and illuminating action, pursuits, studies, feats of arms, the opinions of contemporaries and his judgment of them. An historical thread runs through them . . .; marks the *when* and *where* they were written.

Sidney's achievement in *Astrophel* can hardly be overestimated. His hero is the first fully realized, poetically conceived character in modern English literature. Astrophel's irony and energy are evident everywhere in his verse; the accents of his speech are recognizable from sonnet to sonnet, and are themselves the music of his poetry. In him, Elizabethan literature came of age: a standard had been set, and a living personality who "conversed" in poetry had been created. The level of Gascoigne, or even of Wyatt and Surrey, would never again seem the best that the new English literature could produce. Sidney's success in *Astrophel*, however, was not the result of a new attitude towards style on his part. *Astrophel* was a natural development upon the style which Sidney first began to fashion in the *Certain Sonnets*, at a time when he was still at work upon the *Arcadia*. The same sensitivity to questions of decorum, and the same attempt to wed "manner" to "matter" underlay all three works.

NOTES

1. *The Complete Works of William Hazlitt*, ed. by P. P. Howe, 21 vols. (London, 1931), VI, p. 236.
2. *Ibid.*, p. 320.
3. "Some Sonnets of Sir Philip Sydney," *The Works of Charles and Mary Lamb*, ed. E. V. Lucas, 7 vols. (New York, 1903), II, p. 218.
4. See "The Poetry of Sir Philip Sidney," *ELH*, XII (1945), pp. 251-79.
5. *Sir Philip Sidney as a Literary Craftsman* (Cambridge, Mass., 1935), p. 186.
6. *Ibid.*, p. 52.
7. *Ibid.*, pp. 151-2.
8. *Symmetry and Sense: The Poetry of Sir Philip Sidney* (Austin, Texas, 1961), p. 12.
9. *Ibid.*, p. 64.
10. *Sir Philip Sidney as a Literary Craftsman*, p. 189.
11. *The Correspondence of Sir Philip Sidney and Hubert Languet*, transl. by Steuart A. Pears (London, 1845), pp. 19-20.
12. *Ibid.*, p. 23.
13. *Ibid.*, p. 201.
14. Most scholars, including Sidney's editor Mr. William Ringler, tend to accept Sidney's phrase "My toyfull books" as a reference to the *Arcadia*. Albert Feuillerat transcribes the phrase as "My toyfull booke" in his edition of the letters: see *The Complete Works of Sir Philip Sidney*, 4 vols. (Cambridge, Eng., 1912-26), III, p. 132. All future references to this edition will be cited simply as "Feuillerat."
15. *The Poems of Sir Philip Sidney*, ed. by William Ringler (Oxford, 1962). Quotations from Sidney's verse are from this edition, hereafter cited as "Ringler." I have adopted Ringler's abbreviations, and have in general simply referred to Sidney's poems according to Ringler's numerical system: OA = *Old Arcadia*; CS = *Certain Sonnets*; AS = *Astrophel and Stella*.
16. Feuillerat, IV, pp. 186-7.
17. See AS 1, 3, 6, 15, and 74, as well as the remarks in *An Apologie for Poetrie*, ed. by Evelyn Shuckburgh (Cambridge, Eng., 1891), pp. 57-9. This edition is hereafter cited simply as *Apologie*.
18. Ringler, pp. xxxv-xxxvi.

19. *Apologie*, p. 57.
20. *Ibid.*, p. 57.
21. *Ibid.*, pp. 57-8.
22. See Ringler, pp. 423-4.
23. *Apologie*, p. 57.
24. *Ibid.*, p. 19-21.
25. *Ibid.*, p. 41.
26. *Ibid.*, p. 33.
27. *Ibid.*, pp. 6-7.
28. Shuckburgh glosses the phrase as "putting the words dramatically now into the mouth of one person and now in that of another" (*Apologie*, p. 82). This is a possible reading, but it overlooks the fact that "persons" probably bears its grammatical sense here: first person singular (I), etc. Apostrophe was the rhetorical figure which most obviously involved "changing" of persons. Peacham defined it as "a sudden removing from the third person to the second." See Henry Peacham, *The Garden of Eloquence* (1593), intro. by W. Crane (Gainesville, Fla., 1954), p. 116.
29. *The Art of Rhetoric*, III.ii. 2-III.xi.4.
30. See Louise Osborn, *The Life, Letters, and Writings of John Hoskyns* (New Haven, 1937), p. 126.
31. Julius Caesar Scaliger, *Poetices Libri Septem* (1561), intro. by August Buck (Stuttgart, 1964), pp. 117-18. There is no published translation of Scaliger's discussion of Energia. I am indebted to Mr. John Shea of Harvard for the version used in my text.
32. *Ibid.*, pp. 118-19.
33. *Ibid.*, pp. 116-17.
34. *Ibid.*, p. 117.
35. *Apologie*, p. 26.
36. *Poetices Libri Septem*, pp. 117-19.
37. *Apologie*, p. 18.
38. *Ibid.*, p. 17.
39. *Ibid.*, p. 25.
40. *Ibid.*, p. 27.
41. *Ibid.*, p. 60.
42. For a full discussion of the development of the iambic line in the sixteenth century, see John Thompson, *The Founding of English Metre* (London, 1961).
43. Feuillerat, IV, pp. 12-13.
44. For a discussion of the full details of this development, see my own longer study, *Sidney's Poetic Development* (Cambridge, Mass., 1967).
45. See Thompson's *Founding of English Metre*, pp. 128-38, and Hendrickson's "Elizabethan Quantitative Hexameters," *PQ*, XXVIII (1949), pp. 237-60.

C. S. LEWIS

Hero and Leander

Chapman's four books or sestiads on Hero and Leander are, I believe, very seldom read in conjunction with Marlowe's two. The whole temper of modern criticism, which loves to treat a work of art as the expression of an artist's personality and perhaps values that personality chiefly for its difference from others, is unfavourable to a poem by two authors. It comes naturally to us to treat the total *Hero and Leander* as two separate works. Nor, of course, is there any reason why we should not do so. There are some composite works—for example, the *Romance of the Rose*—which are best dealt with in this way. But there are others such as our composite English *Morte d'Arthur*, where earlier English work and French work and Malory and Caxton so subtly grow together into "something of great constancy" that the modern approach is baffled. I am not claiming that *Hero and Leander* is in that class. We know quite well which parts are by which poet, their styles are clearly distinct, there is no "contamination" (in the textual sense), and pseudo-Musaeus is so far in the background that we can ignore him. Yet I think we shall be richly rewarded if we obey the apparent invitation of the old editions and read the poem, at least sometimes, as a whole. For here, as I shall try to persuade you, collaboration has produced an extremely fortunate result. Each poet has contributed what the other could not

Reprinted by permission from *Proceedings of the British Academy*, XXVIII (1952), pp. 23-37.

have done, and both contributions are necessary to a worthy telling of the story. For the difference in style and outlook here corresponds to the two movements of which that story consists. If we feel young while we read the first two sestiads and feel in the remaining four that youth has died away, our experience is very like Hero's. If Venus dominates Marlowe's narrative and Saturn that of Chapman, the same may be said of the events which each narrates. It is almost, as it ought to be, like passing from a Song of Innocence to a Song of Experience.

Of course, when we speak of "innocence" in connexion with the first two sestiads we are using the word "innocence" in a very peculiar sense. We mean not the absence of guilt but the absence of sophistication, the splendour, though a guilty splendour, of unshattered illusions. Marlowe's part of the poem is the most shameless celebration of sensuality which we can find in English literature—unless we extend the category of literature to include such works as the booksellers call "curious." It does not even keep within the bounds of what might be called, either in the older or the modern sense, a "kindly" sensuality. It exults to see

> the gods in sundrie shapes
> committing headdie ryots, incest, rapes   (I. 143),

and the loves of Neptune in Sestiad II are what Saintsbury called "Greek style." The point need not be laboured. A critical tradition which can stomach the different, but far worse, depravities of *Tamberlaine*, can well put up with *Hero and Leander*. The question which Marlowe's sestiads invite is not a moral one. They make us anxious to discover, if we can, how Marlowe can write over eight hundred lines of almost unrelieved sensuality without ever becoming mawkish, ridiculous, or disgusting. For I do not believe this is at all easy to do.

Marlowe's success is most easily seen if we compare him with other sixteenth-century specimens of the erotic epyllion. Lodge's *Scillaes Metamorphosis* is hardly good enough: despite its frequent beauties it is too static and too lacrimose. Drayton's *Endimion and Phoebe* suffers from discordant aims and even discordant styles. We shall have to come to *Venus and Adonis*. And I must frankly confess that, in so far as the two works are comparable at all, Marlowe seems to me far superior to Shakespeare in this kind. *Venus and Adonis* reads well in quotation, but I have never read it through without feeling that I am being suffocated. I cannot forgive Shakespeare for telling us how Venus perspired (175), how "soft and plump" she was, how moist her hand, how Adonis pants in her face, and so forth. I cannot conceive why he made her not only so emphatically older but even so much larger than the unfortunate young man. She is so large that she can throw the horse's rein over one arm and tuck the "tender boy" under the other. She "governs him in strength" and knows her own business so badly that she threatens, almost in her first words, to "smother" him with kisses. The word "smother," combined with these images of female bulk and strength, is fatal: I am irresistibly reminded of some unfortunate child's efforts to escape the voluminous embraces of an effusive female relative. It is, of course, true that there are touches of reality in Shakespeare's poem which cannot be paralleled in Marlowe's. But I am not sure that reality (in the sense of naturalism) is what a poem of this type demands: at any rate, naturalism such as Shakespeare gives. Shakespeare shows us far too much of Venus' passion as it would appear to a third party, a spectator—embarrassed, disgusted, and even horrified as any spectator of such a scene would necessarily be. No doubt this unwelcome effect comes in because Shakespeare is, in general, a far profounder and more human poet than Marlowe. His very greatness prevents his succeeding in the narrow and specialized world of erotic epyllion. But it suits Marlowe exactly. He does not see beyond the erotic frenzy, but writes from within it. And that, curiously enough, is his poetic salvation.

In reading *Venus and Adonis* we see lust: in reading Marlowe's sestiads we see not lust but what lust thinks it sees. We do not look at the passion itself: we look out from it upon a world transformed by the hard, brittle splendour of erotic vision. Hence all that sickly weight and warmth which makes unrestrained appetite in the real world so unpleasant to the spectator or even, perhaps, in retrospect to the principals themselves, does not appear at all. Instead of Shakespeare's sweating palms and poutings and pantings and duckings and "lustful language broken" and "impatience" that "chokes the pleading tongue" we have a gigantic insolence of hyperbole. The real world, which Shakespeare cannot quite forget, is by Marlowe smashed into bits, and he makes glory out of the ruin. Hero has been offered Apollo's throne. The brightness of her neck makes a collar of pebbles shine like diamonds by reflection. The sun will not burn her hands. The ladies of Sestos, walking in procession, make the street a "firmament of breathing stars." In that world there are boys so beautiful that they can never drink in safety from a fountain: the water nymphs would pull them in.

If you compare these hyperboles with one of Shakespeare's you will easily see the difference. His Venus promises Adonis that her hand will "dissolve or seem to melt" in his. That, of course, is hyperbolical, but it is in touch with fact—with the fact that hands may be hot, moist, and soft. But Marlowe's hyperboles are so towering that they become mythopoeic. They have, none the less, their own wild consistency and co-operate in building up such a world as passion momentarily creates, a topsy-turvy world where beauty is omnipotent and the very laws of nature are her willing captives. This mythopoeic quality is reinforced by Marlowe's use of what may be called the aetiological conceit, as in his passage about Mercury and the fates at the end of I, or his explanation why "since *Heroes* time hath halfe the world been blacke." Though the whole two sestiads celebrate the flesh, flesh itself, undisguised, rarely appears in them for long. Leander's beauty is presented half mythically: he is a prize like the golden fleece, his body is as "straight as Circe's wand," and the description of him shines with the names of *Nectar, Pelops, Jove,* and the cold *Cinthia.*

With this style there go two other characteristics. One, of course, is the metre—a ringing and often end-stopped couplet, compared with which the stanza of *Venus and Adonis* is unprogressive and the enjambed couplets of *Endymion* invertebrate. I suspect that the masculine quality of the verse, in fruitful tension with the luxury of the matter, plays an important part in making so much pure honey acceptable: it is a beautiful example of Wordsworth's theory of metre. The other is the total absence of tenderness. You must not look in Marlowe for what Dryden called "the softness of love." You must, indeed, look for love itself only in the narrowest sense. Love here is not "ful of pittie" but "deaffe and cruell": his temple is a blaze of grotesques. Leander woos like "a bold sharpe sophister." The male and immortal lover who first tries to ravish him, ends by trying to kill him. Hero is compared to diamonds, and the whole work has something of their hardness and brightness. Marlowe sings a love utterly separated from kindness, *cameraderie,* or friendship. If female spiders, whose grooms (I am told) "do coldly furnish full the marriage breakfast," wrote love-poetry, it would be like Marlowe's. But, however shocking, this treatment is an artistic success. We know from some terrible scenes in Keat's *Endymion* how dangerous it is to attempt the mixture of tenderness and sensuality in verse. Licentious poetry, if it is to remain endurable, must generally be heartless: as it is in Ovid, in Byron, in Marlowe himself. If it attempts pathos or sweetness an abyss opens at the poet's feet. Marlowe never comes near that abyss. His poem, though far from morally pure, has purity of another sort—purity of form and colour and intention. We may feel, as we come to the end of the Second Sestiad, that we have been mad, but we do not feel that we have been choked or contaminated. And yet I believe that the final impression left on an adult's mind is not one of madness or even of splendour, but, oddly enough, of pathos. If we had caught Marlowe striving after that effect in such a poem we should perhaps have turned from him in contempt. But it is not so. What moves us is simply our knowledge that this passionate splendour, so insolent, so defiant, and so "unconscious of mortality," is "desperately mortal."

That it was doomed, for Hero and Leander, to end in misery Marlowe of course knew well. He wrote only the first movement of the story, the ascending movement; how he would have handled the descent we do not know. If he was to do it successfully, he would have had to use powers not found in the first two sestiads: would have had to "change his notes to tragic." The necessity of this change, even had he lived, renders tolerable the still greater change, the change to another author, which now meets us at the beginning of the Third Sestiad. If ever one poet were to "take over" from another, no happier juncture could be found. At the very moment when the theme begins to demand a graver voice, a graver voice succeeds.

In his Dedicatory Epistle Chapman describes himself as drawn "by strange instigation" to continue Marlowe's work. From a line in the Third Sestiad (195), when he describes himself as "tendering" Marlowe's "late desires," some conclude that Marlowe had asked Chapman to finish the poem. But it is not at all clear why this should be called "strange instigation." Perhaps Chapman poetically feigned, or (quite as probably) actually believed, that he had been strangely instigated by Marlowe since Marlowe's death. I am certainly inclined to think that when, in the same passage, he sends his own genius ("thou most strangely-intellectual fire") to "confer" with Marlowe's "free spirit" in the "eternall clime,' he is speaking seriously: believing, like Scaliger and others, that a man's *genius* is a personal, immortal creature, distinct from himself. But the question is not of great importance. The poetic impulse which moved Chapman to write is quite clear from his own sestiads as a whole, and especially from the open-

ing lines of the Third. And it was essentially an impulse to continue,
to finish. We cannot doubt that he had entered into Marlowe's erotic
poetry with the fullest (temporary) sympathy. But, to his graver
mind, it cried out for its sequel. As he says

> Joy grauen in sence, like snow in water wasts.   (III. 35)

It had fallen to Marlowe to tell of joy graven in sense, it fell to him to
tell of the wasting. Love, or such love as Hero's and Leander's, is in
Chapman's eyes "a golden bubble full of dreames" (III. 231): he will
show how it burst.

I do not think we should regard this as a "cauld clatter of morality"
officiously and unpoetically added to a poem which does not require
it. There are several reasons against doing so. The most obvious is the
fact, already mentioned, that the myth itself already contained a tragic
ending. The second is that the picture of headlong love presented by
Marlowe demands some nemesis poetically no less than morally.
Every man who sees a bubble swell, will watch it, if he can, till it
bursts. A story cannot properly end with the two chief characters
dancing on the edge of a cliff: it must go on to tell us either how, by
some miracle, they were preserved, or how, far more probably, they
fell over. I do not mean that Chapman would have put it to himself
quite like that. Conceiving poetry as a kind of philosophy, he would
have been content with a purely ethical justification for his sestiads.
I mean that even if we banish, as he would not have banished, all
moral considerations, our aesthetic interests would still demand a second, downward, movement. Finally, we must remind ourselves that
the particular moral content which Chapman put into his part of the
poem was not nearly so platitudinous for him as it would have been
for a nineteenth-century poet.

Chapman's sestiads are a celebration of marriage in contrast to, and
condemnation of, the lawless love between Hero and Leander. We
are in danger of taking this as a thing of course. It was not so in Chapman's day. When writers like Lyly and Greene fall into a fit of moralizing they are quite likely not to make a distinction between lawless
and wedded love, but to attack love and women altogether in the old
ascetic, misogynistic manner which goes back to St. Jerome. When
Sidney's heroes struggle against love they too are concerned less with
the distinction between lawful and unlawful than with the baseness
or unmanliness of the passion itself as something contrary to the heroic ideal. In taking the line he does, which is the same as Spenser's,

Chapman is therefore doing something not without importance. It may have given him more trouble than it gave Spenser, for there are passages in his plays which suggest that the old conceptions of courtly love could still come to life in his mind. His part of *Hero and Leander* is to be taken as the product of serious thought.

It is especially to be noted that his doctrine is no facile warning against enchantments which he could not feel. This is one of those things which a poet can show only by the actual quality of his writing, and Chapman does so. Time and again he writes lines of an extravagant sweetness which Marlowe could not surpass. As this:

> Musick vsherd th'odorous way,
> And wanton Ayre in twentie sweet forms danst
> After her fingers.
> (V. 42)

Or when the Athenian maidens have been carried off by robbers and, at the same hour the stars are coming out,

> the yellow issue of the skie
> Came trouping forth, ielous of crueltie
> To their bright fellowes of this vnder heauen.
> (ibid. 171)

When Hymen hands the lily to Eucharis,

> As two cleere Tapers mixe in one their light,
> So did the Lillie and the hand their white.
> (ibid. 221)

A girl's skin is "softer than soundest sleep." Leander, dripping from his swim, runs to his sister "singing like a shower," and as the white foam drops off him

> all the sweetened shore as he did goe
> Was crownd with odrous roses white as snow.
> (III. 81)

I am not saying that the quality in all these is exactly like Marlowe's. Chapman has his own slower movement and his own type of conceit; he is nearer than Marlowe to the metaphysical manner. But they are not less rapturous and exalted than Marlowe's. If Chapman does not permanently abandon himself to "golden bubbles," it is not because he could not. He knows what he rejects.

This rejection is not in any way that I can discover based on Christian grounds. And this is not to be explained by the fact that the story is Pagan and involves the Pagan deities. That would have presented no difficulties to a medieval or Elizabethan poet if he had wished to christianize it. The gods and goddesses could always be used in a Christian sense, as they are in *Comus* or in *Reason and Sensuality*. If Chapman had wished to theologize, chastity embodied in Diana or divine reason in Minerva would have descended to rebuke Leander. The figure who actually appears to him is someone quite different—the goddess Ceremonie. To a modern Englishman, I suspect, no abstraction will seem less qualified for personification and apotheosis. We do not—at least that class of Englishmen who study literature do not—perform ceremonies gracefully, nor attend them with much enthusiasm, and we doubt whether any ceremony can modify the nature of the act which it accompanies. The Elizabethan sentiment was very different. About ceremonies in the Church there might be some dispute: but even there the Puritans objected to them not so much because they desired a pure, individual inwardness as because they thought that a Divine positive law excluded certain ceremonies. In secular life ceremony reigned undisputed. The chroniclers describe ceremonies at length as if they were equal in importance to the gravest political events. And so perhaps they were. Pageant, masque, tournament, and emblem book taught men to expect a visible and formalized expression of every rank, emotion, attitude, and maxim. One quarrelled, loved, dined, and even played by ceremonial rule. The Ciceronian in Latin and the Euphuist in English made prose a ceremony. The universe itself with its noble and base metals, its sublunary and translunary regions, and the nicely graded hierarchy of planetary intelligences, was a vast ceremony proceeding in all space and all time. It is in ceremony that Shakespeare's "Degree" and Spenser's "Concord" are manifested.

Chapman condemns the loves of Hero and Leander not because the pair were ill matched, nor because they lacked the consent of parents, nor because he admires virginity, nor by the Christian law, but only because, being hasty and not waiting for marriage, they had defied *Time* and *Ceremonie*. *Time* must, of course, here be understood as meaning "the right time," "timeliness," the Latin *opportunitas*: it is very close to Elyot's virtue of *maturitie* (*Boke of the governour*, 1. xxii), and its connexion with Ceremonie becomes plainer if we remember that it is one of the virtues which, in Elyot's scheme, we learn

from dancing. Chapman takes great pains to make us understand his
point of view. Ceremonie, for him, is what distinguishes a fully human action from an action merely necessary or natural. As he says, no
praise goes to the food which "simply kills our hunger" or the dress
that "clothes but our nakednes." We reserve praise for "Beautious
apparell and delicious cheere." Thus unexpectedly the goddess Ceremonie, who forbids lawless *luxuria*, is from another point of view almost the patroness of luxury—the ordered, humane luxury of evening
dress, and choice wines, and good cookery. The embraces of Hero and
Leander were, after all, only a coarse meal snatched by ravenous
hunger "with ranke desire" (III. 49). Here, as everywhere else, it is
the humanized and "ordred" procedure that "still giues pleasure
freenes to aspire" and

> Vpholds the flowrie bodie of the earth
> In sacred harmonie.
> (ibid. 61)

The whole "bench of Deities" (the planets) hang in the hair of this
goddess. Devotion, Order, State, Reuerence, Societie, and Memorie,
are her shadows. Chapman sees her as our defence against utter ruin
and brutality: as Shakespeare sees Degree. And, as in the *Dunciad* the
enemies are always creeping on, so here we see Confusion, and (close
on her heels)

> Barbarisme and Auarice
> That followd eating earth and excrement
> And humane lims.
> (ibid. 138)

We are told that they would soon storm the palace of the gods "were
Ceremonie slaine." It is tempting to say that Ceremonie is simply
Chapman's name for civilization. But that word has long been prostituted, and if we are to use it we must do so with a continual reminder
that we mean not town-planning and plumbing and ready-cooked
foods but etiquette, ball-rooms, dinner-parties, judges' robes and wigs,
Covent Garden, and coronations in Westminster Abbey. In a word,
we must realize that what we should regard as the externals of civilization are, for Chapman, essential and vital. The simplest way of
doing this is not to use the word *civilization* at all but to retain his
own word *ceremonie*, remembering what he meant by it.

It is early in the Third Sestiad that Ceremonie appears to Leander.

The remainder of that sestiad and the whole of the next are concerned with Hero's remorse and deterioration—a passage to which I
must presently return. Up to the end of the Fourth, Chapman is occupied with his negative theme, the condemnation of lawless, uncere-
monial, love. In the Fifth we have the positive side, the celebration
of the lawful and ceremonial alternative, marriage. The contrast is
pointed for us first by the fact that Hero (who has now resolved on a
life of consistent hypocrisy) exercises her priestly function by marrying two young lovers and afterwards attending their marriage feast.
To this feast, apparently unbidden, there comes a very curious person. She is called a nymph but has rather the characteristics of a sixteenth-century English fairy. She is a "little Siluane," known as
Apollo's "Dwarfe," a haunter of "greene Sestyan groues," a prophetess.
Her name is Teras: that is *monstrum*, portent, prodigy. From that
point of view she continues, in a personified form, the sinister omens
which have harassed Hero in the preceding sestiad; and her function
at the banquet is fulfilled when she left the company and

> the turning of her back
> Made them all shrieke, it lookt so ghastly black.
> (V. 489)

Seen from the front she had been beautiful: in other words, the one
omen that had appeared to be good turns out to be bad, and Hero's
fate is sealed. But between her pleasing entry and her terrifying exit
she has exercised another function. Perched on an altar she has entertained the marriage party with the tale of another marriage, which
marriage in its turn (this sestiad is constructed like a Chinese nest of
boxes) was between Marriage himself, Hymen, and Eucharis, was in
fact the archetypal marriage. Much of it is concerned with mystical
explanations of Pagan marriage ceremonies: a sort of learning dear to
the Elizabethans. The only thing in it which calls for comment is the
part played by the girl Adolesche—Garrulity, or Chatterbox, who had
a face

> Thin like an iron wedge, so sharpe and tart
> As twere of purpose made to cleaue Loues hart.
> (ibid. 299)

This unpleasant young woman hurried off to Athens to spread the
news of the love between Hymen and Eucharis, but arrived just as
their marriage feast was ending and found no market for her scandal.

She sank beneath her disappointment and was promptly metamorphosed into a parrot. The meaning of this little fable is, I suppose,
obvious. Adolesche tries to play the part played by the tale-bearer or
losengier in an affair of courtly love, but fails because marriage comes
in between her and her hopes. Chapman is pointing out that marriage
settles the old problem of the *losengier*. From this tale Teras, her terrible back still hidden, turns to sing her Epithalamion: in a sense the
heart, though not the climax, of Chapman's story, and perhaps the
finest lyric he ever wrote. He never praised Night more deliciously;

> O come soft rest of cares, come night,
> Come naked vertues only tire,
> The reaped haruest of the light,
> Bound vp in sheaues of sacred fire.

This summary is intended to make clear that Chapman's part of
Hero and Leander is, as we should expect, a doctrinal and philosophical poem, very seriously meant by the poet. Much invention has gone
to the creation of a new mythology which embodies his doctrine.
Venus' motive for treating so sternly an offence which she, of all goddesses, might be expected to have pardoned is too trivial and too
merely mythological for so grave a story: but with that exception the
"plot" (if one may so call it) is watertight and enables Chapman to
say what he wanted to say. But, of course, all this will be unavailing
if the actual texture of the writing fails to please.

It must be admitted that Chapman has his bad moments. The
worst is when, in Sestiad VI. 197, Neptune suddenly jumped up and
"for haste his forehead hit Gainst heauens hard Christall." We might
at least have been spared the adjective *hard*; it is for most of us too
painfully, and therefore too comically, reminiscent. Of course, what
Chapman means is to tell us, in conceited language, that the waves
rose heaven-high. The influence at work here is, I have little doubt,
that of Du Bartas. Chapman is trying the Bartasian technique which
consists in representing things great and superhuman in the most
humdrum and anthropomorphic terms. I do not think we should continue to laugh at that technique as our fathers did. The French poet,
after all, bequeathed it to our admired Metaphysicals. Marvell's vigilant *patrol* of stars, Donne's liberated soul that "baites not at the
Moone," Herbert's representation of Christ as an innkeeper, are all
Bartasian in character. Elsewhere Chapman is more successfully
Bartasian. To tell us that the moon rose, he says:

> The saffron mirror by which Phoebus loue,
> Queen Tellus decks her, now he held aboue
> The clowdy mountaines.

(V. 406)

It should be noticed that the lines which I quoted a moment ago from the Epithalamion are really of the same sort:

> The reaped haruest of the light,
> Bound vp in sheaues of sacred fire.

The image, when we work it out, is Bartasian; daylight is mowed like a field at evening and the harvest is tied up into those sheaves which we call stars.

Of course, Chapman is not more conceited than Marlowe had been: he is conceited in a different way. His style admirably exemplifies the transition from the pure Elizabethan manner to that of the Metaphysicals. It can, as earlier quotations have perhaps shown, display on occasion all the old abandonment and sweetness. But in general it is slower, weightier, more difficult. And Chapman, when he first comes on the stage at the opening of Sestiad III, very wisely explains the difference so that, with a little goodwill, one may take it as a change arising from the story itself and not merely from change of authorship.

> More harsh (at lest more hard) more graue and hie
> Our subiect runs and our sterne *Muse* must flie.
> Loues edge is taken off. . . .

The last phrase is curiously happy, for it applies not only to the experience of Hero and Leander but to that change in English poetry with which Chapman's succession to Marlowe coincides. The old love for a poetry of pure deliciousness was, indeed, losing its edge. Honey began to pall. That is why a movement either to the more violent and knotty poetry of Donne or to the harder and severer poetry of Milton was necessary. In that way the composite *Hero and Leander* is a kind of bridge. The English Muse herself loses her innocence in the process of telling how Hero lost hers.

The new effect "more hard, more graue and hie" depends on several changes. The most obvious is that of metre. Marlowe uses some enjambment, but I think he is happiest, most irresistibly himself, when he is most end-stopped: here, as in his plays, the superb single line is his characteristic glory—"The sweet fruition of an earthlie crowne," "To entertaine diuine Zenocrate," "Who euer lov'd that lov'd not at first sight?" When there is a run-over it seldom adds much music. But Chapman can write true verse paragraphs in couplets, and the pauses are well managed. There is also a far greater intrusion of philosophical and reflective matter: fifteen lines on optics in the Third (235 et seq.), nine on the nature of beauty (99 et seq.), and eighteen on the properties of numbers (323 et seq.) in the Fifth. These will be unwelcome to the modern reader, but the last is relevant to Chapman's intention, and if we cared as much as our ancestors did for Arithmosophy (so to call it), it might please. We can also find in Chapman passages of a saturnine realism, which, in their own way, strengthen and, as it were, thicken the poem: the sketch of Adolesche has already been mentioned. You may add the description of women talking at a funeral in the tale of Teras (V. 185 et seq.). Yet after all, these detachable passages count for less than that habitual cast—by no means a pale cast—of thought, which mixes with the normal flow of the narrative. A phrase like "forme-giuing Cypria's siluer hand" (V. 314) is typical. Silver connects it with the old style, the style of Marlowe: but forme-giuing lets in the whole doctrine of the archetypal Uranian Venus and the influence of the third heaven. Chapman is taking his Venus more seriously than Marlowe would have done. When he has to describe a woman yielding to a wholly legitimate love, he says

> The bribde, but incorrupted Garrison
> Sung Io Hymon.
> (V. 253)

There is a concentration of thought in "bribde but incorrupted" which it would be hard to find in Spenser, Sidney, or the young Shakespeare. If we could purge the word "cleverness" of the sneering overtones that it has unfortunately acquired, I should say that Chapman's poetry is almost everywhere cleverer than Marlowe's: his imagination not less stimulated by the senses but more stimulated by ideas. The following describes the moment at which Hero's remorse weakens and a reaction in favour of Leander begins.

> And all this while the red sea of her blood
> Ebd with Leander: but now turnd the flood,
> And all her fleete of sprites came swelling in

With childe of saile, and did hot fight begin
With those seuere conceits she too much markt,
And here *Leanders* beauties were imbarkt.
He came in swimming painted all with ioyes
Such as might sweeten hell: his thought destroyes
All her destroying thoughts.
(III. 323 et seq.)

The splendour of the first line and a half has been praised before.
What I would rather draw your attention to is the manner in which,
throughout, the ideas and images catch fire from one another: how
the ebb leads to the flood, and then the flood no longer exists for itself but carries a fleet, and the swelling of its sails leads to "with
childe of saile" and thence to a sea fight, and thence back to Leander,
now swimming again; but all this not for ornament, as it might be in
a long-tailed epic simile, but closely presenting the movement of
Hero's mind.

This passage comes among the lines—there are nearly five hundred
of them—which Chapman devotes to Hero in her solitude, in the
Third and Fourth Sestiads. This is on the whole the high-light of his
poem. The process of her degeneration is well conceived. It begins in
blank despair, at first neither hopeful nor desirous of concealment,
then passes to a long stillness, then to the reaction which I have just
quoted which leads at once to the delusive belief that all will yet
(somehow) be well. After that comes the resolution to be a hypocrite.
It is, as I say, well conceived: but it is presented not after the fashion
of the novelist nor even as Chaucer would have done it. It reaches us
through an intricate pattern of conceit, symbol, and myth, much commented on and generalized. The method seems to me highly successful. The first despair is expressed in a tragic conceit which could not
be bettered—

She was a mother straight and bore with paine
Thoughts that spake straight and wisht their mother slaine.
(III. 227)

The prolonged and static misery which follows is not directly described at all. What we are actually shown is simply Hero's dress and
Hero's pose—the robe of black "Cypres," "exceeding large," the left
hand clasping it at her breast, the bent head, the knees "wrapt in
vnshapefull foulds." It is a method proper to painting but equally

proper to narrative poetry: we respond to it with our muscular as well
as with our visual imagination. In the next sestiad we see her tricked
out again in her priestly garments and working with her needle. We
are told little about what she felt during this period of false hope, but
we are made to feel it for ourselves because every picture her needle
makes is truer than her conscious mind will confess—

> These omenous fancies did her soule expresse,
> And euery finger made a Prophetesse.
> (IV. 108)

After that comes the ill-omened sacrifice, the resolve to act a part, and
the apparition of Venus. Out of Hero's torn robe and torn hair there
rises up in the altar fire a new creation, a "mayd most fayre," girdled
with snakes and ending in the scorpion's tail. It is Eronusis, Dissimu-
lation. The thing that Hero's mind has conceived now stands before
her, like Athene sprung from Jove's head or Sin from Satan's. We are
in the world of nightmare. Yet still

> Betwixt all this and *Hero, Hero* held
> *Leander's* picture as a Persian shield.
> (ibid. 345)

The truth and unexpectedness of this conclusion are surely admirable.

It will be seen that Chapman has his own, highly personal, technique for narrative poetry. It stands about midway between the continuous allegory of Spenser and the phantasmagoric poetry of the
moderns. He can mingle at will direct psychological description, full-
blown allegory, and emblematic picture. Once we accept it, we do not
find ourselves confused. For me at least it has great potency. I do not
know that I can find exactly the same sort of power anywhere else.

I must, of course, be careful not to claim too much. Neither Marlowe's nor Chapman's part of *Hero and Leander* is anything like a
faultless poem. Here, as always (most inexcusably in his Homer),
Chapman is too digressive: he is often obscure, always mannered,
sometimes ridiculous. He clogs his lines with consonants. He indulges
in that curious sort of false rhyme to which Mr. Simpson devoted an
article. As for Marlowe's part, it is, after all, a beautiful monstrosity:
a thing which, even if no moral objections are felt, can win admission
to the mind only in a particular mood. Even in that mood we shall
admit, if we are quite honest, that it lasts just a little too long. But
heaven forbid that we should never read—and praise—any poems less

than perfect. Marlowe's part, with all its limitations, is a very splendid and wonderful expression of accepted sensuality: Chapman's a very grave and moving reply—an antithesis, yet arising naturally, almost inevitably, out of the thesis. My main concern is not to assess the absolute merit of either but to suggest the propriety of reading the composite poem as a whole. I first made that experiment twenty, or it may be nearer thirty, years ago: repeating it the other day, I found my old delight renewed and even deepened. Hence this lecture. I ask you to admire the lucky accident, if it was no more, which, at that particular moment in the history of poetry, brought together upon that particular story two poets so necessary to one another for enabling us to live through the process which that story embodies. I recommend all who have not done so to read the old book, for once, in the spirit of children to whom a book is an ultimate and who, never thinking even of one author, would not care whether two or twenty-two had written it.

Shakespeare's Banquet of Sense

Alas! why lent not heaven the soul a tongue?
Nor language, nor peculiar dialect,
To make her high conceits as highly sung?
But that a fleshly engine must unfold
A spiritual notion.   .   .   .   .
O, nature! how dost thou defame in this
Our human honours, yoking men with beasts,
And noblest minds with slaves; thus beauty's bliss,
Love and all virtues that quick spirit feasts
Surfeit on flesh; and thou that banquet'st minds,
Most bounteous mistress, of thy dull-tongued guests
Reap'st not due thanks.

CHAPMAN, Ovid's Banquet of Sense

"Self-schooled, self-scanned, self-honored, self-secure," Arnold calls Shakespeare. These epithets have poetic validity, though we no longer, like critics of the seventeenth century, consider Shakespeare a literary changeling, owing parentage and schooling only to Nature and Fancy. But in establishing his real parentage and the probable

From *Shakespeare and Spenser* (Princeton, 1950), pp. 3-24. Reprinted by permission of the Princeton University Press; Copyright, 1950, by Princeton University Press. A concluding section on *Antony and Cleopatra* has been omitted.

extent of his schooling, in the whole process of humanizing him, historical scholars sometimes unintentionally give the impression that Shakespeare's real aim in writing was obligingly to illustrate all the literary and social conventions of his day. Ever since Theobald they have been invaluable in revealing sources and analogies, usually less convincing in determining the metamorphosis of those sources in Shakespeare's own work. And this second task, though it can be accomplished with only relative success, is more important. The citation of a source or analogy is but the starting point for literary criticism.

At least we know now that Shakespeare was not a genius operating in a literary vacuum, and not so untaught as Ben Jonson's "small Latin and less Greek" implies. No University Wit himself, Shakespeare knew many of that select circle; however difficult to demonstrate satisfactorily, he must have been deeply affected by personal and professional associations with them. The safest evidence is in his own writing, and the most illuminating is that which shows the impact of a current literary mode on Shakespeare's individual poetic temperament, so far as we can deduce that temperament from the constant study of the whole body of his work. Evidence of this kind is the player's speech about Hecuba in *Hamlet*:

> But who, O, who had seen the mobled queen
> Run barefoot up and down, threat'ning the flame
> With bisson rheum, a clout about that head
> Where late the diadem stood, and for a robe,
> About her lank and all o'er-teemed loins,
> A blanket, in the alarm of fear caught up;—
> Who this had seen, with tongue in venom steep'd,
> 'Gainst Fortune's state would treason have pronounc'd. . . .[1]

This speech, significantly based on the *Aeneid*,[2] reduces the player to tears and draws an extraordinary panegyric from Hamlet:

> For the play, I remember, pleas'd not the million; 'twas caviare to the general; but it was—as I receiv'd it, and others, whose judgement in such matters cried in the top of mine—an excellent play, well digested in the scenes, set down with as much modesty as cunning.

Such commendation of an extravagant, bombastic vein by the most intellectual of Shakespeare's characters has bewildered thoughtful students of the play; the tone of the praise is so personal that it seems to be Shakespeare himself speaking. Bradley analyzes in some detail many suggested interpretations.[3] More recently, Grierson maintains that the speech represents "Shakespeare's conception of classical tragedy, something that moved on loftier buskins than would suit a play at the Globe Theatre or his own taste for life and reality."[4] That Shakespeare had a taste for life and reality does not preclude an interest in more formalized "literary" modes, or the implication that he may really have wanted to write in this vein; in fact, the genuineness of his desire is attested by his two early, self-consciously literary poems, *Venus and Adonis* and the *Rape of Lucrece*, and it can readily be proved that his interest in current literary modes never left him, though the modes are more perfectly assimilated in his mature work.

In *Venus and Adonis* Venus is so shocked to discover Adonis wounded that she sees double:

> "My tongue cannot express my grief for one,
> And yet," quoth she, "behold two Adons dead!
> My sighs are blown away, my salt tears gone,
> Mine eyes are turn'd to fire, my heart to lead:
>   Heavy heart's lead, melt at mine eyes' red fire!
>   So shall I die by drops of hot desire."

This anticipates the high wrought Hecuba vein, and such a line as

> Variable passions throng her constant woe

is exactly the sort of rhetoric deplored in eighteenth century poetry by the Romantic critics who have a neat way of blaming un-Shakespearean passages in Shakespeare on other men—"This is not Shakespeare; let the chips fall where they may."

We find in *Venus and Adonis* this elaborate yet beautiful image:

> Or, as the snail, whose tender horns being hit,
> Shrinks backward in his shelly cave with pain,
> And there, all smother'd up, in shade doth sit,
> Long after fearing to creep forth again;

followed by a couplet which is dubious:

> So, at his bloody view, her eyes are fled
> Into the deep-dark cabins of her head.

To explain precisely why I find the first four lines successful poetry and the final couplet dubious would require an elaborate analysis out of place here; for, while it is an essential critical technique, intellectual analysis, unless it is constantly and somewhat tediously tested against the poem, is liable to become skillful rationalization, self-indulgence of the intellect at the expense of the poem. A few suggestions will suffice.

Venus instinctively recoils from the realization of her anticipated dread, Adonis' death, shutting her eyes at the sight of his wounds.[5] The snail image, though a daring conceit, shows both emotional and imaginative correspondence with Venus' recoil; if there is any emotion at all in the following couplet, it is melodramatic violence inconsistent (despite the equivalence suggested by *so*) with the preceding emotion, while the imagistic correspondence is literal and rationalistic. We are led away from Venus' closing eyes by the snail image, so delicate and elaborate that it draws attention to itself; even so, the tenderness and timorous shrinking from pain fuse both images, the snail and Venus' eyes, and the incidental correspondence between shell and skull we absorb without visualization. In his attempt in the couplet to bring us back to Venus, Shakespeare makes unfortunately explicit and visual what the snail image had subtly suggested; we see too clearly the eyesockets of her skull—"'the deep-dark cabins of her head" —into which her personified eyes are fleeing. However ingenious the conception may be, it is frigid; and the elaboration through two more stanzas anticipates Cowley's cold-blooded, protracted autopsy of a conceit.

The fault in this couplet is not the conceit, which is successful in the snail image; nor is it the highly wrought language. All his life Shakespeare indulged in rhetoric from time to time, either for its own sake or to indicate a certain quality of emotion; but the rhetoric in *Venus and Adonis* is disconcerting because it does not seem to be always intentional or under full control. Much of the poem fails where *Hero and Leander* succeeds, yet the partial failure of *Venus and Adonis* is illuminating.

Shakespeare at this period is immature and overambitious. He is straining for effect and consequently ill at ease. One suspects that his head is in the poem but not his heart. He seems carried out of his own element by his admiration for Ovid and for Marlowe's recapture of the Ovidian spirit in *Hero and Leander*. Marlowe's Ovidianism, like classic drama, is as much caviar to Shakespeare as to the general, though I think he would have been reluctant to admit it, just as some ten years later the *Hamlet* passage suggests reluctance to give up entirely a drama moving "on loftier buskins than would suit a play at the Globe Theatre."

Ovid unquestionably affected Shakespeare profoundly. "The whole character of Shakespeare's mythology," according to Mr. Root, "is essentially Ovidian."[6] But in *Venus and Adonis* he is at once too close to Ovid and Marlowe and too far removed from them. He could not accept the Ovidian spirit either pure or in Marlowe's Italianate version, and he had not yet learned to transmute it. Marlowe seems to be the immediate cause of the difficulty. Despite Shakespeare's immense debt to him, the minds of the two poets, their imaginations, their emotional quality, their interests, are on the whole fundamentally different. Both are passionate and intense, but in different ways and about different aspects of life. Marlowe is more intellectual; his mind is more single in focus and narrow in range. Literary allusion and imagery have for him, for Spenser, and for Milton deeper imaginative meaning than they ever have for Shakespeare, who is more emotional than intellectual, more interested in people than in books. The Ovidian tradition is essentially literary. Marlowe is completely at home in it; Shakespeare is not, though he tries to be in *Venus and Adonis*.

It has often been remarked that what vitality the poem has[7] is due to the nature imagery drawn from firsthand observation of fields and woods. Shakespeare is inferior to Marlowe in intellectualized, artificial imagery; Marlowe is incapable of the Shakespearean type, such as the snail image, the hare, the hounds, the horses, the divedapper, the caterpillar, the blue-veined violets, and especially this:

> Lo, here the gentle lark, weary of rest,
> From his moist cabinet mounts up on high,
> And wakes the morning, from whose silver breast
> The sun ariseth in his majesty.

The artifice of "moist cabinet" is in keeping with the poem; yet it is interesting to find the more characteristically Shakespearean expression of the same image not long after in *Sonnet 29*:

> .   .   .   the lark at break of day arising
> From sullen earth, sings hymns at heaven's gate,

and many years later, in *Cymbeline*, the final transmutation:

> Hark, hark! the lark at heaven's gate sings,
>   And Phoebus 'gins arise,

> His steeds to water at those springs
> On chalic'd flowers that lies.

Quite apart from growth in poetic maturity, this last passage shows perfect assimilation of a literary image with one of natural observation, an assimilation conspicuously absent in most of *Venus and Adonis*. In attempting to combine a conservatory atmosphere and the out-of-doors, an ornate style and simplicity of observation, Shakespeare may have had in mind something more than merely another Ovidian poem, or something different, but he fails to bring it off.

The limitations of Marlowe's *Hero and Leander* are the limitations of its genre, the full imaginative, sensuous, and humorous possibilities of which he exploits; the poem embodies, as Mr. Bush says, the best qualities of the Italianate Ovidian tradition, along with its vices.[8] This tradition derives as much from the *Amores* as from the *Metamorphoses*, as much from the sensualist as from the excellent storyteller. *Venus and Adonis*, for instance, combines two fables from the *Metamorphoses*, Venus and Adonis and Salmacis and Hermaphrodite, while its motto is from the *Amores*.[9] In *Hero and Leander* Marlowe sacrifices characterization and flow of narrative to sensuous elaboration for its own sake and to contemplative sensuality. He does not care about consistency. Leander is sexually innocent part of the time merely for the piquancy of the situation; otherwise he speaks with the authority of the "Professor of Love." Both lovers, in fact, are hardly presented in individual terms at all; they are primarily instruments for subtle sensuous and sensual impressions. And for this reason Marlowe, unlike Ovid, removes all prosaic traces, so that the sensual is presented as unadulterated beauty. Miss Ellis-Fermor says: "The poet of *Hero and Leander* does not 'look before and after,' much less does he 'pine for what is not.' . . . Beauty is enough, and the love of beauty is neither an instinct in conflict with moral preoccupations and dark, obscure fears, nor a poignant devotion to a threatened and possibly doomed cause."[10]

Curiously enough, of the other Elizabethans Spenser rather than Shakespeare comes closest to catching this spirit, only of course in moments when he is morally off-guard, as in a few stanzas of the Bower of Bliss and the Gardens of Adonis, or in his description of Leda and the Swan in the House of Busyrane:

> Then was he turnd into a snowy Swan,
> To win faire Leda to his lovely trade:

O wondrous skill, and sweet wit of the man,
That her in daffadillies sleeping made,
From scorching heat her daintie limbes to shade:
Whiles the proud Bird ruffing his fethers wyde,
And brushing his faire brest, did her invade;
She slept, yet twixt her eyelids closely spyde,
How towards her he rusht, and smiled at his pryde.[11]

Even in these unguarded moments Spenser sometimes shows, if not explicitly, at least in the tone of his verse, an unconscious repulsion in the fascination—a repulsion totally absent from *Hero and Leander*. This portrait of Cymochles is the true Spenserian sensualist:

He, like an Adder, lurking in the weeds,
His wandring thought in deepe desire does steepe,
And his fraile eye with spoyle of beautie feedes;
Sometimes he falsely faines himselfe to sleepe,
Whiles through their lids his wanton eies do peepe,
To steale a snatch of amorous conceipt,
Whereby close fire into his heart does creepe:
So, them deceives, deceiv'd in his deceipt,
Made drunke with drugs of deare voluptuous receipt.[12]

We have only to compare Cymochles with Leda to see the difference; his sensuality is more mental than physical. The sense of moral danger and the emotional connotations of *adder* are not found in Spenser's Leda or in Ovid or in Marlowe. They are not present in Spenser's account of Venus and Adonis in a tapestry of the Castle Joyous in the first canto of the Third Book of the *Faerie Queene*:

And whilst he slept, she over him would spred
Her mantle, colour'd like the starry skyes,
And her soft arme lay underneath his hed,
And with ambrosiall kisses bathe his eyes;
And whilest he bath'd, with her two crafty spyes,
She secretly would search each daintie lim,
And throw into the well sweet Rosemaryes,
And fragrant violets, and Pances trim,
And ever with sweet Nectar she did sprinkle him.

So did she steale his heedelesse hart away,
And joyd his love in secret unespyde.

Though this is as non-moral as the Leda passage, it has a peculiar innocence lacking in Leda. Later, in the sixth canto, Venus and Adonis
become philosophical symbolism in a poetic account of creation, for
Spenser's allegory is protean. In the actual telling of the story Shakespeare owes him nothing, and the influence of Spenser's Ovidianism
is impossible to estimate. Shakespeare knew Spenser's poetry. He is
closer in spirit to Spenser than to Marlowe. But, while his debt to
Marlowe is abundantly evident, his relationship to Spenser is less susceptible to textual proof.

Miss Ellis-Fermor, tacitly assuming that progression in time is inevitably progression in quality, considers *Hero and Leander* the final
and perfect fruit of Marlowe's genius; she is troubled because she
finds it "beautiful and seductive, but not passionate or profound," and
insists that we do not know what he would have done with the poem
if he had finished it himself.[13] One thing is certain: he could hardly
have made the continuation more serious and profound without destroying the delicate balance of sensuality and humor which gives the
fragment that we have its miraculous tone.

This blend of pagan delight in sensuality, kept in bounds by the
polished restraint of verse, and urbane humor is rare in English poetry. It is achieved by Chaucer and Marvell and attempted by Byron
in *Don Juan*. Byron's sophistication, however amusing and witty,
seems immature when compared to that of his elders. Consider this
passage from *Hero and Leander*:

> To Venus, answered shee, and as shee spake,
> Forth from those two translucent cesternes brake
> A streame of liquid pearle, which downe her face
> Made milk-white paths, whereon the gods might trace
> To Joves high court.

Translucent cisterns for eyes and *liquid pearl* for *tears* are certainly
artificial; yet they are effective in Marlowe's poem, where all the imagery is artificial, highly wrought, as if by Yeats' Grecian goldsmith.
This aureate style is difficult to sustain without risking the absurd.
The tone established must be under complete control; it must be complex—serious delight in extravagance together with humorous awareness of that extravagance. The hyperbolical description of Hero's
buskins, with their chirruping water-filled sparrows, strains credulity;
but when we come shortly after to these lines describing Leander:

> His dangling tresses that were never shorne,
> Had they beene cut, and unto Colchos borne,
> Would have allur'd the vent'rous youth of Greece
> To hazard more than for the golden Fleece,

we begin to suspect latent humor, and our suspicions are confirmed by such couplets as this:

> And many seeing great princes were denied,
> Pyn'd as they went, and thinking on her died.

Any lingering doubt is banished by the deft ironic touches, which Byron should have envied:

> Still vowd he love, she wanting no excuse
> To feed him with delaies, as women use,
> Or thirsting after immortalitie—
> *All women are ambitious naturallie—*
> Impos'd upon her lover such a taske,
> As he ought not performe, nor she to aske.
>
> . . . .
>
> Albeit Leander rude in love, and raw,
> Long dallying with Hero, nothing saw
> That might delight him more, *yet he suspected*
> *Some amorous rites or other were neglected.*
>
> . . . .
>
> Where seeing a naked man, she scriecht for feare,
> *Such sights as this to tender maids are rare,*
> And ran into the darke herselfe to hide.
> *Rich jewels in the darke are soonest spide.*
> Unto her was he led, or rather drawne,
> By those white limmes, which sparckled through the lawne.
> The neerer that he came, the more she fled,
> *And seeking refuge, slipt into her bed.*

Shakespeare in *Venus and Adonis* is no more elaborate than Marlowe. Superficially considered, he seems to be trying for the same effect:

> Her two blue windows faintly she upheaveth,

and

> Once more the ruby-colour'd portal open'd,
> Which to his speech did honey passage yield;

> Like a red morn, that ever yet betoken'd
> Wreck to the seaman, tempest to the field.

Something may be said for the first image, despite the conceit; the second is both more frigid and more cloying than Marlowe's extravagances. As in Marlowe, there is often humorous awareness in the exaggeration. Desire lends Venus strength

> Courageously to pluck him from his horse,

and there is even Byronic colloquialism and bathos:

> "Sweet boy," she says, "this night I'll waste in sorrow,
> For my sick heart commands mine eyes to watch.
> Tell me, Love's master, shall we meet to-morrow?
> Say, shall we? shall we? Wilt thou make the match?"
> He tells her, no; to-morrow he intends
> To hunt the boar with certain of his friends.

Marlowe surpasses Byron in this sort of effect; Shakespeare only equals him. But the important point is that the humor in *Venus and Adonis* is sporadic and incidental rather than interfused throughout. Shakespeare wavers between taking himself too seriously and not seriously enough.

This wavering is symptomatic of his lack of perfect control; whether we attribute this to ignorance of exactly what he was after or to a failure in achievement makes no real difference. The same wavering is apparent in his handling of the two characters in the story. If the embryonic playwright intended to dramatize two conflicting points of view, as he does frequently in his plays with complete success, the result is fumbling; and we are profitably concerned only with the result.

Mr. Wilson Knight, preoccupied with what he calls "in-feeling," finds that "Adonis's blood-life is felt through his physique; he is, as it were, a body lighted from within, and you get more of a real physical existence than in Marlowe's description of Leander's nakedness."[14] He is right to the extent that Shakespeare does not limit himself to the beautiful but recognizes other aspects of physical relationship, though his recognition is not completely Ovidian. The most that can be said for the "real existence" of Adonis, physical or otherwise, is that he is an incomplete sketch of what might in a less confusing poem have been a characterization. Leander has no personality.

Shakespeare seems to have begun, like Marlowe, with the idea of frankly exploiting all the possibilities of the innocent young man in a sexual situation. Then, like Leander, Adonis suddenly and unexpectedly becomes a mouthpiece for wise aphorisms on love; we are not made to feel that these sentiments motivate his aversion from the beginning. The sacrifice of characterization in Marlowe we accept because we recognize a purpose; in Shakespeare the imperfect characterization remains confusing to the end, for the stated purpose appears accidental—one of several improvisations—and we are left wondering whether at certain critical points the poet is not using Adonis as a mask for his own conflicting emotions. I do not think that Mr. Knight clarifies the issue by calling the sensuousness of *Venus and Adonis* healthy "in the sense that Lawrence is, or tried to be, healthy"; and I completely disagree with his belief that "in *Venus and Adonis* and *Lucrece* Shakespeare gets his main sexual, and general, poles of reference clear."[15] Clarity of pole or reference is precisely what is lacking.

Venus is reminiscent of the sixth elegy of the Third Book of the *Amores* when she protests:

> "Fie, lifeless picture, cold and senseless stone,
> Well-painted idol, image dull and dead,
> Statue contenting but the eye alone,
> Thing like a man, but of no woman bred!"

She is right to an extent that Shakespeare can hardly have intended; throughout most of the poem Adonis is a "well-painted idol, image dull and dead," and the fact that the conditions of the story impose unresponsiveness on him is not sufficient explanation.

Mr. Knight points out that the poem "is written from the woman's view and the sensuous attractiveness is masculine."[16] He suggests a relation to the "heterosexual" sonnets, an explanation like Mr. Wyndham Lewis' that Shakespeare's "sex organization, his sentimentality was directed towards other men and not towards women."[17] Applied to *Venus and Adonis,* this generalization is facile, not taking sufficiently into account either the conditions of the story or the nature of the imagination. The "sensuous attractiveness" of Venus is by no means overlooked, though repugnance is stressed occasionally in a manner not fully explicable by a dramatic conception of Adonis' predicament. The modern tendency to go beyond a work of art to the "sex organization" of the artist should be judged with considerable

skepticism when it is so blandly confident as in Mr. Lewis. In his
book on the sonnets Mr. Young combats the psychoanalysts in their
own terms;[18] whether he or anyone can settle so delicate a matter with
complete success is debatable. Mr. Hubler considers the question with
admirable common sense.[19] It is not my purpose to enter the controversy beyond pointing out that, though as a man of the Renaissance
Shakespeare was cognizant of homosexuality, there is nothing in
Venus and Adonis comparable to the Neptune-Leander passage in
Marlowe's poem, and nothing in *Richard II* so frank and sympathetic
in treatment as the Piers Gaveston portrait in Marlowe's *Edward II*.[20]

The possibility of revulsion from the physical fact of sex is more
germane to the issue, and is a plausible explanation of the confused
emotional quality of *Venus and Adonis,* though not wholly convincing, since soon after Shakespeare writes with extraordinary frankness
Sonnet 151 to the dark lady:

> Love is too young to know what conscience is;
> Yet who knows not conscience is born of love?
> Then, gentle cheater, urge not my amiss,
> Lest guilty of my faults thy sweet self prove:
> For, thou betraying me, I do betray
> My nobler part to my gross body's treason;
> My soul doth tell my body that he may
> Triumph in love; flesh stays no farther reason,
> But, rising at thy name, doth point out thee
> As his triumphant prize. Proud of this pride,
> He is contented thy poor drudge to be,
> To stand in thy affairs, fall by thy side.
> > No want of conscience hold it that I call
> > Her "love" for whose dear love I rise and fall.

And much of the beauty of Juliet's speech on her wedding night
comes from her frank recognition of the physical:

> Come, civil night,
> Thou sober-suited matron, all in black,
> And learn me how to lose a winning match,
> Play'd for a pair of stainless maidenhoods.
> Hood my unmann'd blood, bating in my cheeks,
> With thy black mantle; till strange love grow bold,
> Think true love acted, simple modesty.[21]

The answer seems to be not so much refusal to accept the physical facts of love as inability to accept them entirely in Ovid's or in Marlowe's terms.

Shakespeare, who was to become the supreme master of emotional intensity, expresses Venus' passion thus:

> By this the love-sick queen began to sweat,
>
> . . . .
>
> Her face doth reek and smoke, her blood doth boil.

Adonis has a "sweating palm"; his breath is a "steam" on which Venus feeds "as on a prey." She denies that she lacks juice, and her heaving bosom is an earthquake. This suggests pantomimic portrayal of passion in the silent movie and is equally unconvincing. There is nothing wrong with sweat in a love scene; it adds to rather than detracts from Britomart as Spenser portrays her after her fight with Artegall, her helmet off and her hair loose. And it is not enough to say that Shakespeare, in moving the Ovidian poem outdoors, is seeking greater realism in showing the effect of a beating sun. He must have been aware of the humor of his exaggerations; but it is nervous, adolescent humor, not fully controlled. Partly he seems to be horsing in order to conceal his inability to preserve detachment. The whole tone of these passages suggests neither intensity of passion nor mock-heroic, but the satire of Donne's

> Ranke sweaty froth thy Mistresse's brow defiles,[22]

or Aldous Huxley's humorous repulsion:

> Two lovers quietly sweating palm to palm.[23]

It is difficult to accept *Venus and Adonis* as conscious, sustained satire on the Ovidian tradition, and occasional satire is probably an accidental result of the strained tone of the poem. There is an opposite view. "Study of this poem alone, therefore, reveals the psychological centre of Shakespeare's work," according to Mr. Knight: "a love rather than a lust; a vital identification rather than a confined sense-relation whether of eye or touch, as in Marlowe's Leander; and this not limited to the beautiful, and thence by a rebound to the satirically ugly as in Marlowe, but dispassionately universal."[24] Though love considered as a vital identification rather than a confined sense-relation is characteristic of the later Shakespeare, it is not of *Venus and Adonis,* taken as a whole; and the rebound from the beautiful to the satirically ugly is consistently more characteristic of Shakespeare (especially in *Hamlet, Troilus and Cressida, Othello*) than of Marlowe. A further comment of Mr. Knight's on Shakespeare—that his "physical descriptions work outside sin-consciousness"—is not in the least applicable to *Venus and Adonis,* but fits perfectly *Hero and Leander.*

Physical contact, real or contemplated, which forms so much of the substance of the *Amores* and which Marlowe exploits to the full, Shakespeare either makes frenetic or shies from. Take this passage from the *Amores* (1.4):

> And don't allow him to place his arms about your neck, don't let your yielding head be on his rigid breast; and don't let your hidden charms submit to his touch; and, more than all, don't let him kiss you—not once. . . . Bring not thigh near thigh, nor press with the limb, nor touch rough feet with tender ones.

The closest parallel is not Venus' athletic exertions but other passages of Shakespeare's quite different in import, such as Hamlet's speech to Gertrude:

> Let the bloat king tempt you again to bed,
> Pinch wanton on your cheek, call you his mouse,
> And let him, for a pair of reechy kisses,
> Or paddling in your neck with his damn'd fingers,
> Make you to ravel all this matter out,[25]

and Iago's account to Othello of Cassio's supposed dream:

> And then, sir, would he gripe and wring my hand,
> Cry, "O sweet creature!" then kiss me hard,
> As if he pluck'd up kisses by the roots
> That grew upon my lips; then lay his leg
> Over my thigh, and sigh, and kiss; and then
> Cry, "Cursed fate that gave thee to the Moor!"[26]

The passage from Ovid portrays eminently natural sexual jealousy, together with a slightly perverse pleasure in that jealousy; the Shakespearean passages are an extreme combination of attraction and repulsion—the repulsion not latent, as in Spenser's description of Cymochles, but savagely dominant in imagery and emotional tone. In *Hamlet* and *Othello* the tone is clarified by the context; it is close to that of some parts of *Venus and Adonis* where, not completely clarified by context, it indicates a partially repressed or not fully recognized emotional current.

This current emerges in the most astonishing moment in any Ovidian poem, when Adonis with a passion and eloquence suddenly acquired turns finally on Venus:

> "Call it not love, for Love to heaven is fled,
> Since sweating Lust on earth usurp'd his name;
> Under whose simple semblance he hath fed
> Upon fresh beauty, blotting it with blame;
>   Which the hot tyrant stains and soon bereaves,
>   As caterpillars do the tender leaves.

> "Love comforteth like sunshine after rain,
> But Lust's effect is tempest after sun;
> Love's gentle spring doth always fresh remain,
> Lust's winter comes ere summer half be done;
>   Love surfeits not, Lust like a glutton dies;
>   Love is all truth, Lust full of forged lies."

This is the tune of moral Spenser or of Milton in *Comus,* not of Ovid or Marlowe; and the *quality of the poetry* shows the depth of feeling behind this speech. Yet the speech does not have the inevitability that it would have had in Milton, who knew from the beginning exactly what he was doing in *Comus.* It is hard to believe that the full dramatic surprise of this outburst is an effect calculated by the poet, or that Venus is meant to typify lust only.

II

In the *Rape of Lucrece,* his second poem, Shakespeare is concerned with lust, but in *Venus and Adonis* Venus is not consistently lust; she is fitfully an Ovidian, non-moral embodiment of sexual love, to which he is yet unable to add an indefinable purity. Shakespeare in his dilemma is responding to the current of his age; of all the poets of the Elizabethan Ovidian school, Marlowe alone accepts and embodies the Italianate Ovidian tradition. The clearest example of the northern humanist's divided loyalty to the classics and to morality is Golding's refuge in allegorical interpretation, the medieval solution. In the address to the reader prefixed to his translation of the *Metamorphoses,* which Shakespeare knew well, he cautions:

> By Bacchus all the meaner trades and handycraftes are meant:
> By Venus such as of the fleshe to filthie lust are bent.

Unlike Shakespeare, Golding was a Puritan. Still, if we judge from other poems in this tradition, the temper of the age was against taking Ovid straight. The first of the group, Thomas Lodge's *Scillaes Metamorphosis* (1589), a tepid pastoral, has little suggestion of Ovidian voluptuousness, first introduced boldly by Marlowe. Drayton's *Endimion and Phoebe* (1595), while showing familiarity with both *Venus and Adonis* and *Hero and Leander,* gives Ovidianism a Spenserian turn. According to Mr. Hebel, Drayton "introduces a conception of love different from both the courtly idealism of the sonnet and the voluptuous materialism of the mythological poem; he presents in concrete story the 'way of love' of traditional Platonism."[27] The most individual twist is given by George Chapman, who in *Ovid's Banquet of Sense* (1595) intellectualizes sensuality. With remarkable suavity Chapman weaves on a warp of philosophic idealism a woof of delicate but purely sensuous gratification.

Shakespeare in refusing to accept unmodified the Ovidian tradition is more typical than Marlowe of their age. We should make due allowance for historical considerations, but if we regard this ambitious early poem in the light of his subsequent work we shall find in Shakespeare's own poetic temperament an important explanation of these waverings and inconsistencies. He manifestly tries, yet cannot assimilate either the aureate style or the spirit of Ovid beyond a certain point. After Venus emerges from all the sweat and steam as a momentary apotheosis of Lust, she becomes in desertion a more sympathetic figure, though the poem still shifts disconcertingly from frigid conceits to moving pathos. For instances, she is guilty of this extravagance (an admiring imitation on Shakespeare's part):

> " 'Tis true, 'tis true; thus was Adonis slain;
>   He ran upon the boar with his sharp spear,
>   Who did not whet his teeth at him again,
>   But by a kiss thought to persuade him there;
>   And nuzzling in his flank, the loving swine
>   Sheath'd unaware the tusk in his soft groin. . . ."

But she can be more moving:

> "For he being dead, with him is beauty slain,
>   And, beauty dead, black chaos comes again."

Black chaos comes again is not Ovid's or Marlowe's phrase; it suggests another Shakespearean context which accomplishes with immediate success what these lines try to do:

> Excellent wretch! Perdition catch my soul,
> But I do love thee! and when I love thee not,
> Chaos is come again.

In this speech of Othello's Shakespeare has found himself. Love has become the principle of cosmos, a conception first dominant in Spenser.[28] Extreme physical passion, which fails of expression in Venus' Ovidian-styled speeches, is supreme here:

> O thou weed,
> Who art so lovely fair and smell'st so sweet
> *That the sense aches at thee. . . .*[29]

And seldom has intensity of the senses been so perfectly expressed as by Troilus, who is not Ovid's or Marlowe's but Shakespeare's sensualist:

> I am giddy; expectation whirls me round.
> The imaginary relish is so sweet
> That it enchants my sense; what will it be,
> When that the watery palates taste indeed
> Love's thrice repured nectar? Death, I fear me,
> Swooning destruction, or some joy too fine,
> Too subtle, potent, tun'd too sharp in sweetness
> For the capacity of my ruder powers.[30]

Shakespeare is no longer trying to master voluptuousness intellectually and present it in a style alien to him, as he was in *Venus and Adonis*; he is writing with perfect control in his own idiom about a kind of sensuality, less philosophically perceived than in *Ovid's Banquet of Sense*, but perhaps closer to Chapman than to Spenser, and certainly closer to both than to Marlowe or Ovid. Not only the expression but the spirit is transmuted. Troilus describes in anticipation an imaginary sensual gratification, which has, therefore, the mental contemplation characteristic of Ovid and Marlowe and Spenser's Cymochles. The effect is subtly different.

In Ovid there is basic cynicism, fear of satiety and tedium; desire again and again must be whetted by obstacles, even if those obstacles have to be created:

If you feel no need of guarding your love for yourself, O fool, see that you guard her for me, that I may desire her more! What one may not do pricks more keenly on. . . . What care I for the fortune that never troubles to deceive? May nothing be mine that never wounds! . . . I give you warning now in time: unless you begin to watch your lady, she will begin to cease being mine.[31]

All the husbands, guarding eunuchs, barred doors, gnawing jealousies are cultivated, for they are essential to what has become an elaborate game. And the obstacles are physical or mental, not moral, though morality enters in a curious way as part of the general awareness. However disarming in its frankness and humor, there is theatrical pose in such Rousseau-like confidences as this:

I would not venture to defend my faulty morals or to take up the armour of lies to shield my failings. I confess—if owning my shortcomings aught avails; and now, having owned them, I madly assail my sins. I hate what I am, and yet, for all my desiring I cannot but be what I hate; ah, how hard to bear the burden you long to lay aside!

For I lack the strength and will to rule myself; I am swept along like a ship tossed on the rushing flood. . . .[32]

Shakespeare attains a sophisticated fusion of wit, semi-seriousness, and mockery in *Twelfth Night* and other romantic comedies; he is temperamentally too intense and serious for Ovidian urbanity or a complex semi-serious tone where sensuality itself is concerned. In Troilus the mental and imaginative refinement of sensuality—"love's thrice repured nectar"—depends not even partially on artificial stimulation; it is a natural, irresistible force.

Mr. Stoll says that Shakespeare did not follow the tradition of Ovid that love is a game or chase, "the young man pursuing and the young woman fleeing—piteous or enticing when neglected, merry and scornful when wooed"; that "Shakespeare's lovers are faithful and constant, and despite some proverbial sayings in his text, the women are not fickle." He finds them free from Platonism and the love-philosophy of Dante, engaged in no subtilizing; he places them in the tradition "partly dramatic, as represented by Robert Greene and in some measure John Lyly, his predecessors, partly literary, as represented by Spenser in Una, Florimel, and Britomart, by Ariosto and the English and French chivalric and pastoral romances in prose and verse."[33] There is truth in this, especially since Mr. Stoll is primarily concerned with the lovers of the romantic comedies and tragi-comedies, though what he says is distorted by his protesting much too much against any taint of psychology.[34]

The comedies and tragi-comedies are not relevant to my purpose, since for the most part they do not stress the physical relation of love; still, it is significant that instinctive chivalry and faithfulness, emphasized by Mr. Stoll, are characteristic of middle-aged Othello as well as of youthful Troilus. Their nobility and idealism are just as instinctive as their sensuality. Both give an impression, if not of naïveté, at least of basic simplicity and of candor different from the artful candor of Ovid. That the characterization of Troilus is partly modified by the ironic outcome in preparation for him intensifies this typical Shakespearean blend of chivalric idealism and physical passion:

> O that I thought it could be in a woman—
> *As, if it can, I will presume in you—*
> To feed for aye her lamp and flames of love,
> To keep her constancy in plight and youth,
> Outliving beauties outward, with a mind
> That doth renew swifter than blood decays!
> Or that persuasion could but thus convince me
> *That my integrity and truth to you*
> *Might be affronted with the match and weight*
> *Of such a winnow'd purity in love,*
> How were I then uplifted! But, alas!
> *I um as true as truth's simplicity,*
> *And simpler than the infancy of truth.*[35]

This is far removed from Adonis—that mixture of Leander and prig and passionate protest.

Troilus, though no actual development of Adonis, resolves many of the tentative formulations and discordant emotions which were probably Shakespeare's when he sat down to rival Marlowe's Ovidian strain.[36] In Adonis, even apart from the conditions of the story, desire seems inhibited; in Troilus it burns with intense yet pure fire. Equally instinctive is his constancy, with no touch of Adonis' prudery. Cressida, understandably a little piqued at reiterated demands for a pledge of faithfulness, turns on her lover: "My lord, will you be true?" He answers:

Who? I? Alas, it is my vice, my fault.

. . . .

Fear not my truth. The moral of my wit
Is "plain and true"; there's all the reach of it.[37]

Troilus is no green youth; he knows the ways of the world, the temptations that Cressida will meet in the Greek camp; he is in his complexity, as Mr. Knight says, something of a "metaphysical lover."[38] But this sophistication he can apply only to others, not to himself, and it does not alter his instinctive idealism, a characteristic element of the Shakespearean sensualist, a beautiful and moving trait not without danger. Despite Shakespeare's care that we sympathize little with Cressida, human nature being what it is, such extreme intensity and seriousness in love almost asks, from all except an equally unusual woman, for the treatment which Troilus receives from Cressida. "Cressid, I love thee *in so strain'd a purity*" is an invitation to disaster.

Mr. Oscar Campbell dismisses brusquely what he calls the "pseudo profundities" of "contemporary searchers for the absolute in Shakespeare's works"; he is himself close to another kind of absolutism when he remarks that Shakespeare "has composed a chapter in a new *Ars Amatoria*" and that "a more realistic observer" would pronounce Troilus' speech in anticipation of the fruition of his passion simply " 'the agony of unsatisfied desire.' "[39] While Mr. Campbell speaks with more confidence about this and the reaction of the Elizabethan audience than one would expect from a historical critic, his study of the play is valuable, and his insistence on the weakness in Troilus' peculiar sensuality is in some measure justified. It is impossible to determine exactly how far Shakespeare himself was conscious of this weakness. Troilus is set off by the satirical tone of the play as Romeo is set off by the indecency of Mercutio and the Nurse; but in a complex drama Troilus' love is only one element. Its shipwreck is mainly due to circumstances beyond his control and to Cressida's nature; he does not share responsibility for the catastrophe to the degree that Romeo shares in the ruin of his love.

Othello, whom I consider to be another Shakespearean sensualist, so far as one is justified in isolating the type,[40] does show Shakespeare's awareness of the inherent weakness of "strain'd purity" yoked with physical passion. Mr. Stoll begs the question when he insists that jealousy in Shakespeare's lovers, specifically Othello, is the result of "no inner maladjustment or misunderstanding" but "injected into them."[44] It is profitless to imply that a lover like Othello might remain innocent in an environment as carefully controlled as the Garden of Eden before the Fall. That jealousy finds such rich soil in Othello's pure and idealistic mind is just as significant as that it took Iago to plant it there. The whole play shows Shakespeare's recognition of the danger as well as the beauty of this precarious balance of physical and spiritual.

NOTES

1. *Hamlet*, 2.2.525-34.
2. R. K. Root, *Classical Mythology in Shakespeare,* Yale Studies in English, XIX, p. 100.
3. A. C. Bradley, *Shakespearean Tragedy*, Macmillan, 1905, Note F, p. 413.
4. H. J. C. Grierson, *Cross Currents in English Literature of the Seventeenth Century*, Chatto and Windus, 1929, note, p. 102. Mr. Dover Wilson has contributed much perception and ingenuity to the debate.
5. "His bloody view," besides being unprofitably ambiguous, is even more inept than "passions throng her constant woe."
6. R. K. Root, *Classical Mythology in Shakespeare*, p. 3.
7. Coleridge's famous passage purportedly on *Venus and Adonis* and the *Rape of Lucrece (Biographia Literaria,* 15), except for commendation of the shooting-star image, which Shakespeare borrowed, defeats expectation. If Coleridge blankets the poems with approval, Swinburne is too severe, though more cogent, in his *Introduction* to the *Works of Chapman* (1875). "With all its overcrowding beauties of detail, Shakespeare's first poem is on the whole a model of what a young man of genius should not write on such a subject; Marlowe's a model of what he should."
8. Douglas Bush, *Mythology and the Renaissance Tradition in English Poetry,* University of Minnesota Press, 1932, p. 124.
9. R. K. Root, *Classical Mythology in Shakespeare,* pp. 31-32. Adonis' reluctance is not explicitly stated in any Continental version of the story, classical or Renaissance. It is transferred from Salmacis and Hermaphrodite, possibly at the suggestion of Lodge, who also uses the same verse form employed by Shakespeare in *Venus and Adonis.*
10. U. M. Ellis-Fermor, *Christopher Marlowe*, Methuen, 1927, p. 123.
11. *Faerie Queene,* 3.11.32.
12. *ibid.,* 2.5.34.
13. U. M. Ellis-Fermor, *Christopher Marlowe*, p. 127.

14. G. Wilson Knight, *The Burning Oracle,* Oxford University Press, 1939, p. 31.
15. *ibid.,* pp. 30-31. Mr. Knight has a tendency, curious in a critic so imaginative and sensitive to poetry, to abstract a mass of images from their context and to re-create from them, partly by rationalization, a luminous but sometimes baseless fabric.
16. *ibid.,* p. 34.
17. Wyndham Lewis, *The Lion and the Fox,* G. Richards, 1927, p. 153.
18. H. McC. Young, *The Sonnets of Shakespeare, a Psycho-Sexual Analysis,* Banta, Menasha, Wisconsin, 1937.
19. E. L. Hubler, Shakespeare, *Twenty-three Plays and the Sonnets,* Charles Scribner's Sons, 1938, pp. 1086-87. Mr. Hubler is preparing an edition of the sonnets.
20. Mr. Knight's and Mr. Lewis' statements, for instance, would be more applicable to Faustus' speech to Helen, quoted below, p. 127; Marlowe's focus seems to be primarily on Jupiter rather than on Semele and Arethusa.
21. *Romeo and Juliet,* 3.2.10-16.
22. John Donne, *Elegie VIII, The Comparison.*
23. Aldous Huxley, "Frascati's," *Leda,* Chatto and Windus, 1920.
24. G. Wilson Knight, *The Burning Oracle,* pp. 31-32.
25. *Hamlet,* 3.4.182-86.
26. *Othello,* 3.3.421-26.
27. J. W. Hebel, *Endimion and Phoebe,* Shakespeare Head Press, 1925, p. xiii.
28. This Platonic conception of love as the principle of cosmos is not only more dominant in Spenser; it is the basis of his idea of married love, which is considered in *Marriage Song,* pp. 207-8.
29. *Othello,* 3.3.90-92; 4.2.67-69.
30. *Troilus and Cressida,* 3.2.19-26.
31. Ovid, *Amores,* 2.19.
32. *ibid.,* 2.4.
33. E. E. Stoll, *Shakespeare's Young Lovers,* Oxford University Press, 1937, pp. 45 and 47.
34. *ibid.,* pp. 4, 5, 7, 13, 24, 98, 108, etc.
35. *Troilus and Cressida,* 3.2.165-77.
36. Adonis is *potentially* a serio-comic but sympathetic study in adolescence, like the early Romeo.
37. *ibid.,* 4.4.103 ff.
38. G. Wilson Knight, *The Wheel of Fire,* Oxford University Press, 1930, p. 69.
39. Oscar Campbell, *Comicall Satyre and Shakespeare's "Troilus and Cressida,"* Huntington Library, 1938, pp. 209-13.
40. Those who regard Falstaff as a type must consider him an exception

here. Though a great sensualist, Falstaff is not even remotely Ovidian; sex is less important to him than drink and food. And he is impervious to all but one idealization. As for Othello, he differs from Troilus and Antony in being a married lover; as such he is considered in *Marriage Song*, pp. 193 ff.

41. E. E. Stoll, *Shakespeare's Young Lovers*, p. 2.

L. C. KNIGHTS

Shakespeare's Sonnets

I

That there is so little genuine criticism in the terrifying number of books and essays on Shakespeare's Sonnets can only be partly accounted for by the superior attractiveness of gossip. A more radical explanation is to be found in certain widespread, more or less unconscious assumptions. In the first place, although consciously we may not believe that the Sonnets—even the first hundred and twenty-six—form a continuous and ordered collection, we tend to assume that the collection is more homogeneous than in fact it is, and we tend, therefore, to make rather sweeping generalizations about "The Sonnets" as a whole.[1] A second assumption was made amusingly explicit in the words that John Benson, the publisher of the 1640 edition—who had an eye on changing taste—addressed to the Reader: "In your perusall you shall finde them SEREN, cleere and eligantly plaine, such gentle straines as shall recreate and not perplex your braine, no intricate or cloudy stuffe to puzzell intellect, but perfect eloquence." Many of the Sonnets were written about the time of *A Midsummer Night's Dream* and *Romeo and Juliet;* the verse is therefore essentially unlike the verse of *King Lear*—it is incapable of subtleties; the meaning is on the surface. No doubt this is an exaggeration, but the effects of an assumption not very dissimilar to this can be seen in such essays as keep

From *Explorations* (London, 1946), pp. 40-65. Reprinted by permission of Chatto and Windus Ltd., and The New York University Press.

decently clear of William Hughes the sea cook, and the rest, and that attempt to approach the Sonnets directly, as poetry. George Wyndham, for example, in his essay on "The Poems of Shakespeare" does not entirely confine himself to pointing out the more picturesque aspects of imagery and the melodic effect of certain lines; but his criticism encourages the belief not only that such things have an intrinsic importance, but that visual imagery, "the music of vowel and consonant" and so on, have much the same function in the Sonnets as they have, say, in Spenser's stanzas on the Bower of Bliss. "Apart from all else, it is the sheer beauty of diction in Shakespeare's Sonnets which has endeared them to poets." Maybe (though they were endeared to Keats and Coleridge for other reasons, and Spenser, we remember, is the Poets' Poet); but the sentence illustrates the kind of limitation that the second assumption imposes: criticism is confined to a surface approach; it remains inappropriately and unnecessarily naïve. It is unfortunate that most readers are familiar with the Sonnets only in modern editions in which, as Laura Riding and Robert Graves pointed out, "the perversely stupid reorganizing of lines and regrouping of ideas"—all in the interests of "clarity"—is achieved by the simple expedient of altering the original punctuation.[2] In the Arden Edition the majority of deviations of this kind are not even recorded in the textual notes. The assumption is thus imposed and perpetuated by the common text.

If we can rid ourselves of these two presuppositions we shall have gone some way towards a revaluation of the Sonnets. "Shakespeare's Sonnets" is a miscellaneous collection of poems, written at different times, for different purposes, and with very different degrees of poetic intensity. (Gildon's edition had the appropriate title, *Poems on Several Occasions*.) The first necessity of criticism is to assess each poem independently, on its merits as poetry, and not to assume too easily that we are dealing with an ordered sequence. The second necessity is to know what kind of *development* to look for—which is a different matter.

I may as well say here that I believe all the Sonnets to be comparatively early in date—roughly from 1592 to 1597 or 1598; none of them is likely to have been written after the second part of *King Henry IV*.[3] We have no means of knowing how they came to be published by Thorpe in 1609 (J. M. Robertson made some attractive guesses), but the evidence suggests that the publication was unauthorized by Shakespeare, that the poems therefore had not been revised for publication, and that the arrangement adopted in the Quarto, except for the grouping of certain Sonnets that obviously go together, has no particular validity; although the printed sequence seems to represent a rough approximation to the time order in which they were composed. The possibility that some of the Sonnets—like *A Lover's Complaint,* which was published with them—are not by Shakespeare, is not likely to be disputed on *a priori* grounds by those who are familiar with the habits of contemporary publishers and the fortunes of authors' manuscripts in the sixteenth and seventeenth centuries. (The fate of the MS. of *Astrophel and Stella* is a common instance.) One can point to such things as the seventeenth-century poetical miscellanies with their haphazard assignment of authorship; and Cowley's Preface to the 1656 edition of his Poems begins with some interesting remarks in this connexion. But since there is no room for argument of this kind I assume a high degree of authenticity.

I I

I do not of course propose to employ my slender resources in the long-standing Southampton-Pembroke controversy and its subtle ramifications; but the popular view that the Sonnets are in some way "autobiographical" demands some notice. The eloquent chapters in which Frank Harris melts out Shakespeare's personal history from the poetic alloy ("The Sonnets give us the story, the whole terrible, sinful, magical story of Shakespeare's passion") are merely an exotic development of a kind of writing that is common among more eminent critics. "No capable poet," says Dr. Bradley, "much less a Shakespeare, intending to produce a merely 'dramatic' series of poems, would dream of inventing *a story like that of the Sonnets,* or, even if he did, of treating it as they treat it."[4] Now the first point that I wish to make against the common forms of biographical excursion (leaving aside for the moment more important considerations) is that the foundations on which they are built have not, to say the least, been the subject of any very discriminating attention. Those who are unwilling to accept the particular validity of Mr. Eliot's remark that "the more perfect the artist, the more completely separate in him will be the man who suffers and the mind which creates; the more perfectly will the mind digest and transmute the passions which are its material," backed though it is by the authority of Coleridge (compare *Biographia Literaria,* XV, 2), have only to turn to the Sonnets of supposedly highest biographical significance and consider them as examples of personal poetry: that is, as expressions by a powerful mind of reactions to a situation in which the man himself is deeply concerned.

Sonnets 33 to 42 are headed by Sir Israel Gollancz, "Love's First Disillusioning," the various sub-titles ending with "Forgiveness." Sonnet 42 runs:

> That thou hast her it is not all my griefe,
> And yet it may be said I lov'd her deerely,
> That she hath thee is of my wayling cheefe,
> A losse in love that touches me more neerely.

Since the obvious is sometimes necessary, we may say that if Shakespeare had suffered the experience indicated by a prose paraphrase (for some of the biographical school the Sonnets might as well have been in prose) it would have affected him very differently from *this*. The banal movement, the loose texture of the verse, the vague gestures that stand for emotion, are sufficient index that his interests are not very deeply involved. (Contrast the run and ring of the verse, even in minor sonnets, when Shakespeare is absorbed by his subject —"Devouring time blunt thou the Lyons pawes . . .") His sole interest is in the display of wit, the working out of the syllogism:

> Loving offendors thus I will excuse yee,
> Thou doost love her, because thou knowst I love her,
> And for my sake even so doth she abuse me,
> Suffering my friend for my sake to approove her,
>
> .   .   .   .   .
>
> But here's the joy, my friend and I are one,
> Sweete flattery, then she loves but me alone.

This, I admit, is a particularly glaring example, though it has its parallels amongst the False Friend and Faithless Mistress sonnets of "Group B" (Numbers 127-152) to which the notes commonly refer us at this point, and the complete insipidity of one "autobiographical" sonnet is enough to cause some honest doubt. Sonnets 78 to 86, dealing with the rival poets, are superior as poetry, but here also it is plain that Shakespeare derived a good deal of pleasure from the neatness of the argument:

> I grant (sweet love) thy lovely argument
> Deserves the travaile of a worthier pen,
> Yet what of thee thy Poet doth invent,
> He robs thee of, and payes it thee againe.

Wyndham remarked that these nine sonnets are "playful throughout, suggesting no tragedy"—though "playful" hardly does them justice. They are rather fine examples of an unusual mode of compliment and complaint, at once courtly and ironic. Those who picture Shakespeare as completely enthralled by his love for a particular friend or patron, and therefore deeply wounded by neglect, can hardly have noticed the tone of critical, and sometimes amused, detachment adopted towards himself ("Cleane starved for a looke"), the rival ("He of tall building and of goodly pride"), and the recipient of his verses ("You to your beautious blessings adde a curse, Being fond on praise, which makes your praises worse").

Of course I do not mean to imply that Shakespeare had never felt love or friendship or exasperation, or that his personal experiences had no effect on his poetry. One can hardly say of the Sonnets, as Johnson said of Cowley's *Mistress*, that "the compositions are such as might have been written for penance by a hermit, or for hire by a philosophical rhymer who had only heard of another sex." I am merely insisting that those who are attracted by biographical speculation should be quite sure of what Shakespeare is doing, of the direction and quality of his interests, before they make a flat translation into terms of actual life: that is, even the biographers must be literary critics. Some of the most interesting and successful sonnets may well have had their context in a personal relationship; but whenever we analyse their interest (further illustration at this point would involve a good deal of repetition later) we find that it lies, not in the general theme or situation, which is all that is relevant to a biographical interpretation, but in various accretions of thought and feeling, in "those frequent witty or profound reflexions, which the poet's ever active mind has deduced from, or connected with, the imagery and the incidents," in the exploration of a mood or discrimination of emotion. If this is so, the attempt to isolate the original stimulus (which in any case *may* have been an imagined situation—"Emotions which the poet has never experienced will serve his turn as well as those familiar to him") is not only hazardous, it is irrelevant. After all, even if Shakespeare had assured us that the Sonnets were written under the stress of a friendship broken and restored and an intrigue with Mary Fitton, the only importance they could have for us would be as poetry, as something *made out of* experience.

With this criterion of importance we can see in proper perspective a second argument—commonly offered as the only alternative to the biographical theory—that the Sonnets are exercises on conventional themes, embellished with conventional ornaments. The argument has a place in criticism, and we should be grateful to Sir Sidney Lee for his exhaustive collection of parallels. When we read

> Not marble, nor the guilded monument,
> Of Princes shall out-live this powrefull rime

it is perhaps as well that we should know that the lines have an ancestry reaching back at least as far as Horace; it is as well that we should be familiar with the theme of mutability and the various forms of diluted Platonism that were common when Shakespeare wrote. But a convention is a general thought, a general attitude, or a general mode of presentation, and a discussion of Shakespeare's Sonnets in terms of the "typical" Elizabethan sonnet sequence tells us no more about them than an account of the Revenge Play tells us about *Hamlet*.

III

The most profitable approach to the Sonnets is, it seems to me, to consider them in relation to the development of Shakespeare's blank verse. There are certain obvious difficulties: the Sonnets take their start from something that can, for convenience, be called the Spenserian mode, whereas the influence of Spenser on the early plays is both slighter and more indirect; and the dramatic verse naturally contains a good many elements that are not to be found in any of the Sonnets. But it is only by making what may seem an unnecessarily roundabout approach—even then at the risk of over-simplification— that one can hope to shift the stress to those aspects of the Sonnets that it is most profitable to explore.

No account of the development of Shakespeare's blank verse in general terms can be very satisfactory. A comparison will help to point my few necessary generalizations. Richard II's lament at Pomfret is a fairly typical example of the early set speeches:

> And here have I the daintiness of ear
> To check time broke in a disorder'd string:
> But for the concord of my state and time
> Had not an ear to hear my true time broke.
> I wasted time, and now doth time waste me;
> For now hath time made me his numbering clock:

> My thoughts are minutes; and with sighs they jar
> Their watches on unto mine eyes, the outward watch,
> Whereto my finger, like a dial's point,
> Is pointing still, in cleansing them from tears.
> Now sir, the sound that tells what hour it is
> Are clamorous groans, which strike upon my heart,
> Which is the bell: so sighs and tears and groans
> Show minutes, times, and hours: but my time
> Runs posting on in Bolingbroke's proud joy,
> While I stand fooling here, his Jack o' the clock.

The only line that could possibly be mistaken for an extract from a later play is the last, in which the concentrated bitterness ("Jack o' the clock" has a wide range of relevant associations, and the tone introduces a significant variation in the rhythm) serves to emphasize the previous diffuseness. It is not merely that the imagery is elaborated out of all proportion to any complexity of thought or feeling, the emotion is suspended whilst the conceit is developed, as it were, in its own right. Similarly the sound and movement of the verse, the alliteration, repetition and assonance, seem to exist as objects of attention in themselves rather than as the medium of a compulsive force working from within. Such emotion as is communicated is both vague and remote.

Set beside this the well-known speech of Ulysses:

> Time hath, my lord, a wallet at his back,
> Wherein he puts alms for oblivion,
> A great-siz'd monster of ingratitudes:
> Those scraps are good deeds past; which are devour'd
> As fast as they are made, forgot as soon
> As done: perseverance, dear my lord,
> Keeps honour bright: to have done is to hang
> Quite out of fashion, like a rusty mail
> In monumental mockery. Take the instant way;
> For honour travels in a strait so narrow
> Where one but goes abreast: keep then the path;
> For emulation hath a thousand sons
> That one by one pursue: if you give way,
> Or hedge aside from the direct forthright,
> Like to an enter'd tide they all rush by
> And leave you hindmost.

The verse of course is much more free, and the underlying speech movement gives a far greater range of rhythmic subtlety. The sound is more closely linked with—is, in fact, an intimate part of—the meaning. The imagery changes more swiftly. But these factors are only important as contributing to a major development: the main difference lies in the greater immediacy and concreteness of the verse. In reading the second passage more of the mind is involved, and it is involved in more ways. It does not contemplate a general emotion, it *lives* a particular experience. Crudely, the reader is not told that there is a constant need for action, he experiences a particular urgency.

This account could be substantiated in detail, but for my purpose it may be sufficient to point to a few of the means by which the reader is influenced in this way. Oblivion, at first a kind of negative presence, becomes (via "monster") an active, devouring force, following hard on the heels of time. ("Forgot," balancing "devoured," keeps the image in a proper degree of subordination.) The perseverance that keeps honour bright introduces a sense of effort, as in polishing metal, and (after a particularly effective jibe at inactivity) the effort is felt as motion. Moreover, "Take the instant way" and "keep then the path," involving muscular tension, suggest the strain of keeping foremost. In the next two lines the roar and clatter of emulation's thousand sons are audible, and immediately we feel the pressure of pursuit ("hedge aside" is no dead metaphor) and—in the movement of the verse, as though a dam had broken—the overwhelming tide of pursuers. The short and exhausted line, "And leave you hindmost," is the lull after the wave has passed.

This line of development, continued in the plays of complete maturity, is central. Primarily it is a matter of technique—the words have a higher potency, they release and control a far more complex response than in the earlier plays—but it is much more than that. The kind of immediacy that I have indicated allows the greatest subtlety in particular presentment (The thing "which shackles accidents, and bolts up change" is *not* the same as "The deed which puts an end to human vicissitude"), whilst "the quick flow and the rapid change of the images," as Coleridge noted, require a "perpetual activity of attention on the part of the reader," generate, we may say, a form of activity in which thought and feeling are fused in a new mode of apprehension. That is, the technical development implies—is dependent on —the development and unification of sensibility. It is this kind of development (in advance of the dramatic verse of the same period in

some respects and obviously behind it in others) that we find in the
Sonnets, and that makes it imperative that discussion should start
from considerations of technique.

Those aspects of technique that can to some extent be isolated as
showing "the first and most obvious excellence . . . the sense of
musical delight" have been well illustrated by George Wyndham, but
his belief that "Eloquent Discourse" is "the staple of the Sonnets and
their highest excellence" precludes the more important approach.

After 1579 the most pervasive influence on Elizabethan lyric poetry
was that of Spenser. *Astrophel and Stella* may have been the immediate cause of the numerous sonnet cycles, but it was from Spenser that
the sonneteers derived many of their common characteristics—the slow
movement and melody, the use of imagery predominantly visual and
decorative, the romantic glamour, the tendency towards a gently
elegiac note. In the Spenserian mode no object is sharply forced upon
the consciousness.

> Of mortall life the leafe, the bud, the floure,
> Ne more doth flourish after first decay,
> That earst was sought to decke both bed and bowre,
> Of manie a Ladie, and many a Paramoure:
> Gather therefore the Rose, whilest yet is prime . . .

As music this is perfect and one is forced to admire; but one is only
mildly affected by the vision of the passage of time, and even the in-
junction to pluck the rose has no urgency. Now there is in Shakespeare's Sonnets a quality that, at a first reading, seems very near to
this: Sonnets 98 and 102, for example, are successful as fairly direct
developments of the Spenserian mode. But if we turn to Sonnet 35
we see the conjunction of that mode with something entirely new.

> No more bee greev'd at that which thou hast done,
> Roses have thornes, and silver fountaines mud,
> Cloudes and eclipses staine both Moone and Sunne,
> And loathsome canker lives in sweetest bud.
> All men make faults, and even I in this,
> Authorizing thy trespas with compare,
> My selfe corrupting salving thy amisse,
> Excusing thy sins more then thy sins are:
> For to thy sensuall fault I bring in sence,

> Thy adverse party is thy Advocate,
> And gainst my selfe a lawfull plea commence,
> Such civill war is in my love and hate,
> That I an accessary needs must be,
> To that sweet theefe which sourely robs from me.

The first four lines we may say, both in movement and imagery, are typically Spenserian and straightforward. The fifth line begins by continuing the excuses, "All men make faults," but with an abrupt change of rhythm Shakespeare turns the generalization against himself: "All men make faults, and even I in this," i.e. in wasting my time finding romantic parallels for your sins, as though intellectual analogies ("sence") were relevant to your sensual fault. The painful complexity of feeling (Shakespeare is at the same time tender towards the sinner and infuriated by his own tenderness) is evident in the seventh line which means both, "I corrupt myself when I find excuses for you" (or "when I comfort myself in this way"), and, "I'm afraid I myself make you worse by excusing your faults"; and although there is a fresh change of tone towards the end (the twelfth line is virtually a sigh as he gives up hope of resolving the conflict), the equivocal "needs must" and the sweet-sour opposition shows the continued civil war of the emotions.

Some such comment as this was unavoidable, but it is upon the simplest and most obvious of technical devices that I wish to direct attention. In the first quatrain the play upon the letters *s* and *l* is mainly musical and decorative, but with the change of tone and direction the alliterative *s* becomes a hiss of half-impotent venom:

> All men make faults, and even I in this,
> Authorizing thy trespas with compare,
> My selfe corrupting salving thy amisse,
> Excusing thy sins more then thy sins are:
> For to thy sensuall fault I bring in sence . . .

The scorn is moderated here, but it is still heard in the slightly rasping note of the last line,

> To that sweet theefe which sourely robs from me.

From the fifth line, then, the alliteration is functional: by playing off against the comparative regularity of the rhythm it expresses an important part of the meaning, and helps to carry the experience alive into the mind of the reader. With Spenser or Tennyson in mind we should say that both alliteration and assonance were primarily musical devices, as indeed they are in many of the Sonnets:

> Noe longer mourne for me when I am dead,
> Than you shall heare the surly sullen bell
> Give warning to the world that I am fled
> From this vile world with vildest wormes to dwell.

Here, for example, the sound, if not independent of the meaning, usurps a kind of attention that is incompatible with a full and sharp awareness. But that which links the Sonnets, in this respect, with the later plays is the use of assonance and alliteration to secure a heightened awareness, an increase of life and power:

> Your love and pity doth the impression fill,
> Which vulgar scandall stampt upon my brow.

> Cheared and checkt even by the self-same skie.

> All this the world well knowes yet none knowes well . . .

> So shall I taste
> At first the very worst of fortune's might.

> And made myselfe a motley to the view.

In reading the last line the nose wrinkles in disgust, and we hear the rattle of the fool,—but I hope the reader will be inclined to look up the examples in their context (112, 15, 129, 90, and 110 respectively).

A slight shift of attention brings into focus a second aspect of development connected with the first. If we open any of the great plays almost at random we find effects comparable in kind to this, from *Lear*:

> Crown'd with rank fumiter and furrow-weeds,
> With hor-docks, hemlocks, nettles, cuckoo-flowers,
> Darnel, and all the idle weeds that grow
> In our sustaining corn.

The rank and bristling profusion of the weeds is there, in the clogged movement of the first two lines, whilst the unimpeded sweep of the

verse that follows contributes powerfully to the image of never-failing
fertility. In many of the Sonnets we can see Shakespeare working
towards this use of his medium, learning to use a subtly varied play
of the speech rhythm and movement against the formal pattern of the
verse:

> Ah yet doth beauty like a Dyall hand,
> Steale from his figure, and no pace perceiv'd.

> And on just proofe surmise, accumilate.

> Then hate me when thou wilt, if ever, now,
> Now while the world is bent my deeds to crosse . . .

> That it could so preposterouslie be stain'd . . .

In the steady movement of the first extract, in the slightly impeded
progress of the second,[5] in the impetuous movement of the third, and
the rising incredulity of the fourth, the verse (if I may borrow the
phrase) "enacts the meaning." Perhaps one can hardly miss this kind
of effect, but a development connected with it—the use of speech
movement and idiom in the Sonnets to obtain a firmer command of
tone (a matter of some importance in determining their meaning)—
seems to have been fairly consistently overlooked. The sonnet form is
a convention in which it is only too easy to adopt a special "poetic"
attitude, and to the four "strong promises of the strength of Shakespeare's genius" which Coleridge found in the early poems might well
be added a fifth: the way in which, in his Sonnets, he broke away
from the formal and incantatory mode (convention and precedent
being what they were) to make the verse a more flexible and transparent medium. Sonnet 7 has a typically stylized opening:

> Loe in the Orient when the gracious light,
> Lifts up his burning head, each under eye
> Doth homage to his new appearing sight,
> Serving with lookes his sacred majesty.

Contrast, say, Sonnet 82:

> I grant thou wert not married to my Muse,
> And therefore maiest without attaint ore-looke
> The dedicated words which writers use
> Of their faire subject, blessing every booke.

In the first line we hear the inflexion of the speaking voice, and it is the conversational movement that contributes the equivocal note of amused irony, directed towards the fulsome dedications and their—inevitably—fair subject. (Compare the "precious phrase by all the Muses filed" of Sonnet 85.) Sometimes a similar effect is used for deliberate contrast, as in

> Thus have I had thee as a dreame doth flatter,
> In sleepe a King, but waking no such matter,

where after a line and a half of yearning the offhand colloquialism shows us Shakespeare detached and critical. It is of course only by exploiting speech movement that any kind of delicacy of statement is possible (reservation is an obvious case, as in "I found—or thought I found—you did exceed . . ."), but it is the fairly frequent use of various ironic inflexions that it seems particularly important to stress:

> He nor that affable familiar ghost
> Which nightly gulls him with intelligence . . .

> Farewell thou art too deare for my possessing,
> And like enough thou knowst thy estimate . . .

—and there are other examples more or less immediately apparent.[6] To be alive to modulations of this kind is to recognize—which is what one would expect—that the *intelligence* that created, say, *Troilus and Cressida,* is also at work in the Sonnets.

I have already suggested that the critics who reconstruct a Shakespeare hopelessly and uncritically subjugated by a particular experience must be quite deaf to variations of tone. It is the same incapacity which causes them to read the Sonnets in which the touch is lightest with portentous solemnity and to perform various feats of legerdemain with the meaning. In Sonnet 94 the irony is serious and destructive.

> They that have powre to hurt, and will doe none,
> That doe not do the thing, they most do showe,
> Who moving others, are themselves as stone,
> Unmooved, could, and to temptation slow:
> They rightly do inherit heavens graces,
> And husband natures ritches from expence,
> They are the Lords and owners of their faces,
> Others, but stewards of their excellence:

> The sommers flowre is to the sommer sweet,
> Though to itselfe, it onely live and die,
> But if that flowre with base infection meete,
> The basest weed out-braves his dignity:
> > For sweetest things turne sowrest by their deedes,
> > Lillies that fester, smell far worse then weeds.

This is commonly taken with Sonnet 95 and read as an exhortation to chastity—"'Tis a sign of greatness to be self-contained" is Gollancz's summary, and J. Q. Adams glosses: "The friend has fallen into a life of gross sensuality, and the poet finds it necessary to rebuke him in the strongest language." If nothing else, "Lillies that fester" (an image suggesting less the excesses of sensuality than "the distortions of in-grown virginity") might cast some doubts on this simple interpretation. The opening is coldly analytic (I at least am unable to detect any symptoms of moral fervour), and the unprepossessing virtues of those "who moving others, are themselves as stone" can hardly be held up for admiration; they remind us rather of Angelo, "whose blood was very snow-broth." If we remember Shakespeare's condemnation, in the early Sonnets, of those who husband their riches instead of acting as stewards of their excellence, we shall hardly be able to mistake the second quatrain for unambiguous praise; in any case the image suggested by "They are the Lords and owners of their faces" is unobtrusively comic, and the comma after "Others" suggests that Shakespeare is ironically repeating the opinion of the self-righteous. The Sonnet may have been intentionally equivocal, but there can be little doubt of Shakespeare's attitude—it is the attitude of *Measure for Measure*—and the poem (though not altogether successful) forms an interesting complement to the more famous Sonnet 129. Perhaps I had better add that I do not regard the earlier sonnet as an encouragement to incontinence.

The vivid and surprising "Lillies that fester" has been commented upon as typically Shakespearean, and indeed the image, whether borrowed or not, is typical of the way in which contrasted sets of associations are fused in the verse of the later plays. But it is hardly representative of the imagery of the Sonnets. In the later plays a wide range of relevant associations, both of thought and feeling ("relevant" being clearly a matter for specific illustration), are compressed into a single image ("The bank and shoal of time"). Images of sight, touch,

muscular adjustment and so on follow in rapid succession (no catalogue of "visual," "tactile," etc., is sufficient to cover the variety), and
different modes may be combined in our response at any one point.
And there are those unexpected and startling juxtapositions of contrasted images:

> The *crown* o' the earth doth *melt*.

> This sensible warm *motion* to become
> A kneaded *clod*.

Now in the Sonnets not all of these characteristic uses of imagery
are developed: it is largely this which justifies us in assigning them a
date earlier than *Troilus and Cressida* or *Measure for Measure*. With
the exception of the striking line, "Mine appetite I never more will
grind On newer proof," we can find no parallels to "Lillies that
fester." Such lines as

> Gor'd mine own thoughts . . .

and

> To bitter sawces did I frame my feeding

indicate an important line of development, but there is little of the
intensely physical impact that we find in *Macbeth* ("The blanket of
the dark," "We'd jump the life to come"). Most of the images—even
when finely effective—arouse only one set of vibrations in the mind:

> Full many a glorious morning have I seene,
> Flatter the mountaine tops with soveraine eie . . .

> My nature is subdu'd
> To what it workes in, like the Dyers hand.

If we place "the dust and injury of age" (108) and ". . . whose million'd accidents Creep in 'twixt vows . . ." (115) beside Macbeth's

> Tomorrow, and tomorrow, and tomorrow,
> Creeps in this petty pace from day to day . . .
> And all our yesterdays have lighted fools
> The way to dusty death

and ask ourselves exactly why "creep" and "dust" are used in each
instance, we shall have a fair measure of the later development.

But even when we have made these qualifications the stress remains on the positive achievement; there is a clear advance on the early plays. In the Sonnets no image is *merely* decorative, as in Romeo's "Two of the fairest stars in all the heaven . . ." Few are excessively developed, as in the laments of Richard II or even as in the Bastard's "Commodity, the bias of the world . . ." There is indeed a constant succession of varied images, which, because they are concrete and because they are drawn from the world of familiar experience, give precise expression to emotion:

> Beated and chopt with tand antiquitie.

> Incertenties now crowne them-selves assur'de.

> But makes antiquitie for aye his page.

> And captive-good attending Captaine ill.

What it comes to is this: in the Sonnets, as in the later plays, the imagery gives immediacy and precision, and it demands and fosters an alert attention. But the range of emotions liberated by any one image is narrower, though not always less intense. We have not yet reached the stage in which "the *maximum* amount of apparent incongruity is resolved simultaneously."[7] That is, the creating mind has not yet achieved that co-ordination of widely diverse (and, in the ordinary mind, often conflicting) experiences, which is expressed in the imagery no less than in the total structure of the great tragedies. Put in this way the conclusion may seem obvious, but it is a point to which I shall have to return when I deal with Shakespeare's treatment of the Time theme in the Sonnets.

A complete account of technical development in the Sonnets would include a detailed discussion of ambiguity—a technical device (if we may call it that) of which, since the publication of Mr. Empson's *Seven Types* and the Riding and Graves analysis of Sonnet 129, one can hardly fail to be aware; though the word seems to have caused some unnecessary critical shyness. But the argument would raise fundamental issues with which I do not feel competent to deal, and all that I have to offer—after a very brief indication of the way in which the language of the Sonnets is "charged" by means of overlaying meanings—is some caution.

There is a clear difference between the kind of compression that we find in "The steepe up heavenly hill"(7), "The world without end houre" (57), or "Th'imprison'd absence of your libertie" (58), and in such lines as "So thou, thy selfe out-going in thy noon" (7), or "That I have frequent binne with unknown mindes" (117). The first three are forms of elliptical construction requiring no unusual agility in the mind accustomed to English idiom. In the last two the context demands that we shall keep two or more meanings in mind simultaneously: "thy selfe out-going" means both "over-reaching yourself" and "you yourself going further on"; "unknown minds" are "strangers," "nonentities," and perhaps "such minds as I am ashamed to mention" (the Arden Edition gives precedents for all these interpretations). In the same way as two or more meanings are fused in one word, different constructions may be run together, as in

> None else to me, nor I to none alive,
> That my steel'd sence or changes right or wrong.   (112)

or they may be overlaid:

> My selfe corrupting salving thy amisse   (35)

There can, I think, be no doubt that Shakespeare deliberately (though "deliberately" may be too strong a word) avails himself of the resources of the language in this way; I have chosen what seem to be the most incontrovertible examples, and they are clearly in line with his later development. In Sonnet 40 and one or two others we have something very like conscious experimenting with simple forms of ambiguous statement.

Now the important point is this: that when ambiguity occurs in successful verse it is valuable in much the same way as successful imagery is valuable, as representing a heightened, more inclusive and more unified form of consciousness. One need hardly say that the mere presence of ambiguities is not necessarily an indication of poetic value—they may equally represent unresolved contradictions in the poet's mind—or that the estimate of success is a more delicate matter (concerned with the whole poetic effect) than the working-out of alternative meanings. There is no need for me to praise Mr. Empson, though I may say that he is the only critic I know of who has detected the equivocal attitude which Shakespeare sometimes expresses towards his subject, and that some of his analyses (of Sonnet 58, for example) seem to me immediately convincing. But in perhaps the majority of cases (I am confining my attention entirely to the pages he devotes to the Sonnets[8]) his lists of meanings seem to me to be obtained by focussing upon a part of the poem, almost one might say by forgetting the poem, and considering the various grammatical possibilities of the part so isolated. His analysis of Sonnet 83, for example (pp. 168-75), is valuable as suggesting the conscious and subliminal meanings that may well have been in Shakespeare's mind at the time of writing, but only a few of them are there, in the poem. It is very unfair to make this charge without substantiating it in detail, but to do so would add many pages to the already excessive length of this essay; I can only hope that the reader will look up the analysis for himself—and my account of Sonnet 123, below, is relevant here. Mr. Eliot has remarked that the Sonnets are "full of some stuff that the writer could not drag to light, contemplate, or manipulate into art."[9] The sentence might be taken by the biographers to refer to an especially painful personal experience lying behind the Sonnets. But it suggests more profitable speculation if we interpret it *in the first place* as meaning that Shakespeare had not yet fully mastered the technique of complex expression.

IV

These imperfect considerations of technique will perhaps have been sufficient to establish the main point, that in the Sonnets, within the limitations of the imposed form, Shakespeare is working towards the maturity of expression of the great plays. But having said this we need to remind ourselves of two things. (The prevailing conception of technique as having something to do with the place of the caesura and hypermetric feet may justify the repetition.) The first is that the kind of technical development that we have been discussing is in itself an attempt to become more fully conscious (just as Spenser's technique is a method of exclusion), an attempt to secure more delicate discrimination and adjustment. The second is that technique does not function in a vacuum, it can only develop as the servant of an inner impulse. I shall conclude this essay by pointing to one or two of the major interests that lie behind the Sonnets.

I have already said that I do not think "The Sonnets" in any sense an ordered collection; they vary from the most trivial of occasional verses to poems in which a whole range of important emotions is involved, and in the latter we find in embryo many of the themes of the later plays; there is variety enough to make discussion difficult. But it seems to me that two interests predominate, making themselves felt, often, beneath the ostensible subject: they cannot be altogether disentangled from each other or from other interests, and they are not quite the same in kind; but the artificial grouping seems unavoidable. One is the exploration, discrimination and judgment of modes of being—attention consciously directed towards the kind of integration of personality that is implied by the development of technique. The second is an overwhelming concern with Time.

The first of these is not only expressed directly. Sonnet 30 is one of those concerned with "Friendship in Absence."

> When to the Sessions of sweet silent thought,
> I summon up remembrance of things past,
> I sigh the lack of many a thing I sought,
> And with old woes new waile my deare times waste;
> Then can I drowne an eye (un-us'd to flow)
> For precious friends hid in deaths dateles night,
> And weepe afresh loves long since canceld woe,
> And mone th' expence of many a vannisht sight.
>
> .   .   .   .   .
>
> But if the while I thinke on thee (deare friend)
> All losses are restord, and sorrowes end.

The Sonnet seems to be an early one, but even here beneath the main current of elegiac emotion (the tribute to friendship is gracefully conventional) there is a counter-current of irony directed by the poet towards himself. In the eighth line Shakespeare is conscious that the present moan, like the sighs [sights] previously expended, involves a fresh expense ("Every sigh shortens life"), so that the line means, "I waste my time and energy regretting the time and energy wasted in regrets"; and the slight over-emphasis of the third quatrain adds to the irony. In other words, Shakespeare is aware of what he is doing (after all, "sessions" implies judgment), and therefore achieves a more stable equilibrium. This is a minor example, but the implicit self-criticism is pervasive (we may compare the previous Sonnet: "Yet in these thoughts myself almost despising"); and—although the poem quoted is far enough from anything by Donne or Marvell—the constant reference of the immediate emotion to a mature scale of values reminds us that Shakespeare—Nature's Darling—is not far removed from the Tradition of Wit.

In many of the Sonnets ostensibly concerned with a personal relationship we find there is something of far greater interest to Shakespeare than the compliments, complaints and pleas that provide the occasion of writing. Sonnet 110 is in the form of a plea for the restoration of friendship:

> Alas 'tis true, I have gone here and there,
> And made my selfe a motley to the view,
> Gor'd mine owne thoughts, sold cheap what is most dear,
> Made old offences of affections new.
> Most true it is, that I have lookt on truth
> Asconce and strangely: But by all above,
> These blenches gave my heart an other youth,
> And worse essaies prov'd thee my best of love,
> Now all is done, have what shall have no end,
> Mine appetite I never more will grin'de
> On newer proofe, to trie an older friend,
> A God in love, to whom I am confin'd.
>> Then give me welcome, next my heaven the best,
>> Even to thy pure and most most loving brest.

There can be no doubt that here the most powerful lines are those recording self-disgust,[10] and that there is a drop in intensity when Shakespeare turns to address the friend directly, as in the final couplet. The Sonnet is important as a direct approach to sincerity—it records the examination and integration of character. Indeed in many of the Sonnets in which the friend is given something more than perfunctory recognition it is hard to resist the conclusion that Shakespeare is addressing his own conscience.

> You are my All the world, and I must strive,
> To know my shames and praises from your tounge,
> None else to me, nor I to none alive,
> That my steel'd sence or changes right or wrong,
> In so profound Abisme I throw all care
> Of others voyces, that my Adders sence,
> To cryttick and to flatterer stopped are. . .

—"Like the deaf adder that stoppeth her ear; which will not hearken to the voice of charmers, charming never so wisely." The reference is important; in the Sonnets Shakespeare is working out a morality based on his own finest perceptions and deepest impulses.[11] Sonnet 121, which has caused a good deal of perplexity, seems to me mainly a protest against any rigidly imposed moral scheme, a protest on behalf of a morality based on the nature of the writer. But that morality can only be discussed in terms that the poetry supplies.

An essay might well be written on the Time theme in Shakespeare. Starting from an examination of *King Henry IV, Troilus and Cressida* and the Sonnets, it would illuminate some important aspects of Shakespeare's genius and of the Elizabethan mind. But before discussing Shakespeare's handling of this theme some distinctions must be made.

In the Sonnets Shakespeare's interest in the passage of time and the allied themes of death and mutability is sufficiently obvious. Not only does it provide the main theme of many of the more important Sonnets, it continually encroaches on other interests and overshadows them. And there is a clear difference in intensity, tone and treatment between Shakespeare's "Time" sonnets and other Elizabethan poems dealing with "Time's thievish progress to eternity"; between

> When I consider everything that growes
> Holds in perfection but a little moment   (15)

or

> Like as the waves make towards the pibled shore . . .   (60)

and such typically Elizabethan things as

> In time the strong and stately turrets fall,
>   In time the rose and silver lilies die,
> In time the monarchs captive are, and thrall,
>   In time the sea and rivers are made dry

or

> Soon doth it fade that makes the fairest flourish,
> Short is the glory of the blushing rose

or anything to be found in Spenser's Mutability Cantos.

Now "the problem of Time" is a metaphysical problem, and in various forms it is a preoccupation of some of the Metaphysical Poets. Moreover, between Shakespeare's mature verse and Donne's there are similarities which it is important to recognize—the immediacy, the images generating intense mental activity ("the intellect at the tip of the senses"), the exploiting of speech rhythm and idiom, and so on: a good deal of Mr. Eliot's account of Metaphysical Poetry applies equally—as he points out—to the blank verse of Shakespeare and other late Elizabethans. This being so, it is all the more important to stress that in the Sonnets "the problem of Time" is not a metaphysical problem at all,—and the discussion of Platonic Forms and Ideal Beauty is irrelevant. Wherever we look, Shakespeare is concerned merely with the *effects* of time on animate and inanimate beings, on persons and personal relationships. As a poet, he reports and evaluates experiences, but he does not attempt to *explain* them, nor do they arouse speculation in his mind. So, too, the plays "explain" nothing; they are experiences to be lived. Indeed if Time had presented itself to Shakespeare as a metaphysical problem it could not have been dealt with in the verse of the Sonnets. Mr. James Smith has made a necessary distinction.[12] He points out that "verse properly called metaphysical is that to which the impulse is given by an overwhelming concern with metaphysical problems; with problems either deriving from, or closely resembling in the nature of their difficulty, the problem of the Many and the One," and that in Metaphysical Poetry it is the conflict arising out of the perception of such problems that is resolved by means of the metaphysical conceit, in which there is both unity and "high strain or tension, due to the sharpness with which its elements are opposed." Shakespeare's imagery in the Sonnets, as I have pointed out, rarely involves a high degree of tension; and when, in the later plays, we find images that not only possess richness of association but embrace conflicting elements, those elements are invariably drawn from experience and sensation, never from speculative thought: they make finer experience available for others, but they offer no resolution of metaphysical problems.

The temptation to look for the development of a metaphysical mode in the Sonnets is not perhaps very common. A second temptation has not proved so easy to resist, and most accounts of the Sonnets point to certain of them as showing "Love's Triumph over Time," without bothering to explain what this may mean. Certainly, if we isolate those sonnets in which a reaction to the passage of time and the inevitability of death provides the main emotional drive it is permissible to look for a coherently developing attitude culminating in a solution that shall be at least emotionally satisfying. There is an obvious advance in maturity, an increasing delicacy in exposition, but unless we are prepared to accept assertion as poetry (that is, bare statement

deliberately willed, instead of the communication in all its depth, fullness and complexity, of an experience that has been lived) we shall
not find that solution in the Sonnets. An example may make my
meaning clearer. Sonnet 123 is commonly taken to show that "Love
conquers Time":

> No! Time, thou shalt not bost that I doe change,
> Thy pyramyds buylt up with newer might
> To me are nothing novell, nothing strange,
> They are but dressings of a former sight:
> Our dates are breefe, and therefor we admire,
> What thou dost foyst upon us that is ould,
> And rather make them borne to our desire,
> Then thinke that we before have heard them tould:
> Thy registers and thee I both defie,
> Not wondring at the present, nor the past,
> For thy records, and what we see doth lye,
> Made more or les by thy continuall hast:
> > This I doe vow and this shall ever be,
> > I will be true dispight thy syeth and thee.

It is upon the ambiguity of the first two quatrains that I wish to direct
attention. *Sense 1*: "Time cannot make his boast that I change with
his passage. The admired wonders of modern architecture are not
novelties to me (since my conscious self is, in a sense, outside time);
I have seen them all before, and I know that the modern examples are
only variations on the old. Man's life is short; therefore he tends to
wonder at things, foisted upon him by Time as novelties, which are
really old, preferring to believe them newly created for his satisfaction
[born to our desire] than to see them truly as repetitions of the old."
Sense 2 (Wyndham's interpretation): "Time cannot boast that I
change. The pyramids—built with a skill that was new compared with
my age-old self [with newer might to me]—were, I saw, no novelties
even in ancient Egypt, but merely dressings of a former sight. Man's
life is short; therefore he tends to wonder at the antiquities foisted
upon him by Time, preferring to accept as absolute the limitations
imposed by birth and death [to make them (dates) the bourn to his
desire] than to think that the years of his life have been counted
[told] before." A rough paraphrase of the last six lines is: "I refuse to

accept as ultimate truth either history (recording that time has passed) or the present passage of time; neither novelty nor antiquity move me; the evidence of universal change given by history and the present time is false: only in appearance are past and present governed by time. I vow that I will be myself (and—perhaps—true to some person) in spite of death and time."

The purpose of the Sonnet is clear: to affirm the continuous identity of the self in spite of the passage of time. But, though a remarkable achievement, its failure is indicated by the unresolved ambiguity. That *Sense* 1 is intended seems clear from line 10—"Not wondering *at the present,* nor the past"—as well as from the Elizabethan use of the word "pyramids"; and even if we do away with the maladroit pun on "borne" by interpreting it as "bourn" in *Sense* 1 as well as in *Sense* 2 (and I find it impossible to exclude the meaning "born to our desire") we are left with "that is old" fitting awkwardly into the first interpretation. Moreover—and perhaps it is more important to notice this than the conflicting meanings which somehow refuse to resolve themselves into unity—the poem *asserts* rather than expresses a resolved state of mind: "Thou shalt not boast," "I defy," "This I do vow," "I will be true."

In the manner of its assertion the Sonnet is in line with the more famous Sonnet 116 ("Love's not time's fool")—a poem of which the difficulties have never, I think, been squarely faced—and with those sonnets promising some form of immortality. And, we may remark in conclusion, in all the Sonnets of this last type, it is the contemplation of change, not the boasting and defiance, that produces the finest poetry; they draw their value entirely from the evocation of that which is sad to be defied or triumphed over. In the plays—from *Henry IV* to *The Tempest*—in which the theme of Time occurs, there is no defiance; the conflict is resolved by the more or less explicit acceptance of mutability.[13] I should like to give this remark precision in terms of literary criticism by examining the second part of *King Henry IV,* a play of which the prelude is spoken by the dying Hotspur towards the end of Part I:

> But thought's the slave of life, and life time's fool . . .

But perhaps enough has been said to show that, in this respect as in all others, the Sonnets yield their proper significance only when seen in the context of Shakespeare's development as a dramatist.

NOTES

1. The tendency is encouraged by the fact that the Sonnets are printed in a numbered sequence, without titles. And remembering the part played by verbal habit in directing thought, we may consider the effect of the mere repetition of the phrase, "The Sonnets."

2. See their analysis of Sonnet 129 in *A Survey of Modernist Poetry*, pp. 63-81. No one need suppose that, in complaining of wanton "emendation," I am claiming complete infallibility for the Quarto, of which, by the way, there is an admirable facsimile edition published by Noel Douglas at 5s.

3. "The mortal moon hath her eclipse endur'd" (107)—the only "external reference" of any difficulty—is more likely to refer to the ending of the Queen's climacterical year (1596) than to her death—as Dr. G. B. Harrison has pointed out.

4. I have italicized the phrase that forces the dilemma: *either* autobiographical *or* "merely dramatic" and conventional.

5. "Surmise" is object to the imperative "accumilate"; the separating comma seems unnecessary.

6. Of course the tone is not determined solely by the movement; often, for example, the degree of seriousness with which Shakespeare is writing is indicated by the imagery. Consider the roses of Sonnet 99 which "fearfully on thornes did stand," or the poet's thousand groans, "one on anothers necke," in Sonnet 131.

7. The phrase is Edgell Rickword's (*Towards Standards of Criticism*, ed. F. R. Leavis, p. 120).

8. *Seven Types of Ambiguity*, pp. 65-73 and 168-75.

9. *Selected Essays*, p. 144.

10. To take the first three lines as referring merely to the profession of actor and playwright is too narrow an interpretation; the reference seems to be to the way in which a sensitive intelligence has displayed its wares of wit and observation in common intercourse.

11. "But we have to know ourselves pretty thoroughly before we can break the automatism of ideals and conventions. . . . Only through fine delicate knowledge can we recognize and release our impulses." —*Fantasia of the Unconscious*, p. 60.

12. "The Metaphysical Note in Poetry" in *Determinations*.

13. An acceptance, I should now (1944) add, that comes to be closely associated with the complementary recognition of new life and of values that are not subject to time. This has been admirably brought out by D. A. Traversi's *Approach to Shakespeare*, which also shows the essential continuity of development—a continuity of developing experience—between the Sonnets and the greater plays.

C. L. BARBER

An Essay on the Sonnets

Everyone who reads poetry knows a number of Shakespeare's sonnets well, but many readers have been put off from the whole collection by the biographical questions it raises and the accumulation of unsatisfactory answers proposed by commentators. The sonnets not only include some of the most beautiful poems ever written, but they have the additional interest that they are the only poems we have which Shakespeare wrote out of his own life, in his own person—a remarkable, indeed astonishing collection. People often wish that a diary or correspondence might turn up from which we could learn about Shakespeare; in the sonnets we have, by a fluke, something of this kind. But they are cast in the mold of his age, not ours, and they do not oblige our curiosity about circumstantial facts. The *who, where, when* are beyond knowing, despite the tantalizing closeness of the poems to Shakespeare's personal life. The many theories that have been proposed were all expertly reviewed in 1944, in the hundreds of pages of the New Variorum Edition, by the late Professor Hyder Rollins, a master of objective literary scholarship; his conclusion was that "nothing worthy of the name of 'evidence' has been produced to substantiate any of them, and probably nothing ever will be."[1] Yet this barren tradition of biographical speculation has led many to assume—

even when they see no answer—that *the* question about the sonnets is "What is the story behind them?" The poems are usually discussed not as poems but as evidence—and insufficient evidence at that.

People who care about poetry usually react to this tendency by making a point of ignoring all questions as to what the sonnets express of Shakespeare's life and attending only to what they are as autonomous poetic achievements. Shakespeare, in finding words for his love, often evokes what is loveliest in the world at large:

> Making a couplement of proud compare
> With sun and moon, with earth and sea's rich gems,
> With April's first-born flowers, and all things rare,
> That heaven's air in this huge rondure hems.   (21)

Such sonnets are products of the brief golden age of English poetry when the magic of the simplest, most fundamental things could be conveyed in unforced words. The sonnets are also, within their forthright form, among the most exquisitely wrought creations of sound and syllable in the language. Frequently they give compelling utterance to experiences everyone goes through in love—anguish, elation, joy, dismay; and they realize with directness and fullness basic conditions of existence which love has to confront—the fact of mortality, the separateness of human beings, their need of each other, the graces that come unsought and undeserved.

It is better to read the sonnets for these universal values than to lose their poetry by turning them into riddles about Shakespeare's biography. But to block off consideration of what they mean as an expression of Shakespeare's own experience is a needless sacrifice, which leads in practice to ignoring those many sonnets which hinge on the stresses of the poet's personal life, and to losing an important part of the meaning and beauty of the whole collection. We can turn our backs on the unanswerable questions of fact, and read the poems not as tantalizing clues but as *expression* of a man's experience. When we do so, we find that, though they do not tell a story, they do express a personality. They are gestures of love, concern, disappointment, anger or disgust, profoundly and candidly conveyed. That we cannot know who was actually addressed does not prevent our feeling and understanding the gestures. What is communicated in this way is not, of course, "the whole truth about Shakespeare." The sonnets are only Shakespeare at certain times in certain kinds of relations, with a young man or several young men (1-126), with a dark-complexioned

married woman of loose morals (127-152). And in them we see
Shakespeare only where he is living by writing poetry to people, rather
than living in other ways. But within these limits, we do encounter
his personality, and it is an extraordinary one. Shakespeare exhibits,
like Keats, astonishing "negative capability." He realizes others with a
selflessness or lack of self that is sometimes poignant, sometimes desperate, even ugly, sometimes sublime. To look at the sonnets in relation to their author does not mean turning away from their qualities
as poetry; on the contrary, the poems gain meaning and beauty—
even the ones most familiar. We can see in them a great artist en-
countering, in love, the predicaments of his temperament and his
part in life. And we can see what he loved, turned into the substance
of poetry.

I   "His Sugared Sonnets among His Private Friends."

To read the sonnets most effectually one must keep in view the place
they had in the poet's life. They were not written for publication, but
to present to friends, not written all together, but singly and in groups
at intervals over several years. In 1598, a schoolmaster, Francis Meres,
surveying current writing, praised Shakespeare as the time's leading
dramatist and poet, listed his plays and his published narrative poems,
and then referred to "his sugared sonnets among his private friends."
Two sonnets (138 and 144) were appropriated for an anthology in
1599, but the other one hundred and fifty-two were not published
until 1609, late in Shakespeare's life, long after most of them must
have been written. This was the only edition, brought out by a marginal publisher, clearly without Shakespeare's permission or super-
vision. The cryptic dedication to "Mr. W. H." was the publisher's, not
Shakespeare's. It seems likely that this one edition was soon sup-
pressed, for in spite of Shakespeare's established fame there is almost
no notice of the sonnets in the decades following their appearance: in
1640 they were so little known that a publisher ventured to pretend
that he was bringing out unpublished poems of Shakespeare in issu-
ing a rearranged version of the 1609 text.

The writing of sonnets was a short-lived literary fashion in the
1590's, beginning with the posthumous publication of Sidney's *Astrophel and Stella* in 1591. Sonneteering was a polite accomplishment;
Shakespeare makes game of the fashion in *Love's Labour's Lost*,
where the elegant young lords "turn sonnet" when they turn from

study to courting: they compose sonnets, recite them, talk them, and finally forswear them as part and parcel of "spruce affectation." A number of sonnet sequences were published between 1592 and 1596 by Daniel, Watson, Drayton, Spenser and others; then the vogue was over. Shakespeare's sonnets are often spoken of as his sonnet sequence, though they are not in fact such a production, indeed not one production at all. They were probably begun in the period when the rage for sonnets in private life was at its height, and when Shakespeare was making much of sonnets in his plays. There are a particularly large number of parallels in imagery and phrasing between the sonnets, especially those numbered below one hundred, and *Love's Labour's Lost, Romeo and Juliet, A Midsummer Night's Dream, Richard II*, as well as the two narrative poems published in 1592 and 1594. These facts suggest that the bulk of the sonnets were probably composed between 1593 and 1597. Many of them, however, including most of those numbered above one hundred in the collection, seem later in style, with affinities to the plays of the "problem" period, and so may have been composed later—unless, as some think, Shakespeare went through rapidly in the close form of the sonnet a development which came more slowly in the larger form of his plays.

C. S. Lewis has made the point that the typical Renaissance sonnet was a *public* form of poetry. "A good sonnet . . . was like a good public prayer: the test is whether the congregation can 'join' and make it their own, not whether it provides interesting materials for the spiritual biography of the compiler. The whole body of the sonnet sequences is more like an erotic liturgy than a series of erotic confidences."[2] Many of Shakespeare's sonnets are drastic (and unparalleled) exceptions to this rule: they refer to complicated and very private relations. But in his sonnets, as elsewhere, he uses the current idiom and goes beyond it or puts it to new uses rather than rebelling against it. He starts out with sonnets of ceremonial praise, seeking

to say
The perfect ceremony of love's rite.   (23)

At intervals he makes astonishing explorations of passion, not because Shakespeare is telling a story, or writing a "confession," but because in living out his life he encounters complications which then become the subjects of sonnets. Occasionally the use of the sonnet as part of the poet's life seems to damage it as art—we sometimes sense distortion serving ulterior purposes, especially in the poems, addressed to the friend as patron, which seek to counter the bid for patronage of a rival poet (78-86). But an extraordinary honesty predominates.

II   The Sonnet as an Action

To read through the sonnets at a sitting, though it is useful for surveying the topography they present, does violence to them and to the reader—it can produce a sensation of hothouse oppression. Each poem needs to be dwelt on; each requires the kind of concentrated attention which could have been given when they were received singly or in small groups. To read and reread is essential if we are to enjoy the way each moves, the use it makes of the possibilities of the sonnet form, the particular development in it of a design of sounds and images. The sonnets ask for a special sort of attention because in them poetry is, in a special way, an action, something done for and to the beloved. Indeed sometimes the activity of the poetry alone makes endurable the passivity of the attitudes expressed by the poet.

Many of the sonnets are wonderfully generous poems; they *give* meaning and beauty. The generosity is at once personal, a selfless love, and impersonal, the glow upon the world at the golden moment when Shakespeare began to write. The poems create a world resonant with the friend's beauty:

> Thou art thy mother's glass, and she in thee
> Calls back the lovely April of her prime;
> So thou through windows of thine age shalt see,
> Despite of wrinkles, this thy golden time. (3)

The curious theme of the first seventeen sonnets, which urge a friend to marry and have children, works partly because it provides occasions for saying simple things beautifully: how lovely April is; how fine it is that age, in spite of wrinkles, has windows through which to see its golden time renewed. The poet's vicarious interest in the young man's sexual fulfillment is not queasy because it is realized by evoking the creative power generally at work in nature:

> Those hours that with gentle work did frame
> The lovely gaze where every eye doth dwell . . . (5)

The phrase "gentle work" is typical of the direct cherishing of the processes of life. The feeling about the destructiveness of death is equally direct:

> For never-resting time leads summer on
> To hideous winter and confounds him there . . .   (5)

There is no holding back from obvious words or metaphors: the sun's
light is gracious, music is sweet, the buds of May are darling; death
is winter, darkness, Time's scythe; beauty is all the usual things, for
example a flower. But the meaning of the usual things is renewed:

> Since brass, nor stone, nor earth, nor boundless sea,
> But sad mortality o'ersways their power,
> How with this rage shall beauty hold a plea,
> Whose action is no stronger than a flower?   (65)

That a flower is a fragile thing is familiar enough. But that a flower
has its own kind of power too—this comes as a poignant realization. It
often happens that the metaphorical vehicle in which Shakespeare
conveys the tenor of his love absorbs our chief attention, so that the
love itself is left behind or fulfilled in what it is compared to. We
dwell on the fact that "summer's lease hath all too short a date," that
the earth devours "her own sweet brood," that the morning flatters
"the mountain tops with sovereign eye," that black night is "Death's
second self," and "seals up all in rest." Consider, as a summary example, the direct descriptions of the seasons in 97 and 98, "old December's bareness every where," "teeming autumn big with rich increase,"
"proud-pied April, dress'd in all his trim," and summer when we
"wonder at the lily's white" and "praise the deep vermilion in the
rose." The world is full of value that can be looked at front-face.
Shakespeare could get more of this gold into his poetry than anyone
else in the golden age because he had the greatest power of admiration.

To quote isolated phrases or lines from the sonnets is unsatisfying,
because every line or phrase is, in the act of reading, part of a single
movement: when you know a sonnet well, an individual line, quoted
alone, rings with the sound that it has in its proper place. Each sonnet
is one utterance. Shakespeare's use of the form is simple and forthright and also delicate and subtle. He never varies from three quatrains
followed by a couplet, *abab, cdcd, efef, gg:*

> Why write I still all one, ever the same,
> And keep invention in a noted weed,
> That every word doth almost tell my name . . . ?   (76)

Other Elizabethan sonneteers showed more technical restlessness.
Shakespeare not only uses nothing but the Shakespearean form (it

does tell his name!), but for the most part he uses it straight. He does not run his syntax against the line endings or rhyme scheme. There are exceptions, but normally the sentences close with the close of each quatrain, or else are balanced symmetrically within the four-line unit. Within sentences, grammar and thought typically pause or turn at the end of the line; where they do run over, the enjambment is rarely emphatic. Shakespeare does not exploit the more outward forms of variation because within the pattern he is making astonishingly beautiful designs with sound and syllable and cadence. He is like an accomplished figure skater who sticks to the classical figures because what he cares about is what he can make of each evolution. (Shakespeare had, after all, unlimited opportunities in the plays for freestyle improvisations, swoops, spins, leaps.) Each sonnet is different, but the difference is achieved not by changing the framework of form but by moving in fresh ways within it.

It seems clear that Shakespeare wrote by quatrains. In coming to know a sonnet by heart, you find yourself recalling it one quatrain at a time and often getting stuck trying to move to the next, for lack of a tangible link. The imagery does not regularly carry through; what does carry through is the momentum of the discourse. The movement from quatrain to quatrain is usually a shift of some sort, though it can be simply a continuing with fresh impetus. The figure skater starts each evolution by kicking off from an edge, and can move from one evolution to another either by staying on the same edge of the same blade, or changing from inside edge to outside edge, or from left foot inside to right foot outside, and so on—each of these technical moves focusing a whole living gesture on the balancing, moving body. People praise Shakespeare's sonnets because each one is about one thing: one should add that each is *one motion* about one thing, the motion normally being composed of three large sweeps and the shorter couplet. (The very different serial movement of 66 is a revealing exception to prove the rule.)

It is important to recognize that in most of the sonnets the couplet is *not* the emotional climax, or indeed even the musical climax; where it is made so, either by Shakespeare's leaning on it too heavily, or by our giving it unnecessary importance, one feels that two lines are asked to do too much. This let-down or over-reach in the couplet is the most common defect in the sonnets, though with tactful reading it usually can be kept from being troublesome. One needs to attend to the motion and the imaginative expansion which the sonnet achieves in the quatrains, realizing that the couplet is often no more than a turning around at the end to look from a new vantage at what has been expressed.

The main line of the sonnet as Shakespeare writes it is the patterned movement of discourse, not the imagery. The voice rides the undulation of the meter, gaining remarkable power and reaching out in ardent or urgent or solemn gestures defined by rhythmical variations. The criticism of our time has been fascinated by the way poetry can explore experience by carrying out the implications of a metaphor or conceit, as notably in Donne's work. Shakespeare in the sonnets occasionally does something like this—most perfectly in the three paralleled metaphors of 73: "That time of year . . . the twilight of such day . . . the glowing of such fire." But the progression by extending metaphors in 73 is most definitely not typical. He is responsible to rhythmical, not metaphorical consistency. The sonnet often starts with something like a metaphorical program, but usually it is not carried through; metaphors are picked up, changed, mixed, dropped *ad lib* while the sonnet runs its strong course as an utterance.

One often finds, as one penetrates the poetic texture of a particular poem, that it holds together by determinate rhythm and sound several almost independent strains of meaning, or a cluster of ambiguities which, worked out logically, are almost mutually exclusive. A case in point, which also will be of interest to us in considering the relationship of Shakespeare to the friend he addresses, comes in 16, where the poet urges that children can provide reproductions of the friend "much liker than your painted counterfeit," and then goes on with an extraordinarily rich use of the word "lines":

> So should the lines of life that life repair,
> Which this Time's pencil, or my pupil pen,
> Neither in inward worth nor outward fair,
> Can make you live yourself in eyes of men.

The suggestiveness of "lines of life" appears in the variety of commentator's paraphrases recorded in the Variorum edition: the "lines of life" can be the lines life etches on a face, or the lines of descent in a genealogy, or the lines of the living pictures presented by children, or the lines of children as living poems (as opposed to the mere written lines of the "pupil pen"), or even perhaps, as an echo at the back of the mind, what one commentator defends in urging unconvincingly that "lines of life" is a misprint for "loins of life" (compare the sonnet's conclusion: "And you must live, drawn by your own sweet skill"). Shakespeare had a supremely wandering mind! To ravel out such associations can of course be misleading. In an actual, live reading of a sonnet such clustering ideas as these are felt together, not sorted; they are the opening out of mind and heart into the plurality of the world's riches. What keeps us from coming to a standstill in wall-eyed contemplation is the flow of the poem's movement as it gathers in meaning in the service of the poet's love.

One can instance even more dramatic places where the poetry makes a thick harmony out of wool-gathering multiplicity—the most famous is "Bare ruin'd choirs, where late the sweet birds sang," thanks to William Empson's discussion at the outset of his *Seven Types of Ambiguity*. What criticism now needs to stress, I think, is not the interplay of imagery but the interplay of sound. (A case in point is the chord of vowels and of "r's" in "bare ruin'd choirs," sounded in three successive long, slow syllables—the mystery of the line comes from this music as much as from the wonderful complex of metaphors it holds in solution.) We need to consider, not a special case like 73, but the much more common case where there is great richness of metaphor but metaphorical consistency is not regarded:

> O how shall summer's honey breath hold out,
> Against the wrackful siege of battering days,
> When rocks impregnable are not so stout,
> Nor gates of steel so strong but Time decays? (65)

These are splendid lines—but it is the design of sound that chiefly carries them, the open-breathing *o* and *u* sounds and flowing consonants of "how shall summer's honey breath hold out" followed by the battering lines, with "wrackful" and "rocks impregnable." One can understand summer's honey metaphorically as provision for a siege—but one cannot carry the metaphor further, one cannot "batter" honey! And the summer-winter opposition, as well as the battering, have been lost by the time we get to "Time decays."

Sound and rhythm again and again give life to statements or figures which might otherwise be banal: so in a quatrain from 97 selected almost at random:

> How like a winter hath my absence been
> From thee, the pleasure of the fleeting year!
> What freezings have I felt, what dark days seen,
> What old December's bareness every where! (97)

A rich use of various *e* sounds emerges: the poignant sense of absence from "thee" is developed as we encounter the same sound in "fleeting" and "freezings"; the open *a* sounds in "What dark days" feel cavernous against the prevailing *e* tones; "December's bareness" includes the three vowel sounds present in "every where," so that the bareness seems to spread out "every where"—and the meter makes "every where" larger than it would be in prose by stressing two of its three syllables. Consonants of course are also put to work reinforcing the meaning, for example by linking "fleeting and freezing" to "felt," "old" to "December," "December" to "bareness." One can go on and on in this fashion, once one starts looking for such tangible patterns—and though it is not always possible to know where to draw the line between cases that really matter and cases that are far-fetched, such texture of physical relations among words is clearly fundamental to the beauty *and* the meaning of the poetry. When we shift from quatrain to quatrain, turning to lean into a new evolution, part of the newness is often the sound of a fresh set of dominant vowels; or again, we sometimes recognize a set of sounds carried all through a sonnet to give it its distinctive tune.

The sonnets often would be "witty" if it were not that the wit in them goes along with sound and cadences that hold feeling—the wit is rarely isolated to be felt separately, as Donne's so often is, but enters into the whole motion. If we read them in isolation, we would be amused by the virtuoso alliteration and assonance in lines like

> And with old woes new wail my dear time's
> waste. . . .
> And heavily from woe to woe tell o'er
> The sad account of fore-bemoaned moan.   (30)

But when we read them as an integral part of the lovely sonnet "When to the sessions of sweet silent thought," the huddled sounds serve to convey the pressure of the past on the present as a thickening or troubling of speech. Where we feel a twinge of amusement, it is usually in combination with feelings dictated by the underlying rhythm, as with the ruefulness of

> But ah, thought kills me that I am not thought . . .   (44)

It would be wrong to suppose that the sonnets are without humor. There are places where Shakespeare positively romps, but the fun is almost never unmixed with serious feeling:

> Let not my love be call'd idolatry,
> Nor my beloved as an idol show,
> Since all alike my songs and praises be
> To one, of one, still such, and ever so.
> Kind is my love to-day, to-morrow kind,
> Still constant in a wondrous excellence;
> Therefore my verse to constancy confin'd,
> One thing expressing, leaves out difference.
> Fair, kind, and true, is all my argument,
> Fair, kind, and true, varying to other words . . . (105)

This gay whirl is an extreme example of the repetition common in the sonnets, the same words rolled round, each time with added life because they fall differently each time within the poem's progress. In 105 this sort of fun is indulged in almost by itself, in celebration of a moment's carefree confidence. But even 105, which is as near to a *jeu d'esprit* as we come, has its serious side, for it raises a question about idolatry which it does not settle.

III   *"Two Loves I Have . . ."*

The publisher who pirated the sonnets in 1640 changed the pronouns in 15 to 126 so as to make the poems seem to be addressed to a woman; he was the first of many editors and commentators who have been troubled by the fact that a man is addressed in these love poems. Whether there was only one young man, or several, cannot be definitely settled: what is clear is that there was one role, of beloved younger friend or "lover," corresponding to a need in the poet to live in and through another person. It is usually in the beauty of a person of the opposite sex that we experience, incarnate, the sum of life's powers and perfections. But here we find that the twenty-five sonnets addressed to a woman, "the dark lady," dwell on her imperfections and falsehoods and the paradox that nevertheless she inspires physical desire; in the poems addressed to a man, by contrast, there is exultant contemplation of the beloved's beauty and cherishing of his whole identity, but nothing of specific bodily prurience. The "higher" love is expressed toward a man and the "lower" toward a woman. Poems to both, moreover, deal with a strange and troubling situation: Shakespeare's friend is lured into an affair by Shakespeare's mistress (40-42, 133, 134, 144); the poet's concern, in the midst of anguished humiliation, is to keep the man's love, not the woman's!

Various explanations have been offered. It has been suggested that the friend and mistress are fictions created in the process of an exercise in conventional sonneteering, but this notion has not stood up. A fiction, especially a fiction by Shakespeare, would satisfy our curiosity where the sonnets frequently baffle us by speaking of things which the person addressed is assumed to know but to which we have no key. And much of what is expressed concerning the friend and the mistress is most definitely *not* conventional sonneteering. The claim that passionate sonnets addressed to men were conventional, with which Sir Sidney Lee and others attempted to allay Victorian anxieties, is simply not true.

It is true that there was a cult of friendship in the Renaissance, and that writers often set ideal friendship between men above love for a woman. Professor Edward Hubler, whose valuable book *The Sense of Shakespeare's Sonnets* judiciously explores this and other problems, points out that Elizabethans used the term "lover" between men without embarrassment: thus Menenius, trying to get through to see Coriolanus in the Volscian camp, does not hesitate to say to a guard, "I tell thee, fellow, Thy general was my lover." Mr Hubler, with others, makes the further point that homosexuality, except for a passing slur about Thersites, is never at issue in the plays, either as a trait of character or, what is more revealing, as a latent motif in the imagery (Marlowe's plays provide a striking contrast). We do get in Shakespeare's comedies a series of places where boy actors play the parts of girls disguised as men; but this playful transvestism, convenient in a theater where boys played the women, is never queasy. We are never shown a man pretending to be a woman. What is dramatized is the fun of young women, Portia, Rosalind, Viola, zestfully acting as youths for a while and then falling back gladly and gracefully into their womanliness. This game reflects, not perversity, but the fundamental Elizabethan security about the roles of the sexes. The same security permitted Shakespeare to present the Duke in *Twelfth Night* delighting in the page Cesario's fresh youth and graceful responsiveness, and so falling in love without knowing it with the woman beneath the page's disguise. The sensibility of Shakespeare's age was open to appreciating qualities which youths and women have in common. This openness probably goes with the fact that homosexuality had no place in Elizabethan social life. Because their masculinity never was in doubt, men could wear their hair long, dress in silks and ruffles, pose for portraits "leaning against a tree among roses."

These facts should be kept in mind in reading sonnet 20, where Shakespeare praises "the master mistress of my passion" for possessing feminine beauty without feminine fickleness. The bawdy joke at the end acknowledges that the friend's sexuality is masculine and directed to women; such a pleasantry could only be pleasant where physical relations of the poet with the friend were out of the question. And yet the fact remains that the relationship expressed is a most unusual one: "Mine be thy love, and thy love's use their [women's] treasure." What Shakespeare's metaphor of capital and interest here proposes is that he should enjoy the whole identity of the friend while women enjoy what this capital yields of specific sexuality. And such is indeed the sort of relationship which the sonnets to the friend express, while those to the mistress present an obverse relationship concerned with the use of her sexuality rather than with her love.

Why then do we read the sonnets if the affections they express are so unusual? In the first place, because the love expressed for the friend *is* love, a most important kind of love which is ordinarily part of a relationship but here becomes the whole and is expressed with an unparalleled fullness and intensity. It is love by *identification* rather than sexual possession. Such cherishing love is a leading part of full sexual love between men and women. And it is central in other relations of life, notably between parents and children: the early sonnet (3) which says "thou art thy mother's glass," is followed by one where the poet is in the mother's place:

> My glass shall not persuade me I am old,
> So long as youth and thou are of one date. (22)

In another place (37) he compares himself to a father who "takes delight / To see his active child do deeds of youth." The strangely special theme of the first seventeen sonnets ("What man," C. S. Lewis asks, "ever really cared whether another man got married or not?") gives Shakespeare occasion to cherish the friend's identity and, beyond that, to envisage generously, in the idea of having children, a process by which one identity is re-created in another, as the poet throughout the sonnets finds himself renewed in his friend.

The universality of the part of love which here becomes the whole makes it easy for us to "join," as congregation, in all those sonnets, among them the most familiar and most beautiful, where the poet expresses how the friend's being galvanizes his whole consciousness. A lover's experience is the same, whoever the beloved, when absence makes a winter (97), when "thy sweet love remember'd such wealth brings" (29), when "descriptions of the fairest wights" in "the chronicle of wasted time" seem all to be prophecies of a present beauty (106). These poems make one very conscious of the active transmutation of experience by passion (e.g. 114), and of the lover's imagination straining at the limitations of physical existence: "If the dull substance of my flesh were thought . . ." (44).

Loving by identifying with the person loved can have a special scope for Shakespeare which it does not have for people who are not poets, because he can realize his friend's beauty and value in words. To realize the relationship by turning it into poetry gives a fulfillment which actually is physical, in that the poem, as utterance, is a physical act. That the writing of a sonnet provides a kind of physical union with the friend explains at least in part, I think, the recurrent emphasis on the sonnets as rescuing the beloved from death. Taken literally, the talk of conferring immortality seems rather empty—the friend, after all, is never named, and he is given no determinate social identity, indeed no personality. (It is because all this area is left so blank that the curious have been free to bemuse themselves with conjectures of every kind about the friend's identity.) But the sustaining reality in the theme of immortality is that the poet, in the act of writing the poem, experiences a lover's sense of triumphing over time by becoming one with great creating nature as embodied in another being. We have dwelt on the comparison made in 16 between different kinds of "lines of life." When the poet turns from urging children on his friend to addressing him directly, he uses the same metaphor to say that Death shall not "brag thou wander'st in his shade, / When in eternal lines to time thou grow'st." (18)

Such claims for poetry's power are of course a universal commonplace of the Petrarchan tradition—Shakespeare regularly links them with poignant, inclusive reflections on mortality. In reflections on mortality in *carpe diem* poems like Marvell's "Coy Mistress," there is often a suggestion, verging on a kind of metaphysical cruelty, that dissolution will come anyway, so it may as well come, delightfully, in sexual surrender. Shakespeare's sonnets often enhance the beauty of his friend and the mystery of life in him by reflections that he "amongst the wastes of time must go," (12) like "the wide world and all her fading sweets." (19) The sense of helplessness in the face of time is more profound and poignant than in most love poetry, partly because Shakespeare looks to no sexual resolution. A great weight is thrown on resolution in the creative act of poetry—and so on poetry's promise of immortality. Not infrequently, as in 19, claims made in a concluding couplet, after large reflections on devouring Time, have not weight enough to make a satisfying balance. But a massive poem like 55,

> Not marble, nor the gilded monuments
> Of princes, shall outlive this powerful rhyme . . .

makes us realize anew art's power of survival; in 74 and elsewhere we are made to feel how a man's spirit can be preserved in poetry, whereas "the earth can have but earth."

IV.   Eros Tyrranos

The concern to realize and live in the identity of another is just what we should expect, if we think about it, from the man who, beyond all other men, created other identities. And the difficulties with love expressed in the sonnets are also congruous with the capacities demonstrated in the plays. One difficulty, which grows more and more obvious as one reads and rereads the poems to the friend, is that the action, in such a love as this, is almost all on the poet's side. In 53, Shakespeare asks the arresting question,

> What is your substance, whereof are you made,
> That millions of strange shadows on you tend?

The poet's powers as a dramatist at once come to mind when he goes on to say

> Describe Adonis, and the counterfeit
> Is poorly imitated after you;
> On Helen's cheek all art of beauty set,
> And you in Grecian tires are painted new.

It is clear that the strange shadows come not from the friend, but from the poet, who costumes him now in one role, now in another. Sonnet 61 recognizes this fact in answering another arresting question,

> Is it thy will thy image should keep open
> My heavy eyelids to the weary night?

The conclusion is a troubled recognition that it is the poet's will, not the friend's:

> For thee watch I, whilst thou dost wake elsewhere,
> From me far off, with others all too near.

One is tempted to answer for the friend that after all, not being a poet, he cannot beguile the long night with a companion composed of images and words!

There are sonnets which recognize, too, if only playfully, that such identification as the poet feels with his friend involves selfishness or self-love. Thus 62 exploits a double take as to who is who: "Sin of self-love possesseth all mine eye, / . . . Methinks no face so gracious is as mine, / No shape so true, no truth of such account." The turn comes with the third quatrain: "But when my glass shows me myself indeed, / Beated and chopp'd with tann'd antiquity. . . ." The same game is played in 39, this time with "worth" and "self": "What can mine own praise to mine own self bring? / And what is't but mine own when I praise thee?" It is easy to dismiss this sort of reasoning, when we read a sonnet in isolation, as sonneteer's logic. But when we come to understand the sort of relationship Shakespeare is expressing, we realize that these poems mean what they say in making equations. The poet's sense of himself hinges on the identification: elation in realizing himself in the friend's self is matched by desolation when he is left in the lurch of selflessness. There are a number of poems where he proposes to do anything, to set himself utterly at naught or injure himself, if by so doing he can contribute to the friend's wishes and give him meaning: "Upon thy side against myself I'll fight, . . . /That thou, in losing me, shall win much glory." (88) "Speak of my lameness, and I straight will halt. . . ." (89) Commentators have been silly enough to conclude from this that Shakespeare was literally lame; they have argued from "beated and chopp'd with tann'd antiquity" that he wrote the sonnets when he was old. Of course in both cases what is conveyed is not literal incapacity but the poet's sense that without the younger friend he is nothing. Indeed the action of making himself nothing is, for him, a way of making love real by making the beloved everything.

With the woman, things go just the other way: Shakespeare makes love to her by telling her she is naught! At the best, he tells her that she attracts him even though she is "black" instead of "fair" (127); more commonly, he asks for favors in the same breath that he tells her he loves her in spite of his five wits and his five senses (141); most commonly, he spells out her falsehood and exclaims at the paradox that "in the very refuse of [her] deeds" she somehow makes him love her more "the more I hear and see just cause of hate." (150) These are outrageous poems: one wonders whether in fact most of them can have been sent to the poor woman—whether many of them were not off-stage exercises in hate and despite written from a need to get something out of the poet's system. To tell a woman that since she is promiscuous, she may as well let you put in among the rest, especially since your *name* too is Will (135), does not seem a very likely way to win even a hardened profligate. Several poems, notably 151, present a sequence in which degrading the woman and his relation to her frees the poet for an impudent phallic self-assertion:

> For thou betraying me, I do betray
> My nobler part to my gross body's treason;
> My soul doth tell my body that he may
> Triumph in love; flesh stays no farther reason . . .

One cannot avoid the conclusion that, for Shakespeare, in the constellation of relations with which the sonnets are concerned, specific sexual love was disassociated from cherishing and adoring love: sonnet 144 summarizes these "two loves," one of "comfort," the other of "despair," one "a man right fair," the other "a woman colou'rd ill." The psychological implications have of course been variously interpreted, most recently by a Dutch psychoanalyst, Dr. Conrad V. Emde Boas. I understand that his large book, which has not yet been translated, sees in Shakespeare's cherishing of a younger man an identification with the mother's role, and a displaced narcissism which in praising the beloved enjoys the contemplation of an ideal image of the poet himself. Such a theory can only be rightly evaluated by mobilizing the whole system of thought which gives its concepts meaning. But common sense can see, I think, that the sonnets reflect only one patterning of a kaleidoscopic personality: the tenderness which here is attached to a man or several men might well, in other phases of Shakespeare's life, have been felt for women.

And without resort to psychoanalytic formulations, our knowledge of Shakespeare's qualities as an artist can help in understanding the attitudes expressed in the sonnets. James Joyce, in pursuing his own obsession with the artist as a natural cuckold, was much preoccupied with the triangle in the sonnets. In *Ulysses*, Shakespeare emerges as a shadowy double for Bloom and as an omen for Stephen Dedalus: the flickering suggestions about Shakespeare center in the notion that he was betrayed because as an artist he would rather see than do, not asserting himself in actual life but taking the lead in love from others, while fulfilling himself in creating the various persons of his plays. Joyce is riding his own concerns, but he provides a useful perspective on the sonnets which deal with the double infidelity. In 40-42, where Shakespeare struggles to find a way of resolving in words the injury that his friend and mistress have done him in deeds, the idea of his identification with his friend is carried to a bitter *reductio ad absurdum*:

> But here's the joy, my friend and I are one;
> Sweet flattery, then she loves but me alone.   (42)

These tortured and tortuous sonnets adopt and abandon one strained interpretation after another, including the ironic suggestion that the two others are behaving as they do only to satisfy Shakespeare vicariously:

> Loving offenders, thus I will excuse ye,
> Thou dost love her, because thou know'st I love her,
> And for my sake even so doth she abuse me,
> Suff'ring my friend for my sake to approve her.   (42)

How much simpler it would be if friend and mistress were both of them in a play! Indeed, bitter as these sonnets are, they express a response to the humiliation life has brought which moves in the direction of art. Most men would bury the event in silence, or else turn injury into anger. Shakespeare turns injury into poetry. The very act of writing about the betrayal is a kind of acceptance of it—which goes with the extraordinary effort to accept the friend even in such circumstances. Thus 41 excuses "Those pretty wrongs that liberty commits, / When I am sometime absent from thy heart," only to exclaim poignantly, "Ay me, but yet thou might'st my seat forbear." In 40 the poet attempts a gesture of total self-abnegation:

> I do forgive thy robb'ry, gentle thief,
> Although thou steal thee all my poverty;
> And yet love knows it is a greater grief
> To bear love's wrong than hate's known injury.
>> Lascivious grace, in whom all ill well shows,
>> Kill me with spites; yet we must not be foes.

The whole metrical force of the sonnet is mobilized in the uttering of "Lascivious grace," a phrase which brings into focus the anguish and enjoyment of Shakespeare's continuing identification with the friend. The poet's artistic sympathy encounters the ruthlessness of another living identity and remains open to it.

These are disturbing and unsatisfying poems, despite their great power, because they do not achieve a stable attitude toward the experience. We encounter the same irresolute quality in some of the sonnets where the young man's dissoluteness or vanity are both rebuked and accepted (e.g. 95, 84). The poems are twisted on the rack of a sympathy "beyond good and evil," the sympathy which is organized in the plays, flowing into opposites and antagonists so that, as Eglington phrases it in *Ulysses,* "He is the ghost and the prince. He is all in all." Stephen Dedalus takes up the point:

> He is, Stephen said. The boy of act one is the mature man of act five. All in all. In *Cymbeline,* in *Othello* he is bawd and cuckold. He acts and is acted on. . . . His unremitting intellect is the hornmad Iago ceaselessly willing that the moor in him shall suffer.[3]

These are wild and whirling words, describing Shakespeare through Stephen and his preoccupations. But in them Joyce brings out how much Shakespeare needed the drama.

V. Self-knowledge

The most satisfying of the sonnets which deal with Shakespeare's difficulties in love are those where he is using the sonnet primarily to confront what love reveals to him about himself. Thus in 35 we get, in the midst of excuses for the friend, a recognition that

> All men make faults, and even I in this,
> Authorizing thy trespass with compare,
> Myself corrupting, salving thy amiss . . .

The most impressive explorations come in sonnets which are late in the numerical order—poems which have a complexity of texture and tone which set them apart from most, though not all, of the first one hundred, and so were probably composed later. Among those to the woman, I find most satisfying the ones which, forbearing hymns of hate, define the cheapness of the relation—cheapness being one of the hardest things to get into poetry (or indeed to face up to in any fashion). Symmetrical lies are laid out in 138, hers to him and his to her, tea for two and two for tea:

> Therefore I lie with her, and she with me,
> And in our faults by lies we flattered be.

A stimulating criticism by Mr. Patrick Cruttwell, which relates these late poems to the plays of the period of *Hamlet* and *Troilus and Cressida*, sees this sonnet as "perhaps the most terrible of the whole sequence," climaxed in the "grim seriousness" of the pun on lie.[4] "Grim" seems to me wrong: I find the poem jaunty as well as devastating, and more honest so. Where the sonnets to the woman do become completely grim, there is usually a certain falsifying simplification in resorting to unmeasured abuse, as in the couplet which ends, but does not resolve, the analysis of love's fever in 147:

> For I have sworn thee fair, and thought thee bright,
> Who art as black as hell, as dark as night.

In the poems of self-analysis addressed to a man, there is a far deeper facing up to the poet's own moral involvement—and to the paradoxes of passion where morality seems no longer to apply. In 109-112 and 117-121 the poet, acknowledging infidelities on his side, confronts directly the polymorphic responsiveness of his own personality:

> Alas 'tis true, I have gone here and there,
> And made myself a motley to the view,
> Gor'd mine own thoughts, sold cheap what is most dear,
> Made old offences of affections new.   (110)

Here "made myself a motley" suggests the actor's impulse and his humiliations, and in 111 Shakespeare explicitly asks his friends to forgive in him the "public manners" which are bred by the "public means" from which he must provide for his livelihood:

> Thence comes it that my name receives a brand,
> And almost thence my nature is subdu'd
> To what it works in, like the dyer's hand.

Commentators have emphasized, indeed exaggerated, the ignominious status of the acting profession in the Elizabethan age, seeing in this outward circumstance the source of Shakespeare's self-disabling humility toward his friend. No doubt it was a factor, just as part of the appeal of the young man or young men was superior birth, a heritage the poet did not have and could enjoy through identification. But the temperament which made Shakespeare an actor and dramatist is more fundamental than the matter of status, as these sonnets make clear: they present a complex, resonant personality which, for most purposes in life, is over-responsive, over-eager, drawn on to act unworthy parts and unable to avoid living out in new relationships what has already been found shameful. His fluidity, his almost unbearable openness to desire and to life, are described in 109 in the course of a moving plea:

> Never believe, though in my nature reign'd
> All frailties that besiege all kinds of blood,
> That it could so preposterously be stain'd
> To leave for nothing all thy sum of good.

The sort of knowledge of the heart and its turnings which finds expression in the plays appears in these sonnets with a special if limited intensity—the intensity involved in seeing, in one's single life, the broken lines made by Eros. In the same moment when he asks forgiveness for making "old offences of affections new," Shakespeare has the courage to recognize that there is value, as well as humiliation, in selling "cheap what is most dear":

> Most true it is, that I have look'd on truth
> Askance and strangely. But by all above,
> These blenches gave my heart another youth,
> And worse essays prov'd thee my best of love.   (110)

There is no set posture in these poems against morality or convention: if they simplified things by adopting a romantic or bohemian rationale, they could not be so serious in exploring the way passion turns corners that it cannot see around and moves in directions contrary to the will. Sonnet 121 confronts in a frightening way the breakdown of moral categories in this territory: "'Tis better to be vile than vile esteemed. . . . No, I am that I am." The pressure of experience on received categories is so great in this sonnet (and at places in others of this whole group), that it is impossible entirely to comprehend the meaning—though we can apprehend it obliquely. In the dramatic form, Shakespeare could present directly, in several persons, what here is looked at askance from one vantage.

These poems reckoning with himself are not the greatest sonnets
Shakespeare wrote, though they are profound and moving. The poems
which gather in life with a lover's delight have more sensuous substance than these inward-turning pieces; and the poems which generalize out from love have more that each reader can make his own.
There is not space to consider some of the most wonderful of the generalizing sonnets, such as the tough yet poignant evaluations of
worldliness, 124 and 125 ("Pitiful thrivers, in the gazing spent?"),
the analysis of lust as "Th' expense of spirit in a waste of shame" in
129, the large-souled gesture of fidelity in 116, "Let me not to the
marriage of true minds / Admit impediments," or the urgent religious
revulsion from life in 146, "Poor soul, the centre of my sinful earth."
These great poems, because they generalize, can be appreciated in isolation. The sonnets confronting his own nature, by contrast, grow in
meaning as we set one against another—and as we see the whole
group in relation to what Shakespeare did in his plays. Few poems
have expressed so close to the heart and nerves as 120 the transformation of suffering into compassion:

> That you were once unkind befriends me now,
> And for that sorrow which I then did feel
> Needs must I under my transgression bow,
> Unless my nerves were brass or hammer'd steel.
> For if you were by my unkindness shaken,
> As I by yours, y'have pass'd a hell of time. . . .
> O that our night of woe might have remember'd
> My deepest sense, how hard true sorrow hits. . . .

Here we see particularly clearly how the capacity for identifying with
a person loved, sometimes disabling, perplexing and humiliating, also
gives Shakespeare his "deepest sense, how hard true sorrow hits."

NOTES

1. Rollins summarized his judgment thus in a brief introduction written
   in 1951 (*Sonnets*, New York, 1951, p. ix.).
2. *English Literature in the Sixteenth Century*, Oxford, 1954, p. 491.
3. *Ulysses*, Modern Library Edition, p. 210.
4. *The Shakespearean Moment*, New York, 1955, pp. 13-14.

T. S. ELIOT

Sir John Davies

Chief Justice John Davies died on December 7, 1626. He left a number of poems, a philosophical treatise, "Reason's Academy," some legal writings, and several long State Papers on Ireland. As a public servant he had a distinguished career; but very likely the poem which has preserved his memory, *Nosce Teipsum*, was what commended him to King James. Possibly James was more appreciative of learning than of poetical merit; but, in any case, he recognized merit in a poet who was, in some respects, as out of place in his own age as he is in ours.

Davies's shorter poems are usually graceful and occasionally lovely, but they are so completely eclipsed even by the modest reputation of *Nosce Teipsum* and *Orchestra* that they are never chosen as anthology pieces. *Nosce Teipsum*, by its gnomic utterance and its self-contained quatrains, lends itself to mutilation; but a stanza or two is all that has been anthologized. Probably all that most readers know of Davies is represented by the two stanzas in the *Oxford Book of English Verse:*

> I know my soul hath power to know all things,
> Yet she is blind and ignorant in all:
> I know I'm one of Nature's little kings,
> Yet to the least and vilest things am thrall.

Reprinted from *On Poetry and Poets* by T. S. Eliot, pp. 149-55, by permission of Faber & Faber Ltd. and of Farrar, Straus & Giroux, Inc. Copyright © 1957 by T. S. Eliot. Originally published in *The Times Literary Supplement* in 1926.

> I know my life's a pain and but a span;
> I know my sense is mock'd in everything;
> And, to conclude, I know myself a Man—
> Which is a proud and yet a wretched thing.

Fine and complete as the two stanzas are they do not represent the poem, and no selection of stanzas can represent it. Davies is a poet of fine lines, but he is more than that. He is not one of that second rank of poets who, here and there, echo the notes of the great. If there is, in *Orchestra*, a hint of the influence of Spenser, it is no more than the debt which many Elizabethans owe to that master of versification. And the plan, the versification, and the content of *Nosce Teipsum* are, in that age, highly original.

The poem of *Nosce Teipsum* is a long discussion in verse of the nature of the soul and its relation to the body. Davies's theories are not those of the later seventeenth-century philosopher, nor are they very good Aristotelianism. Davies is more concerned to prove that the soul is distinct from the body than to explain how such distinct entities can be united. The soul is a spirit, and, as such, has wit, will, reason and judgment. It does not appear as the "form" of the body, and the word "form" appears in the poem rather in the sense of "representation" [*similitudo*]. The soul is in the body as light is in the air —which disposes of the scholastic question whether the soul is more in one part of the body than another. Nor are the problems of sense perception difficult to resolve: Davies is not troubled by the "reception of forms without matter." His contribution to the science of acoustics is the explanation that sounds must pass through the "turns and windings" of the ear:

> For should the voice directly strike the braine,
> It would astonish and confuse it much.

Whether or not Davies borrowed his theories—if they deserve the name of theories—from Nemesius or from some other Early Christian author, and whether he got them direct or secondhand, it is evident that we cannot take them very seriously. But the end of the sixteenth century was not a period of philosophic refinement in England— where, indeed, philosophy had visibly languished for a hundred years and more. Considering the place and the time, this philosophical poem by an eminent jurist is by no means a despicable production. In an age when philosophy, apart from theology, meant usually (and especially in verse) a collection of Senecan commonplaces, Davies's is an independent mind.

The merit and curiosity of the poem, however, reside in the perfection of the instrument to the end. In a language of remarkable clarity and austerity Davies succeeds in maintaining the poem consistently on the level of poetry; he never flies to hyperbole or bombast, and he never descends, as he easily might, to the pedestrian and ludicrous. Certain odd lines and quatrains remain in the memory, as:

> But sith our life so fast away doth slide,
> As doth a hungry eagle through the wind,

(a simile which Alexander borrows for his *Julius Caesar*), or

> And if thou, like a child, didst feare before,
> Being in the darke, where thou didst nothing see;
> Now I have brought thee torch-light, fear no more;
> Now when thou diest, thou canst not hud-winkt be.

Davies has not had the credit for great felicity of phrase, but it may be observed that, when other poets have pilfered from him or have arrived independently at the same figure, it is usually Davies who has the best of it. Grosart compares the following two passages showing a simile used by Davies and by Pope:

> Much like a subtill spider, which doth sit
> In middle of her web, which spreadeth wide;
> If aught do touch the utmost thread of it,
> She feels it instantly on every side.

Pope:

> The spider's touch, how exquisitely fine,
> Feels at each thread, and lives along the line.

Davies's spider is the more alive, though he needs two more lines for her. Another instance is the well-known figure from the *Ancient Mariner*:

> Still as a slave before his lord,
> The ocean hath no blast;
> His great bright eye most silently
> Up to the Moon is cast—

where "most" is a blemish. Davies has (in *Orchestra*):

For loe the Sea that fleets about the Land,
    And like a girdle clips her solide waist,
Musicke and measure both doth understand;
    For his great chrystall eye is always cast
Up to the Moone, and on her fixèd fast;
    And as she daunceth in her pallid spheere
    So daunceth he about his center heere.

But the mastery of workmanship of *Nosce Teipsum* and its beauty are not to be appreciated by means of scattered quotations. Its effect is cumulative. Davies chose a difficult stanza, one in which it is almost impossible to avoid monotony. He embellishes it with none of the flowers of conceit of his own age or the next, and he has none of the antitheses or verbal wit with which the Augustans sustain their periods. His vocabulary is clear, choice and precise. His thought is, for an Elizabethan poet, amazingly coherent; there is nothing that is irrelevant to his main argument, no excursions or flights. And, although every quatrain is complete in itself, the sequence is never a "string of pearls" (such as was fashionable in the next age, as in Crashaw's *Weeper*); the thought is continuous. Yet no stanza ever is identical in rhythm with another. The style appears plain, even bald, yet Davies's personal cadence is always there. Many critics have remarked the condensation of thought, the economy of language, and the consistency of excellence; but some have fallen into the error of supposing that Davies's merit is of prose. Hallam, after praising the poem, says:

"If it reaches the heart of all, it is through the reason. But since strong argument in terse and correct style fails not to give us pleasure in prose, it seems strange that it should lose its effect when it gains the aid of regular metre to gratify the ear and assist the memory."

Hallam's criticism is topsy-turvy. Hallam's heart must have been peculiarly inaccessible, or his reason very easily touched. The argument is not strong; had Davies entered the ring of philosophical argument his contemporary, Cardinal Bellarmine, could have knocked him out in the first round. Davies had not a philosophical mind; he was primarily a poet, but with a gift for philosophical exposition. His appeal is, indeed, to what Hallam calls the heart, though we no longer employ that single organ as the vehicle of all poetic feeling. The excellence of the theory of body and soul which Davies expounded is, however, irrelevant. If someone had provided him with a better theory the poem might have been, in one aspect, a better one;

in another aspect it does not matter a fig. The wonder is that Davies, in his place and time, could produce so coherent and respectable a theory as he did. No one, not even Gray, has surpassed Davies in the use of the quatrain which he employed for *Nosce Teipsum*; and no poem in any similar metre (compare *The Witch of Atlas*) is metrically superior to *Orchestra*. Even his little acrostic poems on the name of Queen Elizabeth are admirable in grace and melody. And with this genius for versification, with a taste in language remarkably pure for his age, Davies had that strange gift, so rarely bestowed, for turning thought into feeling.

In the effort to "place" Davies, who appears anomalous, critics have compared him on the one hand to the Senecals, to Chapman and Daniel and Greville, and on the other hand to Donne and the metaphysicals. Neither classification is quite exact. Davies' only direct debt as a poet seems to be to Spenser, the master of everybody. The type of his thought, and consequently the tone of his expression, separates him from the Senecals. His thought, as we have said, is inferior as philosophy, but it is coherent and free from eccentricity or pose. He thinks like a scholastic, though the quality of his thought would have shocked a scholastic. Chapman, Daniel and Greville, so far as they can be said to have thought at all, thought like Latin rhetoricians. Like the other dramatists, they imbibed from Seneca a philosophy which is essentially a theatrical pose. Hence their language, even when pure and restrained—and Daniel's is astonishingly pure and restrained—is always orotund and oratorical; their verse is as if spoken in public, and their feelings as if felt in public. Davies's is the language and the tone of solitary meditation; he speaks like a man reasoning with himself in solitude, and he never raises his voice.

In the same way Davies may be said to have little in common with Donne. It is not merely Davies's restraint in the use of simile and metaphor. The verbal conceit, as used by Donne, implies a very different attitude towards ideas from that of Davies, perhaps a much more conscious one. Donne was ready to entertain almost any idea, to play with it, to follow it out of curiosity, to explore all its possibilities of affecting his sensibility. Davies is much more mediaeval; his capacity for belief is greater. He has but the one idea, which he pursues in all seriousness—a kind of seriousness rare in his age. Thought is not exploited for the sake of feeling, it is pursued for its own sake; and the feeling is a kind of by-product, though a by-product worth far more than the thought. The effect of the sequence of the poem is not to diversify or embellish the feeling: it is wholly to intensify. The variation is in the metrics.

There is only one parallel to *Nosce Teipsum,* and, though it is a daring one, it is not unfair to Davies. It is the several passages of exposition of the nature of the soul which occur in the middle of the *Purgatorio.* To compare Davies with Dante may appear fantastic. But, after all, very few people read these parts of Dante, and fewer still get any pleasure out of them: in short, these passages are probably as little read or enjoyed as *Nosce Teipsum* itself. Of course they are vastly finer, for two quite different reasons—Dante was a vastly greater poet, and the philosophy which he expounds is infinitely more substantial and subtle:

> *Esce di mano a lui, che la vagheggia*
> *prima che sia, a guisa di fanciulla*
> *che piangendo e ridendo pargoleggia,*

> *l'anima semplicetta, che sa nulla,*
> *salvo che, mossa da lieto fattore,*
> *volentier torna a cio che la trastulla.*

> *Di picciol bene in pria sente sapore;*
> *quivi s'inganna, e retro ad esso corre,*
> *se guida o fren non torce suo amore.*

> From his hands who fondly loves her ere she is in
>   being, there issues, after the fashion of a little child
>   that sports, now weeping, now laughing,

> the simple, tender soul, who knoweth naught save that,
>   sprung from a joyous maker, willingly she turneth
>   to that which delights her.

> First she tastes the savour of a trifling good; there she
>   is beguiled and runneth after it, if guide or curb turn
>   not her love aside.

It is not in any way to put Davies on a level with Dante to say that anyone who can appreciate the beauty of such lines as these should be able to extract considerable pleasure from *Nosce Teipsum.*

PART III

The Faerie Queene

The Spenserian Fluidity

Through Spenser Elizabethan England first becomes fully vocal. His frequent excess, though sometimes deplorable, is of the stuff nevertheless that fills the mould of *Twelfth Night* and *Othello*. He offers a fountain of Elizabethanism, neat. Ideals of Queen-worship and courtiership, especially clear in his admiration of Sidney, are strong in him; also an English pastoralism entwined with Greek mythology; and a sensuous love. He is both national and lyric. Part of his life a civil servant in Ireland, he aspired to be more, and his disappointment has left poetic records of satiric bitterness. But failure did not stifle his more vivid apprehensions, and it is that more positive and characteristic quality that I shall emphasize.

The Shepherd's Calendar (1579) shows a typical profusion, an upgushing of poetic life. Each eclogue is a miniature lyric playlet, the sequence patterned on the procession of the twelve months. In his archaic language Spenser is here self-consciously English, acknowledging Chaucer and attempting to repudiate other, especially continental, sources. Hellenic mythology is, as in Lyly, a natural expression for a native voice. From out a medley-setting of Theocritus and an English spring, Queen Elizabeth is hymned with extravagant praise and shower-garlanded with a stanza of flowers. One of E. K.'s[1] notes to *April* is valuable:

From *The Burning Oracle* (London, 1939), pp. 1-18. Copyright, 1939, by G. Wilson Knight. Reprinted by permission of the author and the publishers, Methuen & Co. Ltd. The author has made some minor revisions in the essay.

> So that by Pan is here meant the most famous and victorious
> king, her highness' Father, late of worthy memory, King Henry
> the Eighth. And by that name, ofttimes (as hereafter appear-
> eth) be noted kings and mighty potentates: and in some place
> Christ himself, who is the very Pan and god of shepherds.

Notice the close texture of Greek mythology, Christianity, and the
throne of England. *The Shepherd's Calendar* is both delicately autobiographical and allegorically allusive: "By the kid may be understood the simple sort of the faithful and true Christians" (E. K.'s note
to *May*). The Roman Catholic Church, Gabriel Harvey, Spenser's
own love-affair, appear in turn and in fancy dress. The close-entwin-
ing of royalistic and heraldic meanings within the flower-stanza of
April has been skilfully analyzed by Janet Spens (*Spenser's Fairie
Queene: an Interpretation*, 1934, 74-5). Red and white roses bind
civil warfare into an offering to Tudor supremacy, a miniature forecast of Shakespeare's historic succession culminating in *Henry VIII*.
Complexity of symbolic or allegoric suggestion enmeshed in the contemporary and actual fact or event, whether of the poet's own life or
the nation's. Contemporary reference is native to the Elizabethan
mind. Abstractions are not, as in medieval literature, allowed dictato-
rial rights over it: they are twisted into a close texture of a new sort.
To the Elizabethan poet the ideal is incarnated and at hand; politically in the Queen, personally in his own love. Neither the medieval
nor the modern distinction between the actual and the imaginative
can properly be supposed to exist.

Inspection of Spenser's four *Hymns* (pub. 1596; the first two purportedly composed much earlier) illustrates the humanistic Eros-cult
which is his belief-core, and, indeed, almost central to Renaissance
poetry. From them we can pass to *The Faery Queen*.

The *Hymn in Honour of Love* addresses its deity with all the fervour of a pagan worshipper, the love being of the sexual-romantic
kind. Eros is a "great godhead" "thou mighty god of love," "great god
of might that reignest in the mind," a phrase neatly pointing a recognition of psychological sovereignty. The analogy is frequent: "sovereign king," "sovereign lord of all," "lord of truth and loyalty," "victor
of gods, subduer of mankind." There is stress on love's power, yet the
god is at heart gentle, inspiring a "gentle fury," taming lions and ti-
gers. It is that first creative force playing on chaos, the Holy Spirit of
Genesis; Venus, beauty-goddess, the life-former, blends the four ele-

ments in harmony. Notice the replacing of Biblical by classical deities. Spenser distinguishes his ideal from lust: it appeals to man's "immortal mind," is a matter of "eternity" and "beauty." Such Platonic intuitions would perhaps silence too glibly a profound problem, but Spenser does not shirk the unrest of an unsatisfied aspiration which drives men to distraction through "enravished" sight of a divine excellence, till "all other bliss seems vain." He realizes its tragic quality and attendant evils, plunging the lover in "hell" and that worst monster jealousy that turns "all love's delight to misery"; the thoughts forecast *Othello* as the greater part of the poem recalls Berowne's defence of love in *Love's Labour's Lost* (IV. iii. 290-365) and kindred Shakespearean imaginations. The whole is heavily charged with light imagery. There is perhaps too facile and adjectival a use of it. A line such as "the flaming light of that celestial fire" illustrates an extreme of what is here an habitual over-stress, almost a technical vice. There is not enough housing of his fire in continually new, concrete, shapes, but the experience transmitted is clear. The poem ends in flowery delight and with a prayer that the lover may, after his pains, attain paradise:

> Then would I sing of thine immortal praise
> An heavenly hymn such as the angels sing,
> And thy triumphant name then would I raise
> 'Bove all the gods, thee only honouring,
> My guide, my God, my victor, and my king. . . .

His adoration is theologically uncompromising.

The *Hymn in Honour of Beauty* is similar, and strongly Platonic. Christian thought is present, but the goddess is "Cyprian Queen" of "sovereign might." This beauty of "goodly pattern" ignites love, it is a "light," a "lively fire" shining in a face and darting "amorous desire" into the beholder's soul. The inwardness and physical transcendence of it is argued from our not falling in love with pictures or natural scenery: the beauty which inspires love must involve vitality. The externals of human beauty seen as "white and red," "golden wire," "sparkling stars" must fade, but not so the spirit-fire moulding the physical form in its likeness. Spenser does not altogether shirk the crucial problem of beauty of face joined to evil of soul; but neither does he solve it. He again waxes fierce against "that hellish fire-brand disloyal lust"; as well he may, since it is the main reason why the cult of Eros has not ages ago been royally established. The trust is, however, finally in the true lover, who sees more profoundly than others, admires "a more refined form," in a sense focusing "the mirror of his own thought": an act of knowledge channelling full subjective instincts. A reciprocity is set up between lovers' eyes:

> For lovers' eyes more sharply sighted be
> Than other men's, and in dear love's delight
> See more than any other eyes can see,
> Through mutual receipt of beames bright. . . .

It is a revelation, a "dawning day." Something is created, or apprehended. This sense of the significance of lovers' eyes is paralleled in Lyly and Shakespeare. Spenser ends his *Hymn in Honour of Beauty* with more regal touches: "thy great majesty," "great sovereign," "great goddess of my life." It is a force that "can restore a damned wight from death." It could scarcely be more highly honoured.

The two Heavenly Hymns parallel and complement these. The four together neatly balance opposing principles in the Elizabethan mind. Janet Spens (p. 51, 111) observes that the *Hymn of Heavenly Love* describes a downward giving rather than an upward reaching: *agapè* rather than *eros*. It is, as Father E. C. Le Bel has shown, a fairly direct transcription of Christian doctrine. Love starting from the Father begets the Son, and from them is derived the Holy Spirit. Spenser phrases as best he can the illimitable bright splendours of angelic life, stress falling on the infinite and, as before, on light. He discusses the Fall, Incarnation, and Redemption. King-imagery, as before, is potent: "high heaven's king," "sovereign might." Christ is "eternal king of glorie" with "sovereign bounty" and "sovereign mercy." The Hymn ends with exhortations to rise above lesser loves to Christ, couched in the usual blaze of fire-imagery and Platonic excitement. Although the reverse movement and explicit doctrine contradicts the earlier pagan aspirations, they remain only part of the poetry. In so far as we attend to the massed impressions, the substance appears not so very different. It is characteristically Platonic, characteristically scintillant. Spenser's explicit repudiation of his former "lewd lays" while offering to sing of "true love" for a change may be nearer an artistic device than a confession of conversion. The Elizabethan poet was not normally convertible, since both terms of the opposition were with him comfortably together from the start, and to the end. This balance the four *Hymns* in turn express. The Elizabethan is only doing on purpose what many poets since have done by instinct, aiming to eat his cake and have it too. This is often a poetic necessity.

Poetry cannot be entirely theological and transcendental. God must be continually imagined in ever new materialist terms: as some sort of "sovereign," "high eternal power," "maker," or, in the Hymn to *Beauty*, "this world's great work-master." In the fourth hymn Spenser has a neat problem: how to sing of that Beauty which transcends nature? What do we mean by "eternal," "divine," "spiritual"? The concrete quality of poetry cannot rest content with such abstractions. The same road is taken by poet after poet: his mind-structure being naturalistic and yet his final aim being transcendent, he focuses a reality best termed "universalistic." The holistic tendencies of poetry are well seen in such instances.

So we are asked to look on the frame "of this wide universe," and thence to dream others "infinite in largeness." We are told of "endless perfectness" and "infinite delight." Impressions of space are expanded:

> First th' Earth, on adamantine pillars founded,
> Amid the Sea engirt with brazen bands;
> Then th' Air still flitting, but yet firmly bounded
> On every side, with piles of flaming brands,
> Never consum'd nor quench'd with mortal hands;
> And last, that mighty shining crystal wall
> Wherewith He hath encompassed this All.

Contemplation of the universe rather than "nature," of *Antony and Cleopatra* rather than *King Lear*, is the way to divine apprehension, spurning earth:

> Air more than water, fire much more than air,
> And heaven than fire appears more pure and fair.

Though all elements are finally transcended, the Heavenly Beauty is frequently imaged as a sun. We are to concentrate on the "king" and "queen" of the sky who "the heavens' empire sway." "King" and "sun," as so often, touch metaphorically: "their Captain's flaming head" is a good phrase. There are regal suggestions, as in "the glorious face of the divine eternal Majesty" and the "sovereign Powers and Potentates" which are said to contain "all mortal Princes and imperial states." This Beauty is a "majesty divine" compared with which Sun and Moon are dark, itself a "bright sun of glory." Therefore throw yourself humbly "before the footstool of his Majesty," whose "throne" is built on eternity and whose "sceptre" is righteousness. Sapience is his queen, "the sovereign darling of the Deity," she is "clad like a queen in royal robes," on her head is set "a crown of purest gold," and all is "subjected to her power imperial." "Beauty sovereign," "sovereign praises," "sovereign light"—the poem is dense with royalistic impressions and imagery, perhaps over-insistent, of sun and fire.

What Spenser is doing should be clear. To read any absolute division into the two halves of the sequence is to read that sequence as something other than poetry. His impressionism remains constant, and though this is not the whole of his poetry it is a great part of it. The human is first seen as divine; the divine is later imaged in human, and in Sapience feminine, terms. At one extreme there are sexual, at the other Christian, apprehensions. They are different-coloured beads threaded on the one golden string of royalistic and fire-impressions intertwisted with a Platonic idealism. This balance in opposition or synthesis of Christian and erotic feeling is vital throughout Renaissance and post-Renaissance poetry. Only less interesting is the close relation, almost equation, of kingship and personal aspiration. A king is, as it were, a super-self, and the term may be used to suggest a super-apprehension, or its object. It blends naturally into a sense of the divine, being soaked in centuries of sacramental feeling.

In *The Faery Queen* (1590-96) Spenser seems to have taken all poetic impressionism as his province. It is stocked with folklore, myth, and legend of all sorts and crammed with influences Italian, medieval and classical. The poem is peculiarly rich in pagan lore. Spenser's metaphysic of fertility and creation is often nearer to the pagan and the naturalistic than to the Christian. *The Faery Queen* is more a storehouse for poets of the future than itself a poem. In this, if in no other sense, he is, "the poets' poet," and a study of *The Faery Queen* in detail should help any one who finds Colin Still's interpretation of *The Tempest* in terms of ancient legendary and ritualistic correspondences a fantastic conception.[2] Behind all our poetry there is a communal store of semi-consciously possessed legendary material: Spenser seems to have possessed it consciously. As so often, the Elizabethan is fully aware, his mind flooded, where later poets rely on mysterious, not-to-be-accounted-for promptings, controlled or otherwise, from unconsciousness.

But *The Faery Queen* is not concerned mainly with ancient recollections: it is supremely Elizabethan as well. Its forked meanings are clear from Spenser's own statement in *A Letter of the Author's expounding his whole intention in the course of this work:*

> In that Faery Queen I mean glory in my general intention, but in my particular I conceive the most excellent and glorious person of our sovereign the Queen, and her kingdom in Faery Land. And yet in some places else, I do otherwise shadow her. . . .
>
> *Poetical Works*, ed. J. C. Smith and
> E. de Selincourt, edn. of 1924; p. 407.

A neat statement of the universal and particular in poetic blend, though so tight and exact a fusion as is suggested applies more generally to the work of Lyly than to that of Spenser, whose significances are often arbitrary and laxly related, as his final phrase suggests. But he is throughout more than a fancy-poet, and also more than a medieval allegorist, though both these he certainly is too. He builds a nationalist and royalist purpose into the scheme. It is "the eulogy of a patriot addressing a united people," writes B. E. C. Davis (*Edmund Spenser*, 1933, p. 75), "the nearest approach to a national epic in the cycle of English poetry." He suggests that the constitution of Spenser's Faery Land presents a happy medium between monarchy and oligarchy that reflects "in vague outline" the commonwealth of Tudor England. The poem is dedicated to the Queen, who as Gloriana is supposed to dominate. In the introduction to Book II there is praise of the Queen; reference to recent explorations and discoveries; and a final sense of mystery and magic in the immediate and actual projected into the equation of England and Faery Land under the "fairest Princess under sky." The Queen's chastity, so often found to make a neat blend in the Elizabethan mind of its two dominating positives —royalistic splendour and sexual excellence of one divine sort or another—is to be related elsewhere to Belphoebe and also to Mercilla. Prince Arthur is, in part, Leicester. Arthur's "magnificence" is the Renaissance ideal in full show:

> The general end therefore of all the book is to fashion a gentleman or noble person in virtuous and gentle discipline.
> (*Poetical Works*, as above; p. 407)

Not, be it noted, to make a saint. The search for eternal truth (Una), the supplanting of deceitful semblances (Archimago and Duessa) are aspects of the humanistic ideal. Again,

So in the person of Prince Arthur I set forth magnificence in particular, which virtue for that (according to Aristotle and the rest) it is the perfection of all the rest, and containeth in it them all, therefore in the whole course I mention the deeds of Arthur applyable to that virtue, which I write of in that book.

(*Poetical Works*, as above; p. 407)

That holiness would not have been one of Aristotle's "virtues" need not trouble us. Renaissance poets try to *include* Christianity in a new, humanistic, comprehension. This is their poetic instinct, whatever their religious assertions. With them the present and actual incarnates the divine; from that sense is born their poetry. This is true equally of their royalistic and their erotic perceptions, which are not finally distinct. Both are blended with Christianity rather than subject to it.

Besides the specifically ancient or contemporary there are throughout *The Faery Queen* essences of the universal and the timeless. I mean the vivid naturalism and imagistic grace, the luscious stanzaic woodlands and glades of impressionism and event, the featuring of beasts and people, good or evil; of lovely life and hideous fears; the use of cosmic forces, sun or earth; of the seasons; of night and day; death and life in interdependence; and of divine purposes generally.

Nevertheless the poem is, as a whole, unsatisfying. It claims more than it fulfills. The various knights and their quests are surely too shadowy, too slightly distinguished and objectified. And even if they were not, the dominating and binding presences of Gloriana and Arthur do not dominate and bind as they ought. It is difficult to feel the poem as a whole and would be even if it were finished. We get from it a vague quality rather than a structure. This is partly because the symbolic technique is faulty. Although Spenser attempts to inweave his general thinking with the national life of his day, yet, faced by his vast self-proposed scheme, he falls back on a medievalistic allegory which he never quite controls. When one of his monsters vomits pamphlets we are shocked; too much realism in the beast's creation renders his deeper significance ludicrous; the blend of allegory and realism has not been properly performed. He misses symbol of the more profound sort: that incarnation of significance in fictional person, or beast, so exactly true that every bend of the mould fits, in its degree, the desired shape of the contained fluid. Spenser's moulds are themselves undisciplined and variable. Dante had his rigid theological beliefs and the medieval allegorists normally started with some precise and ruling intellectual structure. Shakespeare has his realism, his unswerving sense of the way things happen, as well as his sources. Spenser has no such discipline: there is nothing to stop his poem going on for ever, and, worm-like, its organic perfection suffers little from its having been chopped off halfway. It is true that in Shakespeare various meanings can be drawn from one symbolic figure: Caliban, for example. But Caliban is first a unit. "This is the law of symbolism," writes Charles Williams in discussion of Spenser, "that the symbol must be utterly itself before it can properly be a symbol" (*Reason and Beauty in the Poetic Mind*, 1933, p. 55). Whatever Caliban may mean, he is first Caliban, a rounded artistic whole. Spenser's significances are flat, and however many flatnesses are superimposed you do not create a multifacial globe. One sees in his work a transition between old-style allegory and a more rounded symbolism. He is struggling for it. He talks well of "general" and "particular" intentions, but in the completed result these are not tied up in a tight knot, it is all loose. His seeming complexity is never a complex profundity.

Though the main plan is, it seems, a magnificent failure, this does not preclude excellences in the parts. Its national, religious, and social implications are probably weaker than those personal and psychological, but these are often exquisite.

The poem is concerned heavily with man's erotic and sensuous nature, the problem of good and bad love. "Love," writes B. E. C. Davis (pp. 217, 220), is "a cardinal motive" in all Spenser's poetry; it "lies at the very foundation" of his "cosmos." In *The Allegory of Love* C. S. Lewis has well analyzed Spenser's meticulous impressionism in conveying states of decadent and healthy sex-instincts. In the Bower of Bliss there is stress on idleness, artificiality ("metal ivy"), eye-lust, and an excessively conscious sex-appeal, as in the bathing nymphs:

> Then suddenly both would themselves unhele,
> And th' amorous sweet spoiles to greedy eyes reveal.
>
> (II. xii. 64)

In contrast, the Garden of Adonis offers nature rather than art, frank sex-intercourse and a stress on creation (*The Allegory of Love*, 1936, pp. 324-6; 330-333). The naked Graces at VI. x. are, comments Lewis (331), "engaged in doing something worth doing"; that is, dancing in a ring "in order excellent" (VI. x. 13). Lewis analyzes another related and tricky opposition: of passionate yet adulterous love, persistent in medieval poetry, to married faithfulness. The end and aim of the sex-substances in *The Faery Queen* seems to be this marriage-ideal: a thought with manifold implications for the study of Elizabethan drama. Chastity to Spenser "means Britomart, married love." The "romance of marriage" replaces the "romance of adultery" (*The Allegory of Love*, p. 340).

We must therefore not complain too readily that Spenser's attractive evils, as in the Bower of Bliss, prove him a dangerous moralist. Rather he is at work on a very subtle problem. Certain stanzas may suggest a failure, such as we find in *Comus*, to be sure about his own judgements; but then he may not be sure; which, of course, may be an artistic limitation. C. S. Lewis writes: "The Bower of Bliss is not a place even of healthy animalism, or indeed of activity of any kind. . . . It is a picture, one of the most powerful ever painted, of the whole sexual nature in disease" (p. 332). The attraction—and the accompanying descriptions are often attractive—is part of the disease, and the problem as old as the Garden of Eden. It is similarly insistent in Marlowe and Milton, though there is no trace of it in Lyly or Shakespeare. The puritan, whether Spenser or Milton, opposes, as did D. H. Lawrence, not a physical instinct but an insidious mind-perversion from which few of us can claim complete freedom. It is the enjoyment of an idea rather than a reality, and ideas can have an attractive intensity no reality quite touches. Properly to act and live an experience the mind must be subdued, dissolved, itself unpossessing; creative things are often accomplished half-aware; while excessive awareness tends to the immoral. Nevertheless some intensity of perception may perhaps be known in the very mental twist of such evil, some sense of the life-fire not known otherwise, depending partly on the breaking of conventional codes, whatever they be; an enjoyment of daring, parasitic on traditional principles. In so far as we describe or imagine an ultimate paradise, where neither creativeness nor ethical codes are properly relevant, a degree of essential freedom may again be helpful, if only to suit the perversions of our minds. Both the Bower of Bliss and the Garden of Adonis have their rights, and maybe this is why Spenser allows so much exquisite description, involving bird-song, to accompany temptation. The problem is obscure. We shall meet it again in study of Milton.

Spenser's puritanism is, in a sense, sex-flooded. In the Garden of Adonis we hear: "Frankly each paramour his leman knows" (III. vi.

41); which is not true of the Bower of Bliss. The Temple of Venus is a place of "joy and amorous desire" (IV. x. 38) where, writes B. E. C. Davis (p. 219), "every object serves to stimulate passion and the instinct to reproduce, unchecked by moral or religious scruple." Again (p. 228), "No moral law or religious inhibition mars the 'sweete love' and 'goodly merriment' of the Garden of Adonis, the 'spotless pleasures' and unbridled Hedonism of Venus' Isle." This is Spenser's central hope: untainted creative joy outside and beyond the world of good and evil, from a Shakespearean height where the Bower of Bliss will perhaps appear an insubstantial rather than an evil dream. The continual search in Spenser's narrative for truth and reality, the supplanting of impostors and righting of erroneous choice, is an aspect of our problem. The deceits of lust correspond within Spenser's story to deceptive occurrences: though these may have ecclesiastical references, there are psychological references too. Spenser's humanism asserts that virtue is finally the only realism: a fulfillment of nature, not a thwarting of it. This he knows, and describes; yet does not, like Shakespeare, reveal.

His poem does not quite live the gospel it preaches. It lacks architectonic strength. It is fluid. Of the two qualities needed, that of a time-sequence and a strong, controlling, spatial design, it valuably possesses only the first. Its spatialized scheme, though vast, is insubstantial. Exquisite descriptions of human art and various rich solids are frequent, but the poem as a whole has neither architectural stability nor solid richness. There is an addition of image to image, of verbal music to verbal music, a diffusion rather than concentration, an essentially stanzaic sequence, but no complex intertwisted multiplication of significances. There are modifying contrasts, but no dramatic intensity. Often Spenser seems more interested in his abstract doctrines than in his created world; or, if his world grips him, he seems to forget, for a stanza or two, his message, which is temporarily smothered by the luxuriant impressionism. The nature of his creation changes indecisively. Aristotle's idea that the constructing of a weighty central plot is a greater art than characterization or rhetoric comes to mind. Spenser's fluid, shifting significances make a boneless, piecemeal work. There is a lack of tough moral fibre in his constructional technique. Any amount of things happen, but you get slight sense of vital action. It is a dream-world, a "faery" world, perilously near decadence. It is sensuous, yet unreal. Janet Spens writes (pp. 69-70) that "he never deals so much with the sensuous fact as with the mental translation of the fact—with the use which the soul's faculty makes of the impact and stir of the physical sensation; and he is more excited by the infinitely various web which man has woven to adorn and clothe the physical than by the simple physical facts themselves." She notes elsewhere (pp. 122, 130) that the root evil in Spenser's world is the medieval *accidie*: that is, sloth, melancholia, inactivity. If this be true, there is an interesting relation between the poem's technical weakness and those sensuous and mental errors the poet so skilfully diagnoses. *The Faery Queen* is an eye-feast, an ear-feast, a mind-feast: but it is not a shared action, it is without dramatic suspense. People do things, but at a distance, like figures on a tapestry. It is hard to feel events in relation to the whole. There is really no organic heart. Though Gloriana and Arthur are meant as such, they do not so function, do not receive from the whole action and pump back living significances. Consequently the body-structure lacks organic warmth. It tends to split, dissolve: the whole into books, books into cantos, cantos into events, events into descriptive luxuriance. The proper organic process is reversed. To compare it with a contemporary: in Thomas Sackville's Induction to *A Mirror for Magistrates* (1563) we have at least fine separate imaginative blocks (death, hell, Buckingham) in whose service images are powerfully used, thronging all their joint force into each little whole. Even in Spenser's shorter movements each whole is liable to obscurity by its parts. It is less than the sum of its parts. Instead of building up and cohering, the poem is always decomposing. Its finest units, being so independently fine, are, even if in themselves organic, rich rather with a cancerous and upstart vitality, drawing attention from that whole they should serve. Hence the baggy, bulgy, loose effect, the fluidity. "Flowing water," writes Miss Spens (p. 78), "always fascinated Spenser." Naturally. This fascination corresponds to a relaxed sensuousness, and that to an immorality of technique which just misses conviction, is over-mentalized and all but decadent. Spenser may explicitly favour his Garden of Adonis, with its upsurge of creative life; but we must go elsewhere for that. *The Faery Queen* is itself one vast Bower of Bliss.

That is, it may be, an overstatement. I admit that I do not feel at home here. Possibly, were the poem complete and I had it in all detail and as a whole thoroughly comprehended, its design might appear satisfactory and its parts contributory. But it is very difficult to reach this, and difficult in a sense that the mental possession of Dante's poem is not. Spenser asks, and I think has undertaken, too much. It is a transition poem, aiming at an epic or medieval-heroic manner not deeply suitable to the age. Greek tragedy stands between us and Homer; the New Testament between us and Vergil; and Shakespeare between us and the *Morte d'Arthur*. The dramatic and complex continually supervene on the epic and the adventurous. A new dimension of significance interwoven with every action is, in the Renaissance world especially, urgent for expression. Spenser's poem has no *active* meaning, is not dramatically alive, because he has not found the action he believes in: action which, as in Shakespeare, is newly created, not a legendary reminiscence of a past chivalry. Greek tragedy and the New Testament are both powerfully realistic and metaphysical. Spenser's story is usually unworthy of his thought, of his metrical and stanzaic skill, of his impressionistic profusion. The action, as such, is weak.

True, Spenser with his subtle and comprehensive designing and his intention of a Gloriana and Arthur centrality attempts the typical patterning and dominant, fusing symbol that so often lend meaning and power to long works: he has the idea, though his vast scheme is too unwieldy for it. Many Shakespearian essences, moreover, are here. The heritage of the ages is combined with a contemporary royalism; human instinct, and especially Renaissance sensuousness, subtly analysed; pagan and Christian mythology entwined. Shakespeare's political thinking is forecast. I quote again from B. E. C. Davis (p. 228): "The national pests disfiguring the land of Faerie—Error, Deceit, Tyranny, Anarchy, Lust, Detraction—all spring from the cardinal evil principle, Disorder." The various knights are at work quelling the various forces of disorder. Spenser is, like all poets, at home among cosmic forces of all sorts; but something is wanting.

That "something" is to be related to (i) the New Testament and great tragedy generally; (ii) individual human personality as an indissoluble and realized unit. The two are clearly related. Often in *The Faery Queen* there is a subtle sensuous inconsistency, or if not that, an artistic indecision: he can insert a lovely bird-song stanza in his Bower of Bliss, or associate the most ghoulish horrors with an *intellectual* heresy. There is a certain want of imaginative common sense, and perhaps sincerity, as though ethical principles were not in the wider issues of this work perfectly integrated with aesthetic associations into his imaginative scheme. Though it witnesses a certain integrity, this indecision—when he is sure of evils he leaves you in no doubt, as in the masque of sins at the end of Book I—precludes the creation of strong human action and a convincing artistic structure. There is not that impact of terrific importance and native direction in the human adventure found in the New Testament drama and in Shakespeare. These generally force a dramatic, often tragic, expression. Conversely dramatic form helps to force creative profundity. Drama, with its close plot-texture and disciplinary limits, its centralized and realistic human concern, was the condition of full Elizabethan expression. The Elizabethan mind was too flooded with a diversity of ideas and images; Shakespeare knew no more than Spenser, but gained by being forced to say less. Steep banks make a stream deep, swift, and forceful—"forceful" rather than "fluid"—which without them is slothful, leisurely, and expansively shallow. Moreover the greatest dramatic expression depends also on a sense of human personality which I feel Spenser, to a final judgment, lacks. He is rarely inside his fictions, enduring their joys and terrors. Shakespeare writes from a hard core of trust in human personality, his own or others', which Spenser's fluid impressionism does not reach, so getting underneath his dramatic figure or action, creating from within and forcing others to share from within; and finally, the structure of his art-form has, with little explicit doctrine, the tough-corded sanity of an unswerving experienced realism.

The Hymns present Spenser's visionary thought, while his sensuousness is most perfect in *Epithalamion,* wherein his fluid tendency, which becomes an explicit river-symbolism in *Prothalamion* and the union of Thames and Medway in *The Faery Queen* (IV. xi), functions beautifully in torrential celebration of his own marriage; but in referring these twin impulses, intellectual and emotional, to epic action, he fails. *The Faery Queen* has nevertheless certain passages of deep tragic meditation; its recurrent metaphysic of fertility is important; and pieces of symbolic description presenting pictures, legends in static design, sculptured figures, and so on, hold profound psychological meanings.

The poem perhaps improves after the more famous, but perhaps less powerful, first two books, moving from religious polemic towards, at times, a blazing humanism, a pagan-ritualistic apprehension wherein the closely related glories of sun-fire and human love are finely advanced. The praise of Venus, sovereign of creation, is especially valuable (IV. x. 37-47). Spenser's ranging cosmic intuition draws level with Bacon's *Advancement of Learning* and Pope's *Essay on Man,* as in the dialogue between Artegall and the Giant concerning the divine ordering of the physical universe (V. ii. 30-50). The poetry grows more plain, virile, and athletic (as at III. xi. 25); with similes of sharp, realistic observation and sense of elemental vigour (see IV. vi. 14; V. ii. 50), and a remarkable projection of animal life in fierce action (see V. ii. 15; V. xi. 12). There is, once at least, a Shakespearian inwardness of dramatic sympathy in description of Britomart's varying anxiety and distress, compared finally to a child's wayward grief (V. vi. 1-14); and once strong action becomes itself significant in Britomart's penetration of fire to rescue Amoret from sensuous enchantment (III. xi. 21-xii. 45). Britomart is Spenser's most satisfying person. She is a comprehensive conception, in her masculine dress and armour signifying an integration of sexual principles, as does Venus at IV. x. 41; a creature of romantic action, challenging purity, and—we are told, though perhaps scarcely made to feel—ardent love. Dedicated to a dream-lover, she is meant to attain successful human consummation, though her attractiveness symbolizing the feminine and finally matrimonial ideal is rather strained by her twice conquering in fight her future lord before their union. Artegall cuts a sorry figure: "Ah, my dear Lord," says Britomart to him during a characteristic rescue, "What May-game hath misfortune made of you?" (V. vii. 40). She herself, however, accurately personifies what the fiction as a whole does not attain: the marriage of strong action with emotional purity.

Spenser's expressly *gentle* humanism, which precludes any convincing presentation of heroic conflict as such and leads to excessive reliance on spiritual content as opposed to realistic form—and this is what we mean by allegory—nevertheless itself draws him finally nearer to the consistently trusting humanists, Lyly, Shakespeare, and Pope, than to the somewhat aesthetically turbulent and variously forceful distrusters, Marlowe and Milton. His attempt to convey in philosophic and epic form a flooding sensuousness which penetrates so many creeks and ramifications of human desire, good or bad, heralds a new line of poetry to be concerned with (i) the erotic impulse as the central drive to an expanding apprehension of man's at once earthy-natural and fiery-cosmic setting, and (ii) the problem of action, involving conceptions royalistic and communal; while both are to be related to man's tragic destiny and the spirit, though not necessarily the dogmas, of Christianity.

NOTES

1. The poem appeared in 1579, edited and annotated, by an authority signing himself "E.K." [1967]
2. I refer to Still's *Shakespeare's Mystery Play*, 1921; revised, as *The Timeless Theme*, 1936. See my study *The Crown of Life*, p. 226. [1967]

A. S. P. WOODHOUSE

Nature and Grace in *The Faerie Queene*[1]

I am to present for your consideration an hypothesis regarding Spenser's *Faerie Queene*.

Historical criticism is, I believe, more than a mere corrective. It may have for its object to restore, so far as possible, the conditions essential to a full communication between artist and audience, which include a common understanding of the potentialities and limits of the genre and, for the purpose of the poet's argument, the acceptance of a common frame of reference. Historical criticism, thus conceived, entails the use of hypothesis, which must submit to experimental verification. Besides the obvious tests of covering the principal phenomena and not running counter to any of the known evidence, a critical hypothesis is verified whenever it serves to bring into clearer relief the poem's aesthetic pattern and demonstrate its consistency. This is a criterion which we shall have occasion to apply. It involves, of course, an assumption, frequently rejected as hampering to scholarly ingenuity, that a great poet is a conscientious artist and knows what he is about.

The particular hypothesis which I am to advance turns upon one of the intellectual frames of reference common to Spenser and many other writers of the Renaissance, namely, their recognition of two levels of existence and experience, traditionally known as the order

From *ELH*, XVI (1949), pp. 194-228. Reprinted by permission of The Johns Hopkins Press.

of nature and the order of grace. A few years ago I found that to read Milton's *Comus* in the light of this frame of reference was to sharpen, and also to modify, one's sense of the poem's pattern and its meaning;[2] and I promised myself that some day I would try the experiment of re-reading the *Faerie Queene* with this frame of reference, this apportionment of experience to the order of nature and the order of grace, in mind, and would see whether here also it might not serve to sharpen, and perhaps to modify, one's sense of the poem's pattern and its meaning. Let this be my excuse for the present delivery of coals to Newcastle, and for the temerity of a mere Miltonist in lecturing on the *Faerie Queene* in the home of the great *Variorum Spenser*.

In Spenser's day, as still in Milton's, the two orders of nature and of grace were universally accepted as a frame of reference, whether they were specifically named or not. Within this frame of reference[3] there was room for every degree of difference in attitude and emphasis: it was a frame of reference, not a body of doctrine. To the Christian, of course, both orders were subject to the power and providence of God, but exercised in a manner sufficiently different to maintain a clear-cut distinction between the two. In the natural order belonged not only the physical world, what is commonly called the world of nature inanimate and animate, but man himself simply as a denizen of that world. The rule of its order was expressed not only in the physical laws of nature, but in natural ethics (in what was significantly called the *law of nature*), and even in natural as opposed to revealed religion. This order was apprehended in experience and interpreted by reason; and it had its own wisdom, for upon the law of nature had been erected the ethical system of a Plato, an Aristotle or a Cicero. It had its own institutions, of which the highest was the state, but this is an aspect of the order of nature which need not detain us here. . . . To the order of grace, on the other hand, belonged man in his character of supernatural being, with all that concerned his salvation, under the old dispensation and the new. The law of its government was the revealed will of God, received and interpreted by faith, and it included a special kind of experience called religious experience. The order of grace had also its appropriate institution, the Church, which, like the state, need not concern us here.

The relation between the order of nature and the order of grace was a problem which admitted of various solutions. One group of answers insisted on the contrast and wide divergence of the two orders, and these answers were returned by individuals and sects of opposite tendencies.

The ascetic and rigorist would emphasize the divergence, in order to depress nature and exalt grace; the naturalist, in order to exalt nature and depress grace, finding the demands of the higher order "unnatural" and denying their validity. Still in the same group were others who insisted on the divergence of nature and grace with the intention of accepting them both, but at the same time of avoiding inferences from the one to the other: such was the fideist, who took the order of grace on authority, but in the order of nature pursued his experimental and sceptical way, the Baconian, with his two philosophies, natural and divine, and (though this lies outside our present scope) the Puritan extremist, reactionary in the realm of grace, progressivist in the realm of nature. All these, though for different ends, apply what I have elsewhere called the *principle of segregation.*[4]

Opposed to them were all those thinkers who, with many different shades of emphasis and inference, agreed in responding to the profound human instinct for a unified view of life. They insisted that the order of grace was the superstructure whose foundations were securely laid in nature; that there was no interval between the two orders; that grace came to perfect nature, an idea including discipline and a miraculous remedy for man's fall; that well-being must be defined in terms of the two orders simultaneously, and that what was for man's good as a natural being could not be to his detriment as a supernatural, or *vice versa.*

These, with varying degrees of modification, were the assumptions of Christian humanism, whose dominance in the Renaissance, and whose importance for Spenser, will hardly be questioned. These were the assumptions of that long tradition which was about to receive its most majestic English expression in the first book of Hooker's *Laws of Ecclesiastical Polity* (1593). But the stormy waters upon which the Church of England was already entering are alone sufficient to warn us not to underestimate the variety and strength of opposing currents of Christian thought released and accelerated by the Protestant Reformation, and specifically by the impressive formulations of Calvin, whose influence upon Spenser Padelford has demonstrated.[5] Underlying the struggle of parties in Church and state were opposing ideals of the Christian life, and supporting these ideals were divergent views of the character and the relation of the order of nature and the order of grace.

The frame of reference is everywhere, explicit or implied; and if we ignore it, we neglect an important part of Spenser's, as of Milton's, intellectual background, and a valuable instrument of critical analysis.

Such at least is the contention of this lecture, which asks, and (so far as time permits) will try to answer the following questions: What light does this frame of reference throw upon the *Faerie Queene*? How does it sharpen and perhaps modify our sense of Spenser's aesthetic pattern (for, whatever be true of some other poets, the aesthetic patterning of Spenser and Milton is based upon ideas, upon conceptual thinking)? Does a recognition of the frame of reference help us at some points to see further into Spenser's allegory? Does it help us to appreciate relations of parallel with contrast (for similarity with dissimilarity, parallel with contrast, are of the essence of an aesthetic pattern)? Does it even serve to explain more adequately than heretofore the significance, intellectual and aesthetic, of certain characters and episodes? Does it, finally, give us any indication of the direction which the poem may have taken in those last six (or is it five and five-sixth?) books which have not come down to us? I would ask you to remember that whatever I assert is tentative, and that the purpose is exploration and the testing of an hypothesis.

II

Some fifty years after Spenser published the second instalment of the *Fairie Queene,* an eloquent contemporary of Milton's, whose name has not come down to us, wrote:

> Christ Jesus, whose is the kingdom, the power and the glory both in nature and in grace, hath given several maps and schemes of his dominions . . . : both of his great kingdom, the world, . . . and also of his special and peculiar kingdom, the kingdom of grace. Which kingdoms, though they differ essentially or formally, yet they agree in one common subject-matter, man and societies of men, though under a diverse consideration. And not only man in society, but every man individually, is an epitome either of one only or of both these dominions. Of one only: so every natural man (who in a natural consideration is called *microcosmus,* an epitome of the world), in whose conscience God hath his throne, ruling him by the light of nature to a civil outward good and end. Of both: so every believer who, besides this natural conscience and rule, hath an enlightened conscience, carrying a more bright and lively stamp of the kingly place and power of the Lord Jesus, swaying him by the

light of faith or scripture, and such a man may be called *micro-christus,* the epitome of Christ mystical.[6]

I suggest that some such relation between the order of nature and the order of grace is likewise present in Spenser's mind, and some such distinction between the motives and sanctions of virtue on the natural level and on the specifically religious, and that these are consistently applied in the part of the *Faerie Queene* which we possess; or, to be quite concrete, that Book I moves (as has been generally recognized) on the religious level, or (as I should prefer to describe it) with reference to the order of grace, and the remaining books (as has *not* been recognized) on the natural level only: that the Redcross Knight is indeed *microchristus,* but Guyon, and each of the other heroes of individual books, *microcosmus* alone.

This hypothesis runs completely counter to one recently put forward,[7] that each of the knights is, as it were, the heir of his predecessors' victories, and together they form a composite picture of the Christian gentleman, or that Guyon, for example, achieves his virtues of temperance and continence, and is able to discharge his task, because he starts from the vantage point of holiness achieved by the Redcross Knight. Few perhaps will accept this hypothesis, which ignores the obvious fact that while the motivation and sanctions of the Redcross Knight's virtue are specifically religious, those of Guyon's, just as clearly, are not. But there is still a middle course, the refuge of vagueness, which recognizes the religious character of the Redcross Knight, and the impossibility of finding in Aristotle, or in Aristotle read in the light of Plato, any equivalent for holiness, which further recognizes the essentially Aristotelian character of Guyon and his virtues, but which breaks down when it comes to Britomart and, in the effort to account for the evident difference between her and Guyon, decides that she must represent a religious virtue, a specifically Christian conception of chastity and love.[8]

We are concerned with testing my hypothesis, and in the degree to which it is verified it will, of course, disprove the other two. All recognize the necessity of some synthesis between the contentions of the various books, but the other two try to provide for the synthesis piecemeal as the poem moves along, while mine, remembering that we have only the first half of the pattern of the *Faerie Queene,* is content that synthesis should be prepared for, but held in solution, perhaps even till Book XII. Spenser's preparation for his final synthesis, as it appears to me, consists, first, in sharply differentiating between the two orders; secondly, in presenting the virtues of natural ethics in a form which Christianity can assimilate, and has in fact assimilated, and, thirdly, in indicating the limits of nature and the points at which it requires to be supplemented or corrected by grace. It is the second of these three steps that has led the critics without exception to conclude that all or some of the heroes and their virtues are specifically Christian. But the question is not whether the natural virtues can be ratified by religion before being transcended by it (for all of them can), but whether in the particular instance the motivation and the sanctions of the virtue are from nature or from grace.

In the part of the poem which has come down to us, such is my hypothesis, Spenser is careful to differentiate the two orders of nature and grace. He emphasizes the parallels between them, and the differences which only these parallels can bring into relief, and he builds both into his pattern; for parallel with difference is (as we said) of the essence of aesthetic patterning. No doubt he interprets the virtues of the natural order as a Christian would interpret them; but he scrupulously abstains from assigning to them a religious motive and from invoking in their behalf the supernatural sanctions so freely drawn upon in Book I; nor does he bespeak in their support any infusion of divine grace. The natural order, the level on which the remaining books move, is also, it is true, under the power and providence of God, which may intervene to protect the natural man from external evil; but nowhere save in Book I (as we shall see) does Prince Arthur figure forth the grace that works inwardly upon the heart and will.

III

Though it sometimes seems to raise as many problems as it solves, every re-examination of the *Faerie Queene* must commence with the Letter to Raleigh. For whatever its relation to the composition of the poem, the Letter is clearly Spenser's introduction to a reading of it. As such the purpose of the Letter is severely limited. It is not to anticipate the whole meaning of the work, that would be an almost impossible task, and so far as it were successfully executed, an error of judgment; it is simply to set the reader's feet on the right path, to make clear that the poem is an allegory, that each book deals with one of the private virtues (holiness in the person of the Redcross Knight, temperance in the person of Guyon, chastity in the person of

Britomart), that Prince Arthur represents in the whole poem the sum of the virtues, or (as it is called in the Aristotelian scheme) *magnanimity*,[9] and in the separate books its application to the particular virtue under discussion, and, finally, to give a very necessary indication of the structure of the poem and the occasion of the various adventures recited. The incompleteness of the Letter is evident from the absence of any allusion to the historical allegory, whose existence, and whose importance to Spenser, no one can doubt. This, and much else, the reader is left the pleasure of discovering for himself. The Letter tells him what he needs to know at starting: it does not tell all he will know when he has finished the twelve or even the three books. Thus Spenser may well have foreseen a function for Book XII, which it would have been premature to disclose. Perhaps, in addition to supplying belated explanations, the twelfth book was to have completed the pattern of the whole and, like the Epilogue in *Comus,* to have furnished the vantage point from which all that went before might be seen in its true relations and its full significance.

It is not surprising, then, that in the Letter the frame of reference is merely hinted, not set out in detail. The reader is told that the virtue of Book I is holiness, which he would instantly recognize as a specifically Christian virtue, outside nature and belonging to the order of grace; that the armour which the Redcross Knight assumes "is the armour of a Christian man specified by Saint Paul," and that this fact alone marked him off, set him above, all the other knights, for when he had donned the armour, this clownish young man, this son of nature, innocent of any cultivation, "seemed the goodliest man in all that company." The reader is then told of Sir Guyon, the knight of temperance, a virtue which (though it had certainly been adopted, like the other natural virtues, into the Christian scheme) belonged in origin and essence to the order of nature, and was, in fact, with justice and magnanimity, the most characteristic of the Aristotelian virtues. He would observe the absence of any reference to religion, and might be expected to take the hint that Books II and I moved upon different levels, and to be rendered sufficiently alert for the contrast which the two books present, and which is an essential element in the aesthetic pattern of the poem.

IV

It need no longer be argued in detail that Book I moves upon the level of grace. Padelford's demonstration is conclusive, that holiness is a purely Christian virtue, and that the *Institutes* of Calvin furnishes a relevant gloss, while the *Ethics* of Aristotle does not.[10] The attempt of DeMoss to extract Spenser's holiness from Aristotle, and of Miss Winstanley to extract it from a blend of Aristotle and Plato, patently break down.[11] It will suffice to recall in rapid summary the essential features of Spenser's first book: (i) the emphasis upon the Christian's armour, and especially upon the shield of faith; (ii) the character of the Knight's companion and guide, Una, the single and all-sufficient religious truth, in whose presence alone he is safe; (iii) the whole tenor of the Knight's adventures up to canto 10, which are not an education in virtue in any ordinary sense, but an illustration of the bankruptcy of the natural man and of the essentially Christian doctrine that only grace can save; (iv) in conformity with this, the special role assigned in this book to Prince Arthur, who certainly does not represent the Aristotelian magnanimity, but on the contrary the operation of divine grace; (v) the completion of the Redcross Knight's education in the House of Holiness:[12] cleansed by repentance, taught by Faith,[13] healed by Hope, led through the works of Charity to the hill of Contemplation, vouchsafed a vision of the New Jerusalem and his own niche as a saint therein, and returned to the world, prepared at last for active service. When Bunyan read the first Book of the *Faerie Queene,* and especially this episode of the House of Holiness, he did not mistake their purport, but recognized it as purely evangelical and gathered from Spenser hints for his own allegory of salvation.[14]

Something of the relation between the two orders of nature and grace is already apparent in Book I, whose central episodes all move upon the level of grace. The lion which accompanies Una to the dwelling of Abessa, and there slays Kirkrapine, represents (it has been suggested) the law of nature, and the action symbolizes the agreement between natural ethics (so far as natural ethics can go) and true religion: their joint condemnation of a superstitious asceticism and of the corruptions which inevitably attend it.[15] A different relation appears in the two encounters of the Redcross Knight with pride. Spenser is sometimes criticized for suffering his hero to escape from the palace of Lucifera, who represents pride, only to fall a victim to Orgoglio, who also represents pride.[16] A clearer sense of the two orders would show how idle such criticism is, and how sound and consistent is Spenser's allegory. For Lucifera represents worldly pride which leads alike to vice and to disaster. But the vices, the seven deadly sins, are such as the moral sense is perfectly competent to detect and condemn: they impinge upon religion only as religion adds its prohibitions to whatever is condemned on grounds of natural ethics, just as religion (in Spenser's view) assumes and ratifies all the natural virtues before transcending them. And for the disasters, they are such as the world regards: the loss of position, of possessions and of life. It is significantly the Dwarf, who represents worldly prudence or common sense, and no celestial visitant, that warns the Redcross Knight of his danger and prompts his escape. The pride represented by Orgoglio, however, is of a very different sort. It is spiritual pride, which assails the Knight in his religious character when he has laid aside the armour of a Christian man. From it he is powerless to rescue himself. The keyless prison-house will yield to nothing but the onslaught of Prince Arthur, that is, to the violence of grace.[17]

There are subtler relations between the two orders than the rather obvious examples which I have chosen; and these relations will, I hope, become apparent as we proceed. But to turn now to the comparison of Book II with Book I.

V

Every reader must recognize the similarities of the second Book to the first, in structure and episode, and must believe, when he contrasts them with Books III and IV, that Spenser intended each group to form one of the larger units in the pattern of the whole.

In each of the first two books, a knight (the Redcross Knight and Guyon) is assigned a task by Gloriana and is accompanied as companion and guide by the person at whose instance the task was assigned (Una in the one case, the Palmer in the other). Each knight passes through a series of adventures which are, in one sort or other, an education in the virtue for which he stands and a preparation for his final task. The adventures involve conflicts with single adversaries (the brothers Sansfoy, Sansloy and Sansjoy in Book I, the brothers Pyrochles and Cymochles in Book II), the temporary separation of the Knight from his companion, the encounter with some analogous temptations (the palace of Lucifera, and the cave of Mammon), the rescue of the hero by Prince Arthur, the completion of his education in a retreat (the House of Holiness in Book I, the Castle of Alma in Book II), which affords the final preparation for his assigned task (the slaying of the Dragon by the Redcross Knight, the overthrow of Acrasia and her Bower of Earthly Bliss by Guyon). These are commonplaces of criticism; for the parallels are so obvious as to be inescapable.

But what of the differences which the parallels should bring into relief, and which should rescue the parallelism from monotony? They likewise (as I believe) are so obvious as to have seemed to Spenser inescapable; but to them less than sufficient attention has been paid, and the reason is not far to seek. All the differences depend upon, and derive their significance from, the fact which has been generally overlooked: that whereas what touches the Redcross Knight bears primarily upon revealed religion, or belongs to the order of grace, whatever touches Guyon bears upon natural ethics, or belongs to the order of nature.[18]

This difference leaves its mark upon the whole character of the education which the two knights receive. Guyon's trials and temptations, for the most part successfully surmounted, have the effect of rendering his virtue habitual. At an early stage, in the episode of Medina and her two sisters,[19] Spenser sets forth the Aristotelian doctrine of the mean—the idea that virtue and well-being lie in a mean between the two extremes of excess and defect—a doctrine applied, indeed, throughout the *Faerie Queene,* but especially in the treatment of temperance.[20] The episode of Medina has been recognized, however, as having a second significance: it is an allegory of the Platonic doctrine of the soul, with Medina and Guyon standing for the rational soul, and the sisters, with their knights, for the two divisions of the irrational, the irascible and appetitive, or (as we might say) for wrath and desire.[21] Temperance and continence (for Spenser combines the two Aristotelian virtues[22]) can be achieved only by the ascendency of the rational over the irrational soul, and it is this ascendency that becomes habitual. Reason dominates Book II as revealed truth dominates Book I, and these are personified in the companion figures of the Palmer and Una.

The education of the Redcross Knight differs markedly (as we have implied) from Guyon's. It proceeds by trial and error—principally by error: indeed until his entry into the House of Holiness he appears to have learned almost nothing, but to have blundered on, despite his innate nobility, from one error into another. The sum total of his education to this point has been one lesson: the bankruptcy of the natural man and his utter dependence for spiritual virtue upon the grace of God:

> What man is he that boasts of fleshly might
> And vain assurance of mortality,
> Which all so soone as it doth come to fight
> Against spirituall foes, yields by and by,
> Or from the field most cowardly doth fly!
> Ne let the man ascribe it to his skill
> That thorough grace hath gained victory:
> If any strength we have it is to ill,
> But all the good is Gods, both power and eke will.[23]

Only as this conviction is borne home to him is St. George ready for the education of the House of Holiness, the vision of the New Jerusalem, and the fulfilment of his task. There is nothing remotely like it in the experience of Guyon.

Fortified by the practice of temperance and continence, Guyon comes to the Castle of Alma, not for correction, and not to receive a vision of higher things, but simply that he may understand more fully the humanistic ethic which has been his guiding principle from the beginning and which will suffice him to the end:

> Of all Gods workes which do this world adorne,
> There is no one more faire and excellent
> Then is mans body both for powre and forme,
> Whiles it is kept in sober government;
> But none then it more fowle and indecent,
> Distempred through misrule and passions bace:
> It growes a monster and incontinent
> Doth loose his dignity and native grace.[24]

One must observe in passing that by Spenser the word *grace* is used in different senses, which are always sufficiently clear from the context: (i) it may refer to the grace of God working inwardly upon the will and infusing power, as in the stanza quoted above from Book I, and this sense alone is peculiar to the order of grace; (ii) it may refer to God's overflowing bounty in bestowing outward benefits or in intervening as providential care in the natural order; (iii) it may refer to native endowment or to natural excellence, as in the stanza last quoted, from Book II; or (iv) it may refer to grace of disposition, bearing, or manner.[25] But to return.

At the same crucial point in each of the two books, the poet pauses to sum up in a single stanza the purport of all that has gone before, and thus to prepare for what is to follow, for the orientation afforded by the Castle of Alma and the House of Holiness respectively: in the one, virtue achieved by man's own effort, by establishing the rule of reason over the passions, and thus realizing the potentialities of his nature; in the other, man's impotence to rise above himself, and thus his utter dependence upon the grace of God. Our knowledge, or rather our faith, that for Spenser these two positions were not incapable of final reconciliation must not blind us to their strong opposition until the reconciliation is reached. If it does, feature after feature of Spenser's pattern will be blurred for us, and we shall fail to appreciate his art as well as his thought. We shall miss the consistent contrast of Guyon with the Redcross Knight, and the dual or (as I would suggest) the triple role of Prince Arthur in the poem. We shall fail to recognize how fully Spenser exploits what I will call the difference in vertical range between the classical and the Christian scheme of things: in the one, man can rise to the specifically human or sink (like the followers of Acrasia) to the level of the beasts; in the other, he can rise (like the Redcross Knight) securely to heaven or fall irrecoverably, and forever, to the bottomless pit. We shall fail, furthermore, to understand why in Book I the supporting imagery comes from the romances *and the Bible,* with scarcely a single draught on Spenser's large accumulations of classical lore, and in Book II, from the romances *and the classics,* with no significant reference to the Bible at all. Finally, we shall misapprehend the purport of Book II itself. For besides the contrast of nature and grace established by the first two books, Book II commences to explore the realm of nature with a new contrast in that realm between nature truly and nature falsely conceived, and this contrast (as we shall presently observe) carries us on from Book II to Book III.

VI

We have mentioned the dual role of Prince Arthur, now very generally recognized, and have suggested that in reality he plays not a dual, but a triple role.

In those books of the poem which deal with the classical or natural virtues he stands for magnanimity, but just as clearly he stands in Book I for God's grace in its inward operation upon the heart and will. Here then are two distinct roles. What is the significance of each, and where is the propriety of having them discharged by the same person?

How does magnanimity, the crowning and inclusive virtue in the natural order, parallel heavenly grace in the religious order, which is clearly not man's virtue, but (if we may use the term at all) God's? The point of comparison, and the justification of the parallel, lies in the respective roles played by magnanimity and grace in the two systems. Magnanimity, in its Aristotelian sense, means knowing yourself equal to anything, and being so: knowing yourself worthy of the highest things, and being so. It is of the essence of grace, on the other hand, that, in a terrifyingly literal sense, you know yourself equal to nothing and in yourself utterly without worth. The classical scheme of ethics turns upon self-reliance: there is nothing else to rely upon; but the Christian relies upon God. Thus it is in Spenser's poem.

It might be argued that while the roles of magnanimity and grace in the two contrasting systems justify the emphasis on each and a parallel treatment of the two, this very fact would rather suggest the propriety of assigning them to different persons. But Spenser is, no doubt, preparing for an ultimate synthesis of nature and grace in the person of Prince Arthur. Clearly, Spenser would not have been the first to attempt a reconciliation of nature and grace: a long tradition of Christian humanism had worked out a Christian conception, not only of temperance, justice and the other natural virtues, but of magnanimity itself.[26] This fact is certainly relevant to Spenser's final synthesis, but it can obscure his pattern if too early invoked.

It is not the specifically Christian version of temperance that Guyon represents, nor is it Christian magnanimity that intervenes in his rescue, because in neither case is a religious motive or a religious sanction introduced. When this fact is clearly established, it is safe, and necessary, to recognize another. There were features in the hard self-sufficiency of Aristotle's magnanimous man which were incompatible as well with the chivalric as with the Christian ideal:[27] at moments one feels that he would have been more at home with Lord Chesterfield than with either St. Paul or Sir Lancelot; and these features Spenser wisely alters in his portrait of Prince Arthur, in whom self-reliance is never arrogant, and who is always a very perfect gentle knight. But Prince Arthur *as magnanimity* is not a specifically Christian figure: at most, he is a figure rendered compatible with the ideal of Christian knighthood. When he intervenes to rescue Sir Guyon from the stealthy attack of Pyrochles and Cymochles,[28] it is no longer as the symbol of heavenly grace intervening to save from inward evil, but as the symbol of magnanimity, swift to recognize a kindred spirit and to protect him from the outward depredation of his foes. For this attack of the brothers upon the unconscious Guyon has evidently a very different symbolic value from the attack of Orgoglio upon the Redcross Knight, and from Guyon's earlier battle with Pyrochles, where that embodiment of irascibility menaces, not Guyon's life, but his integrity, damaging his shield and inflicting a slight wound.[29] Spenser, it would seem, was perfectly well aware that the effects of evil are not confined to the human heart: it stalks abroad with fire and sword to plunder and slay the innocent.

But though this be true, is it not also true, it may be asked, that Prince Arthur's intervention is *providential* in the strictest sense, so that Spenser has merely exchanged one religious conception for another? It is indeed true that the intervention is providential; and this, I submit, is the third role of Prince Arthur, *to figure forth the power and providence of God in the natural order.*

Here, as occasionally in the *Faerie Queene*,[30] Spenser offers in rapid succession two symbolic presentations of the same truth. For the angel who stands guard over the unconscious Guyon[31] is likewise, and even more obviously, the minister of God's providence, of the overflowing grace which extends its protection even to the natural man:

> And is there care in heaven? And is there love
> In heavenly spirits to these creatures bace,
> That may compassion of their evills move?
> There is; else much more wretched were the cace
> Of men then beasts. But O! th' exceeding grace
> Of highest God that loves his creatures so,
> And all his workes with mercy doth embrace,
> That blessed Angels he sends to and fro,
> To serve to wicked man, to serve his wicked foe.[32]

Such a description would apply only to the natural man, and would by evangelical standards apply to him equally whether morally virtuous, like Guyon, or the reverse.[33]

Prince Arthur, it would seem then, represents, in the order of grace, the grace of God in its fullest extent as it works upon the will of the converted; in the order of nature he represents the virtue of magnanimity, which is as central in classical ethics as is grace in the Christian scheme; but, also in the order of nature, he represents the power and providence of God as they intervene to protect his creatures from outward evils.

VII

Only after the elementary distinction between the two orders of grace and nature has been accepted will one be prepared to appreciate the complexity and consistency of Spenser's findings respecting the second realm, the order of nature, as these are developed in the second and subsequent books of the poem.

In Book II there is (as we have remarked) a contrast between nature truly and nature falsely conceived, and this contrast is carried on in Books III and IV and serves to connect them with Book II. Acrasia's Bower of Bliss represents nature falsely conceived. For there nature's provision for the replenishment of life is prostituted to sensual pleasure and is without issue. The Genius of the Bower is a lord of misrule, and in truth no Genius at all, no spirit of nature, though falsely so called by Acrasia and her followers;[34] and the contrast with nature truly conceived is emphasized (as Mr. C. S. Lewis has shown) by the intrusion into the Bower of a false art whose aim is to deceive[35] and whose effect is to heighten and at the same time to misdirect natural impulse. But if one paused at the end of Book II, one might easily mistake Spenser's meaning. Whatever part nature really has in the Bower of Bliss is rescued and rehabilitated in Book III, in Spenser's account of the Garden of Adonis.[36] There, under the auspices of the true Genius, the veritable spirit of nature, life replenishes itself. It is an allegory of the principle of generation in all things, and pleasure, rejected when it usurps the role of end, is frankly admitted in its proper role of natural accompaniment. The Garden of Adonis thus furnishes the cosmic setting, not indeed for the ideal of chastity represented by Britomart, but for the view of love and marriage associated with it, which is likewise presented in terms of the order of nature and without reference to grace.

As compared with Guyon (representing temperance and continence) Britomart is positive and dynamic, representing the chastity which is coupled with love, which finds its principal motive in love, and which reaches its goal in marriage. But if this is true, and if it is Spenser's sufficient reason for proceeding from the subject of Book II to that of Book III, it is not because the argument is shifted from the order of nature to the order of grace, but because it is more fully elaborated, and under proper qualifications, on the natural level. Granted that the ideal presented in Britomart can be assimilated by a

Christian view of love and marriage, it still remains true that at this stage it is not thus assimilated. In other words, there is no more reason to regard Britomart as an embodiment of a specifically Christian ideal of chastity and love than to regard Belphoebe as the embodiment of a Christian ideal of virginity. For in neither case is there the slightest hint of a religious motivation or sanction.

Since Spenser presents his idea of nature in connection, more or less immediate, with his treatment of love, it is desirable to scrutinize carefully his argument on this subject, which extends from the final canto of Book II through Books III and IV, and includes the journey of Britomart in rescue of her lover Artegall, in Book V, cantos 6 and 7, an episode too seldom related to the argument of the preceding books. In broadest outline, then, there are four representations of chastity in these books, Britomart, Belphoebe, Amoret and Florimell, and each is also a representation of beauty and its evocative power.

Of these representations Belphoebe is the simplest, stemming (as her name implies) from the Diana of classic myth, and embodying, like Diana, all the beauty, all the free activity and all the positive human development that the ideal of chastity conceived as virginity, and moving on the natural level, without motivation and direction from religion, will permit. The situation is, if you will, artificially narrowed: the response to it is not artificial, but natural; and Belphoebe, certainly, is no starved and thwarted personality. She and her twin sister Amoret are (as the story of their birth is intended to symbolize) children of nature;[37] but Belphoebe is adopted by Diana and brought up among her nymphs, while Amoret is placed by Venus in the Garden of Adonis, there to be brought up by Psyche with her daughter Pleasure "In all the lore of love and goodly womanhead."[38]

If Belphoebe and Amoret are contrasted in their fortunes, each is again contrasted with Britomart, the central figure of the whole argument. Britomart is as positive and dynamic as Belphoebe, but over a far wider range of experience: as perfectly adjusted but to a far more complex situation. For she is as chaste as Belphoebe, by including in theory and action the principle of generation and its human expression, wedded love, and not by excluding them. From the first Britomart is dedicated to the love of Artegall,[39] and like a Shavian heroine (or, for that matter, Shakespeare's Helena) she sets out to get him, obedient to a principle at work through all nature and symbolized for Spenser by the myth of Venus and Adonis and, on the human level, by the myth of Cupid and Psyche. Like other central figures in the

Faerie Queene, Britomart has her companion, old Glauce, who certainly does not symbolize any religious directive,[40] as does Una, but moves, like the Palmer, on the natural level, though with a significant difference. For Glauce does not represent reason or any principle of control, but rather yields to the motive force of love which drives Britomart forward, and from which nothing but Britomart's own spirit, passionate but pure, can derive a principle of control and direction. It is sufficient; and Britomart not only passes scatheless through every danger, and unassailed by any temptation, but wherever she goes brings rebuke to the unchaste and aid to the incomplete or insecure in virtue. The crowning instance (as Padelford has shown) is her rescue of Amoret from the wicked enchanter Busyrane.[41]

Amoret is as deeply in love with Scudamour as Britomart with Artegall. By nature she is as chaste as Britomart, or as the twin sister Belphoebe. But her education in the Garden of Adonis, while true to nature, has yet been incomplete: it has not contained all the elements requisite for love true and chaste *at the human level.* There is some failure in integration. She cannot securely transcend the merely physical in her passion for Scudamour; hence her imprisonment by Busyrane. Her natural chastity insists that she must do so; hence her tortured resistance to the enchanter. Assigned the task of her rescue, her lover is powerless to effect it. Perforce he resigns the task to Britomart, who thus in Book III assumes the function of Prince Arthur, or something more, but in his role of magnanimity, not of heavenly grace, and with this role his pursuit of glory:

> Ah! gentlest knight alive (sayd Scudamour)
> What huge heroicke magnanimity
> Dwells in thy bounteous brest! . . . .
> Life is not lost (said she) for which is bought
> Endlesse renown, that, more then death, is to be sought.[42]

Britomart is able to effect the rescue because she has by nature the attitude which Amoret must struggle to attain. In Amoret what is required is transcendence, but transcendence on the way to unification. Essentially, it is this unification that Britomart represents.

Britomart is the ideal embodiment of love as well as chastity, and not, like Belphoebe, of chastity alone. She is the Spenserian equivalent of Milton's "Hail, wedded love." In this ideal whatever is natural, so far from being rejected, is ratified and comprehended. There is room in it for all the raptures of Spenser's own *Epithalamion.* Part of the significance of Britomart's vision in the Temple of Isis (that wonderful piece of dream psychology and symbolic art) is to show how securely grounded in nature is the ideal structure of Britomart's life and love.[43] They comprehend, and give appropriate human expression to, a principle of generation at work through the whole range of nature. That is why the Garden of Adonis may be said to furnish the cosmic background of the human ideal represented by Britomart.

But that the ideal and its expression are specifically human is of the first importance. There are different levels in the order of nature, and a principle of ascent. The highest level within the natural order is the specifically human level; and (again within the terms of this order) success in living means the secure achievement of the specifically human. It means (to borrow Arnold's phrase) the development of our humanity proper as distinct from our animality. Nature, said Renan, knows nothing of chastity. And of nature on her sub-human level, this statement (as Spenser would agree) is perfectly true. She knows no more of chastity than she does of temperance and continence, of friendship, of justice, of courtesy or constancy or magnanimity. She does not know them because she does not need them, having her own sure law, adequate to each level of existence. But this does not mean that the human virtues are unnatural. On the contrary, they are natural in a double sense: because they belong to the nature of man, and because nature, adequately conceived, is seen to furnish their base and to lend them her sanction. Nowhere does this fact appear more strikingly than in Spenser's conception of love and chastity as represented by Britomart. Here the principle of generation common to the whole natural order reaches its appropriate human expression in wedded love, and here it meets and is harmoniously united with the specifically human virtue of chastity.

The cause of Amoret's predicament, from which only Britomart can rescue her, is not that her education in the Garden of Adonis has run counter to nature, as it would have done, for example, had it been carried on in the garden of Acrasia. The cause is that it has failed sufficiently to distinguish the different levels in the natural order. Her education has failed to unite the human virtue of chastity to the natural principle of generation because it has failed to recognize that on the human level the virtue is as natural as the principle: that the virtue is as natural is attested by Amoret's instinctive and tenacious hold upon it, as well as by the triumphant naturalness of Britomart.

The fourth and final character, Florimell, is dedicated, like Britomart and unlike Belphoebe, to love as well as chastity. But she altogether lacks the magnanimity (in Aristotle's and Spenser's sense of the word) which distinguishes these two heroic figures: she is always in flight from danger and always in danger, real or imagined. Florimell has, however, a second role in the poem. In special degree she represents beauty and its evocative power, so that everyone whose path she crosses is drawn after her, impelled by love in some one of its forms, impure or pure, base or exalted, according to his own nature: the witch's son, the boatman, old Proteus, Sir Guyon, even Prince Arthur, who believes or hopes that she is (or at least is like) the Gloriana of his dreams, and at last the resistance of Marinell himself is broken down. Beauty, as Spenser sings in the first two of his *Fowre Hymnes,* is the universal principle which evokes the universal passion, love. In the *Faerie Queen* it is Florimell pre-eminently who illustrates this principle and its evocative power.

All these ideas, and more, Spenser develops in his treatment of love and chastity on the natural level, and one result is to give us our principal insight into the poet's reading of the order of nature.

VIII

Under the term *nature* is comprehended the whole range of existence from formed but still inanimate matter up to and including man, save as man in his religious character belongs also to the order of grace. Nature, thus conceived, is an ascending scale, at whose successive levels are added, first, life, then consciousness, then rationality and a moral sense, and finally religious feeling, which last marks the transition to the order of grace. At every level nature connotes a principle of dynamism, a law and a norm; and on the human level the law and the norm are recognized as rational and moral. Thus, as Hooker was soon to argue, the law of nature holds sway over the whole natural order, though its rational character can be apprehended, and its dictates consciously consulted, only at the highest level, that is, by man. Everything seeks its appropriate perfection, and man finally can achieve his, only by a reference on to the order of grace; but so far as it goes nature is a sure guide and her law part of the divine law. These assumptions, made familiar to us by Hooker, Spenser in some measure shares. They underlie his antithesis between the natural and unnatural, and between nature adequately and nature inadequately conceived. Everywhere in the *Faerie Queene* the unnatural is condemned as absurdity, as defiance of fact or as perversion of the appointed order of things; and, avowedly or by implication, the natural is accepted and approved.[44]

Acceptance, however, and approval are not unqualified. There is in Spenser a much sharper line of demarcation between nature and grace than any that can be discovered in Hooker: there is a Calvinistic sense of the bankruptcy of the natural man, and a conception of grace as entailing not so much a perfecting of nature as a new start. Even in his treatment of the natural order, there is more than a suspicion that nature may on occasion prove for man a delusive guide. In the garden of Acrasia the antithesis between nature and the unnatural as represented by an art intended to deceive, is crossed by another idea: up to a point nature herself seems willing to second Acrasia and her art.

> The joyous birdes, shrouded in chearfull shade,
> Their notes unto the voice attempred sweet. . . .
> The silver sounding instruments did meet
> With the base murmure of the waters fall. . . .
> The gentle warbling wind low answered to all.

Such is the accompaniment furnished by nature to the singer of the Rose Song; and, when he ceased,

> then gan all the choir of birdes
> Their diverse notes t'attune unto his lay,
> As in approvaunce of his pleasing wordes.[45]

And in the Garden of Adonis itself, where nature alone prevails, the lesson taught, as Amoret proves to her cost, is insufficient for life on the human level until the ideals peculiar to that level are recognized as likewise natural, and as modifying for humanity the principles common to the whole order of nature.

At certain points, moreover, natural and humanistic ethics require to be rectified by Christian. A striking instance is furnished in Book V. There Spenser's treatment of justice is strictly Aristotelian, and justice, the justice of natural ethics, is stated to include equity. But natural ethics, unrectified by the example of Christianity, is incapable of furnishing the principle which must temper justice. By itself human nature cannot rise above the uncertain and unorganized sentiment of pity. Only Christian teaching and example can afford the principle of mercy. Thus in the court of Mercilla there is introduced a specifically Christian note. Mercilla (who represents Elizabeth in her judicial function) administers justice tempered by mercy, and Artegall (who represents natural justice) and Prince Arthur (who represents magnanimity) visit her for instruction. Spenser makes his point by one of his happy adaptations of classic myth. With the daughters of Jove and Themis, Justice, Good Order and Peace, who attended upon Mercilla, he associates the *Litae*, whose office is to plead the cause of human frailty and to turn aside the wrath of Jove.

> They also doe, by his divine permission
> Upon the thrones of mortall princes tend,
> And often treat for pardon and remission
> To suppliants, through frayltie which offend.[46]

Lest we should miss in this symbolism the Christian reference, Spenser introduces it with an allusion to the angels that encompass the throne and support the canopy of Mercilla, who herself is angel-like.[47] And of mercy indeed he categorically declares that

> in th'Almighties everlasting seat
> She first was bred, and borne of heavenly race,
> From thence pour'd down on men by influence of grace.[48]

Thus Christian teaching must on occasion be called in to rectify natural ethics, just as grace must intervene in rescue of nature. Book II (as we have seen), in contrast to Book I, moves on the natural level: Spenser's treatment of temperance and continence, like his treatment of justice, is strictly Aristotelian. But there is one episode, baffling to the commentators, which becomes, I think, perfectly plain and highly significant if one reads it as symbolizing the limit of man's natural powers and the necessary intervention of grace. In canto 11, Prince Arthur, in his character of magnanimity, is defending the Castle of Alma (that is, the human mind and body) against the assaults of sin and sensuality led by Maleger. It is in this strange and sinister figure that the difficulty of interpretation is met. He bears upon him every mark of disease and death, and is attended by the two hags, Impatience and Impotence; but he is a swift and resourceful adversary who all but overcomes Prince Arthur himself. The sword Morddure proves useless, and Arthur, attacking the fiend with his bare hands, crushes the life from him and casts the dead body to the ground. But, like the giant Antaeus, at the touch of earth Maleger leaps to his feet and resumes the fight. Repeatedly he is slain and as often revives, till at last Arthur, recognizing the cause, bears the body to a standing lake and hurls it in. Maleger has been variously interpreted:[49] his name (it has been contended) means *evildoer* and he represents sensuality or perhaps sin in general or perhaps Satan himself; his name (say others) means *sick unto death*, and he represents disease which results from the sins of the flesh, or again disease, not as the result of sin, but as a circumstance favourable to it, as lowering resistance to temptation. But none of these interpretations is satisfactory.

What is required is something that will draw the ideas of disease and perennial evil into more intimate relation, and will cover all the details, including Arthur's narrow escape of defeat, the fruitless effort to destroy Maleger, repeatedly restored by the touch of earth, and device by which the destruction is finally compassed, with water standing in symbolic antithesis to earth. I suggest that Maleger is original sin or human depravity, the result of the fall, and that the marks of physical disease and death are the symbols of the inherited taint, the moral and spiritual malady, which man is powerless to remove, and which may betray the strongest and most secure in the natural virtues. It is in his character of magnanimity (of natural virtue) that Prince Arthur barely escapes defeat, and then only by providential intervention. The rescuer stands in need of rescue. How better could the limits of nature be enforced? But this is not all. Nothing can destroy Maleger, nothing can finally remove the inherited taint, but the exercise of grace in its fullest extent. The manner of his destruction by water is significant. It is intended to suggest baptismal regeneration, that is to say, it moves in the same area of symbolism as does the sacrament of baptism. This I am persuaded is the correct interpretation of the episode of Maleger and the only one which will cover all the phenomena.[50] The image of earth is as significant as that of water. Maleger, though momentarily brought under control, revives at the touch of earth. As water symbolizes grace, earth symbolizes nature; and among the various ideas shadowed forth in the *Faerie Queene* is the presence of some principle of evil in nature itself, and especially in matter, a relic of the dark forces which ruled in the chaos before it was reduced to cosmos, and which still struggle to reassert their sway.[51] With these forces of evil in nature, the evil in fallen man enters into alliance, and in them it finds a support. Hence the necessity of grace to rescue and rectify nature.

Apart, however, from this suggestion of forces of evil in nature, which must not be overemphasized, the two orders of nature and grace are contrasted in another respect: the order of nature is temporal and transient; the order of grace is eternal. In the much debated Cantos of Mutabilitie, which I am inclined to accept as furnishing the cosmic setting for Spenser's treatment of the Aristotelian steadfastness or constancy in the *Faerie Queene,* three important points about the order of nature are clearly made. First, that mutability holds sway through all the natural order, not even the stars and their courses being exempt from change. Secondly, that change, however, does not connote dissolution merely, but also replenishment. It is true, says Nature,

> that all things steadfastnesse do hate
> And changed be; yet, being rightly wayd,
> They are not changed from their first estate,
> But by their change their being do dilate,
> And turning to themselves at length again,
> Do worke their own perfection so by fate:
> Then over them Change doth not rule and raigne,
> But they rule over Change and do their states maintaine.[52]

If change is the rule of death, it is also in the natural order the rule of life. In Spenser's account of the Garden of Adonis, in Book III, the true Genius presides at once over the two processes of dissolution and replenishment, of death and life.[53] But this is not the end. Man is in nature, but not wholly of nature: man the immortal spirit craves for permanence, and not in vain. For—and this is the third point that is abundantly clear—nature, by her very deficiency, points on to that time when

> all shall changed bee,
> And from thenceforth none no more change shall see.[54]

To this pointing on from time to eternity, from change to permanence, from nature to grace, Spenser instantly responds. He feels, like Shelley, the pathos of change, but he does not conclude that "Nought may endure but Mutability." Like Wordsworth, he hears its rhythm as a "musical but melancholy chime," yet recognizes that amid the ruins "Truth fails not." But the truth to which Spenser has final recourse is the truth of another order:

> Then gin I thinke of that which Nature sayd
> Of that same time when no more change shall be,

> But stedfast rest of all things, firmely stayd
> Upon the pillours of Eternity,
> That is contrayr to Mutabilitie;
> For all that moveth doth in change delight:
> But thenceforth all shall rest eternally
> With him that is the God of Sabaoth hight:
> O that great Sabaoth God, grant me that Sabbaths sight![55]

By accident indeed, not design, these are the last words we have of Spenser's *Faerie Queene*. And, like the first words, they are about the order of grace.

IX

This, like the other facts we have adduced, seems to support our hypothesis that Spenser wrote with the concept of the two orders as a principal frame of reference. Nor is this all. At some points (as we have noticed) a recognition of the frame of reference enables us to see further into Spenser's allegory and, what is more important, to appreciate more fully his aesthetic pattern by understanding its conceptual basis. Not only does it help us to explain, that is, to see more significance in, Maleger and Mercilla, in Britomart as contrasted with Amoret, in the Redcross Knight as contrasted with Guyon and Artegall, in Prince Arthur, and by implication perhaps even in Gloriana herself: it also tends to justify the poet where his art has been called in question. It completely justifies the parallel structure of Books I and II, and the repetition in episodes; for parallel is necessary to bring out the essential difference. Or, to take a single example of the clearing of the aesthetic pattern in Book II considered alone: critics have complained of the division of labour in the final cantos, with Guyon going forward to his destruction of the Bower of Bliss while Prince Arthur is left to defend the Castle of Alma against Maleger and his host.[56] But once we invoke the frame of reference, and understand the meaning of Maleger, we see that the episodes are complementary, and one as necessary as the other. For Guyon, moving upon the natural level, and guided only by reason, can discharge his particular task; but nature and reason have their limits, and when these limits are reached, as by Arthur in his battle with Maleger, only grace can save. And this use of contrast is highly characteristic of Spenser's whole mode of patterning in the *Faerie Queene*.

In broadest outline (as we have observed) Book I moves upon the level of grace and deals with a specifically Christian experience and virtue (call this Spenser's thesis); and the subsequent books which we possess move upon the level of nature and concern themselves with the natural virtues (call this the antithesis). Somehow, before the poem was completed, Spenser must achieve his synthesis, and a synthesis that would, of course, recognize the priority of the order of grace.

No doubt the task was rendered more difficult by Spenser's partial adherence to two different traditions. If, like Hooker, he had been content to emphasize the unity of the whole creation under God, and the steady and relatively unimpeded ascent through nature to grace: if he had simply emphasized one law of perfection operating throughout the whole natural order, as physical law, as biological and, on the human level, as rational and moral: if he had regarded revelation as merely supplementary, as completing this natural law by pointing man on to that fuller perfection which his nature demanded but to which the order of nature could carry him only part of the way: if unequivocally, Spenser had taken his stand in this tradition, his task would have been easier, though his record of human experience would have been less complete. To this tradition indeed he did respond, and strongly (let there be no mistake about that). But in him it was crossed and partly cancelled by another: by the tradition which we may associate with Calvinism, and which tended to emphasize the insufficiency of nature, and indeed, since the fall, its depravity, and to regard grace as necessary, not merely to complete, but to correct nature and to supply its patent deficiencies. In the one tradition grace could build on the sure foundation of nature. In the other it seemed, rather, to demand a new start. Spenser tries to do justice to the facts of human experience which support these two rival views. And the synthesis at which he aimed in the *Faerie Queene,* whatever its precise character, must somehow have included them both.

That it did so, we have sufficient indication in the part of the poem we possess. Guyon, Artegall and Britomart achieve their natural virtues of temperance, justice and chastity just as surely as does the Redcross Knight his supernatural virtue of holiness; and just as successfully they fulfil their tasks. In so doing they are supported by nature adequately conceived, that is, by a nature in which human wisdom, deliberate or instinctive, can find a guide; but the manifestations of nature are multifarious, and the guide therein must be sought with discrimination. Once it is found, Spenser emphasizes the harmony of nature with grace so far as nature goes, and extorts from nature herself a recognition of the higher order and its claims. Here, plainly, are facts relevant to any attempted synthesis. But there are others. Despite the success of Guyon and Artegall in achieving temperance and justice as natural virtues and without recourse to grace, Spenser's sense of the limitations of nature comes out in their books. In Book V, the natural law of justice includes equity, but has no place for mercy, which can be learned only from the Gospel. In Book II, the sufficiency of nature in Guyon is balanced by the necessity of grace for Prince Arthur's destruction of Maleger.

In Books III and IV, however, this pattern is not maintained. In Britomart, as in Guyon and Artegall, nature is sufficient, but here there is no added appeal from nature to grace, either to modify the ideal of chastity and love or to remove obstacles to its fulfilment: the whole story moves on the natural level, without reference to grace. Yet in some ways Britomart seems more readily adoptable into the Christian scheme than does either Guyon or Artegall, and the ideal of wedded love which she represents seems to require an addition merely. In *Paradise Lost* Milton, adapting to a conception of Christian marriage the Platonic scale of ascent, sees the possibility that chaste love, such as that of the unfallen Adam and Eve for each other, may become a ladder leading to the heavenly love. In Britomart nothing of the sort is suggested. For all we are told, Spenser might here entertain the opinion strongly suggested by the last two of the *Fowre Hymnes,* that heavenly love could not be based on earthly, but required a new start. Clearly it was a problem for the poet, as not only the *Fowre Hymnes* but the hesitations and contradictions of the *Amoretti* show. But despite the studied silence of the Britomart-Artegall story on this subject, there is perhaps the hint of a solution if we bring that story into relation with the very different one of the Redcross Knight and Una. At the end of Book I, as a symbol of holiness achieved, and a reward for his task accomplished, the Redcross Knight is betrothed to Una. It is, of course, a common device in moral allegories, which Spenser has here adopted; but it clearly presents earthly love as a symbol of heavenly and so far prepares for, if it does not effect, a synthesis of the two.

This, I believe, illustrates a possible relation of the order of nature to the order of grace, which was essential to Spenser's synthesis. One thing that we miss in his explanation of allegory in the Letter to

Raleigh is any allusion to Dante's four levels of meaning: possibly because, like other things omitted, it is unnecessary to an intelligent commencement upon the poem: more probably, because Spenser did not adopt in its entirety the Dantean scheme. But the idea that the earthly is a symbol of the heavenly, he clearly does adopt. It is of the very texture of Book I;[57] and, noting the evidence of symmetry in the half of Spenser's pattern which we possess, we should expect this relation to be reasserted in or before Book XII. If there was to be a book devoted to wisdom, with Sophy as hero, where more appropriately could the reassertion occur, since there is a heavenly wisdom as well as an earthly? There is also an earthly and a heavenly glory. The magnanimous man, says Aristotle, desires glory because he alone is worthy of it. Thus Prince Arthur is in search of Gloriana, of whom he has had a vision. But Arthur has his role in the order of grace as well as in the order of nature, and there Gloriana must signify not the undifferentiated glory of the Letter to Raleigh, but that glorification which cannot be achieved by man's worthiness, but only through God's grace. Book XII (as we said) must do more than furnish belated explanations: it must complete Spenser's synthesis, and with it his pattern: like the Epilogue in *Comus*, it must furnish a vantage point from which everything falls into relation. Among the resources which Spenser had at his disposal was one peculiarly adapted to poetry, the sense that the inferior order stood (as Newman was to phrase it) in a sacramental relation to the higher order: that nature in one aspect might be viewed as "the outward and visible sign of an inward and spiritual grace."[58]

NOTES

1. Annual Tudor and Stuart Club Lecture, April 29, 1949.
2. The Argument of Milton's *Comus, University of Toronto Quarterly,* 11 (1941). 46-71.
3. The account of the frame of reference is adapted from my article on *Comus.*
4. *Puritanism and Liberty* (London, 1938), introduction, pp. 57-60.
5. F. M. Padelford, The Spiritual Allegory of the *Faerie Queene,* Book One, *Journal of English and Germanic Philology,* 22 (1923). 1-17. Cf. P. N. Siegel, Spenser and the Calvinistic View of Life, *Studies in Philology,* 41 (1944). 201-22. In effect, though not explicitly, Padelford discriminates between nature and grace. In pursuance of his own principle that "in studying the relationships and interconnections of

man's intellectual history, it is well not to be too schematic" (p. 215), Siegel confuses the two orders, finding Puritanism in Guyon's rejection of Mammon's offers of wealth as, "above all, distraction from the pursuit of a righteous life" (p. 203), and talking of Calidore's return, after his pastoral interlude, "to the service of Gloriana *and God*" (p. 204). Obviously the principle is wrong. What is required is the highest degree of precision (which involves schematism) in the formulation of positions and their consequences, and the ability to determine when an author recognizes these consequences and when he does not.

6. *The Ancient Bounds* (London, 1645): reprinted in my *Puritanism and Liberty* (spelling, etc., modernized), pp. 247-8.

7. By Professor Fredson Bowers, at the M.L.A., December, 1948, Group English IV (see multigraphed summary).

8. Thus Padelford in The Allegory of Chastity in the *Faerie Queene, Studies in Philology*, 21 (1924). 367-81: *Variorum Spenser* 3. 324.

9. Spenser's word in the Letter is, of course, *magnificence,* but in the poem *magnanimity*.

10. As cited in n. 5.

11. W. F. DeMoss, Spenser's Twelve Moral Virtues 'according to Aristotle,' *Modern Philology*, 26 (1918). 23-8, 245-70; Lilian Winstanley, in introduction to her edition of Book II (Cambridge, 1914).

12. 1. 10.

13. It has not, I think, been noticed that in Spenser's description of Faith the serpent in the chalice (1. 10. 13) bears a double significance, both in the order of grace: besides being the symbol of healing (the emblem of Aescalapius) and of salvation (Moses' serpent on the staff—Numb. 21. 9—the type of Christ on the Cross), it is also a symbol of menace, doubtless with reference to 1 Cor. 12.27-9. and its doctrine as repeated in the *Book of Common Prayer*.

14. Harold Golder, Bunyan and Spenser, *P. M. L. A.*, 45 (1930). 216-37.

15. 1. 3; H. S. V. Jones, *Spenser Handbook* (N. Y., 1930), 159. The two orders are again brought face to face in the meeting of Una with the satyrs and Sir Satyrane (1. 6), which yields a similar result: the friendship of uncorrupted nature for grace, but the limits, nevertheless, of merely natural perceptions.

16. 1. 4-5; 1. 7.

17. 1. 8. 37-9. Another and less significant juxtaposition of the two orders occurs in the encounter with Despair (1. 9): Sir Terwin is reduced to despair and impelled to suicide by a sense of earthly misfortune: it is an offence against nature (and of course against religion, which is not invoked); the Redcross Knight, by a sense of sin and spiritual shipwreck: it is an offence against religion (and of course against nature, which is not invoked).

18. Guyon's encounter with the Redcross Knight (2. 1. 26-34) has for its general significance a further note on the relation of the order of nature to the order of grace: the harmony of natural ethics with religious, so far as the former can go (cf. 1. 3, as explained above, and n. 15) and the recognition of the claims of the higher order by the lower and by reason (cf. 7.59 as explained below, and n. 55). Guyon is more swift to recognize and bow to the symbol of the cross on St. George's shield than is the latter to recognize Guyon as the worthy representative of one of the natural virtues. The Palmer (reason), coming up later, confirms Guyon's judgment. Guyon's reference to "The sacred badge of my Redeemers death" might seem at first to run counter to our hypothesis that Guyon stands for natural as distinguished from Christian virtue, but the distinction is not between pagan and Christian, but between unconverted (natural) man and converted (regenerate). Though denied by some extreme Calvinists (cf. Prynne, in my *Puritanism and Liberty*, p. 233), Christ was generally held to have died for all men and so might be referred to, even by the unconverted, as "my Redeemer," though confessedly Spenser momentarily obscures his pattern by the phrase. It is but momentarily, however; for, as I shall argue below, a large part of the significance of Book II turns on the assignment of Guyon to the order of nature, consistently maintained throughout. And to deny it in this early episode would be to rob the episode itself of much of its meaning. Observe that the Palmer recognizes the Redcross Knight for a saint, a being of a different order, but characteristically attributes his reward to his own merit, which the Redcross Knight, also characteristically, is swift to deny, with gentle reproof, "His be the praise that this achievement wrought." The Palmer speaks of Guyon as having to set out from the point at which the Redcross Knight started, not from the point which he reached (i. e., not with his virtue achieved) as would be demanded by Professor Bowers' hypothesis, and he prays that God may guide him in his task, the God (no doubt) who presides over the order of nature as well as over the order of grace.

19. 2. 2.

20. Medina's house is described as "wondrous strong by nature, and by skilful frame" (2. 2. 12).

21. J. S. Harrison in *Variorum Spenser*, 2. 416.

22. Cf. F. M. Padelford, *ibid.*, 420.

23. 1. 10. 1.

24. 2. 9. 1.

25. It is significant that virtually all the instances of "grace" meaning the grace of God in its full extent (i. e., (i) and closely related senses) occur in Book I. For example: "heavenly grace" (which supports) (1. 7. 12; 1. 8. 1); "of grace" (doctrine of grace) (1. 10. 19); "Where justice growes there grows eke greater grace" (1. 9. 53); "perfection

of all heavenly grace" (state of grace) (1. 10. 21). In the more extended sense of (ii) and related meanings (God's bounty in bestowing temporal gifts or providential protection, in the natural order), "grace" occurs in all six books. For example: "heavenly grace" (divine protection) (1. 5. 31); "wondrous grace" (providential intervention) 1. 6. argmt.; "God's sole grace . . . To send her succour" (6. 4. 10.); Britomart is saved from disaster "by God's grace and her good heedinesse" (5. 6. 34); "grace" intervening to check the natural man for his protection, without external instrument (1. 9. 26), with external instrument (2. 11. 30); "Providence hevenly passeth living thought, / And doth for wretched mens reliefe make way; / For loe! great grace or fortune thither brought / Comfort to him" (3. 5. 27) (interesting as suggesting that what is really God's providence is sometimes mistaken for chance by the natural man); "his Creators grace . . . The guifts of soveraine bounty" (2. 7. 16); "The grace of his Creator [he] doth despise / That will not use his gifts" (4. 8. 15); "If goodnesse find no grace [divine favour] nor righteousnes no meed" (3. 11. 9). The meaning (iii) of natural endowment is not frequent, and in its examples it is probable that the word "grace" actually refers to some natural quality (as goodness of disposition or beauty): 2. 9. 1 (quoted above); Belphoebe was born with "all the gifts of grace and chastity" (3. 6. 2); Radigund seemed a "miracle of natures goodly grace" (5. 5. 12); "deckt with wondrous giftes of natures grace" (6. 7. 28); "Whether such grace were given her by kynd" (6. 6. 43). In what is the commonest meaning, (iv) grace of disposition, bearing, manners, or simply beauty, the adjective "heavenly" is sometimes added: thus of Una's "grace" (1. 3. 4; 1. 6. 18) where the primary reference is certainly to her beauty; Belphoebe was a "goodly Maide full of divinities / And gifts of heavenly grace" (3. 5. 34). Our classification is not exhaustive. There are a few doubtful examples to be noted: Mercy is born in heaven and "thence pour'd down on men in influence of grace" (5. 10. 1), probably to be classed under (ii); God planted the flower of chastity in Paradise, "to make ensample of his heavenly grace" (3. 5. 52), and thereafter did it "in stocke of earthly flesh enrace / That mortall men her glory should admyre" (probably to be classed under (iv), but as a disposition which God specially approves); "Nepenthe is a drinck of soverayne grace / Devized by the Gods" (4. 3. 43): as also in the preceding example, the phrasing appears to be so calculated as to make it available for shadowing forth a religious meaning, which renders it difficult to classify; "grace" would here seem to mean native property (iii), but with the added idea of a divine cause; similar is the remark about fountains, how some have natural properties, and others special properties "by guifte of later grace" (2. 2. 6).

26. H. S. V. Jones, *The Faerie Queene* and the Medieval Aristotelian Tradition, *Journal of English and Germanic Philology*, 25 (1926). 283 ff.; V. B. Hulbert, in *Variorum Spenser*, 2. 424-6.

27. The highminded man (Aristotle, *Ethics*, 4. 8) is apt to appear supercilious, though affable to his inferiors; he is justified in his contempt for ordinary people, whom he is apt to treat with irony. "He is not given to admiration as there is nothing which strikes him as great." He is in the highest degree courageous, of course, when stirred to action, but "there are few things which he values enough to endanger himself for them." He would rather confer than receive benefits; and those received he tries to repay with interest and then forget, "for the recipient is inferior to the benefactor, and the highminded man always aspires to superiority." He is dignified in his movements, with a deep voice and a sedate speech, and is never in a hurry. It seems evident that by a Christian standard he would be condemned as self-sufficient and proud, and by a chivalric, as lacking in generosity and a spirit of adventure.

28. 2. 8. 23 ff.

29. If one is to interpret correctly the allegories of the *Faerie Queene,* one must bear this obvious distinction in mind. Some encounters are dramatic projections of an inward struggle in the mind (e. g., the Redcross Knight's meeting with Despair, 1. 9); others are conflicts with some outward evil (e. g., his fight with Error, 1. 1).

30. The most striking example is the twofold presentation of the principle of generation in the whole natural order, in 3. 6., first in the account of the operation of the Genius with matter and forms, then in the myth of Venus and Adonis, which effects the transition to the human level in the myth of Cupid and Psyche.

31. 2. 8. 1-8.

32. 2. 8. 1.

33. Legouis (*Variorum Spenser*, 2. 271) complains bitterly of Spenser's thoughtlessness in applying these terms to the virtuous Sir Guyon. It is not the poet who is thoughtless.

34. 2. 12. 46-9.

35. 2. 12. 46, 50, 55, 58, 59, 61; C. S. Lewis, *The Allegory of Love* (London, 1936) pp. 324 ff.

36. 3. 6. 29-50. I have deliberately refrained in this lecture from going into the details of Spenser's allegory of matter and the forms, since it would carry me too far afield. The rival interpretations are summarized in the *Variorum Spenser*, 3. 340-52. Of these I still prefer, as a basis for further consideration, Dr. Brents Stirling's (*ibid.*, 3. 347-52). I have already recorded my reasoned conviction that Spenser's treatment of the myth of Venus and Adonis refers simply to the principle of generation in the natural order, and his treatment of the myth

of Cupid and Psyche to the operation of this principle at the human level in the institution of marriage, in other words, that both are in the order of nature (The Argument of Milton's *Comus*, *University of Toronto Quarterly*, 11 (1941). 67-9).

37. 3. 6. 4-11.

38. 3. 6. 28, 51.

39. 3. 2. 22 ff.; 3. 3. 26.

40. It is perhaps unnecessary again to emphasize the fact that the natural does not necessarily connote the pagan. Britomart and Glauce go to church, Britomart thinking only of Artegall, and Glauce only of Britomart, or (as Spenser remarks) "With great devotion, and with little zele" (3. 2. 48). Glauce's appropriation for Britomart of armour, captured from the pagan Angela, and deposited in a church (3. 3. 58-9), certainly does not mean that Britomart is clad, like the Redcross Knight, in the armour of the Christian, but perhaps symbolizes the idea that the natural principles (available even to the pagan) on which Britomart proceeds harmonize with, and can be assimilated by, Christianity. This is not Spenser's synthesis of the two orders, but necessary in preparation for any synthesis. It is important that we should be clear on this point. For in her rescue of Amoret, Britomart's shield protects her from the flames, and her sword parts them and makes way for her (3. 11. 25); but it is not "the shield . . . wherewith ye shall be able to quench all the fiery darts of the wicked," nor "the sword of the Spirit, which is the word of God" (Ephes. 6. 16, 17). But this too may prepare for the final synthesis in another way, which I shall suggest at the end of the lecture, by rendering nature eligible as a symbol of grace.

41. F. M. Padelford, The Allegory of Chastity in the *Faerie Queene*, *Studies in Philology*, 21 (1925). 367-81; to whose exposition I am deeply indebted.

42. 3. 11. 19.

43. 5. 7. 12-16. In addition to the interpretation of the dream (5. 7. 22-3), one should observe that four basic facts condition its development and imagery as dream. (i) Britomart's love for Artegall is the dream's directing motive, as appears in its conclusion. (ii) Her memory of her first sight of Artegall in the magic mirror (3. 2. 17 ff.) and of Merlin's explanation (3. 3. 21 ff.) have their strong influence. In the latter the child that Britomart is to bear to Artegall is likened to a lion (3. 3. 30), and again the image of a lion occurs, followed immediately by the image of a consuming fire (3. 3. 47-8). In Britomart's dream these images are reproduced in reverse order. (iii) Then there is the whole course of Britomart and Artegall's love story, and especially their fighting against each other (4. 6), with Artegall's fierce and impetuous wrath, first stayed, then turned to love, by Britomart's

beauty: this too receives symbolic presentment in the dream. (iv) Finally, all is combined with images derived from Britomart's vigil in the temple of Isis. From neophite she herself is transformed to queen or goddess: the moon-shaped mitre, to a royal crown, and the white vestment to a royal robe of scarlet, blazing with jewels. And here is added the nightmare touch as in a flash the image suggestive of fire becomes the image of fire itself—the fire on the altar of Isis which seems to spread to the temple. But the fire-image has also its place in Merlin's well-remembered prophecy, and so dimly, as it were, and afar off, Artegall is introduced into the dream. Thus when the crocodile, roused from sleep, does battle with the flames, he becomes the symbol of Artegall; for the animal is Osiris, the lover of Isis, and Britomart and Artegall parallel Isis and Osiris. At first, in his pride and impetuosity, the animal seems more like enemy than lover. Here is reflected past experience, when Artegall fought against Britomart; but to this antagonism love had quickly succeeded, as it does when the animal is rebuked by Isis. What follows is prophetic of the consummation of their union and the birth of their child.

44. The pronounced vein of idyllicism in Spenser has been often remarked. It influences his treatment of nature, especially in Book VI, but also at other places, as in 2. 7. 15-16, where a reference to nature as norm suggests the reflection that "At the well-head the purest streames arise" and leads on to the famous description of the "antique world in his first flowring youth." In a characteristic reference to the unfallen state (1. 11. 47) the doctrine differs (since one passage bears a reference to nature only, the other to nature and grace), but not the tone: Spenser describes Eden as

> that soile where all good things did grow,
> And freely sprong out of the fruitfull grownd,
> As incorrupted Nature did them sow,
> Till that dred Dragon all did overthrow.

45. 2. 12. 71, 76.
46. 5. 9. 32.
47. 5. 9. 29.
48. 5. 10. 1.
49. See *Variorum Spenser*, 2. 343.
50. Throughout this episode Prince Arthur retains his role of natural virtue, of magnanimity. Even at the end, it is the water, and not the Prince, that symbolizes grace. The providential intervention which earlier effects the temporary rescue of the Prince is described as an act of grace in the second meaning of the term (see n. 25, above). Its instrument is the Prince's Squire; and, like the treatment of Despair (1. 9), the allegory adds to the firm handling of a proposition genuine

psychological insight. The Prince is almost borne down by his subtle inward foes, when the Squire appears, and it is his example that recalls the Prince to himself and to the pursuit of virtue and honour which is the mark of the magnanimous man:

> The whiles the Prince, prickt with reprochful shame,
> As one awakte out of long slombring shade,
> Reviving thought of glory and of fame,
> United all his powers to purge him selfe from blame (2. 11. 31).

And Spenser's comment makes it clear that the Squire's arrival is the effect of Providence, which can on occasion use the weak to save the strong:

> So greatest and most glorious thing on ground
> May often need the helpe of weaker hand;
> So feeble is mans state, and life unsound,
> That in assurance it may never stand,
> Till it dissolved be from earthly band:
> Proofe be thou, Prince, the prowest man alyve, . . .
> That, had not grace thee blest, thou shouldest not survive (2. 11. 30).

51. 1. 5. 20-3; 4. 2. 47; 1. 1. 37.
52. 7. 7. 58.
53. 3. 6. 31-3.
54. 7. 7. 59.
55. 7. 8. 2. I adopt the correction Sabbaths for Sabaoths; but see D. C. Allen "On the Closing Lines of the *Faerie Queene*," *M. L. N.*, 64 (1949). 93-4.
56. J. W. Bennett, *The Evolution of the Faerie Queene* (Chicago, 1942), p. 134.
57. Because the action of Book I (as of the other books) takes place in the material world, the order of nature, while its allegorical content is experience in the order of grace, the lower order stands to the higher throughout the book in the relation of shadow to substance. In his "Spenser and the Enchanted Glass" (*Johns Hopkins Alumni Magazine* 19 (1930. 23-8: *Variorum Spenser* 1. 442-5) Professor C. G. Osgood has shown how penetrating and consistent is the psychology of Spenser's story on the literal (i. e., the natural) level.
58. In his Anglican days Newman had developed this idea (with, of course, no thought of Spenser) as a corollary of Bishop Butler's concept of analogy, read in the light of Keble (see Newman, *Apologia pro Vita Sua*, Everyman edn., p. 42). The quoted phrase is not Newman's, but from the *Book of Common Prayer*, added thereto after Spenser's death, but from Nowell's *Catechism* (1570). Apart from

Book I (see n. 56), we can, in the unfinished state of the poem, have only scattered hints of this last relation between the two orders which I have suggested. They would be best gathered by a close reading of the other books in relation to Book I, as we saw in considering the parallel between the Britomart-Artegall and Una-Redcross Knight stories. That the parallel may extend to some of the details we observed in noting the similarity in the description of Britomart's natural equipment to the Christian's armour (see n. 39).

PAUL J. ALPERS

Narrative and Rhetoric in the *Faerie Queene*

I

Whenever we interpret a narrative poem, we must decide how narrative action reveals poetic meaning.[1] In this essay, I want to propose a new way of seeing the relation between poetic meaning and narrative events in the *Faerie Queene*. The usual view of this relation is based on what I would call a confusion between narrative materials and poetic narration. Spenser's narrative materials are stories, settings, and characters, while his poetic narration is a sequence of stanzas. Confusing the two produces interpretations like Ruskin's analysis of Book I—one of the first reactions against the romantic tendency to dismiss or minimize Spenser's allegory:

> [Holiness], in the opening of the book, has Truth (or Una) at its side, but presently enters the Wandering Wood, and encounters the serpent Error; that is to say, Error in her universal form, the first enemy of Reverence and Holiness. . . . Having vanquished this first open and palpable form of Error, as Reverence and Religion must always vanquish it, the Knight encounters Hypocrisy, or Archimagus: Holiness cannot detect

From *Studies in English Literature*, II (Houston, Texas, 1962), pp. 27-46. Reprinted with permission of the editor. This article is part of the author's forthcoming *The Poetry of "The Faerie Queene,"* to be published by Princeton University Press.

Hypocrisy, but believes him, and goes home with him; where-
upon, Hypocrisy succeeds in separating Holiness from Truth;
and the Knight (Holiness) and Lady (Truth) go forth separately from the house of Archimagus. Now observe; the moment
Godly Fear, or Holiness, is separated from Truth, he meets
Infidelity, or the Knight sans Foy. . . .[2]

Ruskin simply translates the narrative materials of Book I into abstract terms. Characters and settings are given consistent symbolic
identifications, and the narrative action indicates their conceptual relations. Ruskin makes what is still the fundamental assumption of
Spenserian criticism—that the sequence of stanzas in the *Faerie
Queene* is equivalent to the narrative materials of the poem. Since
"narrative materials" is too bulky a term for frequent use, I shall refer to the stories, settings, and characters of the *Faerie Queene* as
Spenser's *fiction*—that which is feigned to exist and happen.

Ruskin's method of interpretation is still accepted as valid for allegorical passages in the *Faerie Queene*; it is usually qualified by saying that some episodes are not allegorical, but are to be considered as
exemplary or dramatic narrative. All recent critics define Spenser's
technique by the poles of narrative and allegory.[3] As exemplary or
dramatic narrative, Spenser's fiction is taken to be real, according to
the conventional suspension of disbelief we grant to any romance or
novel. As allegory, the fiction is understood to be less real than its
conceptual translation, but it nevertheless provides both the terms
and the syntax of the translation. "What happens" poetically is taken
to be identical with, or at least determined by, "what happens" fic-
tionally. Whatever the specific content or meaning, it is expressed by
the characters and settings that constitute and the events that take
place in the putative reality of the poem.

However, when we read the poem on this assumption, we find numerous inconsistencies, some of which produce major interpretive
difficulties. We find inconsistencies, I suggest, because our criterion
of consistency is not valid. In turning narrative materials into stanzas
of poetry, Spenser's attention is focused on the reader's mind and
feelings and not on what is happening within his fiction. His poetic
motive in any given stanza is to elicit a response—to modify or complicate feelings and attitudes. His stanzas, then, are modes of address
by the poet to the reader. For this reason, I call his use of narrative
materials *rhetorical*.

The most striking instance in which this approach resolves a fictional inconsistency is the problem of why the figure of Time is in the Garden of Adonis. According to Spenser's myth, the flowers in the garden are souls or forms that are sent out into the world; having lived and died on earth, they return to the Garden of Adonis to be replanted and reborn. The garden itself is a spontaneously flowering paradise and projects the idea that nature is permanent because its change is orderly. Literally, then, it is simply a mistake to place wicked Time with his scythe in the Garden of Adonis: the realm he rules is the earth below, and he represents a principle of sudden and final death that is presumably resolved by the orderly cycles of the garden.[4]

Yet poetically Time's presence is perfectly valid. The potency of the image of a natural paradise depends on our understanding the idea of change that it corrects and resolves. In order to make us aware of earthly mutability, Spenser is willing to neglect both his fable and its philosophic coherence. He sets these aside in order to introduce a concept or feeling that is relevant to our understanding of the Garden of Adonis. In the stanza preceding the description of Time, Spenser explains the continuity of matter. "The substance is not chaunged," he says, but forms are:

> For formes are variable and decay,
> By course of kind, and by occasion;
> And that faire flowre of beautie fades away,
> As doth the lilly fresh before the sunny ray.
>   (III.vi.38)[5]

Spenser returns to the flowers of the garden by means of an image developed in the course of direct address to the reader. In the next four stanzas, he lays out the double suggestion of the image of the lily—on the one hand the inevitability of decay, and on the other the sense of benignity and naturalness given by "sunny ray."

The first of these stanzas is the presentation of earthly time:

> Great enimy to it, and to all the rest,
> That in the Gardin of Adonis springs,
> Is wicked Time, who with his scyth addrest,
> Does mow the flowring herbes and goodly things,
> And all their glory to the ground downe flings,
> Where they doe wither, and are fowly mard:

> He flyes about, and with his flaggy wings
> Beates downe both leaves and buds without regard,
> Ne ever pittie may relent his malice hard.
>
> (III.vi.39)

Time is more the activated abstraction of a sonnet than a fictional personage. The striking details of the stanza impress us primarily as emphatic diction, and not as the attributes of an emblematic character. "Wicked," "mow," "to the ground downe flings," "wither," "fowly mard," "beates downe," "malice hard"—this series runs through the stanza and is juxtaposed with the language of delicate pastoral— "flowring herbes," "glory," "leaves and buds." Spenser is multiplying statements about the action of earthly time. But the stanza, although more like a sonnet than a mythical narrative, is not exactly like a sonnet. In accordance with his rhetorical aim—to give a comprehensive sense of earthly time—Spenser presents Time as both mower and winged. These two versions are quite distinct, but Spenser accommodates them by turning Time's wings, which ordinarily represent swiftness of flight, into instruments of destruction. He thus creates a quasi-fiction that gives continuity and movement to his statements: fictional action is in the service of direct address to the reader.

The stanza that follows is also organized and developed as an address to the reader:

> Yet pittie often did the gods relent,
> To see so faire things mard, and spoyled quight:
> And their great mother Venus did lament
> The losse of her deare brood, her deare delight:
> Her hart was pierst with pittie at the sight,
> When walking through the Gardin, them she spyde,
> Yet no'te she find redresse for such despight.
> For all that lives, is subiect to that law:
> All things decay in time, and to their end do draw.
>
> (III.vi.40)

The first line directly echoes the last line of the stanza on Time and produces an important shift of tone. "Ne ever pittie may relent his malice hard" has a note of finality and rigor. "Yet pittie often did the gods relent" conveys tender solicitude for Time's victims. In other words, Spenser presents Venus's mourning for her flowers within the framework of our responses to his diction and verse rhythms. Between the image of the lily and this stanza we have undergone a cumulative verbal experience, so that Spenser now returns to the pathos of the lily with increased command and weight. At the end of this stanza, he elicits from Venus's fictional tenderness a tone of direct address that is both delicate and grave. His explanation of the goddess's help-lessness is really a summary statement of Time's dominion over na-ture. It is from this rhetorical point that he presents the garden as a paradise (III.vi.41-2). And even here he begins by saying, "But were it not, that Time their troubler is." In a strict philosophical sense, this concession is absurd, but poetically it places the vision of "con-tinuall spring, and harvest . . . both meeting at one time" in a wider context of human feeling about time.

The poetic coherence of the *Faerie Queene* is usually described in terms of fictional consistency; but it is rather to be found in the co-herence of the reader's feelings and attitudes. One of the great puzzles of the poem is the ending of Book I, when the Red Cross Knight leaves Una. Spenser does not explicitly address the reader, but we can solve the interpretive dilemma only by recognizing that the mode of his narration is rhetorical:

> Yet swimming in that sea of blisfull ioy,
> He nought forgot, how he whilome had sworne,
> In case he could that monstrous beast destroy,
> Unto his Farie Queene backe to returne:
> The which he shortly did, and Una left to mourne.
>
> (I.xii.41)

If the knight's separation from Una does not mean separation from Truth, as it did earlier in the book, then what does it mean? The question is unanswerable if we assume that Spenser's fiction is the main vehicle of his meaning. But surely Spenser's intention is clear enough. The holy knight still bears his burden of flesh, and therefore must resume a life of heroic action. Marriage to Una symbolically tells us about the knight's election and his moral condition, but it is not the literal truth about his human experience. As literal experience, the marriage is a "sea of blisfull ioy" and suggests permanent earthly happiness—precisely what is not possible for man since the Fall. Una's mourning suggests the pathos of the fact that the servant of God does not enjoy the eternal bliss of the saints in heaven. It would be ab-surd to say that Truth mourns: both the marriage and Una have sim-ply their literal meanings, human marriage and human wife. But although they are demoted to non-allegorical status, Spenser uses them to modify the reader's understanding of issues that have been presented allegorically.

There is a further fictional inconsistency in the departure of the Red Cross Knight. He has already promised the hermit Contemplation that he will forsake arms and take up a "Pilgrims poore estate" (I.x.64), and this vow is directly contradicted by the vow to return to the Fairy Queen. Yet both vows serve the same poetic purpose: each in its context enlarges the reader's sense of the conflicting imperatives that involve the elected man. The vow to the Fairy Queen, which is not mentioned until the last canto, is introduced simply to be used as a poetic device in the conclusion of Book I. In fictional terms, this conclusion must seem clumsy and almost meaningless. But it is entirely true to the reader's sense of Spenser's central concern—human experience seen under the aspect of man's relation to God.

When we assume that Una retains a specific identity and is therefore always Truth, or that Spenser holds a mirror up to a putatively real garden that is external to him, we assume that the narrative poem is a world. This idea underlies the interpretive assumptions that I have been questioning. For our purposes, the most pertinent statement of it is by Tasso:

Sì come in questo mirabile magisterio di Dio, che mondo si chiama, e 'l cielo si vede sparso o distinto di tanta varietà di stelle, e . . . l'aria e 'l mare pieni di uccelli e di pesci, e la terra albergatrice di tanti animali così feroci, come mansueti, nella quale e ruscelli e fonti e laghi e prati e campagne e selve e monti sogliamo rimirare; . . . con tutto ciò uno è il mondo che tante e sì diverse cose nel suo grembo rinchiude, una la forma e l'essenza sua, uno il nodo dal quale sono le sue parti con discorde concordia insieme congiunte e collegate; e, non mancando nulla in lui, nulla però vi è che non serva a la necessità o a l'ornamento: così parimente giudico, che da eccellente poeta (il quale, non per altro è detto divino, se non perchè, al supremo artefice nelle sue operazioni assomigliandosi, della sua divinità viene a partecipare) un poema formar si possa, nel quale, quasi in un picciolo mondo, qui si leggano ordinanze di eserciti, qui battaglie terrestri e navali, qui espugnazioni di città, . . . là opere di crudeltà, di audacia, di cortesia, di generosità; là avvenimenti d'amore, or felici or infelici, or lieti o compassion-

evoli: ma che nondimeno uno sia il poema che tanta varietà di
materie contegna, una la forma e l'anima sua; e che tutte queste
cose sieno di maniera composte, che l'una l'altra riguardi, l'una
a l'altra corrisponda, l'una da l'altra o necessariamente o veri-
similmente dependa, sì che una sola parte o tolta via, o mutata
di sito, il tutto si distrugga.[6]*

Interpretations of the *Faerie Queene* characteristically assume that
Spenser's poem is a world in Tasso's sense. All the narrative materials
are selected and developed in order to make the poem an ordered
creation that is obedient to its own laws. My argument, on the other
hand, is that Spenser's poetic motive is consistently to elicit responses.
In the *Faerie Queene,* poetic meaning is defined with reference to the
reader's awareness and not to the coherence of a self-contained and
internally consistent fiction.

When Tasso says that a poem is a world because it is single, the
single soul or form he refers to is what he calls the fable—the comprehensive and controlling action that is assumed to exist in each book
of the *Faerie Queene*.[7] But there is no reason to think that Spenser
shared Tasso's concept of the heroic fable. Tasso says that the *Aeneid*
has an ideal action for an epic: "Oltre tutte l'altre è nobilissima azione
la venuta di Enea in Italia, perchè l'argumento è per sè grande ed
illustre; ma grandissimo ed illustrissimo, avendo riguardo a l'Imperio

* As in this wonderful realm of God, which is called the world, one sees the
sky scattered or highlighted with such a variety of stars, and the air and sea full
of birds and fish, and so many animals, both fierce and gentle, inhabiting the
earth, in which we are accustomed to wonder at brooks and fountains and lakes
and fields and meadows and woods and mountains; . . . for all that, the world
is single which holds in its lap so many and so diverse things, its form and
essence are single, the knot is single with which its parts are brought together and
bound in discordant concord; and, with nothing lacking in it, yet there is nothing
there which does not serve for either necessity or ornament: so by the same token
I judge that an excellent poet (who is called divine for no other reason than
that making himself like the supreme maker in his workings [*al supremo artefice
nelle sue operazioni assomigliandosi*], he comes to participate in his divinity) can
make a poem in which, as in a little world, here we read of armies drawn up,
here of battles on land and sea, here of sieges of cities, . . . there deeds of
cruelty, of boldness, of courtesy, of magnanimity, there the events of love, now
happy now unhappy, now joyous now pitiful: but that nonetheless the poem is
single that contains so much variety of material, its form and its soul are single;
and that all these things are composed in such a way that one thing looks to another, one thing corresponds to another, one thing depends on another either
necessarily or plausibly, so that if one single part is taken away or has its place
changed, the whole is destroyed.

romano ch'ebbe origine da quella."[8] English critics of the sixteenth century do not speak of Aeneas's travels and their destiny; the "argument" of the *Aeneid* is always stated in terms of the moral qualities of its hero. Thus Sidney calls Aeneas "a vertuous man in all fortunes" and describes the *Aeneid* as a series of moral exempla:

> Only let Aeneas be worne in the tablet of your memory; how he governeth himselfe in the ruine of his Country; in the preserving his old Father, and carrying away his religious ceremonies; . . . how in storms, howe in sports, howe in warre, howe in peace, how a fugitive, how victorious, how besiedged, how besiedging, howe to strangers, howe to allyes, how to enemies, howe to his owne; lastly, how in his inward selfe, and how in his outward government.[9]

Similarly Spenser, in the Letter to Ralegh, classifies epic poems by the type of virtue, ethical or political, their heroes exemplify.

The *Apology for Poetry* provides considerable support for our view of the *Faerie Queene* as a continual address to the reader rather than as a fictional world. Sidney justifies the poet's use of fiction, but he does not describe or analyze poetic fictions. For example, he does not raise what is, for Tasso, a central question—whether the narrative of a heroic poem should be historically true. Sidney's criterion of truth is not the nature of the fiction in itself, but its didactic efficacy. He consistently describes poetry as a moral influence operating on the reader's mind. Hence his golden world is entirely different from the world of the poem that Tasso describes. At first "golden world" refers to poetic landscape and is really a metaphor for the attractiveness of poetry ("Nature never set forth the earth in so rich tapistry as divers Poets have done"). Sidney then goes on to say that Nature never produced such excellent men as the heroes of epic poetry:

> Neither let this be iestingly conceived, because the works of the one be essentiall, the other, in imitation or fiction; for any understanding knoweth the skil of the Artificer standeth in that Idea or fore-conceite of the work, and not in the work it selfe. And that the Poet hath that Idea is manifest, by delivering them forth in such excellencie as hee hath imagined them. Which delivering forth also is not wholie imaginative, as we are wont to say by them that build Castles in the ayre: but so farre substantially it worketh, not onely to make a Cyrus, which had

been but a particuler excellencie, as Nature might have done,
but to bestow a Cyrus upon the worlde, to make many Cyrus's,
if they wil learne aright why and how that Maker made him.[10]

For Tasso, the poet resembles "il supremo artefice nelle sue operazioni" because he creates his own little world, the poem. For Sidney,
the poet "substantially worketh" by creating virtuous men. If this defines a golden world, it is a world of heroic readers.

II

I call the mode of narration in the *Faerie Queene* rhetorical, because
each stanza is an address to the reader. But we do not feel, as we do
in *Paradise Lost*, that a decisive voice speaks to us. Spenser's manner
of address is much more self-effacing than Milton's—so much so that
C. S. Lewis finds it possible to claim that "outside the proems to the
books and cantos he scarcely writes a line that is not for the story's
sake."[11] Nevertheless, Spenser's style is not, as Mr. Lewis proposes,
"to be judged as the style of a story-teller"; it makes sense only as a
rhetorical instrument, a means of modifying the reader's feelings.
Without attempting a comprehensive discussion of Spenser's style, I
want to examine a crucial phenomenon in his poetry—the pictorial
effects in which his well-known verbal sensuousness seems to be in
the service of fictional narration.

It has always been assumed that in his pictorial stanzas, Spenser's
purpose is primarily imitative or descriptive: his language is chosen
to suggest a "real" object, which of course can be symbolic or emblematic.[12] But we often find that a striking pictorial effect is not identical
with visual description:

> For round about, the wals yclothed were
> With goodly arras of great maiesty,
> Woven with gold and silke so close and nere,
> That the rich metall lurked privily,
> As faining to be hid from envious eye;
> Yet here, and there, and every where unwares
> It shewd it selfe, and shone unwillingly;
> Like a discolourd Snake, whose hidden snares
> Through the greene gras his long bright burnisht backe declares.

> (III.xi.28)

Several words and phrases that support a pictorial effect are not at all descriptive—for example, "unwares," "unwillingly," and most notably "faining to be hid from envious eye," where Spenser directly suggests the kind of feeling that Busyrane's tapestries induce. Other phrases that do have a visual reference are persuasive because they are suggestive moral formulas—"close and nere," "lurked privily," "hidden snares." A great deal of quasi-visual effect is achieved through verse rhythms, particularly in the sixth and ninth lines. Spenser is using all the verbal resources of his poetry; our sense of physical immediacy comes specifically from our experience of words and their poetic disposition, and not from any optical illusion. The last line is the most distinctly pictorial, yet we are not meant to see the color green at all. The effect of the line comes from the rhythmic crowding of words, and we are to hear the alliterated formula "greene gras." Literally, the "long bright burnisht backe" of the snake is like a fitfully gleaming golden thread. But through alliteration, rhythm, and the concluding "declares" with its strong rhyme, Spenser makes us feel we are dazzled, our field of vision filled—nor do we remember that the snake is "discolourd." The stanza has a pictorial effect because Spenser wants to achieve a certain psychological impact, not because he wants to render real visual experience.[13] He impresses upon us, as if it were a direct sensation, the sinister moral atmosphere of Busyrane's palace.

This stanza is not a description, but a "speaking picture" in Sidney's sense:

> Whatsoever the Philosopher sayth shoulde be doone, hee [the poet] giveth a perfect picture of it in some one, by whom hee presupposeth it was doone. . . . A perfect picture I say, for hee yeeldeth to the powers of the minde an image of that whereof the Philosopher bestoweth but a woordish description: which dooth neyther strike, pierce, nor possesse the sight of the soule so much as that other dooth. . . . No doubt the Philosopher with his learned definition, bee it of vertue, vices, matters of publick policie or privat government, replenisheth the memory with many infallible grounds of wisdom, which, notwithstanding, lye darke before the imaginative and iudging powre, if they bee not illuminated or figured foorth by the speaking picture of Poesie.[14]

We ordinarily understand "speaking picture" to mean "a picture that speaks." But Sidney does not attribute to poetry any formal analogies with painting, nor does he think poetry is vivid because it imitates the visual experience of external objects. He is speaking of the psychological effect of poetry. The poem enables the reader's imagination to function properly: he can, as Sidney says elsewhere in this passage, "satisfie his inward conceits with being witnes to it selfe of a true lively knowledge." Poetry immediately implants in the mind images that the completely sound and regenerate man would produce by his ordinary psychological activity.[15] Observe that Sidney does not limit the resources of poetry in order to make it pictorial. All that he says assumes the full exploitation of the verbal resources that specifically belong to poetry and have nothing to do with painting. "Speaking picture," then, means "speaking that is so vivid, has so much of its own life, that it gives immediacy and clarity to its subject matter." In using the traditional phrase as a metaphor for the psychological effect of poetry, Sidney deals with the crucial problem in any didactic theory—to show that the knowledge conveyed by poetry is necessarily dependent on the emotional force and quasi-sensory immediacy of verse.

The relation between Spenser's pictorial language and his rhetorical use of narrative materials becomes very clear in Calidore's vision of the Graces, where pictorial experience is part of the fictional action. Spenser attempts neither a real description nor a dramatization of the hero's visual experience, but rather directly conveys the vision and its significance to the reader. Hence at the climax of the passage, the observing hero and what he sees vanish into a heroic simile. The vision begins when Calidore comes to an open green on the top of Mount Acidale:

> There he did see, that pleased much his sight,
> That even he him selfe his eyes envyde,
> An hundred naked maidens lilly white,
> All raunged in a ring, and dauncing in delight.
>
> (VI.x.11)

Spenser does not paint a picture or portray Calidore as first seeing, then responding. Descriptive elements are absorbed into a rendering of Calidore's response, which is completely identified with our experience in reading the passage. Thus two clauses that render quality of response intervene between the verb "see" and its object "naked maidens"; feeling and rhythm are dammed up so that the release will imitate Calidore's surprise and delight. This rhythmic effect and the shift of tone it produces in the next to last line account for the extraordinary impression the word "naked" makes on most readers. From the remarks of critics, we would gather that the vision of the Graces is the healthy analogue of the long erotic description of Acrasia's damsels (II.xii.63-68).[16] Not at all—this single line is almost all we see of the dancing maidens. There are, after all, a hundred of them, and we are not meant to see a naked human body any more than Wordsworth meant to describe, or meant us to see, the leaves and petals of the ten thousand daffodils that danced in the breeze. Pictorial description renders real visual experience, while Spenser's diction uses visual suggestions to make us experience the words themselves.

The next stanza decisively shows the difference between pictorial description and the rhetorical use of pictorial diction:

> All they without were raunged in a ring,
> And daunced round; but in the midst of them
> Three other Ladies did both daunce and sing,
> The whilest the rest them round about did hemme,
> And like a girlond did in compasse stemme:
> And in the middest of those same three, was placed
> Another Damzell, as a precious gemme,
> Amidst a ring most richly well enchaced,
> That with her goodly presence all the rest much graced.
>
> (VI.x.12)

Clearly there is no pictorial equivalence between the two images in this stanza: if the lady is in the center of a ring of dancing maidens, she cannot be described as the jewel set into a ring for the finger. But it would be absurd to complain that Spenser is visually confusing, for he has no desire to be visually convincing. He uses sensory suggestions in order to give a quasi-physical presence to images and words that express value.

The rationale of Spenser's sensuousness is exceptionally clear in the profound and breath-taking stanza that concludes the vision. Although it is a heroic simile, it is not announced by the usual "like" or "as": the modification of the poet's voice does not suggest that he is turning from the narration of action (which scarcely exists at this point) in order to state an analogy. Spenser begins with "Looke," and his simile continues and intensifies our experience of the preceding stanza:

Looke how the Crowne, which Ariadne wore
Upon her yvory forehead that same day,
That Theseus her unto his bridale bore,
When the bold Centaures made that bloudy fray,
With the fierce Lapithes, which did them dismay;
Being now placed in the firmament,
Through the bright heaven doth her beames display,
And is unto the starres an ornament,
Which round about her move in order excellent.

(VI.x.13)

The significance of the Graces is not expressed by the hero's fictional experience, nor by a symbolic vision that we see within a fictional framework. We understand the Graces' dance by responding to a simile that develops our previous responses to imagery and diction. What Spenser makes us "see" is not a fixed image, an emblem in the usual sense, but a sacramental transformation of turbulence and fury into order and beauty. Our experience is specifically an experience of words and is modulated and developed in the very act of reading. The process is quite explicit in this stanza, for the crux of the simile has no iconographic or fictional reason for being there. The Centaurs and the Lapithes are not at all necessary to Ariadne's crown—they belong to another myth—nor does their bloody fray correspond to any part of the Grace's dance. Yet once there, the bloody fray is both relevant and necessary—as the syntax, which directs our reading, makes us recognize.

III

There is a temporal dimension in our reading of any poem, and in a narrative poem it is conventionally identified with a sequence of fictional events. But in the *Faerie Queene*, as our last example shows, time is the dimension of verbal events—the lines and stanzas that create and modify the reader's responses. An episode in the *Faerie Queene*, then, is best described as a developing psychological experience within the reader, rather than as an action to be observed by him. By heeding this distinction, we can solve the most perplexing interpretive problem in the poem: why is Amoret tortured by Busyrane? As W. B. C. Watkins remarks, "Her captivity and torture by Busyrane seem sadism unrelated to her character or desert, since as Belphoebe's twin, she is clearly designed to represent a second kind of chastity closer to Spenser's heart—married faithfulness."[17] The puzzle arises because the meaning of the episode is taken to be a simple translation of the story into abstract terms. Thus, "Britomart rescues Amoret from Busyrane" means "Chastity rescues Amoret from Lust." We are then led to search for what Mr. Watkins calls an "indefinable . . . fault"[18] in Amoret that is symbolized by her torture. If we take Amoret not as a dramatic individual but as an embodied concept, we are in the same dilemma, because we must find a concept that is in need of rescue from Lust.

There seems to me no way of juggling fictional terms to produce a plausible interpretation of the episode, much less one that adequately suggests its vastness and intensity. In this episode a series of speaking pictures that creates our psychological experience as it unfolds has a clear priority over the narration of an action. The moment Britomart enters Busyrane's castle, she completely disappears, and Spenser presents directly to the reader the series of mythological tapestries (III.xi.28-46). More important, we feel no break between this long set piece and the end of canto xi, in which Britomart reappears and fictional action nominally begins. There is complete continuity from one part to the other, because the end of the canto develops and expands the poetic experience begun in the presentation of the tapestries. The image of Cupid's darts is carried over to the description of his statue (III.xi.48), and it is in the context established by the tapestries that we feel the menacing brilliance of that description. Taken by itself, Spenser's parenthetical "Ah man beware, how thou those darts behold" is a merely pious exclamation; in the context of his continual admiration of the persuasive liveliness of the tapestries, it brilliantly records the intensification of our involvement as we move further into Busyrane's palace. When we proceed into the next room, the living walls of gold and the spoils of mighty conquerors (III.xi. 51-52) again intensify images of the tapestries.

The role of fictional action in this canto is to support the reader's psychological experience of images and their transformations. Spenser makes this explicit by reintroducing Britomart in the middle of the reader's exploration of the first room:

> And underneath his feet was written thus,
> *Unto the Victor of the Gods this bee:*
> And all the people in that ample hous
> Did to that image bow their humble knee,

> And oft committed fowle Idolatree.
> That wondrous sight faire Britomart amazed,
> Ne seeing could her wonder satisfie,
> But evermore and more upon it gazed,
> The whiles the passing brightnes her fraile sences dazed.
>
>   (III.xi.49)

Britomart's daze is not something to be observed; it intensifies the reader's reaction to the dazzling effect of the palace. Britomart's actions in this episode never have the fictional independence that would place the reader in the role of an observer of an action. Rather they are poetic devices that develop the reader's responses and that frequently merge with a direct rendering of them. Britomart's vigil in canto xii is absorbed into Cupid's masque, an emblematic procession of the psychological impulses that are engendered by and characterize erotic feeling. Action in these cantos consistently turns into images that speak directly to the reader.

The nominal action at the beginning of canto xii is Britomart's lying in wait to observe her enemy and Amoret, the object of her quest. But in fact Britomart is no more present as the masque marches by than she was when the tapestries were presented. It is the reader who first sees Amoret, and Amoret is primarily identified with her torture, the image Spenser wishes to impress upon us:

> Her brest all naked, as net ivory,
> Without adorne of gold or silver bright,
> Wherewith the Craftesman wonts it beautify,
> Of her dew honour was despoyled quight,
> And a wide wound therein (O ruefull sight)
> Entrenched deepe with knife accursed keene,
> Yet freshly bleeding forth her fainting spright,
> (The worke of cruell hand) was to be seene,
> That dyde in sanguine red her skin all snowy cleene.
>
>   (III.xii.20)

The whole stanza is a preparation for the visual directness of the last line. In the first three lines, Spenser develops the suggestion of artificiality in the commonplace comparison of skin to ivory. He praises Amoret's beauty in terms that recall the sinister glamor of the palace, and thus suggests the puzzling presence of a beautiful woman in Busyrane's masque. When he presents Amoret's torture, Spenser directly identifies our psychological experience with the process of reading. Subordinate clauses and exclamations intervene between the major grammatical elements, "a wide wound" and "was to be seene"; each is a separate unit that presents a single aspect of a multiple response to Amoret's wound. The strikingly simple last line emerges from a context of deliberate confusions with which Spenser draws us in more closely.

Once what we may call the emblematic presence of the wound is achieved, Spenser continues to involve the reader:

> At that wide orifice her trembling hart
> Was drawne forth, and in silver basin layd,
> Quite through transfixed with a deadly dart,
> And in her bloud yet steeming fresh embayd:
> And those two villeins, which her steps upstayd,
> When her weake feete could scarcely her sustaine,
> And fading vitall powers gan to fade,
> Her forward still with torture did constraine,
> And evermore encreased her consuming paine.
>
> (III.xii.21)

After fully presenting the emblem, Spenser does exactly the reverse of allowing us to observe it as complete and amenable to decisive understanding. In the final lines, he makes us participate in Amoret's pain; we have a sense not only of the fact that she is tortured, but also of her endurance of torment. This stanza is the last we see of her for the moment, and we are left at a peak of tension. By thus heightening the sense of mystery that characterizes the verse throughout this episode, Spenser makes it explicit that Britomart's quest is not an action we observe, but is identified with our experience of reading. When Britomart finally enters Busyrane's inner chamber, all the figures of the masque disappear, and we see only Amoret, bound and still tortured (III.xii.30-31). The object of our quest is the image of the pure heart transfixed by the cruel dart of desire, and Britomart's "rescue" of Amoret is a resolution of this image:

> The cruell steele, which thrild her dying hart,
> Fell softly forth, as of his owne accord,
> And the wyde wound, which lately did dispart
> Her bleeding brest, and riven bowels gor'd,
> Was closed up, as it had not bene bor'd,

> And every part to safety full sound,
> As she were never hurt, was soone restor'd.
>
> (III.xii.38)

The poetic meaning of these lines lies in the profoundly erotic sense of relaxation, wonder, and wholeness after the terrors of the palace have reached their height in the preceding stanzas (III.xii.36-7). By bringing the reader into intimate contact with his verse, Spenser creates feelings and awarenesses that cannot be stated by a conceptual translation of fictional action.

Amoret's torture is a conventional image that has occurred throughout Book III. It now emerges as the culminating symbol of the major issue of the book—the compatibility of sexual desire and spiritual value in human love. The meanings the image carries are most succintly indicated by Spenser's exclamation at the sight of Busyrane tormenting Amoret: "Ah who can love the worker of her smart?" (III.xii.31). "Worker of smart" is an epithet for the object of desire, and Spenser's sententious outcry asks, "Who can be a human lover?" Human love must involve the flesh and hence must involve desire and pain. Spenser's conception of chastity as marriage rather than virginity demands that he keep this point firmly in view, and Amoret's torture is the most drastic and comprehensive statement of it. Her torment presents something characteristic of all human love and not the unique suffering of an individual. The healing of her heart, then, expresses the resolution of problems with which the whole book is concerned, and in which Britomart—rocked by the storms of love and wounded by Malecasta and Busyrane (III.i.65; xii.33)—is fully implicated. Amoret's torture and release are not the action of the final episode, but its poetic climax. They are a direct rendering of awareness that have developed in the reader throughout the book, and particularly in those passages of the final episode that have very little to do with fictional action—Busyrane's tapestries and the masque of Cupid.

Amoret's torture is a crucial problem in the *Faerie Queene* because it is confusing on a very simple level where Spenser's meaning is usually clear. In this episode, Spenser was able to find and express vast symbolic significance in a story that has no clear allegorical translation. The moral is that what we usually think of as Spenser's allegory should be considered part of his narrative materials, and should not be identified with the meaning of his poetic narration. Ruskin's corrective to romantic criticism was perfectly just, but he was simply pointing to the obvious. Allegorical encounters and emblematic figures were simply the raw material of story to Spenser.[19] In its general outlines, Spenser's allegory is usually plain enough; confusion sets in when we try to elaborate its significance by treating poetic details as if they were fictional details. It is perfectly clear what Spenser means by Guyon's resistance to Mammon and his destruction of the Bower of Bliss. But we should not be content with dull and simple meanings in episodes of such impressiveness and length. In all the climactic episodes of the *Faerie Queene*, Spenser brings us into extraordinarily close, almost physical contact with his verse, in order that our psychological experience be identified as closely as possible with the direct experience of language in the activity of reading. The immediacy of the reader's psychological experience is the sign of all these episodes —the Red Cross Knight's misery in the Cave of Despair, the menacing glitter of Busyrane's palace, the oppressiveness of Mammon's cave, the seductive *otium* of the Bower of Bliss. Simply to recall what is surely a general feeling about the high points of the poem does not in itself prove that Spenser's narration is rhetorical in its mode—a continuous address to the reader, rather than an internally consistent fictional narration. But I submit that when we examine these or any other episodes in detail, we shall find that their symbolic material serves to enrich our responses in the way I have described, and not to complicate the significance of a translated or rationalized fiction.

NOTES

1. Part of this paper was read before English Group IV at the MLA meeting in Philadelphia, December 1960.
2. *The Stones of Venice*, Appendix 2. ("Theology of Spenser"), in *Works*, ed. E. T. Cook and A. Wedderburn (London, 1904), XI, 251-2.
3. See W. B. C. Watkins, *Shakespeare and Spenser* (Princeton, 1950), p. 130; C. S. Lewis, *The Allegory of Love* (Oxford, 1936), p. 334, and *English Literature in the Sixteenth Century* (Oxford, 1954), p. 381; Hallett Smith, *Elizabethan Poetry* (Cambridge, Mass., 1952), p. 335.
4. Brents Stirling maintains that "there is nothing inconsistent in Time mowing down the 'flowring herbes and goodly things,' " "The Philosophy of Spenser's 'Garden of Adonis,' " *PMLA*, XLIX (1934), 526. Stirling is primarily concerned with charges that Spenser inconsist-

ently places Time in a changeless garden, and he is entirely correct
in pointing out that Spenser never represents the Garden of Adonis
as changeless. But it is still necessary to explain how the figure of
Time is compatible with the depiction of "continuall spring, and
harvest . . . both meeting at one time" three stanzas later. The
problem is not that Spenser places a figure named Time in the Garden, but that he depicts Time as a destroyer, an agent of death not
of change. The words that describe Time's actions—"mow," "flings,"
"wither," "fowly mard," and "beates downe"—all suggest final destruction; there is a sharp contrast with the terms of preceding stanzas,
all of which suggest a process—"chaungefull" (stanza 33, which ends,
"so like a wheele around they runne from old to new") and "decayes"
and "fade," which appear jointly in both stanzas 37 and 38. Stirling's
argument, as it stands, depends on identifying change and death.
But the depiction of Time will not support, as the rest of the canto
will, the formula used of Adonis, "eterne in mutabilitie" (III.vi.47).

5. My text is that of J. C. Smith, 2 vols. (Oxford, 1909). In all quotations, contractions are expanded, proper names are not italicized, and
u, *v*, and *w* are made to conform to modern usage.

6. *Discorsi del Poema Eroico* in *Le Prose Diverse*, ed. Cesare Guasti
(Florence, 1875), I, 154-5. For a penetrating history of the idea of
"the poem as heterocosm," see M. H. Abrams, *The Mirror and the
Lamp* (New York, 1953). pp. 272-85.

7. See *Prose*, I, 126, 135-6, 142.

8. *Prose*, I, 121.

9. *An Apologie for Poetrie* in *Elizabethan Critical Essays*, ed. G.
Gregory Smith (Oxford, 1904), I, 166, 179-80.

10. *Elizabethan Critical Essays*, I, 156-7.

11. *English Literature in the Sixteenth Century*, p. 389.

12. The most extreme statement of this view is Joseph B. Dallett, "Ideas
of Sight in *The Faerie Queene*," *ELH*, XXVII (1960), 87-121. Dal-
let treats Spenser's reader as an "ideal spectator" *within the fiction*,
and he argues that "many of the descriptions (including those with
optical 'absurdities') are analogous to methods of representation found
abundantly in the fine arts" (98). See also W. B. C. Watkins,
Shakespeare and Spenser, pp. 223-58 ("Spenser's Palace of Art");
Rudolf Gottfried, "The Pictorial Element in Spenser's Poetry," in
That Soueraine Light, ed. W. R. Mueller and D. C. Allen (Baltimore, 1952), pp. 123-33; Carl Robinson Sonn, "Spenser's Imagery,"
ELH, XXVI (1959), 156-70. Watkins's chapter is an engaging and
sensitive essay in the tradition of comparing Spenser to various paint-
ers. Gottfried complains that Spenser's "pictures" are very bad paint-
ings, and therefore concludes that the pictorial element in his poetry
is insignificant. Sonn argues that Spenser does not attempt to paint

pictures, but uses concrete details in formal images that convey abstracts or universals. But he assumes that when Spenser's language is pictorial it renders the sensory experience of objects in the external world. He recognizes that some of Spenser's sensuous imagery offers "no chance of sensuous identification with the object" (166), but he so completely explains these images in terms of abstractions that he is unable to account for their sensuousness, which he describes as "transient," "superficial," or "sublimated" (167-8).

13. The following lines from the *Divine Comedy* genuinely attempt to render real visual experience. Tasso cites them as an example of *evidenza* or *energia*, "quella virtù che ci fa quasi veder le cose che si narrano" (*Prose*, I, 257):

> Come le pecorelle escon del chiuso
> Ad una, a due, a tre, e l'altre stanno
> Timidette atterrando l'occhio e 'l muso,
> E ciò che fa la prima, e l'altre fanno,
> Addossandosi a lei s'ella s' arresta,
> Semplici e quete, e lo 'mperchè non sanno.
> (*Purg.* iii.79-84)

14. *Elizabethan Critical Essays*, I, 164-5.

15. For an excellent account of Renaissance psychological ideas that are relevant to this passage, see Perry Miller, *The New England Mind: The Seventeenth Century* (Cambridge, Mass., 1939), chs. ix and x. For another example of a "speaking picture" as it is defined here, see the presentation of Time in the Garden of Adonis (discussed above, p. 28, *et seq.*).

16. Lewis contrasts "the naked damsels in Acrasia's fountain and the equally naked (in fact rather more naked) damsels who dance round Colin Clout" (*Allegory of Love*, p. 331). Similarly, Maurice Evans says, "The symbol [Spenser] chooses in Book VI for supreme perfection is that of naked maidens dancing without shame" (*English Poetry in the Sixteenth Century* [London, 1955], p. 147). H. J. C. Grierson praises Spenser's "flowery meadows of irrelevance—pageants and processions and the marriage of rivers and Colins piping to their naked loves" (*Cross Currents in English Literature of the XVIIth Century* [London, 1929], p. 60).

17. *Shakespeare and Spenser*, p. 206.

18. *Shakespeare and Spenser*, p. 66.

19. The phrase "continued allegory, or dark conceit" in the Letter to Ralegh refers to the symbolic nature of Spenser's materials, but it does not guarantee or even imply that a fiction with a continuous double significance is the main vehicle of poetic meaning in the *Faerie Queene*. Spenser would have found exactly this notion of

allegory in Tasso's preface to *Gerusalemme Liberata*, which he certainly knew but from which he borrows nothing in his own prefatory letter. Spenser's formula "dark conceit" is based on the rhetoricians' definition of allegory as the local device of continued metaphor ("dark" is the stock epithet for the figure in rhetorical handbooks). Furthermore, in his remarks on *Gerusalemme Liberata*, Spenser does not follow the allegorical interpretation of the heroes that Tasso develops by rationalizing the fiction of his poem. The only possible conclusion is that Tasso's division of a heroic poem into the imitation of actions and the allegory hidden beneath this surface (*Prose*, I, 301) meant very little to Spenser.

THOMAS P. ROCHE, JR.

The Nature of the Allegory

In Books III and IV of *The Faerie Queene* Spenser breaks the pattern of expectation set up by the narrative structures of Books I and II, turning from the epic structure of Virgil to the episodic romance structure of Ariosto. The shift in narrative technique has been attributed to Spenser's ineptitude in handling the virtues of chastity and friendship or to his returning to an earlier plan to make use of material already written.[1] These explanations, it seems to me, do not suggest recognition of the amazing brilliance and vitality of Books III and IV or of Spenser's superb ability to integrate apparently disparate materials. They rest on the judgment that "the narrative" and "the allegory" have somehow gone awry, all coherence gone, as if narrative and allegory were two separate and parallel functions of the poem we find before us. In what sense can we complain that Books III and IV do not "present a continuous story on the allegorical level"?[2] How can a story be told on any level but that of story? Stories may delight, and they often instruct, but they always tell us about some action. It is with the action of the narrative that any inquiry into allegory must begin.

Prince Arthur goes in search of the Faerie Queene, Guyon meets Mammon and captures Acrasia. This action is embodied in a narra-

From *The Kindly Flame* (Princeton, 1964), pp. 3-31. Reprinted by permission of the Princeton University Press. Copyright © 1964 by Princeton University Press. The illustrations referred to in the text have been omitted.

tive, whose words present to the reader the meaning that the author wanted this action to convey. The allegory is part of the meaning presented by the narrative and may either be intended by the author or discovered by the reader or both.[3] At no point is the allegory independent of the action as presented in the narrative. If the critic grants independence to the allegory, chaos is come again, for he is in fact denying the primacy of that golden world we enter when we read literature.

Renaissance rhetoricians showed their awareness of the dependence of allegory on narrative by defining it as "continued metaphor," the use of which "serueth most aptly to ingraue the liuely images of things, and to present them vnder daepe shadowes to the contemplation of the mind, wherein wit and iudgement take pleasure, and the remembrance receiueth a long lasting impression. . . ."[4] Here the emphasis is decidedly on "the liuely images of things" that give rise to the allegorical meanings, that is, on the tenor of this continued metaphor which the vehicle (narrative) illuminates. Only through the "daepe shadowes" of particulars can the universals, which are the repository of allegorical meanings, be presented to the human mind. This is not to say that the universal allegorical meanings are stuffed into the particulars of the narrative. The allegory is contained by the narrative in the same way and to the degree that universals are contained by particulars. Particulars figure forth universals; the narrative figures forth the allegory. The narrative presents itself and under the guise of its deep shadows lures the mind toward a vision of those lively images it embodies, toward those universals that are the ground and form of *these* particulars.

In this sense, of course, reading narratives allegorically does not differ in the least from reading them symbolically, and we have no way of distinguishing a proper reading of *The Faerie Queene* from a proper reading of *The Scarlet Letter,* or *The Golden Bowl,* or *Finnegans Wake.* However, to bring allegorical reading within shouting distance of symbolic reading tends to correct our jaded and erroneous opinions about the relation of the allegory to the narrative text. No one would think of saying that the scarlet letter equals   or that the golden bowl means   or that Anna Livia Plurabelle represents   —without relating these statements to the text that complicates, enriches, and makes them significant. Yet how few critics of Spenser feel obliged to carry their remarks beyond this "predicate nominative" stage of criticism? In part our modern over-simplification of allegorical reading is due to the common and traditional metaphor of rind and pith to explain the relation of the allegorical senses to the narrative text. Sir John Harington, for example, despite the implications of the metaphor, does not doubt that the relation is "organic":

> First of all for the litterall sence (as it were the vtmost barke or ryne) they set downe in manner of an historie, the acts and notable exploits of some persons worthy memorie; then *in the same fiction,* as a second rine and somewhat more fine, as it were nearer to the pith and marrow, they place the Morall sence, profitable for the actiue life of man, approuing vertuous actions and condemning the contrarie. Manie times also *vnder the selfesame words* they *comprehend* some true vnderstanding of naturall Philosophie, or somtimes of politike gouernement, and now and then of diuinitie: and these same sences that *comprehend* so excellent knowledge we call the Allegorie, which *Plutarch* defineth to be when one thing is told, and *by that* another is vnderstood. [Italics mine except for Plutarch][5]

The senses are contained (*wrapped* or *comprehended*) in the narrative, and *by that* do we come to understand the fuller significance of the text. Harington is talking about the way an Elizabethan discovered meaning in narrative poems, and for this purpose the metaphor of rind and pith is valid. He is not talking about the enjoyment of poetry, the pleasure of entering that golden world of narrative—unless we are to visualize the Elizabethan reader surrounded by empty nutshells or orange peels. In general, critics have not been careful to observe that Harington and the other Renaissance writers who use this metaphor are not thinking of two separate and divided entities; the allegorical senses reveal themselves when one "gets into" the work. As soon as the critic begins to talk about poets telling stories *on the allegorical level,* he confuses the tenor and vehicle of this continued metaphor and misses the beauty and economy of the allegorical mode. To leap at random from the concrete embodiment of the universal in the narrative to an abstract statement of it can only flatten out the narrative and dull the experience that the allegorical narrative is attempting to create in the reader. Like other men the readers and writers of allegory cannot serve two masters.

At this point one should beat a hasty retreat from the kinship with modern symbolic reading lest we trick ourselves into applying the criteria of the novel or the drama to an entirely different type of literature. Red Cross is a character, but he is neither "round" nor dramatic. Guyon's bloody babe should not raise the question of what to do with our orphans, nor should Busyrane's wounding Britomart arouse the slightest trace either of pity or of fear. *The Faerie Queene* is symbolic, but its allegorical narrative is not trying to do any of these things.

Allegorical reading (or more simply allegory) is a form of literary criticism with a metaphysical basis. It postulates a verbal universe at every point correspondent with the physical world in which we live, that is, a Realistic view of language. The history of allegorical interpretation of the Bible and secular literature is too long and complicated to relate here, but by the time of the sixteenth century allegory had attached itself firmly to the image of the universe created by Ptolemy and Dionysius the Areopagite and familiarly known as the "Elizabethan world picture." According to this theory there are in reality three worlds: the *sublunary*, the fallen world in which we live, subject to change and decay; the *celestial*, the unchanging world of the planets and stars; the *supercelestial*, the dwelling of angels and the Godhead. These three worlds are held together by God's Love and are analogically correspondent. Thus, in the sublunary world fire burns, while in the celestial world its analogue the sun not only burns but by its burning nourishes life, and in the supercelestial world the seraphim burn with love for their Creator.[6] The three worlds are a progression away from the material and toward the spiritual, and just as our image of the purely spiritual seraphim is drawn from our knowledge of the visible fire and sun, so too is our knowledge of universal truths drawn (in part) from our reading of the imitation of the visible worlds. Pico makes this quite clear in the introduction to his *Heptaplus*:

> For euen as the . . . three worlds being girt and buckled with the bands of concord doe by reciprocall libertie, interchange their natures; the like do they also by their appellations. And this is the principle from whence springeth & groweth the discipline of allegoricall sense. For it is certaine that the ancient fathers could not conueniently haue represented one thing by other figures, but that they had first learned the secret amity and affinitie of all nature. Otherwise there could bee no reason, why they should represent this thing by this forme, and that by that,

rather then otherwise. But hauing the knowledge of the vniuer-
sall world, and of euery part thereof, and being inspired with
the same spirit, that not onely knoweth all things: but did also
make all things: they haue oftentimes, and very fitly figured
the natures of the one world, by that which they knew to bee
correspondent thereto in the others.[7]

The basis of allegorical reading is this analogical nature of the universe. In an hierarchical universe where each thing has a fixed place
the relationship of any two things in the same world or sphere may
adumbrate the relationship of two other things in another world or
sphere. The original pair do not lose their identity or relationship by
such adumbration; they simply call attention to other possible relationships through the fact that they themselves are related in such a
way. The analogies are validated by the fact that the whole hierarchical structure with its often unseen web of interrelationships is contained within the mind of God, Who sees the relationship of all
things one to another. In allegorical reading a further step is taken:
since words represent things, words must represent this basic analogical relationship.

The whole matter will be made clearer by returning to Harington's
Apology for Poetry. Immediately following his definition of allegory
is an example: "*Perseus* sonne of *Iupiter* is fained by the Poets to haue
slaine *Gorgon,* and after that conquest atchieued, to haue flowen vp
to heauen." Harington gives an euhemeristic interpretation as the
"Historicall sence" and continues with several more senses:

Morally it signifieth thus much, *Perseus* a wise man, sonne of
Iupiter endewed with vertue from aboue, slayeth sinne and
vice, a thing base & earthly; signified by *Gorgon,* and so mount-
eth vp to the skie of vertue: It signifies in one kinde of Allegorie thus much; the mind of man being gotten by God, and so
the childe of God killing and vanquishing the earthlinesse of
this Gorgonicall nature, ascendeth vp to the vnderstanding of
heauenly things, of high things, of eternal things; in which
cotemplacion cosisteth the perfection of man: this is the natural allegory, because mā [is] one of the chiefe works of nature:
It hath also a more high and heauenly Allegorie, that the heauenly nature, daughter of *Iupiter,* procuring with her continuall
motion, corruption and mortality in the inferiour bodies, seuered

it selfe at last from these earthly bodies, and flew vp on high, and there remaineth for euer. It hath also another Theological Allegorie; that the angelicall nature, daughter of the most high God the creator of all things; killing & ouercomming all bodily substance, signified by *Gorgon,* ascended into heauen: the like infinite Allegories I could pike out of other Poeticall fictions, saue that I would auoid tediousnes.[8]

The final, almost parenthetical comment is worth the consideration of any one piecing out the Elizabethan idea of allegory. Many poetical fictions adumbrate more than one allegorical meaning, and these meanings, as the Perseus example shows, need not conform totally with every detail in the narrative (vehicle of the continued metaphor). Perseus, the son of Jupiter, may become in an allegorical reading the *daughter* of God, as in the "more high and heauenly Allegorie." Perseus is not the name or personification of the heavenly or the angelical natures; he is an allegorical representation of these beings because in his narrative he is the offspring (not son or daughter) of Jupiter, and hence because of the poetic statement of this particular adventure the whole statement may adumbrate these and any other heavenly mysteries that follow this particular pattern. There is no relation between narrative statement and allegorical meaning except the "secret amity and affinitie of all nature." When the structural patterns of the narrative coincide with the structural patterns of any other events of nature or supernature, we as readers are entitled to view the conformity or analogy as an allegorical meaning.

This, I take it, is what Elizabethans meant when they called allegory a "continued metaphor." They do not mean a point-for-point correspondence between the narrative events and any meanings they may derive from the narrative; that is, the continuity is not vertical but horizontal. In reading a metaphorical statement one does not jump from the vehicle to the tenor at every stage; such reading calls to mind the old adage about changing horses (or vehicles) in midstream. This point is best illustrated by turning to proverbial statements, which the Renaissance rhetoricians saw did not drag along the problems of imaginative literature. "A bird in the hand is worth two in the bush." Try a vertical or one-for-one translation: An opportunity in the (bank?) is worth two opportunities in the (neighbor's bank? other hand?). One sees at once the distortion of translation and the enormous difficulty of arriving at a satisfactory equivalent for the original statement, yet no one (I think) would miss the point. If this is the case with such a simple metaphorical statement, surely the allegorical narrative will demand more complicated reading.

To see the difference, let us consider two passages from *The Faerie Queene*. The two passages I have chosen are allegorically worlds apart. The one—the flight of Florimell in Book III, canto 1—is the beginning of a new narrative, clearly indebted to the first canto of *Orlando Furioso*, where Angelica rushes madly away from her rash of lovers. The narrative is brisk, and we are apparently not to fret about "allegorical meanings." The other is the key allegorical episode in Book IV, Spenser's continuation of Chaucer's Squire's Tale with its insistent allegorical demands from Agape and her three sons Priamond, Diamond, and Triamond. The allegorical intention is obvious, but the conceit is extremely dark. On the surface they are both simple narratives, but one cannot help feeling the vast difference in the narrative of Florimell's scattering Britomart and her companions and of Cambell's encounter with Triamond. The difference felt in reading these two episodes can be attributed to Spenser's allegorical intentions, and these intentions are embodied in the narrative itself. How, then, do the two narratives differ?

The opening of Book III differs markedly from the opening of Book I. The gentle knight, lovely lady, milk-white lamb, and lagging dwarf passing by present an iconic, two-dimensional vision like that of a medieval processional. Within the first five stanzas we know the purpose of their journey and the sad history of the lady's parents. All is simplicity and clarity. Book III begins with ambiguity. Arthur and Guyon, having finished their work with Acrasia, meet a knight and an aged squire. The strange knight and Guyon fight, but Guyon is dissuaded from a further trial—by the Palmer, of whose presence the reader has not been aware. In a moment Florimell flashes by pursued by the "griesly Foster," and we begin to realize that there were six people riding together after the opening encounter: Arthur and Timias, Guyon and the Palmer, Britomart and Glauce. Neither Florimell nor Glauce has been named; Britomart has been identified simply as a "single damzell." As quickly as the group was assembled, it is dispersed, and we are left with Britomart riding on unknowingly to Malecasta's castle (apparently with Glauce, although she is never again mentioned in the early adventures of Britomart). Britomart comes upon a single knight beset by six knights, who twenty-two stanzas later we are told is Red Cross. Things are not what they seem, but this is not the thematic development of the novelist nor the ineptitude of Spenser as a narrator. It is the method of allegory.

Sometimes there is an evocation of the setting; here there is not. Sometimes there is a careful delineation of character; here there is not. Sometimes there is a decided "point of view"; here there is not. The manner of the narrative is dictated not by a set of rules but by the effect the poet wants to create, and in this respect the allegorical poet is freer even than his modern descendant the novelist. We do not need to know where the characters are nor who or how many they are nor how we are to view them. The narrative will tell all, until the poet wants to focus the meaning. Then he may bring in these other ways of declaring meaning. The technique of the allegorical narrative lulls the reader into its meaning. If the reader should feel on occasion a paucity of allegorical significance, he may be absolutely right. Many things are necessary to keep a story going, or to get it started, which is the case with the opening episode of Book III.

This is all very pedestrian, but Spenser's technique as a poet has fared so badly in the hands of the critics that it may be worthwhile to examine his skill in handling a simple narrative passage. Harington's translation of Ariosto presents Angelica's flight from her own point of view. Everything in the description points to her inner fears.

> But follow we *Angelica* that fled.
>
> That fled through woods, and deserts all obscure,
> Through places vninhabited and wast,
> Ne could she yet repute her selfe secure,
> But farder still she gallopeth in hast.
> Each leafe that stirs in her doth feare procure,
> And maketh her affrighted, and agast:
> Each noise she heares, each shadow she doth see,
> She doth mistrust it should *Renaldo* be.
>
> Like to a fawne, or kid of bearded goate,
> That in the wood a tyger fierce espide,
> Killing her dame, and first to teare the throate,
> And then to feed vpon the hanch or side,
> Fearing lest she may light on such a lot,
> Doth seeke it selfe in thickest brackes to hide,
> And thinks each noise the wind or aire doth cause,
> It selfe in danger of the tygers clawes.
>
> (*Orlando Furioso*, I. 32-34)[9]

Spenser handles the scene quite differently. Florimell is described in some detail; we are told that she is afraid, but everything in this description points to the effect she has on her observers.

> All as a blazing starre doth farre outcast
> His hearie beames, and flaming lockes dispred,
> At sight whereof the people stand aghast:
> But the sage wisard telles, as he has red,
> That it importunes death and dolefull drerihed.
>
> (3.1.16)

We know even less of Florimell's motivations than we do of Angelica's. At that point Spenser brings the "griesly Foster" out of the woods, and part of Florimell's motivations is revealed. We know only that she is a damsel in distress and that her flight is patterned on Ariosto's Angelica.

Guyon and Arthur ride off after her and Timias after the Forester, the significance of which will be revealed in later cantos, although Spenser does not tell us so at this point. Only "faire *Britomart,* whose constant mind, / Would not so lightly follow beauties chace, / Ne reckt of Ladies Loue, did stay behind. . . ." With the disappearance of the others the point of view changes. We cannot suppose that Spenser intends the reader to think ill of Arthur and Guyon. They have gone, and now we are focusing on Britomart, whose thoughts these are.[10] We are not to build up any kind of animosity between Britomart and her companions. The motivation attributed to Britomart is one way of emphasizing the fact that she is a woman, which is the subject Spenser is about to undertake.

This opening episode of Book III is typical of one style of allegorical narrative. The allegorical meaning is exactly the meaning presented by the narrative—no more, no less. We may say that two chivalrous knights attempt to rescue a beautiful woman in distress, but if we should proceed one step further and say that beauty pursued by lust must be rescued by magnificence and temperance, we leave out much of the pleasure of the narrative and dispel the air of mystery that Spenser is apparently using to arouse interest in his new narrative. We also raise questions that cannot be answered: why is it that chastity does not (or cannot) rescue beauty? Such a question is a dreadful burden for a poem to bear, since it takes us immediately out of the realm the poet is creating.

A more interesting and fertile clue to the meaning of this first episode is the fact that Florimell is patterned on Ariosto's proud, coy, flirtatious Angelica. With this perception another question arises: is Florimell to be a repetition of Ariosto's heroine? Once more we may take a hint from Harington's treatment of the allegory in the beginning of *Orlando*. Even with the more fully developed characterization of Ariosto at hand (and before him Boiardo) Harington is cautious about labelling Angelica: *"In the hard adventures of* Angelica, *we may note how perilous a thing beautie is if it be not especially garded with the grace of God, and with vertue of the mynde, being continually assayld with enemies spirituall and temporall. In* Orlandos *dreame we may see how vnquiet thoughtes are bred in the myndes of those that are geuen ouer to the passion of loue or ambicion or whatsoeuer else may be vnderstood by* Angelica."[11] The point is not that Angelica has no meaning, but that her meaning or meanings have not been specified at this point in the poem. The reader must be patient; he should not try to assign meanings to Florimell until the poem warrants it.

At the opposite extreme of Spenser's allegorical technique is the episode of Cambell and Triamond. Here Spenser loads his narrative with every indication that the episode should be read allegorically. At that point in Book IV where the futures of the major figures are darkened by the hellish power of Ate, Cambell and Cambina, Triamond and Canacee seem almost a pledge of Ate's defeat, for immediately after their appearance Spenser devotes the second half of canto 2 and all of canto 3 to the story of their initial conflict and eventual concord. He further separates this episode from the main narrative by beginning it with his famous invocation to Chaucer, whose unfinished tale he is apparently taking over as his own.[12] Most important are the names Agape, Priamond, Diamond, and Triamond, which clearly point at the concepts they represent. (The tenor has been drawn over into the vehicle in what the rhetoricians would call a mixed allegory.)[13] Agape is, of course, the Greek term for Christian love; the names of her sons mean first, second, and third world. Any reading of Spenser—in particular, the *Fowre Hymnes*—will tell us that Love did, in fact, create the three worlds: terrestrial, celestial, and supercelestial. Spenser realized that the mysteries of Christianity could not be loosed on his Faeryland too freely, but here he is clearly demanding that the reader view this episode as a metaphysical conflict as well as a literal battle between some knights. This much of the meaning is clear, but how do the details fit together and what do the actions of these figures mean?

An important hint occurs in the original title of Book IV: "The Fovrth Booke of the Faerie Queene. *Containing* The Legend of Cambel and Telamond, or Of Friendship." Each of the other books follows the same pattern and includes the name of the titular hero or heroine. Unless we are to doubt the authenticity of these titles, we should be prepared to accept the episode of Cambell and Triamond as the major exemplum of friendship in Book IV. A further problem arises with the name Telamond. All the early editions read Telamond until the 1734 edition of Jortin, who emended this word to Triamond. It is a sensible emendation, but unnecessary. Spenser's etymologizing instincts would easily have led him to conflate the first syllables of the names of the three brothers into one word that might suggest their meaning. Such a word is the Greek *téleios*—perfect. Thus the title would run "Cambell and the Perfect World," which is consonant with the action of a story devoted to the miracle of perfect amity and concord achieved between enemies. The legend of Cambell and Telamond is in one allegorical sense a metaphysics of friendship and in another the symbolic statement of the metaphysics of *discordia concors,* as interpreted by Christian philosophers of the Middle Ages and the Renaissance. To see how Spenser's myth exemplifies the emergence of order from chaos and of friendship from enmity let us examine the action of the narrative, keeping in mind the kind of analysis that Harington gave to the Perseus myth.

At the beginning of the narrative Cambell sends out his challenge to those who desire his sister. We do not need to know what they represent specifically; he is a brave and temperate knight; she is a learned and chaste lady and a much sought prize. The challenge is accepted by the three brothers, who we learn have a strange fate. At this point it will be useful to recall two popular Renaissance symbols: (1) an emblem from Alciati, and (2) the nature of Demogorgon as popularized by Boccaccio.

(1) Spenser devotes three stanzas to the description of the three brothers, in each of which he emphasizes their triune nature. In 2.41 he explicitly states that they were "All three as one." Stanza 42 recapitulates this statement in an elaborate rhetorical pattern of repetition and inversion. The third stanza elaborates the initial statement:

> These three did loue each other dearely well,
> And with so firme affection were allyde,
> As if but one soule in them all did dwell,
> Which did her powre into three parts diuyde;

The fortieth emblem in the expanded version of Alciati is called "Concordia insuperabilis" and pictures a man with three heads, six arms, and six legs. The quatrain explains this grotesque by saying that such concord as well as piety and love existed among three brothers that they could not be overcome and that they held kingdoms under the one name of Geryon. Despite the facts that Spenser concludes his stanza with a different simile and that Geryon appears in a much different context in Book V, Spenser's and Alciati's brothers do benefit from comparison. The Paris 1584 edition of Alciati comments: "De cecy nous apprenons que ceux qui sont de bon accord & vnanimes, se rendent inuincibles: lesquels estans separez & en discord, ou qui ne se veulent entendre ensemblément, se rendent du tout debiles, & aisez à surmounter."[14] This elaborate development of the essential unity of the brothers not only explains the relationship of the three worlds they represent, but it also heightens the dramatic impact of the story by suggesting their invincibility.

(2) Boccaccio follows the authority of the mysterious Theodontius in making Demogorgon "summum primumque deorum gentilium," presumably a corruption of Plato's Demiurge. He is coeternal with Eternity and Chaos and the father of an innumerable brood including Discord, Pan, and the Fates. According to Boccaccio his name is Demogorgon in Greek and god of the earth in Latin: "For *demon* means god, as Leontius says, and *Gorgon* means earth. Or rather wisdom of the earth, since often *demon* means knowing or wisdom. Or, more pleasing to others, the terrible god, because it is written of the true God Who dwells in heaven: Holy and terrible is His name."[15] Thus two radically different interpretations could be given to the figure of Demogorgon: he could be (a) a variant on the name of Plato's Demiurge, that dark and mysterious creator of the universe and by analogy a name for the Christian God in His role as creator, or (b) an equally dark, mysterious, and idolatrous perverter of true worship, invoked by Faustus.[16] The latter interpretation is used by Spenser when Archimago invokes the spirits from hell (1.1.37).[17] Agape's trip to the Fates in the deep abyss of Demogorgon partakes of the hellish mystery and dread of this figure without being idolatrous blasphemy. It is rather an attempt on Spenser's part to foster an awed respect for those dark forces that constitute the material source of our being. Anything more than this would involve us in heresies too obvious to be endured.

The same may be said of the conception of Agape's sons. If we even begin to speculate on what the "noble youthly knight" represents or why Agape should be combing her golden locks by a crystal stream, we are not reading allegorically, and it is very possible that we are not even reading poetically. The extraordinary loveliness of the few stanzas describing the incident preserves the decorum of nymphs being taken by handsome young men and at the same time reinforces the basic theme of the episode as a whole. He "oppressed" her, and from the conflict of the oppression come "these louely babes, that prou'd three champions bold." If a poet chooses to write about the ineffable mysteries of universal creation, the figures in his myth had better be able to sustain themselves without the puppet-string of one-for-one equivalents, for there are none.

Agape's trip to the Fates belongs to the same world of romance as her conception. Part of the pleasure of this incident comes from the very fact that Spenser chooses a vehicle that reduces the scope of the tenor. The charming incongruity of the lovely nymph seeking out the ominous Fates for love of her children images the loving care of Agape in all its meanings, and her amazement at the shortness of the threads of their lives is a figure for the grief felt by all fathers and mothers at the discrepancy between the desired achievements of their creations and the actuality. Her humble yet shrewd petition to the three Fates assures her an ultimate victory over the forces of chaos and disorder. It begs for life in another form, and for more than this no Christian reader would inquire. The double vision of this enigmatic petition echoes the double vision of Spenser's "mixed allegory" without transgressing the limits of either tenor or vehicle. In view of the essential unity of the three brothers already stated in the poem Spenser probably knew that Agape might be comforted by the fact that the created universe "we may also call [One,] (sic) not onely because the three worlds doe proceede of one onely and selfe cause, and tend to the like end; or else because being duly tempered by numbers, they are ioyned together by an harmonious accord and affinity of nature, and by ordinary succession of degrees: but also because that that which is in all the three is likewise comprised in one of them, and that there is not one wherein all things, which are in the other three, do not remaine."[18] Thus Agape can leave the house of the Fates, as Spenser tells us, "with full contented mynd."

The third canto begins with two stanzas of Spenserian irony on the question: "O why doe wretched men so much desire, To draw their dayes vnto the vtmost date. . . ?" The answer is implicit in the irony of the second stanza:

> Therefore this Fay I hold but fond and vaine,
>   The which in seeking for her children three
>   Long life, thereby did more prolong their paine.
>   Yet whilest they liued none did euer see
>   More happie creatures, then they seem'd to bee,
>   Nor more ennobled for their courtesie,
>   That made them dearely lou'd of each degree;
>   Ne more renowmed for their cheualrie,
> That made them dreaded much of all men farre and nie.
>
>   (4.3.2)

The fond vanity of Agape finds ample compensation in the lives of her sons; the general misery of most lives is contradicted by the nobility and courtesy of the three brothers. The ironic apology is necessary because of Spenser's myth. By explicitly identifying his nymph with the concept she represents Spenser places a double burden on his myth, which he eases by ironies such as these stanzas and the fact that after the initial act of naming Agape he always refers to her merely as "Fay."

The past history of his heroes explained, Spenser can give his full attention to the battle for Canacee, which is the most bloody in the poem, no doubt to suit the occasion, "the dreddest day that liuing wight Did euer see vpon this world to shine. . . ." The battle is meant to be exciting, and accordingly Spenser varies the description of each succeeding joust with epic similes and with ever increasingly hideous wounds. The air of unreality is maintained by the magical powers of Canacee's ring to restore Cambell and by the mysterious process of traduction that translates the soul of one brother into the next. This process requires some comment since its physiology is more complicated than the physiological architecture of Alma's Castle. Priamond is struck such a blow that "His weasand pipe it through his gorget cleft," and his soul enters Diamond, "In whom he liu'd a new, of former life depriued" (4.3.12-13). Diamond is beheaded, and the spectators are amazed to see his trunk still standing. Except for the fact that his body had been dismembered his soul would have remained. As it is, the soul enters Triamond, filling him with "double life." The phrase is ambiguous, but from later events we must assume that the "double" refers to the dual soul of Priamond and Diamond, and thus Triamond's life is trebled. Two of these souls are lost in the ensuing joust, and the third is saved by the sudden appearance of Cambina.

It should be mentioned at this point that I am entirely conscious of the fact that we have not determined a single allegorical meaning for any event in the narrative so far. This is as it should be. The appearance and description of Cambina is the culmination of these most obscure battles, and although we may have inklings of what this or that detail means, we (and therefore the allegory) will be better served if we defer to the poet's story and wait until his meaning is fully declared in the figure of Cambina. She is not so much a character as an aggregate of iconographical details, all of which have long histories that enrich and consolidate the larger issues that Spenser's narrative is meant to suggest. Spenser's description of her and her chariot contrasts with the painter's use of iconographical details. A picture makes an immediate total impression, after which the viewer may pick out various attributes and (if he is lucky) may see how and why they relate to the central image. The verbal description can give no immediate total impression; it is a linear progression of details. The process is additive rather than total, and the difference between the two media will be apparent to those who have turned from the immediate impact of one of Ripa's images to his verbal description. The difference is primary and intellectual and should be observed whenever one is tempted to extol Spenser's pictorialism.[19] A picture is no doubt worth a thousand words—but only to the trained observer. The poet can bring into his conception of any figure any number of details that enrich his presentation but would obscure a picture.

So it is with Cambina. She arrives in a chariot drawn by two lions. In her right hand she holds a caduceus, and in her left a cup. So much the artist could give, and we would know (if we were trained to read the figure correctly) that this female figure was meant to represent Concord or Peace. Spenser's verbal description can go deeper.

The relation of the lions to Cambina recapitulates the basic theme of *discordia concors*. Through the power of Cambina these two most wild beasts of the wood have been made to "forget their former cruell mood" and call to mind the figures of Love and Hate held together by Concord at the entrance to the Temple of Venus in canto 10. It is obvious that these animals by their very presence in the narrative add to the air of wonder and mystery, but they also relate this wondrous chariot to others of more venerable history. Alciati has an interesting emblem, entitled "Potentissimus affectus amor," which pictures a blind Cupid riding in a chariot drawn by two lions, to show that Love does indeed conquer all. The chariot of Cybele, Magna Mater, goddess of civilization, is drawn by two lions, who (we are told) are the

transformed Atalanta and Hippomenes.[20] The three sets of lions exemplify an initial discord overcome by the figure whose chariot they
draw. The relationship among the three is not that of source or of
parallel. The fact that Alciati did invent his emblem and that Cybele's chariot is traditionally drawn by lions allows Spenser to use his
lions to point us toward a context in which his Cambina benefits from
our recollection of these other figures without any kind of explicit
identification. She is not Love, and she is not Nature, but her function in the poem is amplified if we have these other figures in mind.

The lion-drawn chariot simply sets the stage for the other two attributes. The caduceus Spenser explicitly identifies as "the rod of peace."
The entwined serpents, as Lotspeich points out, are suitably allegorized by Natalis Comes as *"concordiae securitatem."*[21] The cup is filled
with nepenthe, "A drinck of souerayne grace," which has a history
extending back to Homer.[22] In the fourth book of *The Odyssey* Helen
gives nepenthe mixed with wine to drown cares and anger. Chapman
refers to "Sacred Nepenthe, purgatiue of care." This is the usual way
of treating the drink, but Spenser goes beyond this tropological sense:

> Few men, but such as sober are and sage,
> Are by the Gods to drinck thereof assynd;
> But such as drinck, eternall happinesse do fynd.
>
> (4.3.43)

Christian meanings begin to infiltrate this apparently pagan drug, especially when Spenser ends his description with an allusion to a similar magic potion in Ariosto:

> Much more of price and of more gratious powre
> Is this, then that same water of Ardenne,
> The which *Rinaldo* drunck in happie howre,
> Described by that famous Tuscane penne:
> For that had might to change the hearts of men
> Fro loue to hate, a change of euill choise:
> But this doth hatred make in loue to brenne,
> And heauy heart with comfort doth reioyce.
>
> (4.3.45)

Once more Spenser overgoes Ariosto in turning a magic potion from
merely tropological to metaphysical ends. Spenser's nepenthe drives
deeper into the essential nature of man.

Cambina's attributes are the handles by which we catch her meaning, and if we now proceed to call her Concord, we do not mean to specify an abstraction. Just as the figure of the statue of Liberty calls forth all that we know and mean and feel by saying "American," so Cambina figures forth all the associated meanings of Cybele and Love driving their lions, of Mercury taming the "hellish fiends" with his caduceus, of Helen's and Ariosto's magic potions to purge care. She means the bond of friendship wrought from discord. She means the universal bond of harmony that sustained the world in which Spenser lived. She means the metaphysical mystery of love evolved from hate, and many other related concepts that we need not name because she contains them all in the essence of her being. The relationship of mother and daughter established in the poem between Agape and Cambina (4.3.40) suggests the deeper metaphysical grounds of her being. She is not to be understood merely tropologically. She is basically an abstraction, but we should remember that to name a *quiddi-tas* was and is a more real activity of the human mind than to recreate a particular embodiment by enumerating particulars. Much of the work of modern criticism has been the naming of the essential quality of particularized beings in literature. We call it practical criticism; Spenser was writing practical poetry.

To complete his description of Cambina Spenser calls these attributes into action. The exhausted warriors, touched with the caduceus, spring back to life and drink from the offered cup of nepenthe.

> Of which so soone as they once tasted had,
>   Wonder it is that sudden change to see:
>   Instead of strokes, each other kissed glad,
>   And louely haulst from feare of treason free,
>   And plighted hands for euer friends to be
>
> (4.3.49)

The reconciliation is almost anticlimactic, but if we refer once more to Alciati, we shall see that Spenser is simply adding another emblem of his basic theme. Emblem XXXIX pictures two warriors shaking hands, and the title is appropriately "Concordia." One might also refer to the emblems called "fictus amicus" and "verus amicus."

The episode is simply an allegory of concord, but we should remember when we name the meaning of the episode that it has taken all our literary skill and tact to discover Spenser's meaning, and that in naming the quality that Spenser is exemplifying we are not forgetting the means by which Spenser led us to his meaning. At this point we can once more enter the main stream of the narrative, knowing that we have been lulled into a knowledge and new awareness of the forces that will eventually triumph in Spenser's book of friendship. "Allegory is a method of reading in which we are made to think about things we already know."[23] This is a more positive way of speaking about abstractions in our older literature.

We may now attempt to specify allegorical meanings for the various incidents in these cantos, but we shall still find that the essential toughness of the narrative will not allow us to make easy leaps between tenor and vehicle. Let us postulate that Cambell is man and that his name represents the warring elements of *bellum intestinum* and that Canacee represents those human elements that sustain man in his battle against himself and the world, whether we call this mind or soul or reason. The magic ring then would become the sustaining link between the two. Cambell's battle with the three brothers figures man's battle with the three worlds to find his place in the universe, to establish harmony in God's creation, and ultimately to achieve salvation.

But since in any metaphysics regulated by analogy and mathematical proportions, any triad may be the analogue of another, the three brothers could become the three worlds of man's soul, in which the defeat of Priamond and Diamond figure the defeat of the vegetative and sensitive souls and the eventual harmony of man with the angelic mind. (This would account for the death of the two brothers, which cannot be understood if we accept them merely as the three worlds.) Already we are getting far from Spenser's myth and the basic generosity of charity that urges one brother without his knowledge to give his life to another, but from our more simple tropological apprehension of Spenser's exemplum, we can begin to understand the difficulty and necessity of seeing this story as a "likely tale" of the workings of that mysterious process that brings concord out of discord.

My explication of the allegory in this episode is not meant to be conclusive; indeed, no explication can be conclusive owing to the very nature of allegory. We began this examination of allegorical reading by suggesting that the entire narrative of an allegorical poem is the vehicle of a continued metaphor and that the tenor may be any concept or object outside the poem that conforms to the pattern or patterns inherent in the narrative. Such a definition of allegory extends the commonly accepted meaning of the term. We cannot restrict ourselves to a sterile hunt for one-for-one relationships. There is no single meaning, at least no single meaning to be stated apart from the experience of the poem. The heresy of paraphrase applies as much to allegory as to other forms of poetic expression. Nor should we complain about the blurring of large concepts. Allegory, as I read it, is not trying to present clear and distinct speculations about philosophical niceties. There is no single object to receive the entire energy of the vehicle; there are always complexes of large and simple ideas, which are illuminated and realigned. These allegorical meanings, when explicitly stated by critics, become a part of the history of the poem in the same way that the allegorical accretions to the Song of Songs belong to that poem. Allegorical poetry is in the best tradition of meditative poetry and finds its source in Biblical exegesis and its latest manifestation in Hopkins' theory of inscape and instress. We may learn from this comparison that the images of allegorical poetry are inexhaustible both in themselves and in the fact that the poet has received these images as a rich and varied vocabulary with a long and venerable history.

NOTES

1. Josephine Waters Bennett, *The Evolution of "The Faerie Queene,"* Chicago, 1942, pp. 138ff. *The Works of Edmund Spenser: a Variorum Edition,* ed. Edwin Greenlaw, C. G. Osgood, F. M. Padelford, *et al.,* 11 vols., Baltimore, 1932-1957, vol. 3, pp. 310-29 (hereafter cited as *Var.* 3.310-29). All quotations from the works of Spenser are taken from this edition and will be cited in the text.

2. Joshua McClennen, "On the Meaning and Function of Allegory in the English Renaissance," *Univ. of Michigan Contributions in Philology,* No. 6, April 1947, p. 9.

3. I am aware that I am begging a rather large question of aesthetics in this definition, but I want to include as allegory both the intentional allegory of *The Faerie Queene* and the probably unintentional allegory of the Song of Solomon.

4. Henry Peacham, *The Garden of Eloquence,* Scholars' Facsimiles and Reprints, Gainesville, Fla., 1954, p. 27. Cf. also Ambrogio Calepino, *Dictionarivm Octo Lingvarum,* Basle, 1584, s.v. "allegoria"; Thomas Wilson, *The Arte of Rhetorique,* ed. G. H. Mair, Oxford, 1909, p. 176.

5. Sir John Harington, *Orlando Furioso,* London, 1591, sig. ¶iiij. Reprinted in G. Gregory Smith, *Elizabethan Critical Essays,* 2 vols., London, 1937, vol. 2 pp. 201-2.

6. *Iohannis Pici Mirandvlae . . . omnia . . . opera*, Venice, 1557, sig.
   **4. "Elemétaris urit: coelestis uiuificat: supercoelestis amat." The
   quotation may also be found on p. 188 of *De Hominis Dignitate,
   Heptaplus, De Ente et Uno*, ed. Eugenio Garin, Florence, 1942.

7. The translation is that of the English translator of Pierre de la Primaudaye, *The French Academie*, London, 1618, p. 671. De la Primaudaye in his discussion of the division of the universal world simply translates the second proemium to Pico's *Heptaplus*. The original
   Latin text is on sig. **4 of the Venice, 1557, edition and on p. 192
   of the Garin edition. The passage also occurs in Fornari's *Della Es-
   positione Sopra L'Orlando fvrioso Parte Seconda*, Florence, 1550,
   vol. 2, p. 3.

8. Harington, *Orlando Furioso*, 1591, sig. Piiij-Piiij^v. Reprinted in
   Smith, vol. 2, pp. 202-3. For an earlier interpretation of the Perseus
   myth that follows the method employed by Harington but finds different meanings see Giovanni Boccaccio, *Genealogie Deorum Gentilium*,
   ed. Vincenzo Romano, 2 vols., Bari, 1951, vol. 1, p. 19 (Book 1,
   chap. 3).

9. Harington, *Orlando Furioso*, 1591, sig. Aiij. Hereafter all quotations
   from this poem will be from this edition and will be cited in the text.

10. Although this interpretation explains the present situation, the figures
    in Spenser's poem are not characters in that they do not have con-
    tinuous interior feelings, nor are they required to react to situations
    with psychological realism.

11. Harington, *Orlando Furioso*, 1591, sig. Fiij.

12. In fact, he borrows the names Canacee and Cambalo (significantly
    changed to Cambell or Cambello), the magic ring, whose properties
    are reduced to the "power to staunch al wounds, that mortally did
    bleed," and the fact that Cambalo fights with brothers (their number
    increased from two to three). The rest of the tale is Spenser's, a fact
    unsurprising since the brevity of the Chaucerian original makes re-
    construction impossible.

13. Puttenham's comment on the following lines will illustrate:

    > *The cloudes of care haue coured al my coste,*
    > *The stormes of strife, do threaten to appeare;*
    > *The waues of woe, wherein my ship is toste.*
    > *Haue broke the banks, where lay my life so deere.*
    > *Chippes of ill chance, are fallen amidst my choise,*
    > *To marre the minde that ment for to reioyce.*

    "I call him not a full Allegorie, but mixt, bicause he discouers withall
    what the *cloud, storme, waue,* and the rest are, which in a full alle-
    gorie should not be discouered, but left at large to the readers iudge-

ment and coniecture." (*The Arte of English Poesie*, ed. G. D. Will-
cock and A. Walker, Cambridge, 1936, p. 188.)

14. Andrea Alciati, *Emblemata*, Paris, 1584, sig. G12ᵛ. See also Collucio
Salutati, *De Laboribus Herculis*, ed. B. L. Ullman, 2 vols., Zurich,
n.d., vol. 2, p. 378.

15. Boccaccio, *Genealogie*, vol. 1, pp. 14, 15 (Book 1, Prohemium).
"Sonat igitur, ut reor, Demogorgon grece, terre deus latine. Nam
demon deus, ut ait Leontius, Gorgon autem terra interpretatur. Seu
potius sapientia terre, cum sepe demon sciens vel sapientia exponatur.
Seu, ut magis placet aliis, deus terribilis, quod de vero Deo qui in
celis habitat legitur: Sanctum et terribile nomen eius."

16. The invocation to Demogorgon in act 1, scene 3, of Marlowe's *Dr.
Faustus* probably is due to a comparable invocation in the *Thebaid* of
Statius (4.512ff) in which Tiresias is too terrified to cry out the name
of Demogorgon. Boccaccio quotes this passage. The most familiar
parallel to this understanding of the heathen gods is the catalogue in
Paradise Lost, I. 356ff.

17. Spenser demonstrates his mythical eclecticism here because in 1.5.22
Duessa invokes Night as "most auncient Grandmother of all, / More
old than *Ioue*, whom thou at first didst breede, / Or that great house
of Gods celestiall, / Which was begot in *Daemogorgons* hall. . . ."
See Maurice Castelain, "Demogorgon ou le barbarisme déifié," *Bulle-
tin de l'association Guillaume Budé*, 36 (July 1932), pp. 22-39.

18. Pierre de la Primaudaye, *The French Academie*, p. 671. Also found
in Pico, *Heptaplus, loc. cit.*

19. A brilliant discussion of this problem may be found in Paul Alpers,
"Narrative and Rhetoric in the *Faerie Queene*," *SEL*, 2 (1962),
pp. 36, 41-2.

20. The lions are mentioned in Ovid, *Fasti*, 4.215-218; Lucretius, *De
rerum natura*, 2.600ff., Vincenzo Cartari, *Imagines Deorum*, Lyons,
1581, see "Magna mater"; Cesare Ripa, *Iconologia*, Rome, 1603, see
"carro della Terra." The story that the lions are the transformed
Atalanta and Hippomenes is found in Ovid, *Metamorphoses*, 10.681-
707. All these commentators emphasize the initial discord of the
beasts overcome by the power of Cybele.

21. H. G. Lotspeich, *Classical Mythology in the Poetry of Edmund Spenser*, Princeton, 1932, p. 44. See also Abraham Fraunce, *The third
part of the Countess of Pembrokes Yuychurch*, London, 1592, sig.
K4.

22. Homer, *Odyssey*, 4.219-25; Milton, *Comus*, 675ff.; Chapman, *Ovid's
Banquet of Sense*, stanza 10, line 1.

23. Rosemond Tuve in the Christian Gauss Seminar, Princeton University, May 1959.

Spenser's Undramatic Poetry

The Faerie Queene is not a "difficult" poem in the sense that "The Extasie" or "The Garden" or "Le Monocle de Mon Oncle" are "difficult" poems; indeed, a frequent complaint is that it is too simple, especially in proportion to its great length. Yet much in our culture shows us how to read Donne, Marvell, or Wallace Stevens, whereas at first blush *The Faerie Queene* seems to demand great learning and many sympathies not easily acquired. Yet people without this learning or these sympathies do read Spenser with pleasure, and as they do they often realize that it is not his poetry but his reader's expectations about poetry that make him seem so impossible. This essay will begin with one such set of expectations, those surrounding the words "dramatic" and "undramatic," and try to develop a description of Spenser's poetry based upon a sense of the kind of undramatic verse it is. For if, as sometimes happens, we assume that "dramatic" is a term of praise, then "undramatic" will imply flatness, monotony, and flaccidity, and Spenser will seem an undramatic writer guilty of all these faults. If, however, "dramatic" and "undramatic" only describe two different ways of looking at the world, then what is so obviously bad dramatic poetry may begin to seem great poetry of a quite different kind.

Originally "dramatic" referred to a literary work that was of the stage and "undramatic" only described a work not suitable for acting. In time, however, "dramatic" became a synonym for "exciting," and at the same time "theatrical" became a dyslogistic rather than a descrip-

This essay appears by permission of the author.

tive term so that "dramatic" referred to excitement of a rather elevated sort. "Dramatic" also came to be used as more strictly literary term to describe moments, events, passages, and even whole works in which were genuine and grand confrontations between discrete and clearly defined characters. In the novel the omniscient narrator gave way to one who was himself a participant in the action, and a "dramatic" novel was not only one in which the action was scenic and approximated action on a stage, but one in which the mystery created by human confrontation was not sullied by a director constantly telling the audience what to look at and how to think. Historically, then, as our sense of the failure or absence of higher powers in the universe increased, so did our implied praise of "dramatic" works in which the human agents were left alone to face each other and their destinies. At this very time *The Faerie Queene,* which is obviously not dramatic in this sense, began to seem old or old-fashioned, sport for antiquarians and "the eccentric few who are born with sympathy for such work." What happened to our sense of Spenser happened as our sense of what is good or relevant changed. It may be true that the reader of *The Faerie Queene* finally needs only trust Spenser's verse in order to learn how to read it, but it is also true that most readers cannot do this without first becoming aware of the many dramatic works that have created their sense of what poetry should be long before they ever come to Spenser.

In a dramatic work a character or a narrator speaks, but what he says is not the whole truth. Another character answers or the narrator takes a different position. What he says is not the whole truth either, but it clarifies for us what the first speaker did not and could not know. A gap appears between two characters or between character and narrator: Heathcliff speaks, Nelly Dean comments and we, as readers, know more than either will ever know; Claudius tries to pray but fails, and Hamlet, because he believes the prayer successful, vows his most demonic revenge. In what is probably the fullest and most explicit rendering of this dramatic sense of gaps between people, George Eliot in *Middlemarch* appeals to our "common sense" belief that each person is only his own candle held up to the random scratches on a pier-glass, unable ever to cross the bridge between a person and our view of that person:

> If to Dorothea Mr. Casaubon had been the mere occasion which had set alight the fine inflammable material of her youthful illusions, does it follow that he was fairly represented in the

minds of those less impassioned personages who have hitherto
delivered their judgments concerning him? I protest against any
absolute conclusion, any prejudice derived from Mrs. Cadwalla-
der's contempt for a neighbouring clergyman's alleged greatness
of soul, of Sir James Chettam's poor opinion of his rival's legs,—
from Mr. Brooke's failure to solicit a companion's ideas, or from
Celia's criticism of a middle-aged scholar's personal appearance.

"I protest against any absolute conclusion" is the implicit attitude of
the writer of dramatic literature, and when we look at the most highly
praised passages in the literature of the last three centuries we find
most often dramatic moments that are supremely expressive of our
sense of the mystery in the human condition. The gaps create irony
and drama, and the author who makes us aware of gaps earns our
highest praise because we admire authors who know they do not know
all the answers.

It follows from this that in a dramatic work the story will "really be
a story," and it will shift and turn as the characters' or the narrator's
view of the world changes. An omniscient narrator will work to maintain evenness of tone and point of view; Thackeray, say, has his range
in *Vanity Fair,* but once we have learned what the range is little that
Becky or Amelia can do affects it much. The book is governed by the
idea of Vanity Fair and almost everything that happens serves to demonstrate once again that all is vanity. But in a more dramatic work
like *Emma,* the narrator must change her stance at every stage in the
education of her heroine. At the beginning Emma is very young,
selfish, and blind so the narrator can be quite neat in her ironies,
quite simple in her covert disapproval. But a tone appropriate towards
an Emma who does not realize Mr. Elton is making love to her is
quite inappropriate towards an Emma recovering from the humiliations of Box Hill. That is why, in a dramatic work, context is so important. We cannot speak of Hamlet without also specifying which
Hamlet we mean, for the Hamlet of the first soliloquy is not at all
"the same man" as the Hamlet who asks Horatio to "absent thee from
felicity awhile." Even in a work with only one character this is often
true; in "Ode to a Nightingale" our sense of who "Keats" is depends
almost entirely on where we are in the poem, for the "Ode" is a journey and the central figure shifts and turns much as a Shakespearean
tragic hero or a Jane Austen heroine does.

If in a dramatic work we have clearly delineated characters created by gaps in understanding between each other and/or the narrator, if we have a story that renders the fullest possibilities of change as expressive of its sense of life, then an undramatic work is one in which no such striking change is possible, no marked differences among characters exist, no shifts in point of view occur. The author of a dramatic work is sceptical and uses his story to discover his sense of life. The author of an undramatic work is certain and does not need his story to discover a sense of life he already commands. The dramatic work expresses differences, usually discords, while the undramatic work emphasizes likenesses, usually harmonies. Most undramatic authors are in some sense visionary; they know their world and move freely within its boundaries. C. S. Lewis has a description of Spenser that can serve as a preliminary definition of all undramatic writers:

> He discovered early the things he valued, and there is no sign his allegiance ever wavered. He was of course often, perhaps usually, disappointed. The actual court did not conform to his standard of courtesy: mutability, if philosophically accepted from the outset, might yet prove unexpectedly bitter to the taste. But disappointment is not necessarily conflict. It did not for Spenser discredit the things of which he was disappointed. It might breed melancholy, or indignation, but not doubt. . . . He was often sad, but not, at bottom, worried. (*English Literature in the Sixteenth Century*, p. 392)

Of all the major English poets Spenser is perhaps the most undramatic, or most consistently so. For later undramatic poets with anything like Spenser's genius had to face, at least implicitly, what Spenser did not have to face until the end of his career. Spenser inherited a view of the universe that was still harmonious and still able to engender a common culture which gave him all the materials he needed. But for Milton, Blake, and Shelley (to name only the most obvious examples) the inheritance was increasingly less secure, and historical forces were at work to create an increasingly secular, sceptical, dramatic world. The language, imagery, and revelation quite easily available to Spenser was technically still "there" for Milton, but Milton could not work at ease with these materials, for what he believed and what he saw were not always the same or even reconcilable. By the time of Blake and Shelley the visionary poet was driven more and more to private language in the case of Blake and to ecstatic mistiness in the case of Shelley in order to maintain the primacy of the vision.

For a critic like F. R. Leavis, who looks for poetic language really used by men, these poets are bound to be seen as having paid too high a price. Dr. Leavis has history on his side if not all responsible literary criticism, and his Great Tradition of more dramatic authors has been the mainstream of our literature since the death of Spenser and the decisive force of Shakespeare.

Anyone who comes to *The Faerie Queene* having been, in effect, raised on Shakespeare, Donne and (what is more likely) the novel is almost certainly going to be baffled and annoyed at first. Many put it down after a few cantos or one book as a work lifeless and probably confused; it is seldom a work its enemies even pay the honor of denouncing. For, after all, if one is looking for scenes, for characters, even for allegory as clearly articulated as it is in *Pilgrim's Progress*, then *The Faerie Queene* is hopeless. There is no "there" *there*, to use a phrase of Gertrude Stein's, and furthermore Spenser seems totally undisturbed by this fact. On and on it goes, battles, castles, streams, and tapestries, with never more than a slight break in the monotonous evenness of the tone. One tries to find a story and parts of Book I seem possible, but the rest is more instead of less diffuse. Characters come and go unannounced and undescribed, good fights endlessly against evil, the poem goes on forever. Now those who know and love the poem know better than this in one sense, but often in trying to explain to the sceptical or uninitiated why someone looking for a dramatic work is looking for the wrong things they turn to the allegory, the thought, the conceptual framework:

> . . . for, whatever may be true of some other poets, the aesthetic patterning of Spenser and Milton is based upon ideas, upon conceptual thinking. (A. S. P. Woodhouse, "Nature and Grace in *The Faerie Queene*," *ELH*, 16 (1949), 197)
>
> The governing principle of Spenser's poems is intellectual and thematic rather than narrative, dramatic, or symbolic. (William Nelson, *The Poetry of Edmund Spenser*, VII)

Accordingly the emphasis in Spenserian studies has always been on the themes, the ideas, and the way the allegory extends the dark conceit.

To some extent this emphasis is correct and unavoidable. Spenser certainly is not dramatic or novelistic and, if we are careful with the way we place the stress, we can say that Spenser's aesthetic patterning is *based upon* ideas. It is altogether proper to say that the subject of Book III is not Britomart or Venus but Chastity and to add that the stories, characters, and scenes are Spenser's materials rather than, as tends to be true in dramatic works, his goals. But still, those who are bored with the poem have a point too, and one most Spenserians ignore. Their sense is that the ideas in *The Faerie Queene* are commonplaces and that the poem seems not so much a large intellectual framework but an endless series of the same or similar events. The governing principles seem too obvious, apparent in every stanza; they also seem hopelessly lost in a jungle of words. It is for this reason that I want to call *The Faerie Queene* undramatic rather than thematic or allegorical. In principle at least the poem is endless, and there is nothing in its framework to prevent it from going on and on as long as Spenser can think of events to relate. It is quite clear, from internal evidence and from the Letter to Raleigh, that Spenser had at some stages of the composition an extremely vast structure in mind. But the point about it was its vastness rather than its dimensions. Whatever the frame it had to allow for as many shifts in apparent direction as there are shifts in syntax, characterization, and narrative. For what holds *The Faerie Queene* together, and here the enemies of the poem seem more correct than its friends, is not so much a conceptual idea as a state of mind. No matter how long one has been away from the poem, no matter where one picks it up, no matter how long one reads, it always seems the same.

It should not be concluded, however, that there is no coherence in the poem or that one can rearrange the stanzas, cantos, or books and end up with the same poem. Just because the story of Britomart exists as a narrative independently of the story of the Squire of Dames (to say nothing of the stories of Guyon or Calidore), just because in some ways the story of Britomart in the Castle Joyeous exists independently of her subsequent rescue of Amoret, the poem is not therefore a hodgepodge. But in a poem as long, as even in tone, as repetitious in its events, the major organizing fact is going to be sequence, pure and simple. In a dramatic work, as we have seen, context, the specific point in the story, is extremely important as one quotes and discusses character, tone, or atmosphere. In *The Faerie Queene* we move from forest to castle, from the House of Pride to the dungeon of Orgoglio, from defeat to triumph, but Spenser writes as though none of these events had any effect on his tone or manner. This evenness does a great deal to make *The Faerie Queene* among the hardest poems for a reader to remember. Ask a man who is reading through as quickly as time and energy allow and who is in the middle of Book IV the following questions: "What is the name of the bloody-handed babe and when does he appear?" "Does Belphoebe rescue Timias before or after the witch remembers the false Florimell?" The chances are good that, even if he has read the poem before, he will blink, back off, smile, try to rub thoughts of Lust or Corflambo from his mind, and slowly go about piecing together the things which seemed so indelibly clear just a brief while ago. Nine out of ten readers in the midst of Book VI cannot remember if it was Artegall or Arthur who fought the Soldan at the end of Book V. Whatever the structure, whatever the large-scale organization, Spenser has deliberately militated against our being aware as we read of much more than the preceding few cantos. The large formal structure of the poem is almost never the operative structure of the reader. It is for this reason that so much Spenserian commentary even at its best always seems rather unreal, drawn as it is from the detached impulse to make the poem diagrammatic rather than from the experience of reading the poem.

For instance, in *The Structure of Allegory in "The Faerie Queene,"* A. C. Hamilton outlines what seems a very persuasive argument that the structure of the extant six books repeat the structure of Book I. In many places the argument is impressive, especially in the account of the transition from Book II to Book III as the result of an awakening to the chaos of living. Mr. Hamilton, quite simply, was able to point to things no one had seen before. But the fact that no one had seen them is, I think, significant; what Mr. Hamilton points to is there, of course, but it is not something a reader can make much of as he returns to the poem. When he tries to keep such a large and detailed structure in his head, he simply fails to read what is in front of him and ends convinced either he or it should not be there. The effort to make patterns inevitably tends to flatten and simplify the myriad shifting details of the endless stanzas. That assertion of formal organization which cannot be made part of one's experience with the poem is bound to seem beside the point. Over and over in Spenserian commentary we are asked to compare the Garden of Adonis with the Temple of Venus, or the Bower of Bliss with the Castle of Busirane. But we can make such comparisons only long after we have finished the poem and we go back to discover, in a detached way, what it all means, where it is all going. The Garden of Adonis is in the middle of Book III and the Temple of Venus is near the end of Book IV, so that if we take them and put them side by side, we are making the structure, not Spenser. In the poem they are 6000 lines apart.

What is most obviously needed, then, is a commentary that relies more fully on the sequence of the stanzas as they are on the page, that relies on using as our means of expressing the poem's meaning the sequence which is all a full scale undramatic work can have for its main means of conveying meaning. Here is another example of recent Spenserian criticism which reveals beautifully how important sequence is and how distorted the poem seems when we ignore it:

> Over against the completely determinate ideal of Medina we have the mysterious three-dimensional ideal of Belphoebe. Belphoebe's instinctive and natural mode of temperance is contrasted to Medina's primarily rational moderation; instinctive aloofness balances Medina's almost frenetic social concern. (Harry Berger, The Allegorical Temper, p. 159)

This seems to me both precise and persuasive and gives us a way that is also Spenser's way to "place" the flatness of the House of Medina in II.ii. What Mr. Berger has done is to see what light the canto following II.ii can cast on its predecessor; the two cantos employ different characters and are not part of the same story, but their sequential juxtaposition makes and perhaps insists upon the comparison. What emerges from what Mr. Berger calls the "conspicuous irrelevance" of II.iii is an ideal of natural temperance that does indeed expand our awareness of the possibilities of virtue beyond anything that the homilies of Medina, Guyon, and the Palmer have allowed us to see. But Mr. Berger then goes on:

> Guyon identifies himself with Medina and sees her as embodying the conscious chivalric ideals he himself espouses; both feel it is their responsibility to maintain justice and order in the world. But Belphoebe's nature also resembles Guyon's and reflects a somewhat different light upon him: though she speaks of honor and decorum and justice she herself is unencumbered by their problems. The unconscious character of her temperance is highlighted more clearly than Medina's, and we are shown the innate self-absorption underlying Guyon's social concern.

This in part only repeats the point made earlier, but when Mr. Berger speaks of the "innate self-absorption underlying Guyon's social concern" he is talking about something he has mined from cantos far removed from those in question—and all come later. It is difficult, even for one looking for what Mr. Berger wants him to see, to read the episode of Belphoebe and Bragadocchio and see in it an illumination or reflection of Guyon's self-absorption. This way of reading both reverses Spenser's sequence and foreshortens it drastically; in effect, it imagines the sequence is not there.

The sequence, thus, is both extremely important and also difficult to remember, but this need not be a contradiction. The sequence one attends to, given the length of the poem, is a relatively local matter precisely because the farther we go on the more the earlier episodes become misty. When the story moves along with one central character in a fairly tight sequence it is not difficult to remember three or four cantos. But when, as in the opening cantos of Book IV, Spenser is constantly shifting his cast of characters and leaving the scenery bare, it is hard enough just to determine who is doing what to whom, to say nothing of what happened sixty or seventy stanzas earlier. This difficulty is quite obviously one calculated by Spenser and we do come to realize that part of Spenser's "point" is that Paridell is here almost indistinguishable from Blandamour and that both are much like Ferramont or Brunchevel. This varying of our sense of the sequence is one of Spenser's major techniques and when he is at his best the sequence is almost always rich and fascinating. For instance, III.v describes the healing of Timias by Belphoebe and his subsequent wounding by his love for her. The episode is "beautiful" according to C. S. Lewis, and most readers have agreed, yet lifted from the context provided by the sequence it would hardly seem so. But the previous canto is a series of laments for lost or unfound loves—Britomart's for Artegall, Cymoent's for Marinell, Arthur's for Florimell and Gloriana —and the resultant aura is one that seems to deny the possibility of any satisfactory human communication or love. After this canto even the silent and painful healing and wounding of Timias seems like a great deal, shines a ray of light in a dark world. So too, after this episode comes the debate between Venus and Diana, a scene far more brightly and warmly lit than the one just before; we gradually are made ready, thus, for the Garden of Adonis, within whose grave joy we find no distinction made between human love and universal harmony: "But she her selfe, when ever that she will, Possesseth him, and of his sweetness takes her fill." The loneliness and despair of the human loves is not denied by the image of the Garden, but our sense of that loneliness is of course modified by it, just as, in turn, our sense of the Garden is modified by the simple and un-abrupt return to "the world" in the following canto. It is one of the most brilliant sequences in the whole poem; deny it, pull any of its parts out of place, and the episode will seem quite different. What connects here is only sequence; there are no causal connections whatever among the episodes. It matters not at all in the "life" of Belphoebe whether she sees Timias or Bragadocchio first, but it makes all the difference to the poem that each meeting is placed where it is.

One final example is perhaps most instructive of all. In *The Kindly Flame* Thomas P. Roche, Jr. offers a fine and detailed account of Britomart's experience at the House of Busirane, after which he concludes:

> What then does this make of Busyrane? Is he not the abuse of marriage just as his house is the objectification of Amoret's fears of marriage? He is the abuse of marriage because his mask of Cupid presents an image of marriage as a sacrifice just as Busiris was a place of sacrifice. He is an abuse of marriage because the mind he possesses cannot distinguish between the act of marriage and adulterous love. He is an abuse of marriage because the falsity of his view of love can lead only to lust or death. His power is derived from the *abusion* of mind in distorting the image of love. The meaning he presents to the wedding guests is trivial, at the most, lust; the meaning he presents to Amoret is the sacrifice of personal integrity. (*The Kindly Flame*, p. 83)

This seems both excellent and unnecessarily wrong. Busirane is to Mr. Roche an abuse of marriage at the end of Book III because he is coming to these cantos via the descriptions of Busirane in IV.i and at the Temple of Venus. He has rearranged the events in the "life" of Amoret to put them in chronological order. He then interprets the end of Book III in the light of sequentially later (but chronologically earlier) happenings. But no one, I think, coming on the House of Busirane after the episode of Malbecco would ever think as exclusively as Mr. Roche does of Busirane as an abuse of *marriage*. Nor need he do so. Mr. Roche's best sentence here can be easily rewritten to read: "He is an abuse of chaste love because the mind he possesses cannot distinguish between chastity and adulterous love." One needs to make clear what "chastity" means, and chastity perhaps does imply marriage to the extent that our image of chaste love in Book III is the married union of Britomart and Artegall. That is why the emphasis Mr. Roche makes on marriage by transposing the events is unnecessary; we can assume it to the extent that is really needed.

It is almost always in the interest of a conceptual distinction that critics have found it convenient implicitly to rearrange or foreshorten the poem's sequence; what is most obviously "there" as we read has thus been overlooked or underemphasized as though we were meant to read the poem in some conceptually clearer sequence than the poem's. Furthermore the effort to find thematic and allegorical patterns and parallels tends to deny the fact that the conceptual scheme of things is something Spenser is really explaining to us all the time. The allegorical centers like the Garden of Adonis and the House of Holiness are in the poem but the poem does not exist for their sake. What at their best they crystallize is something part of almost every stanza, part of the monotonous yet beautiful tone that keeps assuring us that Spenser knows, that he can clarify, that above all there is no hurry. Here, there, all along, what is most important is always most clear:

> And comming to that fishers wandring bote,
> That went at will, withouten carde or sayle,
> He therein saw that yrksome sight, which smote
> Deepe indignation and compassion frayle
> Into his hart attonce: streight did he hayle
> The greedy villein from his hoped prey,
> Of which he now did very litle fayle,
> And with his staffe, that drives his heard astray,
> Him bett so sore, that life and sense did much dismay.
>
> (III.viii.31)

This is Proteus rescuing Florimell from the fisherman, and if there is nothing particularly unusual about the stanza it shows us the way almost every stanza does what is most important to Spenser. Proteus sees the sight and the sight "smites" him with deep indignation. The metaphor is then stretched as compassion is "smote" as well as indignation, and finally it is lost altogether when the compassion that the sight "smote" is "frayle." Here is that characteristically loose syntax that is the surest sign of an undramatic writer; "frayle" floats free of the verb which controls its noun just as the adverb floats freely in

Keats' "Alone and palely loitering." Compassion is frail; the truth is true regardless of the particular situation. Yet there is reason for calling compassion frail at this point—the sight, Florimell, is frail; it is frail because it is not compassion but indignation which causes Proteus' first move, his beating of the fisherman; it is frail because compassion is thus a weak human feeling. After this comes the beating, and without warning "life" and "sense" appear on the scene to be "dismayed" because the fisherman is near death. We know why they come but we will never know where they "came from" or "go to." But we see that we are not alone, none of us, not even the lustful fisherman; life and sense hover here, compassion is frail, and these are the facts of life. At every point Spenser is there to tell us of these facts. What Proteus, Florimell, or the fisherman know or apprehend is secondary at best, materials of the dramatic writer, important only if we need to stress that each of us sees the world differently.

We read on and on in *The Faerie Queene* not to find out what happens to a particular character but to follow Spenser's sequence, the evenness and unhurriedness of which is the mark of his assurance that he knows what life is like and that he can reveal the wellsprings of that life if we will but look. Faerie land is a misty place because, in one sense, we are always lost in it. We have no bearings and nothing is even tied down, nothing need be consistent. But at the same time we are never lost, there are no gaps and we never feel the excitement and terror and suspense that the uncertainty of what will happen next forces upon us. For Spenser to be uncertain is to be blind because it accepts the consciously apprehended world as the whole truth. Were we to see Florimell and the fisherman in dramatic terms we would see them as uncertain; they would not and could not know that compassion frail smote Proteus' heart or that life and sense were dismayed. They are, like us, limited, tied to themselves. But Spenser insists, in this stanza and in the slowly unraveled sequence of stanzas, that what we see is but "seems" and that he knows what "is." Such is the solemn assurance of the undramatic writer. He knows we may become lost in the wandering wood and fall into mazy error for such is the human condition. Life is wretchedness, Britomart tells Scudamour before the flames surrounding the House of Busirane. But the voice that knows this knows there is more. Spenser is the great priest of our uncertainty, hovering over us, quietly and effortlessly showing us that to be uncertain and lost is to be blind as well as human, and that it is possible to see. Every line he writes is there to show us we are not alone.

II

But if we are not alone, what kind of world do we live in? The discussion thus far has focused attention on the kind of poem *The Faerie Queene* is and the problems of interpretation that thereby most usually arise. But of the nature of faerie land, the stuff of the poem, the sense of life it conveys—what of these? If it is undramatic, Christian, and neo-Platonic, so too are other works of nothing like its scope or stature or peculiar feel. If the sequence is of supreme importance, then nothing less than close analysis of long stretches of the poem can convey an adequate sense of this. But some general points can be made.

Donald Davie once said of Shakespeare and Hopkins that there was no word in the language they might not use should the need arise. Spenser's vocabulary is by these standards limited, though of course it is very large. What we are perhaps most aware of are the repetitions, the apparently incessant use of a relatively small number of words. The Spenser concordance shows a handful of uses of some of his more famous archaisms and racy words almost swamped alongside lists of words that go on for a column or more—to pick words from only one section of the alphabet, we find more than fifty uses of "fayre," "good," "foul," "dear," "full," "force," "hand," "heaven," "gold," "glory," "great," "green," "ground." The adjectives are moral or meagerly descriptive, the nouns are simple objects in daily view, the verbs are simple and active. Above all, the vocabulary is monosyllabic. Much of this is the result of using adjectives as metrical and stanzaic fillers, much too is the result of not working very hard to find the right word when an ordinary one is available. But this is far from the whole story. Spenser is not really a poet of epithets or verbal formulas; what we find instead is a host of words surrounding one repeated word and a word used apparently to signify one fixed thing but actually used to illustrate different things in different contexts. Thus around an abstract noun Spenser will use a constellation of related adjectives: "sorrow" is "dolefull," "lamenting," "fowle," "secret," "thrilling," "pensive," "stupid," "long," and "huge," while "passion" is "great," "stormie," "dredfull," "restlesse," "raging," "troublous," "franticke," "sharp," and, just once, "piteous." The aim seems a suggested range of meanings and associations which will have a hidden but finally telling effect on our sense of Spenser's feeling about the quality conveyed by the noun. The common nouns, however, seldom have

such constellations, and even when they do the appearances may be
deceiving. Day and night, light and dark—these do remain constant
and thereby attain the status of abstractions. But the fountain of
Diana's transformed nymph is "frail" and "feeble," while Chrysogone
bathes in a "fresh" fountain far from all men's view, and while Archimago's fountain beside his hermitage is "sacred" and flows from a
christall streame. Gold is lavishly used in the furnishing of both the
House of Pride and the Temple of Venus. The things of faerie land
can be good, bad, or deceiving.

But more important is Spenser's way of charging almost every
thing, every action, every attribute with a kind of moral valence.
Look at what happens to "emptie" in the description of Orgoglio and
to "rude" in the description of Belphoebe:

> Brought forth this monstrous masse of earthly slime,
> Puft up with emptie wind, and fild with sinfull crime.
>
> (I.vii.9)

> In her rude heares sweet flowres themselves did lap,
> And flourishing fresh leaves and blossomes did enwrap.
>
> (II.iii.30)

Here the words that might seem like filler words—"monstrous" and
"earthly" and "sinfull" in the description of Orgoglio—really are a
kind of lumber making the necessary scaffolding that will support and
define "Puft up with emptie wind," so that the moralizing epithets
really exist to give moral valence to the words around them. No one
readily recognizes this effect taking place as it happens, but slowly
and silently the world of things is made to inhabit a land of profoundly moral weather, a land indeed of faerie, made alive by the
very words that often seem most dead, as in this simile about the
dragon in Book I:

> As burning Aetna from his boyling stew
> Doth belch out flames, and rockes in peeces broke,
> And ragged ribs of mountains molten new,
> Enwrapt in coleblacke clouds and filthy smoke,
> That all the land with stench, and heven with horror choke.
>
> (I.xi.44)

Here "filthy" and "horror" are the easy moralizing words, yet they also
transform our sense of "boyling," "belch," "broke," and "molten,"
words held in moral suspension until the last two lines of the stanza.

In such a faerie land the potential density or complexity of feeling will be modified by the constant moral shadings; things rightly seen are seen morally, but the moral seeing is so constant and effortless that our final sense is not of "moral" as a means of strictly dividing good from evil but of knowing the endless variety of things seen and ways of seeing open to the moral vision. Again, only prolonged analysis can reveal the enormous range of this variety, but even a brief look at two of the poem's great moments can help show Spenser's undramatic inclusiveness and his moral generosity towards his own imagination.

> What man so wise, what earthly wit so ware,
> As to discry the crafty cunning traine,
> By which Deceipt doth maske in visour faire,
> And cast her colours died deepe in graine,
> To seeme like Truth, whose shape she well can faine,
> And fitting gestures to her purpose frame,
> The guiltlesse man with guile to entertaine?
> Great maistresse of her art was that false dame,
> The false Duessa, cloked with Fidessaes name.
>
> (I.vii.1)

At the heart of Book I this question with its answer all too clear illuminates the plight of the Red Crosse Knight. The paynims and the monsters, the enemies that announce themselves as enemies, are relatively easy for the Knight, while the figures who tempt, waylay, and defeat him are all hidden in their evil, masters of their illusions "By which Deceipt doth maske in visour faire." (Incidentally, the moral valence given to "died deepe in graine" and especially to "fitting" are nice instances of the kind of work done by the surrounding flat moral tags.) Just before this opening to Canto vii Archimago, disguised as a pilgrim, has tried to crush Una by telling her the Red Crosse Knight is dead. Though he fails he follows close behind her as she leaves Satyrane to fight Sansloy. Then, just after this stanza, Spenser returns to the Knight who, having defeated Sansjoy and painfully left the dunghill of carcasses in the House of Pride, sits down by a fountain.

Weary, he removes his armor. His horse eats of the grass and he too "feedes," "upon the cooling shade." Duessa finds him and upbraids him a little for having left her in the House of Pride, but soon "they gan of solace treat," and together they "bathe in pleasaunce of the joyous shade." We need not notice, particularly, an irony in that "joyous," for soon Spenser will show how deceitful, temporary, and disastrous that joy is. The shade of the tree protects a fountain that came into being because one of Diana's nymphs, just like the Red Crosse Knight, once when she was "quite tyr'd with heat," "satt down to rest in middest of the race." Diana, angry with the nymph's laxness, made the waters that flow from her "dull and slow" so that "all that drunke thereof did faint and feeble grow." What Spenser is doing here is merging the Red Crosse Knight with the landscape. First the Knight and his horse feed on the grass and shade, then he and Duessa bathe in it. Then he drinks of the nymph's waters, and of course "eftsoones his manly powers gan to fayle":

> And mightie strong was turned to feeble frayle:
> His chaunged powers at first them selves not felt,
> Till crudled cold his corage gan assayle,
> And chearefull blood in fayntnes chill did melt,
> Which, like a fever fit, through all his body swelt.

At first he does not feel what is happening, and then even when he does he does not realize its consequences. The cold of the waters chills the "chearefull blood" which is also his courage, and the transformed liquid swells through his body like a fever:

> Yet goodly court he made still to his dame,
> Pourd out in loosnesse on the grassy grownd,
> Both carelesse of his health, and of his fame. . .

The wonderfully supple syntax here allows the second line, "Pourd out in loosnesse on the grassy grownd," to modify both the subject (he) and the object (his dame) in the first line. Thus both the Red Crosse Knight and Duessa become like the fountain, poured out, both being careless of his health and fame. As he becomes liquefied, as it were, he becomes feeble, faint, and uncaring, so hero, villainness, and landscape all dissolve into one.

Then "at the last he heard a dreadfull sownd," Orgoglio appears and quickly subdues the Knight. He is a giant, proud of his strength, boastful and arrogant, "puft up with emptie wind." He is about to kill the Red Crosse Knight when Duessa asks him to make the Knight his slave and her his mistress. Orgoglio agrees, the Red Crosse Knight is imprisoned, and both victor and vanquished are captured by Duessa. Orgoglio here is like the fountain, an external object that serves as a mirror for what the Knight has become. Careless, without his armor, the Knight drinks and becomes like the fountain. He is now "at one" with Duessa, they are poured out on the ground, so he meets Orgoglio, the very thing he has allowed himself to become; thus, both Knight and giant are ensnared. It is a marvelous spectacle of human degradation; by means of his allegorical figures, his faerie landscape, and his freely inventive syntax Spenser does in less than 150 lines what many novels have taken hundreds of pages to do less well. This way of working, using the external figures and landscape as mirrors, is, we slowly see, superbly appropriate for a book in which the enemies all really lie within and where the fatal vice is believing one has triumphed.

Early in Book I the Red Crosse Knight goes into the wandering wood and defeats the monster Error. If we were committed to a strict allegorical interpretation of events this would be puzzling because while "The Red Crosse Knight defeats Error" summarizes the plot it does not state the meaning of the episode. Nor can we come much closer by making the statement read "Holiness defeats Error with the help of Truth"; the Red Crosse Knight does not defeat error in the abstract sense and he does not fight in a particularly holy way. But we can say that the Christian knight, by himself, because he is mortal, is liable to be "wrapt in Errours endless traine" and that, with the exhortation to "add faith unto your force," he *can* defeat error—the monster or the human fact. The episode, thus, is an emblem of human possibility, a description of what can happen. Yet what is possible is of course not always what is; immediately after defeating Error the Red Crosse Knight "errs" in the hermitage of Archimago. In Canto vii carelessness with himself and neglect of his armor lead the Knight into the clutches of the proud and equally unheeding Orgoglio; this too is an emblem of human possibility. Of course theologically all sins are versions of pride, but this, we notice, is not the point stressed here; what is important is the way Spenser fills the landscape with those very qualities which the Red Crosse Knight cannot see are within him. The illusion evil is best at creating is the illusion that enemies are really external and visible.

Milton's famous pronouncement about Spenser in the *Areopagitica* is not really adequate to Spenser's sense of life in Book I. Undoubtedly Spenser could not praise a fugitive and cloistered virtue either, but neither was he the creator of Abdiel. In Book I struggle is necessary and constant but not, therefore, good and certainly not ennobling. The Red Crosse Knight is purified not in battle but in the

House of Holiness. Milton's epic imagination was more challenged by godly struggle than by holiness, but Spenser casts a continual shadow across the whole idea of such struggle. Evil is disguised and deceitful and is therefore an illusion, but because we are liable to believe the illusion real evil is constantly able to weaken its enemy. The very idea that good can conquer evil is in Book I the most monstrous of illusions and is the one most certain to lead to self-destruction. Over and over the Red Crosse Knight wins only to lose. Being on the plain is debilitating because it puts the Knight where he cannot know what he sees "out there" is an image of himself. That is why the Giant Despair is the greatest of enemies, for he knows all this, he knows the appeal of rest and can sound to the weary ear so much like Contemplation. After a career of seeing triumph lead to error and degradation the Red Crosse Knight by himself cannot distinguish between the two voices that assure him they know how heavily sin can weigh upon a sinner and how eager the sinner must be to be rid of himself. Thus we can see why Book I has more of a story than the other books and why its central figure is least the embodiment of the virtue he represents. We can perhaps see also why there is no need to describe the book as the education of its hero. The process of redemption is clear enough and the separate episodes do not so much form a causally connected narrative as they do a tapestry of emblems the final emphasis of which is that there *is*, really, no education for the Red Crosse Knight because the presumption of such an education would be that one can learn to defeat evil and be holy once and for all. It is for this reason that Book I is stiffer, more stately and uncompromising than the books that follow. This is as it should be, of course, for its goal is only partly of this world and is not attainable on the plain or in the House of Holiness, or in the poem even, except as promise.

But having taken this position Spenser is not committed to maintaining it or discarding it, and it is only in dimly analogous ways that the distinctive techniques of Book I appear again in the poem. The passage that is technically, morally, and emotionally at the furthest remove from it, to which we now turn, is not contradictory of it. It is simply another part of faerie land and, no matter how different it may seem from Book I, no one would ever doubt that it came from the same poem as the episode of Duessa and Orgoglio. The episode is the meeting of Britomart and Artegall in the middle of Book IV. The situation as Canto vi opens is roughly this: Satyrane's tournament has grotesquely collapsed when the false Florimell cannot wear Florimell's girdle; Scudamour has been stupidly victimized by Ate and has wandered into the House of Care; Artegall sits sulking on the plain after his defeat at the tournament by a knight he does not know is Britomart. The canto, thus, opens darkly:

> What equall torment to the griefe of mind,
> And pining anguish hid in gentle hart,
> That inly feeds itself with thoughts unkind,
> And nourisheth her owne consuming smart?
>   (IV.vi.1)

The final result of Ate is unfriendliness to self and both Scudamour and Artegall are thus crippled. Suddenly Britomart appears, the knights attack her, and just as suddenly Spenser shifts his tone:

> Who soone as she him saw approaching neare
> With so fell rage her selfe she lightly gan
> To dight, to welcome him well as she can:
> But entertaind him in so rude a wise,
> That to the ground she smote both horse and man;
> Whence neither greatly hasted to arise,
> But on their common harmes together did devise.

Seldom is Spenser more like Ariosto than this; Britomart's girlishness, her "welcome" and her "entertaining" of knights has never been quite so lethal.

After Scudamour comes Artegall:

> But to himselfe his felonous intent
> Returning, disappointed his desire,
> Whiles unawares his saddle he forwent,
> And found himself on ground in great amazement.

There is no Britomart here, just the return of "his felonous intent" back on itself, which, piquantly, "disappointed his desire," as he forgoes his saddle and finds himself on the ground. But Artegall has only begun. He leaps at Britomart "as doth an eger hound Thrust to a hynd within some covert glade," but when his first success comes the glory is hardly his:

> So as they coursed here and there, it chaunst
> That, in her wheeling round, behind her crest
> So sorely he her strooke, that thence it glaunst

> Adowne her back, the which it fairely blest
> From foule mischance. . .

The "it" that glances down Britomart's back is an unnamed sword, "it" does the fair blessing but because of some "foule mischance" rather than Artegall. Even when, in the succeeding simile, Spenser turns his characters into deities it is not they who are responsible for their actions:

> Like as the lightning brond from riven skie,
> Thrown out by angry Jove in his vengeance,
> With dreadfull force falls on some steeple hie;
> Which battring, downe it on the church doth glance,
> And teares it all with terrible mischance.

In four stanzas Artegall has been transformed from a buffoon who "forgoes" his saddle to a godlike avenger, and Britomart changes from a Brynhild who laughingly entertains the men with blows to a defenseless steeple. Then Spenser backs off and lets the two grow large before our eyes; for two stanzas they fight "heaping huge strokes, as thick as showre of hail," then once again Spenser steps in:

> What yron courage ever could endure
> To work such outrage on so faire a creature?
> And in his madnesse think with hands impure
> To spoyle so goodly workmanship of nature,
> The Maker selfe resembling in her feature?

Artegall is heroic enough, but at the very moment Spenser concedes him his "yron courage" Spenser is expanding his universe beyond such simple heroism. Britomart is now an image of "the Maker selfe," and only after placing her so loftily can Spenser afford his final revelation. Only by seeing that Britomart is a girl can Artegall discover the outrage of his heroism:

> The wicked stroke upon her helmet chaunst,
> And with the force which in itself it bore
> Her ventayle shard away, and thence forth glaunst
> Adowne in vaine, ne harm'd her any more.

Artegall is now nothing, his sword everything. It strikes of its own volition and like a dumb animal stops when it rips away Britomart's helmet, and, obediently, "ne harmed her any more." Presumably what the sword "sees" is:

> her angels face, unseene afore,
> Like to a ruddie morne appeared in sight,
> Deawed with silver drops, through sweating sore,
> But somewhat redder then beseem'd aright,
> Through toylesome heate and labour of her weary fight.

This is done with lovely daring; in the final metamorphosis the "real" Britomart has both an angel's face and much very human and very girlish sweat and flush. But that face that is redder than seemed right is surrounded by the golden hair that lights up faerie land so brilliantly on each of its four appearances:

> And round about the same, her yellow heare,
> Having through stirring loosd their wonted band,
> Like to a golden border did appeare,
> Framed in goldsmith's forge with cunning hand:
> Yet goldsmith's cunning could not understand
> To frame such subtile wire, so shinie cleare.

So Britomart is both a girl and "the Maker self," beyond the power of art to make or, really, to describe:

> And as his hand he up againe did reare,
> Thinking to work on her his utmost wracke,
> His powrelesse arme, benumbd with secret feare,
> From his revengeful purpose shronke abacke,
> And cruel sword out of his fingers slacke
> Fell down to ground, as if the steel had sense,
> And felt some ruth, or sence his hand did lack,
> Or both of them did thinke, obedience
> To do to so divine a beauties excellence.

Only in a world so constantly changing and so filled with unseen powers can the cartoon-like conceit of the sword and the obedient hand seem anything but ludicrous. Before this icon Artegall and sword are reduced to the same level:

> And he himselfe long gazing thereupon,
> At last fell humbly down upon his knee,
> And of his wonder made religion. . .

The magnificent last line is both Spenser's and Artegall's response to Britomart's metamorphosis from rough knight to courageous foe to ruddy girl to divine excellence. Faced with a vision that none of his own earlier roles as buffoon or hero would enable him to understand, Artegall changes once more, sees what Spenser sees, and "of his wonder made religion." Earlier his arm was powerless, "benumbd with secret feare," but now "trembling horror did his sense assayle." It is not the horror that trembles; Artegall sees he has assaulted a deity and so he is attacked by horror and trembles. He knows he does not understand, he wonders, and of his not understanding he makes a religion.

But Artegall's faith is powerless to hold Britomart still, so she is transformed again:

> Nathelesse she, full of wrath for that late stroke,
> All that long while upheld her wrathfull hand,
> With fell intent on him to be ywroke:
> And looking sterne still over him did stand,
> Threatning to strike, unless he would withstand:
> And bad him rise, or surely he should die.

With the last line here we are returned to the Britomart who entertained Scudamour with blows; this command is the gayest she ever gives. Without denying any comic possibilities Spenser continues to show that the gap between "seems" (what the others see) and "is" (Britomart) is wondrous. First Scudamour, always willing to commit himself lavishly, tries to outdo Artegall with his fawning. Then Glauce reappears and, medieval character that she is, seeks an end to all strife and celestial visions. Artegall complies by removing his helmet and so shows Britomart the face she had seen in her glass so long before:

> When Britomart with sharp avizefull eye
> Beheld the lovely face of Artegall,
> Tempred with sternesse and stout majestie. . .

The face that had just been staring at her dumbly now seems stern and majestic and lovely; like Artegall, Britomart does not "see" what is "there," and, like him, makes of what she does see an act of faith:

> Her hart did leape, and all her hart-strings tremble,
> For sudden joy, and secret feare withall,

And all her vitall powres, with motion nimble,
To succour it, themselves gan there assemble.

Britomart also has her secret fear and is beset by powers beyond her
control, and so both Britomart and Artegall make their most important
gestures when they are filled with surprise and wonder. We can see, if
we like, that Artegall is worshipping his mistress in standard courtly
fashion, but what Spenser is emphasizing here is the way such worship is founded not in convention but in natural responses to one's
beloved. Rather than stressing the comedy of the scene, Spenser
creates the comedy and then instead of insisting on the limitations of
the lovers that gives rise to the comedy he stresses the possibility of
acting upon this very limitation. What he knows is that they enact
their limits in a limitless world. At one moment Spenser and Artegall
are together, implicitly praising their maker for showing them a
larger world than they had ever known. But Artegall is only a character, locked in time, and so his moment passes, but instead of working the comedy ironically against Artegall Spenser really continues to
do what he does throughout: reveal the relation between men and an
ordered universe. Given his belief in such a universe it is natural
rather than conventional that Artegall made religion of his wonder.
Given this belief, furthermore, Spenser can easily show that there is
little that is mystical and much that is pragmatic in his vision. To
deny the wonderfulness of what has happened by stressing only the
confusion and the blindness of his characters would be, for him,
simply perverse. To give full play to the mysterious life of his universe
he must show both the disarray of what his characters see and the
shimmering possibilities for human love that lie in the midst of the
very chaos.

So we have the stern and almost moody poet of the liability of the
Red Crosse Knight to fall into error, then we have the mercurial
wondering spirit of human possibility here in Book IV. What makes
them part of the same poem, what makes each in its way true and
important, is simply the freedom that Spenser's undramatic vision
allows him. If we are surprised by anything in these episodes or in the
whole poem it is only because we have unduly limited Spenser's
range by making him consistent in a narrow sense. What gives rise to
such surprise and such limiting, of course, is our more modern inclina-
tion to think of a moral universe as a restrictive universe. We may
know we "cannot do without morality," but much in our life leads us,

for example, to side with D. H. Lawrence when he attacks Tolstoi for denying Vronsky's masculinity for the sake of maintaining his own restrictive social morality. So when we come on a writer like Spenser who fills every stanza with "fayre" and "foul" and shows us a world in which all actions are charged with implicit praise or blame, we naturally are tempted to think he is only old and that his ideas, though perhaps expressive of his earlier age, are merely dead. Even the sternest and most reactionary among us pauses before honoring temperance and a rigid idea of holiness. But to speak this way is to distort Spenser by stressing Spenser's ideas in a very narrow way; such remarks are usually made by those not really interested in reading the poem. Of course Spenser has his narrownesses, and they are almost always the result of his occasional bland acceptance of the medieval allegorical tradition: Kirkrapine in Book I, Medina in Book II, the House of Alma are at best deftly handled and rather mindless reworkings of the allegories of earlier poets. But this is not all of *The Faerie Queene* or even very much of it, and only those interested in maintaining a particular social or religious ideal will stress these episodes in order to praise or attack Spenser. After all, interpreted narrowly a writer's ideas die very quickly, if they ever lived, and if we restricted ourselves to admiring only those authors whose ideas coincided with our own we would only doom ourselves to much rereading in a very small room and to casting the infinite riches outside.

No, the problems in reading *The Faerie Queene* are far different from those small difficulties we may have with Spenser's "ideas." Outside of the cumbersome fact of its great length, the major problem is seeing how a writer writes when he sees human life as his subject but not as the limit of his material. He is careless of much we implicitly admire—time, situation, and character seen dramatically—but we need not work up an argument about the parts of all of us that are undramatic in order to see that such carelessness is not beyond our understanding or our care. We need not be "born with sympathy for such work" to see that great areas of our imaginations can be opened by a writer who feels a solemn joyousness in the fact that man is not the measure. When C. S. Lewis says of Spenser that to read him is to grow in mental health we may perhaps demur and add that C. S. Lewis says this because he believes what Spenser believes. But the freedom of the undramatic writer *is* a wonderful thing to behold in the service of one as inventive as Spenser. This inventiveness is of course a matter of artistic mastery but the mastery is only superficially a matter of technique. It is the result of Spenser's knowledge and of its density and security combined with his constant sense of wonder. The freedom this gave him was clearly profoundly absorbing to Spenser himself and the absorption in turn meant he was never imaginatively in any hurry. His task was not to go anywhere, not to explore the edge of the unknown, but to embody and make imminent the endless aliveness of his received universe. Because it was moral so assuredly it had little need to be didactic. Faerie land is a fact, not a doctrine.

There is a vast difference, then, between loving *The Faerie Queene* and being a Spenserian in the narrow sense, between being baffled, delighted, and bored with its endlessness and being convinced that one has to study oneself into the right frame of mind in order to read the poem at all. It takes study, of course, and even more it takes patience, but both study and patience are necessary only to see what is there rather than to transform oneself into a denizen of the mists. For the central fact about *The Faerie Queene* is not that it is old but that it is unique, and the real difficulty in reading it is simply reading it and not in making oneself an Elizabethan. To call the poem simple, it seems to me, is to be simple; to say it is not very well written is to fail to see what kind of writing it is; to move in quiet excitement with its movement is to be touched in a way that can never be quite eradicated or replaced. Spenser does not ennoble or elevate as later visionaries can do, he offers no sense at all of a personality to be met and felt. But the argument and the few examples of the ways of the poem offered above are designed to begin to show that about the largeness and smallness of being human he makes all other poets seem a little confused. Perhaps more than anyone else, he makes us remember what we forgot we ever knew.

MARTHA CRAIG

The Secret Wit of Spenser's Language

The language of *The Faerie Queene* to most modern readers seems alien and unaccountable. Spenser seems to have overlooked the expressive possibilities of idiomatic speech revealed so magnificently by Shakespeare and devised an artificial language which, in contrast to the artificialities of Milton's language in *Paradise Lost,* seems less significant and less forceful than the ordinary language it replaces. Many qualities may seem unfortunate, but perhaps the most vitiating are the archaisms and an apparently purposeless distortion of words. Even after careful study, Spenser's archaism seems superficial and specious, consisting more in odd spellings and grammatical forms than in a genuine rejuvenation of obsolete words that are needed because they are particularly meaningful or expressive. And his liberties with language, the coinages and peculiar forms seem willful and meaningless; alteration of words for the sake of rhyme seems to betray not only lack of resourcefulness but irresponsibility. It is no exaggeration to say that for many readers the language of *The Faerie Queene* is at best merely curious or quaint, at worst hollow and contorted. And this is especially puzzling because the faults seem not only bad but often utterly gratuitous.

The traditional account of Spenser's language provides no re-assur-

This essay is based on the author's unpublished doctoral dissertation, "Language and Concept in *The Faerie Queene,*" submitted at Yale University, June, 1959.

ance but instead confirms the reader's suspicions. Spenser's diction is said to be "decorative" and to appeal "through spontaneity and inherent suggestiveness, independent of source or application."[1] If so, this has become not a defense but a condemnation. And any other defense of *The Faerie Queene*, of the structure or the allegory, for example, seems ineffectual to the modern reader, for according to his expectations, his implicit hierarchy of literary values, in ignoring the language it presupposes what is primary and most in doubt.

The most influential modern critic of Spenser, C. S. Lewis, suggests that the reader revise these values. Spenser's poetry belongs to an older narrative school in which richness or subtlety of language is not required and would even be inappropriate. It "has in view an audience who have settled down to hear a long story and do not want to savour each line as a separate work of art. Much of *The Faerie Queene* will therefore seem thin or over-obvious if judged by modern standards. The 'thickness' or 'density' which I have claimed for it does not come from its language."[2] This account will not solve the reader's problem, however, for the language seems to call more than usual attention to itself. The peculiarities of spelling and form, the rare words, and the high degree of formal organization in the Spenserian stanza seem to encourage and even enforce close inspection of the language. If Spenser's language lacks the density of Donne or Shakespeare, it also lacks the seeming transparency of Chaucer. A language merely thin or over-obvious might be more generally acceptable, but to many the language does seem dense, not dense with meaning but slightly muddy or opaque in a way they do not penetrate or understand and yet can not ignore.

Another account offered by W. L. Renwick explains the language in terms of the linguistic goals of the Renaissance. Spenser is said to have been influenced by the program of the Pleiade which urged the poet to revive archaic words, introduce foreign words, and construct new ones out of the existing vocabulary. The purpose was to enrich the language, ultimately the language as a whole but intermediately the language of poetry.[3] Spenser certainly shares the spirit of the Pleiade and their belief in the creative right and creative power of the poet. But their program does not explain his style very exactly nor justify his style to the modern reader, for it does not show how the language has been truly "enriched." The vocabulary of *The Faerie Queene* is in general rather circumscribed compared to that of Spenser's contemporaries. Most of his archaisms consist not in the revival of obsolete words to enrich the language but simply in the substitution of archaic forms for modern ones. Though Spenser does adopt some foreign words and invent some new ones, the liberties he takes consist primarily in special modifications of current words, and even these are not consistent in the poem.[4] Why, for example, should the text of the proem to Book I read "scryne" instead of "shrine" as it does in the proem to Book III?

The qualities of style that seem puzzling may be accounted for more adequately if, in place of the specific recommendations of the Pleiade, we consult a more fundamental view of language and reality which the recommendations of the Pleiade only in part represent, that is, the Platonic or "Platonistic" view. A useful document to study in this connection is Plato's *Cratylus*, useful because as an abstract exposition of the fundamental view, it makes the view explicit.

The *Cratylus* is cited prominently by two of Spenser's mentors in their works on language, and references to the dialogue elsewhere during the Renaissance suggest that Plato's discussion had a certain vogue.[5] Spenser must surely have been aware of it and the view of language it presents. The specific question of influence is not primary to an understanding of his poem, however. The dialogue is important to the modern reader as a rationale to account for Spenser's linguistic impulses and to disclose the attitude toward language which *The Faerie Queene* presupposes.

In the *Cratylus* Socrates sets forth the view that words must be not merely conventional and arbitrary, as many believe, but in fact "correct" and "true." For if there is such a thing as reality and knowledge of it, our statements must be about reality, and they must be true to it. And if statements as a whole are to be true, the parts, that is, the words of which they are composed must be true as well. Or, on the analogy of a craft like weaving or cutting, speaking is an action performed for a certain purpose and must be done not according to our own opinion or arbitrary whim but according to nature. We must have the proper instrument correctly suited to the task. In the craft of weaving, the instrument is the shuttle used to separate the web. In the craft of speaking, the instrument is the word.

The instruments of a craft are originally made by someone; so words, too, must have been constructed by an original law-giver or name-maker. An instrument that is good must be constructed according to an ideal. The one who judges whether this has been done successfully, who superintends, is the one who uses the instrument; the carpenter judges the awl. In the case of words the one who judges is the one who knows how to ask and answer questions, who knows how to use words, that is, the dialectician.

What, then, is the principle of "correctness" in words? Socrates says that he does not have the money for a course with the Sophists, so he suggests that the poets be consulted instead. For the modern student of Plato, this advice is tinged with irony, but the Renaissance Platonist, who took at face value the description of poetic inspiration in the *Ion*, Marsilio Ficino, for example, accepts and even approves of the appeal to the poets.

> After thus carefully inquiring from whom the correctness of names, that is, the proper principle by which they are consti-tuted, is to be learned, he mocks the Sophists, and he leads us rather to the poets, not just any of them but the divine ones, as if they had received the true names of things from the gods, among whom are the true names.[6]

In a similar spirit, the Ramist logic acknowledged no fundamental distinction between dialectic and poetry.[7] In respect to words as well as ideas, the poet ideally is a dialectician; he has divinely inspired in-sight into the truth.

If we consult the poet Homer, we discover that correctness of words consists in revealing the nature of the things named. Words reveal reality through their etymologies. The composition of "Agamemnon," for example, shows that he is admirable (*agastos*) for enduring (*men-ein*); the derivation of "Atreus" shows that he is the destructive one (*atēros*). Words contain within them little self-explanatory state-ments. The subject of the statement is the word itself, the predicate is the elemental word or words from which it is made, what we would call the morphemes. Words are "true" because they imply a true state-ment.

The Ramists on these grounds even introduced etymologizing into logic. Words are a form of argument because the "notation" or ety-mology of the word bears some logical relation to the "notion" of the thing.[8] "A woman is a woe man because shee worketh a man woe."[9] As the Ramist discussion reveals, the "etymology" here is not neces-sarily the grammatical one, for this may not furnish a second term: we can not make a significant statement out of "argument" from "argue." The etymology required is the "logical" one which "explains the cause why this name is imposed for this thing."[10] That is, the "etymology" or "true" word is not historically true but philosophically true, and it is not the function of the grammarian but the dialectician to interpret words. Often philosophically true turns out to be what we would simply call "fanciful," but neither Plato nor the Renaissance Platonists had any definite standard for distinguishing the two nor any desire to do so.

The names of Spenser's characters are clearly philosophic and true, for they reveal the nature of the one named through the etymology. The heroes' names, like the names of Homer's heroes, are "composed according to a certain allegorical rationale," as Ficino would say.[11] Belphoebe is the "beautiful, pure one," Artegall is the "art of justice." As a poet-dialectician Spenser also interprets given words truly and philosophically through etymology. "Magnificence" is not properly conspicuous consumption but "doing great deeds" as the etymology shows.

When a suitable etymology is not apparent in the current form of a word, Socrates looks to its archaic form or other archaic words to see if they are more suggestive, for if language has been handed down from some original name-maker, words may have been corrupted in the course of time. If so, the early form should be the right one (*Cratylus* 418-19). Through his theory of language Plato in fact acts out the etymology of "etymology": the true explanation of words is in their origin. The original name-maker in Plato is really a metaphor for whatever principle of order and reason there may be in language. The search for older forms is a search for the true forms that are ideally expressive.

Plato's etymologizing expedient explains the sort of archaizing Spenser does in *The Faerie Queene*. Through archaism Spenser carries out the basic Platonic metaphor of the poem, the metaphor of the antique world, a time in the past when the world was more rational and comprehensible, an ideal time, "ideal" not because there was no evil or difference, but because evil and difference could be more readily perceived and understood. The purpose of his archaisms is not primarily to enlarge his vocabulary, the concern of the Pleiade, but to make it more flexible and expressive. The archaic forms and form words, "-en" endings, "y-" prefixes, and expressions like "ywis" act as a sort of solvent of language, dissolving ordinary patterns and the reader's usual expectation. With archaism established as a mode of diction, Spenser is free to pick out archaic forms that are more suggestive of philosophic meaning.

The state of the language in the sixteenth century made such usage more possible and more likely than it would be now. No fixed standard of spelling and syntax had been established. There was less pattern or expectation to overcome, and the writer was free to choose among many forms available. Spenser simply exercised this freedom more widely than other writers of the time by reviving forms that were obsolete or obsolescent. Because there was no fixed standard, the sixteenth century reader always needed to be more resourceful and interpretive than we. It might not be obvious or indisputable even what word was before him. He would always examine word forms more carefully than we and so would be more apt to see their "etymological" nature, the meaningful affinities which they suggest.

As the analysis of words in the *Cratylus* progresses, it soon becomes clear that even the aid of archaism does not yield a perfect language. The given language is clearly deficient; it is not an adequate or reliable source of truth. But for that very reason language should be improved. Words are only approximations, but as such, they can be perfected. Numbers, because they are images simply of quantities can not be; if we change II to III, we do not refer to the same number better, we refer to another number. But if we change "demon" to "daemon," we improve the word and make it more revealing by showing more clearly the identity of spirit and intelligence.[12]

The poet's alterations are an effort to correct language according to his vision or insight so that it reveals reality more adequately. Forms and spellings are improved in order to disclose the etymological rationale of the word. Slight alterations in sound or spelling are admitted so that connections in meaning may be clearer. Rhyme words are spelled the same, not only implying connection in sound but encouraging comparison of meaning. Portmanteau words are devised to cover complex notions.

The lack of "realism," the uncolloquial, unidiomatic character of the language ultimately follows from Spenser's philosophic realism, his belief that truth is not found in the everyday or in immediate surroundings, the "world of appearances," but in a realm of ideas that are only partially and imperfectly reflected in the everyday world. Ordinary language is not adequate to this world of fuller insight. So Spenser's major heroes are not personifications of common terms, like most of the characters in medieval allegory, but of words he has invented. He writes not of "chastity" but of "Belphoebe," a perfected insight into chastity, not of "courtesy" but "Calidore," a concept something like courtesy but refined and redefined.[13] It is the same basic impulse at work which occasions the form "scryne" to suggest that the shrine the poet seeks in his invocation is, according to the Latin root of the word, a *scrinium* or box of papers where the secret wisdom of the sacred muse may be found.

What the modern reader or the lexicographer sees as a distortion of language is in fact an impulse to perfect it. Like the action as a whole, individual words are allegorical; they contain hidden meaning or implied metaphors. It has frequently been said that Spenser's language suits the poem—a fancy language for a fanciful world. This should at least be supplemented: a more fully significant language for a more fully significant world.

No word even so perfected is ever quite adequate to the idea, however, for words according to Plato are ultimately a kind of image. An image can never be a perfect reproduction, for if it were, it would not be an image at all but the very thing; it would be not the word "horse" but the real horse itself. Such inevitable inadequacy of language might, it seems, lead to despair of ever successfully expressing the truth. In the *Seventh Epistle*[14] Plato vehemently disavows a pupil precisely for trying to state first principles, ultimate realities, explicitly. Yet truth can be reached. It is reached through indirection, through the use of three separate but mutually complementary instruments: the word, the definition, and the image. Each of these suggests different aspects of the truth. By the continual, energetic comparison of the three, the soul rises to a comprehension of the thing itself. The three are constantly rubbed together, so to speak, and the friction ignites and illuminates the soul.

In poetry the definition is dramatized either literally or symbolically by the action. The meaning of "Agamemnon" in the view of classical and Renaissance commentators, is implicit in the etymology, but it is fully disclosed only in the action of the *Iliad*. The reader discovers the meaning of the name by analyzing the action of the poem. Homer, with the aid of divine inspiration, originally discovered the proper name, or the true meaning of the given name, by analyzing the conduct of his character in life. Since the heroes of *The Faerie Queene* are not types but concepts and universals, their proper names must be discovered in the conduct of life as a whole. The author, if a true poet-dialectician, was inspired to direct intuition of the concept, only adumbrated in life. He then invented the proper name, a personification, and a symbolic action through which it is fully revealed.

The action of Spenser's heroes in *The Faerie Queene* continually unfolds an "etymological" rationale, the secret wit of reality which his language is devised to disclose. Nothing, therefore, could be more misleading than the opinion that Spenser's language is negligible in our reading of the poem. In fact "etymological" associations of language are a constant guide to the implicit meaning of the poem and form the very principle of its organization. From the beginning, the poem evolves according to such a rationale: for example, in the action of Book I, a *hero* inspired by *eros* (these terms are explicitly connected in the *Cratylus*, 398 D and make up a traditional "etymology") rides forth as a knight *errant*. His first adventure as a knight errant is, naturally, an encounter with Errour: he defeats her but then proceeds to err through eros, the misplaced affections of his "heroicke" heart.[15] So misled, he goes to the house of Pride from which he emerges safely, only to err again in the *arrogance* of Orgoglio, the presumptuous spirit, the *airs* of man. He is then redeemed from Orgoglio by *Arthur,* the *ardor* and the *art* or efficacy of grace. Yet again he almost errs in *despair* before he is led to the house of Holiness by *Una* where he is restored to *wholeness* and the whole of *holiness* is symbolically revealed.

The action thus proceeds by a series of etymological puns, yet their presence is frequently unobtrusive; the wit appears to us as a secret wit. At the opening of the poem when the knight, his lady, and the dwarf enter the "covert" to find shelter from the storm, we enter into their vision of things. The traditional catalogue of trees becomes a dramatic record of enthrallment, the process of being "led with delight" and so beguiled. The trees, clad with summer's "pride," conceal "heavens light" and the guiding star: what is simply "farre" seems "faire." We are warned by Una that "This is the wandring wood, this *Errours den*," and the double meaning of "knots" and "boughtes" (bouts) anticipate the implication of the knight's encounter with this tortuous beast. Yet the climactic pun drawing so deeply upon the very wit of the language itself takes us by surprise: "God helpe the man so wrapt in *Errours* endlesse *traine*."

With the killing of Errour the knight's first encounter is complete. He proves that he is not in this sense an errant knight: he is not subject to a form of error which, as the language re-asserts again and again, can be made "plaine." He proves worthy of the "Armorie" which first won his heroic heart.

The action then proceeds to show that the knight is "errant," however, in another sense made fully clear when the word is at last used in Fradubio's speech: he is subject to Duessa or duplicity. "The author then (said he) of all my smarts, / Is one *Duessa* a false sorceresse, / That many errant knights hath brought to wretchednesse" (I. ii. 34. 7-9). "*Duessa*" is, of course, associated with *duo*, two to suggest her doubleness or deceit but also with Greek *dus-*, bad, ill and *duē*, misery to suggest the wretchedness she brings.

The Red Cross Knight is parted from Una, the one truth, by Archimago, the arch magician, and can be because "*Archimago*" in his "Hermitage" is the architect of images, of delusive likenesses. Archimago sends to "*Morpheus*," the former or fashioner, for a "diverse" or, etymologically, misleading dream, subtler and more seductive than the "diverse doubt" of Errour because the threat then made "plaine" now becomes an ambiguous "plaint." The "doubtfull words" of the dreamlady make the "redoubted knight / Suspect her truth." Yet "since no' untruth he knew," he is not seduced but interprets her appeal in an honorable way. Sheer ambiguity can not destroy him because if the evil is truly ambiguous, the interpreter must ascertain or supply it, and the knight as "redoubted," reverent as well as revered, has no such evil in him to supply. Archimago must create a definite false illusion of Una as unfaithful which exploits the knight's virtue, his love of her. Una and the Red Cross are thus divided into "double parts" or separated through duplicity and Una left "wandring," the end of Archimago's "drift," leaving the Red Cross to Duessa's wiles.

The nature of the Red Cross Knight's susceptibility is then further dramatized by the difference between Duessa and Sans Foy. The Red Cross defeats Sans Foy; it is not a complete loss of faith on his part which is leading him astray. But he errs, he falls prey to Duessa as Fidessa, a superficially perfect semblance of faith, through his impulse to love, the "heroicke" character of his stout heart. His love for Duessa is certainly a crude bedazzlement revealed in the way he looks her up and down, and in respect to him she is "*Fidessa*" or little faith, but it is significant that his faith is not lost primarily but misplaced: he always believes but he may misbelieve.

The analysis of error which began in the "wandring wood" is completed in the encounter with Fradubio, metamorphosed into a tree or an instance of error in its more refined and significant sense. In the symbolic plant the meaning of the action which began with the earlier "plaints" is "plast in open plaines" (I. ii. 32. 9; 33. 6) and made explicit. Fradubio like the Red Cross was overcome not by doubt per se but by guile, the guile to which doubt as an indeterminate state of mind makes him prey. When he tried to judge between his lady and Duessa, "the doubtfull ballaunce" swayed equally; doubt itself determines in no way. So Duessa intervened with an act of misrepresentation, obscuring his lady in a fog. Fradubio suggests *dubius*, doubting, and reflects its dangers; more specifically, though, he is the victim of "fraud" (I. iv. 1. 3), the active evil to which the uncommitted state of doubt makes him vulnerable.

The Red Cross Knight misled by Archimago's Duessa next appears at the house of Pride, implicitly the palace of hypocrisy, as playfully derived from *Hyper chrysos*, covered over with gold.[16]

> A stately Pallace built of squared bricke,
> Which cunningly was without morter laid,
> Whose wals were high, but nothing strong, nor thick,
> And golden foile all over them displaid,
> That purest skye with brightnesse they dismaid.
>
> I. iv. 4

It is a house, as the *Bible* suggests, not on the strait but the broad way and built on sand, but it is "painted cunningly." The porter *"Malvenu,"* a parody of *bienvenu* or welcome, greets them, prefiguring the evil that will come. Then *"Lucifera"* appears, the bringer of light who like Phaeton proudly burns and bedazzles with light intended "fairely for to shyne" or *phaēthōn* (I. iv. 9. 9).

In the pageant of the Seven Deadly Sins which follows Spenser's wit is comically farfetched in keeping with the gaudy cartoon quality of the parade. The first sin *"Idlenesse,"* dressed like a monk in "habit blacke, and amis thin," which may by some extravagant puns suggest the poet's condemnation, carries his "Portesse," but unfortunately the prayer book is only a "portesse" only carried and rarely read. Certainly the "wayne" is poorly led with such a vacuous and inattentive fellow guiding its "way." Idlenesse "esloynes" himself and challenges "essoyne" "from worldly cares," (*soins* in French); the legal terms suggest his Jesuitical invocation of the letter of the law to free him ironically for "lawlesse riotise."

Gluttony follows with the long fine neck of a crane; "gluttony" in Latin is derived from *glutire*, to swallow. He is depicted as Silenus the satyr (*satur*, full); his drunken "corse" reflects the course he leads. Lechery, who appears on the traditional goat, *caper*, is true to that depiction, capricious; his "whally" eyes, white or wall eyes, are the goat's eye or *oeil de chèvre* in French.[17]

Envy is presented primarily as a vile mouth, stressed by the rare form "chaw" for jaw to reiterate his endless malicious and mordant backbiting. His gown of satin as "discolourd say" seems to pun on the vicious things he says; the snake he carries in his bosom "implyes" his mortal sting. Envy's gown "ypainted full of eyes" reflects the root meaning of envy in Latin, *invidia,* the evil eye. He eyes all with hatred but particularly looks at his precursor "Covetyse" or avarice with covet eyes, reflecting their close connection.

Wrath is depicted through associations in English as rash or rathe; his is a *"hasty* rage." And when Satan tries to drive this "laesie teme" of evils, Idleness is called *"Slowth,"* spelled as if derived from "slow."

The pride of the Red Cross Knight is mettle, spirit and courage (I. x. 66. 7), zeal, not the pride of this house. As the inhabitants go forth to sport, he estranges himself from their "joyaunce vaine" and therefore encounters Sans Joy. By the defeat of Sans Joy he reveals that it is only vain joy, proud and empty pleasure that he is estranged from, however; though his "cheere" seems initially "too solemne sad," his solemnity is not a puritanical joylessness but reverence.

The Red Cross Knight's Dwarf discovers those who have "mortgaged" (I. v. 46. 4) their lives or literally pledged their lives to death through pride and warns his master who escapes. The Dwarf, who is always the "wary" dwarf, the "carefull" dwarf, seems—in part through association with the archaic term "dwere," meaning doubt or dread—to symbolize not common sense as critics have believed but the fear implicit in the reverence of holiness. His first speech of warning epitomizes his nature: "Fly fly (quoth then / The fearefull Dwarfe:) this is no place for living men." (I. i. 13. 8-9).

The Red Cross escapes the house of Pride only to encounter pride in another form, Orgoglio. According to mythographers pride is derived from heaven and earth, *ex aethere et terra,* but Spenser corrects this through a series of puns to suggest that pride as symbolized by Orgoglio is not from heaven and earth but merely from earth and air. As a "Geant" Orgoglio is born of *Gea,* the earth, but his "boasted sire" is "blustring Aeolus" from *aella,* stormy wind, and *aiolos,* shifting, changeable. Pride is man's earthliness blown up by the vicissitudes of his mortal circumstance. Aeolus "secretly inspired" the earth with "stormy yre," a form which suggests both ire and air, creating Orgoglio. Orgoglio takes "arrogant delight," again with a suggestion of air, in his "high descent," but such descent suggests not true divinity but rather how far he has fallen. Orgoglio thus suggests Greek *orgaein*, to swell, to teem, and *orgē*, temperament, wrath, passion, as well as the Italian *orgoglio*, pride.

This association of Orgoglio with air apparently alludes to the Prince of the Power of the Air in *Ephesians*, chapter II, and explains why an encounter with Orgoglio succeeds the Red Cross Knight's rejection of the house of Pride. In *Ephesians* Paul recalls that all men once followed

> the course of this world, according to the Prince of the Power of the Air, the spirit that now worketh in the children of disobedience: Among whom also we all had our conversation in times past in the lusts of our flesh, fulfilling the desires of the flesh and of the mind; and were by nature the children of wrath, even as others. But God, who is rich in mercy, for his great love wherewith he loved us, even when we were dead in sins, hath quickened us together with Christ. . . . For by grace are ye saved through faith; and that not of yourselves: It is the gift of God: Not of works, lest any man should boast. (Authorized Version. The earlier translations contain the same key phrases.)

When he leaves the house of Pride, the Red Cross Knight, wearied by the ordeal, disarms and sits down to rest by a fountain; he thus puts off the armor of faith, to which Spenser in the prefatory letter ascribes all his success, and fails to stand, according to the teaching of *Ephesians* (chapter VI, verses 10 ff.), having done all in the whole armor of God. Instead, like the natural man or the child of wrath in *Ephesians*, he indulges the desires of the flesh and the mind by bathing in the pleasure of the shade, listening to the music of the birds, and taking solace with his lady. He drinks from the fountain, the antithesis of the well of life which is later to renew him in his battle with the dragon, for this makes all who drink from it feeble and faint. It comes from a nymph who "tyr'd with heat of scorching ayre" like the knight sat down in the midst of her race, making the goddess Diana "wroth." So disarmed, the knight encounters Orgoglio. The monster, boasting of his high descent and matchless might, symbolizes the knight's pride and the divine wrath such pride arouses: the pride of indulging himself in the confidence of his achievement. Duessa in-

tercedes with Orgoglio begging him not to destroy her knight but to
make him an "eternal bondslave," the thrall of pride in works, especially works as a sign of "high descent," of election. And he is so
enthralled, erring in the arrogance of the Prince of the Power of the
Air, until he is redeemed by grace.

The Red Cross is redeemed from the wrath of Orgoglio by Arthur,
symbol of the ardor and art of God's grace. Arthur represents not the
magnanimity of God, his potentiality or etymologically his great spirit,
but his magnificence, his actuality or etymologically his doing great
deeds. Arthur's image and geneology are resplendent with the glory
of such greatness. He appears with a headpiece like an almond tree on
the top of "greene *Selinis*"; "*Selinis*" in Greek resembles *selinon,* the
plant from which the chaplets of victors in the ancient games were
made; Virgil calls its "palmosa Selinus" (*Aeneid* III. 705).

A comparison of Spenser's image of Arthur with Marlowe's adaptation in *Tamburlaine* reveals how carefully Spenser's language maintains the suggestions of the almond tree and transfers them to his hero.

> Upon the top of all his *loftie crest,*
> A bunch of haires discolourd diversly,
> With sprincled pearle, and gold full richly drest,
> Did shake, and seem'd to daunce for jollity,
> Like to an Almond tree ymounted hye
> On top of greene *Selinis* all alone,
> With blossomes brave bedecked daintily;
> Whose tender *locks* do tremble every one
> At every little *breath*, that under heaven is *blowne*.
>
> I. vii. 32

> I'll ride in golden armour like the sun;
> And in my *helm* a triple *plume* shall spring,
> Spangled with diamonds, dancing in the air,
> To note me emperor of the three-fold world;
> Like to an almond tree ymounted high
> Upon the lofty and celestial mount
> Of ever green Selinis, quaintly decked
> With bloom more white than Herycina's brows,
> Whose tender *blossoms* tremble every one
> At every little breath that thorough heaven is blown.
>
> Tam. 4092-4101 (Pt. II, IV, iii, 115-24)

In both passages there is a personification; the hero is compared to the personified almond tree. But in Marlowe the personification is incidental while in Spenser it is so radical and persistent that the language seems continuously symbolic of the hero. Instead of "helm" Spenser uses "crest" which suggests not only the plume on the helmet but an identifying insignia, as if the crest were Arthur's sign; "crest" also suggests the summit of a mountain, anticipating the comparison and so suggesting that the almond on Selinis is the sign. Yet because this is merely suggested the tree on the mountain remains natural, free, and alive.

Applied to the ambivalent "crest," Spenser's "loftie" exercises more of its ethical implication than in the Marlowe passage when applied to the more literal "mount." "Haires" in place of "plume" helps to personify the crest; "drest" applies more readily than "spangled" to a person in the sense clothed, to hair in the sense combed, and to the plume in the sense adorned. The line could even be a description of the person instead of the plume. The phrase "for jollity" makes sure that "daunce" keeps its literal as well as its transferred meaning, while in Marlowe's phrase "dancing in the air" the personification is almost dead. Even "daintily" with its association of gentleness seems more human than Marlowe's "quaintly."

The suggestions are further carried out by the term "brave" which in contrast to the phrase "more white than Herycina's brows," suggests the courage as well as the esthetic splendor of the glory implied. "Locks" instead of "blossoms" suggests tufts of hair as well as foliage, maintaining the personification and implying that Arthur himself as the succourer trembles in sympathy at every breath blown. The idea is not clearly controlled in Marlowe's lines; it would certainly be inappropriate for Tamburlaine, yet without it this part of the comparison seems pointless. In Spenser's stanza there is even a slight metaphoric play in the phrase "all alone" between "by itself" and "the only one" which underlines Arthur's pre-eminence and makes an obtrusive explicating phrase like Marlowe's "to note me emperor of the three-fold world" totally unnecessary. We notice, incidentally, that Spenser's Selinis is not "celestial," and his almond tree trembles at every breath blown "under" not "thorough" heaven. Though the almond tree is "ymounted hye" on the mount, it is in this world. Arthur is the highest man and one alone, God's vice-regent, but he is not God.

After his victory Arthur explains to Una and the Red Cross that he was raised by "Timon" or in Greek honor, worth, and he is accom-

panied by "Timias," his squire, "th'admirer of his might," who is similarly derived. He was raised "Under the foot of *Rauran* mossy hore,
/ From whence the river *Dee* as silver cleene / His tombling billowes
rolls with gentle rore" (I. ix. 4.6 ff). The river Dee suggests his divine origin; this is the explicit etymology of the river in the marriage
catalogue of Book IV: "Dee, which Britons long ygone / Did call divine . . ." (IV. xi. 3,4). (The Rauran seems so named because it is
where the Dee gently "rores." Arthur's shield is made of "diamond,"
suggesting its function of representing God in the world.[18] It was
made by the great magician Merlin, the antithesis of Archimago, who
created the shield to expose everything false. Merlin, too, seems related to honor and wonder through Latin *mirus* by virtue of his "admirable deedes." Arthur's sword was made by Merlin from metal
mixed with "Medaewart" or meadwort, so spelled suggesting that it
wards off cunning and magic, *mēdea* in Greek: it is so made "that no
enchauntment from his dint might save." (II. viii. 20. 6).

When Arthur appears to save the Red Cross Knight, the poet pro-
claims the "goodly golden chaine" by which the virtues are linked in
love, and each hero aids the other. This chain is literally "concord,"
the cord that ties all things together (cf. III. i. 12. 8) through *con* and
cor, the uniting of the heroes' hearts.

Arthur departs in search of the Faerie Queene whom he discovered
in the revelation of a dream, the antithesis of the Red Cross Knight's
dream delusion contrived by Archimago in canto one. The Red Cross
and Una set off and are soon accosted by a knight fleeing a ghastly
sight, the sight, we soon learn, of Despair. The knight Trevisan with
his head disarmed and a rope about his neck approaches looking back
continually in fear. His steed flies with winged heels "As he had beene
a fole of *Pegasus* his kind."

The myth of Pegasus and Bellerophon, according to mythographers,
signifies the importance of neither exulting too much in good fortune,
nor sorrowing too much in adversity since God is the governor of all.
Bellerophon, over-elated by his success, decided to fly to the sun on his
horse, Pegasus, but he was struck down for such pride by Jupiter and
so taught the true limits and proper temperament of man. Both "Trevisan" and his companion "Terwin" reflect the topsy-turvy fate and
temperament of Bellerophon in his fall. "Trevisan," however, sees
(*viso*) and escapes.

God brought such a disaster upon Bellerophon, according to mythographers, to reveal his true source and sustainer. As the poet asserts

in the opening stanza of the next canto, "all the good is Gods, both power and eke will." But God is good, as his name itself implies, and he is merciful to man. The "fole" (I. ix. 21. 9) or foal of Pegasus, and his rider, is also a fool thus in his "foltring" (ix. 24. 9) terror of despair.

Pegasus is traditionally the symbol of poetry; the tradition is germane to the depiction of Despair, for his victim Terwin is a victim of Petrarchan despair in love, so closely associated with poetry, and, more important, Despair's appeal is through the power of rhetoric. The Red Cross Knight is nearly overwhelmed by the poetry of Despair, almost charmed by the "inchaunted" rhyme of the "Miscreant," the unbeliever who miscreates or distorts his argument, evoking doom by the omission of God's grace, insisting that the knight will eternally err: "For he, that once hath missed the right way, / The further he doth goe, the further he doth stray." Even the knight's response is the traditional literary one; he begins to "tremble like a leafe of Aspin greene" (the only use of this figure in the poem.)

Like most of the evils in Book I, Despair is associated with division and doubleness. The main accusation he brings is that the Red Cross was false to his faith and served "Duessa." The term first appears in Book I when Una is originally "from her knight divorced in despaire" (I. iii. 2. 8); she herself remains faithful, but she is "forsaken, wofull, solitarie" through his error, his displaced faith. Spenser seems to suggest that despair is the dis-spirited state which occurs when Una or the one truth of grace and the Red Cross Knight are divided or dispaired. At any rate it is Una who now rescues the Red Cross from the rhetoric of Despair, calling him away from vain words and "the accurst hand-writing" of God's justice to action and grace.

The knight then proceeds to the house of Holiness where the whole of holiness is symbolized. In this house he is taught repentence and the way to "heavenly blesse," according to the argument of the canto. The spelling distinguishes "blesse" from "blisse," though the two were often identified in Elizabethan English and come ultimately from the same etymological source. The Bower of Bliss thus lies in contrast to the house of Holiness as the house of Unblessed Bliss, an ironic *Eden* or garden of pleasure in Hebrew. The excess of "*Acrasia*" which we see there is implicitly contrasted with the abundance of "*Charissa*." "*Acrasia*" is presented in Book II as a perversion of *charis* or true grace; she "depastures" delight, a term Spenser coined, as the ironic pastor in her bower who takes life rather than nourishing it, destroying her worshippers.

In the house of Holiness Saint George at last gains his name and full identity as his sainthood is foreseen. He learns that he like Arthur is a changeling. Arthur was taken from his mother and delivered to the faery knight "old Timon" thus, it seems, being taught by time, as Achilles was taught by Cheiron, son of Chronos. Saint George, however, was found where a faerie left him in the furrow of a field.

> Thence she thee brought into this Faerie lond,
> And in an heaped furrow did thee hyde,
> Where thee a Ploughman all unweeting fond,
> As he his toylesome teme that way did guyde,
> And brought thee up in ploughmans state to byde,
> Whereof *Georgos* he thee gave to name;
> Till prikt with courage, and thy forces pryde,
> To Faery court thou cam'st to seeke for fame,
> And prove thy puissaunt armes, as seemes thee best became.
>
> I. x. 76

"*Georgos*" is derived from the Greek term for plowman as "Adam" was derived from the Hebrew term for earth. The etymology suggests their ultimate affinity in the moral allegory. It suggests, too, in retrospect that the earthly giant "*Orgoglio*" is George himself, inspired or blown up with the air of arrogance to which every man in his weakness may succumb.

The etymology of St. George functions also in a very different way: it presents an allusion to English literary history and the career of "holiness" as a topic for poetry. The truth of holiness was lost but then "fond" or found again as invention, matter for poetry in *Piers Plowman,* substantiating the traditional name of the English saint as "ploughman" or man of the soil. Spenser eventually returns the topic to the simple, rural world through the career of "grace" in the poem. "Of Court it seemes, men Courtesie doe call" (VI. i. 1), but Spenser eventually corrects this to show that the court is the source of false courtesy, of "courting;" true "courtesy" is a form of "grace" which thrives best not at court but in the pastoral milieu, or pastoral ideal, of Book VI.

Spenser's secret wit suggests not only the moral implication of the action but political and social instances which substantiate and exem-

plify. A most vivid instance occurs in Guyon's encounter with Phaedria, Book II, canto vi; a series of puns associates her with Italy and
the Italian way of life during the Renaissance. Phaedria's boat is
called a "little Gondelay" and a "little frigot." Both terms had been
introduced into English not long before from the Italian. With his
use of them in the Phaedria passage Spenser seems to be punning in
Italian: "gondola" suggests the Italian term *gongolare*, "to laugh till
ones heart be sore or shoulders ake, to shuckle and be full of joy, or
excessive gladnesse"; "frigot" suggests *frigotare*, "to shuckle, to shrug,
or strut for overjoy." These puns are reinforced by the epithets of her
"shallow ship," "painted bote" (false good), and "flit barke," (meaning airy, insubstantial, as well as swift.) The puns become an allusion to Italy through the meaning of "gondola" which Florio defines
as "a little boat or whirry used no where but a bout and in Venice."[19]

Other references suggest the allusion. In repudiating war, Phaedria
refers to the kind of skirmishes she prefers as "scarmoges." This spelling instead of the usual "skirmish" (IV. ix. 20. 2) associates the term
with Italian *scaramuccia*, the name of Harlequin's companion with
his buffoonish battles in the Italian farce. Phaedria locates her world
"In this wide Inland sea, that hight by name / *The Idle Lake*";
"Inland sea" is a translation of "Mediterranean"; the "*Idle Lake*" is
apparently the Adriatic, which Spenser associates with *adraneia*, inactivity. She lives on an idyllic island suggesting Venice, to the Renaissance Englishman the very land of Venus. The 1590 edition of
The Faerie Queene even carried a proverbial allusion to the pope:
"Sometimes she sung, as loud as lark in aire, / Sometimes she laught,
as merry as Pope Jone." The song she sings is the magnificent perversion of the Biblical "Behold the lilies of the field, they toil not neither
do they spin."

Through such puns the Phaedria incident forms an elaborate commentary on the Italian way of life during the Renaissance and a criticism of the young Englishman's practice of sowing his wild oats there
and affecting the Italianate style. Spenser finds reflected in Italy the
prototype of inane mirth and shallow epicureanism; in the virtual
enclosure of the Mediterranean Sea he finds a symbol of stagnation
and idleness.

Phaedria entertains her companions with stories like those of the
joke-books, the thesauri of merry tales which flourished in the period,
many from Italy, offering crude tales without any formal elegance:
". . . And greatly joyed merry tales to faine, / Of which a store-house

did with her remaine, / Yet seemed, nothing well they her became; / For all her words she drownd with laughter vaine, / And wanted grace in utt'ring of the same. . . ." (II. vi. 6). Part of Spenser's ambition to "overgo" Ariosto was a desire to prevent the epic from descending to this level.

In the Bower of Bliss Spenser continues such allusions but also turns to the goals of the Elizabethan Merchant Adventurers, the ports they sought in ships like the "Delight," the "Desire," and the "Castle of Comfort" as they sailed for the expected sweet life of the West Indies. The "wandring Islands" recall Cuba and La Dominica, called the wandering islands because they wandered all over the map in Spain and Portugal's dispute over their location and thus ownership. "Verdant" may recall Cape Verde; the Bower of Bliss itself suggests Deseado or Port Desire and more generally Florida. It is "goodly beautifide / With all the ornaments of *Floraes* pride, / Wherewith her mother Art, as halfe in scorne / Of niggard Nature . . . did decke her." The art that Spenser refers to would include the art of the voyagers in their hyperbolic accounts which "too lavishly adorne" with wealth and fertility the nature they actually encountered.

The journey to the Bower of Bliss reveals the financial disasters which resulted from adventuring in the hope of perfect pleasure. The most vivid depiction is in *"The Rocke of vile Reproch,"* a dramatization of bankruptcy as the bank on which men break. The rock hovers over its potential victims "Threatning it selfe on them to ruinate"; one sees on its "sharpe clifts the ribs of vessels broke" and the "carkasses exanimate / Of such, as having all their substance spent / In wanton joyes, and lustes intemperate, / Did afterwards make shipwracke violent, / Both of their life, and fame for ever fowly blent." The greedy "Cormoyrants" or moneylenders and "birds of ravenous race" wait there for the "spoyle of wretches," that is, their ruin and so the confiscation of their goods "After lost credite and consumed thrift, / At last them driven hath to this despairefull drift." "Credit" had just recently acquired its specifically commercial sense in addition to the more general moral one, and "thrift," too, contains a comparable ambiguity. *"The Rocke of vile Reproch"* is the counterpart of Homer's Scylla, etymologized to *skyleuein*, to strip, to spoil. The Gulf of Greediness opposite corresponds to Charybdis (*charis hybris*) which Cicero, for example, uses as a metaphor for prodigality in attacking Antony (*Phillipics* II. xxvii. 67).

"The wandring Islands," the counterpart of Homer's Wandering

Rocks, in respect to the commercial and social world etymologically suggest the vagabonds and vagrants, travesties of the knight errant, whose devices Robert Greene was soon to expose. Pictured as "wandring Islands" "seeming now and than" like the classical Delos, which Spenser etymologizes traditionally to *dēlos,* apparent because the islands simply appeared out of nowhere, their seemingly fair and fruitful grounds are seductive but unsure. When Phaedria re-appears on a "wandring Island" with her little boat beside her, the boat is called a "skippet" meaning basket, a nonce usage by Spenser here (N. E. D.), suggesting perhaps the baudy baskets exposed by Greene's precursor Thomas Harman in his *A Caveat or Warening for Common Cursetors, Vulgarely Called Vagabones* (chapter xvi). The basket was a device of Elizabethan prostitutes who first presented themselves as pedlars of notions before they exposed their baudy purposes. Certainly Phaedria at her reappearance is more crudely and clearly just such a wayside prostitute. Spenser's term "skippet" resembling "skipper" and "skiff" accommodates her very nicely to the maritime setting and resembling "skip" implies the frivolity and the insecurity of her mode of travel, her way of life.

It may even seem as if Spenser in calling Acrasia's victim *"Verdant"* was alluding to Greene himself whose demise he thereby predicts and attempts to prevent. Greene at any rate gained a witty benefit from his degradation by moralizing on himself with such a pun in the last stanza of his poem of repentance: "My wretched end may warn *Greene springing youth* / To use delights, as toyes that will deceive / And scorne the world before the world them leaves: / For all worlds trust, is ruine without ruth."[20]

But the development which emerges most strongly moves in the direction of amplifying symbolic implication rather than pursuing social allusions in detail. Like *"Mordant"* (or *"Mortdant"* II. i. 49. 9) his counterpart, *"Verdant,"* the flourishing young man whose spirit Acrasia "depastures," must receive what he gives, though in his case the outcome is happily reversed. Acrasia with her curse enacting *"Mortdant"* gives "death to him that death does give,"[21] the Palmer, through his "counsel sage" enacting *"Verdant"* gives truth to him that truth does give or instructs the victim in the true harm of Acrasia which he depicts and so frees him from her.

The language of the voyage projects a world of the moral imagination above the social scene to which it simply dips in specific allusion with an occasional detail of incident, image, or term. The sea-beasts encountered by Guyon and the Palmer are not the conies and quail of the Elizabethan underworld or their sea counterparts, nor even sea-lions and sea-foxes but the most fantastic monsters imaginable. The catalogue begins by literary allusion: a battle with the "many headed hydra" is Plato's symbol in Book IV of the *Republic* (426 e) for the futility of attempting to legislate the end of fraud instead of converting the spirit of man, since without such a change of spirit new forms of fraud like the heads of a hydra will continually spring forth. The scolopendra, it was thought, "feeling himselfe taken with a hooke, casteth out his bowels, untill he hath unloosed the hooke, and then swalloweth them up againe,"[22] which perhaps resembles certain specific devices of the sharper. But what the chosen epithets depict is images of evil monstrously general. The hazards of the course are immense and indefinable except as threat, the "Ziffius" or swordfish, for example, and its consequence, the morse, which Spenser derives from the Latin *mors* to mean death.

This is the advantage of Spenser's secret wit. He may suggest implications at every possible level of experience without disrupting the symbolic unity and continuity of the moral world. The operation of his style was perfectly described by Spenser's first critic, Kenelm Digby, in a letter of appreciation addressed to Henry May, 1638:

> Spencer in what he sayth hath a way of expression peculiar to himselfe; he bringeth downe the highest and deepest mysteries that are contained in humane learning, to an easie and gentle forme of delivery; wch. sheweth he is Master of what he treat-eth of; he can wield it as he pleaseth: And he hath done this so cunningly, that if one heede him not wth. great attention, rare and wonderful conceptions will unperceived slide by him that readeth his workes, and he will thinke he hath mett wth. nothing but familiar and easie discourses: But lett one dwell a while upon them, and he shall feele a strange fulness and roundness in all he sayth.[23]

The Faerie Queene has disappointed the modern reader, for in an age that admires the difficult and complex it seems "familiar and easy." But, as Kenelm Digby testifies, it offers "rare and wonderful conceptions" to the attentive reader who does not let them slide by. To discover their fullness the reader must heed the language closely, however. The language must be savored for the cunning within its gentleness and ease.

NOTES

1. B. E. C. Davis, *Edmund Spenser: A Critical Study* (Cambridge, 1933), p. 155. "His diction is decorative rather than composite or associative, differing from Milton's as the music of Schubert from that of Bach, appealing through spontaneity and inherent suggestiveness, independent of source or application. It is the surface lustre that has made Spenser the poet's poet."

2. C. S. Lewis, "Edmund Spenser, 1552-99," *Studies in Medieval and Renaissance Literature* (Cambridge, 1966), p. 143.

3. W. L. Renwick, *Edmund Spenser, An Essay on Renaissance Poetry*, (London, 1925). The book was preceded by two articles, "The Critical Origins of Spenser's Diction," *MLR*, XVII (1922), 1-16; "Mulcaster and DuBellay," *MLR*, XVII (1922), 282-7.

4. Bruce R. McElderry, Jr., "Archaism and Innovation in Spenser's Poetic Diction," *PMLA*, XLVII (1932), 144-70, concludes that the number of archaisms and innovations in Spenser's poetry has been greatly overestimated. Yet the list according to McElderry's criteria, in turn, tends to be too inclusive: he regards "keen" in the sense of "sharp" as an archaism, for example (p. 151). What strikes the reader most vividly about McElderry's list is the number of terms that seem to be simple substitutions for terms current in Spenser's day: "allege" for "allay," "blend" for "blind," "eath" for "easy," "forthy" for "therefore." Other terms, like "yfere" for "together," are more formally distinct, yet they still do not seem needed to fill a gap in the Elizabethan vocabulary. There are very few archaisms and innovations with sufficiently distinctive connotation to "enrich the language" as the modern reader understands that phrase.

5. Richard Mulcaster, Spenser's master at the Merchant Taylors' School, cites the *Cratylus* in the peroration to the first part of his *Elementarie*, 1582, proving the existence and importance of "right names" (ed. E. T. Campagnac, Oxford, 1925, p. 188), and Richard Wills, commonly regarded as the Willye of Spenser's *Shepheardes Calendar*, in his *De Re Poetica*, 1573, gives a nearly verbatim rendering of a passage from Marsilio Ficino's introduction to the dialogue for his Latin edition of Plato (*De Re Poetica*, ed. A. D. S. Fowler, Oxford, Luttrell Society, 1958, p. 73). Interest in the *Cratylus* during the Renaissance seems to have been spurred by Peter Ramus (Pierre de la Ramée). He first cites the *Cratylus* in his *Dialecticae Institutiones* (Paris, 1543). The reference is dropped from the text of the famous *Dialecticae Libri Duo* (Paris, 1556) but returns and is greatly elaborated in the commentaries of Ramus' editors, in the edition of Beur-

husius, for example, printed at London in 1581, or in Abraham Fraunce, *Lawier's Logike* (London, 1588).

6. Marsilio Ficino, "In Cratylum," *Opera Omnia* (Torino, 1959, a reproduction of the *Opera Omnia*, Basilea, 1576), II, i, p. 1311, translated by the author. Compare Richard Wills, p. 73:

> So Plato, when he inquires in *Cratylus* who are learned in the true names of things, with good reason ridicules the sophists, and judges it necessary to go to the poets—not indiscriminately to all of them, but to such as are divine; as if they had learned the true names of things from the gods.

7. Abraham Fraunce, for example, makes this clear in *Lawier's Logike*, I, i, p. 4.

> Whatsoever it bee, nay whatsoever thou canst imagine to bee, although it bee not, never was, nor never shall bee, yet by reason it is invented, taught, ordered, confirmed: as the description of fame in Virgil, of famine in Ovid, of Elysian fields, of Styx, of Acheron, of the golden apples, and a thousand such poeticall imaginations. And therefore Logike hath beene of a loong time untollerably abused by those miserable Sorbonists, & dunsicall Quidditaries, who thought there was no reasoning without Arguitur quod sic; Probatur quod non: no part of Logike without Ergo and Igitur. Whereas indeede the true use of Logike is as well apparent in simple playne, and easie explication, as in subtile, strict, and concised probation. Reade Homer, reade Demosthenes, reade Virgill, read Cicero, reade Bartas, reade Torquato Tasso, reade that most worthie ornament of our English tongue, the Countesse of Pembrooke's *Arcadia,* and therein see the true effectes of natural logike which is the ground of artificiall, farre different from this rude and barbarous kind of outworne sophistrie: which if it had anie use at all, yet this was all, to feede the vaine humors of some curious heades in obscure schooles, whereas the Art of reasoning hath somewhat to doe in everiething, and nothyng is anything without this one thing. Some Artes are appliable onely to some certayne subject, but Logike is scientia scientiarum, as I sayd before, not tyed to one thing, but apt for aniething, free from all, yet fit for all, framing orderly, proving strongely, expounding playnly, perswading forcibly, any Arte, any cause, any question, any man whatsoever.

Present day commentators (for example, W. S. Howell, *Logic and Rhetoric in England,* 1500-1700, Princeton, 1956) tend to confuse

the Ramists' division between logic and rhetoric for purposes of exposition and instruction with a division in practice and in fact, or at
least they so stress the former that the fundamental identification of
logic and rhetoric is lost sight of.

8. In P. Rami, *Dialecticae Libros Duos*, ed. Fredericus Beurhusius
   (London: Henricus Bynneman, 1581), I, xxiv, p. 110, "Notatio est
   nominis interpretatio: nomina siquidem sunt notae rerum, nominum-
   que vel derivatorum, vel compositorum, si vera notatione fiant, ratio
   reddi potest ex aliquo argumento primo: ut, homo ab humo Ovid. 6.
   Fast."

9. Fraunce, I, xii, p. 57.

10. Fraunce, I, xii, p. 51. "Grammatica notatio exponit vocū adsignifica-
    tionē; Logica vero causam explicat, cur hoc nomen huic rei sit im-
    positū." "Nomina sunt argumenta, non quatenus ad rem significan-
    dam referuntur, sed quatenus referuntur vel inter se mutuo, ut
    coniugata: vel ad suae originis interpretationem, quae Notatio dicitur.
    Sed sic non considerantur ut nomina, id est symbola, sed ut res quę-
    dam, seu *onta* quędam. Piscator."

11. Ficino, "Inter haec ostendit Homeri poesim allegoricam esse, etiam
    ubi historiam narrare videtur, quemadmodum in nominibus allegorice
    fictis apparet. Refert autem multa apud Homerum heroum nomina
    certa allegoriae ratione composita."

12. Socrates points out that in the old form of the Greek language the
    terms for "spirits" and for "wise" or "knowing" were the same (*Craty-
    lus*, 398 B). Spenser invokes this etymology in his use of "Daemo-
    gorgon" in Book I: Night was begot in "Daemogorgons hall" where
    she "sawst the secrets of the world unmade" (I. v. 22). Spenser sees
    another etymological connection, however, to Greek *demein*, to build,
    which is also present here and elsewhere. In IV. ii. 47 Agape, to dis-
    cover the secret of her sons' fate, descends into the "fatall sisters
    house" where "*Demogorgon* in dull darkness pent, / Farre from the
    view of Gods and heavens bliss, / The hideous Chaos keepes, their
    dreadfull dwelling is."

13. It requires the whole of Book VI to reveal all the implications of
    "Calidore," derived from Greek *kalos*, beauty and *dōron*, gift. The
    most important aspect of Spenser's meaning is symbolized by the
    Graces on Mount Acidale who present their gift of beauty to the poet
    Colin Clout not when he wills but as they will, graciously. Courtesy
    like grace is a gift which the receiver in turn gives.

14. A Latin translation of Plato's epistles with commentary was brought
    out by Peter Ramus at Paris in 1549. The *Seventh Epistle* seems to
    contradict the *Cratylus* because in it words are considered arbitrary
    and conventional; Plato's authorship has even been questioned spe-
    cifically on these grounds. (Cf. Glenn R. Morrow, *Studies in the*

Platonic Epistles, University of Illinois Studies in Language and Literature, XXXII, No. xliii (1935) 69.) But the *Seventh Epistle* describes language as it is, not the ideal which the Renaissance Platonist found in the *Cratylus.*

15. The "heroicke" spirit is an erotic one, Amor and Mars natural companions, as the ambiguity of "courage" and "heart" in the poem confirms. This idea is first suggested in the proem to Book I but is most explicitly elaborated in the defense of love in the proem to Book IV.

> Which who so list looke backe to former ages,
> And call to count the things that then were donne,
> Shall find, that all the workes of those wise sages,
> And brave exploits which great Heroes wonne,
> In love were either ended or begunne:
> Witnesse the father of Philosophie,
> Which to his *Critias,* shaded oft from sunne,
> Of love full manie lessons did apply,
> The which these Stoicke censors cannot well deny.
>
>> IV. Proem. iii

The appearance of *"Critias"* suggests a comparable ambiguity. He is Socrates' chosen, a critic who is not a censour like the Stoics but a discerner, one for whom "philosophie" is the love of wisdom and the wisdom of love, the erotic heroism of the mind.

16. Fraunce, I, xii, p. 57, derives "Hypocrisis, of *hypo,*" (for *hyper,* it seems) "which is over, and *chrysos,* gold, because hypocrites bee cloaked with a golden shew overcast." He regards this as a "monkish" and ignorant definition, however, and gives the proper one as *hypokrinomai,* to dissemble.

17. Randle Cotgrave, *A Dictionarie of the French and English Tongues,* (London, 1611).

18. This word play on *deus* or *dieu,* god, and *mundus* or *monde,* earth, as an explanation for Spenser's deviation from his Ariostan source seems much more satisfactory than D. C. Allen's explanation in terms of the Christian symbolism of stones, "Arthur's Diamond Shield in *The Faerie Queene,*" *JEGP,* XXXVI (1937), 234-43. Allen's explanation for the change from carbuncle to diamond requires that Arthur be seen as a symbol not of grace but reverence, which hardly corresponds to the suggestions of the text.

19. John Florio, *Queen Anna's New World of Words* (London, 1611). (Not included in *A Worlde of Wordes,* 1598.)

20. Greene ends with a very practical moral: "Then blest are they that like the toyling Ant, / Provide in time gainst winters wofull want,"

Groats-worth of Witte, Bought with a Million of Repentance, (1592), the end.

21. R. H. Super, "Spenser's *Faerie Queene* II. i. 490-492," *The Explicator* XI (1953), 30.

22. Bollakar, *English Expositor* (1616), quoted in the *NED*. The idea is traditional from Aristotle, *History of Animals*, 519. 19.

23. As quoted in E. W. Bligh, *Sir Kenelm Digby and His Venetia* (London, 1932), p. 279.

ROSEMOND TUVE

The Medieval Heritage of Spenser's Allegory

It may be interesting and salutary at the outset to exemplify the kinds of relations Elizabethans had with early materials by following visible footsteps—those of some sixteenth-century writer who out-and-out borrowed from the materials and shows it indubitably. We also need a few distinctions and working definitions, merely to get started, although in general it is preferable for these to arise gradually from the materials. We are attempting, for instance, to discover, instead of impose, a definition of allegory (for literary pieces, of this time, and character). The number of words spent defining and delimiting allegory in this decade could never have been foretold two generations ago, and yet certain well-inculcated nineteenth-century assumptions about interpretation cloud the language of theory, and rebellions against them cloud the theory itself. It is well to let the mediaeval works do their own defining. Of the first trouble, the most persistent case is the Coleridgean definition of allegory (and symbol), born of nineteenth-century German critical theory, not mediaeval usage. Of the second trouble, the revolt, a leading instance is the faithful dependence upon the four senses, which in many modern writings are more dogmatically and perseveringly applied than we find them to be by mediaeval writers.

It is mere chance and luck, perhaps, but both clarification through

This essay, with the title "Problems and Definitions," is from *Allegorical Imagery* (Princeton, 1966), pp. 3-55. Reprinted by permission of the Princeton University Press. Copyright © 1966 by Princeton University Press.

an unquestionable case in point, and a few needful distinctions, can be achieved by a short look at a minor writer who made literary use —provable use—of almost every mediaeval "kind" here treated—Lodge. With his fondness for mediaeval materials (which we find duplicated in others but not so well attested by specific evidence), he will point to many kinds of questions and materials we will encounter; he will demonstrate connections without our needing to present evidence for the fact of dependence, for he flatly plunders mediaeval sources. Lodge is a quite sufficiently ordinary figure, and if he read and used the thirteenth-century *De oculi morali,* we need not worry over whether it was too recherché a book for ordinary sixteenth-century writers to read with interest. This simplifies the first presentation of questions.

The striking and well-known example, of course, is Lodge's remaking of the Middle English *Gamelyn* into that *Rosalynde* of 1590 to which we owe *As You Like It.* Manuscripts are generally so neglected as carriers of materials—textually and through illustrations—down into Elizabethan times, that it is right to remark that Lodge had to find *Gamelyn* in manuscript. However, since he probably thought it Chaucer's (the tale intended for the Cook), it would have an untypical eminence. This is scarcely true of some other mediaeval texts which Alice Walker showed Lodge to have used.[1] Both Thomas of Hibernia's fourteenth-century collection of sayings from the fathers, the *Manipulus florum,* and the thirteenth-century *De oculi morali* were common mediaeval books, but their commonness to a late sixteenth-century English author of no great pretensions to learning is not self-evident, and we would have hesitated to claim it as a likely thing. At any rate, Lodge used the *Manipulus* just as some mediaeval predecessor would have, or as Christine de Pisan did nearly two hundred years before him; and he makes neither a flourish nor a secret about using *De oculi.* He found, or could find, both in print.

Miss Walker mentioned two other printed sources of large portions of Lodge's *Catharos* (1591), which, when we examine them, turn out also to have been mediaeval inheritances. The first is a *Somme des Pechez* by the French Franciscan Jean Benedicti; it is an elaboration of so common a type of mediaeval book, one so fruitful for figurative treatment of the virtues, that we shall have to give a whole chapter (Two) to pursuing some of the many and beautifully illustrated forms taken by such *sommes.* The second is the *Dialogues of creatures moralised* which Lodge read evidently in the printed sixteenth-century English version (STC 6815, 1535?).

Since our interest is not so much in later authors' attitudes toward mediaeval materials as in their continued use of them and pleasure in them, we do not care very much whether Lodge realized that the *Dialogues* are an early-to-middle fourteenth-century compilation; he surely did not know that they are probably by a Milanese physician Mayno de' Mayneri.[2] Like so many books which remained accessible, this one represents a whole genre and is but one exemplar of a long roster of similar mediaeval books. We shall see that Elizabethan dependence is upon mediaeval books that were eminently typical, not singular, and not "ahead of their time." The "kind" here exemplified is the collection of moralized exempla. Since the 1100's it had flourished rankly, and Welter's whole detailed volume is needed for mere description of these vastly numerous texts. One thing that astonishes us in his footnotes and data is the frequency with which collections achieved early printings; these books are often hidden in that corner still rather dark to us—sixteenth-century Latin books that were read but did not become classics. The example everyone knows is the *Gesta Romanorum*. But until there is more investigation of the unlighted bridges between manuscript and book publication, we shall not be able to judge how much effect *early* translation into vernaculars, and a manuscript tradition of illustration, had to do with a mediaeval book's chances for extended life into the Renaissance. The *Dialogues* had the latter of these advantages, but its translation into three vernaculars may not antedate printing.

A striking point is that Lodge finds it worth borrowing from for its most "mediaeval" element—he copies the moralizations of the fables. The plan of the *Catharos* (to overdignify that catchall pamphlet) shows that he snatched the stories, amusing as some are, largely because he had use for the morals that follow each. He thus differs from the nineteenth-century revivers and readers who busied themselves with these collections and characteristically omitted or telescoped the "dull allegories" in favour of including all daily-life interest and story motifs. To the sixteenth-century borrower, universality or a usefulness independent of epoch resides precisely in the significancies. I suspect that this is typical. Where we brush off the didacticism or the figurative reading of tales and stress their interest as straight recording or anecdotal narrative, the didacticism was, without any self-consciousness or sense of historical alienness, just as interesting, to a Renaissance reader of old books.

The 122 fables, conveyed as the title says in *Dialogues of creatures*, are often good stories, and occasionally clever, but that is not what

makes this a gay book. The compiler has a turn for vigorous conversation and for the drama of a rhetorical situation, conveyed in tone,
gesture and unobtrusive incongruities. The squabbles he invents are
between such opponents as the Air and the Wind, the Seabanks and
the Sea, the Carbuncle and the Glass, the Ass and the Wolf, the
Dolphin and the Eel. The dialogue in each is followed by its "ditty,"
and this by its expectable, or more often its surprising, moral application or reading. Frequently, barefaced extravagances are presented
with comical decorum. The quality most often felt is a serious-faced
outrageousness, and one is convinced that the book had this from the
beginning, the "morals" so-called being meanwhile intended as quite
sensible, and readable by us as such. The book was, of course, to be
read in snippets, mined for anecdotes, used or read orally. It was
translated into Dutch and French as well as English; but some of the
Latin editions are the most attractive as books. The collection was
thought worth printing in Gouda, Antwerp, Köln, Stockholm (the
first Stockholm-printed book), Geneva, Lyons, Paris, and more than
once in four of these cities. The tradition in the woodcuts, as I have
seen it, varies little as to plan or subject, but greatly in skill; some
have much charm of design.[3]

FIGURE I

Thus begins Fable 23, a dispute between the Lock and the Key: "A
kaye there was som tyme. Which was verye goode / and pleasauntlye
oppynde her locke / and also made it faste / in so moche that the

patrone / and ownar therof reioicyd greately therin. Upon a tyme thys Locke fel in froward mynde and grutchyd agaynst the kay and sayde thus, O wykked creature why pursewyst thow me thus continually, dayly thow entrist into my bowellys and tournyst my stomake uppe and downe. Cece of thy greef and trowble me no more / or ellys I shall caste the awaye or make the crokyd. To whom the kaye answerde & sayde. Sustyr thow spekyst evyll. By me thowe arte conservyd in prosperite. . . ." But notwithstanding, the lock was not pleased; in a fit of petulance it suddenly "stoppyd fast the hole / and wode not suffre the kaye entyr into hym." Then came the owner, could not open the door, and in sudden heat smote off the lock and broke it. "And the kaye . . . sayde"—and here comes the ditty, often not so concise and pert in the vernaculars as in the Latin. And after it, the moralization proper, with quoted *auctores*, in this case admonishing those "that desire to lyve peceablye with ther neybowris" that they should "bere parte of ther charges, as the Apostle wrytythe ad Galat. vi., Every one of yowe bere the burdon of othir."

Or there is the Chayne (Fable 24) that has had quite enough of carrying the Cawdron daily to the flame and never getting even a share of some good morsel that the pot boils up. But he receives the smart rebuke, "Thou servyst me to my hurte . . . holdiste me uppe to the fyre . . . and cawsiste my sydes to be brent and consumyd." The moral of this little encounter is no other than: if you desire to do service to other men, serve them to their pleasure. The Rosemary plant (Fable 25), which can make ground fertile, is begged by the barren Field to come and make it fruitful: "O pastor egregie et bone custos / descende ad me & protege me," says the Latin, echoing liturgical language. She takes up residence there and all things flourish. To our surprise, the moralization of this fable is that commonwealths should choose good and learned governors. The point of the similitude with the fertility-bringing Rosemary is then repeated in the timeworn advice of the Roman king to the French one, to educate his sons "in lyberall seyence" or he will have as successor on his throne *asinus coronatus*. Part of our pleasure is evidently expected to lie in seeing that a governor's learning is to a state as the fertility-bringing rosemary is to a barren field.

Catching sight of a point of mere prudential alertness, of cunning in the true and Baconian sense, is quite as usual a meaning of "moralize" as is the drawing of a moral in our sense. The collection is typical in that its author makes no such distinction, and hands out the "wisdom" of intelligently practical hints through just the same sort of figures as serve to uncover a deeper wisdom. The "creatures" quietly witness to the sense and intelligent rationale of the universe as readily as to its moral laws; all phenomena "discover" not only the probity of their Author, but also shadow all the kinds of wisdom, lower and higher. Trivial as some examples seem, I am not overreading here, as the Prologue will presently show.

The Ass and the Wolf (Fable 107) are sawing together, with the humble Ass ready to work either at top or bottom of the saw, but the envious Wolf, at the bottom, steadily blows the dust into his fellow's eyes. It only hits the timber and falls back into his own eyes, and as we expect, this shows what happens to the malicious who dig pits for their neighbours. It is picked up by Lodge for the same use (under Envy). Yet the serious moral charge brought by the Silver against the Iron—that munitions make wars—and answered sharply with a long accusation that Silver has been behind centuries of evil deeds, from adultery to treachery, is moralized merely to warn that one should know when to hold one's peace or one may be out-argued.

Another oddity to our modern minds is the lameness of some of the story sections, those portions we have been taught to think were the focus of literary interest and the author's real concern, the "moral" being tacked on to satisfy public, church, the stuffy bourgeois—anyone, in short, but the composing author. But we read stories—and several are chosen by Lodge—which consist of how the black Crow, jealous of the whiteness of the Swan, blackens him while he sleeps; or of Laurus, a Bird, who being a shipman too, greedily overloaded the ships he captained so that they sank; or another in which the hawk Osmarillus and his partner, a goshawk, take a quail, to whom they give the seemingly pre-decided choice of being eaten on the spot or guiding them to her nest, where she and her young will be consumed in one multiple feast. There is no struggle between choices, no cunning twist, no revealed novel foible of personality. It is clear that we are expected to take our pleasure in the plain observation of similitude: in noting how clearly this Swan figures a human being taken, when not vigilant, by the devil, who cannot endure the cleanness and purity of God's servants; how covetousness can everywhere be seen meeting its ineluctable end; how the humble quail, deciding to die alone, can elect to set "the commune profite" above "syngler avayle."

Lodge extends the quail story to cover Divines, who if they were right-thinking fowl would die themselves and spare their flocks; in the "Laurus" he copies the original's application to greedy Merchants.

He is engaged in the common mediaeval game of allocating vices-and-virtues class by class, estate by estate—a conventional design Chapman enjoyed using in *Bussy d'Ambois*, and fitfully present in Nashe and Dekker. Like the looser definition of "moralize," the pre-eminence of significance over an interesting story is typical of exempla collections. Hence, if they appear shorn of their moralizations by impatient nine-teenth-century editors, or if we are too largely in search of the modern pleasure in provocative surface or local detail in narrative, the pleas-ure which is often the only one in such stories escapes us. It was clearly shared by mediaeval author and Renaissance imitator: the pleasure in pure seeing-of-similitude, taken in as immediately as an echo, while conceiving the literal story, as one sees a pebble under water with more significance than a pebble. Neither water nor pebble offers any great novelties; what pleases is merely to observe the nature of the world and correspondences one can see in it.

In Lodge's use of the Sea and the Seabanks, whose rambunctious quarrelings he copies outright, we see more of that comical pseudo-realism which is a special attraction of the *Dialogus creaturarum*. That it is a natural concomitant of the genre of fable, we are re-minded by Spenser's example of this precise "kind"—the Oak and the Brier in *Februarie* of the *Shepheardes Calender*. Spenser had read this kind of mediaeval literature and had missed little it could teach him (as *Mother Hubbard's Tale* shows). The pleasure in mediaeval specificity and realism is more apparent in the Renaissance than is our typical interest in mediaeval detail which is "romantically" removed and strange—a connotation not yet in their word "romance"; we shall note this more especially in dealing with romances, where this pithy and matter-of-fact homeliness was a stronger influence on the fights and the conversations of the *Faerie Queene* than was any exotic un-reality. It is barely worthwhile even to notice, as an analogue to *Feb-ruarie*, the Cedar (proverbially ambitious) left unprotected in the blast (Fable 35). Similarity in "kind," which produces similar con-ventions and relation to figurative meaning, had regularly produced the brash conversations, the minute, suddenly actualized details or tones of voice, the super-dramatic drama and super-weighty moraliza-tions. The latter are often unexpectedly specialized: the Brier dies not for Pride but for scorning old age, such as Gods themselves have. The ditty of Fable 35, "Of the hyghe Cedre Tre," reads: "They that be rulers may nothinge avayle. If they that be undyr of helpe doth them fayle."

Just as in Spenser or in Lodge, we are expected to be sufficiently aware of how fables work—and sufficiently alert—to see the "moral" double meaning almost as soon as we embark on the description or tale, the later outright statement of moral point being deliberately heavy-footed. Thus our enjoyment of the doubleness involves tiny details and is subtler. It is typical that the near-irony does not corrode the serious sense of the "moral" ("extended signification" would be more precise), and we catch this habit if we read at length.[4] We, like earlier men, take amusement from the figurative sense long before its statement, and from the fact that fantasy is likely to be more striking in the literal story. For example, the overweening Cedar Tree who ". . . magnyfied hyr self inwardly and sayd within her self: I am gretly spokyn of / and lawdid . . . for my beawte which is worthy to be lawdyd. But I trowe that if the smale plantis and treys that . . . growe rownde abowt me / were cut down or pluckyd uppe I should apere most goodely and large withowte comparyson. [It were best and surest] to mayme them or fell them down betymes / or they ascend so highe / that they take not awaye my worshyppe . . . [hence she caused them all to be cut or pulled up by the root, wherefore] she aperyd nakyd and bare and within fewe dayes a greate wynde blewe . . . & the prowd Cedre was Curvate and overthrowe. . . ."

Making exception for its greater variety and gaiety, the *Dialogus* can typify a considerable body of popular and accessible moralized *exempla* literature that was in its very nature allegorical. It is now time to look more closely at what precise kind of allegorical reading such books induced and the exact rhetorical character of their figures. The general points made about the character, popularity and uses of these books, their combination of narrative and significance and the types of relation made, exactly what they do when they "moralise" (the word which won out over others for allegorical figures), their way of applying figurative power, the assumed correspondences and serious uncovering of universal meanings, the underlying particularity that was simultaneously described and appreciated for its own realistic sake—these various general points could be well exemplified from a Nicole Bozon or a *Gesta Romanorum*.[5]

Some stories or examples have a relation to their morals or significances which even no known misdefinition could admit under the figure of allegory. The Lead (Fable 19) goes to the Gold, and says, "Why art thowe so prowde agayn me. Am not I of the substaunce of metallys as welle as thowe." When, in the suggested trial by fire of the virtue that is in them, the boastful lead vanishes and the meek gold is purified, the notion we are expected to see is that "much prowde people *be in that same case* thinking they have vertewe / which *is not in* them." Or a Topaz (Fable 16), set in a cross in St. Peter's in Rome, was "infectte with bad counsell" and said to himself, "What lyf is this, to continewe alway in the Chirche, I wyll for a season retourn to the worlde that I may have a lytel recreacyn in it." Of course, the monk out of his cloister, the topaz out of the cross, both lose the worth they had in their fair setting, which they gave up so lightly. The first of these stories is not figurative at all, save as inanimate things speak—a prosopopoeia. Strength was not "in" the lead, nor is it "in" the proud people. The second also is technically only a comparison—if it is a figure at all; quite literally, the priest, like the topaz, should have stayed in the place that gave him value. It is interesting, and perhaps unfortunate, that it is apropos of such parallels that editors or describers of texts most commonly remark sagely and with approval, "here the analogy is not so strained." But this is not the kind of analogy that allegorical reading is exercised on. We apprehend a likeness, and from it a moral point; but in several of these cases there is no metaphor to read, the comparison being based upon a property or situation quite literally predicated of the creatures treated. Things talk or act; but only the topaz (and it only if given quite different elaboration) could start off a fiction to which we could give an allegorical reading.

We may recall, to point up the difference, the Rosemary planted in the field, thus figuring the good governor. I am not confusing the question by doubting the rosemary's power to make fields literally more fertile, but pointing out that Fertility has become metaphorical —in a commonwealth and as the result of learning. So too with the Crow-devil, who could not stand "whiteness" in the Swan-soul. So with the envious Wolf, whose blown dust comes back on himself; we immediately metaphorically translate "dust." Not so with Laurus the Shipman-bird, however; he greedily filled his ship too full; so do human captains. We could write about an allegorical ship, but the author has not told that story. The Lock that would not suffer its Key is fully capable of turning into a variety of allegorical forms of the notion that each must help suffer the cost of the other's duty. The difference is not in content, nor is it in the area whence the vehicle is chosen, the type of fancifulness of the tale or the a priori likeness or unlikeness of two objects held in a similitude. Strain has nothing to do with it; lead is not more like a boastful person than a crow is like a

devil or a smooth lock like a loving neighbour. The difference comes
in the logic of the relation made *in this use or story* between the two
terms of the comparison. Lead and the weak talker are merely likened
on the grounds of not having strength to withstand anything, and in
truth they have not; but governors can bring fertility and devils hate
whiteness of soul in the faithful only as these words are capable of
metaphorical meaning. Thus what is said about farfetched analogies
is beside the point. It simply does not matter where the parallels are
fetched from in allegory; what counts is whether a metaphorically
understood relation is used to take off into areas where a similitude
can point to valuable human action, or to matters of spiritual import.

These last two phrases concerning human action and spiritual import describe, respectively, moral allegory and allegory strictly so-
called; although this is a distinction new to our discussion, it can be
observed and defined through the materials in hand. Lodge uses none
but "moral allegories." He always uses quails, intelligent griffons,
clever hare-lawyers and the rest to tell us what we ought to do, or
what someone is doing but ought not to. We may illustrate the allegorical reading he does *not* ask of us (though others of the *Dialogues
do*) by telling a story that is susceptible of a further reading than we
are expected to give it; and we shall see that it is even possible to detect an author's wishes in such a matter.

FIGURE 2

We may consider the fable of the Smaragdus (Fable 14), greenest
of all stones, that was set in a ring of gold. And many came from far

countries to see it. Upon a day, the Ring spoke uncourteously to the stone and said, "Thou haste long contynued / and dwellyde in my stacyon / and nevyr paydest me / for thy standynge. Wherefore delyvre thy dewtye for thyn habitacyon / and goe thy waye. Or I shall take from the all that thowe haste / and putte thee owte of thy lodgynge." The Smaragdus, though maintaining that it is because of him that the Ring has been put on the King's finger, says, "Yf thow wylte nedis expell me," sell me then and from the proceeds "take thy dewtye for my howse-rent." But when the Ring had done so, behold he found himself but "bare and abject." But the moral has nothing to do with the obvious moral drift touching harsh methods toward debtors; it is: The servant of Christ is worshipful in like wise "as long as he retaynyth and kepith precyows vertewys within hym. And if he caste them from him he is to be cast awaye. . . ." The relation of the clear green stone to its significance is metaphorical rather than comparative, figuring virtue; and further, the image is turned aside from moral instruction to say something rather about the ultimate destiny of those who, asking that their virtue should pay off, find that they are become the empty rings whom the King of heaven casts away.

I have made one illegal extension of the figure, to demonstrate that that activity on our parts can be detected and refrained from; at the last I named the King. The text did not direct me thus to bring in the common image of Christ as the virtuous soul's Bridegroom, and I doubt if the author was thinking of it. We have, without it, true allegory. Not instead of, but in addition to, the moral of "it is vyle to be partyd from a worthy thinge," the story is so told as to reach into a signification touching our destiny as souls, to be cast away, or to be worn on the King's finger. This is an "allegorical reading" in the sense that long history and uncountable pages of interpreted texts had developed the meaning of that word; and this text of the fable itself demands it, or parts thereof are left idle.

The basic distinction lies in which particular realm of meaning the figure carries us into. We have only rediscovered the old commonplace, that moral allegory makes us read about how we should act, while allegory more strictly so-called brings us to the view of what we ought to believe. It seems to me unsafe to refer too easily to the traditional four senses in dealing with later allegory; but it is wise to make at least the present distinction, partly because the two sorts of figures operate differently artistically, and partly because the distinction (unnamed) is observed by writers.[6]

FIGURE 3

Another fable (No. 32) will demonstrate how the difference in the desired end governs minor artistic choices. "In a sertayne herbar" there grew a fair Rosier, and a Partridge desired to have some of the roses and said, "O thou beawtyfull flowre of all flowris graunt me of thy Rosys for I desyre to refresshe my self a while in these swete odowris." The Rosier answered, "Come to me moste interely belovyd sustyr . . ."; but when the Partridge had flown thither to gather the flowers, the sharp spines pricked its feet so sore it would gladly have departed without roses. "The Rosier," we are told, "betokenithe *the world*." The moral talks about riches, and, with the exception of one suggestion, this would be straight moral allegory about the unrealized pains that attend worldly desires. But to our surprise, by a quotation from Gregory, riches have thorns since they wound man's mind by the "prykkynge of their inordinate love." Though this underscores the wooing or seduction phraseology of the tale,[7] it is apparent that we must not press too far what could easily have been conventional religious allegory strictly so-called. For this careless sensualist does not wed saeculum; nor is he made a captive of that usurping lover who steals the soul from its real spouse. The image is a lesser one and keeps us within the narrower bounds of didactic warning anent the true nature of mixed evil-and-good (the beautiful, urging to excess). There is no indication that "pluck my roses" is truly symbolic, and this would disturb the narrative as told; in it there is no place for lost honor or for the significances of union and allegiance that made the marriage-image allegorically powerful.

One last fable in which the author fully extends the signification will perhaps make the formal difference which marks such figures quite clear. The reason why even indifferent authors can maintain this distinction lies in the fact that it is a difference in end and purport, not one in skill; a firm grasp of the distinguishing characteristic enables us to recognize a fully intended allegorical figure and will serve us well in reading masters of figurative language like Spenser. "There is a Fissh callyd Regina," says Fable 45, and she is so called "for she rulyth herself very well" (*rego*). "A Water serpent callyd Idrus havynge many hedes cam uppon a tyme to this Fissh and sayde. O Regina most fayre to me before all othir fisshes, thow art . . . most interly belovyd. And therefore I wyll be knytte unto thee . . . in holy matrimony." To whom Regina answered, "That maye not be. For it is not convenient." She means, of course, quoting *Eccles.* xiii, that it is not fitting, and disregards the Lord's command that every creature should seek out his own likeness or kind. The serpent goes home "with confusyon," and the full purport of the word is seen in the moral: "Every Crysten man shulde soo answer to the Devyl/ whan he temptith hym/ for *he is the olde serpent* more subtyle than any thinge lyvynge. . . . And therefore thus shulde every creature saye unto hym. Go thow fro me/ for thowe arte not of my kynde. Nor thow arte noon of them that shal be savyd. And if thou doo thus he cannotte abyde."

This is a fully developed allegorical image, and has to be so read. Every likeness is metaphorical in nature: the old serpent from the sea, the wooing, the non-kinship, the seven heads in the illustrations showing that he was allegorically read, the magical strength of the refusal, which lies simply in recognizing and stating the Adversary's identity. Of course, Regina is man, or Anima. The marriage-image was best suited to draw in the desired ideas—of seduction, devouring, ravishment, pre-eminently of full union and the giving away of the self. This idolatrous allegiance is resisted by Regina, but also the point about not marrying out of her kind is important; Satan has lost his title to heavenly sonship. This conception of man, as that creature whose property it is to be salvationis capax, who belongs to the kind that may be delivered from the ravishment of death and united to the heavenly original whence it sprang, is a conception of man which is of central importance to the question of allegorical reading. It is remarkable that it should have carried over into secular writing, even into allegorized classical imagery, a sort of large popular residue from more careful and precise understandings of allegory in theological materials. For a figure to reach into the area where it is read as speaking of man's metaphysical situation, it must use with clarity the translatio that defines metaphor as a figure of speech—as here the "marriage" immediately conveys to us ideas touching the soul's captivation by evil. There may or may not be need of the systems of analogical correspondences between natural and spiritual reality so often spoken of, but what we do find is reference to man's ultimate destiny or meaning, perhaps his relations to supernatural Being—usually in some ancient similitude or element accustomed to bear this burden of reference.

If we turn to visual images, we find that it is easier to experience, in a way that does not admit of argument, the absence or presence of elements that make us respond to an image at this "allegorical" depth. Obviously we will now walk clumsily over ground that is daily flown over with competence and success both by art historians and readers.[8] Nevertheless, where there is opportunity for cooperation between the two fields of pictorial and literary art (and the use of evidence from iconography has entered English studies to stay), hurry and confusion on the very simplest mental steps and distinctions are the source of some grave difficulties. I shall therefore count no difference or distinction too elementary to mention. The numerous illustrators of the *Dialogues* have pictured the Lock and Key (Fig. 1); so also the Ring and the Stone (Fig. 2). It is obvious that it is not possible to detect the traits in either object which enabled the teller to give the Lock's actions or the Ring's emptiness a metaphorical point. Yet this is what enabled the fictions to constitute comment upon human self-importance or human weaknesses (moral allegory). With a simple comparatio like the Topaz set *in* the cross—if the other term (the priest *in* his church) were portrayed in juxtaposition—a cunning interpreter might conceivably see the naked comparison and jump to a moral point, from general notions about clerics "in" the church. Move to the illustration of the Rosier story (Fig. 3), and not all the ingenuity in the world could extract the metaphorical significance of thorns as that which, in riches, pricks us with inordinate love of them. The sensuous experience of thorns which we share with St. Gregory would carry us as far as "prickly"—the logical base of comparison that allows the metaphor—but it becomes obvious that metaphor works through paralleling concepts that are too abstract or subtle to convey through the shared properties one can indicate visually.

We may observe also that the Rose-tree could be that of the *Roman de la rose*, or that of which Yeats wrote in the Easter Rising poems, or that in the nearest garden; further, we may try to think of any device by which the designer could unmistakably indicate that *this* Rose-tree is not these but *mundus fraudulentus*. Without another image, he cannot tell us to think well or ill of the roses, and even a worm in one would say something else; meanwhile, the metaphorical heart of the *exemplum* lay in an idea that would defy short statement, that the Rosier was *saeculum*, with all the burden that carries to New Testament readers.

FIGURE 4

Yet in this next picture, which illustrates Fable 38, "De syrenella," just such an evaluative distinction is conveyed (Fig. 4). We mistrust her and know why. The reader need not be told that when the boatman leapt into that sea he was destroyed. What the reader already knows is exactly the factor which enables this picture to evoke an evaluating response both sure and clear. I do not mean a "single" response, for even this simple image has the ambiguity of delightful-*and*-noxious, and we all allow the siren, without second thought, the beauty she has not to the eye (Fig. 5). The sole difference between this fable and that of the Rose-tree lies in what the auditor or spectator knows beforehand—some practically universally known story which has given an accepted conventional significance to sirens. This factor provides many of the "moralizations" of fables such as those in the *Dialogus*; the conceptual or evaluative point that enables a figure to say something about *quid agas* (i.e. moral allegory) can even be communicated wordlessly if we already possess the notion which acts as a key. This is true for the unsaid significance of verbal images, too, and is a major objection to modern clichés about depending only on what is "in" the poem. Unstated moral-allegory meanings may be "in" a conventional image in one poem and not in it in another.

FIGURE 5

But it takes something the fable does not have for us to see this boatman's death as the death of the soul; the siren does not represent quintessential evil to most of us, and thus we do not read in it Adam's Fall or any other all-inclusive myth of the origin of man's woe or the meaning of his life. Yet we do read just that in the pictures alone, even, of the Regina fable (Fig. 6). The old Serpent from under the sea cannot possibly be a morally indifferent creature; more than that, he cannot, in our culture, be an allegorically silent one. We cannot catch the Regina-wooing image unaided, but we catch sight of the notions which caused that image to develop, for we realize from recognizing Leviathan, the Apocalyptic Beast, the Adversary, how metaphysically significant a rape or union is here threatened. If, like men of many earlier centuries, we are accustomed to seeing in the seven heads the seven sins that were the chief mode of the capture, and if we have much other knowledge of this "sea," we read still more of the whole complex of ideas and feelings the figure tries to speak of. It may not have power upon us, but it has profundity and subtlety in itself. Most images that undeniably require or allow allegorical reading convey in this manner, through public figures or symbols, the needed concepts which trigger thought. The thoughts are not only judgments or evaluations on moral matters, but are ideas concerning ultimate destiny, divine beings, supernatural forces. These seem to need a surer and richer language than any private or contrived symbolism, since the interpretation of the literal with the metaphysical, as well as the moral, meanings is an element we persistently find in mediaeval allegory.

I suppose it is not necessary to underline the fact that the images do not *equate with* the concepts spoken of (if this were so, no images would be needed). Equation is not quite the process even in late classical and Fulgentian allegories of pagan gods, before different and deeper Christian understandings changed the figure. "Bad allegory" may use a set of concretions to mean nothing more or less than some set of concepts we could write out, and to which they are "equal," but even this is so hard to work out in practice that it is far scarcer in literature than in critical interpretation. Some statable concept or nameable abstraction is generally a key and an indication; but so is the literal "thing." "Leviathan the sea-beast" and the word, "Evil" are, respectively, the closest men have come to the bodies of meaning they refer to. They represent two of the ways we have developed to refer to things too complex to state in full, though experienced by all of us. There are not very many such great public images (quest, pilgrimage, marriage, death, birth, purgation, for example) and not very many such metaphysical problems.

FIGURE 6

It might be useful to point up certain facts through a picture still more undeniably "allegorical." For example: the likelihood that illustrations will use an acquired language of metaphors (acquired by learning, and based on developments taking place through some centuries, but taken for granted as commonplaces in their times); the firm relevance, nonetheless, of the literal meanings of things portrayed, or (in stories) of the plain narrated events; the conceptual solidity or continuity, so that a "continued metaphor" becomes a complex of several ideas symbolically stated; the greater richness and condensation of such symbolic statement, though a brief and general discursive statement is all we can manage if we are asked to say what the image means;

the way in which such pictures (though static as always) can, like literature, reach backward and forward in time. These accomplishments are more complicated in their theoretical statement than in practice; we apprehend very readily such differences between Fig. 7 and the Rose-tree or the Lock and Key.

Figure 7 is a fifteenth-century drawing from a manuscript translation, in MS Bodley 283, of the *Somme le roi*. This is the best known mediaeval text of the popular "kind" represented by the second of Lodge's sources (Benedetti's *Summa*), which we indicated as ultimately mediaeval. One has something of a key, recognizing Christ by his cruciform halo; had we used the parallel picture from the French tradition of late thirteenth-century illumination of this text, the key would not be there, for Christ appears as simply a larger central tree. The text at this point is describing a garden-image which is structurally important in later treatises of the compilation, which underlies many another treatment of virtues and their nourishment or roots, and which uses numerous basic Christian doctrines—Christ in the temple of the heart, the nature of grace, the meanings of "paradise." Mediaeval materials on the virtues and vices prove so important for allegory that they will need a chapter (Two) to themselves, but the quoted image will make the picture at least readable, if not moving and true as it seems in context.[9] "Holy writ likneth a good man and a good womman to a fair garden ful of grene and of faire trees. . . . The grete gardener, that is God the fadre . . . maketh the herte nesche and swete . . . and good erthe al redy . . . to be . . . graffed with goode graffes. These graffes ben the vertues that the Holy Gost gyveth of grace. . . . [He makes the heart as a paradise right delitable, full of good trees and precious.] But rigt as God sett ertheli paradis ful of goode trees and fruygt, and in the myddel sett the tree of lif. . . . Rigt so doth *gostly* to the herte the goode gardyner . . . for he sett the tree of vertue and in the myddel the tree of life, that is Ihesu Crist, for he seith in the gospel, 'Who-so eteth my flesch and drynketh my blod hath lif without ende.' This tree wexeth grene and fair bi vertue ouer al this paradis, and bi vertue of this tree wexen, blowen, and beren fruygt alle the othere trees." (Italics mine.)

Although any of us would probably correctly interpret the water in the foreground, possibly only an earlier audience would divine from the fact that there are seven trees the realization that "This welle is departed in sevene stremes, that ben the sevene giftes of the Holy Gost, that wateren al the garden." And perhaps only the position of the pic-

FIGURE 7

ture at the head of the Pater Noster treatise expected in this compilation would tell even a mediaeval observer that "The sevene peticiouns,
that are askynges, ben as sevene rigt faire maidenes that leven not to
helde everemore water of thilke sevene stremes that wellen alwey, for
to watere wel thes sevene trees of vertue, that beren the fruygt of lif
with-outen ende."

This is an allegorical image by the definitions of its time and kind,
before the entrance of the personification of the petitions. They are
maidens that they may be pictured, or mentally imaged in tangible
shape; seven fountains and conduits that the sinner could himself open
would do as well. It teaches doctrine, "what to believe" (and is, in fact,
more theologically careful than we have time to notice here); it conveys very little moral judgment or evaluative impulse and uses numerous ancient metaphors to read the literal facts of fruitful growth
spiritualiter ("rigt so, gostly").

"Personification of abstractions" is so often thought of as the very
root of allegory that a quick consideration of some complications may
be worth a moment. So much of language is just this—ossified—that
the phrase is not very useful. The phrase cannot turn into allegory a
figure that happens to occur before English developed the use of "it"
to replace the personal pronoun, making it necessary for the Lock in
the fable to say that he would not suffer the Key to enter into "him,"
the keyhole. The visual arts customarily personify to indicate the presence of allegorical meaning, but that element does not provide the
meaning, as is obvious from the banderoles so often needed; and also
something quite different may be indicated. In the illustrated manuscript of the *Dialogus* in Paris MS. B.Nat. 8507*, all the objects are
provided with faces—seabanks and sea, topaz, the stick-like gold and
lead ending in human faces, lock, key and all. Our way of understanding the figurative nature of the fables is unaffected by this, and it does
not help us to distinguish between the simplest moral exemplum and
a metaphorical image of ancient profundity.

The illustrator was faced, in Fable 7, with differentiating pictorially
"The Air" from "The Wind." In this fable the Air goes to the Creator
and complains of being vexed and made "untemperate" by the Wind;
"Therefore I saye to hym yf ever from hensforth he presume to blowe
upon me/ I wyll choke hym and put hym from his lyfe." Figure 8
shows that the designer found the solution we might anticipate—but
the Air is no less personified than is the creature we recognize as
Aeolus. Nevertheless, the poets make the fullest use of such inherit-

ances; Mammon is among other things a Pluto, and therefore some of the threatening and terrible meanings Mammon has will be conveyed without Spenser's mentioning them. What counts is less personification than the kinds of considerations drawn in by the recognized persons, what dramas they had elsewhere been *personae* in and have come to imply, like brief abstracts of much experience and feeling.

FIGURE 8

If personification of abstractions is not a defining or causative element in allegory, there is no doubt that it is a most natural form of it. But instead of personality giving the abstractions life, the figure often works the other way around; the excitement comes when we "conceive" the idea, the person suddenly then becoming charged with meanings of very great depth and extension. Everyone has had the experience of a genre-picture—or so he had thought it—turning into a symbol or allegory before his eyes, by something he learns (usually about the history and thence the deeper significance of the image). The curious inner revolution experienced, as *gestalt* replaced *gestalt*, came from moving out of the area of imitated literal life into an area where universals rather than particulars seem to be met, into an area where ideas themselves confront one or interact. Imagine an illustration of a rose-garden and an angelically beautiful youth which one suddenly saw put in its place at the head of a section of the *Roman de la rose*. Or suppose two pictures wherein a woman gives a garment to a naked man, and a woman sits by a sickbed—and that one finds the other five pictures and recognizes the Seven Acts of Mercy. The different experience that we move into is that of "seeing" all Love (not A Lover) in the God himself, all possible concrete cases of Mercy in the idea of her.

Moral allegory of some depth is possible as soon as we perceive that we can note the nature of universals in action—and this is often as true of genre-pictures as it is of naturalistic writing; bored people would probably stop looking and reading if it were not. But allegory in a stricter sense occurs so commonly that we ought to try to differentiate it; in a picture, it seems to depend on whether the action shows us, or whether an accompanying text or known significance makes us read in the images, something about the relations of Love or Mercy to the ultimate meaning of human life or about a divine source for them or their metaphysical ground. If a picture could show us (as one like Fig. 6 might if elaborated) Misericordia's place as the Fifth Gift of the Holy Ghost, with her nature suggested, as so often, by the Works of Mercy, or some of them—then that image would take on before us the dimension we may as well call by its old name, allegorical.

These are not rules for allegories—with cards to be presented at entrance, texts otherwise not admitted. I merely try to make clear a distinction which is observed in the works written. Spenser uses images which work in all these different ways, very close together, as all literary works do, often indeed transforming one kind into another as we look; but his choices of concretions to use, associations to suggest, and so on, are unselfconsciously apt, and we can damage "an allegory" markedly, for example, by asking it to work like a moralization. Distinctions made in religious exegesis, and therefore familiar for centuries, were responsible for calling this last kind of figure allegory, as some still did. The term was not to hold on even partially for much longer, in spite of the great Pauline passages that everyone knew. But the skill that preserves such distinctions in practice stayed alive at least long enough to show us why Milton's Sin and Death are conceptually and theologically two of the most accurate and fertile images in his poem and to demonstrate a very particular relation between concrete detail and philosophical (not just ethical) meaning. I do not know which we lost first—the terms or the distinctions. I do not think modern writing has a use for either. Surely a differentiation between images based thus on difference in function—whether we are brought to think about how to act or how to believe—would be alien to us.

Visual imagery may have preserved it longest, for it was popularized along with the use of certain truncated allegorical counters.

Poetic examples generally cover some compass, but perhaps an unusually brief climax to one of Spenser's transformations of one kind of image into another may illuminate the theoretical remarks. If one recalls the whole complicated analysis of love in Book III, and the story and characterizations which lead up to the dinner-table scene in Malbecco's house, and the seemingly quite realistic image of Paridell's lascivious use of erotic signs as he spills his wine-cup toward Hellenore (to which she will respond by letting some of hers spill into her lap), one is egregiously startled by Spenser's line: Hellenore read herein *A sacrament prophane in mistery of wine*. With a flash of comprehension we take in all that Spenser believed and might have said about the preservation of the nature of "love" (for example, that Love came down to make that nature clear forever in the sacrifice on the cross, and comes down persistently in the "wine" of the Eucharist); and we take in with shock the wild disproportion between the divine agape and this sensual use of others for self-indulgence. There is nothing but failure to be expected if one tries to explain something Spenser himself could only say by an image (Bk. III.ix.30), but the agency through which the entire two cantos of the story now take on a new relation is unmistakable.

Poets have more varied and numerous ways of making us conceive ideas of such depth and extension than have artists, because of the inescapable conceptual dimension of their medium, words. This is dangerous ground, even if we try to keep close to a poetic example manifestly powerful by reason of its imagery. Two of the great images of Book II of the *Faerie Queene*—like the Rosier which is the world and the Sea Beast who tries to ravish and possess man's spirit—present two of the omnipresent concerns of allegory. Mammon images the first concern, Acrasia the second.[10] The far simpler fables also treated these same matters. We may thus toss ourselves in front of a danger always waiting for readers of allegory—that so many allegories "mean the same thing" that one is as good as another; "the idea" being in them, nothing intrinsic distinguishes a greater image, and bad poets cannot be told from good. This of course is untrue. Having voiced the protest we may leave it to each reader to supply the defense of poetry. We may court a second danger by noticing, in Spenser, the exact nature of some specific advantages which words have as conceptual instruments. The risk we run is that we may be understood to confuse allegory with "a discussion of ideas carried on by having some concrete equivalent stand for each one." This is a confusion met everywhere in commentary.[11] It describes some allegory in English, but later than Spenser's.

One advantage of the conceptual medium, for both moral allegory and the stricter kind, is that comparisons or associations convey directly, without statement, a constant stream of responses—values placed on things, the tiny movements of attraction or repulsion which we share more in language than in sense experience. As we meet Mammon through description of his person and habitat, every detail awakens antipathy by virtue of something Spenser had only to name, not provide. The deserted unordered wilderness, the gloom, the sooty beard and coal-black hands carry evaluative notions about Mammon in themselves—and this is an ineradicable property of language. Words tip the scales of our affections, and we cannot call this rhetorical, but simply a linguistic fact; it has been provided by the long development of words as instruments of communication. Objects themselves are much more ambiguous in effect, as pictures of the wilderness and the beard would show. This semantic fact especially touches words that convey properties; they amplify or deprave (the technical Elizabethan words for *magnify* or *denigrate*) quite securely and almost without our realizing what is happening. This is a great strength when a poet wishes to convey through imagery some great abstraction from large areas of human experience toward which he expects to arouse attitudes of espousal or rejection. One result is that great allegories are usually the most concrete of all writings in texture. It is not only by temperament that Spenser became the painter of the poets.

Poets use this natural advantage (and frustrating disability) of the medium of words in every cunning way, often magnifying in order to deprave or diminish—as the gold and brightness and artful richness (*FQ*, II.vii.4; vii.28) are shown only to be negated by the coverings of "filthy" dust, jet-black clouds, webs of Arachne denominated "cunning," or subtile "nets." Two other plain advantages of the medium show up: first the ease with which a poet can interpolate abstract epithets or value-stating words whose only and proper function is to sway the judgment, and secondly, the natural operation of figures using comparison, which generally do this surreptitiously. Spiders' "nets" are no real danger to any but flies, but as with "nayles *like clawes*" or the "ravenous *pawes*" of the fiend who follows Guyon with "monstrous *stalke*," experiences are drawn in by way of the mere

terms of comparisons which tacitly but inescapably press us to condemn or exalt. These are the simplest forms of a conceptual power
which words have, from their history. It is shown more complicatedly
when a poet loads a simile with some imported notion, one which
frightens, for example, as the light in the cave is like that of the
moon *to him that walkes in feare,* or is like that of a lamp "whose
life does fade away" (as ours will, we half catch from this). Those
who recall the canto stanza by stanza will remember that the cre-
scendo—by which every kind of dark word (physical, moral, intellectual) turns the cave finally into a hell—includes many uses of
dubious or terror-filled light, even that in the eyes of the laboring
shapes.

These shapes brought their pain and terror with them when they
entered, or rather, they brought their history, which is as important as
their forms. In the Acrasia canto the analogue to these uses of darkness is the fearful sea. One remarks the crowd upon crowd of concretions that make the sea journey more fearsome than any experienced
or pictured voyage; but they vary. There are mere "things" which in
their verbal forms are simultaneously appearances and significances,
in this case, of terror (the owls and bats and quicksands and sea-
shouldering whales). There are ancient literary conventions with
trains of associations (the mermaids and ivy and hell-mouth and
squeezed potion, the magnet-rocks and wandering islands and the
fée's Helpful Damsels). There are also inventions not seen but fully
understood, like the carcasses stuck on the rock, but of *wanton* and
ruined men only. All these sense experiences impregnated with meanings deepen the conviction that is usually the ground for reading a
literal experience (verbal or lived) allegorically—that all things though
fully present to the senses are meaningful beyond what sense reports.
In the case of great numbers of the images, their meaning comes with
them, carried by their history.

The images are based firmly on physical and psychological experience, often known individually, but chiefly known and made important by centuries of vicarious experience passed on to us through
earlier literature; hence such images work at a deep associative level,
and we are conscious of not being the first to whom they have reiterated their burden of more meant than is seen. That Spenser counts
upon his images' history is provable from his text; and merely by their
nature, some images themselves reach beyond considerations which
belong (as do moral problems) to our life in the phenomenal world.

Journeys into the otherworld expose, handle, discuss or pronounce upon just such matters of ultimate or metaphysical import as are the concern of allegory strictly defined (or the concern of so many actual allegories which otherwise fit very loosely with the definitions of Christian religious allegorizing). The graphic arts have difficulty matching this sure and concentrated deepening of "spiritual" significance except through literary aids like titles, or known conventions of imagery.

Although both cantos vii and xii of Book II of the *Faerie Queene,* are read as moral allegory, both undeniably talk about man saved or damned. Though Acrasia is a nameable vice, and the adventures of Mordant or Cymochles with her have a more limited moral meaning, Guyon in canto xii looks at the kind of complete seduction which means the final death of the soul; and there is firm evidence for this in Spenser's use of myths and figures which historically had been used thus. The Dantesque and Virgilian imagery and the mediaeval-and-Renaissance Circe figure are but single cases. Perhaps this is one of the reasons why he erects a "goodly frame of Temperance" instead of just forming a temperate person, and why Guyon is a man journeying rather than a tempted protagonist; poets who show us men conducted through hell do not picture them having fights there with their appetites, but discovering what hell is. If it could never *be* a paradise (to men like us), we should already know what Intemperance is, and would not need to have it proved upon our pulses in canto xii.

We add then to the advantages which literature's inescapably conceptual medium provides its good fortune in being able to go backward and forward in time—not only narratively but through images. Literature can mean something about future generations not in the story or communicate meanings found by past generations whose story is not being told, and all without deserting its subject. It is true that outright conceptual statement may be the way to make the extended meanings shine out in character and event most surely, as when we are shaken by Mammon's "God of the world and worldlings I me call" (vii.8) or by the shocking completeness of "Here is the fountaine of the worldes good" (vii.38) or by the doctrinal accuracy of "See the mind of beastly man, That hath so soone forgot the excellence/ Of his creation" (xii.87). But Spenser employs a poetic method almost as firm and sure when he makes the past uses of his images indicate to us that we are to read them with this reach into ultimate questions. We recognize them as instruments for the discussion of just such matters—but able to speak in the present of the timeless, and locally of the universal.[12]

I do not mean that images repeat the story they told in the past. It does not turn Guyon into a "Christ-figure" when in canto vii.9 Spenser directs us to see the parallels with Christ's three temptations. Rather, this indicates the amplitude of the issue and states a doctrine about the relation between all human temptations and Christ's.[13] Spenser uses classical images similarly, to extend through their history the significance of his fiction; the golden apples evoke all those sad stretches of human history when men's concupiscence, for power of all kinds, had brought all the great typical "ensamples of mind intemperate" to their various eternities of frustrated desire. He uses what he calls the "present fate" of these long-dead persons to tell the powerful who have *not* yet left their mortal state for that other, "how to use their present state"; this is evidence that he wishes us to read allegorically of the relation between a virtue Temperance and what can happen to a soul, and not merely morally of a character Guyon and his confrontation of covetous desires.

In the Acrasia canto we are most helped by whatever we know of something common enough to Elizabethans—Circe as an image of man's betrayal of his spiritual allegiances to the intemperance of his natural desires; our familiarity with this conventional Christianization,[14] enables us to catch the many insistences in canto xii that widen the image of yielding to "Voluptas." The basic meaning of man's loss of his humanity has such fundamental implications that no reader can quite miss the allegorical purport of a fatal seduction, breaking man's tie of fidelity. "Fidelity to a divine allegiance" is the continuation fitting both Spenser and *Comus,* for as the image widens from moral to allegorical, it shows its Christian heritage.

It is well to repeat periodically that we do not seek to define allegory as if it were some changeless essence, and then in turn use the definition to admit or shut out poems from the category. We seek something quite limited and historical—what was involved in reading allegorically to certain writers at a given time, and for reasons we can trace. My first conviction, that certain definitions and distinctions were inherited mediaeval distinctions passed down to sixteenth-century writers and readers, arose from reading a late mediaeval book systematically, and consciously handling and exemplifying these matters. Christine de Pisan wrote her *Épitre d'Othéa* at the end of the fourteenth century; she was an esteemed author, and her books, including this one, were accessible in more than one form and in more than one language. The *Othéa* is invaluable for our questions, because the author tells us outright how she expects to be read.

Christine tells one hundred stories, or rather versifies what she calls one hundred "Textes," and they may be mere story-moments or even personages, pagan gods, or dicta from ancient times; all are classical in provenance. She then appends a prose "Glose," and thereafter a short prose discussion she entitles "Allegorie." We read the hundred, each first as a history or straightforward statement (i.e. "in the letter") and up through the Elizabethan period this may embrace such figurative senses as the parabolic meaning, say, of the sower. And then if we read each of the hundred in the two prose interpretations, which are two ways of reading the significance of the letter, we have at any rate

FIGURE 9

one invincible authority providing what our book is trying to find: what distinguished allegory from other ways of reading, to mediaeval and Renaissance readers. Christine satisfies the requirement of being famous and accessible enough for later writers in the mode to have been nourished on understandings she represents. And when one such writer exemplifies definitions before our eyes, in examples whose very phrasing we can check, we know we are reading as someone in truth did read, not as we conjecture "the mediaeval mind" must have. It is very rare to find documentation so precise on a matter of literary interpretation.

We will exemplify from a few of Christine's hundred merely to secure and confirm working definitions; her book as a whole suggests ideas about the imposition of Christian allegory upon classical materials which can wait for another chapter (Four). The *Othéa* has the additional merit of usually being illustrated, so we can observe what conditions permitted or assured the appearance of "allegory" (by Christine's own definition) or of moral meaning in the pictorial presentations of her hundred stories. Some of the manuscripts which illustrate all the hundred are thought to have been done under her surveillance, another lucky circumstance; the tradition in illuminations is interestingly constant, but of the early editions, Wyer's partial English translation does not follow early designs, and the Pigouchet cuts are not detailed.

Figure 9 shows an image we should unhesitatingly interpret narratively; Perseus on Pegasus rescues Andromeda from the Sea Monster. For the interest of an iconographical tradition preserved through vicissitudes, I include the parallel pictures from St. John's Coll.Camb.MS. 208 in English (Fig. 10) and the French MS.Laud misc.570 (Fig. 11) as well as Harl.4431. Christine's Texte (No. 5) tells the aspirant to knighthood to emulate him in this chivalrous behavior. In the Glose, we "make a figure of it according to the manner *of poets*"— and we should notice that both this reading and the third are figurative. Like Perseus, every "bon chevalier" is to rescue those in peril, flying upon his steed of Good Renown; he must win his chivalric good name, then use its strength to succor the distressed.[15] This is a good moral allegory. But Christine proceeds to what she herself entitles Allegorie: Andromeda is his soul which he will deliver from the enemy of hell by conquering sin (in himself, of course, so that this Andromeda, like the other "maiden," may return to her parents). The Pegasus which carries "lesperit chevalereux" is a Good Name since

he desires to please God, for he must have no hint of vainglory, and
his good angel who carries him through dangers here will make good
report of him when his guerdon, like Lycidas', is finally to be enjoyed
amid the singing companies of Paradise. Perseus is to be "read" first
as bon chevalier, but secondly as bon esprit, that within the human
creature which can help it to attain deliverance of its immortal soul.

We may turn to Narcissus, who so traditionally exemplifies Pride

FIGURE 10

FIGURE 11

that we certainly know we are embarking on a series of the seven
deadly sins (Fables 16-22). The moralized figurative reading in the
Glose sees in the fountain where Narcissus looked at himself and was
drowned, that overweening of himself which blinds him and makes
his knightly good deeds of no account; we are instructed on Pride.
But the Allegorie quotes from Origen a reminder of man's creatureli-
ness, the absurdity of pride in one who has his being in so frail and
corrupt a vessel. Then *Job* is quoted on the ignominious destruction
that is the destiny of a soul of such quality—one possessing this
quintessential Pride which sees no irony in the arrogance of mere
creaturely earth and ashes.

Ceres is pictured as a goddess sowing in a plowed field, a goddess of
grains (or, rationalized, une dame who taught men to plow before
seeding). To be a liberal giver who gives with "abandon" is to have

FIGURE 12

the "condition" of Ceres, says the moral Glose; but when we read the Allegorie in Ceres, we see in her the action of the blessed Son of God, chief exemplar of giving with abandon to men of his high good things. The good knight reads chivalric largesse in Ceres; the good spirit believes in, loves and imitates the condition of Ceres read as figure for the agape of Christ and its fructifying influence. Ceres does not "equal Christ." Her condition is agape, and He is that in its essence. When properly read, allegory does not need to turn some personage into Christ or into God the Father. We merely pause to notice that the relation is not quite that of a type either, and in a later chapter of this book we will observe that the distinction is kept, though it is a nice one. Figure 12 shows Ceres' action; the illustrator has not rationalized away her divine nature or there would be no cloud.[16] Rationalizations (like Ceres as teacher of plowing), which are traces of late classical forms of rationalizing divinities through "allegory," are frequent in Christine's Gloses. Though both the moral and the allegorical figurative meaning can persist despite the rationalizing, it does more damage to the classical figure than is done by the translation into Christian-deity terms, much as these might be thought of as a forcing of the meaning. The divinity lies in the loving abandon of the gift; belief in this as the very nature of God is strictly intended here, for Ceres is the second of a series of figures in whom we "read" the Twelve Articles of the Apostles' Creed, and the second is "And in Jesus Christ our Lord. . . ."

In Fable 54 we are shown a figure of Jason, who by Medea's help won the Golden Fleece, but ungratefully and disloyally (the same thing) deserted her. It is Jason's lack of fidelity, of troth owed to her who saved him from the death others met, which puts him outside the pale of chivalry, a warning to the bon chevalier. "Ingrate," "disloyal," "unnatural," are the key words of the figure, and we are not surprised when the Allegorie tells us to read in Jason what the bon esprit must hold to as its first allegiance: it must not forget Who made it. St. Bernard is quoted on the dry wind that shrinks up grace and mercy in a spirit that is ingrate. This is the prime arrogance in a soul, and untroth is regularly a first branch of Pride, as we should remember when we read Una (and Sansfoy).

Two general observations can be made, even with so few illustrations from Christine's hundred.[17] The simplest one touches the design of her book, commonly denigrated as haphazard and eccentric. Her general scheme is to take up classical stories in which we "read" the virtues, thereafter the seven sins, thereafter the Twelve Articles of the Creed, thereafter the Ten Commandments, thereafter a series of virtues and vices (Fables 45ff.). This has been noticed,[18] but nothing has ever been made of the fact that this structural design relates Christine's book to one of the commonest kinds of earlier mediaeval works—to those "Summa's" which were a major source of doctrine on the virtues, their contents being enjoined in concilia as a minimum of knowledge for the faithful, from the thirteenth century onward. This undiscussed fact has many implications. When for other reasons I very shortly take up the most popular of all exemplars of that common group, the Somme le roi (in its English form), we shall notice one of these important resulting similarities: an emphasis upon the "two chivalries," a natural part of a virtues-treatise and a pervasive figure in other forms of mediaeval literature also. It encouraged an understanding of the human situation and of human nature that made a place for the theologian's allegory, reading spiritualiter, in secular literature. In Christine we find the idea of double chivalry giving a kind of rhetorical currency to figures which are just classical images read mystice. Among lesser implications, we remark that the formlessness of mere casual didacticism is removed from Christine's list of demerits. One trait surely enjoyed by her audience is the originality of this use of classical materials to shape a scheme so thoroughly familar in the handbooks, for it surprises, provokes new realizations of the meaning of old doctrines and mnemonically is quite amusingly efficacious.

The second general observation is important because it points to a broad distinction we find silently upheld in other literary works, one that is helpful in determining how allegory as used in literature of the time was usually read. One of our toughest problems is whether allegory strictly so-called, a mode of reading useful for centuries to theologians and suitable primarily for scriptural interpretation, could be drawn over into secular literature, and if it could be, whether or not it was. If it was not, and the modern flurry of interest in such matters has merely produced readings that were no part of the pleasure taken in allegory in its heyday and not intended by authors, it would be salutary to discover this.

When we read all one hundred of the Othéa's sections as innocently as possible, we find that whereas the first reading, in the Glose, has to do with building a character (preparing the Good Knight to enter the moral tournament of life), the simultaneous additional second reading, the Allegorie, does not use literature or vicarious experience for that purpose—though advice on the good life is often near at hand as a by-product. The Good Spirit (bon esperit chevalereux, "soul" often in MS. Harl. 838) reads in figures the reminder of its true condition as a creature, sometimes seeing its need of rescue, often seeing in the figures a repetition of the news of its way of deliverance or some definition of the nature of this deliverance. The author herself is these two readers. Hence the peculiar usefulness and authority of the Othéa, since we are almost ubiquitously in the perilous situation of conjecturing how writers expected to be read, from evidence that is largely implicit.

It may not be practicable to keep Christine's terminology and distinguish allegoria as she does; although I try to maintain roughly such a distinction in this book, mediaeval books do not so limit the word itself. However, many do characteristically so frame their allegorical images, which are thus distinguishable from moralizations, and whose function is to discuss the ultimate destiny of man as bon esprit. Some figures are clearly more amenable to the second reading than others; Christine sometimes flounders as she seeks to supplant a reading concerned with moral conflict and substitute the Good Spirit's fulfillment of some other concern inseparable from being human. Some classical figures resist the natural Christian twist—that human beings not only have moral responsibilities but belong to that Kind which is not debarred from regaining the lost resemblance to the divinity which created them, or belong to a Kind beloved and sought and espoused and owing fidelity to, a loving Creator. This is the aspect which was bound to enter Christian images of Temperance (governing the famous ones created by Spenser and Milton), since these ineluctably chose to speak of the end of temperate behavior. Indeed, it is merely one appearance of the universal stress on wonder and gratitude as the proper "temperate" response of a rightly reasonable man toward the book of the universe, emphases so familiar up through the arguments of Bacon's Advancement and Milton's Paradise Lost, and destined to become so ill-understood soon thereafter. Earlier acceptance of these commonplaces is often phrased in ways that show us that they greatly strengthened habits of "reading" the creatures in the universe allegorically, confirming us in right belief. They emphasized the notion, such as we see in Christine (and I think in Spenser), that the virtuous disposition of the soul is its adornment and beautiful raiment, not only its hard-won guerdon after conflict.

The *Dialogues of creatures,* in a preface, and citing Isidore, states thus this operation of figures which rather than instructing man morally, reveals meanings to him as spirit. Though outwardly the creatures do not "playnly show" their "inwarde meanyinge," yet these are shadowed in them, in order that "by the same path that man erryd from God, he may . . . retourned to him agayne, for as man was "pluckyd by his inordinate love of the creature/ from the greate love of his lorde & maker, so, by inspectyon of the great beawte of creaturys, he owith to be refourmed and to gyve lawde & worshippe to the incomparable Creator." Also quoted is Augustine's great sentence on how all things He made "crye to me, and sece not, that I owe to love the, my lord god and maker above all othir thinge."

Christine has a "Prologue a Allegorie" between her first Glose and Allegorie. What draws us "a ramener a allegorie le propos de nostre matiere" is "l'edificacion de l'ame." Because all things are created by the sapience and power of God, "raissonablement doivent toutes choses tendre *a fin de lui.*" Because nostre esperit is God's image in us, and most noble (after the angels), it is meet (*convenable*) that it be *adorned* with virtues, "parquoy il puisse estre convoye a la fin pourquoy il est fait." She contrasts the droite chevalerie of the struggle here on earth with "l'ennemy d'enfer" with the parfaitte chevalerie whose heroes are "couronnez en glorie"; this speaking of lesperit chevalereux is "fait a la louenge de dieu principalement."

This decking of the soul for its heavenly destiny, this seeing the virtuous action of the bon esprit as a fitting form of louenge de dieu, produces (as we saw briefly) images quite distinct from those urging or portraying moral improvement—however much the decking improves us. The Gloses fasten their attention upon the latter, but the Allegories of Perseus, of Ceres, Narcissus, Jason, had a different end in view, though the same virtuous course was commended. The Caxton translation of the *Somme le roi*—or any form of that popular treatise—[19] makes with great naturalness a similar distinction between man as a moral creature and man as a spiritual creature. Treating of the virtue Prowesse, rooted in us by the Fourth Gift of the Holy Spirit, Fortitudo, Frère Lorens says, "More ferthere coude not the philosophres the vertue of prowesse leden" than simply to "destroie and overcome vices and wikkednesses and to wynne vertues." But "oure gret philosophre Ihesu Crist" and His disciples "gon moche forthere"; for He said "Who-so endureth in-to the ende, he schal *be saved,*" and His disciples seek to be righteous and true *to Christ.* That is, they give their lives "for hym that gaf his lif and his deth for

me," a virtuousness we may desire here but never attain, for though
the motive for virtuous action is a gratitude which simply makes men
try to imitate His acts of love, we shall not match them here, nor
"paie it pleynliche," the debt we owe. This is why the Fourth Beati-
tude, in parallel with the Fourth Gift, speaks of a hunger and thirst
after righteousness which "goes further than" what ethics commends,
the struggle for attainable moral virtues. We have moved from questions of ethics to questions of fealty. Again, in elucidating the beginning of the Pater Noster, the words "Our *Father*" involve a "travaile
to be like hym"—to be "large and curteis, swete and deboner" as He
is, *so that thou go nougt out of thi kynde*" (pp. 169, 99).

It is not by fortuitous chance that we here meet independently the
same turn to the orthodox Christian tenet as we heard in the fable of
the fish Regina. Virtues as qualities natural to a child of God, beautiful in a spouse of Christ, expected of the chevalier Jesus Christ, are
an inevitable result of this conception of man's nature and metaphysical position. For such a notion of his nature and "end"—a familiar
doctrine, but one accommodated in dozens of phrases and in many
books to mediaeval chivalric ideals and society—the imagery is likeliest
to be that of a Quest, of knightly devoir, of Pilgrimage (seeking the
final home of the spirit, born of heavenly lineage). The image of the
two chivalries, briefly seen in Christine and more movingly seen in
romance materials which we reserve for a later chapter, is based on this
understanding of man's moral and spiritual nature and is a common
carrier of the distinction. And Christine's "Prologue a Allegorie"
showed how clear and easy to her were such relations between man's
raison d'être and this figure of allegory—to us a most curious observation. As we have seen, figures of speech that deal with man respectively as moral and as spiritual formally obey the difference in purport.
I think we are justified in interpreting these conceptions as ordinary
popular understandings of the learned differentiations we know well.
Touching figurative writing, the resultant difference is that between
moral instruction and exhortation through tropological writing and
allegory more strictly so-called.

The Pater Noster quotation from the translated *Somme le roi* was
actually part of an image of the higher chivalry. "Gretter nobleie may
non be than to be so gret an emperoures sone as God is"; the imitation
(of God) to which we set ourselves is admittedly impossible, and yet
we say *Our Father* just as "whan a newe knygt goth to a bataile or to
the turnement, men bidden hym thenke whos sone he is."

Although the imagery of the Knight battling for virtue, and the distinguishable imagery of God's Knight imitating a divine original, is structurally fundamental in all the portions of this easily accessible book which were most naturally attractive to later writers (as we shall see in Chapter Two), it is made especially clear in a treatment of another ancient commonplace, the Three Goods. These receive countless statements from the time of Augustine and Ambrose onward, but here they are denominated: small or temporal (ephemeral, of Fortune); the middle or mean goods, of Nature, or acquired by study; and great or "true." *Verray* Lordship, Freedom and Nobility are described, and when we read what constitutes verrey nobleie or true gentillesse, it is proper that we think of Dante, of the 'Franklin's Tale," of the *Roman de la rose,* for these enormously popular didactic manuals, like the *Somme,* were important channels by which patristic and scholastic doctrine or classification flowed into vernacular writing. We are not surprised to hear that verrey nobility comes of "a gentel herte," that there is no gentle heart "but it love God," no nobility therefore but to "serve" Him and no "vilenye but the contrarie ther-of."

The basis for this is always the same:

Non is rigt gentel and noble of gentrie *of body*. [For as far as the body goes] we ben alle of o modre, that is of erthe. . . . [There is not] *rigt gentel ne free but our rigt fadre,* that is the kyng of heuene, that . . . maade the soule to his owne ymage and to his owne liknesse. . . .

[And because like an earthly father he rejoices to have sons like him] . . . he sente vs . . . Ihesu Crist, for to brynge vs the verrey saumple bi whiche we mowe schappe us to his ymage and to his faireness [like those that already dwell in the high city of heaven].

This quest of "the holy men of this world" for "the verrey nobleie that a man bigynneth heere bi grace and vertue" is "fulfilled in ioie," in eternity. But "than hath he the ymage and the liknesse of God, as [much as] a man may have in erthe" when "ther is no thing bitwene God and hym but o wille."

And this is the grettest nobleye and the grettest gentrie that any man or womman may come to . . . (pp. 85-87).

Such, then, is the quest of the chevalerie celestienne. It does not at all preclude, in Christine, in the prose *Lancelot* and in the *Queste del saint Graal,* in moralized fables and books inculcating the virtues, an attention to the Good Knight's earthly combats with vices. But I think it may be apparent that the large literature of virtues battling with vices, which we are accustomed to think of solely as a great tableau of the psychomachia we call the moral struggle, had running through it another kind of image as well—the spirit's quest for a lost but native noblesse, regainable ultimately but not here, a noblesse which every soul had as belonging to the "kin" of the sons of God.

The result of this double attention is especially interesting in Christine because her book also belongs, by direct intention, to a kind—the "regiment of princes"—which had a great Renaissance flowering and development. What Christine wrote was a double courtesy-book. She asks us to read each figure as assisting the Knight, who is a person fighting evil on earth and in his own mind, and as assisting the Pilgram-Knight who is a journeying soul, the chevalier Jesus Christ. One notes that the difference is not between this-worldly and otherworldly; both kinds of courtesy are double-worldly. Both knight-readers read figuratively, for the distinction is neither between literal and figurative, nor between didactic and non-didactic.

Even the Gloses are not mere example; they go beyond "be not like *him*" to universalize faulty or admirable human behavior and thus take in even our own forms of it, though experienced through very different particulars. As with any Spenserian exemplum—Fradubio or Sir Terwin—Christine's personages, being moralized, operate as metaphors to generalize upon experience. Writing as did Spenser, to "fashion a gentleman or noble person in vertuous and gentle discipline," she clearly has in mind a particular social group; these are courtiers who must wage the moral battles described, under conditions localized in the France of 1400. But by the usual action of moral allegory (which is simply a strengthened form of the action of any metaphor), we cannot avoid applying her Gloses or moral readings to all men, who all emulate Perseus, turn from Narcissus' self-love, meet Orgoglio or Mammon or Despair.

The second way of reading the same Textes, "allegorie" in her terminology, while not more universal than this extension of moral meaning, is more profound. It concerns the reasons why the psychomachia is entered upon. The actor is not only a Knight, an Everyman who fights for Christian ethics, but a "spirit," that within any man which is in quest of his ultimate or his timeless destiny. This is why the second reading is—to use one of the oldest words for distinguishing it—spiritual; for moral readings are equally concerned with what are now called spiritual values, editors and commentators to the contrary. I do not think the distinction when it operated in secular literature is quite the same as the familiar distinction between tropological or moral, and allegorical, in interpretation of Scripture; but it does seem to be a more loosely understood or relaxed variant of that distinction.

We are of course entirely familiar with this habit of distinguishing between figures according to their sphere of action, in Scriptural interpretation. Most students of late years, resembling in this no doubt most mediaeval students, have found the famous distich the neatest and most memorable way of reminding themselves of the main difference in few words: "Littera gesta docet, quid credas allegoria,/ Moralis quid agas, quo tendas anagogia."[20] It would be false to think that mediaeval readers always agreed on where the line could be drawn between these two functions we are emphasizing, for they could not always separate quid credas and quid agas.[21] It can be grievously and harmfully oversimplified, as can (and sometimes is) the whole method of reading in the four senses. This was not evolved, or thought of, as a way of reading secular pieces, at least with any rigor or consistency; and when this method is so used in the centuries of its popularity, it is applied with delicacy and restraint, suggestively and not tightly. It seems to me we should try to match this restraint, going only as far as earlier writers give us warrant. The restraint is peculiarly necessary in dealing with the basic conception underlying allegory's power to teach us true belief. This is the relation, caught in the word "type," between history itself (actual persons, events) and revealed truth, so that the actual people and events pre-figure or shadow what later comes to pass, and thereby fulfill the figures. For this is a firmly religious conception, requiring a characteristically Christian conception of God's relation to history, and is tied closely to a necessary other concept, the Old and the New Law. The present ease with which the relation of type is claimed argues a verbal rather than profound understanding. Nevertheless, it seems to me that these long centuries of practice—very common practice—and acceptance of Christian allegorical interpretation left a mark on the ordinary understanding of allegory. The more so because careful theory, New Testament sanction and doctrinally necessary safeguards kept the religious definitions of allegory incredibly pure, moving and deep (considering that we deal with the wide breadth of Christendom and at least twelve loquacious mediaeval centuries).

We should not lose sight of the fact that certain commonplaces of

Christian doctrine have much to do with the current overeasy detection of types (usually of Christ) in some secular writings, often Shakespeare's or Spenser's. It is a doctrinal commonplace to think of the faithful Christian who tries to "imitate" Christ as attempting an image of Christ, as restoring through grace the relation to God which man held before the Fall—when he was truly and recognizably "in His image." Typology is not needed to understand the most important way in which Red Crosse "becomes" or "takes on" Christ; the Pauline terms describe what is supposed to happen constantly in the life of any Christian, and it is a misuse of a word needed for its own meaning to find types in all these. Types properly precede the figure that fulfills them, Moses before Christ. Only a divine Author can so write history that the types foreshadow the revelation of pure truth in another historical occurrence, and the serious use of this figurative relation requires a religious conception of man's reason for being.

As a natural and living figure it could not outlast, in the secular literatures of the Western countries, the unselfconscious acceptance of such basic ideas as universally valid and relevant. If Spenser had not been so much influenced by mediaeval ideals and materials, he might be outside the circle of influence as well, but he seems to me to come just within the time when the long tradition of exegesis and of reading spiritualiter could still impel a secular but Christian author to write images with a truly "allegorical" impulse. The relaxation of definition, which is bound to accompany the secularized use of a figure with such *ends* as this one, makes possible a much more general or large gesture toward the doctrine which we are to realize and believe instead of the exact doctrinal teaching familiar in Biblical allegory. In fact, the chief contribution of its theological background may be not its didactic force (which it shares with many types of figures) but the unrelaxed insistence on the importance of the literal sense.[22] This is absolutely constant during its mediaeval history, and it is easy to see why. If the history itself is not true, the "quid credas" of the figure is nonsense. Herein lies the main difference between it and the grammarian's allegory, the allegory of late classical tradition, which did not undergo this long Christian development. These allegories are frequently content to substitute the allegorical for the literal meaning, having no truth of Old Testament history to preserve, and no such understanding of the relation of revelation (the New Law) to history.

When we learn "beliefs" from non-religious pieces, our lowered demands—almost shrunk to a notion that the image should speak to us insofar as we are souls, or of our eternal not temporal health—admit of application to classical or worldly materials and purposes not ecclesiological or strictly dogmatic. Many among Spenser's figures which truly operate to make us see "what we are to believe" and are strictly allegorical by virtue of this function, yet invite a reading couched more in Platonic than in Christian terms. But the reason for the increased depth, power and permanent interest (the "importance") of the figures are much the same in either case. Usually the well-known commonplaces of both bodies of thought are all that is called upon, and Spenser is not the first poet who has been more Christian by being more Platonic. There is yet a seriousness about the philosophical and metaphysical purport of the images in the *Faerie Queene* which is somehow causally different from the many idealized disquisitions which commend the same virtues or vilify the same vices.

Here lies the power of the change which comes over the *Faerie Queene*, which I should also call a double courtesy-book, when we allow its major fictions and figures to speak with such a double voice. Spenser's design, whereby knights should show forth virtues in their very shape (or look for them), was uniquely suited to the figure of allegory strictly defined, for such "ideas" of the virtues can be seen pure only in deity, but are shadowed in all types and images of deity. The relation to Book I is so evident that I need not take space to particularize it; Red Crosse clearly figures forth both kinds of noblesse—in Christine's terms he is both bon chevalier and bon esprit. The imagery of the House of Holiness, the vision of the Heavenly Jerusalem, the rescue of Una-Andromeda-Regina-Eurydice or whomever you choose, the marriage made in heaven—all this shows both the use of the great expected ancient images and the ambiguity of the chevalier Jesus Christ who takes on a divine (redemptive) office without ceasing to be a human character. But Book I, with its religious direction, its sources in Revelation and in morality plays, its presentation of the basic theme of allegory (salvation through holiness), may be felt to be so special a case that it lies outside discussion.

Guyon and Britomart, too, are images of a quest more than of a conflictus, and their books show not only the confined method of a Guillaume de Lorris staging inner experiences in new and piquant terms—though of course Spenser does this too, and frequently, and well. They show equally well the difficult and dangerous method of a Jean de Meun, a kind of weaving dance-like movement, a dialectic in which no figure is Auctor but in which all the possible positions are shown to us on the great questions of: What is man's nature? Can such a thing as bon amour exist? What are Temperance, and Reason, and Fidelity, and Love? Spenser stresses more often the crying Renaissance problem, What is responsible Power? But even Book V, the one most evidently concerned with the moral discipline of the bon chevalier and good ruler, shows as well, or shows primarily, man's quest for a divine condition—the union of Justice with Love. All the characters, hero and all, constantly only approximate it. They learn what these are and look on them to admire and follow after them.

That Britomart comes closest to approximating this condition is part of a long differentiation of Love from very many things that look like it. In Book V a chief differentiation is self-will, in the relation of love to desire; it is Britomart's own first error, and Radegund's final one. But Britomart's long discipline, her manifest excesses and mistakes, and the kinds of loving acts she nevertheless consistently lays aside in order to perform her own purposes and desires—all point to an allegorical meaning in Britomart's attempt to understand the nature of Love and to pursue it. In Book III of the *Faerie Queene* we are not, nor is Britomart, learning the sex role, to use the modern psychologist's phrase. Neither are we set to re-define this role by translating it into idealistic terms or to re-shape the relation to Artegall by pouring it into Platonic or Christian molds. We are asked to watch Britomart at tasks which turn her away from finding Artegall as her raison d'être, though the place of passionate love between the sexes, in relation to all kinds of love that can be thought of, is always a theme kept before us. Whatever notion Spenser had when he began what has turned out to be the complex of Books III and IV, it is clear that before long he is examining the Idea of Love with the complications which had been brought into it by Christian thought; it is hard to retain the complexities in the one worn English word, but we catch sight of philia and agape as well as eros, or caritas when amor seems to have inextricably entwined it with concupiscentia. It seems to me a most happy part of Spenser's design that Britomart's pursuit of Artegall is interrupted and her union with that Just Knight deferred; he makes good use of these conditions, though I would be surprised if he did not come upon them rather by default, a universal artistic experience.

Allegorically, a Knight of Love is quite properly (and quite traditionally) a Knight who learns chastity, learns the nature of fidelity.[23] Britomart does not cease to be the faithful human lover in quest of a particular person—maintaining the literal sense is understood as an element in the figure of allegory—but the fidelity she comes to under-stand is not simply keeping-to-one-human-attachment; and the misde-finitions of love she meets with go much deeper than the infidelities of lust, to show the root of these infidelities and of others in the an-tithesis of love—self-worship.

All Spenserian figures of this size and importance are both moral and allegorical in a stricter sense; this is absolutely usual, for of course Scriptural figures were not written to be "tropology" or "alle-gory," and for centuries, untold numbers of them were read as both. Mammon's cave is most surely a moral allegory showing the evils of concupiscentia (in its most embracing sense, as well as covetousness in a narrower sense). But both the imagery of the canto and the ex-traordinary freedom and grace of the following vision of Guyon's angelic protector prove us right in our feeling that we have been in hell, where there was nothing *but* concupiscentia, and have seen the Beast himself, who thinks he is a god. It is better not to dilute these poetic experiences to moral allegory only—fictions which convince us we should fight greed or strive for chaste love in marriage; they por-tray men faced with the death of the soul or learning what its free-dom depends upon.

The notion of a double chivalry of course developed quite inde-pendently of these two functions of figurative language. It is interest-ing that Christine should see and use the parallel between two sets of ideas whose relation lies in a common understanding of human ends. The hierarchy of man's allegiances, his two knighthoods, is paralleled in a literary theory which differentiates figures according to whether they are addressed to one sphere of man's spiritual life or another. The two chivalries naturally gained currency in mediaeval writings which wished to show the more than moral nature of man's pursuit of virtue. It is proper to leave until the next chapter (on the virtues and vices) the further demonstration of uses of the double knighthood in connec-tion with specific virtues—especially with the conception of Magnifi-cence as the highest virtue of the Christian Knight, and the one pos-sessed in perfection only by Christ himself. However, although we also give the whole matter of romances a chapter (Five), I would not defer so long the point that in the most powerful of all allegorized ro-mances, the *Queste del saint Graal,* the strictly allegorical reading which is to be given to all important images is attached to a deliberate and declared presentation of the two chivalries.

The *Queste,* which was incorporated into the so-called Vulgate Cycle of the Arthurian romances between the prose *Lancelot* and the *Mort Artu,* is the most open treatment, and one of the most poetic and original treatments, of a fundamental motif in mediaeval writing—the tension between the earthly chivalry and heavenly chivalry. It creates a new Grail Knight, Galahad, and it tells the story of his successful achievement of the queste del graal, here a fully Christianized symbol but not therefore fixedly equated with an historical chalice; it tells of Lancelot's moving, often piteous, failure and of Gawain's utter incomprehension, and Bohort's and Perceval's different kind of success. Neither Christine nor Spenser finds it necessary, as does the *Queste* author, to see the soul's quest as the sum of the human adventure. But quite aside from any subscription to this idea, or to the *Queste's* narrow definition of chaste fidelity in the soul, the long advance through the very many symbolical episodes, which culminates in the final allegories of the marvelous Ship of Solomon and the Grail liturgy in the castle, is better preparation than any theoretical treatment of the nature of allegory for anticipating and understanding those larger metaphysical significances which we cannot persuade ourselves are absent from Spenser's large culminating allegorical images.

I am thinking less of the great mystical scenes of the *Queste* than of the constant double texture and the resulting complexity and variety of human character portrayal—and thence the poignancy with which we realize (always through figurative presentation) what it is to attempt the second kind of noblesse Caxton spoke about. As we take our way through the scores of tiny incidents, they cease to seem like fantastically curious marvels and become, under a surface as puzzling and dark as that of our real lives, a clear record of the meaning of men's half-understood choices. There are the small choices made on grounds of human bravado or self-assurance: Meliant decides to take the left-hand path he is warned against, thus testing his new knightly valor (alas, says the hermit, the warning spoke of the celestial chivalry, and you acted by the code of the chivalry of the world); Hector rides his horse up to all gates, as Knights do, and sees nothing to remark, notes no lack of the humility which marks out the chevalier Jesus Christ. There are the choices made on inadequate grounds which are obscurely blameworthy, or, the choices that are not reasoned but follow upon some commendable habit in the will and affections. We see the first sort in Lancelot as he helps the black knights that seem to need it most. He does by second nature what accords well enough with the codes of earthly chivalry, but is fatally inattentive

THE MEDIEVAL HERITAGE OF SPENSER'S ALLEGORY

to what the battle is about. The second sort can be seen in Perceval naïvely acting rightly—half by habit, half by chance, but protected time and again by the innocent and all but thoughtless way he looks to Heaven in his puzzles or his perils. There are the more complicated dilemmas, like Bohort's anguished hesitation, or there are the characters unaware of the presence of a choice, as with Gawain's courteous blind ironic answers to those who if heeded might reveal to him the secret that makes his journey meaningless.

The usefulness of irony is apparent in figures like these large fictional images where the persons are unaware or only half-aware, or at least less aware than are we, of the significance of what happens to them. Irony is native to the figure, and where significances are so quickly grasped that the mind moves with real freedom (as here), this must have been an important part of the pleasure taken by mediaeval audiences in such works. The same reserve and understatement which makes irony successful is responsible for the fact that the worst illegality in allegorical reading is to re-tell the images as I have just done, making the significances apparent. The hermits of the tale confine their explanations to those who have just lived through the experiences. For we have again in the *Queste* the unimpugnable evidence of readers *within* the work. We soon become accustomed to take the pleasure mediaeval listeners must have taken both in confirming our understandings by the hermits' interpretations of events, and in observing nuances we had neglected. We even learn readily to detect the fake hermits who rise up to apply conventional symbolic mis-explanations and lead knights astray. The allegorical critic we know so well, who announces "represents Evil!" as soon as he sees black objects, would quickly lose his way.

The *Queste* shows with what power the idea of a double chivalry could be used in a great literary work (a description we should never think of using for Christine's piece). But because it is so extreme and so consistent an example of reading a fiction allegorically, it amounts to a kind of discipline in the sort of double comprehension which this kind of figurative writing demands—and which some Elizabethans demanded, some of the time. The Lancelot of the *Queste* is a great psychological creation. That is by no means all. For as we take our way without hurry through all the things that happen to him, taught to see allegorically the double meaning of all that he does and all that the others do and say, we begin to read (as though under the flowing water of events) a great design, not of the drama-in-men's-minds but of the meaning of men's lives, lying there to be read under a transparent veil.

As we see slowly in many happenings what it means that Galahad is an image of Christ, that is, as we slowly take in the allegory (for allegories cannot be arrived at by the short cut of equations), we also see that the way to understand Red Crosse as a Redeemer is similar —though Galahad and Red Crosse are not the same image and do not mean the same thing. All the symbolical dictionaries we could consult will not convey the mode of action of such figures, which takes place phrase by small phrase within a work—but comparably acting figures do illuminate each other.

The double action, and hence the double reading, which I have suggested as typical of figures that can be both moralized and allegorized, was not, of course, spoken of under such carefully distinguished terms, though Christine was useful because she did so distinguish them. But even in the high mediaeval period, when such reading was common, the word "allegory" can refer to either; the *Ovide moralisé* is a prime example of what we must expect, being a tissue of the kind of interpretations Christine (and I following her) called not morals but allegories. I have wished to distinguish between two things, not two terms, and do not recommend trying to maintain Christine's terminology; it is too late. But it is not too late to keep the two kinds of figure roughly separate, since we have indisputable evidence that this was done, and done in secular literary works, much later than we would have expected. These understandings, which were to hand in popular and accessible forms for sixteenth-century men to take in and follow, will deliver such writers as Spenser from the slicing machine which reading on different "levels" has turned into of late. It will sometimes at least restore the depth of a reading that does not reduce human life to a psychomachia, spiritual life to morals and images to axes and hammers.

NOTES

1. Other writers have not had the benefit of the kind of attention given to Lodge in A. Walker, "The Reading of an Elizabethan," *RES*, vol. 8 (1932), 264-81. On my ascription of the first to Thomas "Hibernicus" rather than "Palmer," see P. G. C. Campbell's study on the sources of Christine's *L'Épitre d'Othéa* (Paris, 1924), ch. 6. The article mentions numerous other mediaeval sources used by Lodge;

for example, in *Wits Miserie* he evidently turned consistently for details on the sins to the fourteenth-century Holcot, but I choose rather the uninvestigated works; Holcot's popular pieces have been especially usefully described (for those interested in how images are transmitted) in B. Smalley, *English Friars and Antiquity* (Oxford, 1960), ch. 7.

2. This ascription has seeped into a few catalogues since Rajna's work on this book in the 1880's; see *Giornale storico*, vols. 3, 4, 10, 11 (1884-88); also—depending on Rajna—J. T. Welter, *L'exemplum dans la litt.* (Paris, 1927), pp. 357-60. Rajna in his series of articles, whence we can build up a list of manuscripts, data on illustrations, etc., attributes the *Dialogues* to the mid-1300's physician and author of some note, Mayno de' Mayneri (so attributed in the Cremona Manuscript), and demonstrates various errors connected with attributions in B.Nat. MS.lat.8512 to a Nicholas Pergamenus, evidently nonexistent though become common in catalogues listing this item. The manuscript title is most often *Contemptus sublimitatis*, and many editions appear under the title *Destructorium vitiorum*, not to be confused with a different book of that title—a preachers' manual often reprinted in the Renaissance by Alexander Carpenter?, studied by G. R. Owst in *The Destructorium Viciorum of Alexander Carpenter* (London, 1932). Correction of these facts promoting errors in identification makes it likely that the list of known manuscripts will increase, and earlier forms of the several translations may be found.

3. Miss Walker's mention of at least eight Latin, three Dutch, and two French editions, before the end of the 1400's, can, for us, take the place of listed editions, since we do not have to support the undisputed fact of its availability; Lodge read it. I have used numerous Latin editions, the French, the Dutch and the English (that used by Lodge is STC 6815; the abridged Wyer translation [STC 6816] of the first seven is of little consequence); but I have seen only one MS., B.Nat. lat.8507, one of the mere five or six illustrated copies noted by Rajna (*op.cit.*, n. 2 above, see vol. 11, p. 52n.). It is convenient to quote from an edition more likely to be owned by libraries—Haslewood's 1816 reprint *Dialogues of creatures moralised*, the translation of STC 6815, with cuts from the Gouda edition and not unlike the general series, though unbeautiful. It is worth noting that, if we did not know it to be a fact, the probability of an Elizabethan of the '90's making use of an Antwerp-printed English book *ca.* 1535 would seem like a hazardous guess; I shall indulge in none so shaky.

4. Any rustic raconteur has all these noted characteristics untaught, and of course, Renaissance tellers deliberately highlight the signs of the low style. One is wary of claims about how the Latin was felt by contemporary readers, but it is hard to believe that the pert conversations

were not similarly responded to: the crisp interchanges between Sun and Moon, or the sharp talk of Stella transmontana and the other stars or "De auro et plumbo" (Fable 19).

5. The last-named collection limits its applications to a stricter allegorical reading. What assures us we are looking at common things is not the well-known few titles but the great tribe of now-forgotten exempla collections which were printed, usually after a long manuscript life; Welter's notes hold many such surprises. The stories became proverbial, or were moralized because they were. I have not separated off the beast fables and Aesopian materials and have kept sub-kinds like miracle-collections and political-history exempla out of the foreground.

6. It will be convenient later to quote the common mediaeval saying about quid credas which has done most to keep the commonplace common; see n. 20 below. We should not be rigid about the terms since the periods concerned were not; where the divisions are made with precision and care, there is generally some specific source (as in Harington's Apology; see II, 202 of the edition in Gregory Smith's Elizabethan Critical Essays, Oxford, 1904). The continued life of the distinction pursued in the text is obviously a part of one of our questions, whether allegory, as the usual Renaissance poet understood it, can be secular.

7. There is no indication that the cant meaning of a Partridge as bawdy-house girl or harlot was to be taken, just as there is no warrant for obtruding the symbolical meaning of emeralds in Fable 14, or the fairly ordinary relation of the Carbuncle stone to the Virgin Mary, in Fable 17. When a traditional symbolical meaning is needed by the story and intended by the author, the manner of telling makes this apparent; I would propose that we should wait upon such indications.

8. No originality and no discoveries will be encountered in this attempt to observe when and how allegorical meaning, or even moral meaning, enters seen figures and read figures. I have purposely kept clear of similar attempts not focussed on the literary problems of this present book (like Panofsky's careful introduction to Studies in Iconology, New York, 1939, or Pächt's Rise of Pictorial Narrative in Twelfth-Century England, Oxford, 1962), which can be so much more sophisticated. For identical terminology is not possible, procurable evidence differs and overcomplication in the artistic problems would make the different complication of literary problems harder. Of course, one does not suppose this a chiefly modern question for speculation; Leonardo discussed it. Though its eighteenth-century developments were phenomenally rich, comparisons are not profitable here, given the different grounding of sixteenth-century notions of symbolizing meaning (e.g. the writers had not been nourished on eighteenth-century German classical scholarship).

9. The manuscript apparently translates the *Miroir* redaction; for all such matters see below ch. 2. Nevertheless, since the texts are very similar just here, I used a printed translation of the unrevised "Somme le roi," *The Book of Vices and Virtues*, ed. W. N. Francis, *EETS*, vol. 217 (1942), 92-97. Convenience is important, since allegorical imagery, of all kinds, most repays scrutiny of the whole context. Other illuminations portraying this image (and references to others reproduced elsewhere) will be found in the present author's double article in *JWCI*, vols. 26-27 (1963, 1964), "Notes on the Virtues and Vices," especially Part II.

10. There is in one sense only one allegorical theme—loss and salvation. Hence our feeling of starvation if literature's variety is boiled down to statement and re-statement of that theme. There is nothing monotonous about the shapes that body it forth. Mammon's difference from Acrasia is sufficient demonstration, even if both "mean" the same loss, to the same enemy.

11. It creeps back under some disguise even among defenders of allegory, and of course denies the whole nature and point of the figure, which *embodies* ideas and thereby makes them manifest; if the critic who tells us what everything stands for were right, we could do very well without the allegory. This conception comes closer to the truth with allegories imposed afterward, as were late classical and Stoic interpretations. The insistence that the literal is true, and figures or means (rather than "stands for") the further spiritual reading is a legacy from centuries of habitual Biblical allegorizing. At any rate, the Elizabethans can still *write* so (the literal being the historical, i.e. the fiction standing up as narrative). Recent nervousness about conceptual elements in poetry make untendentious phrasing difficult. One is sure that modern touchiness about words similarly felt to be dangerous or obscurely associated with guilt is very temporary—words like "intention," "statement," "conceptual discourse," "static." They are used in this book as if they were not famous coterie-words.

12. I claim these extensions without in the least giving up what various studies have shown in these cantos: moral exposition more than usually indebted to Aristotle's *Ethics* (see Sirluck, "FQ II and the Nicomachean Ethics," *MP*, vol. 49, 1951-52); warnings to Elizabethan England to maintain a middle way; the evidences of the metaphor "British England: Fairyland" which Greenlaw brought out as long ago as 1918 in "Spenser's Fairy Mythology," *SP*, vol. 15. These largest images simply go farther.

13. The point about the triple temptation was made in an interesting context in R. Durling's "Bower of Bliss and Armida's Palace," *Comp. Lit.*, vol. 6 (1954), 335-47. A recent comparison is Kermode's in "The Cave of Mammon," *Elizabethan Poetry* (London, 1960), where the parallels are numerous and clear and the relation suggested is not

that of figura. My statements do not quarrel with the idea that Guyon "is imitating both Hercules and Christ." The relation of imitatio Christi, not that of "a Christ-figure," is the reason why we require no recherché theories to account for the next scene, where Guyon needs and receives the grace which all followers of the tempted and victorious Christ are promised—"And angels came and ministered unto him" as readers recall, and expect (Mark 1).

14. This inherited Christianization of temperance comes out with special clarity in *Comus,* late and by a learned and conscious artist; much was pointed out by Bush in 1932 (*Mythology and the Renaissance Tradition*), but the essential Circe article is Merritt Hughes's in *JHI* for 1943, and we may save ourselves the numerous citations here since they are clustered and the problem discussed in R. Tuve, *Images and Themes in 5 Poems by Milton* (Cambridge, 1957), pp. 130ff.

15. Pegasus as fame and good repute is discussed at pp. 189f. of M. M. Lascelles' "The Rider on the Winged Horse," which examines many other points, such as the connection with poets and with Bellerophon, and in much more important literary texts (see *Elizabethean and Jacobean Studies presented to F. P. Wilson*, Oxford, 1959, 173-198). Christine's source is the *Ovide moralisé;* our concerns here, definition and the setting of problems, discourage the complication brought in by source treatment, but citations to Campbell and other investigators appear in ch. 4 below. My descriptions and quotations are from the MSS., for there is no edition of the French text (one of Scrope's translation is promised by Curt Bühler), but Gordon's edition cited below n. 18 or the Roxburghe Club edition of Scrope's translation (ed. Warner, 1904) can be consulted.

16. As is said in the verbal descriptions accompanying pictures in several manuscripts described in the article (Part II) cited in n. 9.

17. Christine's deliberate action of directing us toward multiple readings of classical story finds an interesting analogue in Enrique de Villena's *Los doze trabajos de Hércules,* ed. M. Morreale (Madrid, 1958), facs. edition of 1499 edition, Madrid, ca. 1879, extant in numerous fifteenth-century manuscripts and editions of 1483, 1499, 1502?. But its divisions into *Historia nuda, Declaración, Verdad, Aplicación,* do not offer us so comprehensive a view of the ways of interpreting classical figure as we find in Christine's less pretentious piece.

18. By James Gordon in his very useful edition and discussion (unfortunately out of print) of *The Epistle of Othéa to Hector* in the translation in MS.Harl. 838 (Philadelphia, 1942).

19. One can quote from Caxton (1486), or Frère Lorens' French text widespread in manuscript and print, or from the only convenient modern printing of an English version in *EETS,* vol. 217, as I have ordinarily done, with references in text to pages; in sections which ap-

pear in all, differences are minimal. I do not take up Christine's sources, but for example, the Prologue mentioned is paralleled in the *Livre de Sagesse*.

20. The distich was popularized by appearing in Nich. de Lyra, but they are twelfth-century phrases, already used in the *Catholicon*, and evidently originating with Augustine of Dacia; see the careful and well-documented "Introduction" to H. de Lubac's *Exégèse médiévale: Les quatre sens de l'Écriture* for the history of this ubiquitously quoted tag (2 parts; Paris, 1959-64). There has been an extreme growth in the very last few years in the materials available for accurate study of religious allegory; I cite but this here, for its completeness and its inclusion of the Latin so that we may assess points of view, and because its recentness insures citation of others. I might add the English translation of J. Daniélou's *The Bible and the Liturgy* (Notre Dame, Ind., 1956), and studies cited therein (cf. also his *Sacramentum Futuri*, Paris, 1950; or V. C. Spicq's *Esquisse d'une histoire de l'exégèse latine au moyen âge* (Paris, 1944), introductions to the pertinent texts in the *Sources chrétiennes*, ed. H. de Lubac, and J. Daniélou). Given this plenty, and because the figures we study show the influence of general understandings not theological information, I do not discuss subtler aspects or religious materials, but count upon readers' study of these.

21. It would seem to me not only unnecessary but harmful in our context to attempt to accommodate the differences concerning four, or three, or more, senses, with English terms, or to fence off the three other senses from the allegory. Influence was too unselfconscious and too loose for this. An anagogical sense sometimes looks confusingly like what I keep the word "allegorical" for; though we admit overlapping in all categories, religious writings, which alone allow truly anagogical imagery, would show its difference ("religious" passages like the image of Lycidas in heaven with the saints, are as close as secular works come).

22. It seems wise to take every pertinent opportunity of reiterating this fact, for whether in ignorance or in wilful disregard of the care taken by mediaeval theory and instruction on this point, even mediaevalists can be heard to characterize a "typical mediaeval allegory" by its *substitution* of allegorical for literal senses, its disregard of historical, literal, or fictional reasonableness, or its schematized and devitalized paralleling of abstraction with concretion. There is no protection against an unwillingness to separate unimaginative, or decadent, or careless allegorical writers from good ones, especially if we will not consider what men advised or intended to do, but only what they do for us. There was the usual number of run-of-the-mill pedestrian writers making use of popular modes, then as now. A chapter (vii)

citing texts is in de Lubac ("Importance de la lettre," part 1, 2), but treatments of single writers and their texts can be more specifically informative (e.g. Hugo of St. Victor, III, ch. iv). See also "La nouveauté chrétienne" in part 1, 2, ch. viii.

23. Virginity as one of the forms of fidelity, "the sage and serious *doctrine* of Virginity," has its place, though this would not be as eminent as in Milton's *Comus* where the Lady's part was written for the young girl Alice Egerton; far less had to be conveyed by the allegory and its figures, and the nature of Temperance is the focus, only one of the elements to be known about the nature of Love. But no one learns so much as Britomart, and in the end it turns out to be what allegorical doctrine thinks of as saving knowledge. If Britomart were chiefly faithful just to *Artegall*, she would have acted very differently in the actions of the two books; and she *learns* how to deliver him. Of the many explanations of one of her great lessons, the delivery of Amoret, none is perfectly satisfying and perhaps none is utterly without contribution to our understanding (except those which see lustful flaws in Amoret to be cured); see most recently T. P. Roche's *The Kindly Flame, A Study of the Third and Fourth Books of Spenser's Faerie Queene* (Princeton, 1964), for a felicitious explanation and also for a very clear exposition of allegorical reading as this century could still understand it.